Radio Journalism
in America

Radio Journalism in America

Telling the News in the Golden Age and Beyond

Jim Cox

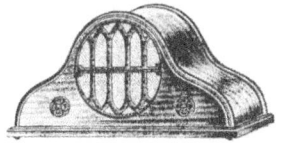

McFarland & Company, Inc., Publishers
Jefferson, North Carolina, and London

All photographs were supplied by Photofest

LIBRARY OF CONGRESS CATALOGUING-IN-PUBLICATION DATA

Cox, Jim, 1939–
Radio journalism in America : telling the news
in the golden age and beyond / Jim Cox.
    p.   cm.
Includes bibliographical references and index.

ISBN 978-0-7864-6963-5
softcover : acid free paper ∞

1. Radio journalism — United States — History — 20th century.
I. Title.
PN4888.R33C69 2013   791.44097309'041—dc23   2013007685

BRITISH LIBRARY CATALOGUING DATA ARE AVAILABLE

© 2013 Jim Cox. All rights reserved

*No part of this book may be reproduced or transmitted in any form
or by any means, electronic or mechanical, including photocopying
or recording, or by any information storage and retrieval system,
without permission in writing from the publisher.*

Front cover image: *CBS Midday News with
Douglas Edwards*, 1968–1979 (CBS/Photofest)

Manufactured in the United States of America

*McFarland & Company, Inc., Publishers
Box 611, Jefferson, North Carolina 28640
www.mcfarlandpub.com*

For the family of the late
James R. Newton,
a cherished comrade and
professional newsman who joined
integrity with proficiency every day

Table of Contents

Acknowledgments ix
Introduction: Cool Stuff and History Light 1

1. Hard Copies: The Origins of American Newspapers 5
2. The Origins of Electronic Journalism 12
3. "Millions Are Out Here Listening Every Day!" 30
4. Who Owns the Ether? It Belongs to Us All 40
5. Censorship: Pressures from Without, Within 50
6. The Art of Persuasion: Everybody Has a Bias 65
7. Nights of the Roundtable: Clashes, Conflicts Courted 72
8. At All Hours: News Achieves Parity, Perceptibly Prospers ... 83
9. Journalism's Inducement in a Rise of Local Stations 95
10. Consequences of Radio's Reliance on Print 104
11. The Fanzines: Trade Issues to Perpetuate the Industry 113
12. Optical Illusions? News Fix? Boosting Aural Text with Pix 122
13. Magazine of the Airwaves: News in a Novel Format 139
14. When It's Time for News, the Big Hand Is on the 24 153
15. Baubles, Bangles, Gadgetry: New Marvels Dispatch News 165

Biographical Dictionary of Radio Journalists 171
Notes 225
Bibliography 243
Index 249

Acknowledgments

When my children were small, one Halloween night a car pulled up in front of our house and parked. The front passenger door opened and a ghostly figure got out. With a bag for stuffing treats in, the eerie form started across the front yard to our door. I was observing from the shadows beside the house. Before our unidentified visitor arrived on the porch, I heard an unmistakably recognized bass voice bellow from the car: "Tell 'em thank you, Patty!" She was the daughter of friends who lived quite some distance from us. Her daddy's admonition — by name, no less — clued me in to who this well disguised child was. Our family has recalled that incident many times in the ensuing years. We return to it when someone does something for somebody else in the family and is reminded: "Tell 'em thank you, Patty!"

Thank you is, for me, one of the indispensable expressions in the English language. There is no substitute for applying it frequently, generously, and eloquently. (I try to remember to offer similar zest with *gracias* to the wait staff in Mexican restaurants.) We taught our kids early to faithfully express their thanks just as we had been taught. As my mother put it: "Use it any time somebody does something for you." Repeating "thank you" a few hundred thousand times was second nature in the households of my birth and my present family. And I try to say it with gusto.

Thus I count it a heartfelt privilege to express appreciation to the folks who contributed something of substance in this volume: Dave Arnold, Mike Biel, Jimmy Cox, Doug Douglass, Ryan Ellett, Jack French, Bob Gibson, Martin Grams, Jr., Paul Urbahns, and Jim Widner. Without them, it just wouldn't be the same. I highly prize their comradeship and thank them profusely for their help.

The chief researcher on this project, Irene Heinstein, has performed in an extraordinary manner. There is absolutely no one I have ever known who approaches her assignments with the fervor and steadfastness that Irene exhibits with every pursuit. Her ability to ferret out the most elusive details is classically stunning. So many times she has made me look good by her tenacious drive to uncover never-before-revealed matter that other historiographers have clearly overlooked. In the profiles in the Appendix of this book and in the biographical sketches of the main body text, Irene has created magic once more with some heretofore obscure material from the recesses of various personalities' lives. Be assured that this author couldn't begin to accomplish what he does without Irene's labors in the background. Her amazing gifts, as well as her allegiance to the tasks, is fundamental as well as incalculable. I am genuinely grateful to have someone behind me with her manifold qualities.

I'm also deeply appreciative to my family, and in particular, to my life's mate, Sharon Cox. She gives me up to endless hours of research and writing because she knows how satisfying all of this is to me. I'm extremely grateful for her supportive encouragement and love.

And thank you, dear readers, for investing in works like these. It is my strong desire that we vintage radio preservationists offer something of inherent usefulness for present and future generations. Hopefully, you will not only make new discoveries here but also find it an enjoyable read.

Introduction:
Cool Stuff and History Light

To our early morning, morning, midday, afternoon, evening, late-evening, overnight, and weekend newscasts, we may add a plethora of newspapers, magazines, satellites, round-the-clock cable news channels, and computers, plus a proliferating mixed bag of handheld electronic devices keeping us connected 24/7. With all of these resources figuratively and literally at our fingertips, I'm certain that Americans living in the early decades of the 21st century are far better informed about what's happening than anyone who maybe inhabited this planet before us ever thought possible. We're also getting the word (whatever it might be) instantaneously and simultaneously, too, so much of the time — often as it transpires, but definitely accessible to us within moments after it occurs. If there is a means of improving on this — and I have little doubt that some creative minds are fashioning flashier gadgets to tempt us in that exercise now — we'll be the objects of colossal marketing schemes designed to lure us into upgrading our superseded stuff. How cool is that? And while much of this electronic wizardry can net innumerable functions and process them all with speedy reliability, one of their diverse provinces is our stimulus for introspection here — that of news dissemination.

Would it surprise you to learn that just three centuries ago our friends, the English — deprived of radio, television, satellite, cable, computer, Internet, smartphone, ebooks, and all the rest of the gear that keeps us so well informed now — remained in touch with what was taking place in their world by gathering at the local Starbucks to hear it every day? (The venue went under alternative nomenclature, of course.) I was startled to learn that those commoners thought of *their era* as manifesting an excess fascination with news! In a 1712 newspaper account, their obsession with finding out what was going on of interest to them was depicted as "a furious itch of novelty." According to that published report, chasing current events had become such a fixation with so many Britishers that it "proved fatal to many families; the meanest of shopkeepers and handicrafts [artists and laborers] spending whole days in coffee-houses, to hear news and talk politicks, whilst their wives and children wanted bread at home...."[1] My, my! And our consumption with the news in modern times can be satiated with the mere flick of a wrist or the push of a button that may not even be visible to the eye or felt by the finger. Just allow a few centuries to rumble by and see how we upgrade the transmission systems!

This little volume first and foremost spotlights radio journalism. It seeks to validate the strategic contributions that the aural medium's newscasts and their related forums have accorded us in keeping abreast of the pertinent details about events, decisions, and people in our world of paramount or passing interest. As radio was the first mass medium with an ability to bring us all together — metaphorically on the same page and essentially in the same instant — it continues to play a fundamental role in providing our nation's denizens with information we can use, rapidly, reliably, and responsibly. Like almost everything else, radio has transitioned through several permutations since its arrival in the 1920s, too. Distinct periods in its history can be traced that embrace its roots, the golden age, and the well-defined eras dominated by the disc jockey, talk, and news, all of which are explored in these pages. Along with the time zone emphases, the reader's attention is directed to our utter dependency on radio as a source of cheap entertainment during the Great Depression and the critical information we solicited from it during the Second World War. We'll survey its diminished effects in the wake of television's start-up, too. That resulted in radio's shift from being at the very core of many families' activities to more individualized applications. In making the changes from its earlier programming — directed to a general audience composed of compound age groups — radio transformed into reaching a much more narrowly defined contingent of listeners. In the process, many of those began to turn elsewhere for the news they had relied upon for decades from large consoles, small table models, and handheld transistor units. Then we broach the introduction of some amazing technological revolutions that have significantly altered what we hear and how, when, and where we hear it. All of these transitions and innovations have impacted the news, commentaries, and public affairs programming that have emanated from our radios across the last nine decades. And all are considered in some detail.

You should know that the text is heavily slanted to the golden age encompassing the time period roughly extending from the early 1930s to the late 1950s and without any apologies for it. In that epoch radio became our most reliable source of instant news and information. That's when the journalism "stars" emerged to dispatch the details for which we waited, occasionally with great expectancy, knowing that they would arrive in timely fashion and at the same time confident that they would be accurate, impartial, comprehensive, and coherent. The news would also most often be delivered by familiar voices in which we placed heavy trust. Radio news was ultimately responsible to us (and not purely to station and network owners). Its messengers were then (as well as now) considered purveyors of the truth. While the remainder of current radio programming may have gone to hell in a handbag in the estimate of some listeners, we can still fairly well count on the accuracy and objectivity of the news reports we hear there. It's a reassuring feeling in a contemporary age, far removed from the broadcasting values and constraints back in the day.

A quartet of communication disciplines is highlighted in this tome, all of which supply us with a steady flow of news. In order of their chronological appearance, they include print journalism (mostly newspapers and magazines — tools that work in primarily hard copy formats), radio (AM, FM, satellite), TV (broadcast, cable, and satellite structures), and computer technology (with a host of developments in electronic wonders that transmit the news while performing tasks in many additional capacities). It's obvious that all of these avenues for bringing news to us impact one another. As radio journalism's pilgrimage is recounted, you may witness manifold routes by which other media navigate those same waters.

Let me suggest that you not overlook the Appendix to the book. It's composed of biographies of more than a hundred national radio analysts, commentators, newscasters, and public affairs moderators who prevailed at the quartet of transcontinental chains in the golden age. Many of them were recognized names in millions of American domiciles while some may have been fairly obscure. All made a contribution, however, and the achievements of their working lives are exhibited there.

Journalism has been much more than a passing fancy for this author since adolescence. Indeed, my entire professional career embraced an assortment of its multifaceted diversions including advertising, editing, promotion, public relations, teaching, and writing. In absolute satisfaction, the intrinsic rewards far outweighed those that met the requirements for survival. ("Do what you love and the money will come.") My enduring passion for journalism dates all the way back to when I was about seven years of age. My father came home from work one evening bearing an antiquated L. C. Smith-Corona manual typewriter model, although I couldn't discern how archaic it was at the time. He allowed that his office was discarding it as surplus equipment and he had bought it for me. Frankly, I was totally uncertain about what it was, what it did, and how it did it. Patiently he showed me how to press the keys that tapped against an inked ribbon and resulted in letters appearing on a sheet of paper that had been inserted into the machine's carriage. Bingo! I was soon creating printed text on paper!

I had no way of knowing that I was to spend zillions of hours in front of a keyboard, of course, earning a livelihood from both vocational as well as avocational pursuits. But my early fascination with those magnetic keys has netted just that. Eventually I was applying the typewriter (later supplanted by a surplus Royal manual machine while still in the pre-computer eon) to compose homework assignments for school, pen dramas which my classmates performed before other students, produce neighborhood newspapers, and author some early freelance articles for magazines. I adopted journalism as a full time profession after my original intent—network radio writing, acting, and/or announcing—fell by the wayside, becoming virtually extinct by the time I earned a college degree in 1964, then ready to go to work. This volume presents a chance to combine the dual loves into one venture. I offer that background so you can know that both subjects are far more than mere fleeting challenges with me.

Not so long ago, I authored a tome about the history of the passenger trains that have crossed the Deep South since 1830. Shortly after its publication a rail fan who's been active in that hobby for decades told me that the members of his local railroad historical society had found my book "refreshing and intriguing" (his words). I thanked him and inquired, "Why is that?" His rejoinder was: "Because, while it is a history book, you make it interesting." After my seventh grade social studies teacher, Miss Phoebe Reynolds, turned me on to history, it became a subject I've had fun with ever since. She was an old maid schoolmarm of advanced years. But she loved history perhaps as much as she loved her students and she had the ability to make her subject come alive as much as anyone I've known. Her class was all the inspiration I needed to turn "all things history" into a fascinating reverie. Although I can't possibly communicate it as well as she, I hope my love for history is evident as I try.

History needn't be torture for those who have never especially embraced it as their holy grail. It simply doesn't have to be cut and dried. Adding some spice through anecdotes, illustrations, comparisons, levity, narratives, and so forth, can make even the most mundane facts palatable to those who prefer not to wallow in the past. Now you've been forewarned what to anticipate. My purpose within these pages hasn't been to make light of history but, more precisely, to make history light. It's my earnest desire that this accounting of media's progression will rise above the usual drab and dullness to soaring heights for you. Well, maybe soaring is a little high but, could you settle for a few inches off the ground?

1

Hard Copies: The Origins of American Newspapers

"I would rather live in a country with newspapers and without a government, than in a country with a government but without newspapers," wrote Thomas Jefferson, author of the acclaimed *Declaration of Independence* and the nation's third chief executive.[1] As it turned out, Jefferson had little to fear regarding the loss of printed news in Revolutionary-era America. The colonists sampled the efforts of plenty of journalists whose publications were popping up across the land; it hardly seemed likely that newspapers were in danger of extinction any time soon. By 1825, as a matter of fact, the U.S. had more newspapers circulating to more subscribers than any other nation on the planet.[2]

Jefferson's ostensible apprehensiveness, if indeed it was that, might have been better served in a modern setting. That's based on the rapid and ostensibly endless innovations of electronic marvels that variously arise to threaten the existence of hard copy communications in the future. Referencing what has been termed the "most powerful medium of global interactive communications," one authority asserted: "The Internet should be understood as the first instance of a global communication system. That system, in turn, is displacing a national system of communications which came into existence at the end of the nineteenth century as a result of the railroad and telegraph, and was 'perfected' in subsequent innovations through television in the network era."[3]

A second scholar responded that the Internet has been on the way for quite a while and is the sum of several parts: "In many ways the Internet is merely a product, or symptom, of a more fundamental technological change that has been under way for the past half-century and only now is beginning to crystallize: the convergence of telecommunications, computing, and traditional media. Together, this new media system embraces all forms of human communication in a digital format where the rules and constraints of the analog would no longer apply."[4] There will be an opportunity to explore some of these modern age marvels in a cursory examination of them in Chapter 15.

> Bear in mind that news and information, let alone computers, are actually quite new. If you consider the time frame of human life on earth and imagine it as a twenty-four hour day, the information age is a fraction of that day. The invention of speech, which occurred about 100,000 years B.C., would not take place until 9:30 P.M. Writing occurred about eight minutes before midnight. The ability to store and transmit speech and writing electronically through the telegraph, telephone, radio, and television happened about eleven seconds before midnight.

The digital computer just made it under the wire two seconds before midnight in our communication day.[5]

For now let us contemplate where all we are going as we initiate an extraordinary journey through the information age, beginning with those well-worn hard copies.

Acta Diurna, a hand-lettered "daily gazette" reporting senate votes and popular events in the Roman Forum between 59 B.C. and A.D. 222, is considered man's first methodical crack at collecting and dispatching data in an orderly style.[6] Copied by scribes and borne throughout the empire, this news of government decrees, legal notices and gladiatorial outcomes was a progressive stab at making storage and distribution of information convenient to the populace. The efforts of the *actuarii*, thought to be the earliest news writers, were still preceded by numerous rudimentary activities with comparable intents.

About 3500 B.C., for instance, the Sumerians of the Middle East concocted their own technique of conserving records. Applying cylinder seals to inscribe signs and symbols in wet clay tablets, they subsequently baked their tangible results in the sun.[7] There are, in fact, legions of similar fascinating tales in the annals of written communication that embrace diverse forms of crude drawings of familiar objects or primitive alphabets created from unpretentious symbols or carved wood lettering that conveyed meaning among ancient peoples.[8]

All of this preceded Johann Gutenberg's successful attempt about 1450 to produce printing from movable type.[9] With the assistance of a well-heeled partner, Johann Fust (ca. 1400–1466), a fellow native of Mainz, Germany, Gutenberg (ca. 1398–1468) applied a mixture of lead and other metals to cast individual letters in reverse and high relief. After printing a few books with an adapted wine press, in 1456 Gutenberg embarked on reproducing the Bible. Unable to pay some loans he incurred to Fust, however, the innovator lost his shop in the following year. It was thus left to Fust to complete the initial printing of the Holy Scriptures. He did so in 1460, although Gutenberg's accomplishments haven't gone unnoticed in the chronicles of printing.

Sixteen years later, in 1476, William Caxton (ca. 1422–91), a native of Kent, England, having spent time observing printing in Belgium, France and Germany, imported the first printing press to English soil at Westminster in London. The popularity of printing itself continued to flourish. By 1490, every leading European municipality had acquired no less than one such press.[10]

The invention of the printing press not only made literature accessible to more people than any previous means, but it appreciably contributed to their edification as well.[11] It began with the fundamentals. Before the printing press was in extensive use, for example, only a handful of citizens could read and write. For the common man — until that transpired, at least — putting a news report on paper would have served no productive meaning. All that changed with the arrival of the printing press, however.[12]

Its introduction into the maturing influence of the English monarchy on society's cultural and commercial aspects offers an arresting study reported in a multiplicity of texts. We may be confident that the printed word ultimately contributed mightily to the progression of Great Britain as a global superpower in the centuries preceding the birth of a sovereign nation in the New World. Although England has no special claim as the habitat of the modern press, that country advanced beyond all other nations journalistically even so.[13]

Long before there was any sense of a newspaper, in reality the English were already exchanging gossip and information at annual fairs during the Middle Ages (1066–1485).[14] Not until 1621, however —145 years after William Caxton instigated printing in England in 1476 — did simplified models of present newspapers begin to be seen on the streets of

London. While supplying a need, the elementary news dispatches of a few pages in length and commonly known as *corantos* offered no reliability in timing, a basic facet of a true newspaper.

Some journalistic academicians, in fact, laid down criteria for a newspaper in the contemporary age.[15] It must be available regularly, on at least a daily or weekly schedule; it must appeal to a broad-interest readership as opposed to one that can be narrowly defined; and it must offer current information. If it doesn't meet those three points, then a publication presumably can't be considered an authentic newspaper. Once newspapers began to be issued in England, they proliferated. The history of these periodicals offers an absorbing pursuit for all who might be intrigued by how we got our modern newspapers.

> Against this backdrop, New England was the birthplace of the American newspaper, but it was not until 1704, or 84 years after the establishment of the first successful colony in that area [Pilgrims, 1620], that a publication meeting all the qualifications of a newspaper appeared....
>
> Massachusetts Bay colonists were concerned about the education of their children. Having enjoyed educational advantages themselves, they wanted to pass on the heritage to succeeding generations. In 1636, six years after the founding of the settlement [1630], they established Harvard College. The larger towns had "grammar schools," which prepared boys for Harvard. As part of this educational process, the authorities established the first press in the English colonies at Cambridge in 1638....
>
> It was the colonists' interest in education and cultural dissemination that made Boston famous as the intellectual capital. Here were all the ingredients for the development of a newspaper — high literacy, interest in community matters, self-government, prosperity, and cultural leadership....[16]

Great Britain's American colonies acquired their journalistic craft by copying the practices that had been witnessed in the Mother Country. English newspapers were widely circulated upon their arrival in American harbors, and articles reprinted from their pages pervaded early colonial newspapers. Upon those English models the earliest of the colonial newspapers were formulated, albeit not continually endorsed by the British royals and the governors that they appointed as their advocacy to Americans.

In 1690, Benjamin Harris (fl. 1673–1716) of Boston — that municipality was the largest town in the colonies — put to press what could be considered the first real newspaper of the New World.[17] His 7 × 11–inch folded sheet with dual columns, under the banner *Publick Occurrences, Both Forreign and Domestick*, while short-lived — a single edition was released on September 25, before it was shut down by the English overseers — was an attempt to report current events with immediacy.[18] Until then the colonists were dependent on news journals that were circulated in the Mother Country. Something was lacking in that formula, however: local matters got short shrift in the urbane European press. Harris determined to concentrate on home-based matters of import to his nearby readership, a foremost raison d'être for any general interest newspaper.

Following Harris's failure, nearly a decade-and-a-half was to pass before any flag-waving partisan would decide to proceed down that road again. Fortunately, a successor had better luck in 1704, setting a precedent that others were to imitate as an occupational pursuit.[19]

Eighteenth century news frequently had its origins in the oral and written reports of some privileged travelers who obligingly submitted them to hungry editors or possibly were coerced into sharing what they had observed or overheard. Although by contemporary criterion that comes across as extremely archaic and little more than slapdash, "correspondent" accounts on the news pages nevertheless exhibited a fundamental logic. Printers collected data from published cargo aboard ships as well as from crews. Mishaps at sea and sailing schedule glitches were often a curse of their newsgathering tactics, sometimes delaying the arrival (and release) of information from Europe by weeks or months. Not only did printers devour published journals on their arrival in American ports, they also pressed the captains of seaworthy vessels for their own recollections and eyewitness accounts of newsworthy actions that transpired across the ocean.

One of Benjamin Harris's successors, Henry Ingraham Blake, editor of the *New England Paladium*, is designated as "the father of modern reporting" for the newsgathering techniques he instituted.[20] Blake maintained a fondness for jumping into a boat and rowing out to meet whatever ships he found plying the waters to the Boston wharf. Upon hearing the latest, he raced back to his print shop to set type for news pages from the scribbled notes on his shirt cuffs and hands, as well as from memory. Rowboat reporting was to become commonplace among American news publishers in the years ahead.[21]

Late in the 18th century, meanwhile, horsepower supplemented sea power in assisting the scribes on their newsgathering missions. Post-riders covered dozens of miles, sometimes employing several changes of steeds in the process. At brief stopovers in an assortment of communities, the riders conferred with local printers (often the area's postmasters), gaining fresh fodder for the publications they represented.

The arrival of more and more newspapers in America, including many with greater degrees of permanency than these original harbingers of journalistic endeavors, are documented in extensive detail in many published volumes as well as on the Internet. The compelling histories of specific newspapers, some with durable and revered monikers, also reside on the shelves of myriad municipal repositories and in the personal libraries of many individual collectors. In reality, there is no dearth of substance about the newspaper industry and its objective of recording the daily events that have transpired in America as well as mentioning the people that made them happen.

American print journalism has not just done its job well but — to the modern era — exceptionally so. While there are newspapers that persist in upholding the high standards that have been a beacon to their decision making, objectivity and integrity in the past — and which show only occasional signs now of allowing their historic quality to slip — regrettably that paradigm is no longer universally upheld. In the contemporary age, after decades of offering their readership a comprehensive package of news, features, opinion and advertising, dailies and weeklies have become callously diluted from their fundamental conceptions.

New owners, often mega newspaper-holding corporations, have turned venerated publications with glorious track records in serving local communities into little more than figments of their former selves. By shrinking the number of pages, page size, contents, staffs, bureaus, and services, they've refocused the intent from a trustworthy information source to an enterprise with an overriding bent on earning profits by cutting corners.

The obsession with improving bottom lines has been at the expense of formerly valued readers and reputations. In tough economic times, hundreds of newspapers have folded or combined, particularly those with smaller circulations, evidence of their inability to cope in a frustrating economic squeeze. The traditions of forbear journalists with formidable records of perseverance have been cast aside for some acceptable, as well as unacceptable, reasons to the dismay of a constantly perturbed home audience.

In the mid–1960s, the author's superior at a publishing house insisted, "The time will come when we see the daily newspaper delivered on a screen, much like television is today."

His foresight has become reality in spades through copious diversified platforms. Will there be a place for a hard-copy newspaper at all in another generation or, at the most, two generations? America's news reportage continues to evolve, in both readable and verbal manifestations. Certainly none of the early U.S. postmaster-publishers could have begun to imagine where the occupational pursuits they followed could have transitioned in the modern age.

Journalism as a formal study was introduced in America by an ex-*Chicago Tribune* financial editor, Joseph French Johnson.[22] That pacesetter conducted an organized writing course at the University of Pennsylvania between the years 1893 and 1901. Frank W. Scott directed the country's initial four-year comprehensive journalism curriculum, meanwhile, at the University of Illinois, starting in 1904. Four years hence a school of journalism was established at the University of Missouri (1908) with Walter Williams as dean. Many other institutions of higher learning have since pursued these examples with their own training programs in writing, editing, and a plethora of added journalistic endeavors. Many of them eventually enlarged their concentrations in verbal communications, specializing in that field in particular after the electronic communications age was instituted.

After electricity was harnessed, printed matter like newspapers, pamphlets and books achieved much greater capacity and velocity than was feasible erstwhile. Mechanical power increased the ability of communicators to provide more substance at a far quicker pace. Furthermore, electricity paved the way for newer marvels. In the decades preceding, during and following the second Industrial Revolution (generally ascribed as the latter years of the 19th century and a handful of the earliest years of the 20th), the capabilities for narrowing the gaps in accessing the population was substantially reduced.[23]

A few inventions made reaching out to others much faster, easier, more desirable and practical. Among them were some rudimentary examples of the telegraph (1836), telephone (1876), loudspeaker (1877), microphone (1877), phonograph (1877), tape recorder (1886), wireless (1893), radio signals (1895), sound film (1923), electro mechanical television (1924), programmable computer (1936), and communications satellite (1962).[24] Set in 1876, Tom Stoppard's play *The Invention of Love*, based on the life of English classicist poet A. E. Housman (1839–1956), includes a line that superbly references this highly productive epoch: "Every age thinks it's the modern age, but this one really is."[25] Up to that moment in the history of mankind, could anybody argue with it?

In 1887, German physicist Heinrich Rudolf Hertz (1857–94) found the existence of unseen radio waves analogous to light waves that traveled at the speed of light.[26] Although Hertz failed to see the communications potential of the radio waves, other scientists did. While he and others performed many experiments, it fell to Italian engineer Guglielmo Marconi (1874–1937) in the following decade to successfully dispatch and receive radio-wave transmissions across an expanse of 1.5 miles.[27] When he couldn't get the Italian government to underwrite his creation, Marconi launched the Wireless Telegraph and Signal Company in 1897 to mass-produce it.

> Now came a small and momentous event. In 1898, through facilities provided by Marconi's newly founded wireless company, the *Dublin Daily Express* received minute-by-minute coverage of the Kingstown Regatta. This was wireless telegraphy — no sportscaster's voice was heard over the air. And the name for news heard over the air is broadcast journalism. Because of this success, the *New York Herald* the next year commissioned Marconi to provide wireless coverage of the America's Cup races. With these two yachting events at the close of the nineteenth century, news and radio were joined. Broadcast journalism, in dots and dashes, was born.[28]

Once Marconi sent a signal across the Atlantic in 1901 covering an expanse of 2,140 miles, the "wireless telegraph" (his name for the contraption, using Morse Code without any direct connection) assured Marconi of permanency for his contrivance.[29] Henceforth, wireless telegraphy was in use everywhere and was especially effective in transmitting distress calls from ships at sea.

Radio (another name for it) was on the way! Unlike some other experimenters of that period, Marconi didn't singularly bind his options for wireless telegraphy to military applications and ocean disasters. Instead he was convinced that it could just as easily carry music and speech for the purposes of conversation, information, and amusement.[30] Once the microphone became a widely used apparatus in 1912, it appeared to be a foregone conclusion that Marconi's ideas would come to fruition.

In the next chapter we will witness how applications in the 20th century in print reportage were broadened to audible modes. Then there would be increased options for delivering current events to sustain a nation that possessed an accustomed appetite for information. Keeping it satisfied had grown proportionately.

> In the United States, radio news began to prove that it had arrived as a significant journalistic force when the Japanese attacked Pearl Harbor on December 7, 1941—a Sunday. There were no evening papers on Sunday. From the first bulletin—interrupting a football game on the small Mutual radio network, right after the wires flashed the news at 2:22 P.M. EST—until Monday morning, the news was a radio exclusive.[31]
>
> The Second World War gave radio news what the Civil War had given newspapers: a taste of the medium's power to bring news home.[32]

Of radio's demonstrated abilities and liabilities in dispatching the news during the Second World War, a bystander contrasted print's facility for doing the same thing:

> Half an hour of radio news from Europe did not compare to the depth of coverage still available in the major newspapers of the day, but radio could carry events in real time and analyze them shortly after. Radio also could reach millions of people in rural America and in small towns where newspapers carried little or no foreign news.[33]

In the modern epoch, of course, so much more has been added to a growing inventory of communications tools, much of it in recent decades. An impressive array of devices for instant contact with others persists in rolling from the drawing boards to the manufacturing plants to the retail marketers. In each case the collaborators anticipate outperforming (or at the very least, matching) what has preceded their latest innovations. As a result there is unremitting improvement in speed and quality of contact as technical breakthroughs perpetually occur. A new gadget often appears with enhanced features over previous models, thereby making it attractive to commercial concerns and to a compulsive buying public with the necessary discretionary dollars on hand.

Radio was but one of a multitude of instruments that broadened our communications horizons in the 20th century, resulting in huge benefits to those relying on it. In its time, for no less than a quarter-century, the aural medium was at the top of its game. In those years it faithfully supplied the bulk of Americans with whatever knowledge they had — virtually as it occurred — beyond the confines of the communities in which its listeners resided. In so doing, radio news profoundly enlarged the scope and understanding of the nation's inhabitants.

As the first available wave of sustained mass information and entertainment that could be tapped by practically everybody at the same time, radio broadened sensibilities by delivering unreported snippets of news. With most people then residing in rural districts, radio became a lifeline to the world for learning what was transpiring elsewhere. While most in that audience possessed an innate inquisitiveness for "What's going on?" and had done so since the beginning of time, radio helped to gratify that passion with immediacy. Concurrently it urged recipients to listen for further particulars, enhancing their thirst for more and more news. In the process America as a country became better informed, formulated opinions and focused on conclusions far more than ever before in its brief history.

> In the United States, millions attended radio news reports, as they did such entertainment programs as *Amos 'n' Andy*. This was a national audience. America's citizenry could now be gathered around their radios, and America's chief executive regained a privilege most tribal chiefs had taken for granted: his voice could reach a significant portion of those he governed. War news, the country's news, his news, could be spread among them almost instantaneously. Another significant step had been taken toward unifying this widely scattered nation....
>
> Radio listeners were residents of an ethereal community, populated by familiar, if unreachable, presences whose voices were accessible anywhere in the nation.[34]

Our first glimmer of radio's as yet undiscovered potential is tied to a specific place and event that occurred in 1920. That episode — from radio's informational branch as opposed to the other side of the coin, amusement — was newsworthy. Not only did it inform us, the fact that it was reported at all made news then — and since.

Details to follow.

2

The Origins of Electronic Journalism

Radio news commenced with voices over the ether reading stories from news journals. Ham operators relied on newspapers merely to have something worthwhile to say.[1] Most invariably hoped that distant fellow hams might mail penny postcards acknowledging that their transmissions had been heard discernibly. "In the 1920s," confirmed one wag, "few stations hired reporters. They pirated their news from newspapers."[2] At that moment in time, there would have been only a minimal hint, if even that, that any antagonism between station owners and publishers might eventually emerge.

And now it seems almost humorous to us living in this day that people in the early 1920s were depicting that newfangled phenomena of what we label as *radio* with the charming metaphor "pulling voices from out of the air."[3] It was that, of course. But its potential — to be realized soon enough — proffered a whole lot more.

From its very start, radio and news demonstrated an affinity for one another, a nurtured stance that was to increase into a pretty tight fit. On a date considered by legions of vintage radio aficionados as the birth of commercial broadcasting as we know it, November 2, 1920, Pittsburgh's KDKA carried the results of an event with national implications and beyond.[4] As they became available that evening, returns from the Warren G. Harding–James M. Cox election for U.S. president were dispatched beyond their original confines over KDKA.[5]

Only a short time before, KDKA had materialized out of experimental station 8XK that had been created and operated by Westinghouse engineer Dr. Frank Conrad.[6] During the United States' involvement in the Great War (the First World War), 1917–19, Conrad designed broadcasting equipment for the U.S. Navy, which operated 20 wireless stations as early as 1904.[7] He got a definite upgrading on postwar broadcasting as an explicit result of his naval liaison. Now his test model was the first to commercially beam messages of a current event to those living within a brief geographical range and equipped with receivers.[8]

For that occasion, a restricted telephone line that was added to the premises connected the newsroom of *The Pittsburgh Post* with a radio shack situated on the roof of Westinghouse Building K. William Thomas activated the transmitter while 24-year-old Westinghouse publicist Leo Henry Rosenberg read the returns.[9] At the outset, supplying an entire evening with factual material related to a national election for president was intimidating to those behind the infiltration in early broadcasting. Concerned even then about the possibility of dead air time, the planners supplied a hand-cranked Victrola and a stack of phonograph records on site to be able to fill with music whatever anticipated gaps occurred. In a letter penned April 26, 1976, Rosenberg offered his recollections from that evening.[10]

> As the returns came in to the *Post*, they were telephoned to the station and recorded by R. S. McClelland and handed to me for reading into the microphone. The private telephone line was constantly monitored by John Frazier, manager of the telephone department of Westinghouse.... Periodically, I would say, "If you are hearing this radio broadcast, please send a postcard to L. H. Rosenberg, Publicity Department, Westinghouse Electric and Manufacturing Company, East Pittsburgh, Pennsylvania." Hundreds of cards were received from all over the United States and some foreign countries, even New Zealand. This was remarkable for a 100-watt station. It was due, we were told, to the bouncing effect of the atmospheric waves.

Perhaps the real news on that night was that KDKA's accomplishment portended the briefest of dimensions in which news was to become a leading source of broadcast programming fodder.[11] Within 10 months, for instance, on a recurring basis KDKA was airing bulletins directly from the newsroom of the *Post*. Not only that, a quickly developing trend in electronic journalism was to have an acute hold on all Americans living thereafter. A point not to be missed from the perspective of *this* text, of course, is that — from its most humble beginnings — radio and news were inextricably linked. The two have been so ever since.

That 1920 broadcast over KDKA was also a catalyst for many others who were thinking along similar lines. By the end of 1922, for instance — hardly more than 25 months after that historic ethereal breakthrough — 576 commercial radio stations were operating in the United States or roughly 23 new ones per month. The secretary of commerce issued licenses to all who applied in those days; true regulation of broadcasting began with the Radio Act of 1927 in this nation. In the meantime, obviously convinced that radio was here to stay, Americans bought 100,000 radios in 1922.[12] It was for them clearly the wave (length) of the future.

There were many other early incidents in informing the masses over the ether following the accepted "beginning of radio" in Pittsburgh that a multitude of scholars routinely cite.[13] In July 1921, for instance, another event with mass appeal, albeit one from the sports world, reached the receptive ears of hordes of listeners when "the fight of the century" was staged.[14] Beyond the 90,000 spectators on site focused on a tiny boxing ring in Jersey City, New Jersey, that evening, thousands more tuned in to hear the action as reigning heavyweight prizefighter Jack Dempsey took on the obvious crowd favorite and French war hero Georges Carpentier.

For that occasion, broadcaster J. Andrew White (1899–1966) became what is speculated now as history's initial sportscaster. By relaying his eyewitness account via landline telephone wires, his comments were dispatched to a mammoth radio transmitter in Hoboken, New Jersey. That high-perch apparatus radiated White's commentary from his makeshift "microphone" to a waiting world; or at least to that part fortunate enough to pick up the signal. Actually, more than 300,000 additional fans tuned in at specially equipped "radio halls" in 61 cities scattered about the outlying region as an insuperable Dempsey retained his title by knocking out his opponent in the fourth round.[15] *Wireless Age* concluded: "Instantly, through the ears of an expectant public, a world event had been 'pictured' in all its thrilling details.... A daring idea had become a fact."

The allure of radio was the upshot of a series of celebrated scientific advancements that had occurred during the previous half-century. Most notable was native Scottish inventor

Alexander Graham Bell's (1847–1922) concept that in 1876 furnished the telephone. It was followed in the 1890s by Italian initiator Guglielmo Marconi's (1874–1937) legendary testing of the wireless.[16] What both of the 1920s events — the Harding-Cox election and the Dempsey-Carpentier prizefight — demonstrated to the individuals pursuing their early experiments in radio was that their pastime (this novel, fairly recent means of communication) had attracted an audience of considerable and passionate proportions.[17]

In truth, radio's popularity with a generation of proletarian hobbyists cannot be underestimated. In the main, the crowd was comprised of two distinct clusters: (1) the amateur aficionados who had built their own receivers and transmitters to become wireless hams, and (2) the crystal set owners who had the capability of picking up broadcasts on their headphones.[18]

The apparatuses they employed in *surfing the airwaves* (one of the earliest applications of that expression) varied. The devices were usually completely homemade or resultant out of a kit that early manufacturers supplied along with a simple instruction guide. Either way, the final assembly of multiple parts of early radios was generally left to the ultimate user of same. Thus, it was commonplace in those days to encounter pieces of odd-looking equipment strewn over living-room floors and on kitchen tables at someone's home before the gadgets were fashioned into their intended functional motif.

A few months after "the fight of the century," in April 1922, the doyen of news broadcasters, Hans von Kaltenborn (1878–1965), launched his vocation as a radio personality over New York's WEAF.[19] Commentaries made Kaltenborn an enveloping authority of the airwaves during an impressive career that extended 33 years. Five months after he went on the air — in September 1922 — tiny Norfolk, Nebraska's WJAG may have been the very first station to inaugurate a *daily* newscast.[20] Not long afterward, Newark's WJZ went WJAG one better. In February 1923, WJZ crafted the *daily quarter-hour* news summary. Soon Portland, Oregon's KOIN was billing its newscast as "The Newspaper of the Air" (1925). And before the decade ended, Manitowoc, Wisconsin's WOMT was airing news "every hour on the hour."

It's not all that difficult to see a pattern emerging here. Indeed wasn't all of this laying the groundwork for everything that was to follow? Even though formulas that would be practiced for generations were being created, "the twenties were the 'sandbox' years," an academic suggested. Radio definitely hadn't grown up. "It was fun, and so was most of the news, befitting a prosperous time when America was at peace and many of its people were at play."[21]

Another radio historiographer insists that broadcast journalism was "the most important development in twentieth-century reporting."[22] It affected not only listener opinion and a broad spectrum of data digested by the public, that wag maintained, but also "the direction of governmental policy and the evolution of the nation." In time, newspapers would be superseded by radio as the country's primary source of current events data. Like health care in the contemporary age, radio offered an inroad to economic development. "For most industries," observed an author and editor, "the '30s were a cruel decade. But broadcasting thrived."[23] And newsgathering and reporting was among its most admired facets.

During those early years no unanimous blueprint existed for establishing precisely how a newsroom fit into an average station's organization. Conversely, it was "fairly common and certainly logical and desirable" for the news department to report directly to top management although this plan wasn't practiced universally.[24] Many times a program director was also a station's news chief. News simply didn't furnish enough of the broadcasting schedule to merit what might have been viewed as a disproportionate amount of management's consideration. The actual duty of delivering the news, depending upon a station's size, was often dispersed to various available members of the interlocutory staff.

> Announcers had no authority to edit copy. They read on the air what was given them to read. When they presumed to revise a newscast without consulting someone in the newsroom, they were reprimanded. In some instances, those who persisted in taking liberties were fired. On the other hand, writers appreciated the announcer who, while rehearsing a script, brought mistakes to their attention.
> There was an informality in the newsroom which disappeared as staffs grew larger, and salaries and competition for position increased.[25]

All of the talk about news programming developments in radio's formative years to the contrary notwithstanding, the current events information genre ran a distant third to comedy, drama, and musical features — at least, on the transcontinental chains. By the early 1930s, some observers were noting that radio news was almost oblivious to the discerning ear of its most enthusiastic adherents. One wag's assessment was typical:

> With rare exceptions — such as *The March of Time*, the work of *Time* magazine — there was a blackout on current problems. The leading network, NBC-red, had not a single daily news series. NBC-blue had only Lowell Thomas. CBS had Boake Carter and (scarcely a newscast) Edwin C. Hill in *The Human Side of the News*, with occasional non-sponsored comments from H. V. Kaltenborn and others, largely in fringe hours. Most sponsors did not want news programming; those that did were inclined to expect veto rights over it.[26]

It was widely reported in the advertising trade that a leading soft drink manufacturer shunned all opportunities to underwrite news broadcasts during radio's golden age. A marketing spokesman with the firm affirmed, "We want to be known for happy programs, and much of the time the news simply isn't." Vaudeville veterans like Eddie Cantor, Joe Penner, Ed Wynn, George Burns and Gracie Allen, Al Jolson, Phil Baker and Jack Benny commanded the biggest audiences in Radioland then. Lowell Thomas and Boake Carter were barely afterthoughts.

The newsrooms of a couple of nationwide broadcasting chains were, in the meantime, instituted in ways that scarcely could be classified as *news functions* today. During the early years of transcontinental operations, starting about 1930, perhaps those efforts could more appropriately have been termed something else. They were, after all, almost altogether unrelated to a modern interpretation of newsgathering and transmission. At both Columbia and NBC, what may have purportedly been branded for a little while as a news operation wasn't really much more than a publicity mill for its respective network(s).

An eyewitness who was on the scene at the time recounted some of what occurred during those nascent days of Columbia's "News Department," a misnomer for the service it actually provided. In 1930, Louisville native Edward A. Klauber (1887–1954), an ex-copy editor of *The New York World* (1912) and reportorial alumnus of *The New York Times* (1916–28) — who rose to night city editor at the latter (1927) — was hired by CBS to run the outfit's fledgling news service.[27] He also had been briefly linked with the pioneering PR man Edward L. Bernays in 1929. Klauber left the news business for public relations in the previous year, joining the Lenman and Mitchell ad agency in New York.

More than one media observer characterized Klauber as a model of inflexible perfectionism: stiff, formal, anti-social — in a word *distant*, difficult to get close to, one who perpetually played by the rules and upheld the standards.[28] Not all assessors viewed his no-nonsense stances as detrimental to the health of the organization nevertheless. William S. Paley, Columbia president, was among them. He was unequivocally impressed with his new hire's impeccable credentials.

> Ed Klauber had been night city editor of *The New York Times*. For Paley that was class. The *Times* was the Cadillac of newspapers, just as Paley wanted CBS News to be the finest in radio. When the day came that some critic called us "*The New York Times* of the Air," Paley's dream had come true.
>
> Klauber was disciplined in the best *Times* tradition, which he brought into CBS. He hated tabloids and the yellow press, which proliferated in those days.[29] He laid down basic *New York Times* standards for CBS News: accuracy, honesty, objectivity, coolness, no dramatics, no show biz of any kind. Klauber was a crusty fellow, a curmudgeon and an editor who missed nothing. Even such outstanding men as William Shirer and Ed Murrow winced under his criticism.... Both Murrow and Shirer, not yet the stars they were to become, knew they were lucky to work under so tough and professional an editor.[30]

Another CBS historiographer declared: "Klauber set a tone, created an atmosphere in which an Ed Murrow and many others could work and flourish. By impressing upon Bill Paley the importance of covering the news aggressively and conscientiously, Klauber was responsible for giving an air of seriousness to radio news that it otherwise would not have had."[31]

Klauber stayed put at CBS to March 1942, when he was eased out.[32] Quite early he emerged as CBS's second in command, gaining the title of executive vice president.[33] Not only did he oversee phenomenal growth of the news operation, he was active in facilitating the chain's incredibly swift expansion overall. As a result CBS was repositioned from the also-ran broadcasting enterprise that it had been in radio's earliest years to a viable competitor to the stronger NBC, a challenger admired by audiences, advertisers, artists, and — one suspects — its adversaries as well.

In 1932, John George "Jap" Gude (1902–98) labored in the same CBS news trenches alongside Herbert B. Glover (1898-?), the web's earliest director of special events, and Paul Welrose White, Jr. (1902–55).[34] At different times White was variously designated news editor and director of publicity.[35] At miscellaneous junctures, Gude was an assistant to both Glover and White.[36] Years hence he delineated their concentration of duties:

> In those days there was no [authentic] news department at NBC or CBS ... it was almost all "special events" — speeches, dedications, parades [that we covered on the air]. We did only snippets of news, which came in on the old-fashioned tickers that gave you the stock market quotations. The news was on this paper ribbon, the kind used in ticker tape parades, and you'd paste it up on a sheet of paper for the announcer to read. Pretty soon we got the teletypes, but there wasn't any news department as you know it today, not until Paul White changed it.[37]

A CBS biographer credited Klauber and White — both of whom arrived at the network in 1930 — as "the founding fathers of broadcast journalism."[38] Whether or not that's precise, by any gauge the pair wasn't very far from that sacrosanct apogee.

> At the time, radio news had no identity, no guidelines to define it, and if its basic style had been molded by other men, with other values, it might well have taken its cue from the lurid sensationalism of the tabloids and the worst excesses of the Hearst press. The fact that it did not was largely because of Klauber and White, who brought to radio the best traditions of print journalism and imposed those standards on the newscasters they hired to work for CBS. Under their aegis, the early giants of newscasting flourished — such men as H. V. Kaltenborn, Elmer Davis, Robert Trout, and John Daly, all of whom were part of the Klauber-White team at CBS in the years leading up to World War II. Moreover, the standards established by Klauber and

White made it possible, or at least easier, for the [Edward R.] Murrow group to emerge in precisely the way it did. For while Murrow and his cohorts deserve credit for bringing scope and innovation to radio journalism, they were building on what was already, by then, the start of a worthy tradition....

Paul White was to Klauber what a good quarterback is to a reticent coach: the holler guy, the tactician, the field general with whom the troops more readily identify. A fast-talking, hard-drinking man with a bulldog face, White was yet another journalist who came to CBS from the lean-and-hungry world of the United Press. He brought the competitive spirit of wire-service reporting to the network, and that nicely complemented Klauber's more scholarly or *Times*ian approach.... And in sharp contrast to Klauber, he was an easy mixer, a backslapper who richly enjoyed the camaraderie of his fellow journalists. But he loathed playing the company game, kowtowing to superiors, and that was one of the reasons why White — for all his ability — eventually fell out of favor at CBS.[39]

Born at Pittsburg, Kansas, in a brief but fast-paced life White served on newspaper staffs in Pittsburg and Salina, Kansas; Kansas City, Missouri; and New York (*The New York Evening Bulletin* and *Sunday World*); toured Europe with the Columbia University debate team, an institution awarding him baccalaureate and master's degrees (1923, 1924); married three times; fathered two daughters; moved successively from wire service to radio (1930), writing and teaching journalism at his alma mater (1946), newspaper executive (1948), and local radio-TV news manager (1950). White included stints at *The San Diego Journal* and KFMB in that city. Along the way he picked up a George Foster Peabody Award for news innovations (1945) and penned *News on the Air* (1947), a scholarly text that journalism schools applied for years.[40]

"Most of us had only read about Klauber and White," Roger Mudd confirmed in his memoir more than three-quarters of a century after their arrival at CBS. Yet it was obvious even to the protégés of his newscaster era that that pair had set a high bar for all time. "CBS News was driven by a simple dictum — that excellence produced excellence," insisted Mudd. The implication was clear, that "the excellence went all the way back to the 1930s."[41] It had begun with Klauber and White; Mudd and his colleagues were practitioners in an enduring and venerable tradition.

Returning to the microphones, the first daily network newscaster was Floyd Gibbons (1887–1939). He was an impulsively spontaneous correspondent who lost an eye while overseas in the First World War.[42] Born in the nation's capital, Gibbons was a veteran news journalist by the time he reached radio. With stints on dailies in Minneapolis, Milwaukee and Chicago, he had also linked up with dual global wire services. Thus, well groomed in reportorial skills when a sedate *Literary Digest* picked him for its news spokesman, Gibbons' ethereal opus launched on February 24, 1930. It was heard six nights weekly over NBC Blue, running a quarter-hour at 6:45 P.M. Eastern Time.[43] He was the first daily nationwide newscaster, somewhat astoundingly "a distinction that went unnoticed at the time."[44]

Gibbons' broadcasts were characterized by his reading the news at breakneck speed, once clocked at 217 words per minute or 3.6 words per second. (Try it and see, with expression and sans mistakes.) "Speed reading" and the inevitable patch over his left eye became signifying symbols of the inaugural national daily radio reporter in varied aural and publicity photo/interview/personal appearance venues. One of several radio historiographers who supplied colorful minutiae of his life labeled Gibbons "a swashbuckling journalist":

> He was the very picture of a stereotypical war correspondent. Flamboyant, often drunk, he wore a patch over the eye that had been shot out as he covered a World War I battle. During his exciting career as a war correspondent he rode with Pancho Villa across the Mexican border

and was aboard a ship torpedoed by a German submarine in the mid–Atlantic. In spite of his death-defying experiences, he proved to be overly brash as far as CBS and the sponsors were concerned. In 1930 he was permanently replaced by a worldly commentator of a different sort....[45]

Meanwhile, the public's reaction to Gibbons' dip into emerging waters had not gone unnoticed by competing broadcaster CBS. Without a rescue, an imperiled predecessor chain that first became Columbia and ultimately was commonly renowned as CBS appeared destined for extinction amid financial woes that plagued its ephemeral heritage.[46] By contrast, rival NBC, with two promising nationwide webs under its aegis (Red and Blue), had the good fortune of a safety net — specifically, the deep pockets of the Radio Corporation of America.[47] RCA was not only willing to take risks with its chains but was able to pull them out of the fire should either fall into dire circumstances. Such wasn't the case at CBS.

Let us digress for a few moments to proffer some details about those network launches, including some of their broad operating strategies and achievements. Supplying at least a few of the blanks in the sweeping panorama of broadcasting will help impart an understanding of the webs' actions as they deliberately turned their focus to endeavors of news, information and public affairs.

In 1928, an ostentatious young playboy, the entrepreneurial William S. Paley (1901–90), bought the floundering forerunning operation that segued into CBS. Ultimately to become "the single most important person in the history of broadcasting," according to a biographer, he was just 26 at the time and heir to a cigar-manufacturing fortune.[48] He became "a wizard in an age of superachievers," another observer assessed, citing Henry Ford in autos, David Sarnoff in communications equipment, and Louis B. Mayer, Adolph Zuker, and Samuel Goldwyn in films. The CBS owner soon inked a pecuniary deal with Paramount Studios that instantly boosted his fledgling chain's value from $1 million to $10 million: "Not even Ford, Mayer, or Goldwyn could top Paley's achievement."[49] The chronicler persisted: "He was the right man, at the right time, in the right place, at the birth of an industry. He could grow with it, make all the rules, control it with his wealth and prestige. That, plus his native talents and qualities, is what made him one of a kind. There will never again be the same mix of talent and circumstance that makes giants."[50]

Paley eventually became a formidable and persistent antagonist to NBC, however, a thorn in the side of a most remarkably tenacious opponent. His doggedness may have vastly improved the quality of programming of those rival operations as each one sought to deliver their goods to audiences with high expectations. In so doing, Paley led CBS to nip at the heels of a more popular, better financed, firmly entrenched NBC before overtaking that foe at last as radio's most accomplished broadcaster.

In the meantime, and almost from their start, an urbane, erudite, serious-sided capitalist, David Sarnoff (1891–1971), guided the dual webs of NBC. A member of RCA's lower echelon executive roster in 1919, Sarnoff unwaveringly rose to the corporate presidency by 1930, and to chairman of the board in 1947. Even after he was kicked upstairs it was clear

Opposite: A playboy of the first rank, William S. Paley nevertheless became profoundly serious in maneuvering the ship of CBS through murky waters. He turned what initially he had said would be a brief tenure in control to a lifetime passion, from 1928 to his death in 1990. Along the way Paley channeled a fledgling, also-ran broadcasting unit into a formidable player that ultimately superseded its staunchest rival. The visionary Paley achieved his destiny by identifying and capitalizing on unfilled opportunities such as building a pervasive news prominence that was seldom threatened by any competing chain during the early decades.

to anybody closely watching, both inside and outside the RCA fraternity, that nothing of any consequence transpired at NBC without Sarnoff's sanction. Those networks were his babies and he jealously guarded them across a protracted tenure with the parent firm.

Although Sarnoff and Paley, both Jews, exhibited an abiding respect for one another in a practical sense (and could be found working jointly on issues like limiting further intrusion by federal regulators into their trade), the two men unabashedly coveted the same prize: winning and retaining first place for their respective broadcasting units. Along with that supreme aspiration went not only a momentous financial and publicly perceived increase

to the multimillion-dollar corporate enterprises they fronted but profuse stroking of their own egos as well. At times, the latter might have been equally indispensable to the former. Both tycoons fought tenaciously, relentlessly, and ruthlessly on occasions to achieve the twin trophies. Sometimes they resorted to problematical, devious scheming to gain one-upmanship on the other. The adversarial relationship they exhibited for all of their active careers was never in doubt to their working associates and to media practitioners observing on the sidelines.

While Paley's unbridled ambition to overtake NBC wasn't all that long in surfacing, a protracted period passed nevertheless before his team's collective efforts realized the fait accompli.[51] More than two decades, in fact, went by. In the late 1940s, he instituted some sophisticated surreptitious maneuvers that resulted in several star-studded artists defecting from their long-held perches at NBC and flying the coop to CBS.[52] There those celebrities joined an entrenched roster of primetime celebrities already in residence, markedly raising listeners' partiality to CBS's favor.[53]

Yet there was still more to this coup d'état. Paley's persuasive ploys had the effect of not only thrusting CBS into unequivocal dominance of aural broadcasting — a summit the network subjugated for virtually the remainder of radio's golden age — it concurrently, and unexpectedly, equipped CBS with a profusion of first-rate talent just as television was coming into vogue. CBS was by this means poised to take command of the newer medium from its inception, an unforeseen byproduct of the Paley raids on NBC (their swiftness referred to as "Paley's Comet" by insiders). Suddenly, *Amos 'n' Andy*, Jack Benny, Edgar Bergen, George Burns and Gracie Allen, Red Skelton, and a few more iconic entertainers were on CBS.[54] As a result, that web advantageously capitalized on its unexpected good fortune in Videoland for two decades, for a time outdistancing its competition in not just one but *two* mediums.

On its way to that hard-fought apex, CBS reached yet another prestigious plateau much sooner, one demonstrating express links to the investigative impetus that is the thrust of this probe. Paley was as much a sharp intellect as his chief rival at NBC. Quite early into his foray into broadcasting, the CBS owner-chairman deftly recognized the need for a first class news operation. While establishing it wouldn't produce the notoriety that the talent raids on his opposition generated years afterward, creating an unparalleled news operation could be crucial in a quest to becoming the ubiquitous, universal, all-encompassing broadcaster Paley envisioned for his enterprise.

By 1930, therefore, he set about attracting a staff of first-rate news journalists that exhibited worthy track records in print and wire operations. While the accolades for developing a reliable, fair, comprehensive newsgathering force wouldn't be heard for some time, Paley was nevertheless laying the groundwork for what followed.

> During the half decade that the CBS news organization was developed, spreading its influence throughout the industry, radio news style — both in bulletins and analyses — underwent a transformation.... At first radio news echoed written journalism. An opening sentence usually gulped down the full story, in curiously inverted sequence. The style hung on in wire-service bulletins used on many stations:
>
> AT A BRITISH PORT— *Bringing a welcome cargo of more than 4,000,000 eggs, 120,000 pounds of cheese, and 1000 tons of flour, the first food ship to ferry across the Atlantic under the terms of the lease-lend act has arrived here.*
>
> Radio had learned to handle it thus:
>
> *The first lease-lend food ship from America has reached a British port. The ship carried four million eggs, 120 thousand pounds of cheese, and 1000 tons of flour.*[55]

Testing of wireless transmission in the 1890s by Italian experimenter Guglielmo Marconi (at right) was an omen of radio's future. In 1933, Marconi stood beside David Sarnoff, who — in 1930 — was named head of NBC's parent firm, RCA. Both men commonly appeared with canes. While Sarnoff was accountable for an enveloping industry in which broadcasting was but a small part, he never took his eye off NBC, warily dissecting its moves like playing a game of chess. His strategies kept the network at the forefront of transcontinental radio operations through the 1940s, and he was also a pioneer in TV's development.

Meanwhile, over at NBC Blue, pioneering reporter Floyd Gibbons was plugging away at his daily offering on behalf of *Literary Digest*.

> Gibbons presented the news in a folksy, rough manner — the style of the school of Chicago journalism — booming out his "Hello, Everybody," and launching into a series of vivid descriptions. In late 1930, when he was earning $10,000 per week, an enormous salary for those Depression-era days, he alienated his sponsors with his brusque manner. At that moment William S. Paley decided that CBS should try to convince *Literary Digest* publisher R. J. Cuddihy to switch sponsorship to his network, using another announcer. He had in mind Lowell Thomas, a veteran newsperson whose main claim to fame was his exclusive story of the Arabian campaign in World War I, found in his best-selling book, *With Lawrence in Arabia*.
>
> A test broadcast was arranged, during which Thomas read the news on CBS ahead of Gibbons' NBC show. Cuddihy listened to both broadcasts. He decided to let Gibbons go and hired Thomas, who made his first broadcast September 29, 1930.[56]

From the very outset, Paley meant for his network to earn a reputation as first in news. One of his durable journalistic minions painted this picture:

> Paley learned early on that a major newsbreak, well-handled, would bring him more kudos than the best entertainment show. He used to tell us in later years: "I dine out on CBS News." After giving [later news VP Ed] Murrow his "open budget" and seeing how much it brought back, Paley never worried about the budgets of the News Division. He never insisted, as executives do today, that the news department earn money for the corporation or be severely cut if it loses.[57]

The CBS owner took action to give radio a voice that was consequentially heard throughout America for half a century — Thomas (1892–1981). Born at Woodington, Ohio, the reporter eventually achieved prominence in myriad realms including as author, commentator, entrepreneur, freelance writer, lecturer, movie newsreel narrator, and newscaster. Debuting nationally over NBC in 1929 with *Headline Hunters*, Thomas was subsequently engaged for a daily 6:45 P.M. quarter-hour news spot. For six months, *Lowell Thomas and the News* was carried by NBC in the nation's eastern region and by CBS in its western zone.

Although Cuddihy shifted Thomas to NBC exclusively the following year, Paley had gotten to sample a taste of the good life, savored it, and decided to go for more. He reacquired Thomas in 1947 and kept him satisfied until the newsman hung it up a final time on May 14, 1976. By then Thomas had long been the last of a dying breed of nightly newscasters dating back to transcontinental radio's embryonic age. "Good evening, everybody" at the start and "So long until tomorrow" at the conclusion were enduring trademarks readily recognized and frequently mimicked by legions of loyal listeners.[58]

While NBC's initial attempts in news, information, and public affairs could be depicted as anything but dynamic, by the early 1930s, the web was also creating the underpinnings for a newsgathering organization that would finally extend around the globe. Although small at its inception, the efforts at last delivered gratifying results. "Because of its leading position, NBC probably had less incentive than CBS toward reckless adventure," proclaimed one pundit. All of this spoke volumes about the two men at the top of the two radio organizations and their perception of newscasting as an element of programming.

> The presence of Ed Klauber in the newsroom and a Lowell Thomas at the mike made it clear that Bill Paley was paying attention to news. Much more so than NBC's David Sarnoff, who had little interest in broadcast journalism; he preferred concentrating on cultural programs. Paley thought differently. He sensed early on that putting his resources behind the news operation would help put CBS on the map. After all, NBC had enticed the major entertainment stars

even before CBS had gotten under way. Paley needed a field to make his own niche, and news provided that. And within the news field, the area of greatest prestige, Paley sensed, lay in overseas news broadcasting.[59]

The overseas emphasis would join the CBS portfolio soon enough and play the starring role between the late 1930s and the mid-1940s.

In the meantime, NBC's early pursuit into the journalistic sphere was lodged in one man, Abraham A. Schechter, Jr. (1907–89). Of Russian Jewish descent, the Rhode Island trailblazer became news director of NBC-TV in the early 1950s, and executive producer of the *Today* show, both firsts.[60] He left NBC in 1942 for a stint with Douglas MacArthur in the Second World War as the general's radio and press communications director. Schechter followed it with a vice presidency at Mutual Radio, essentially performing the task he had earlier at NBC. Much earlier — having reported for *The Providence Journal* and *The New York World* and having been a New York editor with Associated Press — Schechter, then 24, joined NBC. Hired in 1932 as director of news and special events, he remained active in radio until called to wartime duty two decades afterward.[61]

> While churning out publicity for the Red and Blue chains in 1932, he evolved into a one-man corporate news division. He occupied space in a joint carpentry shop-storage room at 711 Fifth Avenue, actually a minuscule broom closet ventilated only by an airshaft.... "Each evening Schechter would pick wood shavings from his hair and head home to listen to Lowell Thomas...," a media historiographer noted.
>
> In his strategic post, Schechter revealed just what an individual possessing a telephone — his lifeline to the world — could achieve. For a decade, he gathered news tips supplied by publicity agents working for NBC affiliates.... Prompted by those bits ... [and] what he read in the newspapers, he placed phone calls everywhere seeking follow-up details. Almost anybody, he discovered, accepted a telephone call

From September 29, 1930, through May 14, 1976, Lowell Thomas resided in one time period at 6:45 P.M. Eastern, airing singly on a trio of networks: NBC Blue, NBC, and CBS. Did any other broadcaster possess such a commanding hold on a single weeknight quarter-hour that enduringly? As millions of families gathered around their dinner tables, Thomas dispatched the day's headlines. The scholarly globetrotting journalist was well versed in a background of diverse topics. His beckoning "Good evening everybody" and parting "So long until tomorrow" were familiar in U.S. households among multiple generations.

"from NBC." Many times his efforts paid off.... Becoming the darling of the press agents, he rewarded tipsters with tickets to Rudy Vallee broadcasts.... He fed enough material to Lowell Thomas ... to fill a quarter-hour each evening while saving a few choice morsels for the gossip-mongering Walter Winchell on Sunday nights....

The one-man ... operation Schechter mustered established NBC as a serious player on new turf, ultimately leading to a global newsgathering team that included wizards of electronic journalism like Morgan Beatty, Pauline Frederick, H. V. Kaltenborn, ... Herbert Kaplow, Irving R. Levine, Merrill Mueller and more.[62]

A radio pundit affirmed: "It is no accident that most of the pictures taken of Schechter at the time catch him with a phone to his ear: he was the whole NBC news staff, and his telephone was his ticket around the world."[63] To augment those telephone pursuits Schechter received several foreign newspapers daily by air. He relied heavily on *The London Express* for data. Dubbing himself a charter member of "The Scissors-and-Pastepot Press Association," Schechter cut, pasted, rewrote and handed Thomas a script nightly bearing the impression of originality plus some intermittent scoops. The scoops (absurdity of absurdities) were then bootlegged by the Associated Press, running in U.S. newspapers coast-to-coast a day or two later.

For some years, nevertheless, CBS would be considered the paramount broadcast news operation in the country, the one against which all the others were measured. "NBC tiptoed in," noted one scholar, while "CBS leaped headlong."[64] In September 1933, CBS formed its own Columbia News Service, netting news bureaus in New York, Los Angeles, Chicago and Washington, D.C. At the same time, the web amassed some 800 reporters and stringers — the initial phase of a comprehensive worldwide news organization of the future — placing its correspondents in every American city with at least 20,000 denizens in addition to copious foreign capitals.[65] CBS was demonstrating to the newspapers and wire services that it had both the capability and resolve to successfully override those sources in its news-gathering efforts as electronic journalism continued to expand.

> There can be no doubt that during World War II CBS had built a reputation as a superlative, impregnable news organization. Reporting from the foxholes and front lines wherever a battle raged, the network gained respect from many millions of listeners dutifully waiting by their radios at home for an accurate assessment of what was happening abroad. They got it daily, and CBS's reputation soared. So impeccable was it, in fact, that key U.S. government officials — including a number in the White House, the Central Intelligence Agency and the Pentagon's Joint Chiefs of Staff— began their workday with transcripts of the morning CBS *World News Roundup*. The truth was, nobody came even close to achieving that kind of status.[66]

"We all felt that we worked for the best broadcast news organization in the world, that there was nobody who could touch us," declared CBS newsman Robert Pierpoint (1925–2011). "When CBS was really riding high in news, it wasn't because of ratings. It was because of the reputation of the Murrow Boys, because of the Murrow legacy," he affirmed.[67] Pierpoint wasn't a member of the celebrated confederation of newsmen hired by CBS reporter Edward R. Murrow (1908–65), the one that usually bore Murrow's taxonomy, incidentally.

Nor was another colleague, David Schoenbrun (1915–88), also outside that Murrow inner circle, yet who attested further: "For a few brief years, the Murrow team was nonpareil. There was CBS and then the others.... While it lasted it was dazzling."[68] On another occasion, Schoenbrun waxed eloquently as he expounded further along those same lines:[69]

> Almost from the start of network news in the thirties, CBS News had been the leader, the Cadillac of news. At one point in the forties and fifties, our Murrow team, the "Murrow boys," were not only number one, we were in a class by ourselves. It was CBS News, then the others....

> CBS News was preeminent for so many ... years of network broadcasting on radio and then television that, despite occasional successes of its rivals, it kept its crown.... Young reporters coming up in local stations ... dreamed ... of getting called by CBS News. If they were talented ... and lucky enough to get calls from more than one network, it was CBS News they chose ... sometimes at lower salaries. That is one of the most valuable dividends of being preeminent — you ... recruit the best.

A third broadcast journalist, Bob Edwards (1947-) — of more recent stock — called Murrow "the patron saint of my profession," and further classified him as "the quintessential broadcast journalist."[70]

There was another CBS news vet, Roger Mudd (1928-) — who left a CBS Television perch to pursue his fortune at NBC after being jilted in rivalry to capture the anchor chair vacated by Walter Cronkite (it was awarded to Dan Rather) — and still had a tough time letting go. He recalls what occurred after he decided to make a hasty retreat:[71]

> In 1986, I left NBC to join the *MacNeil/Lehrer NewsHour* on PBS for five happy and rewarding years. What followed that were ten years as the documentary host at the History Channel....
>
> But never was there a doubt during those years about where my heart lay. It lay with the Washington bureau of CBS News....
>
> It was a rare combination of principled leadership at the top; talented and honest journalists; and dedicated and skilled producers, editors, photographers, and couriers.... We felt unique to have been a part of it.... We had no doubts about how good we were; we had no doubts about our values; we had no doubts that our mission was to cover the news without flattering or tricking the viewer. Most of us thought ourselves chosen. It was [as] if we had been lifted up by a journalistic deity and dropped down in the middle of the Washington bureau to serve our country by doing God's work.
>
> Even during the six years I spent at NBC, trying my best to beat CBS, there was always a little hitch, perhaps a slight choke, in saying, "I'm Roger Mudd, NBC News, Washington."
>
> I had never truly ceased being a CBS man.
>
> It was, indeed, the place to be.

Perhaps a disproportionate share of the profession's high honors and accolades were heaped on CBS in those days. Nevertheless, they had been earned through demonstrated innovation, creativity and commitment, often at personal peril, and therefore weren't heedlessly bestowed. "In just fifteen years, Murrow and company ... introduced news to both radio and television — essentially creating broadcast journalism — to complement and compete with the more established media of newspapers and magazines," claimed colleague Bob Edwards, a half-century after the fact.[72]

> Murrow remains the conscience of responsible broadcast journalists because of his relentless pursuit of the truth, his fondness for the English language, and his deep affection for the best in America's heritage. This, of course, includes the First Amendment guarantees to free and vigorous debate, open assemblies, independent gathering of the news, and critical commentaries about public affairs.[73]

Perhaps surprisingly, meanwhile, NBC moved to focus in this period on an altogether different course: "Gradually, NBC left the news commentaries to its rival and concentrated on the more profitable entertainment side of radio."[74] In 1933, for instance, NBC's schedule offered listeners music and drama as 76 percent of its programming. This was followed by talks and discussions (7 percent) and news (2 percent). CBS was providing just about the same. Within six years, however, NBC featured music and drama 77 percent of the time and news 3.8 percent of the time. Simultaneously, in 1939, CBS programmed 62 percent of its schedule with music and drama and 11 percent with news.[75] The figures substantiate the priorities of each enterprise in the varied disciplines.[76]

Lest it become completely and unintentionally shortchanged, it must be noted that a fourth transcontinental chain was created which at times was a formidable challenger to the dual webs of NBC and of CBS. By 1934, NBC's two chains amassed a combined 127 affiliates while CBS attracted 97 to its fold.[77] That year four influential independent outlets, each with powerful wattage, founded the Mutual Broadcasting System (MBS).[78] That web operated differently from the others without national headquarters and relying on members to supply its outlets with locally generated programming. After several sizeable regional hookups joined MBS the network's strength was apparent. It reached its zenith in number of affiliates in 1979 with 950.[79]

Mutual gained traction in news and public affairs with a newsgathering organization originally spearheaded by G. W. "Johnny" Johnstone. He was still getting scoops even as he operated with merely an infinitesimal proportion of the funds that Abe Schechter of NBC and Paul White of CBS had at their disposal. In 1936, for instance, Johnstone temporarily put his rivals to shame by reporting Howard Hughes' global flight as it occurred. "Mutual, which originally entered the picture as a sort of distant relation, and was spending practically no money," Schechter allowed in his autobiography, "was doing very nicely."[80] While his reference related to the Hughes adventure, it might have typified Johnstone's hard-hitting operation in toto.

Born at Plainfield, New Jersey, on January 8, 1900, George Willfred Johnstone, Jr., lived to February 1976, succumbing to death at Rumson, New Jersey. A U.S. Navy radio operator in the First World War, he was variously cited as a publicity agent and public relations manager of the National Broadcasting Company during the early decades of his career, notwithstanding his post as a news chief. Later, Johnstone was radio and television director of the National Association of Manufacturers, promoting that industry's welfare through projects like a weekly *Industry on Parade* video series. Produced from 1950 to 1960, at its peak that quarter-hour TV feature ran on 270 local stations. In 1955, it also won a Peabody Award for national public service programming.

In the meantime, upon the formation of a New York chapter of the Radio Pioneers in 1951, Johnstone was unanimously elected first president.[81] The national body, founded by news commentator H. V. Kaltenborn, included professionals identified with radio for at least two decades. In the following year, 1952, Johnstone was elected second vice president of the Radio and Television Executives Society, Inc., another fraternal organization.[82] Concurrently named president of that group was one of Johnstone's past superiors, Robert W. Sarnoff, chairman of the Radio Corporation of America.

There is a satisfying outcome to all of this. After NBC Blue transitioned into ABC, Johnstone was responsible for ABC's news department while Abe Schechter directed the news operation at MBS and Paul White was a newspaper executive in California. In time what Johnstone had launched at MBS supplied the memorable voices of Cedric Foster, Gabriel Heatter, Fulton Lewis, Jr., Raymond Gram Swing, Westbrook Van Voorhis and other superlatives saturating its portfolio of commentators and reporters. Not only that, in 1938, an innovative MBS added rebroadcasts of news programs originally beamed by the British Broadcasting Company. And in 1946, lest anyone forget, MBS was the birthplace of *Meet the Press* on a coast-to-coast hookup. It became the most enduring interview forum in broadcasting, now approaching seven decades on the air.

Not all that far into radio's advance into journalistic endeavors, nonetheless, considerable friction erupted between the newer medium and the long-established traditional suppliers of current events. The newspapers as well as the wire services (Associated Press, International News Service, United Press were the major players) viewed the growing development of electronic journalism as an intolerable intrusion upon their sacred, previously unchallenged, turf— turf they had habitually subjugated. "There were no newscasters as such," observed one astute historiographer, "until wire services began to object to networks and stations ripping them off— literally, right off the news ticker without crediting the source."[83] Coalitions of newspaper owners and journalists adopted motions deploring the upstart medium. They heavily criticized radio broadcasters for "destroying the surprise value of news."[84] NBC's Abe Schechter had once alluded to radio's becoming "the prize exhibit in American journalism's doghouse."[85]

For the newspaper owners, of course, this was in fact perceived as a danger to their very livelihoods, purporting to siphon off a healthy portion of the revenues they had long commandeered.[86] The threat couldn't go unchallenged. The earliest salvo in what became known as the Press-Radio War was fired in 1922 as the Associated Press told its member subscribers that AP news copy could not be applied to the broadcasting arena.[87] Without the mutual support of INS and UP, however, AP's posit was negligible, proving unenforceable and of little consequence.

There were incidents in which the troublesome conflict found its way into the federal legal system. A couple of instances are cited.

> In Sioux Falls, South Dakota, the AP brought suit against Station KSOO [in 1933], charging piracy of news. A Federal court issued an injunction denying the station the right to use news gathered at others' "labor and expense" during the period in which the news retained commercial value. The injunction fixed this period at not less than twenty-four hours, thus differing from decisions in analogous cases, which usually set the commercial life of news at no longer than the period between publication of a morning and a succeeding evening paper....
>
> Late in 1934 the AP instituted another suit against a radio station which, after long litigation that took it to the United States Supreme Court, resulted in a draw. In October the Washington *Bellingham Herald* obtained an injunction forbidding Station KVOS-Bellingham to use news from the *Herald* and two other AP papers, the *Seattle Times* and the *Seattle Post-Intelligencer*. On December 18 a Federal district court judge in Seattle dissolved the injunction on the ground that publication of the news in the papers threw it into the public domain. A year later the Ninth Circuit Court of Appeals in San Francisco reinstated the injunction, upholding the principle that a news-gatherer (in this case, the AP) retains a protectable property right in news during its commercial life. But on December 14, 1936, the Supreme Court dodged the issue by a decision that the case was not within the jurisdiction of Federal courts....[88]

The war raged on. It was briefly halted following a gathering December 11–12, 1933, at the Biltmore Hotel in New York City that collected wire service representatives, network executives and newspaper publishers in one room.[89] They hammered out a document popularly dubbed the "Biltmore Agreement." Their motivation was clear: the publishers recognized that radio could — and probably would — take revenue away from the newspapers. As a result, the Biltmore treaty severely restricted the upstart electronic medium's journalistic pursuits by favoring the wire services and their long-established clients, the print press.

The covenant rationed the radio networks to two daily five-minute newscasts, one after 9:30 A.M. and another after 9 P.M. local time. Networks were limited to the established wire services as their sole news sources without the ability to add breaking or last minute news. The pact stipulated that news couldn't be aired under the auspices of commercial sponsorship although listeners might (literally: *should*) be urged to "consult your local newspaper for the latest news."[90]

The accord soon withered, however, after some potent independent radio outlets — about 75 percent weren't then linked to any network — solicited their own news, gathered, edited and broadcast it on sponsored news shows of their own. This was completely outside the Biltmore Agreement that, of course, did not apply to them in the first place.[91] To adequately compete in their own markets, however, many of the network-affiliated stations responded to their independent counterparts by ignoring the Biltmore proviso entirely, performing similarly to their local rivals. This resulted in a quick unraveling of the infamous one-sided Biltmore document.[92]

The Press-Radio War raged on nevertheless to the spring of 1939. That year, the Associated Press, the preeminent wire service, at last relaxed its hard-nosed posture that prevented the electronic media from using its services during the preceding 17 years. It had held radio in abeyance and by then presumably would do the same to TV (exhibited to the general public for the first time that year at the New York World's Fair) for fear of offending its major customers, the powerful newspaper lobby.[93] No more. Electronic journalism would have equal access with the print press to AP news copy from that time forward.[94] A permanent cease-fire, at least outwardly so, had occurred.

By then radio was also developing luminaries of the microphone.

> Amused, then annoyed, newspapermen acted to bar them [radio reporters] from Washington press galleries and did manage to keep them out until as late as 1939. But it was a futile gesture. People were listening, as if to oracles, to Lowell Thomas, Floyd Gibbons, Gabriel Heatter, Raymond Gram Swing, H. V. Kaltenborn, Walter Winchell, John W. Vandercook, Fulton Lewis, Jr., and their fellows. World War II brought Edward R. Murrow to the fore. The voices of men like these carried far more emotional authority than cold type on newsprint.
> Radio was competing with newspapers, books, and magazines, and winning hands down.[95]

Citing Murrow's contributions for establishing radio and television as "carriers of powerful news," as well as that of other journalists including some on TV, one scholar duly observed: "Broadcast news made some people stars."[96]

To counter the early discernible trend that threatened their very existences, some newspapers began to operate radio stations of their own, extending their information-distribution systems to verbal as well as visible spheres of influence.[97] Although in mid-1922 less than a dozen stations were subsidiaries of newspapers, within six months that number had soared to 69.[98] More amazingly, by 1939, when the industry's fraternal American Newspaper Publishers Association (ANPA) abandoned its undertaking of cutting radio out of the news business altogether, journal-owned radio stations had swelled to something beyond three in 10. And of nearly one-third of the total number of outlets then in existence, newspapers already controlled more than 80 percent.[99]

To the print media, consequently, radio wasn't to be patently dismissed any longer nor its right to compete fairly be denied. The ANPA radio committee affirmed that radio's reporting of news events stimulated newspaper sales, a belief borne out fully by subsequent investigation.[100] The venerable published press was gradually giving in to radio news and that segment of journalism's privilege to pursue it.

Observing all of this in 1930, a couple of sages opined: "Of course there is some competition between broadcasting and publishing, but newspapers, realizing that broadcasting would take place whether they engaged in it or not, have quite sagaciously taken part so as to steer the new art along lines which would not interfere with the stability of their own field."[101] Another wag remarked: "Newspaper objections to radio news subsided from piercing shrieks to a grumble, then a mutter."[102] And interim National Association of Broadcasters president Mark Ethridge, general manager of *The Courier-Journal*, Louisville's premier paper that also owned a broadcast station, summarized in 1939: "The newspaper business has been fighting a rear-guard action for ten years — and a losing action, at that."[103]

Electronic journalism's unshakable destiny, it seemed, was about to be secured.

3

"Millions Are Out Here Listening Every Day!"

As the third decade of the 20th century neared its conclusion, the U.S. Office of Radio Research (ORR) observed that more than three out of five Americans were deliberately turning to their radios to "catch the news."[1] Although radio had not yet replaced the newspaper as the source of most people's information pertaining to domestic and global episodes, more and more were relying upon a combination of the twin media to gain particulars in regard to newsworthy elements. The dual forms exhibited distinct but overlapping qualities.

> Radio had obvious advantages: it was often first with breaking news, it was "free," you could get the news while doing something else, and listeners often felt transported to the scene of the event. Newspapers, by contrast, provided pictures of many people and events, allowed readers to pick and choose what they wanted to read, and choose the time to read as well, provided more in-depth coverage, and offered specialized coverage of financial news, society, and so forth....
>
> ORR researchers found that radio news was preferred over newspapers as the listeners' economic status went down, and women greatly preferred hearing the news over the radio. So did young people, who constituted the first "radio generation," and those who lived in rural areas. The ORR also found that over 50 percent of high-income and professional men listened to political radio commentators, but only 37 percent of unskilled workers and men on relief did so. *Fortune*, in its 1938 survey, put it slightly differently: "News is welcomed by twice as many of the poor as of the prosperous.... Housekeepers (who like to listen while they work), wage earners, and the unemployed rank by occupation at the head of radio news fans." ...
>
> By the late 1930s radio was giving much more attention to international news than newspapers did, and more than 90 percent of those the ORR polled said that radio news had increased their interest in foreign affairs....
>
> Broadcast news created a sense of intimate participation in "a larger world." "The radio signals, coming instantaneously often from the very scenes of events and entering directly into the home, gave listeners a feeling of personal touch with the world that possibly no other medium could provide." Radio relieved suspense about "what happened" in the course of a news story's narrative, and it did so faster than newspapers. Thus it intensified excitement about the news....
>
> These [radio] men spoke to and for everyday Americans in a conversational, personal style, often using *I*, which some of their counterparts in the print media could not. [Correspondent Edward R.] Murrow's hallmark ... was to create concrete mental images.... Such details made a story told with words but not pictures more vivid and immediate; they also cultivated identification and empathy in the listener.[2]

Broadcast news's development did not come about overnight. Yet it eventually became a major source in satisfying people's hunger for details of what was transpiring in their world. Nevertheless, it took years of assiduous reporting from the scenes of newsmaking activities for the aural medium to establish a persuasive sense of reliability, sagacity, objectivity, and integrity that could not only rival but also ultimately supersede society's longstanding love affair with ink as the habitual source of its information. Several decades later, near the end of the 20th century, an astute reporter, languishing in nostalgic deference to the patently accepted Golden Age of Radio many years before, harkened back to some of radio's earliest newsworthy triumphs as he waxed pensively:

> Early radio news was a catch-as-catch-can affair, thrown together to broadcast major events — disasters, celebrated trials, conventions, title fights, and the World Series. The watershed event for radio news was a marathon sixteen-day Democratic convention in 1924 that required 103 ballots to nominate John W. Davis as breathless listeners clung to their radios awaiting the outcome.[3]

Said another:

> The coverage of news before Murrow came along was event-oriented. Stations and networks assigned staff to broadcast preplanned activities such as speeches, hearings, ship launchings, athletic events, and the like. Most didn't have professional reporters; they had announcers who might host a program of dance music one day and describe a boxing match the next. To be a broadcaster in the early days of radio was to be a person who could handle any sort of assignment one might be given: a garden party, a circus parade, a religious revival, or a news conference. One wonders if today's broadcasting superstars could function as well as NBC's Graham MacNamee or CBS's Robert Trout in rotating daily among interviewing professors, hosting musical recitals, covering Ivy League rowing matches, and doing the talk-up to FDR's fireside chats.[4]

In the year 1931, CBS broadcast 415 special events (typically more than one a day in an average week). Its only transcontinental competition, NBC — with dual chains under its aegis — aired another 256 special events. Together the trio was on the ether with 671 unique occasions that year or more than 1.8 broadcasts per day.[5] These figures underscore the critical role that pre-planned and impromptu proceedings contributed in making up the daily agendas of the networks in their earliest years. If this much was transpiring on a national basis, how many localized happenings did individual stations cover, whether affiliated with transcontinental webs or not? It had to be thousands of political rallies, store openings, award celebrations, school board meetings, mayoral addresses, and the like.

During radio's sterling epoch at the forefront of mass communications in this nation, there was in fact a litany of newsworthy occasions and incidents transpiring that were customarily tailor-made for audio reportage. Many of these were one time only events, some pre-planned and some that escalated purely by happenstance. In the previous chapter, the 1920 Harding-Cox presidential election returns aired by Pittsburgh's KDKA, and prizefighter Jack Dempsey's 1921 bout to retain the heavyweight title over challenger Georges Carpentier — relayed from Jersey City, New Jersey to "radio halls" in scores of cities — were examples cited of these newsworthy "events" that were gaining the attention of many Americans within earshot of a radio set.

Extraordinary news events invariably built audiences, even as radio's golden age progressed. On the evening of December 7, 1941, the day the Japanese struck Pearl Harbor in a surprise and unprovoked assault, between 7 and 10:30 P.M. Eastern Standard Time, 47.2 percent of all radios in the U.S. were turned on.[6] Some 40.7 percent of radios in America were in use during D-Day on June 6, 1944. An overall average of 50 percent reported election results on the day of the Roosevelt-Dewey balloting, November 7, 1944; that escalated to a peak of 56.6 percent between 9 and 10 P.M. Eastern Time. And on V-J Day, August 10, 1945, twice the conventional morning crowd was drawn to a radio, with the evening listeners soaring 65 percent above habitual figures that day.

What is apparent to the perceptive and sharp-eyed student of journalistic endeavor must be how radio's ability to control the immediacy factor appeared to prevail so sensationally. *Today it continues to prevail*, in fact, unequivocally leaving the print media at least to some extent shortchanged in the competition for velocity in news delivery. Newspapers (in traditional hard copy format, at least) are normally clearly at an unswerving disadvantage at the hands of timeliness — incessantly tormented by the physical constraints that relevance imposes. Broadcasting simply cut so sharply into the "wait-time" between a newsmaking incident and at what time the end consumer learned of it (much of it simultaneously) that print was almost invariably trumped in that battle altogether. "It is axiomatic in journalism that the fastest medium with the largest potential audience will disseminate the bulk of a community's breaking news," proclaimed one wag.[7]

On the other hand, print could usually regain some lost ground in another crucial realm, that of detail. By making the most of its ability to provide in-depth reporting — something that was, of necessity, frequently absent in the race against time in broadcasting — the ink-sheets secured a significant plus. On the air there might be little more than a mention of what transpired in a reported incident, given broadcasting's eternal restrictions mandated by the clock.

This might leave the listeners with multiple unanswered questions or at least a thirst for more knowledge than the radio newscast proffered. The printed word could come to the rescue in prolific measure, subsequently filling in the blanks with substantially more information than radio could ever find time to deliver. Both media therefore had something to boast about. How well they applied their strengths made a quality difference in whether their coverage reached a high level of journalism excellence or whether it could be rated only "so-so."

To be intentionally objective, as an aside, let's examine a few figures of a journalism intellect that don't incessantly reflect positively on radio news — especially when judged against the press (print media). Mitchell Charnley's findings generally encompass the postwar period of the mid to late 1940s, when he acknowledges that "just about everybody is likely to pick up some radio news every day."[8] He contrasts the two news media's audiences.

> Qualitatively, the radio newscast has often come out second best. The lower an individual's economic or cultural level, or the younger he is (and probably, therefore, the less informed), the more likely he is to depend on radio for his news. The evidence shows that those who have a sound orientation in current affairs — those who do more than the average amount of reading, who have more than high school education, whose occupations or environments throw them into physical or intellectual contact with the streams of major affairs — rely less on radio than do the less sophisticated. Seventh and eighth grade students, just beginning an acquaintance with news, depend heavily on radio; by the time they become high school seniors, they have started to turn to other news media....
>
> In 1939, a *Fortune* survey showed 63.8 percent of the national population claiming newspapers as the source of most of its news, 25.4 percent claiming radio. But a study by the National Opinion Research Center in 1945 ... showed 61 percent getting most of its news by radio, 35 percent getting most news from newspapers. A second NORC survey in 1947 showed ... 48 percent favoring the newspaper, 44 percent the radio.... It seems likely ... the peak of interest

in radio as a news purveyor in 1945 may be attributed to broadcasting's dramatic development as a war news medium.[9]

Charnley's summary covered more territory comparing the dual media: responsibility for actions, speed, comprehensiveness, prejudice, and believability.[10] In most areas, radio news seemed to have an amazingly strong grasp on the public's confidence. Certainly by that time most radio news was a worthy representative of the traditions of expected professional standards in the trade. It could, according to that academic, hold its own in head-to-head competition with its older brother in the broader newsgathering and dispatching family.

In the meantime, yet another radio news historiographer seemed to simplify precisely when that genre took off, proving itself an unmistakably influential force to be recorded in the annals of journalism.[11] That wag's assumption, at least at this considerable distance, might appear to have been inadvertently misleading nonetheless.

> In the United States, radio news began to prove that it had arrived as a significant journalistic force when the Japanese attacked Pearl Harbor on December 7, 1941— a Sunday. There were no evening papers on Sunday. From the first bulletin — interrupting a football game on the small Mutual radio network, right after the wires flashed the news at 2:22 P.M. EST — until Monday morning, the news was a radio exclusive.

While the unparalleled magnitude of the circumstances referenced may not be surpassed in earlier broadcasts, to a lesser extent but surely commanding in nature are numerous previous instances in which *radio was there* and was thereby making a noteworthy difference. As it beamed its coverage to an audience that had seemingly become "all ears," the newfangled audio medium scooped the newspapers, beating the purveyors of pulp to a pulp (the pun is intended). In this regard radio did its job well, capitalizing on an instantly recognizable superlative as it went head-to-head with its printed peers in newsgathering and reporting.

The examples of radio's greater ability to cope with the timeliness factor give the impression of knowing no end. Here are a few more that stand out in broadcasting's first couple of decades:

- Through radio, President Woodrow W. Wilson's historic address to Congress on January 8, 1918, embodying his Fourteen Points for a just peace, was spread throughout the world in a few hours. A 50-KW transmitter erected by the Marconi Company at New Brunswick, New Jersey, later upped to 200 KW — the most powerful in the world — played a key role in Wilsonian appeals over the heads of enemy governments, accelerating the Armistice. Radio, during the hostilities, was the nation's "main medium of communication with its expeditionary forces," noted a historian. "Even in the forward trenches for radio operators, troops were provided with regular news bulletins."[12] It was a foretaste of what was on the way.
- Verner Alexanderson, age six, son of an experimenter-inventor who devised the alternator, was lured from home on April 30, 1923, in a kidnapping that began with a pledge of rabbits.[13] After Bert Jarvis, manager of some summer cottages at Theresa, New York, heard an emotional appeal by the lad's father, Ernst F. W. Alexanderson, over Schenectady's WGY, he told authorities that a man and woman had brought a child to the cottages fitting the description given over the air. It wasn't long until the boy was reunited with his parents. *Radio Broadcast* titled its August 1923 account, "Radio Repays Its Genius."
- That same periodical reported a month later that President Warren G. Harding achieved what no previous chief executive had by addressing a million subjects simultaneously as

he spoke at St. Louis on June 21, 1923. Three stations carried his speech rejecting the League of Nations — KSD, St. Louis; WEAF, New York; and WCAP, Washington, D.C. (the last two owned and linked by AT&T). Harding fell ill on his westward trek and died on August 2.

- A Ku Klux Klan rally at Kokomo, Indiana, on July 4, 1923, drew the largest crowd in that coalition's existence. It was variously estimated that up to 200,000 people attended, presumably with a great many being little more than gawkers motivated by prying curiosity.
- A few radio events instigated some touching moments celebrated by the countrymen. By autumn 1923, ex-President Woodrow Wilson had been virtually forgotten. His health in decline, he vanished from the stage into isolation at a house on S Street in the nation's capital. When asked to give an Armistice Day talk from his home to air over AT&T-linked outlets in New York, Providence, Schenectady and Washington, however, he responded eagerly. Though there were some lengthy pauses in the broadcast of November 10, 1923 — including times when Mrs. Wilson was heard whispering words to him from a speech he had written and was unable to see — he rose to the occasion, asking at its finish: "That is all, isn't it?" The next day, Armistice Day, to his surprise, 20,000 citizens encircled the S Street house for five blocks in every direction. "It was as though the broadcast had helped to remind them of a ghost that still walked among them," said one wag.[14] Wilson came out to express appreciation, signifying "that we shall prevail is as sure as that God reigns!" A dozen weeks hence his funeral aired over a handful of stations that measured such moments with poignancy.[15]
- All New York City radio stations heard an SOS and ceased broadcasting after the dirigible *Shenandoah*, moored at Lakehurst, N.J., broke free on a stormy night in January 1924, drifting away. The Lakehurst wireless transmitter was toppled, too, leaving ground and blimp crews incommunicado. WOR station manager Joseph Bennett offered to intervene and was authorized to return to the air, gaining a local monopoly. A WOR announcer asked listeners to phone WOR if they heard the *Shenandoah's* motors. Talent set to go on the air as the crisis erupted took calls on phones across Bamberger's dry goods store (WOR's owner). Pins on a map let the station plot the dirigible's moves. With a vast audience tuned in, WOR addressed the blimp's crew that didn't know their position or course. Careening through black clouds they hardly saw the ground; nor could listeners see the ship, only hearing motors whirring as it passed them overhead. The crew was told by WOR where they were. At 4 A.M. — eight hours after it broke loose — the ship landed safely. Radio had performed another incredible feat.[16]
- From July 10 to 21, 1925, listeners to *Chicago Tribune* station WGN remained glued to their sets as they witnessed the live proceedings of the Scopes "monkey trial" unfold in Dayton, Tennessee. They had never heard anything like it. In actuality no American audience had. An enterprising WGN felt it important enough to broadcast, however, that it expended $1,000 daily in wire fees.[17] The conflict at the apex of those daily features arose after a state-mandated biblical view of creation ran afoul of an evolutionary stance. The latter proclaimed that man descended from apes.[18] The courtroom drama included the arguments of stimulating legendary barrister Clarence Darrow (1857–1938), an outspoken activist representing the American Civil Liberties Union. Darrow defended John T. Scopes (1900–70), who taught the evolutionary (apes) theory in a local biology classroom. Holding the opposite posture and consulting with the prosecution was William Jennings Bryan (1860–1925), a widely recognized ex–U.S. Secretary of State and three-time Democratic presidential hopeful. Five days following the famous trial's conclusion

in his (and the state's) favor, Bryan died in his sleep, his higher office bids never realized. While the trial may be gauged as a novelty by some contemporary standards, it was serious business to an awestruck audience tuning in. Although a portion of the crowd's fascination may have had something to do with the colorful figures influencing its outcome, the subject matter was visibly contentious among the trial's followers in that day.

- Following the epic 33.5-hour, 3600-mile flight of aviator Charles A. Lindbergh (1902–74) in his monoplane *The Spirit of St. Louis* between Long Island, New York's Roosevelt Field and Le Bourget Field near Paris on May 20–21, 1927, Lindbergh's return prompted the nation to tune in to a celebration of epic proportions for a newfound hero.[19] His triumphant arrival on June 11 at the base of the Washington Monument in the nation's capital was indeed a spectacular salutation.[20] The six-and-a-half hour, carnival-like marathon aired by the recently formed National Broadcasting Company included the roar of airplanes flying overhead in review and a patriotic address by the eminent American entertainer George M. Cohan. On June 13, a tumultuous ticker tape parade honored the fêted pilot, moving along the downtown streets of New York City and including congratulatory messages from Governor Al Smith and Mayor Jimmy Walker.[21] That momentous occasion, captured by NBC's team of reporters led by Graham McNamee (1888–1942), was beamed to the farthest geographical reaches of the fledgling broadcasting empire. It also initiated the multiple aircast pick-ups. Some journalist eyewitnesses, having reported what they could view from their individual vantage points, switched the passing parade to other correspondents along the route, much as relay runners do in passing a baton. With each event of similar magnitude, not only were radio's operators gaining incalculable experience but introducing unexpected innovations into broadcasting, too.
- The same year that Lindbergh flew the Atlantic, Jack Dempsey (1895–1983) — the very same athlete who was pitted in "the fight of the century" in 1921— and Gene Tunney (1897–1978) were contenders in a prizefight that American listeners heard on 69 stations — the largest "network" put together yet at that point in time.[22] Aired from Chicago's Soldier Field before more than 100,000 spectators on September 22, 1927, it was a rematch of a Philadelphia bout a year earlier in which Dempsey had lost the heavyweight championship. Despite the bulk of a gate of nearly $2.7 million that had been placed on Dempsey, in 10 rounds Tunney — with a unanimous decision — retained the title. (Note how sporting events fascinated the early radio audiences, occupying several of these broadcasts that attracted colossal numbers of aficionados. Athletic competitions became "newsmaking" draws for a developing contingent among audiences from radio's very start.)
- There was aviatrix Amelia Earhart's (1897–1937) tumultuous return as the first feminine passenger aboard an aircraft to cross the Atlantic, on June 17–18, 1928. Like Lindbergh before her, she was treated to a tickertape parade in New York City of her own followed by a White House reception with President Calvin Coolidge — both preludes to an even more dazzling celebration after Earhart soloed across the Atlantic on May 20, 1932, near the close of Herbert Hoover's presidency.
- The completion of the Empire State Building and its formal opening ceremonies on May 1, 1931, netted live radio coverage. At 1,250 feet and 102 stories tall, the literal skyscraper was the world's tallest structure at that moment.
- Following the kidnapping of Charles A. Lindbergh, Jr., infant son of the world famous aviator, from his nursery in the Lindberghs' New Jersey home on March 1, 1932, radio turned the nation's sustained focus to that absorbing story. For 150 continuous hours, more than six days, both CBS and NBC covered the intriguing pursuit that gripped the

nation by providing news bulletins every half-hour.[23] It was a prelude to CNN several decades before the cable service and its equals were envisioned. "No radio drama," wrote *The New York Times*, "ever won such widespread attention ... over such a long period." (The child was found murdered more than two months later. Convicted of the crime in 1935, Bruno Richard Hauptmann was electrocuted on April 3, 1936.)

- Although there was no live coverage of an assassination attempt on the life of President-elect Franklin Delano Roosevelt (1882–1945) on February 15, 1933 (as there most assuredly would be today), radio was quick to react nevertheless.[24] CBS correspondent Edwin C. Hill (1884–1957) was on the air almost immediately with an initial bulletin of the shooting as the impending leader spoke to a crowd at Miami's Bayfront Park. This report was soon followed on CBS by on-the-scene interviews with eyewitnesses. Although Roosevelt was not harmed, several others were, the most serious injury being suffered by Chicago Mayor Anthony J. Cermak, who died from a bullet wound a few weeks later. An Italian anarchist, Giuseppe Zangara, flailing against capitalism, was tried, convicted and—on March 20 of that year—electrocuted for the crime.[25]

- Who could realistically argue that Roosevelt's celebrated "fireside chats" in the 1930s and 1940s weren't "events" in themselves, perpetuating hope in a country mired in the throes of economic depression? Candid "one-on-one" talks by the nation's chief executive aired as he sat by the fireplace in the Diplomatic Reception Room of the White House. His listeners—scattered in living rooms all over America—found compassion and solace in his words. "It was as if a wise and kindly father had sat down sympathetically and patiently and affectionately with his worried and anxious children," noted CBS commentator Edwin C. Hill.[26] Beginning with the first such chat on March 12, 1933, Roosevelt addressed the nation's citizens 30 times altogether through 1944. Not only did his messages restore confidence, they solidified the viability of reaching the populace with electronic transmission, a technique consequently expanded but not yet eclipsed. While Roosevelt's declarations may not always have been news in the strictest sense, they revealed what the government was doing to absorb some of the nation's shock and pain, thereby restoring people's faith in their country. It was one of the greatest services radio could render in a time of national peril and despondency.

- The *Hindenburg* disaster which occurred on May 6, 1937, provided the first recorded matter to be broadcast on a radio network.[27] While docking at the Lakehurst (New Jersey) Naval Air Station, the German passenger airship LZ 129 *Hindenburg* caught fire and was destroyed. Thirty-five persons on board and one in the ground crew perished in the tragedy, bringing an end in public confidence for dirigibles. As it happened, Herbert Morrison (1905–89), an announcer with Chicago's WLS, was in the crowd of eyewitnesses. He was making transcriptions for his station's record library. Morrison's emotional account, played over NBC the following day, is one of the most gripping sound images ever broadcast.

- The coronation of King George VI (1895–1952) in Great Britain on May 12, 1937, became the first worldwide affair to be aired in the United States.

- Finally on October 30, 1938, radio created its own mischief by causing a make-believe scare that legions of listeners took seriously.[28] Dramatist Orson Welles (1915–85) adapted H. G. Wells's *War of the Worlds* treatise into a radio play in prime time on CBS. Despite numerous disclaimers hinting it was a hoax, multitudes believed the repeated radio news alerts that seemingly "interrupted" the dance music program they were tuned to. An announcer confirmed that a Martian spaceship had landed near the eastern seaboard hamlet of Grovers Mill, New Jersey. This set off a reactionary panic the likes of which America had never witnessed, turning a charade into a convincing scenario that enveloped millions.[29] It's been dubbed "the most alarming program in vintage radio history."[30]

In addition to these singularly newsworthy occasions there was a host of inveterate sporting competitions carried on the ether with regular consistency, among them: baseball's World Series, golfing's PGA Championship, horse racing's Kentucky Derby, the Rose Bowl and its myriad counterparts featuring collegiate football teams in end-of-the-season classics, and the Summer and Winter Olympics, all of which were seemingly made-for-broadcast naturals — and destined to be heard at repetitious interludes for decades. Beyond these events, of course, were the presidential elections and inaugurations that came around every four years,[31] plus many added episodes that captured people's attention, providing radio with ready-made audiences during broadcasting's nascent interval.

Radio stepped in to plug a void that existed among messaging dispensaries since the beginning of time. Suitably filling it, the medium's unseen spokespersons supplied patrons with detailed knowledge that they might never have grasped or that they wouldn't otherwise have received until later in the day, the following day, or week, or month after a publication, circular, or piece of mail was deposited on their doorstep revealing what had happened or — perhaps even worse — when someone told them about it ... *whenever*. An informational chasm that had been the bane of every denizen that had ever lived on the planet was broad and durable prior to radio's inception. And that new channel, wherever its transmitters beamed it, was capable of permanently abolishing the curse. Additionally, and remarkably so, radio also delivered its product to everybody tuning in *at the very same time*.

Itinerant wordsmith Robert Hardy Andrews (1903–76), who concurrently penned a handful of daytime radio soap operas throughout the 1930s, composed a few lines under the title *A Voice in the Room*. Although his essay intentionally portrayed the American housewife of that day going about her duties while a radio played in the background, its simplistic message is indicative of all who switched on the new visitor in millions of domiciles.

> The average woman lives by a schedule in which no element changes from one day to the next....
> The accomplishments of such days may be great in their value to humanity, but the hours are — or were, in the past — long, empty, and deadly dull. But now a new thing has happened.
> There is, or can be, a voice in the room. A friendly, unhurried, likable, listenable, neighborly voice that is created by the turning of a dial....
> The housewife turns on her radio. She goes here and there, into her living room, upstairs to make the beds and clean the bathroom, out in the yard to hang up the washing, back to the kitchen to prepare lunch for the children....
> She knows, without thinking much about it, that the voice in her room tells her what is being heard by other women like herself. Therefore, she is a member of a great group....
> She is grateful, because in the world at last she has at least one neighbor, who is many voices in one, who talks to her all day long every day. And it is talking, the sound of a voice, not music or a joke that must be thought about or drama so artistic that she must sit down to listen to it, that the woman wants to hear. That is what she is grateful for: the voice in her room.[32]

Along the way radio established the *theater of the mind*, in which each individual hearing its programs formed his or her own mental images of the action encountered. The tale is told of a young child who was asked whether he preferred adventures presented over radio or television, to which the youngster exclaimed, "On the radio!" His inquisitor prompted, "And why is that?" Quickly the juvenile replied, "Because I can see the pictures better!" It was just such illustrations that netted the infamous theater of the mind that vintage radio addicts cite. Indeed, the pictures *are* better, and the territory isn't limited purely to amusement and entertainment; it can be applied just as readily to hard news and information. The listener might be hearing the action as it transpires or as it was earlier transcribed, or it might be a circumstance in which someone who is viewing it or has firsthand knowledge of it is recounting it to an infinite unseen audience. Its many spokesmen, of course, could include the newscasters. The dimensions of radio's innovative technology are numerous and cannot be bound by any dismissive epithet.

In the province of immediacy of news delivery, however, when compared with daily and weekly newspapers, magazines, newsletters, newsreels, direct mail, billboards, signs, public notices and other methods by which news was dispatched back in the day, there can be little question that broadcasting alone — and in the 1920s, 1930s, 1940s, and in the early 1950s, for most Americans, that meant *radio*— won the battle in getting the word out to large audiences swiftly (and even concomitantly). While for radio, the devil was in the details — which print journalism commonly and competently exploited to its fullest advantage (and rightly so) — radio seized upon its opportunity to tell what happened *first*.

Sometimes while working in tandem, the broadcasting and print modes prompted the very best in one another. As a rule working independently of each other, it forced their staffs to rise to an occasion and deliver their most brilliant efforts out of their collective expertise, talent and creativity. In those situations not only did high journalistic standards prevail, the consumer could realize a win-win outcome. The gift from the dual media to the ultimate user was a total package of news and information. Usually unheralded, the unseen benefit was available many times just the same.

Typical Americans eventually nursed an unmistakable dependency on radio news as their instant lifeline to knowledge of events that were transpiring half a world away. By 1938, several respected authorities signified "radio's emergence as America's chief news medium."[33] This was especially evident during the Second World War. By November 1942, a survey taken in 95 U.S. municipalities concluded that 73 percent of participants received most of their news about the war from radio. At the same time, some 49 percent said newspapers were still a viable supplier for their information about the war. Not so long after, however, in spring 1946, a nationwide poll revealed that radio news was substantially outdistancing newspapers, even beyond the war which had ended the year before.[34] Sixty-one percent of respondents cited radio as their chief news provider while 35 percent listed newspapers as their main source.[35]

At no point in the country's history on any sustained basis was the citizens' reliance upon radio any greater than during this era in which it singularly proved itself so effectively and so astonishingly. In an insightful musing on how vital radio news had become to most Americans, a couple of media historians offered a thrilling memory of CBS correspondent Eric Sevareid's (1912–92) own revelation of radio's widespread acceptance and compulsion by many Americans.[36] The incident occurred during the newsman's homecoming from an overseas station where he had dispatched the news for three years. It's recounted in an essay that reflected his web's coverage under the oversight of chief foreign correspondent Edward R. Murrow (1908–65).

> Sevareid returned to the States in the fall of 1940.... He ... settled easily into the routine at CBS headquarters and began to see how little he and the other [Murrow] Boys understood about the business they were in, about radio's reach, its impact, its importance. The sheer power of the medium had grown phenomenally, and that power would have a radical impact on his life and the lives of his colleagues.

He clearly grasped this for the first time on a street corner in Manhattan shortly after his return from London. It was a warm autumn day. All the cars and taxis had their windows down. As Sevareid stood waiting for the light to change, he realized he could hear [CBS's] Larry LeSueur's voice echoing through Manhattan's skyscraper canyons: Larry was broadcasting from the tight little cabbage-scented closet in the BBC basement [rank with the essence of cabbage from a cafeteria a few steps away], and at almost the same moment his voice was pouring out of the open windows of all these cars and taxis in New York City.

My God, Sevareid thought, *people are listening. Millions of them.* Every *day!* He realized radio was not just "a pantomime in an empty room." Standing there, Sevareid wanted to shout his discovery back to Murrow, LeSueur, and the others with all the passion of a convert: *They're out here, boys! They can hear you!*

The astounding impact of radio news, broadcast from the far flung corners of the earth, *as it happened*, was a discovery that Sevareid — who had been in the trenches outside the country for three years — hadn't put together until then. Yet it was one that most Americans who had been at home during that time had grown increasingly aware of. To learn the facts quickly and accurately, they had merely to turn on their radios. Once its tubes had "warmed up," with the flick of a wrist they could dial to the latest happenings from close to home or around the globe. Reporting the news simultaneously to millions of waiting ears was one of the things radio performed best. The coverage provided to virtually any newsworthy event confirmed it again and again and again.

4

Who Owns the Ether? It Belongs to Us All

A biographer of William S. Paley, the president and principal owner of the Columbia Broadcasting System from its inception under that nomenclature in 1927, referenced the primitive days of network radio. In spite of the noteworthy but sporadic events that occurred during radio's initial decade, so the wordsmith hinted—several of which were enumerated in the previous chapter—in broadcast journalism in particular there wasn't a whole lot going on in any motivating consistency prior to 1930. But then CBS decided to capitalize on that spectrum to discriminate it from its venerated rival for the affections of U.S. radio listeners.

In 1929, Edward Bernays, referenced in the passage below, became the first of several confidantes to gain Paley's ear as his public relations counsel. Edward Klauber and Paul Kesten would carry on the traditions begun by Bernays when they succeeded him in that critical capacity.[1] PR wasn't all the rage in American business then that it is today. But Paley had enough visionary adroitness about him to summon the expertise he knew he lacked and then was willing to apply the sage advice he was given. His forward thinking would be good for the enterprise he represented both then and in the future.

> News and public affairs programs formed the cornerstone of the image-building strategy Bernays and Paley had launched the previous year. Initially neither CBS nor NBC had done much in news broadcasting. NBC ... was reluctant to appear too powerful or influential. The passage of the Radio Act of 1927 had come amid congressional concern that a single corporation—namely, RCA—might dominate the flow of information on the airwaves.... In keeping with its low profile, NBC did not set up a service to regularly report and comment on national news. It merely broadcast important public events....
>
> At first Paley followed NBC's lead. CBS covered official functions to fill time while trying to seem public-spirited and responsible. Like NBC, it broadcast countless campaign speeches as well as the presidential election returns in 1928. But on Inauguration Day in March 1929, Paley began to appreciate the public appetite for news programs. CBS and NBC devoted the entire day to Herbert Hoover's White House reception, motorcade, swearing in, and inaugural ball. The two networks were rewarded with the biggest combined audience up to that time, 63 million listeners.
>
> Bernays, meanwhile, was prodding Paley to create an identity distinct from NBC. His prescription for CBS was to emphasize information and communication. "I recognized the importance of freedom of speech and freedom of the press, so I told him to keep stressing these

elements, which he did," said Bernays. Paley saw that news programs could attract listeners. But he also recognized that CBS's prestige "would depend to a considerable extent upon how well we could provide" radio news.

Paley's appearance on Capitol Hill in 1930 helped create the impression that CBS was the leader in public affairs and news programs.[2]

Indeed, it soon clearly was.

News and public affairs represented one of the pillars on which the House of Columbia would rest, and as much as anything, in many ways it would separate CBS from the various other competing members of the transcontinental broadcasting pack. There will be unmistakable growing evidence to support this theory to be witnessed in the years that followed.

It didn't really matter that America's broadcasting industry pursued a direction that was generally diametrically in contrast with that which was adopted by most of its European equivalents in deriving sufficient resources essential to financially support radio. The bulk of nations on the Continent put their new communications systems wholly or in part under the purview of the governments in each country. While that method satisfied a need for adequate funding of broadcasting operations, at the same time it proffered the very real threat that sovereign overseers could determine what would and would not be heard by the listeners, thereby influencing political machinations.

Although America's radio pursuits eventually went in an altogether different direction — selecting the route of private commercial enterprise instead of one forged by the bureaucrats — even in a capitalistic society, in spite of everything, Big Brother imposed certain restrictions on the new medium. These affected not only the national and regional chains that occasionally emerged but also the local stations as well, some of which were affiliates of those local and coast-to-coast chains. The lawmakers believed that the airwaves were possessions of all of the citizens collectively, and they expected and deserved reasonable safeguards by those entrusted with their protection.

Because the ether was so free and readily accessible (unlike newspapers and magazines, which derived substantial revenues from paid subscriptions, as well as advertising), the feds felt that everybody was entitled to be shielded from substance that could be considered offensive or inflammatory. In the long run their actions netted dual entities (in succession), responsible for broadcasting's sanction.[3] These regulatory agencies, with stated and implied levels of jurisdictional power, meted out restrictions on the airwaves that were commonly accepted for the benefit of all Americans.

This chapter and the two following will examine three large issues that have affected radio broadcasting and its news delivery. They include (1) ownership, (2) oversight, and (3) opinion. The first answers the question, "Who has the ultimate control over the airwaves in the United States?" The second responds to "What form of censorship is applied in radio journalism?" In the third, the subject of "How does radio deal with personal biases among broadcasters?" is processed. Ownership, oversight, and opinion: a case may be made that all three disciplines — at least in the context in which they are presented here — may be tied to the concerns about censorship in one form or another. An exponent of the ether, radio journalism in its multiple manifestations will be scrutinized with a view to drawing objective conclusions.

To lay the groundwork for this exploration, the present chapter provides a history lesson that may refresh memories for some and offer new insights for others as the table is set for what is to follow.[4] One source identified the severity of a growing predicament that was rapidly becoming burdensome to many in the industry. It divulges one of the chief reasons why it became necessary to implement policies for conducting the trade.[5]

> In 1925 the growth of radio began to create problems. In major cities there were too many stations on a limited band for good reception — for instance, 23 in Los Angeles and 40 in Chicago. Receivers were unselective; transmitters tended to drift. With the limited spectrum space and equipment available, the typical large city could accommodate only seven stations without resorting to *share-time* operations. In Los Angeles and Chicago, share-time might allow a single station as little as one hour or two of air time daily, divided into widely separated parts of the day. With four or five stations using the same channel, no one of them could build an audience. Because many of their listeners were DX fans, who listened for distant stations, some cities designated "silent nights," when local stations signed off early to improve distance reception.[6]

Until 1927, radio had been regulated by the U.S. Department of Commerce. Commerce secretary Herbert Hoover, appointed by President Warren G. Harding in 1921, played a strong role in shaping the fledgling industry. From its earliest beginnings, Hoover insisted that radio must not rely on paid advertising to keep it afloat. He believed the commercialization of radio would be a waste of listeners' time, a totally frivolous notion in his opinion. Was he advocating federal manipulation of the airwaves, European style, perhaps?

Not really. He lobbied instead for self-regulation, seeing it as an alternative to governmental control.[7] It was a noble gesture but one with little possibility of coming about given that hundreds of new stations were going on the air to serve a limited number of available frequencies. Inevitably a glut of new broadcasters was simultaneously assigned to the same wavelengths. Each outlet was allowed to air only a few designated hours per day to avoid interference with the rapidly expanding number of entrepreneurs wanting to dive into broadcasting. Nearly all were unhappy and many doggedly railed against the great odds preventing them from enjoying clear-channel status all the time.

While circumstances were perplexing, the reality was that Hoover, as secretary of commerce, who labored with restricted powers, could do very little. Without sufficient cause he couldn't deny a broadcasting license to anybody who applied. This exacerbated the problem at the crux of the dilemma. But Congress at last heard the protestations of the wailing cynics when in due course it created the Radio Act of 1927.[8] This was definitely watershed legislation for it proclaimed for the very first time that *the government owned the airwaves*, and thereby had jurisdiction over that domain.[9]

> *Nothing in this Act shall be understood or construed to give the licensing authority the power of censorship over the radio communications or signals transmitted by any radio station, and no regulation or condition shall be promulgated or fixed by the licensing authority which shall interfere with the right of free speech by means of radio communications. No person within the jurisdiction of the United States shall utter any obscene, indecent, or profane language by means of radio communication.*[10]

The ether was to be licensed in harmony with "the public interest, convenience, or necessity." Upon implementation, the landmark enactment took control of and responsibility for the conduct of broadcasting, allocating it to federal assignees on behalf of the people's trust. The Radio Act of 1927 established a sweeping and powerful precedent that had never before been defined. At the same time it created a five-member supervisory panel known as the Federal Radio Commission (FRC). Congress envisioned that the FRC could complete its work within a year, returning oversight of broadcasting's operations to the Department of Commerce and Labor at that time.[11]

Hindsight is often more sufficient than foresight. We know now that the original assignment proliferated in manifold proportions, growing into complex dimensions that Congress had never imagined. The upshot was that within a few years, no less than nine departments of the federal bureaucracy maintained intermingling activities in radio, dipping into public, private, and governmental sectors. Early in the administration of President Franklin D. Roosevelt, meanwhile, a unifying committee on communications named by Roosevelt urged creation of a component expanding the FRC's duties. The telegraph and telephone industries would be added to radio's oversight if the panel's recommendations were enacted. Congress responded by doing just that. On July 1, the Communications Act of 1934 created a seven-member Federal Communications Commission (FCC) with jurisdictional status over any business relying on "wires, cables, or radio as a means of transmission." Over the years since, the act creating the FCC has often been amended, frequently in response to technical advancements.

If the Radio Act of 1927 had ascribed some landmark language in control of the airwaves — underscoring the government's rights to their oversight — the Communications Act of 1934 went still further. By then all Americans were recognized as authentic stakeholders in the broadcasting enterprise. With guidelines to manage the ether for the populace offered, overseers were given both authority and boundaries for executing their tasks. A radio scholar penned the following observations in 1946; by that time, a dozen years had elapsed since the milestone legislation of 1934 had been enacted.

> The first principle, established by the Congress, was that *the people own title to the wave lengths of the air.* Private persons and commercial companies may use them as lessees for a limited period, but they have no title to them. Every owner of a radio station, before receiving a temporary license to operate, signs a waiver to any permanent claim.
>
> The second principle follows naturally from the first: the people's property must be protected. And the people must be safeguarded not only from any permanent sequestration of their property, but also from immediate abuse of it by those to whom it is temporarily ceded in trust. One hundred and thirty million people cannot take personal responsibility for the day-to-day management of their affairs…. It is the function of government to do this, for government alone is answerable to the people. Hence in 1934 Congress established the Federal Communications Commission as our guardian.
>
> The terms of guardianship are clear. They define the nature of our rights as owners of property. They define also … the limits of the powers of the Federal Communications Commission.[12]

The FCC merged the administrative responsibilities for regulating broadcasting and wired communications under the rubric of one agency. The new operation was given broad authority to establish "a rapid, efficient, Nation-wide, and world-wide wire and radio communication service." On July 11, 1934, seven commissioners and 233 federal employees began the task of merging rules and procedures from the Federal Radio Commission, the Interstate Commerce Commission and the Postmaster General into one agency subdivided into a trio of sectors: broadcast, telegraph, and telephone. That unit today has expanded duties commanding a workforce of 2,000 individuals with oversight for newer communications technologies like satellite, microwave and private radio transmission.[13]

Perhaps it should also be noted that — in rendering one of its enveloping opinions — the U.S. Supreme Court made passing reference to radio as equal under law with press (commonly referencing newspapers) and films in its claim to protection under the First Amendment.[14] Thus, the high court considered the broadcasting province worthy of the same respect shown to other more enduring media.

With that as introduction, let's return to the question of funding that broadcasting pursued in the United States. "How will we finance radio?" was a question proffered as far back as 1921. The following year it was a topic of extensive conversation.[15] With arresting urgency, it was raised again in 1923 and 1924. By 1925, it was of such paramount importance among practitioners and would-be practitioners that some resolution of the matter was deemed an imperative.

"The economic explorations were spurred by a number of factors," one intellect enlightened. "Broadcasts of public events via telephone lines involved seemingly fantastic costs, which had not been foreseen. Demands for payment of artists increased the pressure."[16]

The trade periodical *Radio Broadcast* was already rolling from the presses a few years before the major chains were established. In its inaugural May 1922 issue, it proposed a handful of options for underwriting the new communications medium: "endowment of a station by a public-spirited citizen," "municipal financing" (similar to tax-paid schools, museums and other publicly-funded educational and cultural activities and facilities), "a common fund" derived by solicitations among the public and goodwill gestures by private enterprises, as well as sales of "fantasy seats" in an imaginary radio theater promoted to the public.

Radio Broadcast missed advertising in its litany of funding designs just as it missed one adopted in Great Britain and in a few other nations: a tariff levied on receivers. Nearly three years later, in March 1925, the same periodical published a winning entry in a competition among readers for what it considered to be the best answer to the question, "Who is to pay for broadcasting — and how?" In the opinion of its judges, the idea selected was based on assessing purchasers of radio sets $2 per tube or 50 cents per crystal set. (If you translate that into modern air travel, for example, think so much per bag, so much per aisle seat, so much per set of earplugs, so much per snack, so much per blanket, etc.) The radio industry, according to the calculations of the individual that had that brainstorm, would net $18 million annually from those levies. Nobody ever found out if the wordsmith was right or not as all of those suggestions were shelved and the industry went in another direction.

Those early innovators and speculators in Radioland finally set into motion a system that was to have both enduring and profound effects on a commercial sphere with far-reaching implications. The blueprint adopted then has persisted to contemporary times. While it has been superseded in certain quarters by publicly funded, enterprise-supported, and subscription-only aural programming, the bulk of radio broadcasting in America right now remains underwritten by commercial sponsorship.

The decision that paved the way for the ether to become an avenue of advertising was neither settled hastily or without substantial debate. Secretary of Commerce Herbert Hoover, one of that system's strongest detractors, who was given an authoritarian function over the fledgling medium by the Radio Act of 1927, fought tenaciously against commercialization of the airwaves. He was persuaded that selling time to sell goods, services and ideas would be offensive to the audience. As early as February 1922, at a groundbreaking national radio conference in the nation's capital, Hoover admonished participants:

> It is inconceivable that we should allow so great a possibility for service to be drowned in advertising chatter. I have never believed that it was possible to advertise through broadcasting without ruining the industry. I don't believe there is anything the people would take more offense at.... The average person does not want his receiving set filled with that sort of material.

As time went on Hoover's opposition grew louder. Mincing no words at a subsequent radio conference in 1924, he advocated that direct advertising was "the quickest way to kill broadcasting." There were many others who felt as Hoover did, including some influential publications of the era. *Printer's Ink* proclaimed in its issue of February 8, 1923: "Any attempt to make the radio an advertising medium would, we think, prove positively offensive

Although he would be one of the earliest chief executives to speak to the nation by radio, President Herbert Hoover acquired an understanding of issues related to broadcasting that most of his constituents never encountered. As U.S. commerce secretary in the 1920s, prior to a boost to higher office, Hoover had the assignment of being radio's liaison with the feds, setting parameters for its operation. In that capacity he stood his ground in firm opposition to suggestions that would underwrite the new industry with advertising fees. The oversight he gave radio predated the creation of the FRC and the FCC by Congress.

to great numbers of people." In the year before, *The Radio Dealer* trade paper advocated: "The radio industry itself, the makers of sets as well as parts, and the wholesalers as well as retailers, are opposed to the use of the air for advertising purposes.... The one million set owners haven't paid out money for radio for the purpose of listening to reasons why this or that product should be purchased."

> One of the counterproposals to advertising that was fleetingly considered by some was the so-called European style practiced in a number of nations, though not in Great Britain. On the Continent the predominant pattern of radio operations was to place it under government sanction or control. In that structure, Big Brother owned virtually everything: the properties, the personalities, the programming, and — to be certain — the potential for propaganda. The environment made it fairly easy — lacking sufficient oversight — for a party line to flourish, leading a constituency unhesitatingly along a course of unbridled socialism.

That method was investigated and soundly rejected by radio's American forefathers. It may have been as much for the potential for lack of programming diversity as for the inherent dangers within the system itself. Nevertheless, the concept hinted at possibilities that Americans had rebuffed ever since the Declaration of Independence was signed. To pursue that line of activity did not, in the judgment of those setting the course of broadcasting in that epoch attend the nation and its listeners' interests well.[17]

There were many other suggestions and several were explored intensely. One that was forfeited by default was the hope that an affluent philanthropist might step forward and agree to underwrite the costs involved in maintaining radio.[18] A benevolent Andrew Carnegie, who earlier funded more than 2,500 public libraries, allowed, "There is no sin in getting rich, but there is in dying rich." Although the proposal was proffered that someone similarly endowed should take up radio's cause, no one did.

Another idea included a modified form of user reimbursement for services rendered. In March 1922, the entertainment business publication *Variety* speculated: "Perhaps some way of charging the owners of receiving sets will be worked out." Perhaps that might be done through assessing an annual fee to each user of the service. But it was not to be. Turning the ether into a commercial zone ultimately made the greatest sense to most people connected with the industry, and though not all were happy about it, that plan was ultimately adopted.

> For a time advertisers were baffled as to how to use this new access to public attention.... An association of greeting card manufacturers presented a talk on the history of Christmas cards. The Haynes company presented the story of the Haynes automobile as told by Mr. Haynes.[19] Gillette offered a talk on fashions in beards since medieval times, culminating in the delights of the safety razor. The resemblance to a carnival pitch was close enough to be uncomfortable, and the telephone executives sought to minimize this. A talk on cigarettes was "heavily censored."[20] A "discreet" talk on the teeth and their care, offered by a toothpaste company, was delayed while executives argued whether anything so personal as tooth-brushing should be mentioned on the air. It finally was.[21]

These caretakers of the ether were anxious to make money but were all together determined that radio would maintain the highest decorum feasible at all times. To that end each new case presented new dilemmas. Radio's guiding policy manual was under constant updating. The officials came up with a list of "do nots" for the air: do not mention prices, the color of a commodity's packaging, the locations of dispensaries where an item might be bought, no samples could be given away, and language had to be very strict. A manufacturer of vacuum cleaners, for instance, couldn't embellish with "sweep no more, my lady" in its pitches for that could be offensive to fans of the popular tune "My Old Kentucky Home."[22] The Cialis and Tampax makers, had they existed, would never have had a chance!

In commercializing the airwaves, radio in the United States appeared to hesitate at first, initially dipping its toes into the water before eventually becoming wholly submersed in the sea. At the outset, many program underwriters (sponsors) named their shows, orchestras, comedians, actors and related themes after whatever they were offering for public consumption. Hence, there was ethereal taxonomy resulting like *The Goodrich Silver Masked Tenor, The Ipana Troubadours, The A&P Gypsies, The Cliquot Club Eskimos, The Gold Dust Twins* (Goldie and Dusty), *The Happiness Boys, The Best Foods Boys, The Taystee Loafers*, the Firestone Orchestra and Chorus of *The Voice of Firestone, The Lucky Strike Dance Band*, and Paul Oliver and Olive Palmer of *The Palmolive Hour*, among many diversions capitalizing on product and company nomenclature.

After 1925 ... listings [in newspapers] carried the names of programs by sponsors, i.e., the *Eveready Hour,* the *Sieberling Singers,* etc. In 1927, the New York Publishers Association, representing the principal New York newspapers, moved to eliminate the names of sponsors from such listings. They held that such listings were free advertising for which the newspaper was not being paid. This program was followed for about two months, until the Scripps-Howard interests purchased the *Telegram.* The *Telegram* decided to continue listing the sponsor's name on the grounds that radio programs were news and the public was entitled to all information about them. Other New York papers were then forced to drop their program of censored listings.

But when before 1930, news about radio and radio personalities had been given full publicity in the press as a matter of news, afterward most newspapers dropped not only such news items, but all program listings as well. In many cities, protests from readers who had come to look upon program listings as a newspaper service compelled newspapers to restore the bare listings.[23]

The so-called "indirect appeals," in which a sponsor's or commodity's name appeared — albeit subdued in nature and often sans specific (or direct) advertising pitches — were believed to do little to acceptably sell goods, services and ideas. They were at best "mentions" of a sponsor's offerings, coming in through the back door but not really justifying the expense they had gone to in order to present those on-air performances. The people paying the bills frankly anticipated a better return from the rather large numbers of advertising dollars they were spending. Ultimately discarding the indirect method almost altogether, they spawned a routine of straightforward plugs for their commodities instead, pitching products directly to consumers by readily soliciting purchases (or asking listeners to buy into a concept) for whatever was being proffered.[24]

Sixty-five years ago, a venerated academician and radio historiographer allowed: "Without advertising, broadcasting, as we know it, would not exist. It is our radio's only source of revenue, accepted and acceptable in preference to any other known method of financing a very costly business."[25] There are a few asterisks in the form of alternatives to that nearly universally applied method of underwriting that are being practiced today, although somewhat sparingly, by some elements of the trade in this country. Commercialization remains, nevertheless, the most viable, accepted, and dominant means of sustaining communications on the ether this late in the day — now on radio, television, the Internet, and in some newer applications of advanced technology. Nothing thus far has replaced selling goods, services, and ideas as a more universally acceptable plan. (If it ain't broke don't fix it.)

Even after all of those preliminaries, however, with their due emphasis upon the development of radio and a method of sustaining it, would it be surprising to learn that the great disparity between electronic and print media remained unsettled? Furthermore, would it surprise you that the differences could be clearly witnessed in how those dual factions of journalism were regarded by the federal government? To wit, by the late 1930s,

> only in Washington did the members of radio's news corps operate under the disadvantage of an almost complete official nonrecognition. In the House and Senate, radio correspondents were barred from the press galleries; they had no admission to the press conferences held regularly by the President, cabinet members, senators and congressmen. In the Senate radio newsmen were forced to sit in the visitors' gallery from which they might view the broad posteriors of orating senators. They were refused permission to take notes. On one occasion, a Vice-President had bellowed his protest at sight of notebook and pencil in a commentator's hand.
>
> In glorified contrast, the gentlemen of the [printed] press occupied a gallery of their own fronting the lawmakers. From it, every little aside, gesture, twinkle which gives meaning to a senator's talk was visible.[26]

Censorship could be exhibited in myriad ways. The sting of exclusion often left radio newsmen derelict, at a distinct disadvantage to their "accepted" equivalents, the "gentlemen of the press" representing journalism's more durable society. But after a handful of radio newsmen went to war with congressional leaders over the disparity — in spite of lobbying from print reporters not to do so — both houses of lawmakers passed legislation extending similar privileges to the dual media. Noted one observer: "This breach of a century-long tradition is much more significant than it seems on the surface, for it marked — after a decade of bitter rivalry — the achievement of an at least official equality of radio with the press. Actually, it was a final recognition of the birth of the Fifth Estate."[27] The newscasters of the ether were accorded courtesies that had heretofore been given only to the "press," which in contemporary times itself seems a misnomer.

Broadcasting's fight with the feds over whom and to what extent the airwaves were controlled wasn't settled for all time in the 1920s and 1930s, however. Indeed not, for the politicians persisted through a vigorous, nasty, and scandalous Sen. Joseph R. McCarthy-inspired blacklisting pursuit in the late 1940s and early to mid 1950s. In so doing, they threw their weight around by underscoring anew that "we maintain the authority over the ether." Although some Communist and Nazi sympathizers may have been correctly branded by their vigilant actions — particularly so after the zealots sought individuals in government, the performing arts, media, and other realms within the public notoriety (some of whom were "guilty" by inaccurate linkages) — in the same breath whole careers and lives were wrecked as Big Brother peeked into nooks and crannies once held as private domains.

A couple of decades following that episode, the Washington watchdogs were back at it again, as powerfully intense as they had been on previous occasions. That time they took on the television news industry by aiming their weapons at CBS and its president Frank Stanton. He adamantly refused to comply with their request to provide outtakes (material that didn't get into a broadcast) from a documentary shown on the network. Airing over CBS-TV on February 23, 1971, *The Selling of the Pentagon* had greatly agitated the lawmakers. Six weeks afterward, on April 8, a congressional subcommittee subpoenaed Stanton to produce the leftovers of that show that failed to make the final cut. The resulting flare-up became a defining moment in broadcast journalism.

Only in the timing was radio spared. Television's usurping of the dominant role in news and entertainment delivery made it the target of the congressional probe. But there seemed little doubt that — should the broadcasters falter under the weight of a probing investigation — the consequent intrusion into the ether by rabid watchdogs that would surely result hardly would have been limited to television. A vengeful Congress was poised to do battle, clearly anxious to pounce on the broadcasting industry's journalistic endeavors and to once more teach the industry who really had the ultimate power over the airwaves. To wit:

> Congress believed it had the authority to investigate broadcast news. It also thought the television networks had become too powerful and their news divisions "out of control." At the same time, the Nixon White House was engaged in an active campaign to discredit the networks and news coverage critical of the President and his conduct of the war. It supported the investigation.
>
> After hearings, the Committee voted that Stanton should be held in contempt of Congress. This could have placed CBS broadcast licenses in jeopardy and sent Stanton to jail. The House of Representatives then held an extraordinary constitutional debate of "high privilege" about its power to investigate the electronic press and the standing of broadcast news under the First Amendment....
>
> Stanton's career was marked by a continuing struggle for freedom of information. For example, he not only defied congressional investigation of news judgment at the risk of contempt of Congress, but also secured the suspension of prohibiting legislation to permit the broadcast of

> the Nixon-Kennedy debates; increased the programming devoted to news and provided free time to the opposition political party to balance the President's use of the airways [sic]; and insisted throughout upon the highest standards for broadcast news coverage....
>
> No newspaper, magazine or other part of the press could be required constitutionally to comply with such a subpoena....
>
> The view of many in Congress at the time was put most directly by Representative John Dingell, the powerful Democrat from Michigan who believed deeply ... in the need to regulate what they considered to be the undue power of broadcasters. In the absence of government scrutiny, broadcasters would run riot with no one "to bid them nay" ....
>
> Stanton saw that if Congress could summon television newsmen before congressional hearings and review their editorial news judgment, there would be no end to it. It could be expected that Congress would do so whenever it was politically popular or whenever the government was criticized, or even just to get a headline. And it would judge "fairness" in governmental terms, not in journalistic terms.
>
> To succeed, Stanton had to stand successfully against both the power of the Congress and the Nixon White House.[28]

The author of these words, incidentally, was executive vice president and general counsel of the National Broadcasting Company at one time. His treatise suggests — as has been stated in print elsewhere and verbally on many occasions — that the trade family of broadcasters celebrated the fortitude of Frank Stanton on behalf of all of them. In the end, he won the victory by guaranteeing continued freedom of the ether. When the first vote was taken in the House to cite Stanton and CBS for contempt of Congress on July 13, 1971, the outcome was 151 to return the issue to a Commerce Committee and 147 to cite Stanton and CBS. A subsequent vote on whether to recommit the issue to the Committee on Interstate and Foreign Commerce tallied 226 in favor, 181 against, two answering "present," and 24 abstentions. Several sources confirmed that tremendous arm-twisting by affiliate radio and TV stations in their districts delivered clout that caught the attention of some lawmakers.[29]

The zealots who sought to squash journalistic integrity and freedom were once again disappointed. Had it gone the other way, the impact on journalistic activity on the air would have been "severe," according to the chronicler: "The television press would be subject to continued second-guessing in congressional hearings called to review television news coverage for acceptability. It could not help but become weak, even submissive."[30] And in that environment, radio newscasts — and newscasters — surely would have been subjected to intense scrutiny and investigation, too, if and when the feds deemed it appropriate.

> Stanton's stand in 1971 was a challenge to government to give the electronic press room to do its job....
>
> If the government is permitted to oversee editorial news judgment on the new Information Superhighway, then we can expect, as history has repeatedly shown, that the government will try to control or restrict the news to serve its own agenda. Government arrangements to provide "access," "fairness," "equal time," or "responsibility" all sound useful but all eventually become instruments used to distort news coverage....
>
> If the concept of government involvement in news coverage is accepted, there will neither be an independent press nor the necessary flow of information to the public, particularly about the government itself.[31]

On the day the Congress failed to carry out its threats against a major player in broadcast journalism, it was a good day to be a member of the electronic Fourth Estate.

5

Censorship: Pressures from Without, Within

With all of the aforementioned established as a preamble, let's now focus our attention on intrusion into the transmission of news and information beamed across the air via radio signals — its sources, impact, and limitations on the industry. First, of course, does it exist? And if it does, to what extent? And finally, how has broadcasting — and particularly, radio — responded to Big Brother watching (and listening)?

In a scholarly introspective that pertains in part to the prospect of interference in broadcasting substance, the issue of censorship is deliberated. While the opportunity for censoring had existed since broadcasting's earliest days — and particularly so following the appointment of governmental regulators derived by the Radio Act of 1927 — the question became still more pertinent during the Second World War.

> Despite the heroics and resourcefulness demonstrated by broadcasters in obtaining war news, one of the chief concerns for newscasters and commentators was the threat of government censorship. Even before the war had begun, many in radio felt that once the United States entered the battle, commercial radio would be appropriated by the government and converted into an arm of the national war effort. Such considerations were not new, for as early as 1933 the question of radio and the next war was discussed in a radio fan publication.[1] Although a federal take-over never occurred after American entry into the war in 1941, two governmental organizations were quickly created to supervise broadcasting on the homefront: the Office of Censorship and the Office of War Information. They were kept busy overseeing commercial radio for, as *Variety* reported, by mid–1942 there were 202 weekly broadcasts of war news (CBS, 72; NBC, 40; Blue, 52; Mutual, 38), and 173 war-related commentaries per week (CBS, 49; NBC, 26; Blue, 41; Mutual, 57).[2]
>
> Although censorship was distasteful to newscasters and commentators, it had been a fact of radio life for the years since the Federal Communications Commission had banned blasphemy, profanity, obscene allusions, and the like from the air.[3]

Roosevelt created the Office of Censorship (OC) with ex–Associated Press executive news editor Byron Price as director on December 16, 1941, nine days after the Japanese attack on Pearl Harbor.[4] Ted Koop, a former colleague of Price at AP and a future CBS vice president, became his deputy at OC. Price assigned station owner John Harold Ryan, who eventually led the National Association of Broadcasters as president, to radio relations. The censorship was strictly voluntary; news copy didn't pass under the eyes of a censor before being aired unless a radio station, network or newspaper requested that an item be checked. "Voluntary censorship was a gamble, an expression of confidence in the patriotism and good sense of the people who handled news," an observer wrote, adding, "And for the most part, it worked."[5]

After Edward Bernays had converted CBS's Bill Paley to the inspiration that radio could be something more than a conduit for mere amusement (Chapter 4), Ed Klauber sated the CBS chairman with a sweeping tutorial in the rudimentary elements of comprehensive news coverage and reporting. It's undoubtedly due to Klauber's being there that the chain didn't pursue, in its entirety, Paley's personal penchant for entertainment. Without Klauber in a strategic post to bend the ear of the chairman there is speculation that CBS's news might have originally pursued the hackneyed mock-up of the movie newsreels.[6] Paley's Hollywood chums were then producing that widely distributed form of information (infomercial?), complete with inflated self-promotion gimmickry.

By Paley's own account, he instigated the rules for evenhandedness in the early 1930s — ultimately absorbed into a Fairness Doctrine issued by the Federal Communications Commission in 1949 — that directed broadcasters to not only allocate time to controversial public issues but to also consent to provide time for divergent perspectives. Paley cautioned that, in the early 1930s, he was apprehensive that regular contributors to the airwaves would limit their exhortations to their own partialities. What he was really afraid of was that — stemming from that opportunity — the feds could step in and react. The personal biases could stir investigation followed by rebuke and then sanctions forced onto the broadcast chains. Thus, Paley allowed in an interview, "These guidelines were not imposed on us by government. They were imposed on us by our own volition."[7] It was something he was clearly proud to have accomplished.

A respected examiner cited dual types of broadcasting censoring[8]: (1) direct interference by the federal government to prevent certain types of programming, and (2) editorial selection of what to air by station management or network officials. Statute and constitution prevented federal agencies from interfering in program content as a general rule. Even the FCC, controlling the matter of issuing and renewing station licenses, was prohibited from directly telling those outlets what they should or should not air. On the other hand, editorial selection occurred rather frequently in those days. Three reasons often enumerated in justifying that intervention then would hardly hold water today, almost seeming ludicrous in contemporary times[9]: (1) the fear of antagonizing listeners by airing controversial opinions, (2) the desire to observe the boundaries of good taste, and (3) the fear of offending a commercial sponsor. We shall return to this topic again in a later chapter.

The subject of censorship and its potential implications took center stage in a wide spectrum of readers' opinions published by *Variety* early in 1939. Although they agreed that few incidences of federal interference had occurred thus far, many examples could be given in which station and network editorial selection was present. You may recall from your studies of American history that this was a period in which U.S. citizens were torn between two opposing points of view: (1) supporting European nations that were unified in their efforts to curtail global aggression, and (2) preserving existing freedoms and an opposing isolationist posture among some that kept our nation out of the conflict.[10]

In a little discourse on Ed Murrow, Bob Edwards discerns something that appreciably aided CBS in September 1939, allowing it to leapfrog ahead of its broadcasting equivalents in newsgathering and reporting:

Murrow's competition made a huge mistake. NBC and the Mutual Broadcasting System suspended their coverage of news from Europe. Broadcasting was more rigidly regulated in 1939, and the networks were intimidated by warnings from the Roosevelt administration that the networks should behave responsibly during war. By the time NBC and MBS returned to war coverage a few months later, CBS had taken advantage and asserted itself as the leader in radio news.[11]

In what might be interpreted by some as a plainly partisan valuation — even if his facts are altogether true, and a case may be clearly made for that — about a half-century afterward, CBS newsman David Schoenbrun offered these conclusions of that period in competitive journalistic aggression[12]:

> When the war ended, CBS News was well established as the leader in network news. NBC and Mutual and ABC lagged far behind. CBS had gotten off to a faster start than the others. In fact, when CBS began expanding its European coverage, just before America entered the war, NBC and Mutual canceled their European reports. America had proclaimed its neutrality in the war, and the two networks, behaving as if they were under government regulation, decided that reporting from Europe would violate our neutrality. This absurd conclusion permitted CBS to forge ahead of the others. They worked hard to catch up to CBS during the war and, with excellent reporters, managed to close the gap a bit. But CBS remained the acknowledged leader for a decade. The others kept trying and finally did match CBS, and at times surpass it in the ratings, but never managed to win the prestige and renown of CBS News.

Some observers might insist that — perhaps with only intermittent lapses — CBS's dominance of electronic news media persisted beyond the proverbial decade of supremacy acknowledged by Schoenbrun. Closer scrutiny hints that his reckoning, complete with its time limitation, is about right. Whether NBC Radio news ever forged ahead of CBS's powerful position of reliable trust for a sustained interval is probably debatable — even with an attractive live-action *Monitor* ("going places and doing things") added to NBC's mix in the mid–1950s.

Admittedly prejudiced NBC adherents like Reuven Frank, twice president of NBC News, nevertheless submitted that it was in *television*— not radio — that CBS's principal rival ultimately caught up with the perceived leader of the pack and, finally, surpassed it. It was done by pairing the darlings of the 1956 summer political conventions, Chet Huntley and David Brinkley, as successors to John Cameron Swayze's *Camel News Caravan* on NBC-TV. The *Huntley-Brinkley Report*, with its dual anchors residing in as many cities (Huntley in New York; Brinkley in Washington), premiered Oct. 29, 1956.

And *Douglas Edwards with the News* over at CBS must have felt a slight tremor as the earth began to rumble a little. (While Edwards was able to hang on to his coveted post for 15 years —1947–62 — as Huntley and Brinkley dug in for the long haul the quake that was building for CBS eventually turned into a tsunami.[13]) According to NBC's Frank, who had put the two new newscasters together just for a season of politics: "They carved a hiatus in CBS News's half century of complacency and soothed NBC News's frustration at failing to convince its own superiors that, given support, it could do as well."[14] But all that was out in the future.

Returning to 1939, as a result of the brief lapse that occurred, a reputation was born for CBS that — while definitely challenged on many occasions — may not be seriously threatened on the aural airwaves even yet. In the decades following the golden age of radio, ABC and a few other since debuting newsgathering enterprises built solid brigades of reporters to compete in that arena. Meanwhile, today CBS remains a steady, dependable source for millions who continue to rely on it in an era long after the once powerful voices of MBS and NBC have faded — only a remnant of NBC now remaining and no MBS whatsoever.

Parenthetically, meanwhile, results of a Gallup poll released in September 1940 indicated that just 16 percent of Americans favored providing increased support to Great Britain. One month later, with the destructive consequences of the blitz fresh on their minds — and much of their information acquired from CBS's Ed Murrow — 52 percent of the populace favored more assistance to America's Motherland in a subsequent Gallup survey.[15] By June 1940, practically every news commentator, with the notable exceptions of Boake Carter and Fulton Lewis, Jr., devoted himself to boosting American aid to England beyond what was then being provided by the federal government.

As much is to be referenced to commentators in this chapter, before continuing, it will be helpful to establish a practical definition of what is meant by the discipline in order for all of us to be on the same page. This pithy clarification by radio historian Mitchell Charnley is satisfactory for our purposes:

> Commentary, in radio news usage, is generally taken to be explanation of a news event in the light of the speaker's personal knowledge *and judgment*.... Commentary ... is the expression of judgment.... The commentator ... seeks not merely to inform the audience...; instead he tries to lead the audience's thinking in the direction in which he thinks it should go.[16]

A few of the better known commentators of the day were already familiar to some radio listeners because they penned columns or else contributed to syndicated, wire service, and localized newspaper journalism. Among them were H. R. Baukhage, Elmer Davis, H. V. Kaltenborn, David Lawrence, Fulton Lewis, Jr., Drew Pearson, Raymond Swing, Dorothy Thompson, Frederic William Wile, and Walter Winchell. These analysts believed strongly in their cause and found it increasingly problematical to keep their thoughts to themselves. Assessing it all three-and-a-half decades later, a scribe lamented: "Listeners considered newscasts objective if they agreed with what they heard. If not, they condemned radio's war hysteria."[17] Take away the reference to war and the same application could be made about much of contemporary radio.

Variety was the "unofficial spokesman for the radio industry" in one critic's opinion. Be that as it may, and there is certainly sufficient evidence to make a case for that hypothesis, the organ cited a reversal of attitude among U.S. citizens over a two-year period. In an article appearing in June 1941 under the banner "Words Win Wars," its editors extolled the virtues of the ethereal crusaders of modern justice. Keeping in mind that *Variety*— despite its coverage of the world of amusements — was in print journalism and not electronic, it found justification for lauding the legends from another medium. It was a departure from a segment of the print media's traditional past, which at one time it might have been loath to do:

> There is something both ridiculous and unwholesome in the continuing spectacle of radio broadcasters and commentators being publicly "accused" of the crime of being pro–British when the official policy of the United States is frankly and completely pro–British.... The people's airwaves have some relationship to the people's government and the policy of the latter must, in the pinch, be the policy of the former.... Which side is supposed to win this war? Who doesn't want England to win? Why are we taxing ourselves until it hurts?[18]

"No one can convince me that ... journalists cannot help contribute to the suicide of their own country," Eric Sevareid said on CBS on July 5, 1941. It was as if he was underscoring the obligation that he and his counterparts had at that crucial juncture in the life of the nation. "Such fervent expressions of opinion help suggest where the radio industry stood," noted one historiographer. "The medium best able to present a specific point of view about foreign policy to the entire nation openly urged Roosevelt to increase American involvement overseas."[19] The FCC had solemnly decreed only a month before this that "the broadcaster cannot be an advocate." Oh yeah? Censorship, so it seemed, wasn't working, at least not well. "By the summer of 1941, radio commentators reflected the attitude of most Americans; they certainly shaped their news analyses to agree with what they hoped to be the prevailing consensus — 'Who doesn't want England to win?'"[20]

Meanwhile, in *Variety's* submissions, the preponderance of contributors desired that — if a war crisis surfaced that could result in our nation's involvement — radio would be allowed to regulate itself free of government controls. Ed Klauber, executive vice-president at CBS,[21] ably argued the case for self-censorship of the industry, focusing on a trio of past encounters[22]: (1) every mention of censorship is met with increasing opposition, (2) when the truth is out, broadcasters have been making earnest efforts to handle points of contention with fairness, and (3) the public knows that broadcasters act swiftly to correct their faults, plus the public has always relied on this method of regulation.[23]

Ultimately, when our country did enter the war, the wishes of most broadcasters were met.[24] Instead of confiscation or rigorous control of radio by federal overseers, a pathway that allowed radio officials to practice voluntary self-censorship was pursued.[25] A journalist observed: "The voluntary position on censorship taken by the government was a reflection of both the consensus within the country regarding the war, and the confidence of the New Deal administration that it could withstand a critical appraisal of its war efforts."[26] At the same time the government's preferences in program content were made known to stations and networks. A sizable portion of this impacted what was broadcast on news and public affairs programming.[27]

In September 1939, after war had broken out in Europe, CBS, MBS, and NBC issued a joint declaration of news policy:

No news analyst or news broadcaster of any kind is to be allowed to express personal editorial judgment or to select or omit news with the purpose of creating any given effect, and no news analyst ... is to be allowed to say anything in an effort to influence action or opinion of others one way or the other.... His basis for evaluation should, of course, be impersonal, sincere, and honest.

Before implementing their initiative, nonetheless, the trio of national broadcasters ran their statement by the Federal Communications Commission. The chains wanted to absolve themselves of any potential blame for collusive or antitrust tactics that might subsequently surface and create legal quagmires for them that they simply didn't need. Once that was done, the FCC itself issued the so-called Mayflower pronouncement that disapproved of editorializing by broadcasters, in January 1941.[28] The situation remained fairly rigid for most of the rest of that decade, until 1949, when the FCC unilaterally reversed its position by dispensing the Fairness Doctrine. That directive urged licensees to take editorial stands on public issues.[29]

All of this censorship business affected different commentators of the airwaves differently although all of them might have been just as happy to see the regulator tactics disappear. H. V. Kaltenborn, analyzing the day's news for CBS in the early 1940s, and one of the most popular and respected voices on the ether, brought trouble on himself with repeated outspoken declarations. The hierarchy at the network asked him to soft-pedal his pronouncements and prognostications with more general observations rather than unmistakably issuing his own perspectives. Years later, Kaltenborn remembered:

Vice President Edward Klauber would call me up to his office for a friendly heart-to-heart talk.... "Just don't be so personal," he'd say to me. "Use such phrases as 'it is said,' 'there are those who believe,' 'the opinion is held in well-informed quarters,' 'some experts have come to the conclusion....' Why keep on saying 'I think' and 'I believe' when you can put over the same idea much more persuasively by quoting someone else?"[30]

After capitalist Wendell Willkie, new to politics, joined contention as a presidential prospect in 1940 — on hearing a Willkie speech — Kaltenborn composed a mention for his broadcast: "I listened to Wendell Willkie's speech last night. It was wholly admirable." But before he could act on that, the newsman deleted it, exchanging it for this bit of analysis: "Millions of Americans of both parties listened to Wendell Willkie's speech last night. Most of them agreed that it was a wholly admirable speech."[31]

It wasn't long until Kaltenborn was offered a nightly spot on NBC and — feeling the pressure mounting at CBS and believing the grass was greener on the other side — took it. Kaltenborn's transfer was "somewhat to the relief of CBS."[32] What he didn't realize was that NBC was "moving toward a position similar to that of CBS."[33] He'd soon be regularly summoned by a new set of broadcast officials for the same imperfection.

The business fraternity of radio (and TV, now), the National Association of Broadcasters, supplemented its own code of ethics:

> News shall not be selected for the purpose of furthering or hindering either side of any controversial public issue nor shall it be colored by the opinions or desires of the station or the network management, the editor or others engaged in its preparation, or the person actually delivering it over the air, or, in the case of sponsored news broadcasts, the advertiser.... News commentators as well as other newscasters shall be governed by those provisions.

In January 1942, the U.S. Office of War Censorship announced an official position on programs that might provide information helpful to internal spies and saboteurs, or external military and naval commanders. In a *Code of Wartime Practices for American Broadcasters*, Big Brother appealed for deliberate suppression of some news, ad-lib talk and game shows, and foreign language features. Banned from these broadcasts were references to the weather, fortifications, war-related experiments, troop and materiel movements, casualty lists, and similar revelations which could be exploited by America's enemies. There were several areas pointedly disallowed

One of the most universally admired news analysts of radio's golden age was veteran newspaperman Hans Von Kaltenborn, age 52 by the time his nightly broadcasts aired nationally. Possessing a riveting awareness of international affairs, in some quarters Kaltenborn was dubbed the "dean of American commentators." His staccato delivery was an identifying trademark, initially on CBS (1930–40), then on NBC (1940–55). Kaltenborn protested vigorously to CBS superiors when he was cautioned to tone down his opinionated rhetoric, only to learn later he had traded for the same impediment after jumping ship.

on entertainment programming that could be innocently and unwittingly used to convey coded or secret messages.

When MBS newscaster Arthur Hale unconsciously spoke of atomic research occurring at Pasco, Washington, a handful of armed forces brass was so enraged that it called for an end to voluntary controls, replacing it with military censorship in the country.[34] The record of American broadcasters was nearly flawless, however, and no changes in the system were made.[35] Broadcast journalists adhered to the voluntary standards in credible fashion. Live broadcasts, such as Edward R. Murrow's reports from London, could unintentionally disclose military secrets. The dilemma was settled after a British expurgator was added to a chair beside Murrow while he was on the air. If the newsman began talking about delicate military factors, the suppressor tapped him on the shoulder and Murrow proceeded to another topic.[36]

> All broadcasts originating overseas had to be cleared in advance by government censors in each country. In America a different sort of censorship prevailed. There were pressures, if not outright prohibitions. Roosevelt's press secretary, Steve Early, said that radio "might have to be taught manners if it were a bad child." The President himself, in notes he dictated as the basis for a speech by Early before the National Association of Broadcasters, warned the networks not to let "false news" be broadcast. "The Government is watching," he added ominously, "and will continue to watch with great interest to see whether those who control radio will carry out this public duty of their own accord." The President did not explain what he meant by "false news." The networks understood this to mean news unfavorable to the administration's point of view.[37]

"Objectivity, as it evolved on radio news" allowed one wag, "was embodied in stories that did not routinely displease the White House and those that did not routinely displease corporate sponsors. The war brought public relations and news management into broadcast journalism, and the success of radio news imposed commercial considerations on reporters and network executives alike. For the networks, the ideal of objectivity sounded worthy enough, but it was a very effective tool for disciplining uppity newscasters, keeping further regulation at bay, and keeping the sponsors happy."[38]

CBS persisted with its strategy which wasn't severely defined until 1954, when Ed Murrow voiced his well-remembered denunciation of Sen. Joseph R. McCarthy (R.-Wis.) on television's *See It Now*.[39] "That was the exception, not the rule," a media historian proclaimed.[40] Co-produced by Murrow, that series itself validated the tube as an unremitting stream of ideas that might be expected to flow forever in supplying original journalistic substance.[41] *See It Now*, incidentally, was the second time that Murrow introduced a broadcasting medium to in-depth news, according to one scholar: "He was a pioneer of radio journalism in 1938 and television news in 1951. Techniques he introduced on both are still in use today, from the multipoint radio roundup to the split-screen TV interview."[42]

> Ironically, while Murrow argued for public understanding of the dangers of McCarthyism, there were many within the broadcasting, film, and advertising industries who bowed to pressure and agreed to the "blacklisting" of certain writers, actors, producers, and directors because of allegations that they were somehow linked to Communism.... The monograph [*Red Channels*, 1950] listed more than 150 broadcast employees and suggested that they should not be trusted as loyal Americans. Loyalty oaths were the order of the day.... It was in this grim atmosphere that Murrow ... and other courageous journalists worked.[43]

Parenthetically, and strictly as an aside, Roosevelt took a bemused approach to the press in his dealings with it. He immediately grasped the potential and power of the radio microphone, becoming the nation's first sitting chief executive to put the airwaves to recurring use in communicating with the people who made up his subjects. At the same time—while considering the press corps that followed him wherever he went to be "inevitable"— he wouldn't have missed them had they given him more leeway from their unremitting prying eyes. Roosevelt relished his moments out of their sight. Privately, to his chief of staff, Naval Fleet Admiral William D. Leahy, a trusted advisor and personal friend for 36 years, the president referred to the media frequently as "ghouls who are just waiting for me to fall out of the automobile, or get shot, or something."[44] It was telling evidence of how those who reported his every word and movement were perceived by a man who had by and large gained their confidence.

Attorneys for NBC were hesitant about allowing newsman H. V. Kaltenborn to say anything he wished on the air. Until wartime censoring mandated it, however, he seldom used a script. Kaltenborn's daily NBC commentary beginning in May 1942 received special dispensation, however: "Wartime censors exempted Kaltenborn from the general requirement that commentators not deviate from the script submitted in advance of the broadcast. His reputation and his long experience won him the concession that he could ad-lib an idea

Edward R. Murrow is remembered as the patron saint of his profession, hailed by historians as the father of radio and television journalism (1938, 1951). Unmistakably he achieved iconic status with his daily accounts of the Second World War, his postwar nightly radio newscasts for 15 years, his innovative early TV news features, and his exposé of a powerful senator's demagoguery that stunted the careers of scores of public figures. "The Murrow Boys," a deputation of reporters Murrow enlisted to inform America of the war's progress from vantage points throughout Europe, contributed in personifying his legend, too.

here or there as fresh thoughts struck him in the middle of a commentary. After the war he continued the practice of preparing scripts in advance, but also continued to add material on the spur of the moment."[45]

The U.S. Office of Censorship noted that — of 7,000 network news broadcasts aired in calendar year 1942 — only about two percent defied the voluntary code. In the main these were seen as inadvertent mentions of weather conditions, a "no-no" in that timeframe. Just 17 of 2,000 network news programs included infractions during first quarter 1943.[46] At the beginning of that era federal authorities assured: "Free speech will not suffer during this emergency period beyond the absolute precautions which are necessary to the protection of a culture which makes our radio the freest in the world."[47] That generally appeared to be the case.

Actually, sometimes it was the self-policing itself that became an issue at odds with some broadcasters. Some unhappy campers in several quarters targeted CBS in one flare-up. On its own initiative, perhaps in a spirit of cooperation with Big Brother, in September 1943, the web issued some ultimatums to its newscasters that severely limited what they were to be allowed to say on the air. The newsmen's commentary programs weren't to proffer any personal opinions or editorializing of the news any longer. The new order ostensibly violated not only the soul of broadcast journalism but also the expressed faith of the federal government in commercial radio.[48]

On one occasion Paul W. White, to whom CBS's news department answered in the 1930s, insisted:[49]

> The public interest cannot be served in radio by giving selected news analysts a preferred and one-sided position. [A news analyst] is to marshal the facts on any specific subject and out of his common or special knowledge to present those facts so as to inform his listeners rather than to persuade them.... Ideally, in the case of controversial issues, the audience should be left with no impression as to which side the analyst himself actually favors.

The declaration became a cause célèbre within a matter of days, however.

James L. Fly, at the time carrying some weight as Federal Communications Commission chairman, expressed his thoughts publicly on it. In an address before the Radio Executives Club on October 7, 1943, Fly stressed that CBS's policy gave a single individual "tremendous power and discretion over news."[50] He admonished the ruling by the chain as establishing an "editorial policy." Any directive that required people like Edward R. Murrow and William L. Shirer (1904–93) to "mouth secondhand opinions" could "serve no good purpose" in Fly's judgment.

This new edict didn't sit well with CBS's on-air commentators either, among them Murrow and Shirer, as well as Ned Calmer, George Fielding Eliot, Everett Holles and Quincy Howe. The commentators who were heard on rival networks didn't think much of it also. (What if the CBS policy took hold for them, too?) Walter Winchell of NBC Blue groused: "Aren't we lucky that Patrick Henry's message didn't have to be reported by the Columbia Broadcasting System? The air ain't as free as it used to be. It's subject to the whims of CBS and its highest mucky-mucks."[51] At about the same time, an outspoken H. V. Kaltenborn of NBC admonished[52]:

> No news analyst worth his salt could or would be completely neutral or objective. He shows his editorial bias by every act of selection or rejection from the vast mass of news material placed before him. He often expresses his opinion by the mere matter of shading and emphasis. He selects from a speech, or interview, or public statement the particular sentences or paragraphs that appeal to him. Every exercise of his editorial judgment constitutes an expression of opinion.

Kaltenborn had marshaled a fraternal group of 31 similar-minded radio commentators in New York in 1942. "Several colleagues were excluded from the select company because of doubts about what they were doing and how well they were doing it," a source alleged.[53] This troupe dubbed itself the Association of Radio News Analysts (ARNA). Among the names of its charter membership there could be found a few legends of the trade: George Hamilton Combs, Elmer Davis, George Fielding Eliot, Burnett Hershey, Charles Hodges, Quincy Howe, H. V. Kaltenborn, Denis McEvoy, Waverly Root, William Shirer, Johannes Steel, Raymond Swing, Lowell Thomas, John Vandercook, Linton Wells, and more. Kaltenborn was elected the group's initial president and Davis and Swing were the first vice presidents with Howe secretary-treasurer.[54]

Incidentally, Shirer's name seems to be unavoidably interjected into several matters encountered with this. He hasn't been fully introduced (for more detail you may read his biography in the Appendix at the end of this text). There is much to appreciate about him, however. If Shirer can't be legitimately declared a co-founding father of global news reporting, he certainly made sterling strides in assisting the man who singularly realized that legacy. Among many accomplishments, in 1938, Murrow and Shirer co-created an indispensable segment to the broadcast schedule — the nightly roundup of news (theirs from Europe). Murrow hosted it and the program itself "would change broadcasting and journalism forever," precisely (as it turned out) assured one historian.[55]

Suffice it for now to observe that Shirer and Murrow were heralded for their contributions in establishing radio as "a vital source of news and not just a place to hear game shows, dramas, and comedies."[56] Their input, for a large contingent of listeners, decidedly altered the landscape of American broadcasting that the audience had been accustomed to hearing during the initial decade of network radio. Surveying the participatory summary configuration that they introduced which became a watershed in headline delivery — debuting with the *CBS World News Roundup* on March 13, 1938 — one appraisal credited the model's instigators like this[57]:

> Murrow, Shirer, and company ... devised and executed what became the routine format for the presentation of news. It not only had multiple points of origin, it also ... included both reporting and analysis of breaking news, and was both a journalistic and a technological breakthrough for broadcasting. No longer would radio news consist of announcers assigned to cover carefully pre-planned events as if they were parades or mere curiosities. From this point on, network staff journalists would provide timely reporting and analysis of important breaking news.

In the meantime, despite what Fly, Winchell, Kaltenborn, and others may have said about CBS's comprehensive policy handed down from on high in the fall of 1943, it was a stubborn CBS brigade that took firm exception to it — and made good on their vocal pronouncements. Collectively they decided they wouldn't obey it, persisting as they had always done, infusing personal opinions in what they reported.[58] (Was CBS going to replace the lot of them? It could hardly afford the loss of Murrow and company whose eyewitness war reportage had made CBS News the most dependably trusted fount in electronic journalism.) After all, noted one unreservedly partisan, Murrow confirmed an ability to engage "the high school dropout while not boring the intellectual."[59] Toward the end of 1943, the rather futile and embarrassing effort by a national chain to censor its own newscasters had been effectively snuffed out.[60] For a lengthy interval thereafter, no network superiors would make any further attempts to introduce similar perceptibly foolish notions.

Meanwhile, during the Second World War epoch, Big Brother lost no time in telling the radio industry that it wished to have certain topics introduced on the air. A slate of propaganda themes was to be interpolated in conventional programming. A *Special Features Plan* would provide war messages to national chains and local outlets for public consumption. The feds embraced certain wartime topics that were advocated to broadcasters: the war itself (presumably as opposed to ignoring it), the enemy's nature, the Allied nations' nature, the war's aims, and the condition of fighting, working, and home forces.[61]

While some of these intents could be readily worked into specific amusement and entertainment programming, certainly including dramatic and comedic fare, the area of news appeared to offer a particularly unpretentious approach. There the messages believed to be in the national interest could be communicated unobtrusively through news reports, analysis and commentary broadcasts, and in discussion and public forum programming. Whether subtlety was required or not — and obviously, Big Brother believed that to a certain extent it was probably a wise direction — if handled carefully, it seems that such nuances could be easily conveyed with a degree of aplomb and sensitivity through news and public affairs features.

All of this, incidentally, was coordinated by the joint efforts of the U.S. Office of Facts and Figures, under the direction of Archibald MacLeish, and the U.S. Office of War Information, under the direction of Elmer Davis, a former CBS newscaster.[62] Numerous radio personalities and officials entered government service during the war, enhancing the coordination of government requirements and radio's response.[63]

As an ex-broadcast journalist, Davis was certainly knowledgeable about the perils tied to censorship. Despite this he would most likely have agreed with a contingent of newspaper editors who admitted in February 1943, on the program *American Forum of the Air*, that wartime conditions made occasional censorship of reporting mandatory.[64] Proclaimed one informant: "If the OWI desired to censor information, it accomplished it by delaying dissemination of its news to the media. In most cases, however, what appeared to be censorial conduct by the OWI actually emanated from military officers who refused to keep Davis' organization fully and rapidly apprised of the latest military developments. More than once, Davis clashed with military officers in defense of the right of the public to be informed."[65]

Recalling his experiences of that epoch some two decades later, one of radio's most influential newscasters, Raymond Gram Swing (1887–1968), an ex-newspaperman who offered commentaries initially on MBS followed by the Blue and ABC webs, allowed:

> During World War II, none of my broadcasts was censored, though at the Blue network they were read prior to delivery by someone on the staff. That was, and is, standard procedure in radio and television today; and I find it not only unobjectionable, but proper, since the station is legally responsible for what its broadcasters say.... I am simply reporting that I had remarkably little interference with my freedom to say what I wished throughout my life as a journalist and commercial broadcaster.[66]

One critic determined Swing's assessment of that period to be "the most positive statement that can be made of a nation's communications system."[67] He continued: "It was a significant social achievement for a major combatant to have conducted a war for almost four years without interrupting the flow of entertainment and inquiry that commercial broadcasting had established. It suggested to many that once the battle was ended, radio had a bright and prosperous future."[68]

As a side note, Swing is worthy of additional mention, particularly so of his role as a broadcaster during the Second World War epoch.[69] To British radio audiences he was what

Ed Murrow was to American listeners — a refuge of insightful commentary delivered from New York weekly to his native countrymen, just as Murrow reported to his homeland from London and other hot spots throughout Europe. Swing's scrupulous analyses of American affairs enjoyed a wide following in England. As that nation approached its hour of desolation and despondency, the Swing revelations acquired historic consequence with Britons hanging on his every word. He offered hope without burnishing it with false hope. The *New Yorker* branded Swing "the best-known voice in the world." Among practiced personalities in broadcasting, for a time he certainly may have been that.

Although CBS's Bill Paley never again allowed his sponsors to receive such editorial latitude, for a while at least he permitted them to experience incredible influence over news by agreeing to one-advertiser sponsorship of some programming. Media historian Erik Barnouw noted that it didn't present a problem in the mid–1930s because "Most sponsors did not want news programming. Those that did were inclined to expect veto rights over it." Buying timeslots of 60 seconds or less didn't come into vogue until about 1960; before that programs were largely sold to single underwriters. In so doing, at least on CBS, the guys paying the bills got to pick who delivered their news and commentary. Rival broadcaster NBC had an even more distasteful policy. Sun Oil not only underwrote NBC's world news roundups in the 1930s, but produced those broadcasts in the PR offices at the company's headquarters in Philadelphia! Irrespective of that, an observer commented: "If an advertiser did not like what was said on its news program, the journalist in residence lost his sponsorship — and often his slot on the network as well."[70] There was plenty of incentive, therefore, to please the men who were signing the checks. It couldn't possibly have been considered radio's most objective epoch.

Even before the prospect of war became a matter of import for the government and communicators, censorship — including self-censorship — had become a reality in the interconnections between those dual factions. One instance surrounded the contentious, provocatively arrogant radio commentator Boake Carter. He had not only acquired a berth on the CBS airwaves but — over time — apparently believed it entitled him to a birthright, too. Hence, his outspoken conservative views got him into trouble with not only the Roosevelt administration but his sponsors and superiors as well. Carter's daily broadcasts at 7:45 P.M. were exceedingly popular in the mid–1930s, particularly so with segments of the listening audience embracing low income, rural, Republican, and isolationist blocs.[71]

> Carter's partisanship wasn't his only problem. His commentary was often filled with "innuendo, invective, distortion, and misinformation" instead of facts, and by the winter of 1938 he sounded not like a newsman but like a shrill demagogue. He didn't act as a reporter; he didn't check his sources; he often deliberately misinformed his audience. This didn't upset just those politically opposed to him. It upset important General Foods stockholders, government officials, and other corporate leaders.... Carter became more extreme in his views, and more deluded about his invulnerability the longer he stayed on the air.
>
> By 1937 the White House had three agencies investigating Carter, and administration officials put pressure on [CBS chairman] William Paley to pull him off the air. That same year, during the Little Steel strike, Carter began attacking the CIO, and the union responded by voting to boycott Philco products. Philco canceled its contract to sponsor Carter in February 1938, but CBS received so many angry letters from listeners that when General Foods — whose chairman of the board hated the New Deal *and* organized labor — offered to step in as sponsor, Carter got a temporary reprieve. Now the administration went straight to Paley, suggesting that it might be time for the FCC to seriously investigate monopoly practices in the broadcasting industry. Paley pulled Carter off CBS for good in August 1938.[72]

With a little nudge from the feds, broadcasters could take whatever actions seemed appropriate in censoring themselves!

Would any of this have been softened — or possibly even solved — had the United Nations General Assembly acted any sooner than December 10, 1948, when it adopted the Universal Declaration of Human Rights (UDHR)?[73] In so doing, the UN responded to numerous egregiously unspeakable incidences that transpired during the Second World War. Freedom from censorship was one of the "inalienable rights" guaranteed by the UHDR in Article 19:

> *Everyone has the right to freedom of opinion and expression; this right includes freedom to hold opinions without interference and to seek, receive and impart information and ideas through any media and regardless of frontiers.*

Could producing this document any sooner have settled some of the lingering questions regarding the expression of personal opinions that a handful of American broadcasters encountered in the 1920s, 1930s, and 1940s? Perhaps it would have mitigated the circumstances and been something to interpose in discussions in the controversial cases of commentators like Carter, Kaltenborn, Lewis, Murrow, Shirer, and others of that ilk. Nevertheless, the model and actual practice will often net different outcomes as a perceptive informant discerned: "Censorship, in the sense of interference with free expression, is the rule, not the exception, throughout the world. It is not a new phenomenon. Rather, censorship has been part of human communication vis-à-vis [in relation to] government in varying degrees."[74] And in relation perhaps to the guy overseeing the broadcasting services? And maybe to the one paying the bills for same?

There were many other times when Big Brother was looking over radio officials' shoulders in its manifold efforts to carry out its directive to regulate the industry. One of the best remembered and most widely publicized interventions of that epoch concerned the controversial issue of when a broadcaster seems to have too much control over what the audience is receiving. Specifically, the case of NBC Radio's twin chains, the Red and the Blue, became an intense investigative matter for the Federal Communications Commission in the late 1930s. And it took a while to resolve. Although the resolution impacted everything about NBC's broadcasting operations, news and public affairs were among the forefront of those features whose entire futures hinged on the outcome, and were ultimately altered forever.

The most visible sign of that change instituted in 1943 that is still obvious today exists in the form of the ABC Television network and, specifically, its news division. Had the FCC not broken up NBC's dual platform then (or someone else had done so since), the likelihood is that you wouldn't be watching ABC-TV today and that you wouldn't be hearing news reports on the multiple networks of ABC Radio. The FCC-mandated split within the National Broadcasting Company was indeed that consequential in the annals of broadcasting in the United States.

The complexities of the FCC's ultimatum won't be overstated here. It would take a long while to absorb the full extent of the arguments advanced by the FCC for the breakup. It perceived a monopolistic dynasty of the airwaves by a single operator controlling more than one affiliated outlet in assorted markets. Meanwhile, NBC and its parent firm, the Radio Corporation of America, countered with the stance that NBC did not dominate the markets it served. Citing what it believed to be an unfair advantage over its rivals, potential rivals, advertisers, talent, and all other broadcasting commerce, following a three-year examination of the business climate the FCC nonetheless ruled against NBC. On May 2, 1941, the federal regulatory body ordered the broadcaster to divest itself of one of its two webs. NBC appealed the decision but its vigorous protestations were to no avail: in 1943, the U.S. Supreme Court sided with the FCC, and the earlier judgment stood. The order shook up the whole industry. Its lingering effects — even though we may not readily recognize them without knowing a little of the historical significance — definitely extend into contemporary times.

Given no choice, NBC obeyed the ultimatum by placing its less powerful and less popular chain, the Blue network, up for sale. Within two months it announced that it had a cash buyer. Life Savers candy magnate Edward J. Noble (1882–1958) purchased the Blue network for $8 million. Following mandatory hearings, on October 12, 1943, the FCC approved its sale to Noble. In the deal Noble also acquired a trio of company-owned outlets in New York (WJZ), Chicago (WENR), and San Francisco (KGO). Although the transcontinental web operated under Blue Network nomenclature for a while, on June 15, 1945, it was reclassified as the American Broadcasting Company (ABC).[75] In the year of Blue's divestiture (1943) it achieved time sales of $24.6 million. The following year sales improved to $41.3 million, a 67 percent rise. That implied that the business enterprise was to remain a viable operation.[76]

Staffing his new network was, of course, one of Noble's top priorities. While we'll not dwell on this point, it's worth mentioning that a few sterling newsmen were engaged in those early years, some having been NBC employees in prior service.

> ABC (and MBS) was viewed by some in the trade as also-ran operations; only through a few rare gems was it afforded an equal place at the broadcasting table during the golden age of radio.
> But those gems, nevertheless, as few as they were, stood out like polished stones, shimmering amidst an array of lackluster programming that seldom attained much sparkle. They included personalities like newsmen Martin Agronsky, Elmer Davis, Don Gardiner, Paul Harvey and Walter Winchell....[77]

Radio's — and indeed, broadcasting's — greatest episode of controversy, certainly so up to the mid–20th century, was an industry-wide upheaval surrounding perceived communist and Nazi sympathizers in its midst. Hundreds of individuals, including many well known names in politics and entertainment circles as well as some other public figures, lost employment, the ability of some to earn a satisfactory livelihood in the future, their dignity, and occasionally their homes, possessions, savings, spouses, children, and — in a few rare cases — their very lives (by suicide, alcoholism, drugs, deteriorating physical conditions, or an inability to mentally cope with such debilitating circumstances). Many of the accusations were based on misguided associations and imaginations without solid evidence of support.

Among the individuals caught in the web of suspicion were a few prominent newsmen, including Charles Collingwood, Alexander Kendrick, William L. Shirer, Howard K. Smith, plus several other broadcast journalists not as widely known.[78] Although we won't make an attempt to explore the matter of "blacklisting" further, the incredibly provocative experience that permeated radio in a very dark and foreboding period is investigated in a plethora of published works as well as on various Web sites. One subjective and sweeping source is Rita Morley Harvey's paperback volume *Those Wonderful, Terrible Years*.[79] The consternation caused by this chapter in American life had far greater repercussions in broadcasting than all the earlier attempts by the networks as well as the Washington bureaucrats to censor who said what over the air. It was a chilling phase for many and some of its effects impacted them and their heirs for the remainder of their lives.

Censorship in radio occurred both outside and inside the industry and sometimes its tentacles left lingering impressions on those it affected. Radio wasn't immune to the imbroglios and misfortunes that are sometimes apparent in the workplace. Most of its issues were settled peaceably nevertheless; few made the news itself.

6

The Art of Persuasion: Everybody Has a Bias

Paul White, whom we have encountered on more than one occasion in this expedition, was CBS's director of news broadcasts when he disseminated a duplicated memo to staff members in September 1943. Even though the controversy it stirred was minimally referenced in the previous chapter — including the reactions of his colleagues — the incident illustrates a point worth emphasizing anew and even more pointedly than we have done. White's instructive dispatch was aimed at all of the chain's news analysts, you may recall, and it underscored in part:

> *Columbia has no editorial views.... Those men selected by us to interpret or analyze the news must also refrain from expression of editorial opinion, or our non-editorial position becomes an empty shell ... we ask you to say to yourselves, "We are not privileged to crusade, to harangue the people or to attempt to sway public opinion...." The function of the news analyst is to marshal the facts on any specific subject and, out of his common or special knowledge, to present these facts so as to inform his listeners rather than persuade them.... Freedom of speech on the radio would be menaced if a small group of men, some 30 or 40 news analysts who have nationwide audiences ... take advantage of their "preferred position" and become pulpiteers.*

Can there be any doubt whatever that the personal nuances of even the most passive, dedicated, and objective individuals who are dispensing their clarion calls include some prejudice, partiality, predisposition, preconceived notions — call it what you like — at some times? Will these prognosticators not unintentionally or otherwise every now and then color the material they offer, present it in a manipulative manner with or without realizing it, or justify some action — albeit perhaps unspoken — because of principles they have adhered to behind the scenes? To state the obvious while paraphrasing a line from a tune popularized by the late singer Dean Martin, "Everybody loves some bias sometime." And no one can be totally objective 100 percent of the time.

"Even the selection of one news item over another tended to influence opinion," a media observer insisted. "Terminology and tone of voice influenced opinion. The newsman could scarcely help influencing opinion. To pretend otherwise was a charade."[1] Affirmed yet another: "It was felt that the timbre and tone of the human voice alone could be used to unduly influence listeners."[2] Despite this, a third informant allowed: "The point of view of an analyst, coupled with his expert knowledge of his subject, is what makes him interesting."[3]

One scholar was insistent that the news commentator during the golden age was radio journalism's most fundamental expression. Said he: "At once a reporter and an editorialist, by the mid–1930s the commentator represented the highest form of opinionated broadcasting in a commercial medium where freedom of speech and program content were often secondary to economic profitability."[4] That, of course, projects the individual biases of speakers into a realm not yet explored intensely.

We have established that every commentator on the air — indeed, every individual, on or *off* the air for that matter — has an ax to grind about something (including those who carry out their mission in subtle ways). Some revelations appearing in a *Variety* summary circulated on July 25, 1945, provide a sweeping assessment of the plethora of electronic newsmen then featured over the four transcontinental chains. The contrasts and comparisons between 30 analysts-commentators are provocative. *Variety's* findings determined that 12 of that respected federation exploited a conservative bent. Five of the dozen were branded a "reactionary" or "extreme reactionary." Eight others were labeled liberals, almost all of them pursuing a "middle-of-the-road" stance, with none classified as "extreme liberals." Beyond this score, six more individuals were rated "middle-of-the-roaders" between conservative and liberal leanings; and the remaining four "defied classification." Commenting on those specific findings which reveal much about the slants then heard over the national airwaves, a radio historiographer re-stated the obvious: "The over-all balance is unfairly weighted on the conservative side."[5] A good thing — or maybe not? It depends on your own point of view, of course.

Bringing this forward to today, the radio commentators of the first half of the 20th century have long since vanished from the ether. They have been replaced in the modern era with a sort of "anything goes" performance. In this activity, freedom of speech has been championed to such an extent that — unless there is compelling reason *not* to do so — most advocates on the air (radio, television, the Internet, and all other sound/visual transmission systems and devices) — seem duty-bound to express their personal opinions on any subject (pick one) while crusading many times to win others to their side. They take issue with and exception to the most trivial pursuits while mounting a soapbox for or against causes that could have profound effects on many people's lives. So often this comes at the expense of what someone else's thinking on a given matter might be. More will be said on this subject later.

For here and now let it be noted that the one-to-five-minute newscasts aired by the transcontinental chains today — many of them dispensed by consistent (and familiar) voices usually airing very limited details — provide virtually no forum for the opinions of speakers, sponsors, stations, and service providers. They are what they are: matter-of-fact informative bulletin boards of the air and nothing more. Today the opinionated excesses predominate on radio call-in shows, often over stations with heavy talk formats, and even more profusely on cable television.

For a few moments let's interrupt our train of thought on that topic to explore modern-day talk radio a little further. It may be acknowledged unequivocally that the pervasive format in aural broadcasting currently, talk radio, has a profound influence on the thinking and reaction of United States citizens reaching incredibly massive volumes. One study, a decade ago, found that 22 percent of all Americans surveyed stated that they were regular listeners to these audio channels. It also discovered that those listening habits climbed as high as 40 percent in some major markets.[6] A contemporary source signifies that 48 million Americans now literally *receive their news* from this veritable fount of information.[7]

On many AM radio stations, the model is more apt than not to be dominated by political ideologues.[8] By 2010, the number of stations airing at least *some* talk shows (if not exclusively so) rose to 2,656, a 50 percent increase over the previous year's sum of 1,370 stations.[9] What does this imply? Certainly that Americans are listening more than ever to the purveyors of assorted dogmas who may be conveying their facts correctly or who may not be (and sometimes it's incredibly difficult to know for sure). Eric Alterman and Danny Goldberg, a couple of observers with their own partisan thoughts, advocate that "just about anyone can embrace reactionary ideas if they are exposed to them repeatedly and without contradiction, and talk radio offers a great forum for this."[10] Yet can there be any doubt that the leading personalities of talk radio are persuasively convincing millions of their points of view?

Among the trendiest hosts America has heard on the regional and transcontinental airwaves during this millennium is a handful of redoubtable talkative honchos that includes in part: Neil Boorts, Blanquita Collum, Bob Dornan, Michael Graham, Bob Grant, Ken Hamblin, Sean Hannity, Thom Hartmann, Don Imus, Laura Ingraham, G. Gordon Liddy, Rush Limbaugh, Mike Malloy, Michael Medved, Stephanie Miller, Oliver North, Bill Press, Michael Reagan, Randi Rhodes, Michael Savage, Laura Schlesinger, Ed Schultz, Howard Stern, and Armstrong Williams. Not all of them are still on the air today, however.

Without question most of the politically opinionated spielers uphold the banner of conservatism to one degree or another. By 2010, in fact, nine of the top 10 talk radio shows were presided over by "implacable conservatives."[11] And those right-wingers invariably attract the largest listening audiences, often by commanding the largest share of stations featuring talk-oriented formats either all or part of the time. Included are some local powerhouses in key metropolitan markets that add noticeably to those shows' influence: they provide significant clear-channel signal accessibility and have furthermore earned virtually unrivaled respect across the years in the communities they serve. These factors traditionally translate into bigger audiences.

Conservative Rush Limbaugh's daily tirade was traditionally heard on 600 U.S. stations in 2010, and his closely aligned air buddy Sean Hannity broadcast on 500 stations. Meanwhile liberal talk was carried by just 100 ethereal platforms.[12] Limbaugh's followers comprise the largest draw of any radio program since the dawn of television.[13] In the fall of 2008, as this wordsmith was completing a manuscript for another exposition on old time radio, when the current status of talk radio came up to bat, a few personal observations escaped from psyche to keyboard. Without naming particular hosts — and they exist on both sides of the spectrum — some were referenced as "narrow-minded bigots."

> These individuals ... frequently conduct little more than rants and harangues, often exhibiting bully pulpit tactics. Such ventures on the air are often characterized by intolerance and the host's particular brand of biased, strictly focused interpretation on issues pertaining to a variety of current events. This isn't to say that they don't have huge followings that buy into their invective completely; it recognizes the fact that they are a motivating force within the talkathon mold ... genuinely appreciated by legions of enamored cohorts.
>
> Anybody who thought that the conversational exchanges of the airwaves might run their course in a brief while, possibly even hoping that they would ... has been in for a rude awakening. In some markets talk radio is now well into its fifth decade of broadcasting. The fact that you can pick up talk shows [so easily] ... is a testament to the form's allure, resiliency and profitability.[14]

The disparity between beaming the conservative and liberal agendas means that millions more people are routinely exposed to the party line of the fundamentalist crusaders instead of progressive propaganda. Of course, this would have been impossible in radio's golden age when a news commentator or analyst created a major rift with his superiors if not with his audience and advertisers over any closely guarded nuance that got onto the air, even if he meant absolutely nothing by it. The reason why it's allowed today, and was not then, goes back to the Fairness Doctrine and its predecessor policies referenced earlier, and the repeal of that formal legislation nearly four decades following enactment. A left-winger sees it as opening Pandora's Box, netting the disproportionately biased talk radio environment that many Americans experience wherever they live today.

> Edward Monks, a Eugene, Oregon, attorney, calculates that in his city, conservatives enjoy a 4,000-to-zero hour advantage over liberals on the radio. He wrote in *The Register-Guard*: "Political opinions expressed on talk radio are approaching the level of uniformity that would normally be achieved only in a totalitarian society...." Monks noted that as recently as 1974, such domination would have been not only inconceivable, but illegal. Back then, the Federal Communications Commission was still demanding "strict adherence to the [1949] Fairness Doctrine as the single most important requirement of operation in the public interest — the sine qua non for grant for renewal of license." This view was ratified by the U.S. Supreme Court in 1969 when it reaffirmed the people's right to a free exchange of opposing views, with roughly equal time given to all sides ... on the public airwaves. The doctrine was overturned by the Reagan-appointed FCC in 1987.... Reagan vetoed attempts by Congress to reinstate the doctrine, and the net result has been the complete far-right domination of the nation's airwaves....[15]

But it was a very different environment back in the day. CBS president-owner William S. Paley's cautionary tactics were typical as the industry treaded softly with its big stick.

> Paley had reached the conclusion that opinion should be confined as much as possible to round tables and other programs providing balanced discussion. Sale of time for the arguing of views had already been ruled out by CBS, except in campaigns. Paley felt that the broadcaster should also refrain from pushing his own opinions. "We must have an editorial page," he said as early as 1937. "We must never try to further either side of any debatable question."[16] By the same token, he had reached the conclusion that a radio newsman should not push opinions — his or any one else's....
>
> Paley's concern over such problems generated a CBS policy: CBS would have news *analysts*, not *commentators*. A news analyst, in CBS doctrine, was a newsman who analyzed the news but promoted no view. A commentator was an opinion-pusher — not wanted at CBS.[17]

The lack of objectivity in broadcast news and commentary could be observed as far back as the late 1920s and early 1930s. Father Charles E. Coughlin, the "radio priest," and politician Huey Long were prime examples of biased demagogues. Each one fanned the flames of partiality in efforts to direct the masses to their respective points of view. There were some others, maybe not as well known, who were doing the same thing. By the mid–1930s, news commentators — then more prevalent than news reporters — "felt no compunction to be unbiased or neutral," an academician insisted. "Much of early radio commentary was openly partisan, as when Boake Carter referred to administration officials as 'fat New Dealers' while Walter Winchell fawned all over FDR."[18]

Radio commentary — delivered by colorful individuals — is even credited with creating the image of a man's man! The perpetrator of that notion explicitly dotes by name on Ed Murrow, Bill Shirer, and Bob Trout as shining examples of what the American male aspired to be after radio journalism produced a new model of icons.

> During the 1930s, when broadcast news was being socially constructed and fought over, we hear a genre being invented, and we hear that male archetype — the newsman — being

designed.... Radio commentators and war correspondents became national celebrities — sometimes overnight stars — their voices instantly recognizable, their public images often carefully crafted.... We hear men who sounded like they came from middle America dethroning their pseudoaristocratic predecessors....

Here were serious men sometimes risking their lives to deliver the news, men confident in the American man's place in the world, men affirming that knowledge, rationality, stoicism, courage, and empathy, and an utter disdain for upper-class pretentiousness, were what made men "real" men. By 1941 the apotheosis of American manhood wasn't Boake Carter or Eddie Cantor, it was Edward R. Murrow, the radio version of Humphrey Bogart's "Rick" in *Casablanca*....

Although these men were becoming experts in European politics and warfare, they made it seem normal to discuss such things in everyday terms. They used the first and second person to address their listeners directly and involve them in what the war felt like.... Shirer introduced reports with "Incidentally" or "Well" or "What happened was this," just as you would at the dinner table. He spoke to the audience as if they were equals, explaining what they couldn't know because they were in the States but also addressing them as informed adults.[19]

In the meantime Ed Klauber, William Paley's personal assistant, was frequently reminding those same newsmen and their cohorts about the CBS policy calling for objectivity in its news programming. Commentators mustn't do the judging for the audience, he cautioned, while opinions were relegated to political round table discussions and other fare where opposing views were invited. Klauber insisted, "An unexcited demeanor at the microphone should be maintained at all times."[20] "He was especially emphatic about emotionalism in the news: this was a male preserve, and real men did not show their emotions; they conveyed 'the facts' without revealing what might be in their hearts."[21]

Nevertheless, it became a struggle for electronic newsmen of that day to restrain themselves to the point that the public did not pick up on their individual biases. After returning home from Europe late in 1940, Eric Sevareid discovered that his anti-isolationist leanings roused recurring protests from lawmakers, radio station officials, and his superiors at CBS.[22] Similarly, as early as 1938, Ed Murrow told a chum, "I am finding it more and more difficult to suppress my personal convictions." On the ether he announced that Shirer in Berlin and he in London were "trying to bring you as much news as we can, avoiding so far as is humanly possible being too much influenced by the atmosphere in which we work."[23] Though nurturing a goal of impartiality, Murrow allowed that "any reasonable person would find it impossible to maintain a stance of pure unbias" while laboring in the environment that then encircled them.

> Some, however, were adamantly against America entering a European war. CBS tapped this sentiment when, in 1938, Ed Murrow received permission from French Premier [Edouard] Daladier to visit the Maginot Line to make the first broadcast from that strategic and highly secret fortification.[24] Murrow was not permitted to give the names of towns or to identify regiments, but he could describe the possibility of war, which he did eloquently. NBC felt that Murrow had erred in making such a broadcast, believing that he had glorified the military prowess of one country over another and, hence, had compromised American neutrality. An antiwar outlook had emerged within the NBC inner sanctum, and Ed Murrow and CBS were offering a contrary opinion. As it turned out, NBC benefited from playing down the chances for war. After Murrow's Maginot Line broadcast, the German broadcast authorities responded by improving their relations with NBC.[25]

When Congress commenced deliberation on the question of neutrality in autumn 1939, Murrow circumvented the decrees from on high in regard to evenhandedness by quoting from British newspapers to his American listening audience. On one occasion he read aloud of the possibility of a Nazi-Bolshevik bloc that could extend from the Rhine to the Pacific, then admonished: "If this be so, we shall be justified in hoping that the rest of the civilized nations, and among them, the greatest, who want us to destroy this menace, will lend us aid more material than their prayers."[26] On the same broadcast Eric Sevareid testified that once the French were emboldened with "the new, fast, American planes, the Curtis planes with the Pratt and Whitney motors," they were adept in destroying the German Messerschmitts. In reporting that piece of news which was undoubtedly designed to motivate the masses, Sevareid elated his fellow countrymen who were just then beginning to realize with some pride the intrinsic worth of such fortified measures. Murrow underscored the newscasters' collective opinion when he allowed: "I, for one, do not believe that a people who have the world brought into their homes by a radio can remain indifferent to what happens in the world."[27] His admonishment could be applied to myriad situations, and not simply the extraordinary ones.

In the 27 months prior to the Japanese attack on Pearl Harbor, no satisfactory estimate may be given in regard to the ultimate effectiveness of those newsmen's efforts. The persuasive nuances they applied against an isolationist stance by the U.S. would hardly be considered small, however. Surely hundreds of thousands of Americans and maybe millions who were on the fence over the issue who were tuning in to those daily mostly CBS broadcasts from the varied European capitals must have thought to themselves: "They need our assistance. If they don't get it, the Axis powers will control the continent, and possibly more."

In his book *News for Everyman: Radio and Foreign Affairs in Foreign America*, David Holbrook Culbert maintains that between the Septembers of 1939 and 1940, objectivity on the air rounded a major corner.[28] Calling it "unneutral" in 1939, the transcontinental chains in the U.S. wouldn't agree to allow an air raid to be heard over the ether. A year hence, however, Murrow — broadcasting from London — carried his microphone out of the studio building to let Americans experience the sirens wailing in real time, announcing yet another of the numerous impending bombing raids by the Luftwaffe that England had grown accustomed to.

Deriding some of the instructions pertaining to objectivity that cascaded down from radio's highest echelons to those within their employ, *Variety* admonished: "Who doesn't want England to win?" The newsmen welcomed that kind of unsolicited intrusion into the fray. They were living and working in an environment that was subject to bombing raids at any time. They witnessed the horrors of war in person. In seeking to convey what they saw regularly to the people at home, they had formed legitimate opinions about what America should do. It would have been hard to feel otherwise given their situation. Their equilibrium in practicing the rule — as well as the justification for the rule itself— began to grow thin as time wore on.

> A few days after Pearl Harbor, [news director] Paul White announced a new CBS policy. Where war coverage was concerned, there would be no further insistence on journalistic neutrality. "This is a war for the preservation of democracy," White wrote. "The American people must not only always be kept vividly aware of this objective, but of the value to every man, woman, and child in the nation of preserving democracy." As usual, CBS was following the government's lead.
>
> It is doubtful that anyone, least of all Murrow and the Boys, disagreed with the new policy.[29]

In 1942, radio thespian Arch Oboler, having revealed thinly veiled signs of a staunch anti–Nazism posture well before December 7, 1941, reflected on the frustrating prewar milieu under which he had labored in that period of neutrality. Oboler spared few words as he injected that there was an exclusive spot in the next world set aside for "radio network executives, advertising agency department heads, manufacturers of assorted objects advertised over the airwaves, and — radio writers.... [T]he devil in Hell alone knows what measure of responsibility is theirs for the national indifference with which pre-war America" mulled over the ascent of fascism in Europe.[30]

Much more could be said, and has been written, about the prewar era as regards objectivity in broadcasting. We'll leave it with the initiative that there was continual tension between the broadcast executives and their newsmen in the matter of detachment. It was perhaps most easily recognized in the 1930s and 1940s, but to some degree it has always been there. In the modern age, with its manifold opinion diversions in electronic journalism, it's unmistakably still alive and healthy. There will probably always be uneasiness about fairness on the air.

Recounting some of the positive outcomes of the radio commentators back in the day, an informant observed the edifying effects of the analysts upon the population. Noting that these spokesmen could be documented as representing myriad political persuasions, still — when they are put up against anybody performing in a similar capacity in other lands — the U.S. system invariably seems to end up smelling like a rose.

> Unlike monolithic regimes where only one answer is permitted to broadcasters since it is considered *the* Truth, American radio — even in time of great crises...— tolerated diversity of opinion. Listeners were compelled to learn for themselves the correct position from which to understand the news of the world.... Relative to other political regimes, the commentators who emerged in the 1930s represented the broadest spectrum of ideas in radio of any nation.[31]

When considered in that light, the American radio commentator of the 1930s, 1940s, and 1950s — complete with his admittedly predisposed judgments — can and probably does look pretty good to us, doesn't he?

7

Nights of the Roundtable: Clashes, Conflicts Courted

In spite of network radio's implicit affront toward biases — particularly so when partiality, prejudice, and preconceived notions were overtly expressed by broadcasting personalities — there were times that the industry actually implored expressions of personal opinion in regard to current events — even when those exchanges led to open hostility between participants. They were usually centered in discussions that pertained to social, moral, ethical, political, and religious questions. And much of that conversation readily fit into the broader scope of the journalistic traditions that already have been pursued in this text.

In the midst of radio's heyday, its four transcontinental webs aired no fewer than one such feature each designed to provoke forthrightness from varying persuasions on topics of interest that could range from mildly touchy to arguably contentious, divisive, and — on rare occasions — litigious outcomes. Sometimes the individuals expressing their opinions might be purely ordinary men and women who stumbled upon an opportunity for their proverbial 15 minutes of fame (although it was probably more likely to be closer to 15 seconds for most of them). Sometimes foremost authorities with extensive expertise on a given subject were invited to a debate to furnish relevant substance out of their exceptional reserves, definitely more absorbing than the average Joe could offer. And at other times newsmakers themselves, including public figures from the spheres of government, entertainment, sports, and media worlds, turned up to address the audience or to argue their own outlooks, possibly in heated exchanges with guests touting diverse stances.

The radio programs that beseeched these contributors of assorted stripes projected a multiplicity of formats for their civilized (and sometimes uncivilized) deliberations. While some forums met the same fate as their less serious opposite numbers on the air (in the form of comedies, dramas, musicals, and other fare) — being canceled after pithy, disappointing runs that failed to generate crowds — a small handful of public affairs features attracted hardy followings that translated into satisfactory and sometimes even spirited ratings. Surprisingly, a few typically unsponsored series in this camp persisted for at least a couple of decades. Fewer still segued even further into video extensions as technology and manufacturing capabilities permitted, significantly expanding their impact on the ether and its audiences.

At the same time this handful of features elevated their distinctive networks with respectability; particularly was this so within broadcasting scenarios that were mired in amusement agendas that could generally be classified as lightweight. Debate forums on key issues added prestige to a chain's image among the listeners while at the same time decidedly impressing the Federal Communications Commission. The FCC bureaucrats, it may be remembered, not only issued licenses but also renewals to affiliates of the networks. The FCC was invariably seeking a higher standard of programming to enlighten the masses. Those issues oriented exchanges helped fill the bill.

This chapter focuses on the leaders of the pack, briefly introducing each one and revealing some of the distinctions that made them enduring habits. They are presented here in the order of their initial appearances on the air.

For nearly a decade prior to the inception of *The American Forum of the Air* over the Mutual Broadcasting System, two precursor antecedents were paving the way for that unmistakable Exhibit A among its web's public affairs programming. At the same time those forebears cultivated an appetite among early radio listeners for similar fare which of course bode well for the more permanent manifestation that lay ahead. *American Forum's* pedigree reaches all the way back to 1928, an epoch in which a foremost New York dry goods mercantilist, Gimbels, owned local radio station WGBS.

Theodore Granik (1907–70), then a law student in Gimbels's employ, nurtured a categorical fascination for the broadcasting side of that firm's business. Ultimately assigned to the radio operation, he was given multiple tasks that included penning dialogue for broadcasts, delivering continuity announcements on the air, reporting sports scores, and filling in at the microphone when a scheduled act failed to appear. Working off his "other" pursuit, young Granik proffered a program concept for a panel discussion series regarding legal issues. It debuted under the moniker *Law for the Layman*. In 1932, after Gimbels had divested itself of WGBS, Granik was hired by New York station WOR to continue his broadcast series there.

WOR, coincidentally, was owned by another local dry goods retailer, Bambergers, an operation that had been purchased by yet another New York mercantile emporium in 1929, Macys. Bambergers and WOR were left by Macys to run as ancillary units and persisted under their widely recognized nomenclature. On September 15, 1934, WOR and three more stations in distant locales (Chicago, Cincinnati, and Detroit) organized a fourth U.S. transcontinental network, MBS (beyond NBC Red and Blue and CBS). Although the new chain's design called for its member outlets to create and share programming with other stations in the family, in due course WOR was to become a genuine flagship station for the nationwide hookup similar in fact to the New York-based affiliates of its network rivals.[1]

By the time MBS was formed (1934), Granik's radio feature was airing under modified taxonomy as *The Mutual Forum Hour*. That didn't last forever either. On December 26, 1937, the show was rebranded a second time with its most recognized and enduring title, *The American Forum of the Air*. The change in monikers that time affirmed a shift from legal-only topics and opened the door to many others. Listeners often formed or solidified personal opinions after hearing typical presentations on prohibition, New Deal legislation, labor strife, civil liberties, isolationism, governmental controls, fascism, communism, and innumerable added social and political issues.

Creator-moderator Theodore Granik was never paid for his services. He once estimated that his out-of-pocket subsidies, beyond what the network authorized for expenses incurred for the show, personally cost him a quarter-million dollars over its lengthy run.[2] Not many panel moderators would be doing that on TV today, even for 15 minutes of fame, nor would they have on radio back then. At varied times Granik was assistant district attorney in New York and, in the nation's capital, consulted professionally with the Housing Authority, Selective Service Administration, and the War Production Board.

"Though a staunch advocate of free speech, Granik refused to let Communists on the show, even when Communism was the topic," declared one informant. The fanzine *Radio Mirror* described him as "firm, hard-headed, and diplomatic." Granik saw his mission on the show as one "deflecting personal barbs between the guests and keeping panelists on the issues." It was similar to what his counterparts were doing elsewhere.

American Forum and *The Mutual Forum Hour* drew at least two future U.S. presidents to its panel — Franklin D. Roosevelt and Harry S Truman — as well as many other prominent figures like Fiorello H. LaGuardia, mayor of New York; U.S. senator Robert A. Taft; and radio journalist and newspaper columnist Dorothy Thompson. Broadcast in 30- or 60-minute segments early on Sunday evenings until 1943, the series moved at that juncture to Tuesday evenings in 60-, 45-, or 30-minute portions through January 18, 1949. On that date it left the ether. But it was far from over.

Although silent for the next few months, on October 30, 1949, the program returned in an even bigger and better way than ever: it transferred to NBC and for the next three seasons was simulcast live over that web's radio and television facilities for 30 minutes every Sunday. Although the show left the tube in 1952, *American Forum* persisted in its original sculpt over NBC Radio through March 11, 1956. Thus, with the exception of only a few months of hiatus in 1949, the discussions — and those of its forerunners — aired somewhere for 28 years, including about three-fourths of it over a national network, an enviable tenure by any measure.

Originating since 1937 from Washington, D.C., the *American Forum* was produced in collaboration with the U.S. Department of Interior. As in the case of *America's Town Meeting of the Air*, follow-up discussion groups formed in communities across the nation. By applying the broadcasts as a springboard for subsequent deliberation, such groups create radio's "greatest contributions toward practical democratic processes," allowed one observer. By 1942, Frank Ernest Hill, representing the advocacy coalition American Association for Adult Education, further delineated:

> It seems reasonable to assume that there are in the United States at least 15,000 organized groups meeting together to hear radio programs, and their activities touch from 300,000 to 500,000 Americans.... These groups are born of the impulse to listen together ... and they stimulate, they broaden, they give definite information which is pretty fully assimilated.
>
> Long after broadcasts for which the groups have assembled are over, discussion — frequently heated — takes place. Radio becomes but a starting point from which a well-informed electorate is in process of building, stimulated by broadcast discussion programs which have become the heirs-apparent of the old-time political debate.

For more than two decades, the *American Forum* fit this mold, a key catalyst in a continuing saga that had implications for denizens spread all over the nation. Like some others of its ilk *American Forum* also won a George Foster Peabody Award for excellence in radio broadcasting. Furthermore, it held the distinction of being the only radio series with words printed verbatim in the *Congressional Record*.

The *national* radio forum possessing the honor of becoming its most durable coast-to-coast exponent of the genre (although not by much) is **The University of Chicago Round Table**. The program was initially prompted by lively exchanges between Chicago professors over lunch at the institution's faculty club. After someone suggested that the topics bantered back and forth would make good radio, local station WMAQ offered its facilities. At least some of those broadcasts originated in the college's cafeteria.

The series that premiered on the Windy City outlet on February 1, 1931, went transcontinental over NBC on October 15, 1933. It lasted through June 12, 1955, having aired *continuously*, unlike most of its competing forums. In so doing it set a high standard for all other discussion series on the aural airwaves. With the exception of 15 months in 1950–51 when the *Round Table* broadcast on Saturdays, it was a Sunday afternoon feature and always on NBC.

While some subsequent radio features focused on topical issues aimed at the great substance of the available listening audience (e.g., *America's Town Meeting of the Air*, *The People's Platform*, etc.), in the main the *Round Table* was fashioned for a more scholarly multitude than enveloped the common masses. By and large there were college professors interacting on its broadcasts, deliberating with erudite individuals of similar pursuits and interests. The academicians were rotated with each broadcast, having been selected for a particular topic by virtue of their teaching disciplines, proficiencies and attraction to specific impending concentrations. The *Round Table* usually appealed to a more urbane, cerebral, cultured crowd than that ordinarily found within the general population.

> In its early years, the *Roundtable* was virtually the only network program that was neither scripted nor rehearsed, exhibiting an uncommon spontaneity that was likely the key to its success. More than a week of planning and research went into each *Roundtable* broadcast, and the leader of each week's discussion attempted to keep the participants within the bounds of a prearranged outline. However, panelists, particularly the faculty members, resisted suggestions that they work from scripts.
>
> Panelists were chosen for their outspoken nature, and controversy was a *Roundtable* staple. Several programs prompted the network to offer free reply-time to someone criticized during the discussion. Network officials threatened more than once to cancel the series over particularly controversial programs, but it stayed on the air until the mid–1950s. The program's first moderator, Professor T. V. Smith, became a U.S. congressman.[3]

A few of the subjects faced by the *Round Table* panelists included "Freedom of the Press," "International Law," "Realism in British Diplomacy," "An Annual Labor Wage," and "Help for the Farmer." Discussions covered such disparate terrain as strikes, prohibition, war, politics, communism, and isolationism. By the early 1940s, the series attempted to infuse its broadcasts with profound doses of realism. From time to time the subjects were pumped up with knowledgeable outside guest speakers. Strident efforts were taken to reduce whatever scholastic phrasing might have been injected into conversations of the past, too. In this way the program sought to make the exchanges more personal, lively, and understandable to listeners.

Enduring moderators John Howe (through the mid–1940s) and George Probst eventually became permanent fixtures at the *Round Table*. At different times they presided over a half-hour confab that was potentially a lot less rowdy than one of its rival forums, *America's Town Meeting of the Air*, which was punctuated by an often unruly crowd of spectators. Nevertheless, the *Round Table* supplied "lots of rousing disagreement" anyway, confirmed a media historian. The "round table" itself was actually triangular in shape, customarily including three and sometimes six participants facing one another on its triple sides. A collapsible model of that desk was constructed for occasional broadcasts that the show took on the road. Both furniture units featured time-warning lights facing each chair.

The *Round Table* went to great lengths to methodically anticipate every broadcast, coaching participants and — in a very real sense — practicing what was to be said when the show went live. One source delineated that "meticulous preparation":

> The speakers are limited in number to a normal maximum of three or four [individuals]. Each receives, well in advance, a carefully prepared digest of the subject to be discussed (pertinent data, statistics, and publications on the subject are summarized). The speakers meet a day or two previous to the broadcast to exchange their opinions.... Salient points of difference emerge and a limited few are selected as their agenda on the air. On the day of the broadcast and immediately before "air time," the speakers meet in the studio and from brief notes engage in ad lib discussion. This discussion, constituting a dress rehearsal, is recorded and the record is then played back to the speakers.... The speakers, advised by the producer, take note of roughnesses and obscurities in the record and, with these fresh in mind, proceed to the actual broadcast. During the broadcast, if a speaker tends to monopolize the time, to interrupt too much, to say too little, a card is placed before him by the producer with an instruction in clear print calculated to correct his defect. Thus while a maximum spontaneity is secured (there is no reading from a manuscript) a minimum of wastage of precious time is likewise provided for.[4]

The *Round Table* was the creation of University of Chicago alumnae Judith Waller, who was educational and then public service director for NBC's Central Region, based in the Windy City. The *Round Table* became the first broadcast feature of its type to publish a weekly periodical, incidentally. Its pages contained a transcript of the last show aired, profiles of the show's participants, letters of listener feedback, a current events topic just discussed with some more ideas for locating matter pertaining to the subject, and a calendar of impending broadcast themes. One year the *Round Table* won a Peabody Award for broadcasting excellence. Max Wylie picked a single *Round Table* discussion — on a 1939 Harlan County, Kentucky, coal mining imbroglio — to incorporate in his *Best Broadcasts of 1938–39* (Whittlesey House, 1939).

With an audience *"far in excess of the collective editorial pages of the American press"* (italics mine), **America's Town Meeting of the Air**— launched over NBC Blue on May 30, 1935, and ultimately pulled from the ABC program logs on July 1, 1956 — was an early harbinger of the myriad public affairs discussion forums that were to proliferate on the ether.[5] Failed thespian George V. Denny, Jr., a North Carolinian who had become a leading motivational advocate, moderated the series' first 17 seasons. Denny had been an assistant director of a cause growing out of the suffrage epoch known as the League for Political Education prior to his baptism into radio. He eventually filled the presidency of New York's Town Hall, Inc.

The show itself was witnessed by about 1,500 "average Americans" weekly at its New York broadcast venue — Town Hall at 123 West 43rd Street. In advance of going on the air the studio crowd was warmed up for each week's subsequent debate with lively exchanges between members of the audience on the topic of the evening. That usually persisted for an hour and was normally conducted by one of two added *Town Meeting* staff members. Surveying it in the early 1940s, an observer was clearly overjoyed with a fact we have long taken for granted in modern times.

> A neat arrangement of portable microphones permits people in all parts of the auditorium to take part in the discussion. The same system permits them to question the speakers during the question period following the debate. That the first broadcast — which went on the air without publicity — drew a response of three thousand letters, was due partially to the fact that Denny's handling of a ticklish chore is so precise and tasteful.[6]

For most of its run *America's Town Meeting of the Air* was heard for 60 minutes weekly; for four years it broadcast for 45 minutes; and in the remainder of its life it aired for 30 minutes. The provocative subject of its premier episode in 1935 was "Which Way America — Fascism, Communism, Socialism or Democracy?" There would be many other stimulating and compelling themes considered in fine depth over a timeframe with only minor interruptions that spanned 21 years. They included: "Let's Face the Race Question," "Do We Have a Free Press?," "Are Parents or Society Responsible for Juvenile Crime?," and "Is America Losing Its Morals?" Each was purposely designed to provoke controversy and arouse interest in discussion topic and program.

When Denny created the show he observed that "the very basis of the democracy upon which the various states had been originally founded was the town meeting in which each citizen might have his say." By radio, the initial moderator was convinced, "the entire nation might be converted into one gigantic town meeting in which all shades of political and economic thought could be expounded." Thus in its day it was a sort of CNN of the aural airwaves but with a much larger crowd interviewed following the diverse theories projected.

A distinctive of the *Town Meeting* that separated it from other broadcast forums then was its encouragement of hecklers that were usually forbidden on rival discussion exploits. Open condemnation of the speakers was not only expected but welcomed on *Town Meeting*, a departure from the more civilized productions that competed for the same audience elsewhere. For each broadcast, for example, there would almost certainly be a handful of "irresponsibles, drunks, and crackpots" present, an informant allowed.[7]

> If this wasn't enough, the guests themselves often came to the edge of violence. Heywood Broun and Julian Mason seemed ready to do physical battle on the air. At least one libel suit was brought as a result of the verbal fireworks.... The guests were political and philosophical opposites, their causes heartfelt and of long standing.... It wasn't the first half of the show that worried them: that was when the opposing guests were each given 10 to 20 minutes to make their best arguments. What drove ... [them] to distraction was the free-for-all with the studio audience. "The speakers heckle each other and the audience heckles everybody," *Time* reported in January 1938. "What a chance to make a fool of yourself on a national scale."
>
> Moderator Denny loved it. The last thing he wanted was an orderly, polite meeting. He went into each show prepared, and hoping, for a verbal bloodbath.[8]

Before long, "listening groups" sprang up across the country to pursue the weekly *America's Town Meeting of the Air* broadcasts with follow-up emphasis provided locally. Each week more than 1,000 such conclaves were independently interconnected by the radio series, forming in individual homes, schools, colleges, Young Men's Christian Association facilities, Civilian Conservation Corps public work relief camps, at job sites, and at other fraternal association gathering places. These clusters applied the radio give-and-take deliberations as a catalyst for their own subsequent dialogue. At some of these events outspoken advocates on multiple sides of controversial issues argued their points sometimes well into the late evening.

By pursuing this pattern extensively, the concept of the town hall meeting, the basis for the broadcasts themselves, was extended into local neighborhoods and communities. As a result perhaps the dreams that founder George Denny originally possessed for his program were realized to an even larger extent. The citizens of the nation hadn't been exposed to opportunities like this one for long because network radio had existed less than a decade when *Town Meeting* arrived. It was a novel treatment of a historic local tradition that, in a sense, reached beyond single communities, an application whose timing was aligned precisely in a day during which town hall meetings still held scrupulous relevance.

Some added facets set the series still further apart from other broadcast features that may have sought to emulate its successful design. One was that, within a year of its debut, Denny installed a remote system that allowed the voices of people all over the country to be beamed in for their "take" on an issue under consideration. He got "up close" to his listeners even more by frequently taking the show on the road, broadcasting from auditoriums in cities across America. Finally, during the series' heyday, Columbia University Press published word for word what was said during the program's early seasons' broadcasts. There was such demand for it that by 1939, more than a quarter-million copies were sold.

Following the initial broadcast season, the Women's National Radio Committee (WNRC) identified the *Town Meeting* as the "best educational program" on the ether. Of 500 listeners across the United States whom it polled, meanwhile the WNRC netted a quartet of rather stunning discoveries:[9] (1) 34 percent altered their opinions on subjects following open discussions on the air; (2) 90 percent of respondents searched for further details once they had been inspired by the audio exchanges; (3) 28 percent usually participated in debates that were staged locally following each broadcast; and (4) 85 percent said a speaker's credentials weren't nearly as powerful as an intellectual dialogue of current events.

Media historiographer Charles A. Siepmann, who contributed to our awareness of broadcasting's early decades in spades — an ex-British Broadcasting Company staffer and Harvard University lecturer — said he encountered but a single programming concept that could be labeled unique after he arrived in the U.S.A.[10] That was one that involved inviting a quartet of guests to the dinner table and launching a literal roundtable debate following the meal — one that was almost certain to trigger arguments after the four guests registered their points of view. The hand-picked foursome was selected not only for their sometimes steadfastly held opinions but for their perceived abilities to be interesting conversationalists as well. They were interviewed extensively by telephone before their selection for a broadcast to be certain they could make a creditable contribution.

A hidden microphone, neatly tucked into a floral centerpiece on the dinner table, removed that otherwise overt distraction from the exchanges. Although the participants were aware of its presence, they were never quite certain when it was off or on. It usually resulted in a kind of give-and-take conversational ambiance that the producers had hoped to establish on topical issues when they created the show.

The People's Platform, as it was branded, debuted over CBS on June 22, 1938. Airing most of its run in weekly half-hour installments, the series was mostly an early evening feature presented on various days during a given season and always over CBS. It persisted through August 10, 1952, some 14 years altogether, much more enduring than some other prime time fare. While not as raucous as *America's Town Meeting of the Air* with its accompanying boisterous audience (*Platform* had none), *Platform* could trigger spirited debate anyway as participants sometimes forcefully dug in their heels and held to their partisan views. Some were unwilling to yield to other opinions or even the idea of compromise. All of it was a ploy that onetime Nebraska newspaperman and later Columbia University educator and chairman of CBS's Adult Education Board Lyman Bryson instituted. Bryson, who had earlier been an assistant to *Town Meeting's* George Denny, remained with *The People's Platform* to 1946. He was superseded by Dwight Cooke as host for the remainder of the program's run.

Those confabs featured some very prominent names sprinkled among their four dinner dates, sometimes with only one of them being a recognized celebrity per show. Tallulah Bankhead, Irving Berlin, Samuel Goldwyn, Herbert Hoover, Groucho Marx, Harold Stassen, Robert Taft, Dorothy Thompson, Gene Tunney, and more of that contrasting ilk were typical luminaries seated around the table. Just as often, however, a contributing unit might be comprised of virtual nobodies: people who might possess animated feelings for or against an issue and be feisty in holding their ground, yet whose names wouldn't be known by the majority of listeners outside the communities from which they emanated.

Moderator Cooke thought of himself as an adjudicator, his purpose in being there merely to ensure that each individual had sufficient opportunity to be fully engaged in the conversation. At the same time he could intervene to make sure that no single individual became so overbearing and possibly obnoxious to the other guests that the intent of the program was jeopardized. Typical topical affairs deliberated by the crowd pertained to whether America's military should be beefed up as a precautionary measure following Germany's aggressive behavior across Europe; President Franklin Roosevelt's foreign policies; the extent of U.S. aid to democracies faced with militaristic subjugation; and the scope of United Nations commitment to global peacekeeping. These were themes of course that came to the forefront more and more as war clouds formed across Europe and then after the U.S. declared war on the Axis powers.

The series explored already were among radio's most revered talkathons back in the day. Nevertheless, two more not yet introduced that arrived later in the golden age were to establish legacies that continue to outshine everything that has gone before them. NBC's *Meet the Press* and CBS's *Face the Nation* derived the most popular and durable conversational exchanges in video. Both launched radio versions at their start; CBS's was alongside its TV entry. Cited in contemporary times as "press conferences of the air," this pair of shows is the oldest still running of a breed of similar weekend newsmaker interviews carried by both broadcast and cable systems. The focus of the two series is timely and centered on issues that usually include public affairs, political, and social concerns of fundamental relevance to a wide cross-section of Americans.

The granddaddy of the strain and its leading exponent, **Meet the Press**, was launched over a Washington, D.C., area station on June 24, 1945. About three months into the run on October 5, 1945, the series was beamed over the Mutual outlet (WOL) in the nation's capital. Ultimately it made its way onto that network coast-to-coast (a fact some historians have apparently missed). Celebrated as "a national treasure" by one of its late moderators, Tim Russert, *Meet the Press* was referenced by *The New York Times* as "the template for the Sunday political talk shows."[11] In a piece obviously written to puff up its ego the show's present network claims that it is "the longest-running and most-quoted television program in the world, and the most-watched Sunday-morning program in America."[12] Its co-creators were *American Mercury* opinion magazine editor Lawrence E. Spivak (1900–94) and freelance wordsmith Martha Rountree (1911–99).

Rountree, the show's original moderator and producer (she produced more shows for radio or TV audiences like *Capitol Close Up, Keep Posted, Leave It to the Girls, Press Conference,* and *Washington Exclusive*), was a reporter for *The Tampa Tribune* in her native Florida prior to moving to the Big Apple in 1938. There Rountree sustained herself by writing advertising copy for magazines until breaking into radio in 1940, creating the medium's initial panel dialogue series. She gainfully pursued that blueprint multiple times. For her most notable feature, at times Rountee had to convince some leading newsmakers to sit before the microphones and "meet the press." During her quests she constantly sought scintillating personalities as interview subjects.

> It was no small job for a 30-year-old fiction writer. But Miss Rountree, who had once been on the writing end of the news herself, succeeded in getting such controversial figures as John L. Lewis, Walter Reuther, Mayor Fiorello La Guardia, and GOP chairman Herbert Brownell, Jr., to face the journalists. The show became an instant success as a newsmaker in its own right, and soon was receiving regular coverage by both major news wire services.
>
> Bill Slater served as early moderator for the top journalists of the era, such inquisitors as Tex McCrary and Dorothy Thompson. The newsmakers, subjected to on-the-spot grilling, often reacted with sarcasm and anger. John L. Lewis rattled his union saber on one show, made coast-to-coast headlines by threatening a national coal strike. When McCrary asked La Guardia if he had ever used his position as mayor to try to get reporters fired, La Guardia snapped, "That's a damn lie."
>
> Pretty strong for 1945, but that's what made *Meet the Press* go.[13]

It's still doing so nearly seven decades later.

Lawrence Spivak, on the other hand, whose whole professional experience prior to *Meet the Press* had been with magazines (*Antiques, Hunting and Fishing, National Sportsman, The American Mercury*), purchased the latter slick in 1935. For 15 years thereafter he watched it spiral downward to a $100,000-per-year losing proposition before he finally sold it. In the meantime Spivak became the first permanent panelist of *Meet the Press*, flanked by weekly guest journalists who joined in the questioning of a newsmaker.

In 1953, Spivak won a coin toss with Rountree to determine which would buy the other's interest in the program that had made their names well known in U.S. households (the tele-version was added in 1947). Continuing as a panelist Spivak remained with the feature until he retired in 1975. In the interim he had sold the show to NBC for a seven-figure sum in 1955.[14] As he selected interviewees Spivak maintained a cardinal rule that was copied by rival shows of like persuasion: "Never take anyone who withholds information." That canon perpetuated a longstanding reputation for candor that is still a hallmark of the series in the modern age.

> Known for his terrier-like tenacity as an interviewer and what seemed to be a muted but waspish personality, Mr. Spivak always said he saw himself as nothing more than a devil's advocate. His style and that of the journalists who regularly appeared on his program stand in sharp contrast to a later generation of television pundits who sometimes used their broadcasting time to express their own opinions.
>
> Mr. Spivak's directness in asking questions may have paved the way for the later approach, but he was always in control of himself, much as a prosecuting attorney might be. Thus, the guests on his program were most respectful of the questions he asked.[15]

The show transferred to NBC on November 6, 1947, at the same time the TV simulcast began. The radio manifestation persisted through July 27, 1986, after which only the video version persevered. In recent years the telecasts once again were beamed by local radio stations in some markets, and could be picked up on computer and handheld electronic devices. Currently, after 65 years with NBC (2012), *Meet the Press* is indisputably that web's most durable series. Its full time moderators have included Martha Rountree (1945), Ned Brooks (1953), Lawrence Spivak (1966), Bill Monroe (1975), Marvin Kalb and Roger Mudd (1984), Chris Wallace (1987), Garrick Utley (1989), Tim Russert (1991), Tom Brokaw (interim, 2008), and David Gregory (2008).

The *other* contemporary newsmaker interview show with audio roots, **Face the Nation**, debuted over CBS Radio and TV on November 7, 1954. The aural form persisted into 1970, while its televised manifestation continues to the modern epoch. If the reader's indulgence may be entreated for a few moments, please permit a digression in order for the author to introduce a few personal observations that could be relevant to the discussion on this topic.

Regardless of the detail that *Face the Nation* is the flagship commodity of CBS's current political ideology and public figure exhibitions that are showcased by NBC's chief rival — despite the fact that many if not most of the same talking heads on *Meet the Press* respond to similar questions on *Face the Nation* (as well as on a handful of analogous features aired on other broadcast and cable channels) — and no matter that the CBS show has attained a steady, loyal following over the years — that entry seldom gains the ringing endorsement and exalted levels of influence accorded the original member of the breed. Could *Face the Nation* pale in part because NBC got a nine-year head start on the flourishing program formula?

A substantiation of the conclusion regarding the inconsistency between features may be viewed in the works of most of the historiographers of vintage radio fare. In general, the leading researchers tout the sterling accomplishments of *Meet the Press* prolifically and unreservedly but have given little or no actual space to *Face the Nation* in their published annals of broadcasting history. Is this an oversight? Whatever the reason, it's a fundamental lapse that clearly separates a couple of commendable series with comparable purposes, audience, and substance. Although one forum may pursue its tweaked method better one week and another execute it equally so at a different time, over the long haul can there be that much disparity in the dual endeavors? It's not the author's intent to applaud one and disparage another, incidentally, but to call for parity in acknowledging credible opponents.

Proposed by Frank Stanton, then president of CBS, *Face the Nation* was to be the Tiffany Network's answer to NBC's popular public affairs confab. Stanton wanted in on the headlines that the rival chain was netting from occasional surprise announcements during what was usually question-and-answer exchanges at the NBC forum. Whatever was said often made for stimulating fodder for conversations on Monday morning in office suites, hallways, conference rooms, elevators, and around the proverbial water cooler.

Stanton got his wish and put the new show on both radio and television from the start. Today it is the longest running network TV series, following *Meet the Press*. Its moderators have been drawn from the sharpest minds in broadcast journalism, most with lengthy CBS pedigrees: Bill Shadel (1954), Stuart Novins (1955), Howard K. Smith (1960), Martin Agronsky (1963), George Herman (1969), Lesley Stahl (1983), and Bob Schieffer (1991), as of mid–2012. While *Face the Nation* airs for 30 minutes on Sunday mornings against an hour's duration for its chief competitor, it's no slouch when it comes to putting the screws to politicians and other newsmakers. Like the others, it often gets its guests on record, sometimes over the protests of some of them who simply can't find an easy out.

There were other network radio series with less influence, and usually of shorter duration, which pursued likeminded intents to those already presented here. Among their number: *American Viewpoints* (1938–39, CBS), *Capitol Opinions* (1939, CBS), *America United* (1945–51, NBC), *Capitol Cloakroom* (1950–57, CBS), and several more.

Writing in the mid–1940s, one informant recalled that — as recently as 1941 — five key issues confronted many Americans when they thought of foreign policy. That scribe identified those topics and mentioned that all had been highly controversial in nature, in some cases dividing outspoken denizens sharply as individuals expressed their personal takes on one or more of those subjects. During a five-month timeframe, according to the authority, the country's quartet of national radio chains had given substantial time to presenting the several sides of those five concerns by airing a program on one of them at least every third day.

But the majority of potential listeners were never exposed to those purportedly objective reports, discussions, and commentary it was noted. Of 842 radio stations then on the air, just 388 acknowledged broadcasting even one feature on any of the top five foreign policy questions. And 454 local outlets or 54 percent conceded that they had disregarded all five vital issues affecting the nation altogether.[16]

> Networks, we might say, made an honest, if not superlative, effort to face up to the crisis. Their affiliates invalidated this effort by extensive nonparticipation and failed to compensate by any effort of their own....
>
> Our current situation is roughly this. Each of four networks offers us regular weekly discussion of some national or international problem. (But these programs reach only a fraction of the audiences that might like to hear them because so many network affiliates choose not to carry them.) From time to time Congressmen and others also express their points of view in sequent talks on particularly burning topical questions. The large majority of local stations make little or no effort to promote discussion at the local level. Over these stations controversy, except as piped in from the networks, is almost extinct. This [is] at a time when more issues of greater complexity at the local, regional, and national levels confront us than at any time in our history. It hardly seems enough.[17]

Ah! If these seemingly disadvantaged denizens had only lived a few decades hence — when cable news networks babble 24/7, broadcast "talk shows" are high priorities with much of the populace, and every unimaginable electronic device exudes not merely exposure to a wide range of issues but the personalities behind them as well, plus they convey an unending barrage of opinions of diverse persuasions from both the elected and the self-appointed among us — they might have called for some relief from all the saturation! But then, the grass is perpetually greener somewhere else, isn't it?

8

At All Hours: News Achieves Parity, Perceptibly Prospers

Nearly a quarter-century has elapsed since a practiced writing coach in one of this nation's premier halls of higher learning hypothesized: "It is axiomatic in journalism that the fastest medium with the largest potential audience will disseminate the bulk of a community's breaking news. Today that race is being won by television and radio."[1]

Well, yes, that was positively true at the time the resourceful intellect decreed it. But in the interval since the statement surfaced, broadcasting in its original connotation doesn't wholly cover the waterfront any longer, at least not without some challengers. Radio and TV can continue to be characterized as instantaneous and universal disseminators of breaking news to local communities as well as to the entire country's population. This is true except when a digital video recorder or comparable apparatus or power interruption delays or cancels reception. On some occasions, nevertheless, those transmission systems are matched and even perhaps outperformed by escalating alternative methods which also offer split-second, synchronized delivery.

At their core is the Internet which is directly responsible for a mushrooming explosion of gadgetry that is capable of receiving not only breaking news but at the same time email communications, videos, music, an array of pre-selected feeds of myriad persuasions, social media, purchase transactions, and so much more. The Information Highway has become littered by a technological revolution that is expanding at a relentless clip. Out of this computer-driven methodology derivatives of the physical machinery that once commanded the hill all by itself now proliferate: smartphones and tablets currently in demand will ultimately be replaced by stunning advancements as yet unknown.

The devices we have are capable of receiving the news instantly, even prior to announcements on the ether. Despite the newer and potentially quicker delivery methods that are here or are down the road (but close), radio news persists in fulfilling a role in communications that—were it absent—would leave a significantly colossal void in the instantaneous reception that benefits millions. People at home, at their jobs, in vehicles and hotels, at leisure activities and exercise pursuits, continually depend upon radio—*even when they own other devices and platforms*—for rapid updates of what's happening in their world. This includes the environment they inhabit as well as those across the state, the country, and international borders as well. For the foreseeable future then, at least, radio news will responsibly fulfill an expectation that many current Americans maintain — not merely rely on, but genuinely anticipate.

The history of the dispersal of this form of electronic information offers a fascinating introspective into a unique segment of aural broadcasting. Some of the highlights of that development in the past century are brought to the forefront in this chapter.

Weathercasting over the ether on a recurring basis emerged surprisingly early. In 1912 (a full century before this text was written), at nine o'clock each morning, ham operators at 9YV in Manhattan, Kansas — a transmitter that ultimately was to be reassigned the call letters WTG — projected weather alerts by tapping out the latest data in Morse Code.[2] That exercise is credited with being the preliminary attempt to dispatch weather advisories over the airwaves in the U.S. with some uniformity. Using spark transmitters as early as 1900 meanwhile, by June 1915, the University of Wisconsin faculty was issuing daily weather reports for farmers in its area over the school's educationally focused 9XM outlet in Madison.[3] Two years hence daily weather reports were transmitted by means of Morse Code. Not long afterward this data was conveyed by voice transmission, daily starting January 3, 1921.[4] 9XM evolved into WHA Radio. All of this portended a new day in weather forecasting, providing listeners with some modest anticipation in any case of what to expect from the heretofore unpredictable twists and turns of Mother Nature.

In another dimension of auralcasting, scores of a baseball exhibition game between the New York Giants and the Memphis Turtles were relayed at the end of each inning from its Memphis site to waiting fans via a circuitous route on April 5, 1914.[5] Indeed, sportscasting itself may have been launched that day. The tally at the conclusion of innings was dispatched by telephone from the ball field at Red Elm Bottoms to Memphis' Falls Building. There the voice of announcer Victor Laughter was transmitted by wireless to the steamboat G. W. Robertson. A crowd of voyagers was dazzled by the revolutionary ability of maintaining the game's progress without physically being at the park itself. On October 5, 1921, a World Series game that originated over Newark's WJZ and was fed to a Westinghouse group station hookup featured newspaper sports columnist Grantland Rice (1880–1954) supplying play-by-play action between the opposing New York teams, Giants and Yankees.[6]

But the initial eyewitness account of a baseball exhibition by wireless transmission — between the Philadelphia Phillies and hosting Pittsburgh Corsairs — aired on August 5, 1921, a couple of months prior to that World Series over Pittsburgh's KDKA (formerly 8XK).[7] The Harding-Cox U.S. presidential election, with its infamous broadcast breakthrough, you may recall, had transpired over the same outlet just nine months earlier. It was "news not only gathered but, for the first time, distributed at something approaching the speed of light," explained one candid historian.[8] That was considered the watershed episode of radio's premiere — "the beginning of radio," at least as we have applied that epithet to the industry in the years since.[9] And KDKA became the nation's "pioneer station" as a result.[10]

The introduction of farm reports and market news on the ether also commenced prior to hard newscasting's widespread investiture. Crop information and weather news was dispatched from a physics laboratory at the University of Texas in 1915.[11] The reports were delivered by an experimental station that — during the First World War — was assigned the call letters KUT. In that same period, the school's extension division broadcast updates from the U.S. Marketing Bureau and Department of Agriculture. It was but another example of how narrowcasting allowed broadcasters to focus their emphases on segments of the listening audience, a practice that was to become increasingly more prevalent during the fading and post–golden ages of radio.

As noted in Chapter 2, the earliest semblance of journalistic pursuits by wireless transmission was conducted by recreational radio operators often acknowledged as *amateurs* or *hams*. These passionate aficionados were usually drawn to the hobby by their fascination with communicating across great distances from home (sometimes homemade) transmitters without perceptible connections. At first they used Morse Code to ship their messages but as capabilities grew, the Code was succeeded by one's own voice or a hand-cranked gramophone or possibly with a musical instrument that the operator played.

Frequently these wireless connoisseurs filled "time" by reading to their "listeners" from newspapers and other periodicals as well as books. Most hoped that leisure-minded enthusiasts enveloped with the same demonstrated fervor might drop a penny postcard into the U.S. Mail to let them know how far their humble efforts extended geographically. As a result the "news" (albeit strictly secondhand) was among emerging technology's premier "programming" applications. If one missed it in his own local newsweekly or daily journal, he might hear some of its contents in a news summary offered by a ham operator.

And as the 1920s proceeded with few brick-and-mortar radio stations actually hiring valid reporters, the precedent established by these amateurs stuck around for awhile: radio outlets, by then formalized as legitimate business concerns—either commercial, governmental, educational or other non-profit organizations—plagiarized the news journals as well as a few professional wire services. This supplied their need for news while being, at the same time, cheap to get. Never mind that it was infringing on others' proprietary material, that it violated any semblance of ethics and honesty, and that it consisted of tapping sources that were legally copyrighted. There was little hint that early in wireless transmissions' ritual serious trouble would be brewing soon with the originators of that copy. It would be ultimately focused primarily upon the brick-and-mortar outlets and the connecting chains that represented some of them, erupting into a Press-Radio War that would extend from 1922 to 1939. (Again see Chapter 2 for details.)

Radio historiographers cite WJAG, in the northeastern Nebraska city of Norfolk (24,000 residents in 2010), as the first station to initiate a daily newscast on the ether, at least so with substantiating data.[12] The noon feature was established at WJAG's debut on September 13, 1922. At the time the outlet was an ancillary of *The Norfolk Daily News*, a paper that had been owned by one local family since 1888. From a spare room in the downtown *News* building—out of a crudely fashioned studio—those news reports, plus the sounds of community choral groups, barber shop quartets, and polka bands, regularly emanated. With its strong emphasis on news due to its ties with the local journal, WJAG promoted the paper itself, refusing—for its first five years on the air—to accept any paid advertising. It put news on the map in its geographical territory, launching a daily tradition that has persisted beyond most lifetimes.

Five months following WJAG's premiere, WJZ in Newark, New Jersey, added a quarter-hour news summary to its schedule each weekday. Again, we don't know if or how long it may have lasted. In 1925, meanwhile, Cincinnati, Ohio's WLW instituted an unusual element (to us, at least) that confirmed there was more than one way to skin a cat.[13] In this case it was by signifying an ingenious variation that local stations might adopt as they offered news to their listeners.

Appropriately titled *Musical News*, its brief headline capsules read aloud were separated from one another with live selections performed on a studio organ.[14] The audience reaction was bracing. The format was instituted by WLW station manager Fred Smith who went on to launch a popular network series of dramatized news events.[15] As the creative mastermind envisaging *The March of Time* ("the first radio newsreel") in 1929, Smith saw that program prosper from its local debut to transcription and syndication in more than 100 markets. The feature was to eventually air on the four transcontinental chains at sundry times. It persisted in that embodiment from 1931 to 1945.[16] (In passing, Smith's original play *When Love Awakens* over WLW on April 3, 1923 — when he was then the station's program manager — is considered to be broadcasting's debuting narrative penned especially for radio.[17])

But if Smith can be considered the true father of the radio newscast as some have intimated (and even that can't be absolutely corroborated, leaving the question to some tentative speculation), his inspired tactics were recognized beyond his very humble beginnings in Cincinnati radio. Late in 1928, he joined the *Time* magazine organization (sponsor of the series that was to confirm his most noble and notable legacy). Disturbed by the fact that there was so little reportage of current events then on the air — including no national newscast whatsoever — that same year (1928) Smith projected a 60-outlet syndicated hookup of a daily 10-minute news synopsis. He would later maintain that his *NewsCasting* feature, originating during the dinner hour over New York's WOR, was the earliest application of the idiom *newscast* to foster the schematic combining *news* with *broadcasting*.[18] By the following year Smith was producing *NewsActing*, a weekly five-minute show in which current events were dramatized by actors. The feature was carried by more than 100 stations and was a direct precursor to the expanding concept of *The March of Time* which was soon to be airing nationally.[19]

Columbia (later dubbed CBS) signed on with its initial newscast in 1929. Five-minute capsules were integrated into the 30-minute morning feature *Something for Everyone*. While those news reports were delivered in rip 'n' read style with United Press furnishing the substance, they were nevertheless digging in new turf over what was to become a coast-to-coast hookup. This deviation in traditional programming began to grab CBS majority owner William S. Paley, persuading him that news offered more possibilities for the future than he had first been led to believe. "Radio would never realize its rich potential unless the networks began developing an independent capability, with newsmen well rooted in journalistic principles," Paley became convinced.[20] After hiring Paul White to be his news editor (Chapter 2), Paley elevated news to the level of entertainment, empowering White to break into programming as transpiring news justified it.[21] There were some other mitigating circumstances that figured into Paley's abiding attraction to news reportage.

> CBS did not have an easy time of it during those early years. NBC, the older and far more powerful network, completely dominated entertainment programming and had a tight hold on almost all the big sponsors. Faced with that situation, Paley chose to concentrate on news and public affairs. More than anything else at that point, Paley wanted to infuse CBS with an aura of class and respectability, and an emphasis on news and other "serious" programs was the quickest and surest way to accomplish that.[22] He also reasoned, with customary shrewdness, that such prestige, once attained, could later be parlayed into power and profits.
>
> So the strong commitment to news was there from the start, even before the emergence of [Ed] Murrow and his group. But their work during World War II greatly enhanced CBS's reputation as the leader in broadcast journalism.[23]

Even that close to the beginning of broadcasting's puerile existence, we can certify, the news was beginning to attain parity with radio's amusements in some quarters. News had begun moving gradually on a trek down a lengthy highway that would lead to perceptible prosperity of the number of insertions provided in the daily programming agendas of some stations and webs. Ultimately at some of those the news would proliferate into every broadcast hour of the day and night. Tall oaks from little acorns grow, and this was hardly an exception to that maxim.

The early developments of the radio newscast can be traced in the advent and evolution of news bulletins, headlines, capsules, roundups, summaries, commentaries, analyses, debates, discussions, and a glut of other modes of forums offered. This was prompted at least in part by the public's growing and insatiable hunger for quick information coupled with radio's ability to pacify it. Not only did this development transpire on the webs reaching coast-to-coast audiences but also on lesser influential regional hookups and awesomely so at local stations as wire service machines were installed as part of the technological framework. The rip-'n'-read copy torn off a teletype machine was born. It became another task added to a growing catalog of assignments that could be given to the individual(s) wearing an announcer's cap for at least part of the time. That fellow might also be responsible for spinning records, penning continuity copy and commercials and reading it aloud, playing an instrument if so gifted, reading or telling stories to children, hosting myriad features, and filling in as best he could whenever a scheduled act failed to appear (which might be frequently). News reading, therefore, required little special added skill, particularly if the multitalented performer was already adept at talking into a microphone.

A few stations began to include "News" in the program logs appearing in their local newspapers. Yet during radio's introductory epoch there was very little evidence in most markets that the news was afforded a great deal of credence by broadcasting management. At the start of 1930, for example, in New York City—of 17 AM stations then on the air in the Big Apple (FM wasn't patented until 1933), five indicated a general news program in their daily logs published in *The New York Times*.[24] Together the five broadcast a total of nine news programs per day, several being no more than three minutes in duration. Two of the trio of network flagship stations based in New York, including both NBC affiliates, offered their listeners no news reports whatever in each weekday's programming. Keep in mind that the stock market debacle of 1929 had just transpired two months earlier and the Great Depression and its prolonged recovery were immediately ahead. Yet a dozen stations failed to generate even one news report.

Station and network owners clearly had not come to grips with radio's potential as an information source, evidently seeing it virtually for its amusement value alone. Nor had they realized the need for an informed public (and electorate). And they certainly had not found the dollars that would be necessary to create a respected radio journalism effort that could become a magnet for attracting added listeners and revenues. Somewhat surprisingly (or so it seems now), in those days in New York multiple outlets included *Aviation Weather* among their newspaper program logs, sometimes several times daily. Along with that feature there appeared financial market summaries, farming and crop updates, as well as labor news. But there was little or no place to report the action occurring in the arenas of city, state, or federal governments, politics, crime, the judicial system, business, industry, education, health, welfare, and among local nonprofit organizations, as well as any mention of prominent newsmakers. What's up with that?

It's rather difficult to determine if New York radio improved in the matter of offering listeners news reports over the next three years. At the start of 1933, *The New York Times* had reduced its radio page to focus on six key stations.[25] They included the flagship outlets of the quartet of networks then airing plus a couple of leading independents. Of the half-dozen stations whose complete logs were published, the weekday listings showed only two stations generating local news shows daily, while a third carried the only national news program on the air. All of this added up to four news reports per weekday including three local shows and the network summary. That's not really impressive for the nation's largest metropolitan district in the midst of the national Depression.

The premiere of a daily news summary carried by dual transcontinental networks on September 29, 1929, gave some credence to the future of news reporting on the other hand. For six months *Lowell Thomas and the News* was carried by NBC Blue in the nation's eastern region and by CBS in its western zone. After a six-month trial with the twin-chain model, the publishing sponsor that underwrote Thomas on the air in those days decided to concentrate all its eggs in the NBC Blue basket. But that didn't keep the newsman away from CBS forever. Thomas returned in 1947, persisting far beyond the outer limits of radio's golden age, at last retiring from daily broadcasting on May 14, 1976. By then he had been airing practically non-stop through parts of seven decades, nearly 47 years. It was a record for a coast-to-coast newscast at the time. That epic achievement was ultimately surpassed by Paul Harvey whose own network news tour persisted for 58 years, until death removed him from the microphone in 2009.[26] (For more on these durable newscasters, see the biographies at the end of this volume.)

Not until 1935, in the meantime, was New York City radio beginning to demonstrate a few signs of integrating news reporting into its daily program agenda in any fundamental way. At the start of that year the complete schedules of eight local AM outlets—including four network flagships and four independents—were published in the radio logs of *The New York Times*.[27] A total of 13 general news segments displaying a mixed exposition of formats were broadcast throughout the weekday by five of those eight stations. More than half (seven) of the 13 reports were identified by the nomenclature *Press-Radio News*, ostensibly attempts to maintain the spirit of the Biltmore Agreement signed by wire service representatives, network executives, and newspaper publishers 13 months earlier. That pact, you may recall, permitted network radio affiliates to air news gathered by the wire services and newspapers under some rather stringent conditions. By 1935, nonetheless, it had all virtually unraveled after some unaffiliated outlets failed to cooperate and launched their own news reports. (For a refresher refer to Chapter 2.)

In the New York market at that point station WOR, one of the founding members of the Mutual Broadcasting System, indicated its allegiance to news programming through a much greater manifestation than did any of its rivals. Three times throughout the day, at 8 A.M., noon, and 11 P.M., the station presented 15-minute summaries of newsmaking scenarios. In addition, at 6:55 P.M., WOR aired a daily five-minute news commentary by Gabriel Heatter who was not yet reaching out to the boundaries of the MBS chain. While Lowell Thomas was continuing to report to the full NBC Blue web in a nightly quarter-hour originated over New York's WJZ, Edwin C. Hill maintained a nightly local-only quarter-hour commentary over WABC (the call letters of the flagship outlet of CBS at that time). All of this focus on news signaled a new day was on the way in the proclamation of current events. They were laying a foundation for rapid future developments that would transpire in hundreds of smaller communities as well as the great urbanized centers of America.

Although we are unsure to our utter satisfaction of the question in pinpointing a time and place that the time-honored, habit-forming custom of airing radio news on the hour was launched, we have a fairly credible impression for a contender, if not the actual source. The earliest stimulation may have gained its impetus at a Manitowoc, Michigan, radio outlet. Manitowoc is a city of 33,000 (2010 Census) against the shores of Lake Michigan.

Not long after WOMT there signed on the air on November 8, 1926 — exactly one week before NBC was inaugurated, by pure coincidence — the fledgling station broadcast news "every hour on the hour." We aren't certain just how much content its news reports included, nor their sources, nor their duration in broadcast time in minutes but also encompassing duration in days, weeks, months or possibly years. WOMT's Web site recently indicated that its newscast frequency presently didn't start to equate with that early omen of repetitive tidings: weekday news reports are aired on the hour five times daily plus three times Saturdays and none at all on Sundays. Still, WOMT may have been the catalyst of a form that outlets in scores of additional markets of all sizes have long since adopted, many of whom are still following the prototype today.

In the meantime, a profusion of news shows had made their way onto the schedules of the four transcontinental chains by the late 1930s. Because of its size and influence on radio broadcasting, Gotham is again cited as an example. At the start of 1940, *The New York Times* radio logs indicated that — of nine outlets with schedules the journal included in print — there were no fewer than 69 weekday general news inserts or programs offered to local listeners (non-specialized news features, thus not embracing "European," "Market," "Labor," or "Financial" capsules or any others of such specialized ilk).[28] Some consisted of simple bulletins; some were of the five-minute variety; several were quarter-hour roundups or commentaries. A few well-known analysts headlined some of those nightly features that prevailed in 1940, several of them beamed across the country: Elmer Davis (twice nightly on CBS), Edwin C. Hill (CBS), Fulton Lewis, Jr. (MBS), Raymond Swing (MBS), and Lowell Thomas (NBC Blue). The point worth remembering in this regard is that — by the 1940s — news was an inclusive core element in programming the daily provisions offered by local stations as well as the national chains. It has continued into the contemporary age.

The city in which the headquarters of all four commercial transcontinental webs are/ were based persisted in initiating many of the permanent customs in broadcasting. Certainly it shouldn't be a stretch to believe that the lasting concept of the hourly news reports, still aired in the modern age, initially wended its way through the Gotham ether. We just may be able, in fact, to isolate the precise juncture in which that most durable of current radio programming traditions was spawned.

In a fortuitous but insightful bit of irony, on Monday, December 1, 1941—six days prior to the Japanese surprise attack on Pearl Harbor naval base in Hawaii and the precipitous trigger that catapulted America into the Second World War, also unleashing a prevailing global news topic for the next quadrennial — *The New York Times* integrated a three-minute news capsule into the programming of the Big Apple's WMCA-AM Radio. And it did so 17 times daily on the hour between 8 A.M. and midnight. This insert was ultimately extended to 18 times per day by eventually beginning at 7 A.M. It is the first confirmed experiment to accomplish such a continuous feat in interminable span (thus far) throughout the aircast day.

On weekends the *Times* news inserts appeared during most of the broadcasting hours. Those pithy headlines of local, state, national, and international developments were dispatched from the paper's newsroom to WMCA's studios at 1657 Broadway at Fifty-Second Street situated high above legendary Lindy's Restaurant. The news bulletins persisted over WMCA through June 30, 1946, after which they were aired over WQXR-AM, a station that *The New York Times* had purchased in the interim. At WQXR they were eventually expanded from an original three-minute aircast to five minutes.

In the early 1940s, the *New York Post* negotiated to buy WQXR, an offer [co-owner] Elliott Sanger said he wished had come from the *Times*. As a result of his offhand lament the *Times* soon made a $1 million offer to [co-owner John V. L.] Hogan and Sanger, and on 25 July 1944 the city's most prestigious paper took control..., keeping the existing staff and management.... There was ... one immediate and serious complication. Since December 1941, the *Times* had been providing news to WMCA, which refused to terminate the contract. So "The Radio Station of the *New York Times*" did not begin to broadcast *Times* news bulletins until 1 July 1946. And it was not until Sunday, 16 April 1950, that WQXR moved from Fifty-seventh Street to studios on the ninth and tenth floors of the Times Building at 229 W. Forty-third Street. *Times* newscasts were fired from the city desk to the WQXR news studio by pneumatic tube, and listeners could tell from the swoosh and clunk when a late bulletin arrived (a noise no less intrusive than the clanging chime that opened each hour's news).[29]

Was the hourly effort by *The New York Times* the mechanism that prompted other nearby stations and ultimately the networks themselves to launch their own news on the hour (NOTH) features? It's certainly possible. While the others didn't arrive with any haste, nonetheless before the decade of the 1950s was history, top-of-the-hour bulletins, capsules and updates were prevalent all over the dial in medium- and larger-sized markets. In New York City itself, the hourly news craze was already taking hold by the mid–1950s, turning up at many hours throughout the weekday on network outlets as well as independents. It was a momentous contrast to the lackadaisical approach to news programming that individual stations as well as the national chains had made less than two decades before.

The evidence of the change is reported in the radio logs appearing in the *Times*. By the mid- to late 1950s, of course, a major revamping in the schedules of the nationwide webs had occurred. It was mandated after audiences, advertisers, and artists shifted their allegiance to the newly introduced medium of television which became the first choice in mass communications entertainment for most Americans. That prompted utter chaos in radio's longtime programming that resulted in a loss of many of the familiar stars and shows that faithful listeners had been tuning to for years. In their absence, local disc jockeys captured much of the broadcast time that was suddenly available. It cost little to put DJs on the air while at times they could produce incredible revenues for the stations employing them.

Those waxworks features were occasionally interrupted by news updates which station owners viewed as favorable opportunities to sell more commercial time. Much of the time the newscasts appeared at the top of certain hours of the day and night — or adjacent to those spots — and sometimes in nearly every hour. At the larger outlets with ample news departments boasting multiple writers, reporters, anchors, and production personnel the news inserts might air more frequently, at more designated times such as the bottom of each hour too.

As the 1950s started to fade, the major national chains began to purposefully adopt the NOTH configuration.

ABC Radio had instituted a five-minute hourly news update on weekends in 1954, the first net to do so.[30] That web suggested that such informative reports blended well with the gradually increasing mood of local stations for flexible programming....

"In a changing and frightening world," wrote a couple of media critics, "special news events were to remain radio's forte, as it could deliver flash or bulletin stories faster than television or any other medium.... Radio networks became vestigial. Stations without network affiliations offered a minimum of 'rip 'n' read' or 'yank 'n' yell' newscasts, composed of wire services' five-minute summaries read by a disc jockey. However, in times of great stress or national disaster the networks often allowed independent stations free use of their coverage."[31]

Over at NBC, meanwhile, an utterly brilliant innovator, Sylvester (Pat) Weaver, who rose to network president in the 1950s, is credited with bringing *Monitor* to the aural airwaves (after building status with inspired creativity for *Today, Tonight, Home* and more landmark features at NBC-TV). *Monitor*, running 1955–75, was contrived as a 40-hour weekend "radio service" of NBC Radio.[32] Gradually banished to fewer hours as the years rolled by, *Monitor's* heavy emphasis on current events and key newsmakers, interviewed by sparkling *Monitor* luminaries, drew legions of listeners to their radios each weekend, long after the golden age passed. In Weaver's original design, features were blended in an omnibus model that almost erased the lines of radio's sacrosanct time-zone barometers (quarter-hour, half-hour, hour-long programs were eliminated). But by the 1960s, with NOTH a visible (hearable?) portion of the chain's schedule elsewhere, *NBC News on the Hour*—a five-and-a-half-minute interlude in the flow of the magazine features—became a fixed building block in the *Monitor* arsenal. It validated that news was not merely a triviality in radio's framework but was one of its most critical components. It was a point substantiated by all of the transcontinental chains in chorus as well as most operators of commercial stations.

In this same era, the co-founding MBS station in the New York market (WOR)—which had unconditionally embraced the news at frequent intervals hypothesis in the 1950s, and included news at the top of every hour all day long by 1960—declined to participate further in the Mutual partnership. After a quarter-century with MBS, WOR's 1959 pullout temporarily left the city with no MBS representation. That wasn't remedied until WINS signed with Mutual late in 1960, followed by WHN less than two years afterward.

Looking past Mutual's inconsistent affiliation in that larger metropolis, the remaining trio of flagship network outlets were feeding their listeners more and more opportunities to tune them in for NOTH or in an adjacent timeslot next to it several times daily. By the start of 1960, in fact, those three stations together provided 43 such daily encounters in addition to several more news, commentary, and public affairs programs at other points during various hours (e.g., 7:15, 7:25, 7:30, 7:45, et al.).[33] Here's an accounting of how those Big Apple flagships were handling the "hourly" news each weekday at that stage.[34] Keep in mind that many of these 5-, 10- and 15-minute newscasts and commentaries were beamed well beyond New York City, transmitted to all the affiliates of a particular chain. The hours shown are listed sequentially from early morning to late evening.

ABC/WABC—6:55, 8, 8:55, 10:55, 12:55, 3:55, 5:55, 7, 9:55, 10, 10:55, 11 (12 spots total at or near the top of the hour)
CBS/WCBS—7, 8, 9, 10, 11, 12, 1, 2, 3, 4, 6, 7, 8, 10, 11 (15 spots)
NBC/WRCA–7, 8, 9, 10, 11, 12, 2, 3, 4, 5, 6, 7, 9, 10, 11, 12 (16 spots)

This data projects a pattern that had been spread not merely by independent outlet WQXR, *The New York Times* station—which was still carrying NOTH programming that the newspaper first aired in 1941—but also included these three local flagship stations as well as a few more independents in that market. Newspaper listings in many American cities confirm that NOTH was a trend rapidly being copied by the mid to late 1950s in many markets of every size.

In less than a year, meanwhile, some shifting in the model was discernable in New York. While local listeners still had 42 chances on weekdays to catch the news at or near the top of the hour, some tinkering with the number of times news was presented had occurred. At least two annotations are pertinent:

(1) It's obvious that stations and networks remained profoundly committed to the high visibility given to news, commentaries, and public affairs programming, raising that discipline to rank at the forefront of radio programming, a giant leap from the relative underground doldrums it occupied a decade previously; and

(2) One of the chains, CBS — re-energized after dispatching most of its entertainment shows and returning the bulk of its programming time to its affiliates late in 1960 — substantially amplified its news presence by doubling the airtime assigned to the area. With its broadcast slate then almost clean, CBS expanded its network newscasts to 10 minutes hourly every hour on the hour throughout the broadcast day beginning November 28, 1960.[35] The web's new blueprint was designed to "preserve the physical network for prestige, emergency, and news," a couple of radio history scholars allowed.[36]

Your indulgence is implored for a fleeting digression. In an attempt at providing full disclosure, not everybody in CBS's listening audience thought that adding an extra five minutes to the already existing five minutes of news at the top of the hour was a great deal. In fact, some seemed to resent it, rebelling strenuously, and made their objections known in no uncertain terms. The newscasts essentially had become a scapegoat for something else, a whipping boy for their actual dissatisfaction: the increase in time allotted for news was a direct result of CBS's decision to practically wipe the schedule clean which included the last vestiges of the radio soap operas that had brought familiar visitors into millions of American domiciles for decades. That was the true culprit and a strong reason why 10 minutes of news per hour met with a lackluster introduction in some quarters. One drama's narrator bade farewell to the audience after the curtain rang down permanently on the final episode:

> "And so, after more than 7,000 broadcasts — 27 years — we say 'good-by' to *Ma Perkins*. This is Bob Pfeiffer speaking." Then an unidentified announcer's voice broke in to laud CBS's daytime schedule changes: "Remember," he chortled, "Monday, CBS News goes double to ten minutes an hour weekdays on the hour on the CBS Radio Network." The expanded concept wouldn't survive long. But the vain attempt to pump up an audience that was losing a friend who had visited in their homes daily for nearly three decades fell on deaf ears. Few saw the personal benefit to themselves in ten minutes of news in the face of pulling the plug on *Ma Perkins* and its peers.[37]

The outraged lit up the CBS switchboard like a Christmas tree. Angry callers and letter writers gave the network a piece of their minds, sparing few words. Ten minutes of news in the face of losing a 27-year legacy didn't seem like a good tradeoff to many.[38]

Yet the news departments of the local radio outlets and the networks themselves had never conducted their business in such high cotton as when the golden age of radio was on the way to being snuffed out. When all was said and done — even in a contemporary setting — the news gatherers, writers, reporters, and anchors are the true survivors of vintage radio. They have frequently been (and still are) the final remnants of the once proud performing traditions of the local commercial stations and transcontinental chains, many times being the last holdouts when the end has arrived for some of their outfits. It's the newsmen and newswomen who usually occupy the gilded cages and the lofty perches as radio enterprises have ground to a halt in some settings — the very last on-air voices they almost inevitably couldn't do without.[39]

As 1960 drew to a close, the newscast schedule looked like this for the trio of New York flagship outlets under current scrutiny.[40]

ABC/WABC — 7:55, 8:55, 9:55, 10:55, 12:55, 1:55, 2:55, 7, 9:55, 10:55, 11:55 (11 spots)
CBS/WCBS — 7, 8, 9, 10, 11, 12, 1, 2, 3, 4, 5, 6, 7, 8, 9, 10, 11 (17 spots)
NBC/WNBC — 6, 7, 8, 9, 10, 12, 4, 6, 7, 8, 9, 10, 11, 12 (14 spots)

As time has elapsed over a half-century since, some developments completely unanticipated have transpired. This trio of once nationally powerful and influential stations witnessed some monumental format changes. While hourly news continued as a programming mainstay, the audience focus has been reduced. It's been narrowed to specific segments rather than the entire available population, a trend pursued by hundreds of other U.S. radio stations during this same epoch. The fragmentation of the audience allowed programmers to concentrate their efforts on appealing to a certain type of listener and his or her interests.[41]

This model dates all the way back to 1921, when Chicago's KYW — founded by the Westinghouse Electric and Manufacturing Company — invented programming specialization.[42] KYW aired opera altogether for six days every week. But when the current opera season finished, the station owners faced a dilemma. Although they had pioneered an untried programming style quite successfully, to remain viable they rolled with the times and diversified their schedule. Instead of opera they provided audiences with pop and classical tunes, interspersed with sporting events, lectures, fictional narratives, newscasts, weathercasts, market reports, and political commentary.

In so doing KYW joined a burgeoning mass of colleagues in the broadcasting industry that were already proffering similar fare. The idea of narrowcasting to a limited quantity of the listening audience might have lain dormant for a while but it never totally went away. After the halcyon days of radio elapsed, to be sure — and after the DJs had spun their last grooves — narrowcasting was monumentally revived, returning to make far more than a mere profound impression. Had it not, it wouldn't be so prevalent today.

WABC, which had been an all-music programmer for 22 years following the passing of radio's golden age, became an all-talk station in 1982. WCBS adopted an all-news format in 1967, and follows that strategy still. WNBC introduced the first call-in format to Gotham listeners when it increased its talk identity in 1964, a focus that lasted six years. At that juncture music was again beamed from its transmitter, specializing in first one sound (contemporary) and then another (hits). WNBC ushered in "shock jocks" Don Imus (1972) and Howard Stern (1982) but remained in a ratings cellar while concurrently alienating a large sector of its traditional fan base with the new blood. Oldies were added to its musical mix in 1987. That didn't improve the situation any. Caught in some corporate maneuvers a short time afterward, WNBC Radio was written off as a lost cause by a new owner and it left the air forever in 1988.

> Radio news ... came in for criticism following the 1981 deregulation of radio, which lessened the requirements for stations to present news and public affairs programming. It was feared that many stations would drop their newscasts in favor of less expensive entertainment programming and that radio news would decline in quality and importance as a result.
> The number of radio news jobs dropped sharply, as did the number of all-news radio stations. FM stations especially cut back on hourly newscasts, and overall the amount of news on music stations declined. On the other hand, there was a large increase in the number of stations doing a combination of news and talk formats. Some critics charged that the function of informing the talk show audience was largely handed over to people who were not news professionals but primarily entertainers, such as Rush Limbaugh and Larry King....
> Following radio deregulation, newscast-story selection also came in for criticism on the grounds that the stories' target and format resulted in a skew toward entertainment news and

softer "lifestyle" reporting. Smaller news staffs meant less on-the-scene reporting, it was charged, and thus a greater degree of error in stories.[43]

During the following decade the MBS and NBC radio networks vanished from most people's radar altogether in 1999.[44] At this writing (2012), ABC and CBS continue to function much as they have for manifold decades: both concentrate on news every hour throughout the day, including weekends. ABC split itself into a quartet of focused chains on January 1, 1968, all with news as a staple perpetually offered in roughly five-minute segments some time each hour.[45] CBS became the first network to provide NOTH 24 hours daily in five-minute portions beginning April 2, 1973. Until then CBS had programmed its daily news from 6 A.M. (7 A.M. Saturdays and 8 A.M. Sundays) through 1 A.M. only. NBC soon followed suit, offering news bulletins 24 hours daily beginning January 1, 1974.[46]

The latter web, which had earned a sterling reputation for its news product back in the day, was continuing to make some noble attempts to compete successfully with contenders for audience share. NBC seldom possessed as many of the no-nonsense animated radio voices that filled CBS Radio's news stable and to which a loyal following among listeners was drawn. Furthermore, by comparison, NBC only occasionally exhibited sustained aggressiveness in newsgathering and reporting that perpetually characterized its staunchest rival—both during and in the first few decades after the golden age of radio concluded. With the obvious exceptions of *Meet the Press* and *Monitor*, news and public affairs was a domain in aural broadcasting in which CBS was ever seldom eclipsed. CBS Radio's exalted status in that province continues to persist today after more than eight decades.

The progression of audio news down through the ages is one of compelling fascination to the awestruck addicts of radio history. Characterized by incessant change, the fundamental form of presentation has prevailed even as the delivery hardware has been altered. In contemporary times, millions of Americans continue to rely on radio as a reliable source for finding out what's happening in their world. Although the apparatus to receive it wouldn't be recognized by the forbears that launched current events on the air, the product's substance is similar. It's the messenger—not the message itself—that's been replaced.

9

Journalism's Inducement in a Rise of Local Stations

Imagine this!

In Budapest there is a newspaper that has no printing presses and no newsboys. It is a large and flourishing newspaper and, as far as I know, all its subscribers are satisfied. It has never been "scooped" and there is little likelihood that such a catastrophe will soon happen. It begins to give its news to the public at nine o'clock in the morning and it does not stop until ten o'clock in the evening....

The newspaper is called *The Telephone-Hirmondo* and has been in existence for twenty-eight years.

As its name implies it is a telephone newspaper. It furnishes news direct to its subscribers by an elaborate system of party lines. All a subscriber has to do is to step to the telephone and put the receiver to his ear. To each subscriber is furnished a schedule showing the hours different news goes out: local, national, world news, sports, fashions. Fiction stories are read to the subscribers, speeches are delivered; puzzles are told and English is taught to all who wish to learn it. Even serials running in local motion picture shows are read to subscribers; that night a person may go to the theatre and see for himself the story his newspaper has told him. Budapest's telephone newspaper is not an experiment; not some vague, uncertain, half-baked theory. It has been a success for more than a quarter of a century.

In the wireless age prior to reaching the full extent of that system's integration into the lives of very many Americans, journalist Homer Croy's enticing "The Newspaper That Comes through Your Walls" surfaced in the September 1922 issue of *Popular Radio* magazine.[1] Published in *this* country, his piece was a charming revelation of how a few enterprising innovators found a process to gather, articulate, and disseminate news of the day to subscribers along with amusing and educational sidelight fare. They found a populace eager to hear details of current events almost instantly as they transpired. Budapest's radio-telephone system dated all the way back to 1894. That's ancient history to us; Americans generally think of transmissions of the human voice as starting in the 1920s, not the 19th century. One of the extraordinary discoveries from this appears to be the value we put upon voice communication that originated close to home. As it turned out, the news and features dispatched from local radio outlets were some of the most treasured of our listening experience.

Near the conclusion of his treatise, Croy speculated:

In the future the newspapers will broadcast in their territories. St. Louis will have newspapers sending out their silent appeals on different wavelengths; Omaha will be doing the same; Waco,

Wheeling, Woonsocket. They will send out local news. For example: "George Washington Jones, the millionaire manufacturer of folding wash boards, was arrested this afternoon for speeding and was fined $4." The license numbers of stolen automobiles will be given out and the police departments will be assisted in recovering the missing property.... Local, grain and crop markets will be sent out; whether wheat is up or down, what activity potatoes show and what chickens are doing.... Gossip, sports, local news items will go out.

What a fascinating world to anticipate! And it was then just over the horizon, rapidly arriving at a broadcasting transmitter near almost everybody. Radio news would furnish American citizens with information and trivia they never had access to so promptly before. The implications of the local hometown radio operation extended promises almost nobody could believe.

As we have witnessed much earlier in this tome, radio news commenced with people reading daily or weekly newspapers over the ether. It was certainly the handiest, most recent, and most authentic evidence of current events that these individuals could put their hands on while being yet another confirmation of the axiom of decidedly recent vintage: *If it ain't broke, don't fix it.* Ham operators largely relied upon newspapers to have something of substance to say, hoping that fellow hams — some of them quite distant physically — would respond with penny postcards to affirm at what expanse their "broadcasts" were being picked up.

Few early operators of the successive brick-and-mortar radio stations could afford staffs of investigative correspondents. Each added warm body would have been a luxury that most outfits couldn't bankroll. Purloining the published achievements derived by the legwork of news journal workforces was commonplace in broadcasting's pioneer era therefore.[2] Those were *real* outlets identified by *real* call letters as opposed to the pseudo nomenclature of the wireless experimenters — broadcasters that were assigned amalgamations of numerals and letters as their handles, identifications that primarily lingered among the amateur hobby-struck buddies that, though they were true believers, were also precursors of the authentic stations.

Into this mix a host of station operators arrived, ranging from outright wealthy, often politically connected individuals and families in local communities to other group operators. In their cases their sole or primary business might be ownership of one or more broadcasting outlets. On the other hand, some stations were run by commercial enterprises whose primary capital gains were derived from other possibly unrelated industries. As a means of diversification, their owners got into broadcasting. They included single newspapers and publishing conglomerates, retail dry goods sellers, automotive dealerships and parts manufacturers, banks and other financial institutions, hotels, household and commercial appliance makers and dispensers (radios among them), insurance products distributors, and privately owned utilities (electric, gas, coal, water, telephone); universities and other educational, religious, and non-profit organizations; and municipal government agencies. The trade journal *Radio Service Bulletin* tallied the ownership of American radio stations in its issue of February 1, 1923, and reported:

Educational institutions	72
Newspapers	69
Department stores	29
Religious organizations	12
City governments	several
Automobile dealers, theaters, banks	a sprinkling

Before the year 1923 was history, the American Newspaper Publishers Association surmised that at least 100 dailies were running their own broadcasting operations as a sideline of their principal business interests. Most, according to one sage, followed a standard pattern touting: "Put on a good show, advertise the paper."[3] Stations owned by those publishers sometimes read news over the air from their own papers to promote a dual-pronged objective: subscription sales and the sale of print advertising space.

As noted earlier, the number of applicants for radio station ownership — particularly in the late 1920s and early 1930s — was plainly overwhelming.[4] While the rate of failure after short trial encounters was fairly high, some organizations — and particularly those backed by deep pockets — were able to withstand the pitfalls of running a business in a field in which they often had little or no experience. The fact that so many succeeded is a testament not only to their perseverance, ingenuity and business acumen, but a tribute as well to those who were listening — and finding something worthy of spending time with. The news became a part of that worthiness, particularly news that was aired on the local stations.

Until radio's arrival, the people living in the early decades of the 20th century relied upon the telephone and telegraph as their dual methods of electronic connection with the outside world. What they learned by those systems even then wasn't normally delivered to several receivers at the same time. A possible exception to that incidence occurred with the multiple-user telephone line. In that set of circumstances more than one telephone customer shared a party-line with one, two, three or more other patrons who were assigned the same line. (Those phones, by the way, were usually stationary and wall-mounted and invariably black and ponderous. They consisted of an earpiece held in one's hand connected to the body of the apparatus by a wire, plus a mouthpiece at the front center of the main body which a person stood in front of and spoke into.)

When the phone rang, a subscriber would count the number of rings until his designated numeral occurred; in that way he knew if a call was intended for his household or business. But if a subscriber picked up the receiver at another moment, he might learn all types of information not intended for his ears as he silently eavesdropped on the conversations of others on the same party line. It was a novel approach in acquiring the "news" of the community, sometimes including mere gossip. And it sounds precisely like the relic that it was even though it was a vast improvement over what these customers' ancestors had for verbal communications over great distances: shouting.[5] As a means of interacting with others at some distance — especially when compared with individually oriented smartphones and their myriad features a century later — the cumbersome wall-mounted party line phone in basic black was absolutely primeval.

Into that deprived communications abyss radio was introduced. Suddenly it brought the world — the larger world — to one's door. By opening connections to the community, the state, and nation, and indeed, the entire global body as well as the far reaches of the universe, radio linked man to places he may have only heard of, if even that. And in doing so man's quest to discover what was transpiring elsewhere hastily escalated into something more intense. News — reports of the happenings with a bearing on the lives of others as well as one's own self— became an imperative, no longer an option. Radio ushered in a means of learning instantly, simultaneously, about the past, present, and future of one's environment. Never had so much detail about so many things been available at the flick of a wrist following the compulsory warm-up of the radio tubes.

In passing, the vacuum tube radio replaced earlier crystal sets with headphones, which could be ordered or purchased complete from a variety of sellers, or fashioned at home.

Many boys' magazines encouraged youngsters to take pride in constructing their own radios, supplying step-by-step instructions for making crystal radios. "Thousands of twelve year old boys *and girls*" successfully set up radio receivers for "entertaining their families and friends," advised the authors of *Radio Receiving for Beginners*, a 1922 tome that initiates others into the "magic" of the "radio wonderland."[6] For about six dollars, most supplies needed in their assembly could be gathered from a hardware or general mercantile dealer.[7] While six dollars was a princely sum a little later it wasn't an unthinkable amount for many in the frivolous and flourishing pre-Depression epoch. Although the sound in the crystal sets was often faint and subject to static disturbance, it nevertheless provided an innovative challenge if one was constructing his own receiving device. The sound was vastly enhanced for most receptors with the introduction of the vacuum tube models, pioneers of which arrived on the market as early as 1924. When the automatic loudspeaker was added in 1928, the volume and its control improved even more.[8]

The 1920s began with people listening to crystal sets with headphones that were passed from person to person if more than one individual was participating in hearing a program. Large battery-operated sets with dozens of dials and horn speakers appeared next.[9] These were followed by electric console radios designed as fine furniture, single-knob tuning, and loudspeakers. Until the transistor radio appeared in 1954, superseding the vacuum tube radio in the late 1950s, the lighted tubular affair was the type that people living in the golden age experienced most commonly.[10] The decrease in size and weight of the transistor replica permitted immediate portability, allowing radio to turn up in many places it had never previously traveled. The brief waiting time to hear sound as the tubes "warmed up" was also a thing of the past; the sound boomed out instantly in transistor sets. The change compared to driving a car with a stick shift and one with automatic transmission.

There were only 30 brick-and-mortar radio stations in this country by the start of 1922, all of them using transmitters manufactured by Western Electric Company (WE), a subsidiary of the American Telephone & Telegraph Company (AT&T).[11] A historian disclosed: "There had been earlier transmitters, but most were what were then called radio-telephone apparatus, generally hand-built or put together by the thousands of amateurs whose imaginations were fired by [Italian inventor Guglielmo] Marconi's great triumph and by those who had been exposed to radio during World War I."[12]

In reality, while WE, the manufacturing supplier of AT&T, was in the business of fabricating radio transmitters along with other hardware components, AT&T prevailed on its assembly unit to delay construction of transmitters that would coexist with its own tower in New York. WE had received orders for more than 100 broadcast transmitters for erection in or near the Big Apple. AT&T officials immediately realized not only the potential for signal interference but the intense competition all this would draw. It advised those who had ordered that it could be years until their transmitters were ready. They could, however, benefit right then by purchasing continuing time on the single transmitter already available and owned by AT&T. The encounters with sundry clients as they attempted to acquire transmitters in other ways and the resistance they sometimes met, briefly described, makes for fascinating reading.[13]

There was an additional fray over stations' supposed infringement on AT&T's patent rights, which the company arduously challenged in 1923.[14] It threatened litigation against hundreds of stations while settling on New York's WHN as a representative defendant in a genuine case. To say that station owners everywhere were surprised by the firm's aggressive behavior is putting it mildly; they believed that once a license to operate was secured from federal overseers, a paid certificate from the manufacturer of components they purchased and adapted was unthinkable. For AT&T, in a quest to turn parts buyers for radio sets and transmitters exclusively onto its manufactured goods, the situation developed into a public relations imbroglio.

In the six months from February 1 to July 31, 1922, some 422 station applicants were approved for licenses by the U.S. Department of Commerce.[15] Of 670 outlets licensed by the close of 1922, 576 were alive at year's end.[16] (Fourteen percent of station applicants that year, accounting for 94 outlets, had met early deaths.[17]) By 1923, meanwhile, operating U.S. radio outlets jumped to an aggregate of 550.[18] By 1930, the number of stations then operating rose to 629.[19] Of course, many of those broadcasters took to the airwaves under rather trying circumstances at times, to wit:

> In Vida (pop. 25), Montana, KGCX was launched on October 5, 1926, by the First State Bank of Vida in a back room of the bank. The broadcasting was done by Ed Krebsbach when he could "slip away from the front counter." In San Diego, Lyman Bryson, a young extension teacher for the University of California, was asked to discuss current events on a radio station in the corner of a hotel. The engineer and control equipment were in the same room as Bryson, but during the broadcast someone warned the engineer that a policeman was going down the street with parking tickets. Leaving the equipment on, the engineer dashed off. As Bryson finished reading his talk, no engineer was in sight. Bryson ad libbed twelve minutes until the engineer returned.[20]

Did we say the conditions were also sometimes primitive?

The venerable network news commentator Hans Von Kaltenborn made a tour of radio outlets in the United States in the summer of 1924, well before his name gained widespread household detection. It was an eye-opening experience for the newsman. Returning to New York, he observed, "I spoke from stations in all sorts of out-of-the-way places — barns, garages, fraternity headquarters, shops, office buildings, and stores." A Denver station he found occupied a family dwelling with its control room situated in the kitchen.[21] Some of the early brick and mortar stations were not quickly distinguished to be sure.

Alfred Balk observed that operational routines were just as crude in those days as some of the facilities from which the sounds emanated.[22] At Pittsburgh's infamous KDKA, the announcer for a program would stick his head in the door of the transmitter room and assert: "Well, we're ready, I guess, let's go." At WFAA in Dallas at sign-off time the announcer would instruct the engineer while they were still on the air: "Shut 'er down, Eddie." Equally bizarre, some stations in broadcasting's early years were obliged to "stand by"— be silent— for three minutes in every quarter-hour so any SOSs could be heard. On one occasion, a diva had just finished an aria as an announcer advised the audience: "We will now stand by for three minutes to hear distress calls."

By the mid–1920s, many of the pioneer broadcasters of earlier years had left the airwaves. The mortality rate was high. "A good many stations ran out of money and 'died' in a few months," noted one investigator.[23]

> Who were the fallen? Few case histories are available, but that of KDYS, launched May 19, 1922, by the *Tribune* of Great Falls, Mont., may be typical. The transmitter had been assembled by a local auto mechanic. For the opening broadcast, in which the mayor spoke, 800 people crowded around a receiving set in a local dry goods store a block and a half from the *Tribune* office. A lady sang. The horn speaker vibrated badly in response to her soprano tones. Then mechanical failure at the transmitter ended the broadcast. An informal survey by the station just before the opening revealed fifteen receiving sets in Great Falls. The station persisted, but in its second year closed for repairs and never reopened.[24]

At least some of the industry's early innovators were replaced by more seasoned entrepreneurs who controlled outlets with greater wattage than their forbears. This gave their operations increased power by pushing a signal further across the ether.

In 1923, some three million Americans owned a radio.[25] In 1924, together they spent $358 million on radio receivers (sets) and parts, a rise from the previous year's outlay of $136 million by more than two-and-a-half times.[26] Were they turned on by being tuned in or what? Three-fifths of all U.S. households included a radio of some type among their purchases in the seven years between 1923 and 1930.[27] That boom put manufacturers of the devices on easy street. At the same time it assured that most Americans not only approved of radio and its contents but they had quickly become addicted to the features transmitted to their domiciles and businesses.

Beyond a set's initial cost, of course, radio boasted the advantage of requiring very little additional outlay. Thus it became a home entertainment center, and eventually most American homes sported one as the focal point of their living rooms. In a time warp caused by unanticipated but colossal economic catastrophe, radio was most people's ticket to freedom: escape from the cares of the moment through fantasy and amusement. Only the insertion of news and public affairs and the frequent "Fireside Chats" from the president sitting in the White House confirmed that there was a sense of reality about it all.

To their credit, many local stations acknowledged a responsibility for maintaining an informed listenership on matters of import, including current events, the stuff of which life consisted. Reporting the daily happenings in a nation that had been turned upside down became a compelling priority for many broadcasters. Journalism had a profound effect on radio as early as the start of the Great Depression, increasing in value with the rise of subsequent troublesome issues in the nation's life. A lot of people were responsible for turning the listening public onto radio to become informed. Not all of them occupied network headquarters addresses.

In one study it was discovered that four times as many locally originated news insertions in the daily schedules existed as national ones during radio's heyday.[28] Eighty percent of news reports and commentaries were derived by the staffs of single outlets as opposed to the more readily identifiable and venerated newscasters and analysts. Affecting this revelation is the fact that, in the early 1940s, 43 percent of U.S. radio stations — then an aggregate exceeding 900 altogether — were independents, unaffiliated with any large chain, and thus reliant on their own resourcefulness when news was included in the programming offered.[29] While this didn't prevent any station from subscribing to sundry wire services, it meant — for anything beyond the minimum — it was up to the station itself to generate it.

With four-fifths of all broadcasters providing far more than token news coverage, these statistics indicate that the focus on news, commentary, and public affairs programming at most local outlets was ample. A 1948 survey of the radio audience in Peoria, Illinois, was illuminating: respondents preferred a local newscaster 3 to 1 over H.V. Kaltenborn and Edward R. Murrow.[30] If local radio could be characterized as "good" it was often considered "very good."

In the hamlets and hollows of America, small station operators developed a following with their resolute commitment to news. While the rip 'n' read style may have been pervasive for a while and possibly was all that many outlets that were owned and operated by individuals, or couples, or families could afford, most enduring ventures — in due course, at least — signed contracts with more than one information source to keep abreast of current events essential to their audiences. In time many of those outfits were able to hire one or two news writers who may have had — or may have developed — minimal reportorial skills at least. Larger stations augmented wire services and some stringers who called in with developments by adding full time journalists to their staffs. Eventually news became a strategic programming core as well as a significant profit center for the local stations, a discovery that CBS's William S. Paley had made for his fledgling chain as the 1920s began to fade.

(This is still true today: consider the programming of commercial stations with which you are familiar, including both radio and television. Don't local broadcasters focus heavily on news, weather, sports, and traffic? The preponderance of hires at local stations in several recent decades has been concentrated in these four information-based pursuits. The real money and prestige at local stations is often derived from territory that audio practitioners started to figure out early in the golden age. By the time that epoch had passed, news/weather/sports/traffic and music or talk usually generated enough revenue to maintain an audio enterprise, while making some of those owners affluent individuals.) But, as we know, that didn't happen overnight.

> Stirrings were ... appearing in the field of news. Early newspaper-owned stations were not conceived as news media but as devices to publicize the papers. The "bulletins" were largely teasers to stimulate readership. At the Detroit *News* station WWJ, *The Town Crier*, which opened with horses' hoofs, seems to have had this function. At some stations the bulletins were little more than fillers. At the Detroit *Free Press*, which launched WCX to counter WWJ, reporter Herschell Hart was called on in any talent crisis. "Hart, haven't you some news you could come in and read?" the harried WCX manager would ask. Hart would "grab up" some United Press or Associated Press copy and go in to read until he got the signal the emergency was over.[31]

And while most stations filched news matter from newspapers, wire services, and magazines, often giving on-air credit for it, there were plenty of unforeseen problems in doing so. When someone without a journalistic background, for instance, was added to the mix, respected policies — widely accepted by accustomed reporters — could break down. On one occasion President Warren G. Harding, who served from 1921 to 1923, was to make a public speech. International News Service obtained a copy of his text in advance and distributed the address to its clients, marking it "Hold for Release." It nevertheless fell into the hands of a neophyte broadcaster at Chicago's KYW who didn't understand the meaning of the embargo. Innocently the full text was read over the air the day before the president was to deliver it. There was plenty of hell to pay over that.[32] Such was the life of local radio newscasters in the formative days of commercial radio.

Over the years, many of those ventures were to become prominent, prosperous, and a hometown commercial enterprise to which many of the citizens who patronized it would point with pride. A radio station's attempts to report the news accurately, rapidly, and impartially added to the listeners' faith that it met its obligations with integrity. Perhaps it was the sincerity, openness, and forthrightness of the reporters themselves that projected a local broadcaster to a level of acceptance with the hometown crowd as much as anything a radio station might have done. In the end, the whole community came out winners.

> The next logical step was developing: the installation of newsrooms in scores of stations throughout the country. The networks had started operations of this kind in their key stations — New York, Washington, Chicago, Hollywood — before Munich [1938].[33] A number of the larger independent or chain-affiliated stations, and a few of the smaller ones in cities where keen newspaper-radio competition existed, had also done so. But after Munich, as the necessity for radio news became imperative, newsrooms began to spring up everywhere.[34]

There were growing signs that news was taking precedence in programming in spots. KFAB in Lincoln, Nebraska, launched double "editions" of a radio "newspaper" in December 1928 — twice daily news broadcasts. Hiring George Kline to direct its new venture, KFAB put a veteran journalist in charge of the challenge. Kline left *The Lincoln Star* where he had been city editor to accept the groundbreaking radio post.[35] More and more experienced newsmen would be seen moving in that direction.

Two years afterward, near the close of 1930, KMPC in Beverly Hills, California, added a trio of quarter-hour newscasts to its daily schedule after it appointed a newsgathering staff to develop its own stories.[36] Ten reporters shadowed the regular beats covered by Los Angeles newspapers. They were augmented by a string of more distant correspondents that had been contracted to furnish news items in "friendly competition" with neighboring newspapers.

In this same era St. Augustine, Florida's WFOY began adding local stories to its newscasts, while Peoria, Illinois' WMBD started offering 10 minutes of local women's news daily in 1932. Five years later, Mankato, Minnesota's KYSM hired its own news staff to develop local and regional coverage for its listeners.[37]

If it hadn't been obvious before the early 1930s that news was going to effectively occupy a strategic spot in local programming on commercial stations, by the late 1930s, for sure, it was a definitively settled affair. The passing of time saw the substance of news grow in intensity for many Americans. And the daily details of the looming Second World War, which were aired over outlets controlled by local broadcasters, was of critical interest to most. Laboring in conjunction with the networks and wire services, many of those stations were capable of providing coverage from the battlegrounds almost as it transpired. That tended to underscore the place that news had begun to occupy — and would continue to fill — in the nation's life.

And in postwar America, a land still largely dependent upon radio news as a leading source of information about transpiring global events at home and abroad, respondents to surveys picked "news programs" as their first choice in multiple quests to determine the radio audience's preferences among several categories of popular features.[38] By 1946, 76 percent of U.S. radio stations were airing more local news than at any time in their history.[39] All of this quietly solidified an argument about the public's estimate of instantaneous electronic news: its unparalleled appeal had become indelibly clear to whatever skeptics might still be residing in the ranks.

There are still many more examples of radio outlets' endeavors to elevate, to expand, and to expose their coverage of local and regional news.[40] Here are a few drawn from the first few years of the postwar epoch.

- At WMAZ, Macon, Georgia, news took a giant step forward when the staff was broadened to include a news editor and two reporters on duty from early morning to afternoon plus two more reporters on an afternoon/evening shift. These five created six local newscasts daily with their pursuits, amplifying stories with INS and UP wire service material. In addition, the 10,000-watt station presented nine CBS network news shows each day for a total of 15 newscasts sprinkled throughout the weekday.
- Binghamton, New York's WINR may have been even more astonishing. It insisted that its newscasts be a quarter-hour's duration because less time was "insufficient to present the complete news story." Combining local features with AP wire copy, the 250-watt outlet produced 10 live spots daily including seven newscasts, a single commentary, and two sports shows.

- Maintaining that "our listeners want complete local coverage of news and sports," Jamestown, New York's WJTN, another 250-watter, hired four full-time men to staff its local news bureau. Together they augmented what the station culled from its UP connection with updates much closer to home.
- By making a momentous exploit of stringers who fed the kitty with news tips and features, 5,000-watt WOW in Omaha, Nebraska, retained a cache of 75 correspondents suggested by county sheriffs. Reporters were compensated for the quantity and quality of their efforts as well as demonstrated initiative. Submissions ran alongside the news provided by AP and UP.
- Still another station with a large contingent of correspondents, Ogdensburg, New York's WSLB, scheduled a "Rural Reporter" entry at 10:30 A.M. daily. The 250-watter maintained a force of 60 stringers to furnish local news beyond its UP-dependent newscasts.
- Two enterprising 250-watt Texas outlets lacking any wire services operated their own newsrooms centered altogether on local issues, people, and events. Listeners tuned in the stations "for news of their friends and neighbors" at Brady's KNEL and Laredo's KPAB.
- Yet another 250-watter, Buffalo, New York's WBNY, went all-out for comprehensive local news coverage. With no network affiliation the outlet supplemented its AP, INS, and UP wires with local stories cultivated from a five-man Buffalo staff plus another full-time correspondent in the nation's capital. WBNY proudly boasted a handful of crusades waged against some local exploited dealings.
- 50,000-watt Minneapolis-St. Paul's WSTP, in addition to AP and UP access, marshaled all station staffers as news junkies. It paid $5 for an initial local news tip monthly from employees and $2 for consecutive tips plus an extra $10 for the one voted best. The plan resulted in numerous scoops over competitive air and print media.
- A news editor devoted five hours a day to preparing for a single quarter-hour "Community News Show" broadcast over 250-watt WIGM, Medford, Wisconsin. The editor digested the contribution of the outlet's quartet of reporters who pursued key spot stories as well as personnel news, local births, deaths, social activities, and other happenings of interest to the community. WIGM relied on UP for the substance of its added newscasts.

These are but a few of the measures that transpired in the newsrooms of radio stations of varying sizes scattered about the county during the heyday of the medium's golden age. To the industrious, ingenious, and inventive broadcasters committed to making local news a noteworthy hallmark of a station's existence went the spoils in a never-ending battle with media of both print and ethereal persuasions. Those radio magnates who sensed that local and regional news could be a substantial draw were frequently rewarded for their investments of capital resources, personnel, and time in their schedules. And their appreciative audiences almost invariably reaped extraordinary benefits as a result of their commitment to these pursuits.

10

Consequences of Radio's Reliance on Print

Radio was a user. As we have noted numerous times, the news reported in the formative years of the "wireless," the "radio telephone," and whatever added taxonomy was applicable to the universally branded "radio," relied almost entirely on the efforts of somebody else. What was begged, borrowed, or stolen for the ether (most often, it could be classified as the latter) was largely derived from a handful of sources beyond a few volunteers or contracted stringers or staff reporters (usually at larger outlets) that may have been pooled. Customarily, these broadcasters — of almost any size operation — relied heavily on information gleaned from the newspapers, magazines, and wire services that had been organized to feed the print media with original hard news and feature stories.

The tradition of partiality shown toward print journalism extended back to an earlier period, of course — from the late 1800s to the third decade of the 1900s — when radio's tenderfoot and still more experienced amateur wireless operators prevailed. Their obsession with print matter to read into a microphone was a direct result of having little else to say to their basically unknown recipients residing beyond the blue horizon. Under those conditions the print media became a wireless fancier's habit and addiction; and that dependency was readily transferrable to the individuals running genuine radio stations (those of the brick-and-mortar motif).

Somewhere along the way, and quite early in the creation of those outlets, the need to inform the public of what was currently available on the air turned into a legitimate question. The matter was put to rest after someone was inspired to include a timetable (most often dubbed a "log" during the golden age itself) within the pages of the local daily or weekly newspapers of what was being sent across the ether. They even supplied news fragments for broadcast. *The Philadelphia Public Ledger*— a paper that didn't own a station — went the second mile by recording news bulletins for an outlet situated in the City of Brotherly Love.[1] If that sounds as if the print journalists were doing all the work and getting little in return, at face value that is probably true. One sage even referenced "the marked friendliness of the press to radio," the press meaning, of course, print journalism.[2] This was the era of the Press-Radio War, you will recall, when the bigger siblings of these entities — the American Newspaper Publishers Association (ANPA), the wire services that supported them, and the national radio chains — were in acrimonious disagreement about feeding the news generated by the first two groups to the latter. (The disunity is spelled out in more detail in Chapter 2.)

It's essential to keep in mind that a rather hefty number of early radio stations were appendages of respected news journals which, in theory at least, had their various ancillary units working together in a kind of team approach. For the surfeit of the outlets owned by somebody else, would it still not have been a beneficial service to a newspaper's readership to publish the radio programming that was accessible anyway? It would, of course, and even at the risk of benefiting an upstart rival that — beyond the amusement shows it proffered — could and did habitually scoop print journalists on breaking news items, usually appropriated from the major wire services or by their own staffs. Sometimes the outside sources were credited on the air but definitely not always.

Until some publishers eventually rebelled (in the mid-1920s and thereafter), declaring that this data should be classified as paid advertising, the ink brigade was rather obligingly willing to become enablers of the radio crowd. By including what grew to be popularly identified as the *radio logs, timetables, schedules,* or *listings* within its pages, print journalism gave tacit approval to modern technology's newest delivery system for news and information, albeit one in utter competition with print's very own livelihood.

The *radio listings* (an unambiguous term that will be applied to our use) that appeared in daily and/or weekly news journals in the U.S. have been virtually ignored by virtually all serious radio historiographers. At least this is true until now, with a few exceptions of relatively intermittent, rather skimpy references. Results of any calculated and extensive investigations into this discipline of radio memorabilia has provided precious little beyond hardly more than honorable mentions.

We know that one of the recommendations of the ANPA's radio committee to its membership at the height of the Press-Radio War in 1933 was "that free insertion of radio programs in newspapers [is to] be condemned."[3] That panel with an obviously strong mindset may have been smiling then when it announced in 1939 that the number of dailies publishing radio listings as paid matter had jumped from 14 to 37 percent in the previous year. At the same time, the number of papers that ran trade names of sponsors in those listings had dwindled from nine percent in 1938 to five percent in 1939, probably evoking another smile. In 1948, however, the ANPA declared that "probably less than five percent" of dailies were earning any revenue publishing radio program listings.[4]

Back to the earlier assertion. A dedicated pursuit of the radio listings appearing in newspapers of that period prompted some extensive and rigorous scrutiny of materials in print as well as many databases. Conducting an independent inquiry, although deliberately adding the collective minds to it of a fairly comprehensive brain trust of esteemed researchers in the vintage radio community, we proceeded on a fairly formidable quest. Regrettably we failed together to confirm precisely when and where the radio listings initially surfaced in a daily and weekly newspaper. At the same time, we were able to pinpoint a couple of early contenders for something approaching that venerated honor, and believe now that we may have gotten very close.

On Thursday, January 19, 1922, at Indiana, Pennsylvania, a tiny burg perhaps 60 miles northeast of Pittsburgh (yet still large enough surprisingly to sustain a daily newspaper which intimates the level of residents' reliance on a daily paper), *The Indiana Evening Gazette* exhibits "Today's Radio Program." The published data was for an unnamed station — presumably the only one within hearing range of that distance, logically KDKA.[5] Here's the programming fodder for that date displayed in the *Gazette*:

4:00 to 4:15 — Music
7:00 — Hope Hampton, one of the younger moving picture stars, who is appearing at the Davis and Grand theatres this week, will sing[6]
7:30 — Music and bedtime story
7:45 — Government market reports and a report of the New York Stock Exchange
8:00 — Talk by William H. Walker, Ph.D., dean, Duquesne University, "Own Your Home Day"[7]
8:30 — Music
9:00 — News
9:05 to 9:30 — Music
9:55 to 10:00 — Arlington turn signals

Note that there are breaks in the broadcasting schedule indicating that the station signed off the air more than once per day. This was, in fact, reminiscent of the early years of television when a local channel might air shows for a given period during the day, then sign off once or twice. It would return to the air to present its nighttime features to the largest crowd of viewers it presumably drew each day. This may have been the point when an irregular and widely practiced pattern of aircasting was developed.

Note also the nine o'clock entry for news bulletins. Is this the first recorded evidence of a recurring newscast to appear in a newspaper? To date, our searches haven't led elsewhere. While this little entry nearly escapes one's notice it just may be precedent-setting in the annals of radio history.

Immediately after this listing in *The Indiana Evening Gazette*, the following ad appears in the same edition, again without identifying the apparently isolated station:

> Buy Westinghouse Radio Apparatus
> and Other Radio Supplies from
> Utility Electric Co.
> Marshall Bldg.
> Indiana, Pa.
> Radio Program Every Evening
> Come In

Apparently the firm named provided an early radio mechanism (most likely a crystal set with earphones in that day) for the curious to enjoy (and perhaps purchase or add to a wish list).

The second early discovery of a radio schedule published in a newspaper also appeared in the first quarter of 1922, too, just a couple of months after the previous exposition. This one in *The New York Times* was spread across the majority of three columns on an eight-column page 25 on March 30, 1922. You may recall that much of what old time radio researchers know about radio, including numerous references to local stations and networks, was first cited by the New York press. It isn't a stretch to suggest that the inauguration of the daily listings might have, in fact, readily occurred in the pages of the *Times* or any of its Big Apple counterparts. That would have been prior to *The Indiana Evening Gazette's* display, of course, and something that hasn't been corroborated prior to this writing. In truth, both of these newspapers bore a prelude to what was would eventually appear in widespread use.

The particular listings in the *Times* under the headline "Today's Radio Program" (the identical title hints that the *Gazette* or *Times* copied the other or a third paper) embraced a half-dozen stations, most of which were of some distance from Gotham: WJZ, Newark; WVP, Bedlow's Island, New Jersey (later spelled Bedloe's Island, and still later renamed

Liberty Island); WGY, Schenectady, New York; KDKA, East Pittsburgh, Pennsylvania; KYW, Chicago; and WBZ, Springfield, Massachusetts. The information included was fairly comprehensive providing not only broadcast times and titles (some generic such as "Musical Program") but also performers' names and each show's individual content.

While there were gaps in the broadcast day (WJZ, for example, aired only weather reports at the top of three scattered daytime hours plus shipping news at another hour and agricultural reports at still another), the evenings were mostly complete — when logically more people were available to listen. WJZ offered programming on that particular day from 6:45 P.M. through its last weather forecast at 10 P.M. With the exception of WJZ, KDKA, and WBZ, the remaining stations each offered listeners a single musical feature in the evening hours while furnishing lengthy directories of guest artists expected to perform.

All of this underscored the fact that local radio (for that's all there was in the early 1920s) was very much in its infancy, doing not a great deal more than experimenting with myriad forms of amusement. Notably missing from the *Times* page were any references to newscasts or news bulletins. These early stations in some respects weren't too far removed from the wireless amateurs they were gradually replacing as the public began to grasp the magnitude of radio's potential and was being drawn into the novelty and innovation of mass dissemination of broadcast programming. The features listed in the newspapers offered some sense of legitimacy for the new medium. And whether it was acknowledged openly or not, print journalists were substantiating the fact that radio was there to stay — and that it had the promise of becoming a pretty powerful opponent.

In a later listing under the same banner, "Today's Radio Program," which appeared in *The New York Times* on December 24, 1925, the readers were exposed to the daily schedule of as many as 91 stations. By their locations one is led to suspect that at that time the newspaper was making a valiant effort to include the fleeting agendas of every outlet then broadcasting in North America, possibly with the exception of Mexico as none are named from that nation. (A logical explanation would be, of course, that there might not have been any stations in Mexico by 1925. If not, the *Times*' attempt to be inclusive still stands.)

From October 6 to 10, 1924, the Third National Radio Conference for fans, station owners, engineers, and receiving set manufacturers was convened in Washington, D.C., under auspices of the U.S. Department of Commerce. Following that gathering, a contemporary radio preservationist noted, "There was more stability in the frequency assignment and programming was becoming regular, too."[8] To at least some extent this seems to account for the proliferation of stations then being tracked by *The New York Times* and very possibly other newspapers as well.

You may be confident that many of these broadcasters were on the air for just one or two hours per day at that time (and thus may have aired but one or two features daily, requiring very little newspaper space to note their schedules). You should also know that some of these outfits eventually faded altogether or combined their operations with one or more other stations. Furthermore, be aware that within a short period of time news journals such as *The New York Times* reduced their published radio listings to encompass the outlets serving the metropolitan environs surrounding the Big Apple. Their limited focus was then on stations where reception was fairly strong within the newspaper's immediate geographical territory. And finally, one additional fact: by possibly including every station then on the air in North America in 1925, the *Times* by example was leading the way in showing the stations — and the newspapers serving their communities — how to satisfy patrons' needs for local radio program information. As a paper with an established reputation, enormous circulation, extensive geographical reach, and powerful influence, whatever the *Times* did was often plagiarized by papers in many smaller markets.

As for 1925 and the ubiquitous 91 stations appearing in the *Times* radio listings, here's a breakdown on where those signals were coming from: Chicago, 12 outlets; New York City, 11; Philadelphia, 5; Cincinnati, 3; Detroit, 3; Newark, 3; Atlantic City, 2; Boston, 2; Cleveland, 2; Los Angeles, 2; and Washington, 2. There was also one each in diverse points like Atlanta, Des Moines, Fort Worth, Hot Springs (Arkansas), Louisville, Memphis, Miami Beach, Minneapolis-St. Paul, Portland (Maine), San Francisco, and Seattle. Finally, a half-dozen stations were beamed from outside the U.S. including one at Tuinucu, Cuba, and the remainder in Canada: Calgary, 1; Montreal, 2; Toronto, 2. The insertion in the daily newspaper was categorically an eclectic mix of broadcasters.

In time readers could find an easy-to-decipher schedule of everything aired by local stations within the subscription territory of the journal printing the information. This solved a colossal headache for radio operators who needed to let their impending constituencies know what to anticipate on every day at every hour. In some cases the broadcasters would grease the palms of newspaper magnates for their courtesy — through literal transfer of cash or more likely through services rendered. That may have included mere acknowledgment on the air of the location of those published radio listings. But it may have gone further, like more commercial mentions without financial compensation or possibly even free programming. In multiple ways the backs of the owners of both mediums could be scratched as a situation warranted.

Another scholar confirmed:

> Since the advent of broadcasting, listeners had been dependent upon newspapers for their radio listings — programs to be heard on various stations at various hours during the day. After 1925, such listings carried the names of programs by sponsors; i.e., the *Eveready Hour*, the *Sieberling Singers*, etc. In 1927, the New York Publishers Association, representing the principal New York newspapers, moved to eliminate the names of sponsors from such listings. They held that such listings were free advertising for which the newspaper was not being paid. This program was followed for about two months, until the Scripps-Howard interests purchased the *Telegram*. The *Telegram* decided to continue listing the sponsor's name on the grounds that radio programs were news and the public was entitled to all information about them. Other New York papers were then forced to drop their program of censored listings.
>
> But when before 1930, news about radio and radio personalities had been given full publicity in the press as a matter of news, afterward most newspapers dropped not only such news items, but all program listings as well. In many cities, protests from readers who had come to look upon program listings as a newspaper service compelled newspapers to restore the bare listings, but other news, designed to increase interest in listening, was severely left alone.[9]

And, as we learned in Chapter 2, wrestling for the advertising dollar stiffened in the depression years of the early 1930s, resulting in bitter competition among several parties in the field of news dissemination. Publishers pressured the wire services to cut out the radio stations and networks. The rivalry eventually coalesced into the Biltmore Agreement in late 1933, sharply restricting the broadcasters in how they received and dispensed news. "The press of the nation was unwittingly forcing radio into the very position it most hoped to avoid — the position of a news gathering as well as a news-disseminating medium," one investigator affirmed.[10] That's when the networks began hiring large staffs of news correspondents and local outlets that could afford it expanded to include their own reporters.

In the meantime, as many of the commercial program sponsors whose names had appeared in the titles of the shows they underwrote departed the airwaves in the 1930s, the newspapers revisited their decision to delete the program listings. They decided, individually — and not unilaterally but separately — that offering those listings to their readers was a good thing that ultimately helped to sell newspapers. In the majority of papers those listings were restored.

Writing in the mid–1940s, a media historiographer sharply criticized the inattentiveness that radio had received (in the reviewer's opinion) in the printed press of that day:

> Our provincial press is for the most part silent on a subject that probably touches more people's interests than most. Very few papers indeed even give us more than the bare titles of programs on the air. Press and radio are still playing rivals. There is not only room for both, but the two are complementary. More people would turn to their papers if they could learn more from them about what dates to keep with their radios each day. Many people hear something over the air and turn to their newspapers to confirm or supplement it.[11]

Keep in mind that this was only a few years prior to television's invasion of millions of American domiciles in which, almost overnight, that medium became a pervasive force in the majority of citizens' lives. Until that point in time, the populace was dependent upon radio as its sole means of simultaneous communications, linking inhabitants as a nation for interludes of information and entertainment. In that epoch radio was literally everything to many citizens, equal to and possibly surpassing many possessions, travel experiences, leisure and pastime opportunities. Radio was the lifeline, the connection to the world beyond the farms and rural countrysides, hamlets and townships, medium-sized cities and large urban centers.

And the radio listings furnished by the county weeklies and the city dailies kept people abreast of what they were in store for on any given day. For some, it became routine to check this data every day. For those confined to hospital beds, homes, and institutions where they may have lived out the years in confinement, being able to rely upon the radio listings during radio's golden age was for many undoubtedly a stroke of good luck. Those listings weren't confined to limited areas either, but could be found almost universally. In late 1946, the National Association of Broadcasters ascertained that 96 percent of all stations were represented in daily or weekly newspaper listings at least once, and some outlets appeared in several publications. And 81 percent of those were published free of charge to those outlets.[12]

The many changes that radio encountered in post–golden age decades that resulted in its displacement by television as most people's chief link with the outside world had a profound effect upon the data that daily and weekly newspapers published. As mega media empires bought up scads of homegrown journals across the land, their owners felt little compulsion to provide space for many matters that had been deemed worthy in the past, even if it was a vital service to readers.

By the 1960s, if not earlier, the program listings still being carried by most news journals had been trimmed considerably. In time even these would be figments of their former selves, offering little more than program titles without names of stars, hosts, guests, themes, topics, etc. In some cases only the genres might be named (drama, news, music, mystery, sports, comedy, forum, etc.). An alternative, adopted by more and more papers as time elapsed, was deletion of the broadcast listings altogether. Today they are probably still included by a majority of print news sources but with only the barest of details. And possibly in the majority of markets radio listings were simply banished years ago. One example will suffice.

For decades, *The Courier-Journal* of Louisville, Kentucky, offered its subscribers extensive coverage of radio and television outlets within its prime circulation territory. Included on the staff was a full-time TV-radio columnist whose sole emphasis was on current and future developments in the dual media. His personality interviews were highlights for anyone interested in entertainment and media. For all of this time, a single Louisville family owned the publishing and broadcasting empire that produced two newspapers, ran a multipurpose printing plant, and operated local radio and television outlets.[13] It all began to unravel after more than a half-century when that clan, which had been focused on its constituency across the years, sold its various business interests piecemeal to successor commercial enterprises. *The Courier-Journal* was acquired by an out-of-state newspaper publishing conglomerate which implemented significant changes.

Not only was the news curbed sharply through multiple reductions in staff and content, as a paradigm that is pertinent to our specialized interests, the broadcasting listings were shrunk smaller and smaller until they appeared in a type point that is exceedingly difficult for many people to read. The radio log vanished altogether. And in the most recent round of setbacks, subscribers desiring a tepid television leaflet were told to inform the paper of their wishes — and are currently billed extra for a weekly insert. Additionally, in August 2008 — after some 32 years on the job — the radio-TV columnist was hastily dismissed, one man among a stable of durable wordsmiths who had given the community-focused paper its homegrown flavoring. Shown the door without mercy, the scribe and most of his cohorts weren't replaced, their former columns, beats, and sections suddenly, woefully underrepresented.[14] Of course, what transpired at that newspaper has been emulated by scores of other metropolitan dailies across the nation in recent years. The model is included here as a representative example and not to cite one paper only among numerous peers.

As in other American industries, the "service" factor has become so diluted that it can hardly be recognized in some quarters any longer. Parallel strategies are now practiced in numerous other newspaper markets as large corporations seek to improve their bottom lines at the expense of loyal and valued readership that had existed for decades. As one whose entire professional career has spanned a multiplicity of journalistic disciplines, this author — taking liberties with an automobile advertising slogan — affirms, sadly, in many places "it's not your daily paper anymore."

That declaration is currently being demonstrated in still more obvious ways. In the spring of 2012, the Associated Press announced that *The New Orleans Times-Picayune*, with a venerated 175-year history to its credit, is set to become the largest metropolitan U.S. newspaper to date eliminating daily circulation,[15] moving to a three-day-a-week publishing schedule in autumn 2012. The business decision surrounding that revered journal is based in part on a ready accessibility of proliferating online sources that consumers are adopting in record numbers in modern times. In the same epoch, the media conglomerate that owns the *Times-Picayune*— Advance Publications Inc., which is also diversified into cable television and Web sites beyond its newspapers and magazine brigade — reaffirmed its plans to void the daily publication of three Alabama chronicles it also controls (*The Birmingham News*, *The Huntsville Times*, and *The Mobile Press-Register*). The trio is slated for three-times-weekly publication, too.

We would be negligent to think that no other dailies across the U.S. would join their number. On the contrary, this may be the proverbial tip of the iceberg, establishing a tidal-wave prototype for the future of many established metro organs. The concept of a daily hard-copy news journal may be in peril one day, eventually becoming a thing of the past for millions of subscribers. Certainly it is a crack in the foundation of conventional journalism that is already prompting shudders within the souls of some traditionalists. It's a notion that would have been considered utterly unimaginable in the previous century.

Mention has been made of radio and, later, radio and television columns back in the halcyon days of broadcasting. Once again the local newspapers, both dailies and weeklies, rendered a huge service to their readers by providing behind-the-scenes perspectives on what was transpiring out of the limelight with shows and the celebrities appearing on them. Not only were interviews with public figures to be found there but information on upcoming performances on the air and at live venues, as well as lots of anecdotal items that increased the readers' knowledge about many facets of broadcasting. And these columns weren't relegated to the urban centers altogether; indeed, the county weeklies in some of the hinterland hamlets produced their own columnists who may have developed a kind of cult following in their communities as respected reporters "aware of all things."

Yet it was the larger papers whose broadcasting critics received notoriety from their efforts, their names sometimes recognized far and wide. They were often quoted freely in the columns of other writers as well as in books and on various Web sites today. Among them was John Crosby of *The New York Herald Tribune*, Robert Feder of *The Chicago Sun-Times*, Jack Gould of *The New York Times*, John T. McManus of New York's *PM*, and others. *The Detroit News*, *The Indianapolis Star*, and *The San Francisco Chronicle* were among dailies with popular columns focused on broadcasting.

Then there was a handful of syndicated entertainment scribes whose work sometimes appeared in hundreds of newspapers nationwide. That crowd of luminaries embraced Rona Barrett, Jimmy Fidler, Hy Gardner, Sheilah Graham, Hedda Hopper, Dorothy Kilgallen, Harriet Parsons, Louella Parsons, Ed Sullivan, Walter Winchell, and many more.

In the meantime, in the summer of 1947, New York's WCBS Radio instituted a series titled *CBS Views the Press*, lasting to 1950. Furnished by on-air host and CBS newsman Don Hollenbeck, the discordant feature actually may have been provoked by the newspaper critics of broadcasting. Most of those pundits, in an apparent attempt to remain impartial, incidentally, both commended and skewered Hollenbeck's efforts. Despite the early respect, the life and career of the outspoken commentator eventually began to unravel professionally and personally. During the infamous "blacklisting" epoch, one of his staunchest newspaper detractors figured into his demise.

The radio series itself was considered "a declaration of independence from a print medium that had dominated American newsmaking for close to 250 years," so a biographer allowed. It candidly criticized *The New York Times*, *The New York Daily News*, *The New York Journal-American*, and *The New York Daily Mirror*. "For this honest work, Hollenbeck was attacked by conservative anti–Communists, especially Hearst columnist Jack O'Brian, and in 1954, plagued by depression, alcoholism, three failed marriages, and two network firings (and worried about a third), Hollenbeck took his own life."[16] He died at 49 from gas asphyxiation, apparently pushed over the edge by some glowing remarks he made on CBS-TV acclaiming Edward R. Murrow. "The result was a vitriolic blast from right-wing columnist Jack O'Brian in the *Journal-American* and others," wrote one observer.[17] Demands from high places called for Hollenbeck to be fired.

Fortunately that extreme outcome was an isolated case and uncharacteristic of the typical columns and appraisals of radio (and its journalists) that appeared in the pages of most American newspapers during the aural medium's golden age. On most occasions, in fact, the print journalists were cordial to the radio broadcasters. It was, after all, their line of work to investigate and report on what was transpiring in front of as well as behind the microphones (and eventually the cameras for many who were present in the transitory period). They could do this best by forming partnerships with individuals at local broadcasting outlets as well as with the networks and a whole industry of entertainment-related components. Most did it successfully and weren't preoccupied by perceived rivalry between journalism's diverse units, a distraction that virtually disappeared in most localities with the passing of time.

Certainly, by the middle of the 20th century, a rapport had long been established between newsmen and women of all branches of journalistic activity which was profitable to all parties. The daily or weekly radio program listings and the columns and news stories devoted to broadcasting were a positive mixture for the electronic medium. At the same time, the ethereal personalities were plugging the papers, referencing what they saw there and sometimes quoting directly from those journals. Usually they credited their sources. Electronic and print journalists had come of age and there was much to respect emanating from both sides of the house.

11

The Fanzines: Trade Issues to Perpetuate the Industry

The now omnipresent term *fanzine* that is believed to have entered our language almost three-quarters of a century ago has gradually spread its wings over a much broader scope of spare time distractions than was probably intended originally. Indeed, it has enveloped far more than Louis "Russ" Chauvenet (1920–2003) anticipated. A U.S. amateur chess champion who won state, national, and international citations, on introducing the idiom in October 1940, Chauvenet applied *fanzine* to signify his *Detours* magazine. The publication premiered that month and grew into a trendy science fiction journal.

In articulating that emblem nevertheless, Chauvenet unwittingly coined what was to befit a sweeping category of periodicals of dissimilar persuasions. His descriptive insignia was adapted by many who used it as a kind of bellwether metaphor to cover their own pastime pursuits. Publishers, editors, and contributors of fanzines even today typically donate their labors gratis. The results of their efforts are generally circulated at minimal or no-charge to their readers.

On the other hand, a few fanzines have progressed into professional publications and probably should be more properly dubbed *prozines*. That, too, is yet another handle contrived by Chauvenet, who seemed to be a rather dynamic wordsmith of some repute in addition to earning accolades as a chess champ plus his publishing and editing achievements. Explained one authority: "The term *fanzine* is sometimes confused with 'fan magazine' but the latter term [*prozine*] most often refers to commercially-produced publications *for* (rather than *by*) fans."[1]

In the meantime the pioneering science fiction fans (the genre which gave birth to all of this discussion) were forming some amateur press alliances as early at 1937.[2] Participants in these federations — a few of which are still operating today — contribute to collective publishing ventures that embrace submissions from their membership. Known as *apazines*, such circulated works contain assorted individual perspectives. Some of these existing organizations maintain Internet-disseminated *e-zines* to deliver their goods.[3] And *zine* often suffices for fanzine or magazine in the modern age, most commonly used in reference to a small circulation publication.

With this background awareness, let us peek into a branch of journalistic activity we have not yet broached, at least not in any comprehensive reflection: the fan or celebrity periodical (predominantly magazines but also newspapers, newsletters, pamphlets, etc., in hard copies and/or electronic editions). The precursors of this strain have been with us as far back as the 19th century. Some American literary-minded cohorts instigated proletarian press fraternities for the expressed purpose of disseminating their compilations of commentary, fiction, poetry, and other linguistic quests.

Tabletop printing presses reproduced the first of these fan-backed leaflets. This nascent practice ultimately gave way to a more advanced spirit duplicator which was eventually replaced by the hectograph. The latter apparatus was capable of supplying nearly a hundred copies of a document in a single run, greatly expanding circulation potential. The hectograph was followed by the mimeograph machine — the standard of many decades, even extending past the mid 20th century — when the photocopier almost universally replaced it. (A modern source claims that "The term [*zine*] encompasses any self-published work of minority interest usually reproduced via photocopier."[4])

From all of this we may finally grasp that a line of valid celebrity magazines (you may call them *fanzines, prozines, apazines, e-zines,* or just plain *zines*) proliferated at varying times in the 20th century, some of which paralleled the golden age of Radioland, exhaustively perpetuating it. Such publications were contrived from movie fan slicks that trace their incubation to 1911 with the launch of a pair of pioneering observers: *Motion Picture Story* (altered to *Motion Picture Magazine* in 1914) and *Photoplay*.

The first of that duo — instigated by Eugene V. Brewster — was combined with *Hollywood Magazine* in 1941, and re-emerged as *Screen Life* that year. It persisted through 1977, a 66-year run, a fairly durable survival for a magazine. *Photoplay*, on the other hand, with eventual ties to one of the oldest and largest publishers in America, was bought by Macfadden Publications in 1934. Founder Bernarr Macfadden had gotten into that trade in 1898. Although *Photoplay* debuted as a short fiction monthly, by the mid teens its editors had revamped it and established a format which "set a precedent for almost all celebrity magazines that followed."[5] With circulation topping 200,000 by 1918, the periodical's approbation was fueled by the public's "ever increasing interest in the private lives" of luminaries, leading to its accreditation for "inventing" celebrity media.[6]

Photoplay, in particular, was the result of some noble efforts proffered to capitalize on undisclosed details in the lives of film legends with which an eager and yet unsatisfied segment of the U.S. population had been transfixed. These curiosity seekers wanted to know what really transpired when the cameras weren't rolling. As nobody was pursuing this in a relatively novel industry, co-editors Julian Johnson and James R. Quirk saw an easy way to win fresh converts (translate: added readers and advertisers) and thereby precipitate a windfall for themselves as a byproduct. They set the standards and those who followed with multiplied similar ventures fell into line, slightly tweaking the imaginative initial editors' successful formula to differentiate their goods from one another.

Some of the recurring bylines in *Photoplay* included those of well known journalists and authors like Sheilah Graham, Hedda Hopper, Dorothy Kilgallen, Louella Parsons, Adela Rogers St. John, Sidney Skolsky, Rob Wagner, Walter Winchell, and Cal York. Beginning in 1920, the *Photoplay Medal of Honor* (renamed *Gold Medal* at a later date) dispensed what is believed to be the first noteworthy annual movie award for excellence in acting. Although it and the subsequent Film of the Year honors instituted in 1944 weren't distributed every single year the *Photoplay* recognitions nevertheless heavily impacted the Academy Awards that were created in 1927.[7]

Broadening itself in the years that followed in order to attract readers in still wider realms, *Photoplay* merged with *Movie Mirror* in 1941 and with *TV-Radio Mirror* in 1977. It was renamed in the latter year *Photoplay and TV Mirror*. Three years hence it finally ceased publication, its fan base having largely evaporated by moving on to other interests and methods of learning about the inside intrigue surrounding its favorite celebrities. At that juncture the periodical's staff transferred to another Macfadden publication, *Us* magazine. In the meantime, a British version of *Photoplay* that had debuted in 1950 persisted through 1989. It featured a selection of American and British films and stars in roughly equal proportions.

Aside from the movie fanzines, there was another cult emerging as radio made its way onto the local and national scene. Entrepreneurial industrialists weren't altogether unaware of the triumphs that *Photoplay* and its contemporaries were having in delving into the private lives of stars of the silver screen. With the arrival of a largely unfamiliar national troupe of artists that radio was ferrying directly into people's homes every day and every week, overnight there was suddenly another ready-made opening awaiting the exploitation of venture capitalists and responsive journalists.

Many of those new personalities were initially mere voices to their listeners. Included among their number were actors, newscasters, sportscasters, announcers, comedians, musicians, quizmasters, and so forth. People — and especially homemakers who tuned them in all day, however — were nevertheless inquisitive about what made them tick. Unless they had reached celebrity or notoriety status in the movies or possibly by making public appearances at venues on the road (performing, for instance, on tours, in summer stock or vaudeville), most audiences in Radioland would never have seen these luminaries. Here was an opportunity to introduce them in a more personal way by creating yet another new category of personality oriented journalism.

The early investigative journals scrutinized everything they could find in the way of stage, film, radio, television, music, books, and popular culture. But their coverage wasn't solely confined to the celebrities and their shows. In a broad sweep of an extensive entertainment trade they focused pointedly on research and analysis that examined aspects pertaining to financial, marketing and publicity, sales, producing, writing, directing, performing, arenas, professional reviews, historical data, collectors and hobbyists, technical, and legal aspects of those ventures.

The scribes of the early and mid–20th century seldom inquired about delicate matters in the lives of their subjects or what would have been considered insolent interrogation as would be typical now. Yet their probing laid the groundwork for the all-out assaults that figures of the entertainment, sports, and political worlds often experience in contemporary times. As the envelope is pushed further and further some very personal minutiae that was traditionally kept out of the news is frequently divulged to the public whether an interviewee grants his consent or whether he doesn't.

As amusement venues have proliferated and prospered, skilled inquisitors have cast aside whatever timidity they might have been born with to pry under rocks, in nooks and crannies, in an effort to satisfy the public's insatiable appetite for the skeletons heretofore tucked away in recessive closets. In the modern age, a far more determined and aggressive reportorial society — really only distant kin of those stalwart interrogators who popped the questions during radio's golden age — ask blunt questions of their focuses in print and especially on cable TV. Their grilling is designed to titillate the audience many times. And a readership, listenership, and viewership feeds on red meat questions dispensed in the name of journalistic integrity. It's a far cry from what used to be and the wordsmiths of yesterday wouldn't begin to recognize some of the current practices that are more commonplace than anomaly in nature.

A teeming mix of printed matter — a large portion of it spawned by show business itself — that focused on myriad contrasting branches of the amusement industry sprang up. Much of it, but not all by any means, premiered in the first half of the 20th century. Included in the surfeit of publications were labels expressing divergent emphases like *Advertising Age, Adweek, American Theatre, Billboard, Boxoffice, Broadcasting & Cable, Cashbox, CNN Entertainment, E! Online, Entertainment Today, Entertainment Weekly, The Hollywood Reporter, In Touch Weekly, Motion Picture, Movie Mirror, Music Box, Music Vendor, OK! Magazine, People, Photoplay, Premiere, Radio Age, Radio-Craft, Radio Guide, Radio Ink, Radio Mirror, Radio News, Radio World, Rolling Stone, Rotten Tomatoes, Show Business, Star Magazine, Television Today, TV Guide, Us Weekly,* and *Variety*.

In addition to the popular culture newspapers, magazines and online bulletins destined for a generally broad-spectrum audience, journalists also produced materials for the use of industry insiders. Some of those were just mentioned (*Billboard, Boxoffice, Cashbox, Variety,* and more). Trade publications debuted with the same fervor demonstrated by capitalists who were discovering niches that could be satisfied by furnishing details of the lives of entertainment and amusement stars and productions to a waiting public.

The first known periodical exclusively tailored for radio news staffers bowed shortly after the Second World War came to a close. International News Service produced *The Newscaster,* a four-page monthly that was circulated without charge "in the interest of radio men handling the news." The bulk of its content pertained to items about radio news personnel. Moreover, it addressed specific local radio news concerns. In addition in some of its early issues, *The Newscaster* turned a spotlight on Miss Radio News of 1946.

Although this was a newsletter published solely for professionals of the broadcasting medium — and a limited segment of those were its recipients — it was part of a small volume of enduring print matter that was focused on a specific aspect of the trade. *Inside Radio* and *Radio Business Report* are currently among a handful of industry-focused sources keeping tabs on the industry in the modern era. As these observers and reporters herald what is presently transpiring on the ether, they have all generally been supportive of their business, usually encouraging growth and expansion in both overt and furtive methods.

Getting back to the subject of *fanzines* or, perhaps more correctly, *prozines* or just plain *zines,* in the epoch prior to online delivery hard-copy print periodicals were distributed primarily through subscription and retail sales. They were heavily encumbered with advertising which, of course, kept them affordable to consumers. Their content often classified them as primarily puff pieces providing radio listeners with insider information that most often was unavailable to them anywhere else.

By concentrating liberally on behind-the-microphone examinations of stars and others whose voices were frequently better recognized than their faces (mostly except in the occurrence of movie, political, musical, or sports figures), these slicks revealed secrets that their disciples would never have known outside reading them there. Certainly there was nobody telling such surreptitious tales on the radio, and cable television news wasn't around before the 1980s. Even then, cable's revelations were almost always tethered to the delivery of hard news — domestic and international — in that period and weren't yet trying to exploit public figures of manifold stripes. That would come soon enough, but not in cable's earliest years.

A performer's name might appear in a byline over a piece about that individual and he or she very well might have penned all or much of it. The finished product was nevertheless solidly edited by a ghost writer no matter who the author was. The ghost writer was an unnamed scribe either on the prozine's staff or contracted on the outside to assist in getting the words on paper and bringing it into line with the periodical's style.[8] There is probably even greater likelihood, however, that the piece in question was penned in sum by a staff writer or outside freelancer even though the name of the individual featured (e.g., a performer, director, producer, writer, musician, sound technician, etc.) appeared in the byline.

Such treatises were typically embellished heavily by staff wordsmiths who sought to cast their subjects in a favorable light (ignoring or hastily brushing aside matters like run-ins with the law, gambling habits, drug or alcohol addictions, divorces, abrupt job dismissals prompted by the subject's actions, patterns of poor decision-making, etc.). Instead, their sunny side was enhanced (favorable disposition at all times, family harmony, working history, professional achievements, admiration by colleagues and management, etc.). These periodicals were in the business of making the stars sound attractive when out of the limelight. A side advantage, perhaps uppermost in editors' minds, was that the better a candidate sounded, the more people would subscribe or purchase issues over the counter. There was that underlying motive for everything that was done.

Those articles that were originated by someone other than the individual about whom it was written might come to fruition through any of a handful of methods of pursuit. A scribe may have actually interviewed his subject in a face-to-face encounter. It's far more likely, however—unless he lived in close proximity to the subject of his article—that the interview occurred by telephone or through mail exchange. (Of course, there was no such thing as email during radio's heyday, and no Web site or texting existed for that matter.)

If a direct connection with an individual wasn't possible—and even if it was—the journalist might gain all the details he needed by reading about his subject in sundry secondary sources (resumes, published biographical accounts, newspapers, magazines, books, trade publications, promotional literature, etc.). In so doing, he might acquire enough factual data to put together a profile for publication or at least form questions to be asked during a subsequent interview. The end result often waded into a celebrity's family life, hobbies and side interests, awards and honors, outside business links, educational and training experience, etc., beyond his or her public persona.

The finished piece was usually run under the subject's eyes before it appeared. When that wasn't possible—if there wasn't enough time or a luminary was out of the country on an extended tour, for instance—the article might be read over the telephone to the star or to his agent. The object was to correct anything faulty by stating the facts clearly while weaving a narrative that was going to be enticing and maybe even beguiling to hordes of fans. Woe be unto any publications that circumvented the process by publishing an item without giving a designee opportunity for input before it ran. More than once embarrassing screw-ups resulted from infractions against longstanding policies that supposedly could not be violated at most publications.

To exemplify some of what has just been said, one of the more popular zines of that epoch, *Radio Mirror*, billing itself as "The Magazine of Radio Romances" at the time and dating from its premiering issue in November 1922 (a quadrennial prior to a national network's arrival), illustrates some of these principles. In the heyday of its industry, an enduring *Radio Mirror*—eventually to be renamed *Radio and Television Mirror*, *Radio-TV Mirror*, *TV-Radio Mirror*, *TV Mirror*, and *Photoplay and TV Mirror* before being withdrawn in 1980—58 years following its inauguration—was among the most formidable and fêted of the celebrity prozines.

Selecting at random *Radio Mirror's* 96-page March 1943 edition during a peak war year, the color cover carries an image of uniformed nurse Patricia Ryan and proffers the observation: "If I Dared — The Story of a Girl Who Was Afraid to Love."[9] What feminine consumer magazine buff could hardly resist that piquant bit of fluff? The newsstand price, incidentally, was 15 cents while 12 monthly issues could be delivered by the U.S. mail to one's door for a mere $1.50—12.5 cents per copy, a fraction of the cost of a single first class stamp today. Macfadden Publications, Inc., in Dunellen, New Jersey, circulated the zine. Its editorial director was Frederick Rutledge Sammis who hailed from a clan steeped in print journalism history.

Sammis (1912–2000), parenthetically, was a compelling figure in his craft, worth more than mere superficial reference. A Second World War lieutenant with the U.S. Coast Guard Reserve, he returned to civilian life to become a seasoned veteran in his profession. By the mid–1930s, Macfadden picked Sammis to edit a trio of its national periodicals: *Radio Mirror* (1935–41), *Photoplay* (1942–47), and *Sport* (1952–55).[10] In 1955, he and Jerry Mason co-founded Ridge Press. A few years later Sammis launched another publishing imprint, Rutledge Books.

Three other members of the Sammis clan also selected print journalism as their vocation. Edward R. Sammis, Fred's brother who died at 89 in 1991, edited for various publishing companies, too. Beginning at Fawcett Publications in 1929, he served several more houses before retiring from Macmillan in 1980. Edward also penned plays, short stories, and novels. Fred's two adult children, John and Kathy, followed their father and uncle into the trade, too. John Sammis became associate publisher of Rutledge Books while Kathy penned many children's texts for Rutledge and other publishers.

Back to *Radio Mirror* itself: Patricia Ryan, as it turned out — the smilingly dimpled blonde, blue-eyed cover girl of that March 1943 issue of *Radio Mirror*— had also graced a previous cover as sometimes happens when one's star is rising (or has already ascended). She appeared on the face of the same zine's October 1941 issue, having then only recently completed a pithy primetime run in CBS's serialized *Claudia and David*.[11] That show had filled Kate Smith's half-hour during the singing legend's 13-week summer hiatus. Ryan, who starred opposite Richard Kollmar there, may have peaked in her radio career at the time.[12] But the London-born actress found many other chances to exploit her talent on the air, having begun when she was but six years of age. Many of her roles were portrayed in semi-subdued obscurity, however.

When she was eight she and Estelle Levy debuted in the leads of *The Adventures of Helen and Mary* (Ryan was Mary), a children's fairy tale bowing over CBS June 29, 1929. The title was altered to a more memorable *Let's Pretend* on March 17, 1934. Ryan, 13 then, segued into a repertory company of adolescent thespians for the weekly plays. Later she joined a troupe of juveniles broadcasting over an NBC equivalent children's theater that appeared at varying times under the labels *The Children's Hour*, *Coast-to-Coast on a Bus*, and *Our Barn* (1936–41).

Ryan eventually won the recurring part of Kathleen Anderson in radio's laugh hit *The Aldrich Family* and the role of Elly Parker in *The Parker Family* sitcom. She turned up in character roles in multiple 1940s crime dramas like *The Adventures of the Thin Man* and *Special Investigator* and in dramatic anthologies like *Aunt Jenny's Real Life Stories*, *Grand Central Station*, *Little Women*, and *Manhattan at Midnight*. She also maintained running stints in the daytime serials *Joyce Jordan, Girl Interne* [sic] and *Just Plain Bill*.

While performing in the cast of the *Jordan* drama, her 1943 *Radio Mirror* interview revealed that Ryan — as volunteer nurse Myra Wilder — was impressed that she should be giving something tangible to the nation's collective wartime service. Persuaded that she could become a nurse's aide like the part she was then playing, even as she concurrently pursued her professional goals, Ryan entered training at Manhattan's Misericordia Hospital. After earning a diploma there she devoted three mornings a week from 7:15 to noon at the hospital. Her afternoons were spent on the air and on most evenings she was at the Stage Door Canteen. "In her spare time," according to the 1943 article, "she lectures for the American Theater Wing. She writes three letters a day to soldiers, another three to the mothers of soldiers she meets at the Canteen — and a very special daily letter to a Private overseas. She also entertains for service men, and particularly likes to give parties for British seamen."[13]

It was her final ethereal outing for which Ryan is undoubtedly recalled best. On Monday evening, February 14, 1949 — Valentine's Day — during an NBC broadcast of the *Cavalcade of America*, she appeared as a woman possessed by migraine headaches. Silver screen actor Glenn Ford worked opposite her in a half-hour live drama titled "A Valentine for Sophia." Appearing in the namesake role of Sophia Peabody, Ryan's character suffered blinding headaches prior to her nuptials to 19th century novelist Nathaniel Hawthorne. The yarn ended conversely on a triumphant note nevertheless.

During the brief span that the coast-to-coast show was airing, meanwhile Ryan herself complained of severe pain at the back of her head. A couple of actresses standing nearby (veterans Alice Reinheart and Agnes Young) stepped into the gulch of resulting dead air to read her lines for her until Ryan sufficiently recovered and returned.[14] The stricken actress was treated by a studio physician following the night's broadcast and subsequently returned home.

A short time after arriving at the New York apartment she shared with her husband George Robert Gibson, the 27-year-old Ryan turned in for the night.[15] The next morning she was unresponsive when he attempted to waken her. Gibson summoned a rescue squad that soon declared her dead in her bed. Following an autopsy the press paradoxically reported that she had succumbed to a cerebral hemorrhage during the night.[16] It was one of the most stupefying broadcasting deaths recorded in which life imitated fiction.

The referenced magazine picture story of Patricia Ryan reported something rather odd, particularly in light of what transpired a half-dozen years hence:

> Pat claims nothing very exciting has happened to her in radio, except that once she was knocked out by a microphone when she was twelve. An announcer was adjusting a mike just over her head and it came loose and beaned her. They brought Pat back into this world just two minutes before the program went on the air and she played her part. "Although," she says, "I had a slight headache."[17]

Would that in even the slightest way seem to be related to the circumstances surrounding her death? While no evidence has surfaced that any further investigation was pursued, could the incident when she was 12 have precipitated her demise 15 years afterward? Perhaps not, but knowing that little detail seems to turn the *Radio Mirror* piece into a more intriguing — and even ominous — revelation.

In unrelated features in that issue, the prozine spotlights other celebs, too, among them comics Bud Abbott and Lou Costello, character actor Robert Allen, opera coloratura Josephine Antoine, character actress Ruth McDevitt, master of ceremonies Don McNeill (*The Breakfast Club*), crooner-bandleader Vaughn Monroe, impresario Raymond Paige (*Stage Door Canteen*), announcer Del Sharbutt, pop singer Kate Smith, character actress Ann Thomas, songstress Frances Wayne (with the Charlie Barnet band), and organist-composer

Louise Wilcher. There are also fictionalized vignettes drawn from selected radio dramas then airing including tales adapted from *Abie's Irish Rose, A.L. Alexander's Mediation Board, Manhattan at Midnight, Men of the Land, Sea, and Air, Theater of Today,* and *True Story Theater.*

Invariably the fanzines, which were purchased by housewives and young single girls more than other homogeneous groups, offer at least a single self-help or self-improvement item in every issue. In that issue it pertains to facials. But it could just as easily have been about culinary arts, homemaking, cleaning tips, dieting, nails, hair styles, hemlines, wardrobes, family conflicts, grocery-buying, food preservation, kitchen safety, childrearing, household budgets, pet care, or what have you.

Advertising in the publication supports some of this broad theme with a range of product promotions that embrace personal care commodities especially aimed at women: toilet soaps, feminine deodorants, cold creams, ladies' shampoos, nail polishes, face powders, lotions, hair dyes, lipstick, bobby pins, hand creams, blemish removers, hair depilatories, feminine hygiene, home permanents, perfumes, etc. Then there is a separate category of goods which is more universally applied in households: disinfectants, health food beverages, toothpastes, mouthwashes, candies, laxatives, over-the-counter pharmaceuticals, soft drinks, laundry starches, clothes dyes, vitamins, cigarettes, facial tissues, nerve relaxers, ear drops, tooth and gum pain relievers, magazines, corn removers, etc.

Finally, through multiple tidbit columns in every issue, the readers learn some behind-the-microphone gossip occurring in the lives of broadcasting and recording favorites. For instance, in that month's (March 1943) edition: singer Dinah Shore is dating actress Hedy Lamarr's ex-fiancé, suave actor George Montgomery (Shore and Montgomery were soon wed, incidentally, from 1943 to 1962) ... when variety show emcee Garry Moore beamed to the musicians playing his show that he was about to become a father, his "exclusive" rapidly evaporated: four members of the Irving Miller Band reported that they, too, were going to be dads! ... maestro Ted Weems and all of those in his 14-piece aggregate joined the U.S. Merchant Marine en masse ... variety show host-quizmaster Bob Hawk may be "the most inveterate movie-goer in radio." He usually sees 10 films weekly! ...

And there's still more from that same issue, to wit: announcer Lou Crosby of the *Lum and Abner* show has returned to work after cleaning his shotgun and unintentionally blowing off a big toe ... when character actor Gale Gordon departed *Fibber McGee & Molly,* where he was heard as Mayor LaTrivia (he joined the U.S. Coast Guard), the show partially replaced him with a new figure played by Gloria Gordon, Gale's spouse, a vet of multiple radio sitcoms ... radio director George Zachary and actress Marion Shockley disclosed their secret wedding vows exchanged while the pair was professionally tied on *The Adventures of Ellery Queen.* Zachary has now left the show to accept program directing for the U.S. Office of War Information, hence the "news" revelation. (Five years later, by the way, Shockley wed inexhaustible announcer-quizmaster-host Clayton "Bud" Collyer in more open circumstances: those nuptials occurred before nationwide listeners tuning in to *Bride & Groom.*)

The legacy of the celebrity-studded fanzines and a copious continuum of equivalent substance flanking them sustained an acute impact on broadcast journalism during its halcyon chapter. Such literature proved a tangible expression of what listeners and viewers were exposed to on the airwaves. There it was simultaneously being corroborated and buttressed in print by a diverse tangent of wordsmiths. The knowledge and understanding of the industry they possessed often proved to be very deep and wide. In the hands of skilled practitioners of their craft, the trade was enhanced as investigative reporters ferreted out facts from both the professional and personal existences of legions of airtime personalities — including those onstage and off.

As a hungry public awaited their latest exposés they drew confidence in their ability to report accurately, objectively, comprehensively, rapidly, and naturally. The scribes supplied the kinds of intriguing matter that could satisfy even the most discriminating tastes. While in a sense it was yet another dimension of radio and television news, the prozines provided a critical link that customarily perpetuated the dependency that a large segment of the American public held for the education and enjoyment furnished by the ethereal fountainhead on which those publications doted.

12

Optical Illusions? News Fix? Boosting Aural Text with Pix

The telegraph (introduced in 1837) and the telephone (1876) very well may be leading contenders for the most indispensable communications tools fashioned during the 19th century.[1] Both of these and their technological beneficiaries have been liberally employed by the masses of denizens over this planet who attempted to reach one another across sizable expanses of terrain extending beyond mere shouting ranges. This pair of strategic gadgets arrived after mankind had relied for centuries upon quaint and incredibly primeval methods of communing with one another that encompassed vast stretches of time and space.[2]

Although people worked with what they had, they were limited to crude carvings on cave walls, papyrus scrolls with hand-printed lettering, town criers, lighthouse beacons, smoke signals, lighted torches, and — around the year 1450 — an archaic contrivance which nonetheless transported their ability to communicate light years, the original rudimentary printing press. In its infancy this was a hand-cranked affair and it offered little more than a hint of what was in store. Following perpetual improvements which turned it into something exceptionally functional nevertheless, the press eventually yielded unrestricted numbers of typeset pages.

At the same time these impressively strategic innovations might be considered among the crucial harbingers of still greater transmission systems that consequently emerged. Apparatus resulting from the input of many practitioners during the 20th century built on such foundational paraphernalia and applied some of its principles in novel modes. Further improvements in technological communications appearing in the modern age continue to unveil many more tantalizing marvels. If you were asked to name the three most pervasive tools in this arena that were introduced in the 20th century, could you do so? What would be your answer?

Perhaps you will or will not agree with this author, who has little hesitation in this regard. In chronological order, the radio, the television, and the World Wide Web would be of unconditionally paramount significance in making — or having made — profound differences in the daily lives of most Americans in disparate eras. Indeed, the differences have been witnessed by multitudes of the world's advanced economies. For the majority, life has been permanently altered for the good because of their existence.

Although there are many added rivals that could be mentioned here, it is this observer's opinion that this trio — and the pair of mechanisms identified earlier that was introduced in the previous century (telephone, telegraph) — have demonstrated the most pervasive influence on the scope of human beings' abilities to commune with one another across mammoth stretches of spatial topography. Particularly does this seem applicable when interconnections are appropriated to an "audience" of manifold individuals — possibly hundreds, thousands, or millions of people — who receive its messages all at virtually the same instant. And the likelihood for their expansion today and tomorrow are incredibly promising, almost uninhibited in fact. (Chapter 15 offers a more extensive treatment of this topic.) We can't help pondering where all the potential for still more electrifying wonderment will lead us in the 21st century. You'll stay tuned for sure; who would want to miss this?

In the meantime, man — in his relentless quest for more — gradually grew discontent with a lack of optical illusions to buttress the early structures of mass communications. Some curious, ambitious, restive scientific technologists believed that comprehension of transmitted substance could be perceptibly heightened beyond whatever images were being dispatched with sheer resonance. Dots and dashes and verbal conduction were foundational to this activity but not the end of man's efforts to mollify some manner of enhanced delivery of news, information, data, ideas, entertainment, and other forms of communication.

Consequently, television, the computer, cable, satellite, the World Wide Web, and many other tools became realities and part of our everyday lives as the 20th century progressed. It seems as if something fresh in the way of an upgrade or an innovative device or system is being revealed to us almost every week while staggering the imagination as we contemplate the future. More will be said in another chapter about the implications of the Internet on our lifestyle in regard to the proliferation of electronic wizardry that currently dominates our interactive environment.

Radio journalism, of course, has been the focal emphasis of the present volume. Television, the remaining member of the triumvirate just mentioned, is the absorption of the majority of the balance of the chapter at hand. Video's role in electronic journalism continues to be pivotal, even though its pervasiveness has diminished substantially from the vaunted levels it occupied for several decades in the latter half of the previous century. Just let some local, national, or international calamity of monumental proportions transpire however, and TV instantly regains its unambiguous vaunted status. Habitually it's the place to be all over again.

Although the Second World War put much of the advancement of impending breakthroughs in electronic communications on hold, during the postwar years of the late 1940s, America witnessed a catch-up phase in which lost time was recouped with alacrity. In no fewer than four genres with major implications for news functions, and three of those overtly exhibiting strong semblances based on eye appeal — facsimile broadcasting, news transmission, television, and frequency modulation (FM) — dramatic progress was demonstrated.

The latter member of that group, frequency modulation — the only system of the quartet with purely aural-only provisions — showed striking promise in the 1940s and early 1950s. For a while its star temporarily faded due to its inability to compete against the stronger, established, commercially thriving amplitude modulation (AM) stations that long dominated most markets. That was anathema to the surge of popularity FM would acquire with a proliferation of FM radio stations across the United States later, of course. The innovation is mentioned here parenthetically because it was one of the strategic technological advancements of the period and was, of course, instrumental in the delivery of news.[3] As the mainstream pursuit is focused upon factors with optical provisions however, FM isn't included in further deliberations.

While there is some overlap in these system applications, a succinct estimate of the remaining trio will be enlightening.

- **Facsimile broadcasting:** This is the practice of using radio waves to activate a receiving set that graphically replicates whatever — for the eye instead of the ear — including printed text and images of wide-ranging description. The notion of dispatching print and still pictures by wire or wireless was not new. The newspaper industry used a process labeled *wirephoto* by which a photograph was scanned and transmitted by wire.[4] During the 1930s, the technique of facsimile was touted as an unambiguous competitor to news journals. With radio on one front and facsimile rising on another, the papers had plenty of challengers in delivering the news, a territory they had occupied all by themselves after the town crier faded and the printing press emerged.[5] By the late 1930s, interest developed in the idea of sending whole newspapers by radio rather than having them hand-delivered to the home.

In a trial exhibition, the trade paper *Broadcasting* unveiled the "facsimile newspaper" for all to witness during the National Association of Broadcasters convocation at the nation's capital on February 15, 1938. Shortly afterward the Federal Communications Commission licensed a handful of broadcasting outlets to persist with testing that budding concept. At that time, however, most news journals weren't overwrought by the potential that facsimile proffered: its print was hard to read, the apparatus was complex, and — when compared with radio's natural immediacy in news delivery — facsimile appeared dismally sluggish.

Ah, but a postwar resurgence in ingenuity, technology, and manufacturing began to turn the tide to improve facsimile's lot. A few newspaper-owning stations coalesced in 1946 to try something new.[6] Utilizing FM (Frequency Modulation) transmission, their collective attempts reproduced four newspaper pages onto 8.5 × 11–inch sheets, the upshot of which saw reading quality emerge that was "little impaired from the original." The process was completed within 15 minutes. The following year, *The Miami Herald* revealed its intents for experimental facsimile reproduction of its complete newspaper. At the same time, New York's WGHF-FM beamed United Press news bulletins to aircraft equipped with facsimile units. And by 1948, Philadelphia's WFIL-AM was broadcasting facsimile news continuously.

It was obvious that radio and other forms of communication were standing on the precipice of many breakthroughs not simply in news delivery but in widely diverse avenues of information flow. In the late 1940s, a radio historian observed: "Facsimile is certain to come into general use for specialized reporting such as market news and stock quotations; it may develop much wider importance."[7] Of course we have long seen the effects of that prediction mature, leading to multiple advancements that are light years ahead of its primordial efforts. As this chapter was being put to bed, for instance (*put to bed* is an old newspaper term signifying "finished," for the uninitiated), a contemporary daily devoted almost a half-page one day to scanner apps then on the market that are capable of turning a smartphone into a fax machine![8]

"For the price you might pay to send a fax from the local copy shop," the article's scribe assured, "you can buy an app that scans documents, builds PDF files and exports them without all the hardware headaches." Free apps, "a good entry point for cautious buyers," were cited, too. "The scanning process is fairly consistent, regardless of the app," the writer insisted. "You take a photo of a page, preferably in good light. The software scans the image and lets you crop it before a version is created for sharing."[9] But none of that might have transpired without the steps performed by the obviously motivated proactive pioneers in facsimile way back yonder.

- **News transmission:** A couple of promising developments in news feed diffusion created a stir in radio newsrooms in the midst of the medium's halcyon days.[10] In contrast to a teletype machine's customary funneling of 3,600 words an hour, Globe Wireless, Ltd., brought a mechanism onto the market in 1947 that was capable of dispatching 6,000 words an hour. And while not yet in service, a second device, Radio Corporation of America's Ultrafax — hinting at much greater potential — could reproduce a million words of copy a minute. By adapting TV principles to message scanning, transmission, and reproduction, Ultrafax was being tested in Eastman Kodak laboratories as RCA president David Sarnoff compared its value to that of splitting the atom.[11]

  Ultrafax's hybrid method of facsimile transmission joined properties of photography and TV.[12] Material to be dispatched (text, writing, pictures, diagrams) was initially photographed on a strip of movie film. Next, applying a modified television technique, the film was scanned by a "flying spot" of light (old hat today but definitely novel then). At the receiving end, another flying spot reproduced the material on a second strip of film. The latter strip was then passed through heated chemicals and developed in 15 seconds and compressed by air in 25 more seconds. For that time, this advancement in transmission was unlike any before it.

  Addressing a gathering of "distinguished" guests at the Library of Congress as he announced it, Sarnoff projected the future by weighing in on Ultrafax's capabilities: "It can duplicate movie films (such as newsreels) almost instantaneously at any distance. It can send whole newspapers. Perhaps it heralds the day when the newspaper reader, on his way to breakfast, will stop off in the living room to watch the 'printing' of his morning paper."[13] Or maybe receive the entire paper on a screen?

- **Television:** The New York World's Fair in 1939 signaled the unveiling of TV to the general public after more than a dozen years of concentrated effort by RCA and its NBC ancillary. Although the war delayed widespread exposure of the new medium, there were about 30 stations on the air by mid–1948 with 70 more anticipating similar activity by the year's end.[14] Broad optimism replaced skeptics' doubts about whether television would ever transmit news pictures and live newsworthy action. By 1948, Acme Newspictures and United Press linked their forces to offer TV stations a couple of five-minute daily spot newsfilm features. This was augmented by special event news coverage embracing newsreels and spot "stills." International News Photos and International News Service, meanwhile, combined their resources to provide newsreel and other image-based stories for TV's original 10-minute sponsored Telenews feature every day. (The Associated Press had already tried that. In 1948, AP nonetheless permitted it to fade.)

  At the same time ABC, CBS, Dumont, and NBC were instituting their own newsfilm technicians, relying on affiliates, and focusing express attention on unique events. Telenews, tendering mostly "still" images and backed by dubbed-in voices, hardly drew any prizes (or audiences beyond the curiosity-seekers, for that matter). This was all in its infancy. Today's 24/7 instant coverage anywhere around the globe with live action visuals and accompanying voice descriptions had its origins in those humble beginnings during the postwar years.

The concepts just explored bode well for significantly increased opportunities in photojournalism. Technology steadily improved and added to our sense of eyewitness drama complementing the text that the news audiences had been accustomed to for much or all of their lives.

Of these multiple innovations, the one with the most visible impact on the greatest number of people is, without any doubt, television. Because it is such a powerful influence on people living around the globe today — even though the traditional landscape of the device and even the time of delivery of its offerings has been radically altered for some recipients — TV remains strategic in the diffusion of crucial news and information. As noted already when we recall the newsworthy moments in our nation's history during the last half-century, where have we concentrated for lengthy periods of time, scrutinizing what transpired with momentous impact in our world? For the majority of Americans it invariably has been television — and sometimes it has been almost in virtual disbelief at what we were seeing unfolding before our eyes.

If you were alive when President John F. Kennedy was assassinated in 1963, for some four days there is the strong likelihood that you sat mesmerized in front of a TV set. There, while almost everything else subsided, you were spellbound along with your neighbors in their homes. You followed every revelation of what had just happened, solemnly witnessing the reactions of a totally stunned country in deep mourning. "Because of that weekend, television news would rise to become the major element in American journalism," confirmed one pundit. "Thanks in part to those four days, Americans would turn increasingly to television for their news."[15]

The same was true following the assassinations of some other prominent American figures, of wartime crises, of natural and man-made disasters at home and abroad, of political revelations, and of course — most of all — that incredibly fateful day of 9/11 and its gripping aftermath. Such momentous occasions are etched on our minds primarily because of the pictures we witnessed on television. And even though we may receive newsworthy optics today on some type of handheld device, or check them out on a personal computer, or record them for playback at a later time, for most people TV continues to exhibit an unmistakably commanding lead over all other forms of instant dissemination when news of weighty severity is breaking.

An exploration into and analysis of the myriad facets of electronic journalism could be found wanting if little more than token acknowledgment of TV's rise to prominence sufficed. Exploring its multifaceted ramifications in detail would call for substantial space, going far beyond the scope of this book. However, at least a few of the historical developments from the medium's origins will offer a glimpse of its stimulating maturity.

Writing in 1938, Hugo Gernsback, one of the pioneers of early radio development and eventually editor of *Radio-Craft*, a monthly trade periodical "for the service man, dealer, radiotrician," insisted that "television dates back more than 50 years."[16] That would definitely put its start prior to 1888, about a decade after the invention of the telephone and a few years before wireless telegraphy emerged. And of course, that was earlier than the inception of radio signals (1895) and amateur "ham" radiophiles which prevailed in the early decades of the 20th century. Gernsback, by the way, the avowed "father of science fiction," was selling radio receivers by 1906 at $7.50 out of his New York-based Gernsback's Electro Importing Company.[17] The entrepreneur advertised that those particular commodities came with "guaranteed reception" of about a mile.

Back to the matter at hand: Gernsback cites three inventor-scientist-engineers representing as many nations who *thought* about the possibility of picture transmission — in Gernsback's attribution, at least, *before anybody else*.[18] That's not necessarily the case, of course, for many were involved in laying the groundwork. They *thought* about it — *but they did more.*

Working separately, there was Paul Gottlieb Nipkow (1860–1940) of Germany: he patented a signature scanning device (the *Nipkow disk*) in 1884 that captured transmitted images and reconstituted those opticals for projection, allowing for an electromechanical television system which preceded the all-electric schematics that finally eclipsed it. Then there was George Roswell Carey (1850–1908) of Malden, Massachusetts, who was a Boston civil servant and, in 1877, submitted illustrations for a selenium camera permitting viewers to "see by electricity." Finally, there was Constantin Senlecq (1842–1934) of France who — by the late 1870s — was one of a handful of innovators offering designs for a *telectroscope*, yet another piece of equipment that translated into "seeing at a distance." These were but three who worked out theories that, ultimately, formed parts of a compatible television system. Unfortunately, none of those visionaries lived to see the pervasive applications of their revolutionary hypotheses.

There were many, many others whose contributions to one or more pieces of the finished product eventually brought television to fruition. (A few will be mentioned presently.) Gernsback acknowledged that video's first practical demonstration didn't occur until January 27, 1926. On that date Scottish engineer John Logie Baird (1888–1946) exhibited a true system that he had developed to 50 scientists gathered at London's Royal Institute. His mechanical arrangement employed black and white images with intermediary shades. But there it was!

Baird, incidentally, one of those key innovators involved in early television systems, had been experimenting with communications all his life. His initial crude TV composed of "odds and ends" actually transmitted a flickering image across a few feet in 1924.[19] He achieved still more notoriety, however, when he demonstrated his television across an expanse of 438 miles between London and Glasgow in 1927. The following year he attained his first transatlantic TV transmission between London and New York as well as the first to be dispatched to a ship in mid–Atlantic waters. Baird's mechanical system was declared obsolete in 1937, when it was overtaken by a much upgraded electronic layout that had been produced by many experimenters, principally spearheaded by Italian inventor Guglielmo Marconi (1874–1937).[20]

A compelling treatise, meanwhile, on the actual instigator of television appears in the Paul Pert Screen Collection, a resource "devoted to classics of the golden age."[21] On the topic of "Pioneers of Television," a portion reads:

> The question of who invented television is an eternal debate. Generally, the answer you would get from most people ... would be that it was Scotsman John Logie Baird.
>
> However, the public image of Baird has changed over the years, as those who would seek to discredit his contribution to television as we know it today say their piece, their reason being that his mechanical system was superseded by electronic television — a fact which is definitely true.
>
> The question however, remains — and in order to adequately position one's self to attempt an answer, an understanding or definition of exactly what the word "television" means must first be ascertained.
>
> Records indicate that the word was first used in 1900, to describe an invention that did not yet exist, by people who knew little of exactly how it would effectively be achieved. Their vision was of a system that would transmit images onto a screen over distance.
>
> Therefore, taking all this into consideration, the populist answer to the fundamental question would indeed appear to be correct, as quite simply, Baird achieved this before anyone else....
>
> In an age when TFT screens are rapidly replacing CRT technology, and soon to become the norm, the argument that Baird did not invent television because his mechanical system was superseded by CRT technology rather falls down flat.[22]

However, Baird's televisions — and other subsequent televisions whether mechanical or electronic — utilized components invented by several preceding inventors, all of whom deserve credit for their respective contributions, as without them, Baird would no doubt have only achieved a more limited success.

As noted, many, many others gave rise to television through their individual accomplishments. A few of the more noteworthy are included here.[23]

- **Jöns Jakob Berzelius** (1779–1848), Swedish scientist who, with a colleague — Johan Gottlieb Gahn — discovered selenium at the bottom of a camera in 1817.
- **Alexandre Edmond Becquerel** (1820–1891), French physicist who — having already studied the relationships of electricity, magnetism, and light — found, in 1839, the electrochemical effects of light.
- **Willoughby Smith** (1828–1891), English engineer who confirmed the principle of selenium's photosensitivity and the possibility of converting light into electrical impulses (a theory first suggested by Irish telegraph operator Joseph May); Smith published the results of their experimentations in a professional journal in 1873.
- **Sir William Crookes O.M., F.R.S.** (1832–1919), English chemist and physicist who in 1878 established that cathode rays travel in straight lines and cause phosphorescence in the objects that they invade, which are heated on impact.
- **Maurice LeBlanc** (1857–1923), French engineer who in 1880 proposed scanning a moving image with light beams reflected on a selenium photocell, converting this to electricity and transmitting it to a screen.
- **Shelford Bidwell** (1848–1909), English physicist principally recognized for his concentration on an early prototype of the fax machine (telephotography) who, in 1881, published results of experimentation with selenium photocells for image scanning.
- **Lazare Weiller** (1858–1928), French experimenter who, in 1889, conceived of image scanning with a mirrored drum to reflect light onto a selenium cell; though his device wasn't constructed until 1898, it was applied in early mechanical televisions.
- **Karl Ferdinand Braun** (1850–1918), German inventor and educator; in 1897, he produced a cathode-ray tube for commercial sale, the first person to do so.
- **Sir John Ambrose Fleming** (1849–1945), English electrical engineer and physicist who patented a two-diode thermionic valve in 1904 that netted an electrical signal by controlling electron movement in low-pressure space — the first vacuum tube, in fact, which allowed TV electronics technology to advance.
- **Max Dieckmann** (1882–1960), German experimenter who — with Gustav Glage — produced and patented "raster images" on a cathode ray tube in 1906; it's a design for figure storage and transmission in computer imaging systems in which optics are divided into consecutive sample elements (pixels).
- **Boris Rosing** (1869–1933), Russian inventor who designed an "electronic vision" schematic using cathode ray tubes and mirror drums; with a 1911 German patent for an improved version of a still primitive electromechanical plan (as opposed to electronic), he exhibited the CRT for TV use ahead of most others.
- **Alan Archibald Campbell-Swinton F.R.S.** (1863–1930), a British visionary who published fundamentals of modern television in 1908; he was still advancing the same topic a score of years afterward.
- **Vladimir Kosma Zworykin** (1889–1982), Russian inventor who patented the first practical television transmission tube, the iconoscope, in 1923; in 1929, he patented an

improved cathode ray tube, the kinescope; the next year he took charge of RCA's TV development in New Jersey.
- **Kenjiro Takayanagi** (1899–1990), Japanese lecturer and inventor; he applied CRT technology to build the first all-electronic TV set, demonstrating it for the first time in 1925, telecasting images of a Japanese figure.
- **Charles Francis Jenkins** (1867–1934), American physicist whose recurring 1928 telecasts from Washington, D.C. comprised of silhouette transmissions applied a spinning disc yielding a one-inch square picture with 48 lines of resolution.
- **Kálmán Tihanyi** (1897–1947), Hungarian inventor who patented a fully electronic television system in 1926 that employed CRT technology, yet was bypassed by two major German manufacturers that were already turning out mechanical TVs.
- **Philo T. Farnsworth** (1906–1971), American inventor who transmitted the first image (a straight line backlit from a glass slide) from his image dissector camera tube in 1927, and the first live human images in 1929; he telecast the Berlin Olympics in 1936, and persisted in conveying experimental entertainment features.
- **Boris Pavlovich Grabovsky** (1901–1966), Russian scientist who said he conducted the first electronic telecast in 1926 of "a bright spot" and "the movement of a hand" although skeptics believe this didn't occur until 1928, netting him a patent then.
- **René Bartholomew** (1889–1954), French engineer who demonstrated a 30-line mechanical TV system; improving on it twice in 1935, he returned for both 60- and 180-line definition exhibitions.

To advocate that any single person invented television of course would be a farce as has been witnessed in these multifaceted accomplishments. While a few imaginative entrepreneurs were able to capitalize on the input of some of their peers and predecessors, television — like radio before it — was never the exploit of any one man. Taking nothing from John Logie Baird — who may be dubbed TV's inventor as authentically as any — some concepts and prototypes designed by others were bequeathed to the finished product. Working independently (for the most part), together (figuratively speaking) those innovators at last produced a feasible television configuration.

In the meantime, many of us on this side of the Atlantic have heard the stories and read the tales of the early development of television in the laboratories of the Radio Corporation of America, principally in response to directives of RCA president David Sarnoff. He's the very same Sarnoff who maintained such an intense scrutiny over the NBC Red and Blue radio networks, you may remember, like a mother hen clucking over her young. If you recall, very little of any great import transpired at those chains without Sarnoff's blessing and, sometimes, his wholehearted intervention.

But back to TV: were we mistaken or simply lulled into thinking that video — just as we like to assign every breakthrough of any consequence — can legitimately claim American origins? What's up with that?

Those experiments did occur and were extensively performed at Sarnoff's urging. He seemed to live — eat, breathe, sleep, in fact — for the day that a reliable quality TV system would surface to displace radio as the foremost means of mass communications in this country and around the globe. You'll keep in mind for sure the fact that broadcasting was but a small part of his enterprise's diversified business portfolio; manufacturing electronic equipment produced far more in profits than program diffusion. Wouldn't an as yet unrealized, untapped, potentially unlimited television market portend good things for RCA's future horizon, and justifiably cause dollar signs to dance in the eyes of its executives and owners? (Just a little food for thought there, you understand.)

Barely a year past the formation of NBC Radio, meanwhile, in a lecture to Harvard business students, Sarnoff touted his obviously keen anticipation for the arrival of "sight communication as promised by television."[24] So convinced was he and so early was this man of television's predestined impact on our world that — without being an inventor yet a respected visionary — he was advocating an unavoidable outcome several years prior to his visit to Harvard.

> The dream of adding sight to sound in transmissions over the airwaves was engaging the interest of many scientists. Still or facsimile images had been sent, experimentally, for a number of years, but images in motion were another matter. Sarnoff, however, was among the first who dared talk of it not as a dream but as an inevitable reality. As early as 1922, ... he was assembling in his mind the theoretical ingredients of television. By April 1923, he was ready to put a forecast into documentary form. In a memorandum to RCA directors he wrote in part:
> "I believe that television ... will come to pass in due course.
> "Already, [still] pictures have been sent across the Atlantic by radio.... In the near future when news is telegraphed by radio ... a picture of the event will likewise be sent over by radio and both will arrive simultaneously, thus ... we will be able to see as well as read in New York, within an hour or so, the event taking place in London, Buenos Aires or Tokyo....
> "It may be that every broadcast receiver will also be equipped with a television adjunct by which the instrument will make it possible for those at home to see as well as hear what is going on at the broadcast station."
> His conception of TV was steadily sharpened. Eventually, he said at the University of Missouri in January, 1924, every farm family would be able to "look in" as well as listen in on news events. And in an article [in 1926] he wrote: "The greatest day of all will be reached when not only the human voice but the image of the speaker will be flashed through space in every direction." It is not easy to realize, in the present television age, how unreal such forecasts sounded in the 1920s.[25]

RCA's long crucial intermingling with electronic television's pioneering phase was ultimately to be followed by its extensive involvement in operating equipment manufacture and sales for broadcasters and viewers. All of this is intricately documented by legions of historiographers and won't be pursued further. Television's introduction on a public platform in April 1939 (and for several months thereafter) during the World's Fair in Flushing Meadows, New York (just east of the Big Apple), drew hundreds of thousands of visitors from all over the nation. They were able to witness the transmission of moving human images for the first time. The enormous number of inquiries there about when and where sets could be purchased was sheer affirmation that TV was well received, a fact that the press also generally upheld.[26]

A Sarnoff biographer, meanwhile, lauded his subject unreservedly for the inspiration and resolve he put into making TV an accomplished fact in most American households in the decade between the mid 1940s and mid–1950s.

> One man above all others was responsible for the introduction of television. I do not mean that he was alone or that it would not ultimately have emerged without him. I mean only that David Sarnoff nurtured the development from unpromising beginnings to operational maturity, despite obstruction by segments of his own industry and small support from any source....
> The brains and labors of hundreds of scientists, engineers, and business administrators went into shaping and refining the new dimension in communications. Although the preponderant inventive and development job was done by the Radio Corporation, elements perfected in other laboratories were built into the final apparatus....

> The television system as it exists today is substantially the one perfected by RCA under his [Sarnoff's] direction. Pride and reputation meant a great deal to Sarnoff, and these he put on the line in the big gamble for television....
> Toward the end of 1944 the Television Broadcasters Association, comprising men who knew the story from the inside, would bestow upon Sarnoff the title of "Father of American Television".... Those who awarded it knew ... that for some fifteen years Sarnoff had pitted his faith against the judgment of the majority in the radio community and even in his own company.
> Year after year, in a time of economic troubles and pervasive defeatism, he had gone before the board of RCA to obtain the appropriations for a pale hope called television. Not until 1949 would TV begin to pay its way and return the investment. By then RCA, directly and through NBC, would have sunk close to $50 million into it. Rarely before, up to that time, had a single business organization put so much capital into a single project.[27]

CBS in this period was at work on its own developmental plans for TV. The network was as competitive there as it was in radio. When NBC opened a New York City television outlet in 1930, CBS wasn't far behind, launching a similar operation in Gotham in 1931.[28] And it was Columbia (CBS) that unveiled the nation's first regularly scheduled telecasts on July 21, 1931, over experimental station W2XAB in Manhattan.[29] That same decade there was a rise in television's visibility through the printed page. In May 1938, trade magazine *Variety* offered its earliest review of a televised show. Counterpart periodical *Billboard* permanently added TV reviews to its editions in 1939. With its August 1939 issue, meanwhile, the durable *Radio Mirror* celebrity-based prozine sported a new title, *Radio and Television Mirror*, reflecting an inclusive change in attitude and emphasis. Eventually "*TV*" would appear before *Radio* in its moniker.

Following the public TV exploitation at the 1939 World's Fair, in 1940, electronics manufacturer Allen B. DuMont put yet another TV outlet on the air in Gotham.[30] He revealed plans for a regional station hookup bearing his surname, too (DuMont or Dumont). NBC rallied in 1941, linking New York City, Philadelphia, and Schenectady in still another chain. Each of the three outlets could originate programming that was telecast by the other two. They were testing the waters for eventual widespread hookup operations.

CBS and NBC obtained licenses for commercial programming on their New York outlets as of July 1, 1941. But late that year, when the Second World War erupted, TV growth and innovative programming was instantly nixed. The efforts in manufacturing sets and advancing new technology were instead harnessed into the wartime mechanism. While temporary, it was nevertheless a disconcerting setback for those with enduring screen dreams, visions that had to be put on hold.

When the war ended in 1945, people within the broadcasting industry who were avowed advocates of TV — a product most of the country still had never seen — moved like a house afire to bring into reality. They wanted TV available nationwide. As more stations went on the air, not a lot of programming existed before 6 P.M. local time when a small troupe of those early viewers might be available in a few large metropolitan centers as viewers. That would change dramatically and fairly rapidly.

During this period CBS brought out the first color television receiver ahead of its perceptually more sophisticated high-tech rival RCA. The Federal Communications Commission (FCC) hastily approved CBS's invention. Yet its design was superseded by an electronic color system that was compatible with existing black-and-white picture sets. The FCC approved the latter on December 17, 1953. This preferred model was a mutation of an RCA-originated blueprint. The decision was a disappointing blow for CBS, and especially so for the web's chief, William S. Paley.

In the meantime, if radio had a guardian angel during this epoch, Paley was utterly and unquestionably that individual. A handful of vintage radio historians reported on multiple occasions that saw him step into the abyss to defend the first simultaneous mass broadcasting medium and to do so practically by himself. In proceeding in that manner, for several years Paley staved off often heated opposition that at times threatened to undo it all except for his standing in the way. Sometimes it appeared that radio could have been swept under the carpet by an advancing horde of single-minded video zealots.[31] The real crux of the battle, nevertheless, which was even more sharply focused, was instigated by CBS's local radio affiliate stations.

For several years in the 1950s they called for an unconditional surrender of nearly all network time in order for them (the outlets) to sell their only available commodity (time) themselves. That design proffered a far more lucrative prospect than merely accepting a pittance in funding from the web for the national programs they carried. Until those affiliates finally threatened mutiny by leaving CBS to join another national chain or go the independent route, however, Paley was able to maneuver and thwart their insubordination. Only after they threw down the gauntlet and left him with no other choice did he finally back off and permit the network radio schedule to be virtually wiped clean. (The rival webs had cut back to bare bones programming long before this with CBS being the last one holding on.) As a consequence, in late 1960, CBS proceeded down a road from which it could never return. From that time forward it concentrated almost all of its broadcasting efforts in Videoland. The decision, once implemented, marked the ceremonial passing of an era.

Earlier that decade, on September 10, 1951, significant expansion of American television occurred when the coaxial cable was opened to the West Coast.[32] For the first time coast-to-coast television became a reality. That year, too, more citizens of this country watched television between 9 P.M. and midnight than listened to radio, also for the very first time. "Television was already conducting itself provocatively, trying to get radio to pucker up for the kiss of death," bemoaned radio comedian Fred Allen, who wasn't among those thrilled about its foreboding prospect for established entertainment venues.[33]

Nevertheless, one who chronicled the advancement of television's escalation to near universal proportions during the postwar epoch alluded to a progressively intense enticement toward TV. Although at first it proceeded gradually ("The problem was to convince the public that television had value; the war had dimmed the memory of summer 1941"[34]), once TV was finally established in multiple places with the lure of so much more, the rush was on and it wouldn't subside for several years. In a mighty swoosh it was as if someone had pulled a plug from a hole in a dike and allowed the dam to spill its floodwaters all at once. At the same time, the anticipation of life ever after based on the premise of everlasting prosperity that the home-grown industrialists had harbored for decades faded rapidly. Their hopes and dreams were dashed forever as the fortunes of a promising opportunity shifted away from U.S. shores.

> Television after the war was more mature and ready to serve the world. Thanks to the efforts of many American radio companies, especially RCA, television emerged from the war years full-blown and ready for use. The rise of the American television industry in both manufacturing and programming was phenomenal. American industry dominated the postwar world. This picture, however, was soon to change. The invention of the Ampex video recorder gave the Japanese a chance to build competing machines, and build them with great skill. It wasn't long before the Japanese were dominating the global television market. Helped by the Japanese government, Japanese products were the envy of the world. This led to the demise of the American

television manufacturing industry, and today there are very few American companies to give the Japanese competition.[35]

At that juncture television had surely become a *global* enterprise. With its earliest experimentations conducted in Europe and some of its most pervasive development and early manufacturing ensuing in North America, it had again jumped an ocean to reach new pinnacles in the designs and production of Asian entrepreneurs. The successive growth in the continuing saga of television's evolvement has been recorded by hundreds and maybe thousands of authors seeking to document the successive details of TV's sometimes surprising twists and turns. The story of that advancement is left to others as the remainder of this chapter is pointed toward TV's involvement in the transmission of news.

Reuven Frank (1920–2006), who would ultimately rise to the presidency of NBC News — and in fact do so not once, but twice — insisted that TV news began with the political conventions in 1948. In a 400-page overview of TV news history, Frank dated the genre to May 1 of that year when American Telephone & Telegraph Company (AT&T) launched recurring commercial intercity transmission of video images. "Suddenly, owning the expensive novelty called a television set had a redeeming purpose," said he.[36] Frank also dates the four early television networks from that period: ABC, CBS, DuMont, and NBC. While AT&T's coaxial cable extended to only nine cities between Boston, Massachusetts, and Richmond, Virginia, nevertheless 17 stations were available in those few metroplexes to transmit convention reflections — including "every moment of everything that happened, plus hours of nothing happening at all."[37]

> Born at the conventions, network news departments came to be defined by their convention coverage. Newspeople relished the status they attained within their networks at convention time, and individuals were judged by how well they had done or might be expected to do. Above all, whoever was his network's visible face at the conventions became its symbol, its standard-bearer for four more years — Douglas Edwards, John Cameron Swayze, Walter Cronkite, Chet Huntley, David Brinkley. All this lasted perhaps two decades, a long time in television.[38]

Radio, of course, had never attempted the gavel-to-gavel coverage that TV afforded the conventions in its early years. Radio didn't have to; with profitable programming running smoothly for two decades it could bypass the conventions altogether. During the single week of the Republican meeting in Philadelphia, one national chain's TV coverage exceeded its web's radio airtime for the GOP meeting alone by 40 hours![39] TV exposed an audience to new dimensions of the convention drama itself, something a fawning public first encountered through audio transmissions a couple of dozen years earlier (1924). New turf was categorically broken both years!

A brief discourse on Douglas Edwards (1917–90), veteran CBS correspondent and network television's initial weekday news anchor, will be insightful for an awareness of what was stirring in this period as radio newsmen adjusted their sets.

> Edwards inaugurated a weekend CBS-TV newscast in 1947 and covered the political conventions in 1948.... [In 1948] the chain tapped him to anchor the nation's first nightly network newscast, *CBS-TV News*, renamed *Douglas Edwards with the News* in 1950, indicating his widespread recognition by then.... (NBC's John Cameron Swayze led the competition into the nightly newscast arena, [but] it didn't happen until 1949.) "It wasn't an easy decision for him [Edwards] to make," wrote a biographer, "in fact his initial reaction was to say no to the offer. Television was considered unworthy for serious journalists, a sideshow and dead end, by many in broadcasting and print. Not only that, ... Edwards would have to give up the substantial additional income which radio advertising provided to announcers. [The debuting TV news

After a few years of hands-on preparation as a CBS Radio newscaster, Douglas Edwards was given the chance to move to the forefront of the web's budding video news product. Unsure it was a promising venture, however, he required some assurance that TV would be bigger than radio one day. A pundit credits Edwards as the father of television journalism, affirming that all who followed him owed a part of their livelihoods to the model he founded. For 14 years he was the face of CBS-TV news (1948–62) and a key CBS Radio broadcaster for an enduring 46 years (1942–88). Few surpassed him in either medium.

show was without sponsorship.] It took Frank Stanton, the president of CBS, to convince him that, far from being a dead end, television was the wave of the future."

"The truth is," pontificated Gary Paul Gates, a chronicler of CBS News, "that [Walter] Cronkite and all the other TV anchormen who have come along since are the direct descendants of Douglas Edwards." Gates continued, "For fourteen years, from 1948 to 1962, Doug Edwards was the face and voice of CBS on its evening news show...." After the coaxial cable linked all of the nation's TV watchers in September 1951, the pioneering journalist introduced his daily quarter-hour newscast with "Good evening, everyone, from coast to coast."[40]

In the meantime, Reuven Frank's account of this nascent age of video's weekday news reportage — particularly as it was reflected in accompanying images — divulges a great deal about the inefficiencies of that previously untested turf. An indomitable spirit was necessary to prevail against the foibles it frequently presented. His observations of those days could be priceless:

> Now both senior networks had daily national newscasts, and their contrasts reflected the fundamental differences between the two organizations. The CBS staff modeled television news on radio news, the same structure for writers and editors, the same standards, purposes, and emphasis on words.... After a few unsatisfactory attempts, CBS News gave up its own national and world newsfilm organization and hired a syndicated service called Telenews to supply film from faraway places. CBS gradually hired its own crews to supplement this service, especially with sound film of press conferences, hearings, and major speeches. But what they got from Telenews was the basis of what they showed each night.
>
> At NBC, the term *newsreel* was not a figure of speech but an accurate description of a fact of life.... NBC's management ... tried to put news on television by hiring one of the theater newsreel companies to do it ... but [with] ... each a tiny part of a large motion picture production organization, [they] turned them down. So they hired an out-of-work newsreel executive to set up a department. He ... hired out-of-work newsreel cameramen.... They covered ... newsreel stories — Miss America, ice cream eating contests, press agents' schemes, movie openings, women's fashions, spring training, girls on water skis.
>
> NBC's news cameramen filmed as though for theaters, on 35mm film. Their basic tool was the Eyemo, a handheld camera powered, like a child's toy car, by a clockwork motor wound between scenes by a large key on the camera's side. It made one minute and ten seconds of picture before it had to be reloaded. It took us several years to realize that the 16mm film used by CBS and almost everyone else was lighter, more flexible, and cheaper — and not only the film but also all the associated equipment, the cameras, editing tables, and processors. Such film was also more practical for recording sound, which was becoming more and more important as we tried harder and harder to cover news. In those days, NBC's news film was silent; crews shot almost no sound, not statements, not interviews, not even ambient noise....
>
> At NBC, only Washington filmed sound; Washington stories were all talk, anyway. Our bureau in Washington equipped itself with the early 16mm sound cameras that were being developed for this new television business, and they had to send the film to a nonunion laboratory for processing. Otherwise, NBC's newsfilm was mute, shown against background music chosen from a mood music record library for which we bought rights by the year. (Even here, real music from real records was forbidden to us under the rules.) ...
>
> [NBC sponsoring cigarette-maker] Camel ... assumed the right to pick the name, *Camel News Caravan*. They honestly believed that years of radio big band music had engraved the words *Camel Caravan* on the public's mind. When Camel cigarettes transmogrified from Glen Gray and his Casa Loma Orchestra on radio to John Cameron Swayze and the news on television, no one presumed to ask what was a news caravan. What Camel wanted Camel got — because they paid so much, because they might have gone to CBS, and especially because they dealt with NBC's salesmen and managers, who were paid to sell and manage....
>
> One reason Camel picked NBC was that we emphasized pictures more than CBS, and one reason we continued to do this was that Camel wanted them. As a result, the organization to provide pictures grew rapidly.[41]

Ah, the primitive days of yore!

Things improved gradually (emphasis on *gradually*). For quite some time, there wouldn't be anything resembling what we have become accustomed to in recent decades on our TV screens. Electronic journalists (*radio* journalists, by and large) were wading into unfamiliar waters in the 1950s. Much of what they were attempting to offer in video's fledgling epoch was accomplished by trial and error on sets with rickety walls, collapsible platforms, mike booms overhead that fell into the picture, stage hands that walked into visibility, all conducted under swelteringly oppressive lights.

It was akin to taking swimming lessons: you learned it or you sank. The local newscasters and those at the network level applied themselves to an unaccustomed venue under makeshift conditions at best. They were practicing their strokes in a public arena every day. And without many rescues while on camera, they swam or sank. Conducting business in a glassed-in pool was consistently demanding. The hardiest of the lot prevailed and fostered a new method for us to claim the news.

Fast forward now, skipping over a few intermediate decades between that nascent epoch and today's televised news product. Hit the pause button in the late 1980s. Here's the lament of one well-worn news broadcaster in that period[42]:

> Veteran newsmen who have gloomily watched the decline of network news accelerate in the mid-eighties have concluded that network news is dying, that, within a decade or so, it will have virtually disappeared. They point to the loss of audience from 1984 through 1988, to the mushrooming of stronger local stations, to news syndicates and communications services, to new networks, to the revolution of high technology, to all kinds of dishes and disks, to video cassettes, to transponders priced even for a single local station, to the loss of advertising revenue, to public saturation with the news....
>
> Men and women of the highest intelligence and competence are reporting on network news. But power has gradually passed ... away from the correspondents and newscasters into the hands of producers, accountants, lawyers, and management, people who are bottom-liners, budgeteers, legalists, not news people. They are not committed to news as we once were in the great days of the [Edward R.] Murrow era. The Murrow years remain the standard of excellence. That is why [Dan] Rather, in his *New York Times* column, deplored the fall from "Murrow to mediocrity."

To some who have traditionally maintained a high respect for journalism in its varied compound expressions, in his day former *CBS Evening News* anchorman Dan Rather (1931-) was something of an iconoclastic hero of the strain. To a band of staunch idealists, he represented integrity, fairness, excellence, objectivity, courage, and whatever supplementary superlatives could be attached to Ed Murrow in *his* day in radio. And while not speaking for everybody, Rather did for many and seemed emboldened at times when his blunt remarks could very well have cost him much professionally and financially.[43] (Ultimately, as we know, his words and deeds eventually did cost Rather his post. He details the story in a memoir released not long ago.[44])

The New York Times op-ed piece referenced above ran on March 10, 1987. It surfaced shortly after a new leader in the CBS executive suite — Bill Paley's successor, Laurence Tisch (1923–2003), the mastermind behind Loews, Inc.— brought an end to the careers of more than 200 news division employees with the chain after clarifying six months previously: "Whether the news loses money or makes money is secondary to what we put on the air. I can't picture any point at which profit becomes the main thought in deciding on a news program."[45] This was amid a comparative residue of demoralized employees (1,200 CBS jobs in all divisions received the sting of the hatchet earlier).[46]

Rather's reaction reminded some of a speech by Murrow three decades before. On October 15, 1958, speaking before the Radio and Television News Association meeting in Chicago, the fearless broadcaster jeopardized his own future as he lambasted the three major

At the Louisiana Superdome in New Orleans in August 1988, three of the most prominent faces among CBS newsmen at the Republican National Convention were (l-r) Eric Sevareid, Walter Cronkite, and Dan Rather. For years this trio individually headlined their own radio newsfeatures while concurrently adding to radio news reports. Sevareid's CBS tenure began in the late 1930s with a stint as one of "the Murrow Boys." The revered threesome, with multiple decades of electronic journalism to their credit, regularly appeared on *The CBS Evening News* on television where each one contributed virtually every day.

networks for programming mediocrity, claiming that during peak viewing periods the medium "insulates us from the realities of the world in which we live." When novelist Thomas Wolfe wrote "You can't go home again" it surely applied to Murrow. From that day forward, so it seemed, things were never quite the same for him with the brass at CBS. And a principled Dan Rather said this in 1987:[47]

> CBS Inc. is not a chronically weak company fighting to survive.... 215 people lost their jobs so that the stockholders would have even more money in their pockets. More profits. That's what business is about....
> What we cannot accept is the notion that the bottom line counts more than meeting our responsibility to the public. Anyone who says network news cannot be profitable doesn't know what he is talking about. But anyone who says it must always make money is misguided and irresponsible. We have lost correspondents, producers, camera crews. That means we will cover less news. We will go to fewer places and witness fewer events. For the viewer, that means a product that may inevitably fall short of the quality and vision it once possessed.
> Our concern, beyond the shattered lives of valued friends and colleagues is, How do we go on? How do we cover the world? Can we provide in-depth reporting and analysis with resources so severely diminished? Can we continue to do our jobs in the finest tradition of this great organization? In the tradition of Edward R. Murrow, Walter Cronkite, Eric Sevareid,

> Douglas Edwards, Charles Collingwood? We are determined that our new corporate management not lead us into a tragic transformation from Murrow to mediocrity. We take our public trust very seriously. It is why we are journalists in the first place. Our new chief executive officer, Laurence Tisch, told us when he arrived that he wanted us to be the best. We want nothing more than to fulfill that mandate. Ironically, he has now made the task seem something between difficult and impossible. I have said before that I have no intention of participating in the demise of CBS. But do the owners and officers of the new CBS see news as a trust ... or only as a business venture?

It was certainly a mouthful for the new kid in the executive office to swallow. But is electronic news' output mired in mediocrity or possibly even worse a quarter-century later? That is left to the reader to decide.

On another note, at the risk of stealing thunder from a later chapter, we can now receive our news through systems that few might have dreamed of in the 1980s — and no one would have foreseen in the 1940s, as video news got under way big-time. Nielsen, the people who have been counting heads and keeping tabs on what we do for decades, reported in early 2012 that young people — who admittedly aren't generally perceived as steady TV news-watchers — have bypassed traditional methods of channel surfing to adopt heretofore unorthodox modes of tuning in whatever is on the screen (mostly entertainment, we presume, but who knows really?— maybe even something informative and educational). Citing those in an age range extending from 12 to 34, the numbers trackers allowed:

> Young people are still watching the same shows, but they are streaming them on computers and phones to a greater degree than their parents or grandparents do.
> It has long been predicted that these new media would challenge traditional television viewing, but this is the first significant evidence to emerge in research data. If the trends hold, the long-term implications for the media industry are huge, possibly causing billions of dollars in annual advertising spending to shift away from old-fashioned TV....
> Echoing those comments, executives at several major media companies said their proprietary research affirmed that there had been a dip in overall youth viewership in recent months....
> The television industry has been expecting — and dreading the day — that TV viewing peaks, and then either plateaus or slowly declines in the face of encroaching Internet and phone use.... Television viewing as a whole is steady, in part because older Americans — particularly those over the age of 65 — are watching more than ever before. Digital video recorders deserve some of the credit for the uptick, since they let people stockpile shows.
> But for three straight quarters, there have been declines in viewing among Americans under 35 even when DVR viewership is factored in, according to Nielsen data....[48]

What does this tell us about the future? If this very early trend should persist, as older Americans are replaced by younger generations who aren't addicted to tube-watching, will anybody be gathering around a corporal TV set to witness *Good Morning America*, the *CBS Evening News*, *60 Minutes*, *Meet the Press*, and the residue of their ilk on a consistent basis? Like the transcontinental radio networks during aural broadcasting's golden age, is conventional TV (and especially the enduring TV news and respected public affairs features) headed for a total transformation and possibly extinction when the youngsters grow up? Can't you almost hear an incredulous gasp emanating from the lips of Douglas Edwards, John Cameron Swayze, John Daly, Chet Huntley and David Brinkley, Walter Cronkite, and other TV journalists who filled the anchor chairs in television's embryonic era?

TV or not TV may be the question. And the answer — TV's fate — may be ultimately decided in the hands of people not yet old enough to drive, who (so the most recent data clearly intimates) could be headed down a different road altogether.

13

Magazine of the Airwaves: News in a Novel Format

In the midst of the halcyon days of vintage radio broadcasting — when music (embracing pop singers, instrumentalists, disc jockeys, and concert artists), drama, comedy, variety, mystery, soap opera, quiz, amateur talent, advice columnists, news, commentary, public forums, athletic contests, and still more amusement and information options lit up the dials in American homes — yet another programming format was budding. The innovation gained traction and has endured, in profusion today where it charms vast audiences of faithful television viewers.

Supplying a cornucopia of entertainment and enlightenment with a smorgasbord of choices, the form is reminiscent of a cafeteria line from which one can pick and choose what to tune in to from an assortment of selections being offered. It isn't necessary to invest in the whole shebang in order to gain a portion of the menu's intrinsic rewards. When it was introduced, this style was considered the very antithesis of traditionally established scheduling broadcasting practices. They had been the norm since the beginning of commercial radio, in fact, some two or three decades earlier. The newer mixed bag of goodies is most commonly referenced as the magazine style of programming, with multi-part features usually provided under a single title.

The cafeteria design may have come about as a bona fide corollary of the shifting behaviors of those tuning in to radio regularly as much as to any other plausible rationalization. In the early 1950s, the arrival of TV promptly siphoned off radio artists, advertisers, and audiences in numbers that were debilitating to the industry. At least two additional changes occurred to trigger a profound consequence in the listening routines of Americans who tried to remain faithful to their longstanding aural habits.

One was the introduction of the portable radio, powered by transistor-based circuitry as opposed to tubes which had generally netted a bulky, weighty apparatus with a wire tethering it to an electrical outlet, virtually guaranteeing its stationary status. (Tubes, incidentally, had been used in radios since the early 1920s.) By the 1950s, nevertheless, people could buy battery operated receivers (with electric cords tucked inside for alternate power indoors). These devices were comparatively small, lightweight, and easily transported from place to place.

A second fundamental change of that epoch witnessed upgraded personal transportation vehicles (principally cars and trucks) equipped with affordably priced quality radio receivers. Suddenly, audio was turning up everywhere, particularly outside the home, places of business, and other indoor structures. Radio went outdoors with its owners, on vacation with them, and many could hear it for the first time as they traveled between places in town and on the highway.

These two factors suddenly opened up new frontiers for aural broadcasters. By 1957, the number of automobiles in the U.S. in which radios were installed had risen to 35 million in just four years (40 percent). In that same time, suddenly about 65 percent of all vehicles on the nation's roads were equipped with radios.[1] The point that's not to be missed in the dual arrival of the transistor and the proliferation of vehicle receivers is this: for many listeners, radio had become *a genuinely mobile medium* for the very first time. While the notion may seem quaint to us in the 21st century, many radio fans were just becoming accustomed to hearing the sensation of ethereal sounds wherever they might be — at home or someplace else.

As the price of radios decreased, too, the number of sets in use sharply increased. Fifteen dollars or less was the going rate for small table-model radios complete with scant internal circuitry. By the mid–1950s, legions of U.S. domiciles sported multiple receivers in bedrooms, kitchens, attics, basements, garages, etc., beyond the enduring larger sets (including table models and floor consoles) that had traditionally occupied space in America's living rooms for many years.

All of this appeared to create an opening for new types of programming formats. The magazine style (or cafeteria plan) was one of those that could thrive in such an environment. With the ability to tune in and tune out easily, maybe the table had been set for just such a time as that. Let's proceed to explore the concept in greater detail, giving scrupulous attention to its history. Several antecedents of the widespread adoption of that formula may have popped up in local markets across the country, sharply contrasted with the more familiar genres (comedy, mystery, music, games, and so on). In the 1950s, at many stations a wall of rock 'n' roll spinmeisters stood at the forefront of locally generated programming. Occasionally, the wax spun was interrupted by chronic news dispatches. Certainly the intrusion of a cafeteria plan into the programming mix would have been presumably noticed at once by a station's most ardent devotees.

Although it might be difficult to allege unreservedly that any single area, market, station, or individual can be credited with conceiving the magazine style of broadcasting, there are some clear, robust signs that New York City — that embryonic bastion of so much of that which transpired in radio during its golden age — could very well be the cradle in which this new movement was rocked. As one media academician typified this "enviable location," its early stations "came up with many of the programs and practices that served as prototypes for American radio."[2] And in this examiner's conclusion there is sufficiently enough rationale to designate Bill Leonard as "the Father of Magazine-Style Broadcasting" to validate it without any quibbling. The approbation establishes implications for both the mediums of radio and television. And here's why, in this investigator's opinion, that it well may be so:

William A. Leonard II (1916–94), who ultimately rose to the presidency of CBS-TV's news division (1979–82) was — in addition to CBS chairman William S. Paley — the only further employee of the so-called Tiffany Network to be allowed to remain on duty past age 65.[3] Of great interest to us is the fact that Leonard inherited the local time period on New York's WABC previously held by entertainer Arthur Godfrey. On April 29, 1946, the Old Redhead went national, establishing his iconic presence with millions of soon-to-be fans as Leonard eased into Godfrey's vacated 45-minute slot at 9:15 A.M. Leonard presided over the debuting *This Is New York* aired on CBS's flagship outlet (which within months was to be rebranded WCBS).[4]

A native of the Big Apple, Dartmouth grad, ex-reporter with *The Bridgeport* (Conn.) *Post-Telegram*, and very recently discharged as a U.S. Navy radio man, Leonard had been hired by CBS late in 1945. His substantive introductory project (*This Is New York*) was to shift elsewhere in WCBS's schedule after the broadcast of December 10, 1954. Yet by then it was already set in a 15-year video extension on WCBS-TV under the label *Eye on New York*. Altogether Leonard anchored those dual watershed developments about 17 years, breaking new turf in not merely one but two mediums.

Prior to *This Is New York's* inception the bulk of CBS Radio's Gotham program creations were specifically crafted for network transmission; little of it was ever manifestly focused on the metropolitan district in which it originated. It didn't appear to matter to the chain's brass that it had an infinitely large populace residing there that had no exposure to a CBS station that generated much in the way of local features.[5] That sweeping assessment includes the local news, of all things. The news dispatches referencing the environs of the Big Apple were instigated, procured, written, and reported instead by the web's newsboys.

If one can possibly fathom it, not until the mid–1940s—despite all of CBS's global pioneering, posturing, and enveloping absorption with newsgathering techniques and a brigade of reporters that was second to none bearing instantly recognized iconic monikers (Carter, Kaltenborn, Murrow, Sevareid, Shirer, Trout were a few)—did WCBS finally certify a separate news corps of its own. "If someone was shot on the sidewalk in front of WCBS's (and CBS's) headquarters at 485 Madison Avenue," the station's personnel resentfully articulated, "we'd have to run to the teletypes to learn what had happened after we looked out the windows."[6] Hiring Bill Leonard then was WCBS's preliminary attempt to correct that oversight.

On his way to the presidency of CBS-TV News late in his career, meanwhile, Leonard figured prominently in several impeccable scenarios that were fated to yield an enduring legacy for both him and his efforts. After being a floor reporter during the 1952, 1956, and 1960 political conventions, he directed the new CBS news election unit (1965–70) in which the pattern of exit polling was instituted. Skills in use today were implemented in that era, substantiating an ability to project the outcomes of political contests swiftly with a high degree of precision. Leonard was also a member of a squad of staff newsmen that was responsible for a handful of award-winning *CBS Reports* documentaries.

Passing through a progression of managerial posts he was accountable for creating myriad televised runs that emulated the news journal layout he originally instigated on radio. They included *60 Minutes, Magazine, 30 Minutes,* and *Sunday Morning* (the latter was once aptly depicted as "a news program for people who did not watch television, with a leisurely pace more like that of leafing through a Sunday newspaper").[7] During the capstone CBS news chief phase of Leonard's career in 1981, he picked Dan Rather to succeed the retiring Walter Cronkite as anchor of video's *CBS Evening News*. Rather remained at his post for 24 years and thereby became the longest serving anchorman in television news history.

In sum, the Associated Press noted that Leonard "influenced network media stars from Murrow to Rather."[8] Among his copious broadcasting citations were a George Foster Peabody Award for manifold contributions to radio and TV, a handful of Emmys, and the Albert Lasker Award for medical journalism.[9] Howard Stringer, president of the CBS Broadcast

Group at the time of Leonard's death in 1994, lauded him to the press: "Bill Leonard was the only on-air network journalist ever to be president of CBS News, and his bravura, warm and iconoclastic style reflected his years as a major broadcaster and made him a brilliant, unique executive. He presided over all of the great documentaries of the 1960s and 1970s and was the godfather of *60 Minutes*."[10]

In spite of the professional accomplishments and accolades that came his way in spades, Leonard's triumphs frequently hearkened back to the fundamental and inspired structure he initially exhibited on WABC and WCBS Radio in 1945. *This Is New York* with its cafeteria plan format turned up in easily distinguished exhibitions in many of the subsequent projects that occupied the newsman's time and energy. That series introduced an innovative hypothesis that made prodigious use of the wire and tape recorder in its frequent applications away from the station, one of the symbols of the show.

One reviewer expounded:

Bill Leonard puts on a forty-five-minute show called *This Is New York* at 9:15 each morning over WCBS-New York (50,000 watts) — nine minutes in commercials — which is "more like a magazine than a newspaper," according to Jerry Walker's excellent description of it in *Editor & Publisher* (January 31, 1948). Leonard stresses feature angles of the news and movie, book, theater, and radio criticism.[11]

As a leading exponent of what has evolved into today's electronic magazine format, and by displaying a charmingly witty, yet penetrating interview technique, Leonard was swiftly acclaimed by a sizable fan base. His innovative methods of delivering compelling content attracted a dedicated following while keeping listeners satisfied and prompting them to return for more. *This Is New York* "never lost its way," insisted a few Gotham radio historians, "finding 'the feel and smell of the city.'"[12] Embellishing still further, they admonished: "In the best CBS tradition, it was an authoritative and craftsmanlike hour and an affectionate reflection of both extraordinary and everyday life 'here, in New York.'"

And although none of this may have been Leonard's original brainstorm, he is the guy credited with putting a *face* on the magazine paradigm (and — in the premiering radio version — more aptly, a *voice*). He was and is the front man with whom the cafeteria approach apparently may be lodged. On his own introductory entry over the ether Leonard embraced the feature angles of news, movie, book, theater, and radio criticism. *Editor & Publisher* fittingly classified *This Is New York* as "more like a magazine than a newspaper."[13] It was that certainly. And in being so it firmly established a prototype exposition: it set the parameters for a whole lot of radio and TV programming that was to thrive in the decades that transpired in the intervening years.

Parenthetically, keep in mind that the magazine of the airwaves is a journalistic offshoot in composite materialization. The motif— by perpetually highlighting news, newsmakers, newsgathering, news analysis, news commentary, newsfeatures, public affairs, public opinion, and other facets of journalism — is the consummate ethereal sample showcase. News is unapologetically almost always the spindle around which the magazine's core is constructed. At the same time, some degree of reportorial experience can be detected in the backgrounds of many of the personalities appearing before and behind the microphones and the cameras. Although more programming elements may be discerned on the cafeteria line (drama, music, and comedy come to mind), the effect of a news-oriented environment should never be underestimated on virtually any magazine entry.

Returning to Bill Leonard: if he is at the forefront of this incomparable broadcasting phenomenon as it appears, what or who was next in the line of succession? Ay, there's the rub! Clarifying that factor could be a tad more uncertain. But in New York itself—where so many concepts emerged that eventually found their way into the programming offerings of so many local and network broadcasters everywhere—a candidate ensconced in the wings who's not to be overlooked is John Wingate. Wingate became the baptismal anchorman for an ambitious mid 1950s project at WRCA Radio that, at its introduction, was plainly branded as *Pulse*.[14] (The original concept for it, nevertheless, has been attributed to station manager Steve White.[15]) This two-hour Saturday morning newsfeatures marathon kicked off at 9:30 A.M. on January 8, 1955. It was hastily increased to two-and-a-half hours. The show persisted only briefly in solitary confinement, however, and with good reason. It departed its preliminary time zone after the broadcast of June 11, 1955.

An early morning six-day-a-week WRCA entry anchored by network personality Bill Cullen (1920–90) was subsequently dubbed *Pulse* as well. The Cullen extraction, which debuted on September 19, 1955, persisted to September 29, 1961.[16] That series ultimately filled hours in the WRCA daily schedule between 6 and 10 A.M. with a couple of additional hours on Saturday mornings in varying timeslots.[17] WRCA, incidentally, renamed WNBC in 1960, was the flagship hub of the National Broadcasting Company.[18]

Although it might have copied the longplaying formula that was winning converts over at WCBS for nearly the previous decade, *Pulse* tweaked the recipe to its own tastes. After refining the basic principles of the magazine style, WRCA offered its listeners an equally charismatic potpourri of miscellany that may have been as alluring as the ancestral *This Is New York*. In its expression of the format, *Pulse* played up the *immediacy* factor of what was directly ahead perhaps to an even greater extent.

During the introductory phase with John Wingate, *Pulse* was focused on what was transpiring *that very day* and *that weekend* across the length and breadth of greater metropolitan Gotham: people, places, events, activities, and so on that listeners could actually get to if they cared—and could hear the details about anyway, whether their participation was to be live or vicariously via the media. In the incarnation presided over by Bill Cullen in the meantime, there was a daily mixture of features, interviews, and reports from all over the city in which news and information were emphasized. Music and entertainment, on the other hand—although still circulated in limited quantities—was de-emphasized, becoming minor elements of the daily agenda. This was just the opposite of the philosophy pursued at most other radio stations' morning shows. In contrast most of them were accentuating their turntables as they spun discs interspersed between commercials, amiable banter, and news-weather-traffic-sports reports.

Did *Pulse* adopt its mock-up from *This Is New York*? Maybe it did and maybe it didn't. The producers of *Pulse* were certainly aware of the enduring innovation, still running on WCBS (to the early 1960s, by the way). But there was yet another precursor of the structure that—while perhaps not totally capable of classification as the genuine magazine article complete with a large medley of news oriented pick-and-choose offerings—nevertheless it furnished some vibrant resemblances of the mounting paradigm that was soon to be modeled broadly. At the same time it would have surely offered a blueprint to the forthcoming *Pulse*. Dubbed *Roadshow*, this feature premiering in between *This Is New York* and *Pulse* emanated from the Big Apple as well and was also beamed over WRCA. Moreover, based on rigorous scrutiny of myriad sources, in the absence of anything that is a confirmable precursor, *Roadshow* just may have been the foremost *network* program to lend credence to the magazine machination beyond the confines of New York City.

[Radio's] portability encouraged new forms of programming to complement the more active lifestyles of people on the go. One theorist ... observed it had become obvious by then that "if radio networks were to stay in business they would have to adjust to the needs of the stations."[19] Perceiving such changes, NBC leaped ahead of the competition in providing appropriate responses to the new demands and opportunities. It bode well for NBC in particular and radio in general, and was a reminder to listeners that it could perform certain things a visual medium couldn't do well.[20]

Roadshow initially took to the airwaves on the afternoon of Saturday, January 9, 1954. A full year was to pass before the innovative *Pulse* wafted across the ether on Saturday morning, January 8, 1955, meanwhile. While one of those shows was strictly local and the other a chain-fed production, both originated in the same facility: the 70-story RCA skyscraper in Rockefeller Center (terrain that is comprised of 22 acres between 48th and 51st streets on Fifth and Sixth avenues in midtown Manhattan). Better known to us perhaps as 30 Rockefeller Plaza, that imposing edifice was home to the National Broadcasting Company and one of its subsidiaries — the pinnacle NBC outlet, WRCA. And both of those series invested liberally in the province of news and information, communicating to their respective audiences the very latest breaking developments. News was, from the very start, a hallmark of the magazine conception as had been long demonstrated by *This Is New York*.

Initially airing between 2 and 5 P.M. Eastern Time, *Roadshow* eventually expanded to cover NBC's Saturday matinee landscape from 10:30 A.M. to noon and from 1:30 to 6 P.M. Saturdays. Well-known network personalities like Bill Cullen and Dave Garroway (1913–82) occupied its anchor chair, another foretaste of things to come. *Roadshow* was to remain a pivotal cog turning NBC's radio wheel on weekends through Saturday, June 11, 1955.

Across its 17-month run the presiding officer (Cullen was assigned to the most hours) pursued the cafeteria approach, injecting news, interviews with celebrities, sports and political figures, and other bits and pieces into a mix of recorded music plus fragments of comedy and drama. There were some stress-free games, too, along with how-to tips, common sense advice, road safety ideas, and still more provocative features. All of it was sprinkled with Cullen's absorption with humor — an attribute undetected by adherents of the soap opera *This Is Nora Drake* only a brief time earlier (Cullen was its initial interlocutor). Exhibiting a witty nature was something that was to become even more pronounced when Cullen acquired more and more duties as a radio and TV host. Eventually he would be lauded as the most prolific game show emcee in broadcasting history, with his tenure on that turf transcending a few decades.[21]

A recurring feature on every Saturday outing of the *Roadshow* embraced multiple live telephone exchanges with "Mr. Safety." He was an unidentified motorist in an unmarked car on the nation's highways, seeking someone to recognize weekly for obeying local traffic laws and extending courtesy to other motorists. When "Mr. Safety" encountered a commendable nominee he signaled for that driver to stop and went on the air nationwide. Extolling his discovery, the NBC staffer weighed down an often startled motorist with bountiful gifts. The overarching dynamic, of course, was that "Mr. Safety" might be "in your neighborhood next," as the host reminded listeners sporadically. Motorists were thereby routinely cautioned to comply with local driving regulations and operate their vehicles responsibly.

To promote "Mr. Safety," at various times throughout the Saturday marathon a recorded singing ensemble was inserted into the proceedings. The lilting choristers belted out a bouncy jingle backed by a rollicking piano accompaniment to a catchy tune, reminding listeners — and especially any who might have just turned their dials to NBC — that they had indeed landed on the *Roadshow*.

> There's just one show, it's the *Roadshow*
> When you're driving in your car…
> And there's no show like the *Roadshow*
> For no matter where you are,
> You'll hear music, you'll hear news,
> There are prizes, too…
> "Mr. Safety's" on the road
> Just a-lookin' for you,
> Oh, there's no show like the *Roadshow*
> When you're driving in your car…
> When you're driving in your car!

Looking back from this vantage point now six decades later, *Roadshow* definitely appeared to be setting the table for an incomparable banquet. Was it a harbinger of things to come? Despite its many attributes, nonetheless, it's still *Pulse* that the celebrated chroniclers of network radio traditionally accredit for what became one of the most colossal success stories in aural broadcasting history. The deeper repercussions of the *Pulse* invasion — the formula that appeared to reinvent New York radio and, ultimately, that of stations in many other towns — is freely applied for having plainly saved (delayed, as it turned out) a network from almost certain extinction.[22]

Before continuing, a little background detail on Sylvester Barnabee (Pat) Weaver (1908–2002), who by 1953 was serving as president of NBC, will be insightful. The network, you recall, was an appendage of the Radio Corporation of America (RCA) which was autocratically run by General David Sarnoff (1891–1971). Sarnoff had risen through the ranks of NBC to precede Weaver as its head before ascending to the RCA presidency in 1930 and chairmanship of the parent firm in 1947.[23] Despite his status there, Sarnoff never really relinquished control of the broadcasting empire, intervening in any decision of real consequence pertaining to his beloved chain.

And if copious assessments are to be believed, Sarnoff wasn't regally or widely admired by his co-workers. "As a corporate chairman, surrounded by minions, press agents, lawyers and aides, [to all with whom he dealt] he was a cold unloved authoritative figure," assessed *The New York Times* following his death.[24] Early on, the senior Sarnoff had big plans for his son, Robert (known by all as Bobby), an understudy to Weaver and groomed by him (Weaver) as his eventual replacement. "Pat Weaver knew he would only get along at RCA and NBC if he did what the General wanted him to do and that he would last only until the General saw that Weaver had trained his son," a network biography disclosed.[25]

Weaver, meanwhile, was the boy genius at NBC. He arrived in 1949 from celebratory achievements in West Coast radio and advertising. He soon blazed new trails at the network by setting the woods on fire with innovative programming concepts. The young executive was personally responsible for setting in motion the video series *Today, Tonight, Home, Your Show of Shows, Wide Wide World*, and a litany of 90- to 180-minute TV spectaculars. Some of his creations were unequivocally related to current events with news segments even more pronounced then than in any contemporary stems. At the same time, NBC Radio's *Roadshow* was developed during Weaver's network presidency. You may notice that almost all of these conceptions flaunted a common derivative: the magazine style of programming.

More than any other NBC official, Weaver was determined to affect big changes in how the chain developed most of its prime time shows. He intended to wrest away programming from the advertising agencies that those organizations had controlled for about two decades.[26] The big agencies sold network time to single sponsors and then filled it with shows that the agencies created, produced, directed, and hired performing talent to appear on as entertainers. CBS had been in similar straits over the same period until its chairman, William S. Paley, threw down the gauntlet and cried, "Enough!" He initiated a new procedure in 1948, creating and staffing original comedies and dramas by CBS's in-house workforce.[27] On that matter Weaver and Paley, whose professional rivalry would normally put them at opposite ends of any spectrum, clearly saw eye-to-eye completely. Four decades hence, Weaver remembered:

> The first thing I did at NBC when I took over radio was to introduce the same magazine concept of multiple sponsorship that I had established in television, and it worked fairly well, mostly, I think, because the big radio sponsors had now entered television, dividing their advertising budgets and making it too expensive for them to control entire programs, as they had previously done. The advent of television also left the ad agencies with less time and personnel to think creatively about radio programming. If any new ideas were to arise, it was up to us at the networks to think of them.[28]

Weaver further disclosed the details of his extraordinary brainstorm for radio, evolving out of what was then already on the air. The inspiration that resulted, of course to anyone familiar with commercial network radio's history, was *Monitor*. At its launch in the summer of 1955, the series ran 40 continuous hours on weekends, a "programming service" that revolutionized NBC and what it was feeding its radio affiliates. For a time, furthermore, it altered the scheduling habits at two other transcontinental webs.[29] One advocate urged the disbelievers: "Check out *Broadcasting* magazine in the years after *Monitor's* debut and see how many local stations, even non–NBC affils, copied it."[30] This is how saving the NBC Radio network came about:[31]

> He [Weaver] had put together a group of people to work on the project that would lead to *Monitor*. One of the ideas discussed at the group's ongoing meetings was to produce a radio network program similar to one which was then airing on WRCA Radio, NBC's New York station. There, station manager Steve White had instituted a program in response to a challenge from NBC's vice president in charge of owned-and-operated stations, Charles Denny:
>
> Denny originally had asked for a contest for weekend programming between the program managers of the [NBC] owned radio stations. The ground rules for the contest were to come up with something that was different, that you weren't doing before, that would result in increased sales.
>
> White created a program on WRCA called *Pulse*, which aired on Saturday mornings from 10 until 11:30 A.M. He had an anchor, John Wingate, and several contributing reporters such as Lindsey Nelson on sports and Gabe Pressman on news. The program would showcase events of the upcoming day or weekend and review events of the past week.
>
> Denny liked the idea and presented it to Weaver, who immediately thought it was something that could work for the network. In the biggest decision he would ever make involving radio—the one that would have the greatest ramifications not just for NBC but for the radio industry itself—Weaver "greenlighted" the creation of *Monitor*.
>
> What Weaver knew was that old-time network radio was finished. No longer would audiences sit down for a radio program—they had to be "caught" wherever they were, at whatever they were doing. Weaver wanted a program that could be "taken with" listeners—travel with them to the beach, in their cars, on their vacations. He wanted a show that people could tune into at any time during the hour, without fearing they had "missed" something.
>
> So, to his way of thinking, the new program had to have a wide variety of ever-changing

elements in it — nuggets of information or entertainment long enough to grab the audience's interest but short enough not to bore them. In short, the program had to emphasize radio's increasing strength as a portable medium — something TV was not.[32]

Shortly before the launch of *Monitor* on June 12, 1955, Jim Fleming, the show's executive producer, cautioned local affiliates to anticipate "not a program but a continuous service format."[33] He insisted it was to be "a complete departure from programming of the past."[34] And it was. From the start, most of broadcasting had adhered to a pattern of set time periods that was now to be eliminated. *Monitor* would cover odd-timed sporting events, rocket lift-offs, presidential announcements, world tragedies, and entertainment specials "as long as necessary" and whenever necessary. It would bring its audience "everything important, entertaining or interesting that is happening anywhere," said Fleming.[35] Forgetting all about CNN and its counterparts of today, *Monitor* was a total departure from anything most listeners (and especially those outside New York) had ever experienced. It was characterized by "an ingenious suppleness" that brought about completely new ways of thinking and performing.[36]

Following its debut, a historiographer termed it "the ghost of radio-to-come" and proclaimed *Monitor* radio's "final extravagant effort."[37] It was a "natural rover built for speed" said *Time*, with *Newsweek* calling it "the biggest thing in radio." Terming it "radio's most effective answer to television at the time," an enthused observer cooed: "Weaver had made radio exciting again."[38] Looking back at the golden age with the benefit of intervening years, the pundits seemed to figure it out precisely. Remote pickups were as indispensable of its absorbing pursuits. The longplaying show mixed news, features, music, comedy, advice, interviews, how-to tips, and other elements in a potpourri of habitual treats. *Monitor* was a true magazine cradled in the news and documentary models that had been in evidence at least since the 1940s. Its three-to-five-minute interviews with political and celebratory newsmakers as well as common Americans who achieved something of extraordinary import were stimulating nearly every time out. *Monitor* contained a lot of these with dimensions on the passing news scene that were not readily available elsewhere in that day.

The structure was set in two-, three-, and four-hour segments with mostly well-known "communicators" (later "hosts") officiating in a multi-hour portion. At varying times over a dual-decade run, some of those voices belonged to:

Cindy Adams	James Daly	Dave Garroway	Hal March	Peter Roberts
Mel Allen	Dan Daniel	Ray Goulding	Frank McGee	Don Russell
Johnny Andrews	Hugh Downs	Ben Grauer	Ed McMahon	Dick Shepard
Red Barber	Bob Elliott	Monty Hall	Henry Morgan	Ted Steele
Morgan Beatty	Clifton Fadiman	Gene Hamilton	Robert W. Morgan	John Cameron Swayze
Frank Blair	Art Fleming	Wayne Hamilton		
Bruce Bradley	Art Ford	Bill Hayes	Murray the K	Tony Taylor
David Brinkley	Gordon Fraser	Don Imus	Barry Nelson	J. B. Tucker
Ted Brown	Allen Funt	Wolfman Jack	Bert Parks	David Wayne
Brad Crandall	Frank Gallop	Walter Kiernan	Leon Pearson	Big Wilson
Bill Cullen	Joe Garagiola	Jim Lowe	Gene Rayburn	

Of that company, several had achieved notoriety through their news reportage. Beatty, Blair, Brinkley, and Swayze professed longstanding traditions with electronic journalism, while Downs, Garroway, and McGee were linked to TV's *Today*. In its earliest decades that show was primarily designed as a news-oriented exhibition. Allen, Barber, and Garagiola were sportscasters. Some of the hosts were summoned from a stable of eminent NBC announcers who may have been responsible for reading the news or introducing it to listeners at other times. Gallop and Grauer qualify. Several more were mainstays recruited from New York radio and mostly identified with WRCA/WNBC, where they performed apprenticeships as newscasters, announcers, and disc jockeys, occasionally fulfilling gigs at the flagship station and network simultaneously. They included Brown, Ford, Lowe, Henry Morgan, Rayburn, and Steele. Of all the *Monitor* hosts, Rayburn occupied the air chair more than anybody else. He presided over shifts that encompassed the years 1961–73, eventually "owning" the Saturday morning period until noon weekly.[39]

As time elapsed, the flexibility of the weekend radio service was progressively diminished. At some juncture *Monitor* transformed into a pattern of five minutes of network news at the top of every hour as the rival chains were doing. The magazine format proceeded in the next 25 minutes with a continual smorgasbord of interviews (recorded and live), advice, how-to helps, tips on this and that, *Monitor's* "Ring Around the World" with reports of newsmaking activities abroad, updates on local events and current issues occurring throughout the U.S., snippets of comedy with top broadcasting stars, and all of it separated by intermittent recorded pop music tunes featuring leading singers and instrumentalists of the day. At the half-hour, stations could cut away from the network's five minutes of music to air local news and commercials if they wished. They returned to the web to resume the innovative smorgasbord for the remainder of the hour.

Although the 40-hour weekend format departed fairly early in the run, the show persisted with portions of three- and four-hours' duration every Saturday morning, Saturday afternoon, Saturday night, Sunday afternoon, and Sunday night. It persisted for two decades, to January 26, 1975, a durable stretch that probably startled everybody at NBC. Few series achieved that many years (mostly only soap operas); and no feature of network origination filled anywhere near that many total hours. (On one level it was correctly stamped "the longest show in radio.")[40]

When the plug was finally pulled, *Monitor* was still demonstrating the immediacy factor. It continued going live (although not as often as in its infancy) to the sites of breaking news and developing stories via NBC correspondents around the globe. In the waning years the recorded music remained interspersed between the news, features, interviews, and live reports. And the original hypothesis of being able to "tune in and tune out for what you need" was still evident.

Five years after its demise, on June 1, 1980, a full-time news-oriented CNN went on the air and eventually was pursued by a handful of replicas.[41] Is it so much a stretch to think that the departure of *Monitor* created a void in the human psyche that needed filling? Was *Monitor's* blueprint among the many that logically would have been pondered by strategists who developed CNN? Perhaps *Monitor's* longplaying formula had simply come again. *Monitor* could have been one of the inspirations that led to the species we classify now as broadcasting's cable news networks, don't you really think?

In spite of the fact that just about everything Pat Weaver touched suggested a brilliant mind, he nevertheless experienced one programming blunder of incalculable proportions during his tenure in guiding the NBC ship.[42] Most of the mainstream vintage radio historians have missed this in detailing the creative genius's collapse and abrupt departure from the chain in 1956. Pitching the magazine formula to excess, however, didn't provide the otherwise dazzling executive — sandwiched as he was between two Sarnoffs, papa and his fair-haired son — with any redemptive salvation.

Presumably it was Weaver, then overseeing NBC Radio, who led the audio chain to attempt to emulate *Monitor's* extraordinary overnight triumphs with a daytime extension through the week. There he hoped to capitalize on the portability that was available to listeners as tubes were superseded by transistors, thus making the physical appliance a true carry-along device for the very first time. That was coupled with the tune in-tune out manner of programming ushered in by the cafeteria approach.

To accomplish his aim Weaver literally had to kill the existing pattern of daytime radio scheduling.[43] It meant not only removing several soap operas from the matinee agenda — narratives loved by the stay-at-home housewives, the predominant audience for most of those hours — yet in so doing, he was breaking up some listening habits that had existed for a quarter-century. Sweeping *Just Plain Bill* (since 1932), *Lorenzo Jones* (1937), *Stella Dallas* (1938), and a few more of their ilk out the door (*Backstage Wife*, since 1935, and *The Right to Happiness*, since 1939, were dispatched to CBS) didn't win many friends for NBC among those who had been loyal to it for so long. It had an incredibly devastating effect on the network, in fact.

Weaver and company found themselves wanting when the multiple-hour *Weekday* with its magazine format debuted on November 7, 1955.[44] The almost six hours of time it filled daily was fundamentally overkill: as *Monitor* continued to add legions of new listeners to its fold, new people who stumbled onto it each weekend, *Weekday* fell on deaf ears from the start and persistently spiraled downward. In August 1956, it was removed from the airwaves. It was just too much of a good thing and piped to the wrong audience, a largely stationary one.

Even worse, years of listening habits by the faithful had been irretrievably broken in the intervening months. As NBC scrambled to return a few old daytime serials to its schedule following the hasty cancellation of *Weekday*, the chain soon learned that most of the listeners had moved on — to enduring daytime dramas at CBS (with storylines that had never been interrupted), to budding soap operas on television which were gaining a strong foothold on that turf, and to other interests away from radios and TVs. NBC was never able to recapture the matinee crowd it had once held in its back pocket, and would never again reign as a formidable weekday pacesetter. Something vital had been lost that would never be recovered. It demonstrated that a mishandling of the magazine formula, no matter how phenomenal that creative innovation was, added detriment to a network's health, wealth, and prestige.

As for Weaver, he left NBC on September 7, 1956, in a tiff over a managerial shakeup involving some subordinates he had hired. He was booted out of his role as NBC president the previous December and "promoted" to network chairman in order for Sarnoff the younger to succeed him in calling the shots; Sarnoff the elder had signaled that Bobby was ready for greater visibility.[45] Shielded from much of the decision making processes in 1956, and realizing he was in a precarious spot between relatives, Weaver decided to walk.[46] He is suitably credited with having created *Today* and *Tonight*, permutations of which are still popular on NBC-TV (as well as the simulations running on competing chains).[47]

Weaver also instigated *Monitor*, yet another legacy that outlived his usefulness. Had it not been for that embodiment, some observers believe NBC Radio would have been lost long before it fizzled and effectively vanished from the ether in 1999, so critics conjecture.[48]

Charles Garment, one of *Monitor's* longtime writers, points out that *Monitor* is on the air now — but in a different form and on a different network. He compares *Monitor* with National Public Radio's long-form evening newscast, but only to a point: "They call it *All Things Considered*. They don't have all the things that we (*Monitor*) considered 'all things.' We had music, we had everything."[49]

As this volume was prepared, no less than five network radio magazines were airing in the United States.[50] With their producers in parentheses they included: *All Things Considered*, *Morning Edition*, and *Weekend Edition* (National Public Radio); *Marketplace* (American Public Media); and *The World* (Public Radio International). All were broadcast daily or on weekdays only with the exception of *Weekend Edition*.

Television has made use of the magazine format, too, including some of those early creations under the tutelage of Weaver. The formula has been deeply embedded in television's history, going at least as far back as the debut of the news-oriented *Today* on January 14, 1952, and entertainment-focused *Tonight* on September 27, 1954. The style proliferated, eventually reaching the rival networks in similarly themed early morning and late evening productions. "Television news magazines provide several stories not seen on regular newscasts," clarified one source, "including celebrity profiles, coverage of big businesses, hidden camera techniques, better international coverage, exposing and correcting injustices, in-depth coverage of a headline story, and hot topic interviews."[51]

That cafeteria plan which often jumps from one morsel of information to another (frequently through changing interview subjects) remains fully entrenched on most of the major commercial broadcast chains today. Nowhere is it more zealously demonstrated than in the unremitting offerings of CNBC, CNN, Fox, HLN, MSNBC, and others of their stripe. If there is news of substance that is breaking, as well as tales from which the curiously minded may be in pursuit, you may rest assured that all webs will have it within moments.

Television has adapted the smorgasbord approach to its own usage in the same way it has been drawn to other genres like comedies, mysteries, music, dramas, and others. Although there are far too many illustrations of its application to recall here, a few of the more sterling may suffice. All of those cited flaunted news and information as their nucleus.

Signified by a quartet of relatively young and unknown reporters, CBS's *West 57th St.* (1985–88) gracefully exhibited the newsmagazine technique. It was superseded by *48 Hours* (from 1988) on the same network. That isn't the "true crime" drama running in contemporary times with the same taxonomy, however. At its debut, *48 Hours* presented documentaries of events that arose within a 48-hour window on a specific topic.

There are better replicas of the magazine form nevertheless, including the most polished and decorated of them all, *60 Minutes*. Launched in primetime as a biweekly feature on September 24, 1968, it was presided over by co-anchors Harry Reasoner and Mike Wallace at the start. On the first show Reasoner labeled it "a kind of a magazine for television." Modern followers of the series, now in its fifth decade, attest to it. To extend the magazine motif, "Vol. xx, No. xx" was added to the title display. Long ago the matchless feature became "the most profitable and, in terms of ratings, the most popular news program in television history."[52]

Don Hewitt, executive producer, established a legacy that extended from Douglas Edwards and Ed Murrow in the early years of CBS News to Walter Cronkite and Dan Rather in successive decades. Hewitt displayed a penchant for storytelling and dramatic investigation that turned *60 Minutes* into a provocative, oft-quoted source, frequently delivering the unexpected zinger to its zealous advocates. Sensational ratings for most of the show's run have permitted it to withstand whatever criticism surfaced, sometimes exploiting reporters' notoriety and hinting that the newsmagazine might be acquiring a lurid propensity.[53] *60 Minutes* remains one of the pride and joys of its network and multiple attempts to copy it across the years have never proven quite as fascinating to the public as the original.

Also joining the vanguard of consummate magazine creations is CBS-TV's *Sunday Morning* with a heritage that has also satisfied the masses, enduring since its inception in early 1979. Created by Robert Northshield, *Sunday Morning's* initial host was the poetic observer Charles Kuralt. Charles Osgood, the rhyming pundit who headlines a pithy CBS Radio feature, filled that pivotal anchor chair at Kuralt's retirement in 1994. The program follows a format similar to a Sunday newspaper but is offered in video form. Telecast six days weekly at its start under revolving nomenclature (e.g., *Monday Morning*, *Tuesday Morning*, *Wednesday Morning*, et al.), the series eventually was curtailed to Sunday only. Presenting five or six news feature segments per week following an update of current news, it continues to confirm a ritual as one of the purest and most widely accepted exponents of the cafeteria order on the tube.

Other television networks have engaged in like ambitions with mixed results, too.

The *ABC Close-Up!* (1960–62) documentary series was severely restricted when budgetary constraints overtook its noble aims. Its network's original evening video news anchor, John Charles Daly, presided over the compelling weekly outing.

ABC-TV's *Primetime Live* (1989–2006), under a mixture of blueprints and myriad anchors, experienced a checkered existence as a marginal magazine. Its manifold aims seemingly contenting producers only briefly, the show consisted of live studio crowds reacting to current events, live interviews, hidden camera investigations, and the public's response to various set-up scenarios. Then there were personality features plus a hodgepodge of outings on crime, family secrets, mind games, basic instincts, and medical mysteries. The whole project was eventually rolled into the web's singularly most successful TV magazine, *20/20*.

Since June 6, 1978, *20/20* has been one of the established icons among televised magazines. Although several personnel changes have occurred through the decades (Hugh Downs and Barbara Walters were its most durable co-anchors), the show's customary formulaic design — with only an occasional deviation — remains essentially as it has since its infancy. Patterned after CBS's *60 Minutes*, ABC's hour-long magazine pursues many more human interest features and fewer stories with political and international drama. Although *20/20* sometimes concentrates on a single topic for an hour, particularly if it has immediate newsworthiness, it usually breaks up the hour into three or more segments with a potpourri of issues. Once more that tune in, tune out arrangement comes into play.

NBC Television has also attempted sundry magazine projects over the years with inconsistent outcomes. No series from its fold perhaps has been as well received as the enduring *Dateline*, which launched in 1992 with Stone Phillips and Jane Pauley co-anchoring. *Dateline* has sensationalized news stories and drawn viewers in with multiple installment narratives. As time progressed it proliferated, filling some of NBC's schedule on as many as five nights weekly before diminishing to a single installment per week. In a quadrennial that some sources say were its premier years (1995–99), the newsmagazine majored on covering substantial breaking news. By 1999, in most weeks an hour of *Dateline* had broken into the coveted list of 10 most-watched series.

Inside Edition, which debuted as a special on CBS on October 9, 1988, is at the forefront of a few syndicated newsmagazines on American television. Its anchor since 1995, Deborah Norville, essentially "tosses" stories to six or eight correspondents via pre-taped overtures. Features include current events and rebroadcast pieces that supply a mix of news, bizarre crime, investigations on consumer scams and safety, pop culture features, celebrity news and gossip, offbeat and human interest stories. Originally *Inside Edition* resembled *A Current Affair* (1986–96) and *Hard Copy* (1989–99), previous syndicated series. But presently it imitates, according to one observer, "a condensed version of breakfast television." Live interviews are out; pre-recorded material is in. Sensationalism is the underlying theme of most of the syndicated series of that breed.

These and many other examples of the magazine motif intimate that its introduction on radio as far back as 1945 (and possibly earlier, of course) still wields a big stick. Now showcased 24/7 by an electronic device not very far removed, it persists in grabbing new generations of watchers and listeners as it informs and amuses at near-dizzying intensity. And in its earliest embodiments, it offered some of radio's finest hours, a legacy passed on to successive generations.

14

When It's Time for News, the Big Hand Is on the 24

In the late 1940s, an astute observer of radio — then in its prime — advanced the notion that somewhere down the line at some future time somebody might recommend focusing a local radio outlet's full time extent on a news and information course.[1] While he was thinking outside the box, wasn't he also ruminating far ahead of the industry itself?

> Radio has not *yet* [italics mine] come forward with the station devoted to newscasting alone. Such a station may one day be projected. One can dream up a station, say, with contracts with two or more networks so as to have the advantage of big network names, and with a daily schedule made up entirely of straight news shows, commentaries, interviews, news dramatizations, specialized news of agriculture, sports, business, women's affairs, "cultural" matters and the like — *and* local news. What kind of audience such a station might build is a matter for speculation.

The illusion of news ever becoming a full time broadcasting species (certainly in most people's estimate during the golden age of radio) eventually turned out to be not so far-fetched and so bizarre after all. To us in the 21st century — and now living well within the fourth decade of CNN's deployment (with enough years passing that we can hardly recall when that incessant stream of cable news *didn't* experience competing chains) — the perception of any inaccessibility to information around the clock might seem wholly preposterous. Yet it was so. If you were born within the final quarter of the 20th century, it may be especially difficult to envisage: you may never have experienced a time that there wasn't an all-news channel beaming the headlines to you electronically.

Only if you resided in a small handful of American cities prior to CNN's arrival in 1980, in reality, could you have been exposed to news all the time. (And that didn't extend earlier than the mid–1960s for most.) Those few metropolitan centers weren't airing news on television either — but on *radio*. The sage quoted above in the late 1940s, so it would seem, appears to be hinting that just such an option wasn't completely out of the question for the future. In his opinion, basically, it merely hadn't happened yet.

But first there was the disc jockey fad.

When network radio began to fade in the 1950s — a direct result of the one-eyed monster that had invaded American living rooms and took whole families into its clutches — the schedules of the major transcontinental aural chains and their affiliates were gradually reduced. A hue and a cry had gone up from station owners pleading their case to network executives for a severe reduction in web-based programming so that they might sell their only commodity (time) more profitably closer to home.[2] The individual outlets were no longer satisfied to accept trickle-down remnants of the enormous fees paid to the big chains by corporate program underwriters: these local network partners instead envisioned a mammoth windfall for themselves by selling much of the commercial time in-house to local, regional, national, and international clients, thereby keeping more of the profit for themselves. Independent stations in their communities were already practicing this highly lucrative route to advantageous effect. The web-based affiliates theorized, so why shouldn't we be doing the same?

> In some fashion, the network schedules still resembled the great days of the previous two decades in the mid–1950s. At no time, in fact, before or after the 1953-54 season did the radio networks offer as many programming hours per week. Yet by 1956 that number had begun to shrink acutely. (That was a year in which more hours were devoted to news broadcasts by the chains, incidentally, than any other type of programming.) Desiring to go their own ways, affiliates were by then deleting sustaining musical programming by the carloads. The remaining sponsored programs, except for news, were often next on the chopping block. Clearing time for network shows was no longer a guarantee to their webs. The local stations now possessed the whip hand, and fully realized that they could produce far more revenue by generating their own programming rather than automatically subscribing to whatever a chain was feeding.[3]

When the networks finally reduced their programming and allowed member stations greater freedom in sales and scheduling, the first line of defense most of those outlets pursued was to fill the numerous hours that were suddenly available to them in their daily agendas with disc jockeys. A DJ with a strong following could fill the void at precious little cost. All he needed was some turntables. There was very little overhead. Representatives of record manufacturers paid regular (often weekly) visits to every station to give away their new releases. They hoped for spins on the air so they might sell thousands of copies to listeners. Salaries for the air-chair personality and an engineer were the most tangible costs in the budget and, for what a station could recoup from advertising revenue for those services, those outlays were usually minimal.

Thus, the DJ — who had actually been there even before KDKA in Pittsburgh broadcast those infamous election returns in 1920 — began to widely obtain significant airplay. As network radio faded it was those individuals who occupied the predominant chairs in daytime, nighttime, and weekend programming shifts at hundreds of local broadcasting outlets across the country. The DJ was to thrive and remain a powerfully competitive force on the ether for some years, in fact, until a successive fad in the nation's listening habits replaced that genre. In some quarters DJs persisted even beyond a payola scandal in the late 1950s, which not only threatened but weakened its province, heavily influencing its abolition at some stations.

In the payola occurrence the record producers were compensating certain DJs with benevolent largesse that included prizes of many descriptions — cash, jewelry, trips, vehicles, prostitutes, and sundry added trinkets. In return for their munificence, a manufacturer's latest recorded commodities were guaranteed a precise number of spins on a given station's airwaves during designated hours.[4] They had successfully implemented the old "you scratch my back and I'll scratch yours" routine. When the public discovered the truth after the details hit the front pages of newspapers, however, many of the faithful addicts among a station's clientele faded quickly. To some in the audience it all seemed so appallingly ethically decadent. As a result many personalities were suddenly no longer employed with a few even facing legal consequences. The obsession with DJs was over in many places.

The next surge of programming mania to supersede the DJs and prevail at many local stations in numerous markets could be classified as talk. Even possibly less costly to produce than the DJ epoch that preceded it, talk radio often transcended individual stations that had carried the local record spinmeisters. They frequently beamed telephone call-in exchanges with hosts in far-away places at a fraction of what stations incurred in originating a show at home. (Many of those outlets still carrying music, by the way, were eventually subscribing to automated music services arriving by satellite, virtually completely removed from local listeners and their requests to "play this song." Programming music across wide spans of the ether not only reduced a station's financial expenditure but its involvement with listenership and its community as well. That disconnect with the hometown crowd could be clearly labeled a downside.)

Talk began coming on strong in the 1970s, nevertheless, flourishing at local stations especially in large- and medium-sized metropolitan areas.

> Seeking alternatives, some stations in virtually every major urban market ditched the news-music format in favor of all talk. Such outlets boasted programming schedules that were characterized by call-in programs, public affairs, interviews, panel discussions, and the like. While brief news updates were retained, they were no longer the centerpieces of each hour's broadcast day.[5]

It wasn't long, of course, until the transcontinental chains began to get into the all-talk act. A few highlights[6]:

- **June 18, 1975:** After ending its 20-year *Monitor* run, NBC debuts *News and Information Service* (NIS). It's not choosy, taking any that cough up its fees (one report says they range between $750 and $15,000 per month), affiliate or not.[7] *NIS* offers news/features 55 minutes hourly 24/7 minus brief Sunday lapses. *NBC News on the Hour* precedes it each hour. To make it work NBC needs 150 outlets, starts with 33, pulls the plug at 62 on May 29, 1977.
- **November 3, 1975:** *The Herb Jepko Show* debuts on MBS, a live call-in entry attracting nobodies with whom the host chatted about current events in their lives. It followed *Nightcap*, a warm-up feature with Jepko doing the same on an ad hoc chain linking Baltimore, Denver, Los Angeles, Louisville, Salt Lake City, and Seattle. In the 1960s, Jepko hosted a similar late-night talk show on KSL, Salt Lake City. It may seem primitive when compared to more critical penetrating, sophisticated exchanges today.
- **January 30, 1978:** Larry King follows Long John Nebel, Jepko's successor, in a 5.5-hour post-midnight talk epic on MBS. King, who earlier hosted a trendy call-in show on Miami's WIOD, gains momentum, seeing the MBS feature grow from a handful of outlets airing him to more than 200. It positions him for greater visibility (on CNN).
- **January 21, 1980:** CBS Radio introduces its popular TV star *Captain Kangaroo* (in real life, Bob Keeshan) to listeners for a five-minute weekday audio treatise titled *The Subject Is Young People*.
- **September 1, 1981:** Although it lasts only 16 months, *America Overnight* is RKO's attempt to put a radio talkathon on the air. Its appeal is limited; only 40 stations are airing it when the plug is pulled. Ed Busch in Dallas and Eric Tracy in Los Angeles split a six-hour marathon at the start; Mitch Carr in Dallas succeeds Tracy after a year.
- **November 2, 1981:** NBC Radio lands in the all-night world of words with *Nighttalk*. At 10 P.M. Eastern Time, Bruce Williams tackles the fiscal fears of callers for two hours.

Emotional distresses are sorted out in the next three hours by Sally Jessy Raphael, who moves to daytime TV later. In September 1982, *Nighttalk* evolves into NBC Radio's *Talknet* with experts in sundry disciplines beamed to stations by satellite.
- **May 3, 1982:** ABC Radio launches an all-talk series (*Talkradio*) that links two West Coast outlets initially, adds New York's WABC in a week, and 19 more stations by June 18. It's aired daily from 10 A.M. to 4 P.M. and midnight to 6 A.M. Eastern Time.

These are but a few samples of the talk paradigm that was becoming prevalent on stations around the country. They reflect the categorical shift that was made away from DJ-dominated orientations to a preoccupation with interview, call-in, and ideologically-oriented hypotheses. In the latter form's fourth decade now in most places — and fifth or sixth in some — straight talk, or news/talk (a derivative of the form), has persisted longer than any other programming motif on the aural ether. It is also one of the least expensive structures to produce, inviting the critical notion that the quality of radio you receive today could be tied to the willingness of the station owners (individuals, small organizations, and behemoth conglomerates) to invest in the outcome.

Then, finally, the all-news station arrived.

The inaugural enterprise that at long last accomplished it failed to make a go of it nevertheless as happens so many times. But a trail was blazed that was picked up by others, a few of whom ultimately found a way to implement it effectively.

San Francisco's KJBS, which had been there since its baptism as a five-watt radio outlet at the start of 1925, appears to have been the initial broadcaster to attempt an all-news format. Progressively increasing its daytime power to 50,000 watts by the time Argonaut Broadcasting bought the station from its original owners in 1960 — Willard Storage Battery Company — KJBS had fallen on hard times in the 1950s. After a couple of decades (1930s, 1940s) as an impressive challenger to rivals in Bay Area radio while it pursued an all-music configuration, in due course the outlet was in stiff competition with several that had adopted similar pursuits.

In a do-or-die struggle to regain the audience it ultimately lost, KJBS's new owners decided to try something *totally* new — which apparently hadn't been tried *anywhere* previously. They programmed news *all the time* under revised call letters — then KFAX ("K-Facts") — in a noble gesture to stem a crushing tide that threatened to engulf the station and push it out to drift helplessly in an ethereal milieu. The outfit had already adopted "Top 40" and "Beautiful Music" formats without any appreciable upsurge when new management decided to put all of its eggs in the news basket.

The changeover occurred in May 1960. You may be certain it was watched closely by other broadcasters across the country. At KFAX, the revolutionary format was dubbed "the newspaper of the air." Offering news incessantly patterned after a print journal, it aired headline news stories, a sports page, culinary tips, and a comic page (which included humorous recordings) among multifaceted portions. Each hour began with 25 minutes of hard news, regularly revised as the day elapsed. The other 35 minutes was filled with business, features, and sports news.[8] Despite the zeal and commitment that Argonaut Broadcasting plunked into its ambitious effort, the "experiment" failed just the same. Within four months KFAX had lost $250,000 in revenue plus the added expenses it encountered with operating an all-news service. Advertisers were hesitant to sign on.

"KFAX had attempted to emulate a newspaper, while the later efforts at all-news radio developed a product that was more suitable to radio," rationalized one source. "This may have been the error that KFAX made; or, they may have just been ahead of their time."[9] Although it had been a decent attempt, with the terrain for the future looking dim, suddenly that September the station was refocused on what was deemed "a sure-fire moneymaker." Shifting to a motif tilted toward Christianity, KFAX became profitable once again. So successful was it in beaming religious radio to the environs in and around San Francisco that it persisted in that pristine pursuit for the next 35 years.

The financial imbroglio on the West Coast notwithstanding, none of this seemed to thwart some others from venturing into similar territory to emulate the futuristic thinking of KFAX, albeit even if it didn't click for those pioneers. The second test in a string of all-news supplicants is believed to be Chicago's WNUS ("News") which evolved out of a deeply rooted Windy City radio legacy.[10] WNUS had emerged from WVON, billed as "The Voice of the Negro," and was the Windy City's first black-owned outlet. Chess Records had bought an earlier WHFC in 1963, and adopted the revised call letters of WVON. WHFC initially went on the air in 1926 at Chicago's Flanders Hotel and at one point shared its broadcasting signal with four more outlets. The five stations eventually separated with WHFC finally buying two of them in 1936 (WEHS, WKBI), perceptibly strengthening WHFC's image.

By the mid–1960s, however — in hopes of further distinguishing its purchase from a zillion other Chicagoland broadcasters — Chess officials decided to turn their property into an all-news effort. There is little reason to believe that the switch, made in 1965 to a full-time news pursuit, gained any lasting popularity. Citations surrounding WNUS affirm that it was merely "first news, then ez listening on 1390 from 1965 to 1975," when the broadcasting operation progressed into successive formulas.[11] Despite its presumably pithy run as a news operation (there is little said about it in records that have surfaced to date), WNUS is nonetheless linked with two personalities who achieved far more impressive recognition and accolades elsewhere.

Gordon McLendon (1921–86) was instrumental in the launch of WNUS although an avowal by the Radio Hall of Fame that this was the first all-news station is patently erroneous.[12] McLendon accomplished great feats in the 1950s, well before WNUS came to his attention. Not only was he an instigator of the Top 40 format among radio stations with DJs, he further established a short-lived 400-outlet hookup dubbed the Liberty Broadcasting System. It aired re-creations of baseball games by applying unique sound effects technology and wire service reports. The radio broadcasting innovator is also credited with instigating the "beautiful music" and call-in talk show formats.

McLendon was responsible for fostering the first commercially successful all-news station, too, located in Tijuana, Mexico. With a powerful 50,000-watt transmitter, it beamed its news in English at the large Los Angeles metropolitan market. It had been known as XEAK, a rock 'n' roll station, but McLendon altered the call letters to XETRA.[13] Eliminating the "E" from the name, on May 5, 1961, McLendon's revamped station went on the air with *XTRA News*.[14] An entrepreneurial McLendon — a man apparently never at a loss for unique ideas — applied grand ingenuity to camouflage XETRA's site of origin. While never actually stating it thus, he nevertheless recurrently projected the outlet as being Los Angeles-based.

> XETRA's jingles would say, "The world's first and only all-news radio station, in the air everywhere over Los Angeles," or "at 690 on your Los Angeles radio dial." The only address ever announced was the Los Angeles sales office. The station was required by law to give its call letters and location every hour. McLendon handled this by having them done in Spanish in a soft, feminine voice, backed by Mexican music and followed by a description in English of

Mexico's tourist attractions. He made it all too easy for listeners to assume that they were hearing an ad for Mexico, rather than the call letters of a Mexican station.[15]

And the whole operation was apparently conducted on a shoestring, virtually in bare bones style with precious little capital outlay, belying the premise of a novel and dramatic sensation as the first permanent all-news station.

McLendon had no reporters. He aired no editorials, offered no commentary. The station carried only hard news from the Los Angeles City News Service and the AP and UPI wires. At first, the news was recycled every seven minutes, but this became every half-hour when McLendon realized how many commuters, listening to their car radios, took that long to get to work.[16]

It was only a matter of time before McLendon or someone else reproduced his innovative concepts elsewhere, of course. This led him to implement round-the-clock reporting at Chicago's WNUS, the first successful all-news station situated on American soil. McLendon converted a rhythm-and-blues station operating as WYNR to a virtual copycat format of XETRA. Although WNUS was running in the black within a year, it was never able to supersede other stations in the Windy City. After four years it segued into broadcasting music once more. Its call letters were too good to totally abandon, however; they were transferred to an all-news outlet at West Springfield, Massachusetts.[17]

One of the newscasters who broke into broadcasting over WNUS was destined to gain far greater tributes as an electronic journalist elsewhere. Bernard Shaw, born in Chicago in 1940, moved from WNUS to assignments with Westinghouse Broadcasting Corporation (1968–71), CBS (1971–77), ABC (1977–80), and CNN (1980–2001). He was among the first newsmen hired by CNN as it went on the air, becoming chief anchor at its launch. Shaw garnered many distinguished honors before retiring there.

The next outlet in the line of succession of news-only operations was New York's WINS owned by Westinghouse. The station made the switch to "All News, All the Time," its tell-all slogan, on April 19, 1965, following some weeks of speculation by the trade. With no network affiliation, WINS was all over the local news stories which were updated and repeated every half-hour. Unlike Gordon McLendon's protégés, however, WINS employed a cadre of strong journalistic investigators and reporters.

Did anybody else adopt a full-time news position earlier that is still pursuing that blueprint without a lapse all the way to today?[18] Intense research has failed to supply a viable alternative candidate. We would be remiss nevertheless to declare emphatically that there is no chance another station may exist that may have embraced that scheme earlier. That takes into account nearly a score of U.S. radio broadcasting ventures by 2012 that continued to demonstrate an all-news platform. While there may have been some others within the epoch (although it seems unlikely), WINS now appears to have been the first to achieve it and maintain genuine sticking power.

That station's roots are found in WGBS in 1924, the original call letters signifying Gimbel's retail dry goods store where the broadcasting operations were then based. In 1932, publishing magnate William Randolph Hearst purchased the operation, altering its identity a couple of years hence to WINS, so named after his separate International News Service operation. Throughout its early years the outlet shifted its spot on the radio dial a half-dozen times before finally settling at 1010 in 1943. Cincinnati's Crosley Broadcasting Corporation bought WINS from Hearst in 1946, and then sold it to Gotham Broadcasting Corporation in 1953.

WINS became one of America's first air castles to program rock 'n' roll music a short time later with spinmeisters Alan Freed, Murray the K (Kaufman), and several more of that ilk.

By the 1960s, WINS was facing taut battles with WABC, WMCA, and WMGM for a larger share of the rock 'n' roll brigade. WMGM changed formats and call letters (to WHN) in 1962, the same year that Westinghouse Broadcasting Corporation bought WINS. The latter had fallen woefully behind WMCA and WABC in bidding for the youth market, however. Westinghouse, with deep pockets, a resolute commitment, and an innovative spirit determined to experiment with news alone. And while Westinghouse purchased CBS in 1995, and ultimately ceased to exist altogether under that nomenclature, the news pursuit it set in motion in 1965 continued to produce surprising results. In fact, it shows no sign of abatement as this is written, and can be easily depicted as having proliferated incredibly. Two years following WINS' move, WCBS — the flagship station of CBS Radio based in the same market — also shifted to a news-oriented design (on August 28, 1967).[19]

> The format has remained unchanged, save for minor tweaks, over the years. Currently, WINS regularly programs traffic reports from Metro Traffic every ten minutes on the "ones" (six times an hour), sports updates every quarter-hour (twice an hour, at :15 and :45), weather reports from AccuWeather as much as six times an hour (three regularly scheduled reports at :12, :32, and :52 past every hour with breaking weather news interspersed in the front of each segment), entertainment news once an hour (at :38) and business news twice an hour (at :26 and :56). When breaking news warrants, WINS will break format to provide continuous coverage of any event.
>
> In 1995 Westinghouse Electric purchased CBS, a move which made WINS a sister station to its longtime rival WCBS. Early on, there had been speculation that either station would drop the all-news format, but these notions were squelched rather quickly. In fact, the performance differences in both stations supplement their continued overlap. WINS's ratings numbers are better within New York City, while WCBS's listener strength is greater in the suburbs, possibly owing to its much stronger signal. And, from a programming standpoint, WINS's harder approach is offset by WCBS' lighter, more conversational style. Since the Westinghouse-CBS merger, both stations have continued to perform well in both ratings and advertising revenue.[20]

By 2012, WCBS — proceeding on a half-hour cycle — was formatted less tightly than WINS which operates on a 20-minute cycle.[21] This allowed WCBS a little greater latitude for including occasional lengthy interviews and analysis pieces than it did for its sister station. And while the Arbitron numbers for WINS are usually higher, WCBS generally garners more listeners in outlying suburbs due to its broadcast signal flow. Its traffic reports and news coverage include more of Long Island and the northern and western suburbs of New York than that found on WINS. By early 2012, WCBS's blueprint included "Traffic and Weather Together" every 10 minutes "on the eights." And its two leading meteorologists were in their fourth decades with WCBS.

Westinghouse made similar format changes at a couple of other stations it owned: KYW in Philadelphia in September 1965, and KFWB in Los Angeles in March 1968. Both outfits have lengthy pedigrees.

KYW's origins date to November 11, 1921, when it took to the airwaves under those same call letters in the Windy City.[22] That afternoon KYW offered listeners an inaugural concert from the stage of the Chicago Civic Auditorium presented by the Chicago Opera Company. Preceding the performance, the outfit's general director loped across an almost jet black dais to reach the podium. Not realizing that the microphones were already turned on, she uttered the opening words transmitted over the facilities of KYW, gasping aloud and apparently to no one in particular, "My God, it's dark in here!"

In the centuries shortly before the printing press arrived in the mid–1400s, town criers were widely dispensed to hawk goods and services of European merchants. They also shouted the news, a common means of mass communications.[23] Displaying foresight well beyond its years, KYW applied a similar authority as it adopted "World Crier" taxonomy early and fashioned a precedence that it would return to years hence — one that many others in the trade might also borrow.

> A news arrangement with *The Chicago Evening American* was expanded to a 24-hour service under the title "World Crier." News bulletins were read over the air on the hour and half-hour 24 hours a day. Bulletins were delivered by messenger every few hours and usually there were sufficient bulletins to provide the announcer with enough material for 5 or 6 "World Crier" insertions.
>
> The "World Crier" service started on December 27, 1922, and continued until 1927, discontinued due to complications of program scheduling.
>
> At night, the "World Crier" bulletins were usually read by the operators on duty at the transmitter as the announcers were not always available. This resulted in a couple of embarrassing incidents and the paper from there on sent over material for the "World Crier" which could be put on the air as soon as possible.[24]

Hang on to that thought. It shall return.

On October 27, 1933, the Federal Radio Commission granted KYW's application to transfer its operations from Chicago to Philadelphia. In January 1956, Westinghouse and NBC exchanged their Cleveland and Philadelphia outlets, and KYW relocated in Cleveland, its third metropolitan market. When the U.S. Department of Justice took a dim view of the swap, however, on June 19, 1965, the Federal Communications Commission instructed the dual outlets to return to their previous homes. KYW took up residence in Philadelphia a short time later. There — three months after that ruling — Westinghouse converted its broadcasting operation in The City of Brotherly Love to a news-only voice. KYW has been deeply entrenched in that mold ever since.

In the meantime on the West Coast, KFWB — also flying under the Westinghouse banner — joined the all-news junkies on March 11, 1968. It remained firmly entrenched until September 8, 2009, when the format was modified to a course of news-talk-sports. Sam Warner, the celebrated founder of Hollywood's Warner Brothers studios, commenced KFWB Radio in 1925. In 1946, the station hired a couple of New York DJs, Martin Block and Maurice Hart, to officiate over its turntables as KFWB transitioned to a record-spinning enterprise. Block returned to New York in due time and he and a KFWB colleague, Al Jarvis, credited themselves incessantly for coining the idiom that made both of them wealthy, *Make Believe Ballroom*.[25] The dual DJs adopted it for local shows at outlets 3,000 miles apart, with Block applying it on to a national DJ series later.

Longtime general manager Harry Maizlish bought KFWB in 1950, physically moving it to Hollywood Boulevard from its original Warner Brothers digs.[26] He sold it eight years down the road to Crowell-Collier Broadcasting which revised the programming to a Top 40 format (it was then billed as *Channel 98 Color Radio*). When KHJ and KRLA overtook it in the ratings in the mid–1960s with similar music strategies, KFWB was hitting the skids. That's about the time Westinghouse came to its rescue, buying it in 1966. It repositioned the station altogether in early 1968 as a news disseminator.

KFWB pursued that tack for more than four decades until CBS — successor to Westinghouse — permitted the property to air Los Angeles Dodgers baseball games in 2003. The outlet's "All News, All the Time" motto (the same applied by New York's WINS since 1965) was temporarily cast aside with that innovation.[27] Now, as in some other markets, two L.A. CBS-owned stations (the other, KNX) compete for a principally news-seeking crowd. A source observed: "In comparison to KNX, KFWB ran more sports stories, had longer traffic reports, and updated top headlines every ten minutes instead of KNX, which updates headlines at the top and bottom of the hour."[28]

In 2008, KNX and KFWB were jointly marketed to advertisers and audiences as *CBS News Radio LA*.[29] Certain unique events have been simulcast on both stations, substantially increasing the number of accessible listeners. From 2008 forward, assigning exclusive field correspondents for the dual stations ended. Since then lone reporters file one story for both outlets.

While the stations just explored were generally successful in their bids for news-oriented listeners, even as some competed with sister stations in the same market, quite early Westinghouse found that those pursuits meant tougher sledding in Chicago. In the mid–1970s, the broadcaster attempted to overtake CBS's all-news WBBM in the Windy City by reprogramming its WIND to news part-time. It just didn't work, and after selling the station in 1985, Westinghouse bought WMAQ from NBC in 1988. The new owner converted it to a full-time news outlet and once again secured less than stunning results. Not every time out has a conversion to news programming achieved a desirable response.

CBS was the first broadcaster that attempted to mimic Westinghouse's all-news formula. WINS' triumph as an all-news station was enough to spur WCBS to make the switch in the summer of 1967, yet WCBS didn't engage in full-time news activity until 1970. In the same epoch, however, CBS was moving vigorously to add the same dynamic to five more CBS owned and operated AM outlets: KNX, Los Angeles; WBBM, Chicago; WCAU, Philadelphia; KCBS, San Francisco; and WTOP, Washington, D.C. (CBS owned a 45 percent share of the latter at the time, and all of the others outright.)

One of these — San Francisco's KCBS — is a storied outlet with a claim to fame that hypothetically, at least, extends all the way back to the experiments of Charles David Herrold in 1909. The tie helps boost the commercial enterprise's identity as "the oldest continuously broadcasting station in the United States and maybe the world." The metaphor may be disputed in some circles but it also may have enough validation to be perceived as credibly relevant.

Herrold (1875–1947) was a communications pioneer long before the fabrication of radio stations as we know them. This "father of broadcasting" (as he was prominently attributed following his death) spent his life fascinated by science. He tinkered with copious inventions from an early age and held patents on several mechanisms that he developed. After teaching engineering at a Stockton, California, institution of higher learning for a few years, Herrold relocated in 1909 to San Jose. There he opened Herrold College of Engineering and Wireless. The prof and his students were eventually able to transmit the human voice a distance of 20 miles using primitive equipment they rigged up together.

> The only radio communication that amateur radio operators of the period had ever heard was Morse code. So, it was quite a thrill for them to hear voices coming out of headphones that usually produced only dots and dashes....
> Once Herrold realized he had an audience of eager radio experimenters, he began to entertain them. He would discuss news items and read clippings from the newspaper, or play records from his phonograph. This got to be a more and more important part of the school's operations, and regular programs were heard from the station as early as 1910.
> Herrold's wife Sylvia later got into the act. Using many techniques of the modern disk

jockey, she regularly aired what she called her "Little Ham Program." ... She would borrow records from a local music store "just for the sake of advertising the records to these young operators with their little galena sets.... They would run down the next day to be sure to buy the one they heard on the radio the night before." And she encouraged regular listeners by running contests. "We would ask them to come in and sign their names, where they lived, and where they had their little receiving sets ... and we would give away a prize each week."

This is the basis for KCBS' claim to be the nation's first broadcasting station. In order to be first, a station would have to be on the air earlier than any other, broadcasting on a regularly scheduled basis, and would have to be "broadcasting" in the truest sense of the word. Almost all radio communication up until then had been point-to-point transmissions, with a specific person designated as a receiver. Herrold and his wife and students were transmitting to whoever could receive them. In later years, Herrold himself would claim that he was the first person to use radio for the purpose of broadcasting.[30]

He would discuss news items and read clippings from the newspaper. Would that possibly make Herrold the first electronic journalist in history? If it does the profession could authentically date as far back as 1909, preceding celebrated newsman H. V. Kaltenborn's initial recurring 1923 news commentary over New York's WEAF by 14 years.[31] And Kaltenborn's debut occurred long before the legendary journalistic icons of subsequent epochs were to give their first thoughts to wireless communications as a livelihood for themselves.

Back to KCBS now: Herrold maintained a habit of identifying the several radio stations he started with a variety of call signs including FN (inverted for "National Fone"), SJN, 6XF, and 6XE. He often went on the air in the early days with a simple greeting: "San Jose calling." It was a hint that Herrold was pursuing a radio-telephone model. On December 9, 1921, he received a commercial license under the call letters KQW.[32] When an "arc-phone" that he developed and used more than a decade was scrapped due to its incompatibility with wavelength technology, Herrold created a tube-like transmitter to draw power from San Jose's streetcar lines. Yet he never recovered financially from the loss of his "arc-phone" and ultimately had to put KQW on the market in 1925. Although Herrold remained a technician for the station he created after he sold it, he consequently died in fundamental obscurity a couple of decades hence.

KQW proceeded through several permutations as sundry owners came and went. This included a stint as a member of the Don Lee network (1937–41) and relocating the base of operations in San Francisco. The CBS network's local affiliation in the City by the Bay shifted from KSFO to KQW in 1942. Seven years beyond that CBS bought KQW outright and altered its call letters to KCBS. In 1968, the chain decided to switch the format of its San Francisco outlet altogether to news, which was then coming into vogue but still untried in most markets.

Parenthetically, Westinghouse Electric Corporation — which owned KPIX, the CBS-TV outlet in San Francisco — purchased CBS itself in 1995. This united the Bay Area's oldest radio and television stations in joint ownership. In May 2006, KCBS and KPIX-TV transferred their San Jose news bureau to the Fairmont Office Tower at 50 West San Fernando Street, San Jose. It happened to be the very same site at which Charles Herrold had made his groundbreaking experimental broadcasts 97 years earlier. Although CBS management hadn't been aware of the history of the San Fernando Street address when the move was planned, once informed of it, they touted Herrold's contributions as one of the architects of broadcasting. The pioneer inventor was properly signified during the news bureau's formal opening ceremonial occasion.

By the mid–1970s, all-news — news all the time — was the fastest-growing concept in commercial broadcasting. But it grew too fast. Some station owners, trusting the wide appeal of news, went in over their heads. They had to give up news around the clock and return to lower-budget programming. While about 50 radio stations were all-news in 1985, the number had dropped to 28 in 1990.[33] The trend was to combine news with talk and call-ins. Talk has wide appeal. And it is cheap.[34]

The following schedule seemed to be emblematic of the full-time U.S. radio stations devoting their programming exclusively to news and information near the end of 2011 and the beginning of 2012.[35] This is the weekday cycle sustained by Washington, D.C.'s WTOP-FM. Notice the repetition in the pattern, and obvious extra time inserted for commercials and other pertinent announcements.

12:00 A.M.	*CBS News*
12:04 A.M.	*WTOP Top Local Stories*
12:08 A.M.	*WTOP Traffic & Weather Together*
12:15 A.M.	*WTOP Money News*
12:18 A.M.	*WTOP Traffic & Weather Together*
12:20 A.M.	*WTOP Live Interviews*
12:28 A.M.	*WTOP Traffic & Weather Together*
12:38 A.M.	*WTOP Traffic & Weather Together*
12:45 A.M.	*WTOP Money News*
12:48 A.M.	*WTOP Traffic & Weather Together*
12:50 A.M.	*WTOP Live Interviews*
12:58 A.M.	*WTOP Traffic & Weather Together*

(*Each hour repeats as above throughout the remainder of the 24-hour cycle.*)

There were 13 full-time U.S. commercial radio stations generating most of their own news product 24/7 in early 2012. Four more originated the bulk of their news to air at designated times in each 24-hour period. The latter station quartet engaged in one or more added components (e.g., public affairs forums, personality-driven telephone call-in features, sporting events, syndicated shows, etc.) during a portion of certain 24-hour zones. One more news outlet didn't create its own material but drew on other news sources altogether by simulcasting them over its signal.

At the same time, there were scores of American radio stations demonstrating the news-talk format, many of those 24 hours daily. Weighed against the quartet previously mentioned, most of these *other* news-talk outlets were heavily invested in *talk* with fairly succinct news report deliveries as a rule except in response to major breaking events.

In the meantime, the programming of a few of the 13 full-time news outlets was simulcast on one or more sister stations within the same market or geographical territory. Collectively, a majority of that 13 maintained a fleet of on-air personalities with individuals specifically designated as anchors, news correspondents, newsfeature correspondents, weathercasters, traffic reporters, and sportscasters.

The 18 current clearly identifiable commercial news stations in America (in early 2012) are presented here alphabetically by market.

Market	*Station*	*Owner*
Albany, New York	WUAM-AM*	Anastos Media Group, Inc.
Boston, Massachusetts	WBZ-AM†	CBS Radio, Inc.
Chicago, Illinois	WBBM-AM	CBS Radio, Inc.
Chicago, Illinois	WIQI-FM	Merlin Media

Market	Station	Owner
Dallas, Texas	KRLD-AM	CBS Radio, Inc.
Detroit, Michigan	WWJ-AM	CBS Radio, Inc.
Fort Myers, Florida	WINK-AM†	Fort Myers Broadcasting
Houston, Texas	KROI-FM	Radio One, Inc.
Los Angeles, California	KNX-AM	CBS Radio, Inc.
New York, New York	WCBS-AM	CBS Radio, Inc.
New York, New York	WBBR-AM	Bloomberg L.P.
New York, New York	WINS-AM	CBS Radio, Inc.
Philadelphia, Pennsylvania	KYW-AM	CBS Radio, Inc.
Pittsburgh, Pennsylvania	KQV-AM†	Calvary, Inc.
San Francisco, California	KCBS-AM-FM	CBS Radio, Inc.
San Jose, California	KLIV-AM†	Empire Broadcasting
Seattle, Washington	KOMO-AM-FM	Fisher Communications
Washington, D.C.	WTOP-FM	Hubbard Broadcasting

*Airs simulcast news from other sources.
†All-news in predominant hours, otherwise news-talk or sports formatting.

The financial commitment to round-the-clock news operations with numerous full- or part-time staff members is — as could be expected — quite expensive. If the proof is in the pudding (product), nevertheless, those journalists appear to be accomplishing the intent of their efforts in awesome style. Tuning them in for a while online can be not only mesmerizing but convincing. It hints that they well may be on to something worthwhile. Furthermore, it suggests that it may not be so long before we are witnessing an infusion of all news-oriented aural broadcast formatting in metropolitan centers in many other markets in this country. (When it comes to news, the big hand is on 24.)

You might check out those now engaged in performing in that arena. Then render your own verdict after engaging sufficient time to hear a healthy sample. The professionalism, you may well think, could rival almost anything you have become accustomed to on the nation's transcontinental radio chains across the years.

15

Baubles, Bangles, Gadgetry: New Marvels Dispatch News

The annual International Consumer Electronics Show (ICES) in Las Vegas early in 2012 drew 150,000 sharp industry purchasers and press corps to embrace acres of gleaming technological marvels. In a veritable showcase of glittering baubles, bangles, and bright shiny gadgetry, 3,100 booths were stocked with groovy tablets, thin TV screens, superthin laptops, and automated phones. Legions of stunning creations were destined next for a showroom near you, there to saturate retailers' shelves with never-before-glimpsed imaginative wonders that will whet the appetites of a populace operating largely on credit and freely committed to a buying-binge lifestyle. And many of those beguiling communications-focused devices will diffuse the aural news, information, and amusement that for decades was confined to handheld, battery-operated transistor units or — still earlier — wired table and console models. Are you ready to acquire what's happening instantly in forms that deliver gusto and kick? By the time you read this your opportunity may be waiting (or passed, as newer widgets penetrate retail counters).

At ICES 2012 there were 55-inch awesomely clear, crisp, colorful, expensive OLED TV screens (the largest until then had been just 11-inch). According to one observer with an imagination working overtime, the new ones were "so thin, you could shave with them."[1] There were many more prototypes for future absorption, including TVs on which two people could view two different channels concurrently on the same screen (think special glasses with built-in earbuds for dual users to accomplish the feat). Some other forward-thinking conceptions distinguish their owners' faces and accept voice commands. There were thin, battery-powered, cordless screens in multiple dimensions — and mobile enough to be toted everywhere. "Now when thieves rob your house, they don't even have to unplug anything," a reporter chuckled.[2]

Ultra-thin Android tablets, smartphones that attach to anything (a dog's collar, for instance, to alert you that he's left your yard); that let you unlock your home, remotely control the temperature and lights; that warn you of impending time and locations of law enforcement speed traps; that vibrate your wristwatch when a call, text, or email arrives; that exhibit incredibly lengthy battery life, and even include eyeglasses with progressive lenses that add or subtract magnification with a simple touch — all awaiting your inspection. Some will deliver breaking news — the headlines only, or complete details — to a magnificently crafted superthin tablet you hold in your hand. And who knows? You just might be the first kid on your block to own one!

A quarter-century ago, a leading journalism educator, author, and contributor to the fundamental periodicals of his trade allowed this about how so many of us would be receiving our news bulletins in the future[3]:

> Much of the globe has already been wired. While the electronic conduits promise to become still more numerous and efficient, we already possess the technological capability to collect news instantly from almost anywhere in the world ... and then transmit it instantly to almost anywhere in the world.... It is difficult to imagine the news becoming much faster or more far-reaching. But technology has outstripped our imagination before....
>
> Soon the *news* in magazines, and eventually newspapers, will ... be tailored to the tastes of individual readers. By forwarding their preferences, readers will in essence be able to create their own news magazines or newspapers — including, should they so desire, all the information correspondents have gathered on African politics but nothing on Hollywood or baseball. Customized radio or television newscasts — available at any time of the day — will also be feasible given sufficiently capacious wires and computers.

Although some of that has been refined a little differently, applied in sweeping terms, the academic's notions are right on track.

At the turn of the 21st century, still another prominent journalist-educator, a veteran of both print and electronic media, offered a few predictions about the rapidly evolving technology of *his* epoch and its impending influence on news delivery.[4]

> The union of cell phones and the Internet promises to be a lasting one.... Coming soon will be high-quality streaming audio and video....
>
> The key for all these devices, and for the future of Internet use, is "transparency" — use of the Web as an integral part of daily life. As technology improves and Internet access and use become faster and easier, people will go online as part of their everyday routine.... When this comes about, the Web will be used increasingly for mundane tasks such as getting weather forecasts, checking movie theater schedules, getting traffic reports, and anything else that people want with the least amount of trouble.... Fiber-optic cable will allow a telephone line to serve dual purposes: standard voice communication and "always-on" connection to the Internet....
>
> Presumably, this easier access to the Internet will affect news consumption. In addition to quick hits for nuggets of information, checking the news might become more of a habit. For many people, this will not be a substantial commitment to get detailed background material but just a check to make sure the local community and the world are still in one piece. News organizations must make such news presentation accessible and interesting. Ideally, it will entice the consumer to dip deeper into the reservoir of information, either at first visit or later. The easier the access and the more user-friendly the news site, the more likely it becomes that the rate of online news consumption will increase.

And so it is. Have you been there and done that? Perhaps — many have been experiencing it for a very long while. Plus a whole lot more. The evolving technological revolution that appears to know no deceleration or completion continues to roll along at a dizzying clip. Routinely it delivers newer, faster, more comprehensive phenomena that dazzle our senses with their ability to obtain what's out there. A large part of it is information we now depend upon to fill in details as well as to improve our lives, perceptibly so at least.

"Coming soon will be high-quality streaming audio and video," said the man. Actually it has been here for a while. Although not operating as perfectly in the past as it is today, streaming has been with us for so long that all but the most inveterate novice among computer users has sampled its wares. With an Internet connection, streaming permits the transmission of fragments of information and entertainment from a given source (a video, for instance) to a personal computer, laptop, or tablet. The application is in manifold exploitation: one of its prime uses is capturing what's going out over the ether from radio stations across this country and around the world in real time. Streaming is capable of doing the same for many TV shows once they have been made available for individual access by a network. In so many diverse structures exposition and entertainment have become spontaneous (and possibly indispensable) for tablets, cellphones, computers, and Internet-connected TVs.

The first traditional radio station to broadcast on the Internet, WXYC-FM in Chapel Hill, North Carolina, began to convert us at the inaugural of its new form on November 7, 1994.[5] Meanwhile, Atlanta's WREK-FM similarly launched streaming on the same day but did not advertise it until sometime afterward.[6] Today more people hear online radio than satellite radio, high-definition radio, podcasts, or cell phone-based radio combined.[7] An April 2008 Arbitron survey revealed that more than one in seven aged 25 to 54 in the United States listened to online radio weekly.[8] That year 13 percent of the American populace listened to radio online, an increase of two percent over the previous year.[9] Radio will never be quite the same again.

Just a few years ago a couple of scholars were exploring the changes in store for music in the days ahead. Their focus is altogether on music but with a little tweaking, could what they say not apply to radio streaming as well?

> Wireless networks are going to completely transform the marketing and delivery of music in the future. Internet hotspots, Web-enabled cell phones, handheld computers, portable video-game players, and of course the establishment of a much more realistic and efficient content licensing scheme will converge to create a seamless experience—*music like water*. It is as exciting and transforming as the development of the transistor radio, which sparked a technological revolution that ... drove listener behavior and revenues to unprecedented levels.[10]

Isn't radio teetering on such an enchanting precipice right now? Its seamless experience provokes *sound*— including the human voice—*like water*. It's an appropriate simile for more than a single province.

Early in 2011, News Corporation announced the debut of *The Daily*, a $30 million tablet-only news publication which had been developed under a shroud of secrecy. But a year later that electronic newspaper had failed to meet some of its creators' topmost expectations.[11] With 100,000 subscribers paying 99 cents weekly or $39.99 annually, it appeared on track to break even when projected—after five years. But profitable? The jury is still out, particularly in light of strong competition. Traditional newspapers and magazines have their own apps and free alternatives like Flipboard. While *The Daily* supplies an interesting laboratory experience for its owners, who hope to expand their digital footprint in established brands (*The New York Post, The Wall Street Journal*), not every such business venture is destined to prosper. The wireless age will undoubtedly claim some victims.

Writing of the "always-on" lifestyle that Americans in the modern age have come to embrace, Brian Chen filled his 2011 treatise with sparkling metaphors that survey the technological revolution and its magnetism for us. He references the "anything-anytime-anywhere" future that awaits users of the iPhone, his favorite essential. "In many ways the iPhone is the first gadget to come close to fulfilling our dream of the perfect device—the one that does it all," technological columnist Chen insists. "Such is the undeniable appeal of a device whose minimal hardware disappears and, in the form of an app, becomes anything its owner wants." Chen concludes: "We are unlikely to reach a solid consensus regarding the impact of an always-on lifestyle anytime soon, perhaps because the Internet and 'media' are so broadly encompassing and there are so many different ways to participate."[12]

At that juncture (2011) the iPhone appeared to stand as the foremost mechanism in a vast array of contrivances seeking to persuade an ever-thirsty public that it was something profoundly better than anything previously, and one that we simply *must have*. Millions have already purchased the original iPhone.[13] It's possible, of course — by the time you read this — something may have arrived to eclipse its success. Smartphone users are a fickle lot. The point which you doubtlessly will not miss is that for every newfangled device created, inventor-entrepreneurs stand ready to replace it with something that promises even more to whet the appetites of a quickly disenchanted clientele. Without a complete economic collapse, the surge in that direction would hardly be expected to abate any time in the foreseeable future.

In the midst of this mind-blowing, unrelenting transformation, radio — the first electronic means of getting us all on the same page at the same instant — persists by informing us by way of multiple means. Today "radio remains a primary source of news (particularly during the endless rush-hour 'drive times')," underscores a chronicler of the varieties of transmittable news and information.[14] The traditional table radio and floor console model with the distinguishing lighted tubes at their core — appearing once the crystal sets with their bulky earphones and the loudspeaker systems before them had sufficiently served their purpose — may be found as collectors' trophies now. Sometimes they are discovered in American domiciles and workplaces, often pushed aside in attics, basements, garages, and storage bins. Perhaps on not-so-rare occasions they are still working, serving their original intent.

But the transistor radio that replaced the tubes in the 1950s, and the modern lightweight earbud headphone that emerged universally in the late 1980s and 1990s, dramatically updated what would have almost surely been an altogether flagging industry. These creations are indicative of a plethora of transmission methods that have come to the forefront of technological advancement in recent years. Contemporary Americans now have access to an unending stream of news and information, all generated by modern radio evolution, some of it providing high definition sound. (Not a large percentage of the programming is originated at local radio stations any more, however, which is probably regrettable to a large segment of especially older listeners who recall how "it used to be.") Today, in addition to the varied forms of standard radio usage (including that affixed to moving vehicles, not previously mentioned), such forms as satellite, wireless, and cable diffusion all have places in conveying audio-based news and information.

By the 1960s, television may have superseded radio as the leading dispensary of current news developments.[15] Writing nearly a quarter-century ago, a broadcast news correspondent professed that TV was not only here to stay but could overcome anything in its path. Would he say the same in the present millennium?

> TV news will not disappear, because it is vitally needed. Television network news unites the entire nation and creates the global village. Should the doomsayers be right, should network news die, a majority of the people of America would have no consistent, reliable view of the nation's and the world's affairs. We would all be even less informed than we are now. Such a development could lead not only to the decline of television news but to the decline of our civilization, for the two, television and society, have developed an inseparable symbiosis.[16]

In the modern age, nevertheless, the Internet and a pool of derivatives have subsequently overtaken television to claim a large share of the function of delivering good (and bad) tidings of great joy (and turmoil). As a consequence, television news organizations have had to confront a new reality: "Either move apace with this revolution or be left behind with a smaller and less profitable piece of the information delivery business."[17]

Yet another contemporary authority affirmed:

> It has been said that newspapers are an editor's medium and that broadcasting is a producer's medium.... Today ... the Internet is a journalist's medium. The Internet not only embraces all the capabilities of the older media (text, images, graphics, animation, audio, video, real-time delivery) but offers a broad spectrum of new capabilities, including interactivity, on-demand access, user control, and customization. Thus using the new media tools available via the Internet, online journalists can tell stories using whatever ... features are needed and appropriate for a particular story. Moreover, each audience member can receive personalized news that places each story into a context meaningful to her or him.[18]

Infinite improvements in Web tools, machinery, organisms, and skills in the modern epoch currently allow TV stations, networks and cable systems to become a "bottomless newshole."[19] Properly massaged with "innovative ways to present the news," that 24/7 capability can strike fear in the hearts of traditional newspaper and broadcasting competitors. "We are using the strength of our Web medium to dig deeper on many stories in ways that television and radio stations never could," allowed one wag whose firm contracts with radio and TV stations to manage their Web sites. "On the other hand," he admonished seemingly without a second thought, "we are jumping far ahead of local print outlets by posting live updated information throughout the day."[20]

Such opportunities abound. Beyond their live coverage, TV operators have applied emerging Internet technology that lets them supply services that meet with still greater receptivity.

> WRAL Television in Raleigh, North Carolina, is among the stations with high-quality sites (WRAL.com). It offers live video streaming of its newscasts, which is useful to the viewer sitting at a computer terminal who lacks access to a television set. That service matches what the television viewer gets. But WRAL on the Web also makes its newscasts available from their archives. This is one of the Web's dominating advantages: consumers can decide for themselves when they want to watch the news....
>
> WRAL also offers an interesting gimmick to its Web visitors: a choice of live shots from the newsroom and several area locations (including Animal Cam, showing pets up for adoption at a local shelter). Often nothing is happening at these sites, but the premise is intriguing. The viewer calls up the camera shot he or she wants to see.[21]

Today, in fact, is seems hardly a week goes by that we do not hear or see or read of a new technological marvel that is destined to impact our lives, revolutionizing the way we are doing things now or in the future. Many of these innovations are directly tied to a form of communications. As a result we are discovering faster methods of finding out what is transpiring around the block and around the world.

> Radio is another growing presence on the Internet, also through streaming. The Web's appeal to radio stations and Net-only audio suppliers is largely economic; much of the expensive technology of a broadcast station is unnecessary for the delivery of audio on the Net. This works to the benefit of listeners, since fewer costs mean fewer ads. Also, Web radio is interactive, allowing listeners to chat electronically while listening, read information about the music being played, or order a recording of what they are hearing.
>
> Radio news on the Web possesses much of the same appeal as television carried on the Internet. It can be accessed through a computer when no radio is available, and local stations can be listened to from remote places. For the American traveling in Europe who wants to listen to his or her hometown baseball team's game, streaming audio on the Web is a simple way to do so....
>
> The next step for radio is the Internet-only station. An early example is WTOP2.com, a

twenty-four-hour all-news station created by WTOP AM/FM in Washington, D.C., and the Associated Press. With its own news director and technical staff, WTOP2 initially used WTOP and AP material, later expanding to provide some unique coverage.[22]

Is this any way to run a radio station? The early experimenters who had a hand in inventing radio — including Edwin Armstrong, Frank Conrad, Reginald Fessenden, Lee de Forest, Charles David Herrold, Heinrich Hertz, Guglielmo Marconi, Nathan Stubblefield, and legions of equally zealous dreamers who were able to turn their ideas into solutions — and the respected early airtime practitioners of radio news — Elmer Davis, Floyd Gibbons, H. V. Kaltenborn, Edward R. Murrow, William Shirer, Raymond Gram Swing, Lowell Thomas, Robert Trout, and others of their practiced ilk — could not have imagined such stuff.

But there it is, operating like a beacon in the night, delivering news and information, and myriad amusement and educational forms through the most incredibly amazing, almost instant, superseding applications of "the wireless." Only a few years ago many of us reading this might never have considered that any of it was possible or even imaginable. And what will the historiographers of aural broadcasting have to document in 10, 20, or 30 years? With as much revolutionary development coming down the pike as rapidly as it is, we may be assured that little that is familiar to us now will be on the horizon then — more like an exhaust screen in a rearview mirror.

Hertz and Marconi had no concept of the manifold implications for what they had started. Nor did forward-thinking Kaltenborn and Murrow catch a glimpse of where any of their reporting was headed. We, too, follow in their train, not realizing — only marveling — at what the future may bring.

As writer Brian Chen persisted in gushing over the seemingly limitless properties of and prospects for the iPhone, there were hints that some of the technology could net unexpected opportunities for would-be journalists.

So what's next? Three words: streaming live video. A host of new apps can now turn the iPhone into a video camera capable of live streaming to computers and other phones. The startup Ustream is leading this new space. In August 2009 the company launched the first app to broadcast live streaming video from your iPhone to the web. That's a magnificent feat because live, anywhere broadcasting used to be a privilege reserved for TV reporters [and radio correspondents before them] with access to satellite trucks. Now, however, every fleeting, serendipitous, or breaking moment can potentially be documented in real time. We'll have a world of broadcasting eyes.[23]

John Ham, the co-founder of Ustream, proclaimed: "People always have a cell phone on them. You can't always predict life, and there are going to be moments you want to share. We've seen people take out devices and stream earthquakes or planes landing, and there are going to be all sorts of citizen journalism events now if we have missions with this application over iPhone."[24]

Citizen journalists? Really? It has a nice ring to it and would definitely increase the fraternity of available reporters. Having discovered newer methods of receiving our news, this would turn the matter of investigative pursuits into a hands-on profession for potentially millions of added news-chasers, greatly enhancing the aura and mystique of how we get the news. And we may rest assured that the great visionaries of their day — David Sarnoff, Bill Paley, and those who helped them build the imposing broadcasting networks that the nation has relied upon for more than eight decades — could not possibly have fathomed anything like that.

Biographical Dictionary of Radio Journalists

The following is a biographical dictionary of some of the men and women considered to have been among the foremost figures of news and public affairs programming on U.S. network radio between 1926 and 2012. These profiles are heavily slanted toward those radio journalists that served between the 1930s and the 1980s. In that era, the medium commanded far greater respect as a source of information than it was able to sustain during later decades when radio was appreciably supplanted by newer communications media. There are 115 individuals included below. Be aware that while this list does not purport to be exhaustive it may be one of the most comprehensive such biographical compilations available about people who made their living either partially or wholly as journalists of the aural airwaves. Every precaution has been taken to assure the accuracy of this data. When dealing with this much material, errors are almost impossible to exclude. For any misstatements the reader discovers, the author expresses deep regrets in advance, and asks to be notified. For ease in determining if specific individuals are included, a list of all names profiled appears below.

Agronsky, Martin
Archinard, Paul
Arlington, Charles
Banghart, Kenneth
Barrett, Ray
Bate, Fred
Baukhage, H. R.
Beatty, Morgan
Bourgholtzer, Frank
Breckinridge, Mary
Brokenshire, Norman
Brown, Cecil
Burdett, Winston
Calmer, Ned
Canham, Erwin
Carter, Boake
Close, Upton
Collingwood, Charles
Combs, George

Considine, Bob
Cravens, Kathryn
Daly, John
Davis, Elmer
Dickerson, Nancy
Downs, Bill
Drake, Galen
Dreier, Alex
Edwards, Douglas
Farrington, Fielden
Foster, Cedric
Fraser, Jack
Frederick, Pauline
Freeman, Florence
Gardiner, Don
Gibbons, Floyd
Goddard, Don
Godwin, Earl
Grandin, Thomas

Grant, Taylor
Grauer, Ben
Gunther, John
Hackes, Peter
Hale, Arthur
Hancock, Don
Hangen, Welles
Hanlon, Tom
Harkness, Richard
Harsch, Joseph C.
Harvey, Paul
Hawley, Mark
Heatter, Gabriel
Herlihy, Ed
Herman, George
Hicks, George
Hiett, Helen
Hill, Edwin C.
Hillman, William

Hollenbeck, Don
Hottelet, Richard C.
Howe, Quincy
Howell, Wayne
Jackson, Allan
Jordan, Max
Kalb, Marvin
Kalischer, Peter
Kaltenborn, H. V.
Kaplow, Herbert
Kendrick, Alexander
Kennedy, John B.
Kuralt, Charles
Lesueur, Larry
Levine, Irving R.
Lewis, Fulton, Jr.
Mack, Floyd
MacVane, John
Marble, Harry

Marvin, Tony	Pierpoint, Robert	Shaw, Bernard	Thompson, Dorothy
McCormick, Robert	Polk, George	Shirer, Bill	Tomlinson, Edward
McNamee, Graham	Putnam, George	Singiser, Frank	Townsend, Dallas
Morgan, Edward P.	Saerchinger, Cesar	Smith, Howard K.	Trout, Robert
Mueller, Merrill	St. John, Robert	Strawser, Neil	Van, Lyle
Murrow, Edward R.	Scherer, Ray	Swayze, John	Vandercook, John
Newman, Edwin	Schoenbrun, David	Cameron	Vanocur, Sander
O'Connor, Charles	Schorr, Daniel	Swing, Raymond Gram	Wile, Fred
Osgood, Charles	Sevareid, Eric	Taylor, Henry J.	Wills, Bud
Pearson, Drew	Shadel, Bill	Thomas, Lowell	Winchell, Walter

AGRONSKY, Martin Zama. b. Jan. 12, 1915, Philadelphia, Pa.; d. July 25, 1999, Washington, D.C. A 1936 graduate of Rutgers University, he became well versed in international affairs while living and reporting in Jerusalem, Rome, Paris, London, Geneva, Ankara, and Singapore. His byline appeared often in a handful of leading newspapers and newsmagazines from this country and abroad during his years overseas. Agronsky joined NBC in Europe in 1940; he moved to ABC in 1943 as Washington correspondent. He rejoined NBC in 1957, and served CBS 1964–68. Agronsky seamlessly shifted from radio to TV. From the early 1950s through the late 1980s, he was a fixture to viewers of public affairs and news panel forums at ABC, CBS, NBC, and PBS, capping one of the most enduring runs as an electronic journalist. He earned a George Foster Peabody Award for his radio reportage of Sen. Joseph R. McCarthy in 1952. Agronsky's account of the Jerusalem trial of Nazi war criminal Adolf Eichmann gained him an Alfred I. DuPont Award in 1961.

ARCHINARD, Paul Jean. b. Apr. 1899, Paris, France; d. Aug. 18, 1966, Paris, France. Archinard made numerous trips between his native France and America where his family put down roots in Cleveland, Ohio. His mother accompanied him on his first sojourn in September 1905. His father joined them from Paris five months later. (Ship manifests and Census records reveal that Paul's father had initially arrived in the U.S. in 1890, followed by his mother in 1892. They returned to France by the time of their son's birth. While the senior Archinard cited his occupation as "clerk" in 1906, both parents identified themselves as teachers in the years Paul matriculated in the Cleveland public schools.) Not long after graduating from high school in 1917, Paul joined the "French Fliers" during the First World War. He remained in private enterprise in France after the war, returning to America in 1926. He was an "importer" then, accompanied by his Paris-born wife, and moved to their new home in New York. Joining NBC Radio there in 1927, he shifted to London in 1934 as newsman Fred Bate's sidekick. The chain sent him to Paris the following year as its French correspondent. While Archinard became a naturalized U.S. citizen in 1931, he kept ties to his native France. In December 1938, he reported via shortwave radio from Paris. After the fall of France in the Second World War, he transmitted from Berne, Switzerland. When the Armistice was signed in June 1945, he broadcast from Vichy, France. Continuing to serve NBC in Paris, Archinard revealed in a 1953 newspaper column that he had been present at the start of the chain's *News of the World* in 1939 and was still with it. That same year he was elected vice president of the Anglo-American Press Association in Paris, and was elevated to the body's presidency in 1955. He retired from NBC in 1964, permanently remaining in Paris.

ARLINGTON, Charles G. b. Aug. 16, 1914, New York; d. May 23, 1989, Glendale, Calif. A graduate of Syracuse University and a fixture in Los Angeles broadcast news for 40 years, Arlington launched his ethereal career at Syracuse followed by a progression of stations in key markets: Atlanta, New York City, Charlotte, Detroit, Philadelphia, San Francisco, and Los Angeles, with a brief return to New York in 1961 before settling in L.A. Arlington led a team of reporters for the Armed Forces Radio Service during the Second World War. From the 1940s to the 1980s, he reported on myriad southern California radio and TV outlets. Simultaneously in the 1960s and 1970s his newscasts went nationally over MBS. In the 1940s and 1950s, he narrated West Coast-based features for the transcontinental chains: *Michael Shayne, Voyage of the Scarlet Queen, The March of Time, Tarzan, Family Theatre, The Cisco Kid, The Count of Monte Cristo*, and more. His was a key voice on 1940s Pathé newsreels screened in theaters.

BANGHART, Charles Kenneth. b. Sept. 11, 1909, Paramus, N.J.; d. May 25, 1980, Delray Beach, Fla. Initially in private business, he rose with Thomas Cook & Sons travel agency to become East Coast manager and run Cook's District of Columbia office. Banghart joined NBC in 1942; in two decades he was a multidimensional figure. He announced for the net's owned-and-operated WRC in the nation's capital, was an NBC Radio newsman (weeknights 1946–49), and shifted to NBC-TV in the 1950s with sundry projects. Banghart returned to radio in New York in 1957 as a disc jockey at NBC flagship station WRCA. In 1962, he transferred his loyalty to CBS flagship outlet WCBS and finished his career there. Outside broadcasting, Banghart performed in a handful of regional stage dramas, co-producing a few plays at Olney (Md.) Theatre Summer Playhouse. He also narrated U.S. Navy training films during the Second World War.

BARRETT, Raymond. b. Sept. 1., 1907, New York, N.Y.; d. Jan. 16, 1973, Ft. Lauderdale, Fla. This multitalented individual drifted into radio following three years in vaudeville, teaching English and public speaking in the New York schools with sideline ventures in transcription recordings and commercial films. The year was 1941, and the versatile Barrett persisted in sundry quests. While chief announcer at Hartford's WDRC, he hosted a couple of daily DJ stints and penned continuity copy. He also acted in summer stock. It didn't last long; soon called up by the U.S. Army Air Corps, his return to civilian life took Barrett to New York where he joined NBC as a staff announcer. Over an enduring course he appeared on NBC-TV at early to mid–1950s sporting events (horse races, boxing matches, etc.) and concurrently narrated prestigious live TV dramas. On Oct. 4, 1957, he was summoned before cameras to fill in background for the launch of the Russians' Sputnik I in space. In 1965, Barrett and NBC newsman Merrill Mueller hosted an unscripted four-hour radio epic during a surprise blackout that blanketed the Northeast. One of Barrett's most ubiquitous assignments — where listeners heard him often — came at the top of many hours during the NBC Radio magazine *Monitor*, a 40-hour marathon pervading the ether from 1955 to 1975. Barrett regularly delivered five-and-a-half-minute news capsules from the late 1950s to his 1967 retirement.

BATE, Frederick Blantford. b. Nov. 13, 1886, Chicago, Ill.; d. Dec. 25, 1970, Waterford, Va. At 25, Fred Bate moved to Europe to study art in Paris (1912). During the First World War he served with the Ambulance Corps of the U.S. Army (1918–19). Thereafter, he was with the Reparations Commission (1919–30), including two years in Vienna and nine more in Paris. By then an adopted European, Bate worked for a U.S. bank in Paris (1930–32) before joining NBC in September 1932. After a quadrennial as the chain's European rep, he was stationed in London as bureau chief (1936). He completed a six-year tenure although he was never able to overtake CBS London bureau chief Edward R. Murrow's air dominance. While they were friends, the two fought tenaciously to one-up each other. Murrow and his colleagues won the war of words and became iconic in American households. In February 1942, Bate went to New York to be NBC's director of shortwave broadcasting. Retiring in 1949, he finished his career promoting educational TV under a Ford Foundation grant (1950–54).

BAUKHAGE, Hilmar Robert. b. Jan. 7, 1889, LaSalle, Ill.; d. Jan. 31, 1976, Washington, D.C. By being at the right place at the right time H.R. Baukhage — who preferred "Baukhage" to any other ID and opened his celebrated commentaries with *Baukhage talking*— went on the air from the White House on Dec. 7, 1941, with the announcement of the Japanese attack on Pearl Harbor. While others had already informed the world of the strike, NBC's Baukhage was the first to tell it from the White House newsroom, where a microphone had never resided until that day. Well-prepared for his crucial role as a radio commentator, Baukhage earned a literature degree in 1911 from the University of Chicago and followed it with added studies at several European universities: Bonn, Kiel, Jena, Freiburg, and the Sorbonne. A lieutenant with the American Expeditionary Force in Europe in the First World War, from Paris he reported for the U.S. Army's *Stars & Stripes*. Other moves: assigned to the State Department and embassies by Associated Press in Washington (1914); left to be assistant managing editor of a forerunner to *Life* and *Look* magazines; sales/promotion with Consolidated Press Association (1919), which moved him to bureau chief at Washington, San Francisco, Chicago; contributed to harbingers of *U.S. News & World Report* that carried his byline four decades hence. Baukhage's radio debut was on *The National Farm and Home Hour* as he dispatched five-minute commentaries (1932–37), launching an NBC spot under his own name in 1937, and penning columns for two newspaper syndicates. At his peak 545 stations carried him. He was NBC's Washington rep before switching to ABC where he and Jim Gibbons co-anchored *News and Views*, ABC-TV's first nightly 15-minute newscast (August 1948-April 1951). Shifting to MBS, Baukhage dropped radio after running afoul with a new MBS leader who said they were paying him too much and his comments were too long. He returned to writing for *The Register*, an army-navy-air force journal, and *U.S. News & World Report* (1963–67). Also in the 1960s, Baukhage was on *Pentagon Reports* produced by the Armed Forces Radio Network.

BEATTY, Morgan Mercer. b. Sept. 6, 1902, Little Rock, Ark.; d. July 4, 1975, St. John's, Antigua. Beatty's greatest single news scoop was one that even future president Harry S Truman didn't know: Truman had been tapped by President Franklin D. Roosevelt to be his running mate for a fourth term in 1944, a selection that eventually thrust the obscure Missouri senator into the White House at Roosevelt's passing in 1945. Beatty also scored other scoops. He compiled the first inclusive map of the European western front at the Second World War's outset. It was so thorough that U.S. military strategists used it, later displayed at the Library of Congress. He envisaged the German drive into Russia and stiff Russian opposition as most other analysts forecast total collapse. Beatty delivered an exclusive in May 1945, revealing Heinrich Himmler's plan for unilateral German surrender. From 1919–27, Beatty gained skill as a reporter for multiple newspapers. Joining the Associated Press in 1927, he was soon elevated to bureau chief at Cleveland, followed by Albany, N.Y. That was superseded by two years in Europe on the verge of war. Returning home, Beatty was a military analyst. He joined NBC in 1941 in London. In 1943, he became NBC's Washington correspondent. Three years later Beatty launched the job for which he was recalled best — as editor in chief and commentator of NBC Radio's *News of the World* weeknight quarter-hour. After Lowell Thomas left NBC in 1947 to return to CBS, Beatty's star rose swiftly on the NBC register of news luminaries. He kept his prestigious spot more than two decades (1946–67), until retiring from NBC. For a half-dozen years (1969–75), he was news analyst on *AP Newsbreak*, a syndicated tape series for broadcast outlets. He wrote and taped five commentaries weekly until illness forced him to quit early in 1975. Beatty died a short time later at a Caribbean vacation home.

BOURGHOLTZER, Francis C. (Frank). b. Oct. 26, 1919, New York, N.Y.; d. Oct. 8, 2010, Santa Monica, Calif. The term "veteran correspondent" comes to mind in depicting Bourgholtzer. He arrived at NBC News in 1946 and stayed to 1986, becoming a four-decade eyewitness of the events shaping America and the world in that epoch. At his passing, he was praised as "an exceptional reporter" by NBC-TV news anchor Brian Williams who dubbed him "a renaissance man." A correspondent in dual mediums, Bourgholtzer's tenure encompassed the nation's capital, several foreign hubs, and America's western states. That long odyssey took flight with his early assignment to the White House as NBC's first full-time reporter in 1947. Like competing networks, NBC Radio treated the 1948 battle for the presidency as news, sending Bourgholtzer along with Harry S Truman on campaign swings across the country. During a televised tour of the nation's most famous residence in 1952, Bourgholtzer convinced Truman to pause at the piano bench in the White House East Room to tickle the ivories during an epigrammatic interlude. In reality it wasn't a very hard sell as the chief executive relished those opportunities. At the peak of the successive Cold War, Bourgholtzer took a turn reporting from Europe. As head of the Paris, Bonn, Vienna, and Moscow NBC bureaus in 1953, he covered the news from the continent's Eastern and Western divides. Transferring to Burbank in 1969, he was asked to treat California "like a foreign country" which he did through extensive reporting up and down the U.S. Pacific coastline. Bourgholtzer persisted until he reached mandatory retirement age, staying a few months beyond to complete 40 years with the chimes and peacock chain in 1986. Even then he didn't hang up his reporter's cap as he continued researching and airing stories that frequently pertained to developments in the Soviet Union. He grew up to attend Indiana University at Bloomington where he earned a journalism degree in 1940. Given the lapse of time before he affiliated with NBC a half-dozen years afterward — although the records confirming military service are missing — he very likely was in uniform during the Second World War. For "extraordinary contributions to the profession," Bourgholtzer was inducted as a member of the Fellows by The Society of Professional Journalists in 1987.

BRECKINRIDGE, Mary Marvin. b. Oct. 2, 1905, New York, N.Y.; d. Dec. 11, 2002, Washington,

D.C. Breckinridge was to be the singular feminine member of the famed "Murrow Boys" tribe, an aggregate of 11 attracted by venerated CBS newsman Edward R. Murrow to report on the European war from the late 1930s to the mid–1940s. Her paternal great grandfather, vice president John C. Breckinridge, ran against Abraham Lincoln for president (1860) while her maternal grandfather was tire tycoon B. F. Goodrich. Yet she invested much of her life to humanity with legions of voluntary and work efforts that benefit those who weren't born to privilege. One of her goals to learn still photography refocused her into photojournalism. Selling text and illustrations, her clients included *Life, Harper's Bazaar, Junior League, Town & Country, Vogue* and similar periodicals plus some leading metropolitan dailies. With several assignments in hand she sailed for Europe in July 1939, intending to be gone six weeks. At Lucerne, Switzerland, news reached her that Hitler's troops had crossed the border into Poland. The Lucerne Music Festival she was there for was suspended and all other events she was to cover were cancelled. In London she lined up replacement work. Having met Murrow previously, she contacted him and his wife Janet there. He was so impressed with her that he put her on CBS three times, airing to the home audience. She exhibited "a natural radio voice — strong, clear, and confident, with an upper-class American accent ... cool and self-possessed...." Murrow hired her as CBS's Amsterdam correspondent. She traveled a lot and met up with old friend Jeff Patterson, a U.S. diplomat in Berlin. They fell in love. She returned to Amsterdam and — six months after arriving in Holland — she escaped two days ahead of the Nazi army. CBS moved her to Paris. She wasn't there long; she quit CBS on June 5, 1940, to marry Patterson in Berlin. Breckinridge tempted fate no fewer than three times. She left Lucerne on the last train out after Nazi forces invaded Poland; fled Amsterdam on the last train out in the nick of time; and caught the final train from Paris before France's collapse. Following her nuptials, the U. S. State Department said it would be "unseemly" for her to write journalistically in the delicate prewar and wartime climate. She acquiesced to her spouse's career although there were hints she would have preferred continuing to cover Europe for print media and CBS. "I liked it more than any job I ever had," she said. Instead the couple traipsed the world on State Department business for 18 years.

BROKENSHIRE, Norman Ernest ("Broke"). b. June 10, 1898, Murcheson, Ont., Canada; d. May 4, 1965, Hauppauge, N.Y. In an era in which everybody in radio did (almost) everything, Brokenshire's duties included reading the news during his earliest years behind a microphone. A bulging ethereal portfolio, meanwhile, was also stocked with stints as an actor, announcer, master of ceremonies, and disc jockey. Beyond broadcasting, he was a newspaper editor and publisher, too. "Broke" (as he was often summoned in the industry) maintained a full plate that preceded network radio's arrival and carried him into the TV epoch where he also practiced his craft. Surprisingly, the minister's son had an ongoing affair with alcohol, so fixated was he that he lost multiple jobs when he was unable to control it. His popularity with the public never waned, however. Brokenshire's introduction stemmed from a groundbreaking age in which few patterns and formulas existed for addressing audiences of aural listeners. It was people like him, in fact — after he affiliated with New York's WJZ in 1924 — that literally created whatever traditions came to be. *How do you do, ladies and gentlemen, how DO you do?*— adopted as his signature opening — was uttered hundreds of times. After his peripatetic pastor-father carried his clan from Canada to America in Broke's youth, the lad matriculated at a Boston high school, graduating in 1915. Though he joined a U.S. Army artillery unit three years afterward, the Great (First World) War ended before he saw action. Accepting a post with the Ft. Totten, Long Island, N.Y. YMCA, he pursued a degree at Syracuse University on a YMCA scholarship (1920–22). Fired from an advertising job, he auditioned at WJZ and was hired at $45 weekly, serious money three years prior to the station's designate as NBC's second flagship (Blue chain — WEAF spearheaded the Red one). Broke and his counterpart at WEAF, Graham McNamee, covered the first presidential inaugural ceremony in 1925 in Washington as Calvin Coolidge entered a full term. That projected Brokenshire to a brief turn at sister station WRC in the nation's capital (1926) and exit from WJZ as a freelance announcer, another pioneering terrain. After some false starts in producing talent shows he returned to station employment in 1927 with New York's WFBH at $125 weekly. He was soon fired for excessive drinking. That led him to vaudeville where his addiction rapidly netted the same fate. He moved on to Atlantic City's WPG, Philadelphia's WCAU (1929), and New York's WABC, the latter the flagship enterprise of the fledgling Columbia (CBS) web. Thereafter, he was heard regularly by network listeners (e.g., *The Eddie Cantor Show*, *Elsa Maxwell's Party Line*, *The Gulf Headliners*, *Hollywood Star Playhouse*, *Major Bowes' Original Amateur Hour*, *Uncle Don*, et al.) Voted "King of the Announcers" by readers of *The New York Mirror* (1932), Broke's fortunes improved. He joined NBC in 1935, quickly returning to earth when an early airtime stupor cost him that job. His pursuits took him to New York's WOR (1937), to Washington's WMAL in the same year and — following his expulsion for old habits — to New York's WNEW as a newscaster (1941). More jobs followed: another shot at Washington's WMAL, then Brooklyn, N.Y.'s WBYN (1944). Joining Alcoholics Anonymous, Broke addressed the outfit's units in scattered settings (1945). He earned a substantial feather in his cap when U.S. Steel Corp. picked him to host a prestigious new series, *The Theatre Guild on the Air* (a.k.a. *The U.S. Steel Hour*) which the newscaster-turned-interlocutor stayed with for its full ABC/NBC run (1945–53). Concurrently he was a DJ at WNBC — then the network's flagship. Broke premiered on NBC-TV in August 1948, hosted *The Better Home Show* on ABC-TV (1951–52), moderated a DuMont TV game show *Battle of the Ages* (1952–53), and emceed *Handyman*, a syndicated home repair series (1955). In the same era he owned a Port Jefferson, L.I., newspaper. Freelancing at his death — having at last conquered his foe — he was still heard over a couple of Long Island radio outlets, Bay Shore's WBIC and Patchogue's WPAC. Few in the trade had persisted more than four decades by then. Nor had many received a paycheck regularly from more than a dozen radio stations. He had done both.

BROWN, Cecil. b. Sept. 14, 1907, New Brighton, Pa.; d. Oct. 25, 1987, Los Angeles, Calif. With a 1929 degree from Ohio State University, Brown was a "distant" member of the brigade of "Murrow Boys" hired by CBS newsman Edward R. Murrow to report from Europe in the Second World War. After a stint with International News Service (1937–39), Brown joined CBS in Rome in January 1940. A "hostile attitude" seen by Italy's rulers banished him to other sites in 1941: Cairo, Singapore, Syria, Turkey, and Yugoslavia. "Although Murrow had hired Brown, they were never as close as Murrow and the other Boys were to one another," said Boys' profilers Stanley Cloud and Lynne Olson. "Overwrought and strident much of the time, Brown hardly fit the statesmanlike image that Murrow preferred." Cohorts thought Brown died in December 1941 when Japanese sank the British battleship *HMS Repulse* off Malaya's coast. But he emerged to give a report on the air, earning a George Foster Peabody Award for it. Next he was expelled from Singapore by the British for his "blistering and relentless" comments on alleged "incompetence" by them. To relieve the pressure, CBS sent him to Australia in 1942. In June, Brown took Elmer Davis's timeslot on CBS in New York. But he left CBS abruptly in 1943 in a clash over airing editorial opinion as news. He joined MBS in 1944 as one of its key weekday newscasters, shifting to NBC later as its Tokyo bureau chief (1958–62). In the waning days of his career Brown taught English at California State Polytechnic University and directed news and public affairs at Los Angeles' KCET-TV.

BURDETT, Winston Mansfield. b. Dec. 12, 1913, Buffalo, N.Y.; d. May 19, 1993, Rome, Italy. A CBS news correspondent from 1940 to 1978, Burdett's reports were prominent on *The CBS World News Roundup* in those years plus on a second daily newscast, *The World Tonight*, 1956 to 1978. While newsman Edward R. Murrow didn't hire him, he was a key member of the famed "Murrow Boys" nonetheless, reporting from Europe in the Second World War. Graduating summa cum laude from Harvard with a degree in romance languages, Burdett went to Oslo in 1939 as a stringer for *The Brooklyn Daily Eagle* and the trifling wire service Transradio. When CBS had a vacancy at Oslo, Burdett was hired and soon impressed Murrow. "The young protégé possessed an innate ability to scoot around the continent with the Nazis in hot pursuit," one report disclosed. The Nazis sent him migrating to Stockholm, then Moscow, Rumania, Yugoslavia, and Ankara — all before the war began. It was revealed later that he had been a Communist and Soviet spy prior to his hire by CBS. Summoned from Rome to New York in 1951, Burdett was assigned to the United Nations for CBS. He went public with his life's story in 1955, naming more journalists who had been Communists. Several *New York Times* reporters were fired and Burdett lost the respect of a few cronies. CBS returned him to Rome in 1956: "He was told that he would have every opportunity to reestablish himself there, in exile, but with the clear understanding that he had forfeited whatever chance he had of becoming a big-name correspondent in New York or Washington." He continued to work for CBS in Rome until he retired in 1978, remaining there to his death 15 years later. "Over the years, a whole new generation

... grew up and became ardent admirers of his reporting from Rome, without ever knowing the circumstances that had sent him there." Burdett was lauded for his "pure intelligence," for writing "beautifully," and possessing a "photographic memory." He could "memorize a script in a single reading and speak flawlessly on the air ... an anomaly in the increasingly cutthroat and cynical world of broadcast journalism," affirmed one evaluation.

CALMER, Edgar (Ned). b. July 16, 1907, Chicago, Ill.; d. Mar. 9, 1986, New York, N.Y. Having attended the University of Virginia, Calmer launched his career as a reporter and correspondent for two major international dailies — *The Paris Tribune* and *The Paris Herald*, European editions of *The Chicago Tribune* and *The New York Herald-Tribune* (1927–34). He joined the French Agence Havas bureau in New York next as foreign news editor (1934–40). Calmer was on the CBS payroll as a newscaster 27 years (1940–67). Among his assignments: *Ned Calmer and the News* (1943–44); war correspondent with the U.S. Armed Forces in Europe (1944–45), letting him air from the beaches at Normandy, France, on D-Day, June 6, 1944; newscaster on CBS-TV's daily *Good Morning* (1956–57); and participation in *The CBS World News Roundup* and *The World Tonight* heard daily on radio along with many early CBS-TV series (*First Person, CBS Views the Press, See It Now, You Are There*). Calmer was a prolific fiction novelist: from the 1930s to the 1970s, he authored more than a dozen books for major publishers, retiring from CBS to center on it at age 60. He is thought to be "the only American news broadcaster ... to have subsidized his income by churning out melodrama focused on beleaguered housewives" by penning dialogue for teeming soap opera producers Frank and Anne Hummert's *Backstage Wife* in the late 1930s and early 1940s. Those scripts apparently opened doors for him into network radio.

CANHAM, Erwin Davis. b. Feb. 13, 1904, Auburn, Me.; d. Jan. 3, 1982, Agana, Guam. Canham kicked off a network career by airing nine-minute news summaries over CBS in the late 1930s. He advanced to Washington bureau chief of *The Christian Science Monitor* next. He was that body's radio spokesman for weekly stints over ABC and NBC from the mid–1940s through most of the 1950s. As an executive of the Christian Science church, he became its president (1966–75). Late in his career Canham participated on a panel of Boston TV figures appearing locally on *Starring the Editors*.

CARTER, Harold Thomas Henry (Boake). b. Sept 28, 1903, Baku, Azerbaijan; d. Nov. 16, 1944, Hollywood, Calif. A controversial subject in a brief tenure, Carter's formal career began as a rewrite editor for *The Philadelphia Evening Bulletin* after he settled with his dad in the City of Brotherly Love. Reporting later for rival journal *The Philadelphia Daily News*, he added newscasting to his proficiency in 1930, being hired by WPEN as a radio reporter. The local CBS affiliate, WCAU, engaged Carter in 1931 to deliver a couple of weekday five-minute newscasts from the *Daily News* offices. In 1932, he surfaced nationally, covering the Lindbergh baby kidnapping which catapulted him into full time reporting at WCAU. At the start of 1933, Philco Corporation followed by General Foods put him on the air with a daily CBS newscast. Radio historians dubbed Carter "America's most popular commentator" at the time. An outspoken ultra-conservative, he was soon separated from his $150,000 annual paycheck nonetheless by stepping "on too many toes," criticizing "Franklin D. Roosevelt too often and too harshly." By 1939, he was writing a syndicated newspaper column and had already penned several books. Late in 1940, MBS picked him up as a news analyst and Carter persisted there until succumbing to a fatal heart attack five years later. A handful of electronic journalism assessors slammed him for his alleged lack of attention to professionally accepted expectations as a broadcaster. Stanley Cloud and Lynne Olson, Robert Trout, and Irving Fang disparaged his reporting while Gary Paul Gates altogether overlooked CBS's star journalist of the early 1930s. While Carter gained widespread status he was often vilified by other wordsmiths who perceived several deficiencies in his character.

CLOSE, Upton (né Josef Washington Hall). b. Feb. 27, 1894, Kelso, Wash.; d. Nov. 13, 1960, Guadalajara, Mexico. George Washington University conferred a bachelor's degree on Josef W. Hall in 1915, who served with the U.S. Legation espionage service in China's Shantung province during the Japanese invasion of that nation (1916–19). He submitted pieces to the Shanghai *Weekly Review*, ending his work with the signature "Up Close" to specify where he was in regard to the battle. But the editor ran the idiom as his name and Hall adopted it ("Upton Close") as his moniker. Subsequently, he was a newspaper correspondent in China, Japan, and Siberia; he advised Chinese student revolutionaries; and was an explorer for the National Geographic Society in Asia and the League of Nations. Typhoid fever sent him home to recuperate in 1922; there he joined the University of Washington faculty as a lecturer on oriental life and literature. He appeared on radio for the first time in 1924 with Lowell Thomas, another teeming globetrotter. The duo became radio's first lecturers. In 1926, Close returned to the orient as director of annual American Cultural Expeditions to the orient. From 1926 to 1935, he led hordes of business professionals, instructors, and students to the Far East, India, Russia, the Middle East, and Europe. Returning home in 1936, he was a regular on Newark's WOR. He wrote, lectured, and traveled extensively, including penning seven volumes on Asian and world affairs. Close narrated Fox Movietone newsreels, substituted for an absent Lowell Thomas when he was away from his daily microphone, and was heard now and then on a handful of NBC newscasts (1934–41). In spring 1941, NBC hired him as an ongoing authority on the Far East and gave him two quarter-hour timeslots weekly — one on each of its two webs. Lashing out against all things liberal (Roosevelt, Britain, Russia, labor, Jews, the U.N., allies, and a host of others), right-wing ultraconservative Close angered management at three networks. Relieved of his duties at NBC's dual chains in December 1944 and at MBS in February 1947, he never went back on the air. Close retired to Mexico where he died 13 years later when his car was struck by a train.

COLLINGWOOD, Charles Cummings. b. June 4, 1917, Three Rivers, Mich.; d. Oct. 3, 1985, New York, N.Y. A Rhodes Scholar pursuing international law at Oxford, Collingwood refocused into journalism as war clouds gathered in 1939 and 1940 over Europe. He signed with United Press in London in 1940; the following March, CBS's Edward R. Murrow hired him to be one of the esteemed "Murrow Boys" covering the war. So highly did Collingwood think of his new boss that he said he not only wanted to write and sound like Murrow, he "wanted to *be* Edward R. Murrow." Collingwood excelled, winning a George Foster Peabody Award for his reporting in 1943. For a year after the war he lived in Los Angeles serving CBS and its KNX Radio. In 1947, he relocated to Washington, D.C., as CBS's first United Nations correspondent. By the end of the decade he was White House correspondent. Taking a temporary leave, he worked for Averell Harriman, director of mutual security, as special assistant. Returning to CBS in 1953, the newsman often supplanted Douglas Edwards at Edwards' occasional absences from his network evening news telecasts. At varied times from 1951 to 1964, Collingwood aired TV series of his own: *The Big Question, Youth Takes a Stand, Adventure, Person to Person* (following Murrow's departure from CBS), *Eyewitness to History, Portrait,* and *Chronicle*. When Edwards was replaced in 1962, Collingwood was passed over twice: Walter Cronkite succeeded Edwards and Harry Reasoner was named Cronkite's alternate. Collingwood debated leaving CBS for ABC but determined he preferred to be "a semi-star at a first-class network than become the headliner at an inferior one." Said one observer: "The pull of the old Murrow tradition exerted its force on Collingwood." In 1964, CBS sent him to London as chief foreign correspondent, an ex-Murrow slot. He retired in 1982.

COMBS, George Hamilton, Jr. b. May 3, 1899, Lee's Summit, Mo.; d. Nov. 29, 1977, West Palm Beach, Fla. After matriculating from the public schools of Kansas City, Hamilton attended the universities of Missouri and Michigan, was in the U.S. Navy during the First World War, and graduated from Kansas City School of Law (1921). An assistant prosecuting attorney in his home state (1922–24), he ran as a Democrat to Congress in 1926 and was elected (1927–29). Moving to New York in 1929, he resumed his law practice and — two years hence — became special assistant to the New York state attorney general. In this period Combs became news director of the Big Apple's WHN Radio and founded Radio Press International, a global newsgathering bureau. He also penned several books. Combs was appointed director of the National Emergency Council by President Franklin D. Roosevelt (1936). From 1937 to 1971, he broadcast as a liberal radio news analyst, war correspondent, and writer, speaking on the NBC Blue, ABC, and MBS chains. From 1952 to 1961, he was also on television. Combs capped his career at MBS as chief U.N. correspondent and news commentator (1961–71).

CONSIDINE, Robert Bernard. b. Nov. 4, 1906, Washington, D.C.; d. Sept. 25, 1975, New York, N.Y. "On the Line with Bob Considine" became one of the familiar ethereal billboards Americans recognized during radio's golden age. Considine also applied "On the Line" to a syndicated newspaper column he penned. A messenger for the U.S. State Department while enrolled at George Washington

University at night, he stumbled into journalism inadvertently. Complaining to *The Washington Herald* about the misspelling of his name in a piece on an amateur tennis tournament, he was surprisingly offered a post as sports reporter. That boosted him into drama reviews, editorials, and his own column in 1933. That year he added broadcasting to his growing duties, having transferred a year earlier to a competitor, *The Washington Post*, for print and aural dispatches. In 1941–42, Considine was sportscaster at New York's WNEW Radio. Not long afterward he presided over his own Sunday evening quarter-hour, airing nationally with *On the Line with Considine*. It was named for a column in *The New York Daily Mirror* and scores of other papers. The show — persisting on radio through the years 1947–68 and 1971–75 — sometimes ran under the alternative title *Headline Hunters*. From 1968–71, Considine was a recurring contributor to NBC's *Monitor* weekend radio marathon with pithy features labeled *On the Line with Bob Considine*. He penned his column 42 years to his death. *On the Line with Considine* appeared on NBC-TV (1951–54) and ABC-TV (1954). In quarter-hour gigs the host read news headlines, offered personal insights, and interviewed celebrated figures about newsworthy topics. Between 1955 and 1960, he was a featured participant on multiple entertainment series on three commercial television networks. Considine authored, co-authored, or edited 25 volumes, penned six movie scripts, and wrote a biography. Not long before his death the man who stumbled into journalism unintentionally was named an exceptional writer by the New York chapter of Sigma Delta Chi of the Society of Professional Journalists.

CRAVENS, Kathryn Cochran. b. Oct. 27, 1898, Burkett, Tex.; d. Aug. 29, 1991, Burkett, Tex. She was one of the pioneers among women in electronic journalism and brought honor to herself, her gender, and her profession in a tenure lasting from the 1930s to the 1960s. Cravens received formal training for an anticipated career as an actress at three institutions — Kendall College (University of Tulsa today), Kansas City's Horner Institute of Fine Arts, and St. Louis's Morse School of Expression. She was to become the first feminine radio commentator on a national hookup. At 15 she acted in silent movies as Kitty O'Dare for 20th Century–Fox. In 1929, she was playing in dramas that she wrote which were aired by St. Louis's KWK Radio. She also recited narratives, vocalized, and performed Negro dialect on the air. Transferring to local CBS affiliate KMOX, Cravens was subsequently dubbed the "Voice of St. Louis" for appearing on four daily programs. A pundit proclaimed: "Her flair for interpreting current events, for doing interviews with the great and near-great, in a way that had a special significance for feminine listeners, soon put her on a coast-to-coast CBS network." CBS introduced her to a national audience from New York City in 1936. In the two years she was on CBS she traveled 50,000 air miles pursuing stories to feature. After her run ended there in 1938, Cravens wrote newspaper columns and feature material. New York's WNEW returned her to the ether in 1941. Without a news background, she didn't deliver stories in accepted factual styles but focused instead on the personal sentiments of those in the yarns she spun. Her broadcasts were picked up by MBS in the 1940s and beamed across the nation. In September 1945, *Radio Mirror* allowed: "It was inevitable that as soon after V-E Day as the Army would accredit a woman radio correspondent for broadcasts from Europe, she [Cravens] would be the first woman to receive such accreditation.... It was because, as an actress, she always wanted to rewrite and improve the scripts she was assigned to act, that Kathryn Cravens became radio's most outstanding woman commentator." She published a novel in 1951, and retired in 1962, returning to her Texas ancestral homeplace.

DALY, John Charles, Jr. b. Feb. 20, 1914, Johannesburg, South Africa; d. Feb. 25, 1991, Chevy Chase, Md. He's best remembered as the unflappable moderator of the enduring live panel series *What's My Line?* (CBS-TV, 1950–67). Most of the show's legions of loyal fans forgot, however — if they ever knew it — that Daly was among the first to tell the world that the Japanese had attacked Pearl Harbor on Dec. 7, 1941 (evidently moments following an MBS newsflash). Or, that it was he who initially informed listeners that President Franklin D. Roosevelt had died on April 12, 1945. Nor did any outside the trade realize that Daly had tutored neophyte newsman Douglas Edwards for larger duties in the same arena and era, who was to become Daly's chief competition in a brief while. He trained Edwards for a post that ultimately eclipsed him as both men jockeyed for the viewers of evening newscasts on rival TV chains. This consummate game show host, meanwhile — an affable, impish, urbane moderator — launched his career as an electronic journalist. When he didn't have the funds to complete formal training at Boston College he joined the Peabody Players as a stage performer.

After a brief sojourn in the nation's capital in 1935, Daly returned to Boston to be hired by WLOE Radio. His big break came two years hence as CBS affiliate WJSV in Washington took him on. He soon began a trek of 150,000 miles alongside President Franklin D. Roosevelt as CBS's White House correspondent. Daly covered the 1940 political conventions as a CBS special events reporter. When Robert Trout went to London in 1941 to relieve Edward R. Murrow, Daly replaced Trout on the CBS evening news program *The World Today*. For 15 months in 1943–44, Daly traipsed the world reporting from London, North Africa, Sicily, Malta, the Middle East, and South America. CBS listeners heard him with V-E Day coverage and reports from the Nuremberg Nazi war criminal trials. He jumped ship to ABC in 1949, where he was named vice president in charge of news, special events, public affairs, religious, and sports programming in 1953. Daly gained a George Foster Peabody Award for exceptional radio and TV news coverage in 1954. That same year he received an Emmy from the National Academy of Television Arts and Science as "best news reporter-commentator." From 1948–59, he was host or prominently figured in nearly a dozen TV series (*Riddle Me This, The March of Time, It's News to Me, America's Town Meeting, Who Said That?, The Voice of Firestone*, et al.). Daly quit ABC late in 1960 and directed the Voice of America for a year following the cancellation of *What's My Line?* In his memoir of the imposing panel show, producer Gil Fates exclaimed: "John thought of himself first and foremost as a newsman.... The fact that the public thought of him first and foremost as the moderator of television's most successful game show did not make him happy. I think the greatest disappointment in John Daly's life was that somebody else beat him to being Edward R. Murrow. But there could be only one Murrow in a generation, so John had to settle for fame and money."

DAVIS, Elmer Holmes. b. Jan. 13, 1890, Aurora, Ind.; d. May 18, 1958, Washington, D.C. After graduating magna cum laude from the Hoosier State's Franklin College, Davis went off to Queen's College, Oxford, as a Rhodes Scholar, expecting to devote his life to teaching ancient history. By the time he came home, however, he had chosen writing as his career. In 1909, he found work editing an obscure magazine, *Adventure*, paying him $9 weekly. He bettered himself from 1910 to 1924 reporting for *The New York Times*, penning a history of that journal in 1921. Davis left to do freelance writing, furnishing short stories for *Harper's, The New Yorker, The Saturday Review of Literature*, and others, as well as novels (1924–39). He also occasionally dabbled in radio without much success. On Aug. 23, 1939, however — impressed by his writing — CBS news chief Paul White hired him to replace H.V. Kaltenborn who was leaving for Europe. Suddenly Davis's name was widely known. *Radio Guide* observed that he possessed "an Oxford brain and an Indiana twang that reeked of neutrality"; it was "exactly the kind of homey down-to-earth manner needed in a moment of crisis." Davis was dispatched to England in 1941; in 1942, he left his $53,000 CBS post to direct the U.S. Office of War Information (OWI). By March 1943, he was on four transcontinental chains with a weekly quarter-hour summary. Until OWI was dismantled in 1945, he oversaw a staff of 3,000. Davis aired over ABC from 1945 to 1955, daily to the time his health began to fail in 1953. He had a weekly opinion piece through 1955, some of it on ABC-TV and some of it on radio.

DICKERSON, Nancy (née Nancy Conners Hanschman). b. Jan. 27, 1927, Wauwatosa, Wis.; d. Oct. 18, 1997, New York, N.Y. Like Mary Marvin Breckinridge before her, Dickerson was a capital journalist-turned-society maven. Unaware of her contemporary's feats, however, Dickerson wrote in her memoir *Among Those Present: A Reporter's View of 25 Years in Washington* (Random House, 1976) that *she* was the "first woman reporter at CBS." While she opened doors for feminine broadcasters that may not have been as widely parted when she got there, she followed Breckinridge and a handful of lesser counterparts into the intrepid conquests on which she embarked. Trained for two years at Clarke College, Dubuque, Iowa — an institution that later created the Nancy Dickerson Whitehead Medallion to cite its promising mass communications supplicants — she transferred to the University of Wisconsin at Madison and completed a degree in Portuguese and Spanish (1948). After a couple of years teaching in elementary classrooms in the Milwaukee schools, she relocated briefly to New York before putting roots down in the District of Columbia. Temporarily working at Georgetown University, once she had her bearings she took a research post with the Senate Foreign Relations Committee, gaining zeal for federal operations. She also enrolled at Catholic University to study drama and speech. In 1954, Hanschman joined CBS's Washington bureau as producer of dual radio series — *Capitol Cloakroom* and *The Leading Question*. That same year she became associate producer of *Face the Nation* on CBS-TV, segueing into an on-air correspondent there in 1960. As time passed and she became infinitely more valuable to broadcasting she covered political conventions, election campaigns, inaugurations, Capitol Hill, and the White House while globetrotting to Europe, the Middle East, and the Far East alongside presidents and other government officials. Her surname changed when, at 35, she wed well-heeled real estate investor Claude Wyatt Dickerson in 1962. Five children were born to that union within six years; after entertaining the Washington elite and visitors to the capital for two decades the Dickersons divorced in 1982. She kept her professional name in marrying a second time and added four stepchildren to her brood (1989). The days of being a prominent D.C. socialite essentially ended with the change: while they maintained an estate in D.C., the couple permanently moved to New York City. Much earlier, in 1963, Dickerson shifted her allegiance from CBS to NBC, the chain with which she is best linked in people's minds. She reported for seven years from NBC News' Washington bureau on *The Huntley-Brinkley Report*, *Monitor*, *Today*, and other news and public affairs features. Resigning from NBC in 1970, she anchored a daily news program, *Inside Washington* (1971–74). In 1980, Dickerson established the Television Corporation of America to produce documentaries for PBS and syndicators. She won a renowned George Foster Peabody Award in 1982 for "784 Days That Changed America — Watergate to Resignation," an account of the scandal that drove President Richard M. Nixon from office. Dickerson capped her professional endeavors as a Fox News commentator in the election campaigns between 1986 and 1991.

Downs, William R., Jr. b. Aug. 14, 1914, Kansas City, Mo.; d. May 3, 1978, Bethesda, Md. Downs set his goal to be a journalist early in life and never wavered. He got early practice as sports editor of his high school newspaper, managed the student newspaper at Wyandotte College for two years, and resuscitated a faltering *Daily Kansan* while he was managing editor of the paper at the University of Kansas in his final two collegiate years. United Press hired him for its Kansas City bureau after his 1935 graduation along with fellow reporter Walter Cronkite. Not long after Downs shifted to UP's Denver bureau and later to New York. He gained the wire service's plum spot in 1941, the London bureau, covering the Second World War. There he met CBS newsman Edward R. Murrow who hired him at $70 weekly as CBS's Moscow correspondent. For the next couple of decades Downs was one of the celebrated "Murrow Boys." The National Headliners Club honored Downs in 1945 for "a vivid account of the surrender of German Armies in North Germany, Holland, and Denmark to English forces in Hamburg." He covered Japan's surrender also in 1945 and, in 1946, atom bomb tests off Bikini Atoll in the Pacific. He was given an Overseas Press Club award in 1950 for Berlin blockade and airlift coverage. The latter years of Downs's career were disheartening, however. The duty he most enjoyed following the war, being stationed in Rome, reverted to Winston Burdett in 1956 when that reporter was exiled for the remainder of his career. Downs acquired a fleeting daily radio news summary in 1957, and then went to the U.S. State Department in a miscast role. He resigned from CBS in March 1962, expecting to write novels. But to his dismay publishers weren't buying. He joined ABC as a second-tier reporter in its Washington bureau in November 1963. Downs retired from it having covered the swearing-in of President Lyndon B. Johnson the month he started, perhaps his most notable encounter at ABC.

Drake, Galen (né Foster Rucker). b. July 26, 1906, Kokomo, Ind.; d. June 30, 1989, Long Beach, Calif. Although recalled for something new that he introduced to the ether from the 1940s to the 1960s — a laid-back, easygoing, conversational program style for women focused on household concerns, child-rearing issues, and cooking tips interspersed with folksy tales to keep milady intrigued — after his radio format fell out of favor with the masses, Drake persevered as a newscaster in the 1960s at MBS. While his reputation had already been established in another species, he spent several years delivering news until reaching retirement about 1971. Drake originally intended to be a vocalist and conductor but abandoned his dreams while pursuing law and medicine at the University of California in Los Angeles. Taking a part time post at Long Beach's KFOX to pay his tuition, he was soon offered a spot at the more prestigious KNX in the City of Angels. He took it and went on the air with pal Fletcher Wiley offering a casual chat series. Medicine, law, and music all evaporated from Rucker's career. He was a commentator on the CBS West Coast chain (1942–43) before a weekday talk stint of his own got rolling over KNX. From that humble start, at different times he was ultimately projected over ABC, CBS, and MBS with his chatter patter, spawning a rash of similar features in local markets. Adopting the pseudonym "Galen Drake," his national talkathons emanated from New York.

DREIER, Alexander McDuff. b. June 26, 1916, Honolulu, Hawaii; d. Mar. 12, 2000, Rancho Mirage, Calif. Fleeing Berlin on Dec. 6, 1941, Dreier was one step ahead of the Nazis who detained American journalists that loitered behind when the U.S. declared war on Germany and Japan the following day. Dreier earned a degree in political science from Stanford University in 1939, and was then hired by United Press which sent him to Berlin. In 1941, he shifted his allegiance to NBC in Berlin. Finding growing resistance to his reports, he realized the Gestapo was scrupulously dissecting his moves. Whatever it was that tipped him off, he left in a hurry, arriving in New York City early in 1942. Dreier was soon given his own daily commentary on NBC. He was in London in October 1942 to relieve NBC's Robert St. John. His assignments led to dinners with British Prime Minister Winston Churchill and President Franklin D. Roosevelt. Returning home he was sent to Chicago and by 1944, appeared on national news programs and local newscasts over NBC's Windy City outlet WMAQ. This was expanded in the 1950s and 1960s to encompass farm and rural news reports. Dreier had a quarter-hour NBC newscast daily at 8 A.M. Eastern Time (1951–56) and a second one daily at 7 P.M. (1953–56), suggesting the confidence his superiors had in his ability. "His baritone voice always made him a favorite on radio," said an obituary writer for *The Los Angeles Times* at his death, "particularly as host of the long-running show *Man on the Go*." After being in several televised series on ABC in the 1960s, in the 1970s Dreier launched a new career as an actor in bit parts in a half-dozen motion pictures. He was a character actor in numerous television dramas as well from the late 1960s to the late 1970s.

EDWARDS, Clyde Douglas. b. July 14, 1917, Ada, Okla.; d. Oct. 13, 1990, Sarasota, Fla. Of scores of accolades that Edwards gained across a half-century, the greatest may have been from CBS news biographer Gary Paul Gates: "[Walter] Cronkite and all the other TV anchormen who have come along since are the direct descendants of Douglas Edwards." He elaborated: "For fourteen years, from 1948 to 1962, Doug Edwards was the face and voice of CBS on its evening news show." After the coaxial cable linked all of the nation's TV watchers in September 1951, the pioneering journalist introduced his daily quarter-hour newscast with "Good evening, everyone, from coast to coast." He won a George Foster Peabody Award for reporting in 1955. But before there was TV there was radio and Edwards was at the forefront virtually from the time CBS took off as the leader of the pack. While in preparatory studies at the University of Alabama, Emory University, and the University of Georgia, Edwards gained reporting experience at Troy, Alabama's WHET, Dothan, Alabama's WAGF, Atlanta's WSB, Detroit's WXYZ, and WSB once again before landing at CBS in New York in 1942 at age 25. Initially a staff announcer, he was soon trained as a network newscaster under the wing of John Charles Daly, another CBS vet. A decade hence the two men competed for the same audience: Edwards was CBS-TV's first weeknight anchor while Daly joined ABC-TV to fill a similar capacity. Edwards took over Daly's CBS broadcast duties in 1943 when Daly went to North Africa. For a few months before the end of the Second World War, he was attached to Edward R. Murrow's London staff but never identified as one of the famed "Murrow Boys" (he got there too late). He was CBS's Paris bureau chief after the war followed by an extended sojourn in the Middle East. Returning to America in June 1946, he was soon on the air anchoring the daily radio *CBS World News Roundup*. From 1947–58, Edwards dispatched a three-minute headline capsule weekdays at noon on CBS Radio's soap opera *Wendy Warren and the News*. The narrative hinged on a mythical broadcast and newspaper reporter with Edwards' news injecting a dose of believability into its story line. Edwards launched a weekend CBS-TV newscast in 1947, with his weeknight TV newscast beginning in 1948 (*CBS TV News*, upgraded to *Douglas Edwards with the News* in 1950). He participated in multiple TV series from the 1950s through the 1980s and aired on myriad daily radio and TV newscasts. Shortly after retiring on May 30, 1988, he allowed: "Next to my family and friends, broadcasting is my great love, a romance I've carried on for more than 50 years. Where else are you going to satisfy your natural curiosity, be privy to the great events of your time, be a disseminator of information to a vast audience, be a conduit by which your fellow human beings understand the world?"

FARRINGTON, Fielden. b. July 4, 1909, Clinton, Ind.; d. July 1977, Bayville, N.Y. Though best remembered for a 16-year run as narrator of one of radio's most beloved daytime serials (*The Romance of Helen Trent*, 1944–60), Farrington spent more time delivering the news than introducing shows in the early years of a network career from the mid–1930s to the mid–1970s. His most poignant line, delivered more than 4,000 times, was: "The real-life drama of Helen Trent who, when life mocks her, breaks her hopes, dashes her against the rocks of despair, fights back bravely, successfully, to prove what so many women long to prove in their own lives: that because a woman is 35 or more romance in life need not be over." Other intros: *Armstrong Theater of Today, The Ford Summer Theater, The Green Hornet, Just Plain Bill, News and Views from the Show World, We Love and Learn*. Farrington turned up on NBC's *News of the World* and *World News Today* and daily CBS newscasts throughout the 1940s. But before and after listeners heard his voice on the air he was a scribe. He broke into broadcasting as a writer in 1929, yet it wasn't long until he was in front of a microphone at Detroit's WXYZ as a staff announcer. After narrating *The Green Hornet* in 1936 over MBS, he relocated to New York, joining CBS in 1939. And long after *Helen Trent* bit the dust, Farrington returned to his roots, penning more than a score of original plays for *The CBS Radio Mystery Theater* (1974–76). He authored a couple of novels, too, including one (*The Strangers in 7A*) developed into an *ABC Movie of the Week* and then released as a theatrical film.

FOSTER, Cedric Wilkinson. b. Aug. 31, 1900, Hartford, Conn.; d. Mar. 6, 1975, Denver, Colo. After attending Dartmouth College for a year, Foster quit to "discover America" by traveling across it. He returned for a newspaper job at his hometown journal, *The Hartford Times*, where he was initially assigned to the police beat followed by the financial pages. Hired to manage Hartford's WTHT Radio in 1935, he learned newscasting as a trade. Foster cultivated a weeknight commentary on international affairs that by decade's end was carried by the region's Yankee network. On Jan. 6, 1940, he went on MBS with a weekday matinee news and commentary quarter-hour. Across his lifetime he made a trio of round-the-world jaunts, 50 transatlantic crossings, and another junket to the Philippines. It gave Americans a close-up view of the places from which he reported. Although he maintained one of the most durable radio commentaries that ran 27 years, Foster was never accorded equal status with his counterparts like Morgan Beatty, H. V. Kaltenborn, Edward R. Murrow, Lowell Thomas, Robert Trout, and more of their ilk. They occupied quarter-hours on major networks in the evenings while Foster—the first daytime coast-to-coast commentator—was relegated to a slot on a second-tier chain out of primetime. In his biography of radio analysts Irving Fang gave Foster short shrift, mentioning him in 16 words. That didn't prevent Foster from doing a credible job. He retired from MBS in 1967. Relocating to Denver he went on the air on three local outlets (KFML, KTLN, and KVOD) and was briefly beamed throughout the region by Intermountain Radio Network. He left broadcasting in 1970 to enter public relations.

FRASER, John Gordon (Jack). b. Feb. 4, 1908, Lawrence, Mass.; d. Jan. 1, 2000, Winter Park, Fla. Although he channeled much of his career behind the scenes at radio's most prolific series in broadcast hours—*Monitor*—where he produced, edited, and wrote for virtually the whole run of the show (1955–74), Fraser was a network newscaster for much of the decade preceding that concentration. He had few goals in mind when he went off to the University of Maine and then Brown University but pursued English and music. The latter institution led him to perform a string of concert dates with a varsity quartet where he directed, accompanied at piano, and sang tenor. A few dates on a Providence, R.I., station resulted in a job offer in 1930. Fraser accepted and advanced to New York's WMCA, was a freelance announcer for a year, joined New York's WOR and followed it with NBC in New York in March 1936. There he covered sports and gained his own news and music slots. He handled a historic NBC-TV exhibition during the 1939 New York World's Fair, too. Throughout the 1940s, he dispatched the news on WJZ, flagship station of NBC's Blue chain, as well as intermittently to that web. After his long tenure with *Monitor* he relocated to central Florida. Fraser spent the last dozen years of his working life airing on the radio station of Winter Park's Rollins College (1978–90).

FREDERICK, Pauline. b. Feb. 13, 1908, Gallitzin, Pa.; d. May 9, 1990, Lake Forest, Ill. She was one of the true champs in news reportage during the heyday of transcontinental radio. Frederick had few equals and only a handful of peers among lady reporters. Her distinctive inflection and authoritative analyses instilled confidence in devoted fans, suggesting she was a woman not only well versed in subject matter but capable of objective delivery of facts in a timely, self-assured manner. All of it underscored her believability to listeners. From the mid–1940s to the mid–1970s, Frederick was prominent on the national airwaves. A society reporter for assorted newspapers around Harrisburg, Pa. in high school days, she went to American University at Washington, D.C., intending to become a barrister. Ultimately Frederick altered her plans, selecting journalism as the genre in which she would apply undergrad and master's degrees. She contributed unsolicited material to *The Washington Star* and the North American Newspaper Alliance at first and that got her noticed by the *U.S. News and World Report* which endowed her with correspondent status. One of the offshoots of that was a part time copywriting post for ABC Radio's H.R. Baukhage, an astute broadcaster who advised her to "stay away from radio — it doesn't like women." Down the road a spell that may have been all the incentive she needed to focus intently on the aural ether. A half-dozen years in print had passed when ABC offered Frederick a chance to join up in September 1946 as a full time news correspondent. She was soon airing six morning radio shows and three telecasts weekly, dispatched to the United Nations as ABC's permanent representative. She performed there for 28 years — the first seven for ABC, followed by 21 for NBC. Assessing that opportunity later, she noted: "Since I was a little kid, I was always interested in international relations, and I chose the United Nations because this was the center of international activity. This seemed to be the one place toward which I gravitated all the time." Frederick was the first of her gender to win a coveted George Foster Peabody Award for distinguished reporting (1954) and the first woman to moderate a presidential debate (1976). In 1980, she received the Paul White Radio-TV News Directors Association Award. She was the first feminine president of the U.N. Correspondents Association and, among other tributes, gained 23 honorary degrees from manifold institutions of higher learning. She departed from network TV in 1975, returning to what possibly had been her first love among mediums as she closed out her career as a news analyst with National Public Radio.

FREEMAN, Florence. b. July 29, 1911, New York, N.Y.; d. April 25, 2000, Kankakee, Ill. A radio actress who "played" a print and electronic journalist, as heroine of CBS's *Wendy Warren and the News* (1947–58), Freeman dispatched a *real* "news report from the women's world" daily at noon. Her bulletins about milady's fashions, running a home, caring for family, marketing, and tips extending from diverse newsworthy events appeared behind a three-minute capsule of news headlines dispatched by CBS newsman Douglas Edwards. Following Freeman's comments and a commercial, the quarter-hour narrative dove into the pretend world of the mythical broadcaster-newspaperwoman. It was an unusual mode of presenting news and may have drawn as many males to its audience as females. Before getting into radio in 1933 at New York's WMCA, Freeman earned a bachelor's degree at Wells College of the State University of New York followed by a master's from Columbia University. She taught high school English two years before trying radio. On the air she won recurring roles on more than a dozen daytime and primetime dramas. In addition to the *Warren* saga, Freeman's most enduring yarn was the namesake part on NBC's *Young Widder Brown* (1938–54).

GARDINER, Donald. b. Jan. 10, 1916, New York, N.Y.; d. Mar. 27, 1977, Quoque, Long Island, N.Y. Gardiner spent nearly a lifetime with ABC. He had been a page at NBC in his youth before going on the air as an announcer at WAIR, Winston-Salem, N.C. That was followed by a similar stint at WRC, Washington, D.C., in which he covered the third inauguration of President Franklin D. Roosevelt (1941), one of his more imposing moments. In 1943, Gardiner relocated to New York and affiliated with the Blue network which was then separating from NBC. Two years hence it was permanently re-dubbed ABC. Gardiner remained with his new employer until his death 34 years afterward at age 61. As a staff announcer he carried many duties, at times introducing the dramatic series *David Harding, Counterspy*; *Dick Tracy*; *Gangbusters*; and *When a Girl Marries*. Yet he was probably as much a newsman as he was an interlocutor. From 1944 to 1958, on Sunday nights Gardiner presented *Monday Morning Headlines* news and commentary. In addition, during the 1948–49 radio season, he delivered *Tomorrow's Headlines* to the ABC audience.

GIBBONS, Raphael Floyd Phillips. b. July 16, 1887, Washington, D.C.; d. Sept. 24, 1939, Saylorsburg, Pa. Before being expelled for childish pranks from Washington's Georgetown University, Gibbons failed English, Latin, and Greek. Nonplussed by it all, he joined *The Minneapolis Daily*

News at $7 weekly as police reporter. A succession of newspaper jobs followed: *The Milwaukee Free Press, The Minneapolis Tribune, The Chicago World,* and *The Chicago Tribune.* Five weeks before America entered the First World War he was aboard the *Laconia* en-route to London to transmit dispatches to *The Chicago Tribune* when it was torpedoed by a German sub and sunk. Spared, Gibbons was subsequently wounded while covering U.S. Marines in combat at Belleau Wood, France. There he lost his left eye and wore a signature white patch for the remainder of his life. On Dec. 24, 1925, he was heard in a broadcast over the *Tribune's* WGN Radio in which he recounted some of his overseas tales. Gibbons had covered battles in Russia, Morocco, China, Ethiopia, and Spain. But he was so terrified of the mike that the station manager tried to distract him by hiding it from his view. He was an instant hit with listeners nonetheless. The veteran print journalist's first real opportunity to move into electronic news enduringly occurred after an NBC audition in spring 1929. Gibbons averaged speaking 3.6 words per second or 217 words per minute resulting in his being hired for a Wednesday night series, *The Headline Hunter,* on which he recalled many of his unusual encounters. He spoke "a mile a minute," said a critic. He was also given the duty of overseeing NBC's remote broadcasts. By early 1930, Gibbons was on the air with the first daily network newscast. Still employed by NBC in 1931, he joined International News Service and Universal News Service and, in November, sailed the Pacific to cover the Japanese-Chinese War. He broadcast over NBC in January 1932 from Manchuria, remaining there until he came home for the political conventions that summer. A frenetic lifestyle in work and word brought on a heart attack at age 46; a second at 52 killed him at the outbreak of the Second World War in Europe, "the big one" he most wanted to cover. Over his brief span Gibbons penned a quartet of volumes detailing eyewitness accounts of his far-flung adventures. A biographer cited the newsman as "the premier war correspondent of his generation."

GODDARD, **Donald Gay.** b. July 5, 1904, Binghamton, N.Y.; d. Mar. 20, 1994, Sun City, Ariz. They were the six hardest years of his life, Goddard said later, as he reflected on the half-dozen years at the start of his journalism pursuits while reporting for *The New York World.* When offered a post in NBC's news and special events department, he jumped at it, supplementing his network newscasting income with similar work at myriad New York stations: WEAF (1942), WMCA (1946), and WINS (1947–48). In the mid–1940s, Goddard presented *News at Noon* weekdays to a WEAF audience. He also appeared at numerous single exhibitions on NBC commemorating D-Day on June 6, 1944; V-E Day on May 7, 1945; and False V-J Day on Aug. 10, 1945. Transferring from NBC-TV to ABC-TV in the mid–1950s, Goddard hosted a half-hour health documentary series, *Medical Horizons.* From 1958–60, he further anchored an early evening ABC-TV newscast as he presided over several weekly news features with that web, extending into the mid–1960s. He retired in 1970 as head of ABC's biographical and history archive, a unit he helped to create. In the 1950s, meanwhile, Goddard began to cultivate a growing interest in alcoholism and other addictions. This led him into a second career that produced documentaries on Alcoholics Anonymous and a related print vehicle. Once he retired to Arizona, he connected with multiple alcoholism treatment facilities locally, particularly some focused on geriatric addictions. Goddard and his colleagues were responsible for establishing models for dealing with dependence issues among the aged that were copied at various clinics throughout the nation.

GODWIN, **Earl Thomas J.** b. Jan. 24, 1881, Washington, D.C.; d. Sept. 23, 1956, Rehoboth Beach, Del. When Godwin broke into radio at 55 in 1936 with a daily NBC newscast, he had long been noted for proficiency in print journalism. His father was city and managing editor of *The Washington Evening Star* whose son gained skill in the trade with the same paper (ca. 1910). Within four years he was also covering the nation's capital for *The Milwaukee Sentinel,* a side venture. He became the *Star's* political writer in 1916, yet affiliated with the rival *Washington Times* (1917–19), a period in which he was also in the army during the First World War. Leaving his journalistic post in August 1920, he joined the Washington regional telephone utility as public relations director. Godwin departed to pursue similar duties with the Woman's Christian Temperance Union in Chicago (1927–35). Subsequently returning to *The Washington Times* and rising to associate editor, by 1938 he was elected president of the White House Correspondents Association. Godwin covered all the presidential aspirants from the campaigns of Woodrow W. Wilson (1912) to Dwight D. Eisenhower (1956). From the mid–1930s to the mid–1950s, his most notable NBC series were *Earl Godwin and the News* (1936–41,

1944–49) and *Watch the World Go By* (1942–44). The former was straight newscasting while he offered an analysis of current events during the latter. Godwin maintained such trust in Franklin D. Roosevelt that, at the president's death, he was traumatized to the extent that his colleague H.R. Baukhage was pressed into service to sit in for him. Godwin signed off the air each day with the aphorism "*God bless you, one and all.*"

GRANDIN, Thomas Burnham. b. July 19, 1907, Cleveland, O.; d. Oct. 1977 (last residence Phoenix, Ariz., though records don't indicate the date and place of his death). Sans journalism training or experience, Grandin was nevertheless hired by CBS newsman Edward R. Murrow in 1939 for wartime coverage from Paris. Having attended Yale and studied beyond that in Berlin and Paris, Grandin was an Ivy League nerd who spoke French fluently albeit in an "unmanly" high-pitched inflection. One asset was that he totally understood the French political situation even as CBS news director Paul White hated his voice and tried to prompt Murrow into firing him. Eric Sevareid, a reporter with plenty of journalistic credentials, was hired to direct the Paris office while Grandin was dispatched around the continent for sundry duties. On one of those he wed a Romanian state radio broadcaster who couldn't speak English. To get her on a ship bound for America in June 1940 — she had no passport — Grandin had to go too, so he left CBS's employ abruptly. Some said this "Murrow Boy" (even though a brief one) took the lesser of evils but Murrow steadily defended him. In 1941, Murrow backed him as assistant editor of the Federal Communications Commission's foreign-broadcast monitoring service in Washington. In 1944, Grandin was hired by the Blue network (soon to be ABC) and reported from Omaha Beach on D-Day on June 6. Following the war he left broadcasting altogether to be a sales executive, eventually winding up living in 1953 as a Scottsdale, Ariz. rancher. Still in awe of Murrow, he wrote him a letter thanking him for the faith he had maintained in him during his early career.

GRANT, Taylor (né Grant Taylor Cushmore). b. Feb. 8, 1913, Philadelphia, Pa.; d. Feb. 24, 1998, Glenside, Pa. From 1938 to 1945, Grant was a newscaster and part time sportscaster at Philadelphia's WCAU Radio. In 1945, he joined ABC and aired for a decade on a weeknight quarter-hour newscast. During a portion of that time (1952–54) he was also heard on ABC on Sunday nights. ABC-TV evening news was spotty following its inauguration in 1948. Attempting one of multiple formats, John Daly was given a quarter-hour there four nights weekly in 1953, while Taylor Grant was handed the same time period on Tuesday nights. It lasted through the 1953–54 video season after which Daly — the web's vice president for news, special events, and public affairs — persisted as solo anchorman five nights weekly. Grant's death a few decades later prompted his son-in-law to recall that the broadcaster labored from the 1930s to the early 1970s in sports, TV, and radio. He distinguished his life as "a champion of civil rights and a die-hard liberal."

GRAUER, Benjamin Franklin. b. June 2, 1908, Staten Island, N.Y.; d. May 31, 1977, New York, N.Y. Although much better remembered as a man who introduced legions of popular shows over an extensive broadcast life (*The Boston Pops Orchestra, Grand Central Station, Kay Kyser's Kollege of Musical Knowledge, The Metropolitan Opera Auditions of the Air, Mr. District Attorney, Mr. Keen—Tracer of Lost Persons, The NBC Symphony Orchestra, The Studebaker Champions, Twenty Thousand Years in Sing-Sing, Your Hit Parade*, and many more), Grauer was a borderline newsman — getting close to the subject through *America's Town Meeting of the Air, Information Please, Meet the Press, Monitor, The Jergens Journal*, and similar fare in much of his career. And throughout the 1940s, he was on the NBC ether delivering news that was interspersed with all the amusements. Working as a movie extra at the age of eight, he was a natural for high school and City College of New York productions while editing the literary magazine and being drama critic of the school newspaper. After a few months of performing skits over NBC, in October 1930, Grauer joined it as a staff announcer. Ultimately he surfaced on no fewer than 46 radio series. He tested the waters as a newsman with the 1936 political conventions, gave an eyewitness account of the maiden voyage of the dirigible *Akron*, called horse races at Aquaduct Park, reported from the inaugural of the United Nations at San Francisco, and affirmed New Year's Eve celebrants at Times Square. On hand as NBC initially exhibited TV to huge crowds at the New York World's Fair in 1939, Grauer was tapped by the National Academy of Vocal Arts as "the most authoritative [voice] in the world" (1944). Beyond daily NBC Radio newscasts (1940–48), the announcer-newsman-actor-anchor hosted early video features. He retired from NBC in 1974, persisting on radio's *Voice of America* for a while and furnishing voiceovers for broadcast commercials.

GUNTHER, John Joseph. b. Aug. 30, 1901, Chicago, Ill.; d. May 29, 1970, New York, N.Y. An early NBC news correspondent and commentator, Gunther first exhibited his creativity at age 12 by circulating an encyclopedia for adolescents. Growing up, he took a reporting job with *The Chicago Daily News* which stationed him in Vienna in 1930. He left print to join NBC Radio in 1939, taking a post in London on the precipice of global war. In the midst of the war he accepted a spot as correspondent for the U.S. War Department (1942–44). In the meantime the widely respected authority was a frequent guest panelist on *Information Please* from the late 1930s through the 1940s. Gunther's radio reporting was confined to 1939 to 1945. He returned to broadcasting to host an ABC-TV weekly primetime half-hour travelogue, *John Gunther's High Road*, during the 1959–60 season. Gunther may be better recalled for a series of *Inside* volumes published by Harper & Brothers between the 1930s and 1960s on lands and peoples of the world. He penned several dozen fiction works as well as nonfiction including many travelogues, character studies, and political commentaries. This distinguished him as one of the most comprehensively published of radio's ex-newsmen.

HACKES, Peter Sidney. b. June 2, 1924, New York, N.Y.; d. Apr. 17, 1994, Washington, D.C. For a third of a century Hackes devoted his working life to two network broadcasters with three years at CBS in Washington (1952–55) and three decades at NBC (1955–86). Even then he wasn't done for he persisted another seven years as the voice of the American Association of Retired Persons. As a communications consultant to AARP, Hackes hosted its transcribed daily audio series *Mature Focus* on hundreds of radio outlets (1987–94). In the nation's capital during his tenure with NBC he covered Capitol Hill, the State Department, and the space program. He won Emmies for his reports of NASA Apollo flights (1969, 1970). His labors with NBC Radio's enduring monthly *Second Sunday* documentary (1966–82) aired far beyond the traditional denouement of radio's golden age and earned for him an impressive George Foster Peabody Award. Beginning in 1956, Hackes reported on every national political convention to 1986, the moment he chose for early retirement. For many years he was a fixture in delivering the news dispatches during NBC Radio's 40-hour weekend *Monitor* (1955–75). Not only was he there at the start of that epic news-music-features phenomenon, long after *Monitor* left the air Hackes continued to report "every facet of American society from politics to economics" said a biographical source. A graduate of Grinnell (Iowa) College, he earned a master's degree in journalism (1949) from the University of Iowa at Iowa City. As a captain in the U.S. Navy Reserve he was commanding officer of several reserve units based at the Pentagon and at the Norfolk, Va. Naval Station. Hackes also appeared in two Hollywood flicks, *Broadcast News* (1987) and *True Colors* (1991), both with Washington ties. In 1994, the District of Columbia chapter of the Radio Television Digital News Association created the Peter Hackes Award for meritorious service by local practitioners of the craft. Signifying the namesake journalist for professional contributions, the tribute's annual recipient is selected for efforts "above and beyond the call of duty to advance the broadcast news industry" in that local community.

HALE, Arthur (né Arthur William Glunt). b. Mar. 16, 1896, Altoona, Pa.; d. Oct. 17, 1971, Harrisburg, Pa. Glunt (his early moniker) earned a bachelor's degree in chemistry from Gettysburg (Pa.) College. Amused by melody, the youth's studies were augmented by music education at a couple of noteworthy French institutes: Fontainebleau School of Music and the University of Grenoble. For more than a year he was a second lieutenant in the First World War (1918–19) and was shipped to France. That delayed his degree for a year (1919). The youth became a striking concert pianist nevertheless, performing as a solo artist and accompanying Gettysburg collegians on stage. In 1948, he composed the *Gettysburg College Hymn* for voice and piano for his alma mater. Apparently never married, he accepted a post in the 1920s at WICC Radio, Bridgeport, Conn. He resigned in 1930 to be a commentator at New York's WOR. That is one of the stations instrumental in forming the MBS chain on Sept. 29, 1934. Once the web was under way, Hale (his radio name) disseminated news and his observations to a national audience on dual series, *Calling America* and *Confidentially Yours*. One of his early duties was introducing entertainer Uncle Don to a faithful adolescent following daily. Hale made a career of WOR and MBS — still newscasting in 1957 — and reached retirement age four years afterward.

HANCOCK, Donald. b. Oct. 10, 1910, Anderson, Ind.; d. May 6, 1980, Anderson, Ind. In a career that was dotted with far more entertainment series than news, Hancock was a CBS newscaster even so in the early to mid–1940s. He left to concentrate on introducing features like *The Children's Hour, Front Page Farrell, The Goldbergs, Grand Central Station, The Jack Smith Show, Life Can Be Beautiful, Major Bowes and His Original Amateur Hour, The Romance of Helen Trent, The Shadow, Stepmother, Stop the Music!*, and many more from the 1930s to the 1950s. Being at the right place at the right time Hancock easily crossed into daytime television in the early 1950s, where everything was performed live. He frequently had no fewer than three commercial spots daily on each of two CBS-TV soap operas, *Love of Life* and *The Secret Storm*. It was a formidable challenge but Hancock proved he had the mettle for it for several years. After retiring as a CBS staff announcer in the late 1970s, he returned to his native Hoosier State to announce summer concerts of the Indiana Symphony in 1977, 1978, and 1979.

HANGEN, Putnam Welles. b. Mar. 22, 1930, New York, N.Y.; d. June 3, 1970, Kampot Province, Cambodia. Hangen is immortalized in Charles P. Arnot's *Don't Kill the Messenger: The Tragic Story of Welles Hangen and Other Journalistic Combat Victims* (Vantage, 1994). He gave new meaning to the phrase, so flippantly uttered without regard to its ultimate price. Covering the Vietnam War for NBC, Hangen — in a party of eight journalists, cameramen, and sound technicians — was ambushed by Khmer Rouge and Viet Cong guerrillas on May 31, 1970, about 30 miles below Phnom Penh, Cambodia. Three died at the scene while the others were captured and consequently executed. On Jan. 17, 1993, Hangen's remains were positively identified by an American-Cambodian search team. The newsman's body was interred with honors at Arlington National Cemetery on Jan. 29, 1993. A 1949 graduate of Brown University, Providence, R.I., Hangen had enrolled earlier at the University of Virginia, Charlottesville; at the University of Geneva (Switzerland); and at New York's Columbia University. He left academic pursuits to attend the United Nations' 1948 session in Paris, covering it for *The New York Herald Tribune*. At 18 it was the launch of his life's work. Shortly after graduation Hangen affiliated with *The New York Times*, where his initial byline appeared at 19 on Oct. 15, 1949. When he resigned seven years hence, at 26, his byline had been published more than 500 times, the last on Dec. 19, 1956. In the months that followed he served the U.S. Army as an information officer in Washington, D.C. In 1958, he joined NBC as a foreign correspondent, the globetrotting post he filled at the time of his death. The Overseas Press Club of America bestowed awards on Hangen in 1967 and 1968.

HANLON, Thomas Anthony, Jr. b. Nov. 7, 1907, Fort Scott City, Kan.; d. Sept. 29, 1970, Hollywood, Calif. Hanlon was one of many examples in the heyday of network radio who put almost all their eggs in the amusement basket while presenting transcontinental series. Except for a few years in the early to mid–1940s, he would have missed newscasting (for CBS) altogether. But he left footprints there as many others did. Hanlon replaced announcer Ken Carpenter at Los Angeles' KFI in 1936 when the latter departed to freelance for singer Bing Crosby's *Kraft Music Hall*. By 1939, Hanlon drifted over to KNX, CBS's owned-and-operated L.A. outlet, and was absorbed into duties as announcer, disc jockey, newscaster, and sportscaster. For the network in the 1930s and 1940s, he opened *The Ford Show, The Phil Baker Show, Hallmark Playhouse, Jane Endicott— Reporter, Lux Radio Theater, Paducah Plantation, Red Barber Sports, The Sweeney and March Show, We the People*, and more. Hanlon enjoyed a sizable run in motion pictures, too. From 1926 to 1954, he or his voice turned up in 64 mostly B-films. A few standards were *The Big Broadcast of 1936, It Happens Every Spring, Kill the Umpire, The Pride of St. Louis*, and *The Bob Mathias Story*.

HARKNESS, Richard Long. b. Sept. 29, 1907, Artesian, S.D.; d. Feb. 16, 1977, Naples, Fla. After attending the University of Kansas, in 1928, Harkness (who was invariably introduced on the air as "Richard C. Harkness" for unknown reasons) signed with United Press as a wire reporter. After eight years in offices at Kansas City, Mo., Oklahoma City, Dallas, and Jefferson City, Mo., he was appointed UP's White House correspondent (1936). Harkness left UP in 1937 to affiliate with the Washington bureau of *The Philadelphia Inquirer*. By 1940, he was slogging the countryside covering Franklin D. Roosevelt's and Wendell Willkie's presidential bids. Two years hence the newsman joined NBC's Washington staff, embarking on a newscast airing concurrently over New York's WNBC and the nation's capital's WRC — both NBC owned-and-operated outlets. For several years in the 1940s,

Harkness supplied news to that pair separate and distinct from the models he furnished others in the transcontinental chain. "His decade reporting and observing the Washington scene has earned for Harkness the reputation of being one of the keenest and most incisive minds among the Capital's younger news veterans," an NBC publicist proclaimed as Harkness launched a three-decade tenure at NBC. His nightly NBC newscasts — twice weekly 1948–51 and every weeknight 1951–53 — were underwritten by Pure Oil Company whose memorable motto, *"Be sure ... with Pure!"* was integrated into the vernacular of those addicted listeners. The newsman exploited numerous chances to mold TV news and public affairs. He presided over NBC-TV's *The Richard Harkness Show* in 1948–49, interviewing imposing figures in current events for a quarter-hour each week. Many more opportunities before the cameras confronted him over the years with Harkness turning up intermittently on various NBC Radio and TV news and public affairs series. Following retirement in 1972, he became press rep (1974–77) for a drug abuse effort spearheaded by President Gerald R. Ford.

HARSCH, Joseph Close. b. May 25, 1905, Toledo, Oh.; d. June 3, 1998, Jamestown, R.I. One of many print journalists who joined the electronic side, Harsch was well prepared academically. Having earned two bachelor's degrees — one from Williams College, Williamstown, Mass. (1927) and a second from Corpus Christi College at Cambridge (Mass.) University (1929) — he returned to Williams to gain a master's degree. Harsch's tenure in print consisted of a long siege of reporting for *The Christian Science Monitor* (1929–43), which he continued doing as a sideline after switching to broadcasting. In the early 1940s, Harsch went on CBS from Germany several times occupying the chair normally used by his pal William L. Shirer. Harsch so wowed CBS news chief Paul White with his microphone agility that — in 1943 — he was extended a five-minute nightly news analysis. A pundit opined that Harsch provided "consistently intelligent commentary during and after World War II." In the mid–1940s, he aired over CBS's owned-and-operated WTOP in the nation's capital. Later that decade he filled multiple weekly slots for CBS. In 1950, he and Marquis Childs originated the *Washington Report* over the Labor-Liberal FM web. Harsch shifted to NBC for twice weekly appearances in the mid–1950s, leading to an appointment as one of a handful of news analysts on NBC's 90-minute weeknight *Nightline* hosted by Walter O'Keefe. Harsch's NBC service persisted from 1953–67, after which he became an ABC commentator (1967–71). He then returned to the place where it had begun for him, *The Christian Science Monitor*, as chief editorial writer (1971–74). Harsch also authored new books in 1941, 1950, and 1993.

HARVEY, Paul (né Paul Harvey Aurandt). b. Sept. 4, 1918, Tulsa, Okla.; d. Feb. 28, 2009, Phoenix, Ariz. The electronic journalist who succeeded in enduring as a network newsman beyond all his colleagues — interrupted by a sustained time-out for recovering health issues early in the present millennium — Harvey was on the national airwaves more than a half-century. He surpassed his closest colleague in durability, Lowell Thomas, who was on a coast-to-coast hookup for 46 years (1930–76). Making announcements and dispatching news at Tulsa's KVOO when he was just 14 was an early harbinger of Harvey's life ahead. He became a staff announcer there while enrolled at the University of Tulsa, then moved on to stations at Salina, Kan., Abilene, Tex., Oklahoma City, St. Louis, Kalamazoo, Mich., and Chicago — where he put down roots. At the Windy City's WENR, he was heard twice daily in the late 1940s with quarter-hour news commentaries plus a weekday evening quarter-hour over WGN dubbed *Speak Your Mind*. There listeners voiced their opinions, a foretaste of contemporary talk radio, sans vitriolic outrage and unacceptable speech that is so common now. By the end of 1950, *Paul Harvey News and Comments* was on the air nationally, carried twice daily by ABC Radio. In 1976, he added a third series to the lineup, *The Rest of the Story*. Harvey unapologetically pushed a conservative stance, regularly pocketed $30,000 for personal appearances, penned a syndicated column that ran in 300 newspapers at its peak, and simultaneously reached in excess of 24 million listeners on more than 1,200 radio outlets. A media critic assessed: "He delivered a provocative and entertaining tabloid newspaper of the air in a style of homespun eloquence." Another observed: "Paul Harvey is corny but fascinating, especially in small doses." Still another: "Despite his stylized delivery, he never achieved the dramatic impact produced by the timing of Edward R. Murrow." But nobody can argue that Harvey simply prevailed longer than all the others.

HAWLEY, Mark Hiram. b. Feb. 17, 1910, New York, N.Y.; d. Sept. 5, 1986, San Jacinto, Calif. Although he introduced a handful of entertainment series on radio in the 1930s and 1940s — notably

Death Valley Days, Famous Fortunes, The Fred Allen Show, and *Mr. District Attorney*— Hawley possessed the distinct voice of a newsman and applied it in dual mediums, radio and theatrical newsreels. Invited in 1929 by CBS President William S. Paley to leave Buffalo's WMAK to join CBS in New York, Hawley did so. There he mingled his duties as an interlocutor with news dispatches. He was also labeled "The Voice of Pathé News" for narrating copious newsreels screened in cinema houses during the 1930s and 1940s. In 1935, Hawley moved over to New York's WOR, one of the flagship stations organizing the Mutual Broadcasting System, where he took similar tasks to his challenges at CBS. Nevertheless, he later returned to CBS as a newscaster (1941–43). Hawley created and directed the Fleet Motion Picture Office in Honolulu while with the U.S. Navy during the Second World War (1943–44). In the postwar era he produced spoken recordings and joined NBC-TV to handle myriad capacities (1947–50). Hawley accepted the management post at Reno's KOLO Radio in 1955. His spouse, Adelaide Hawley, also gained some notoriety: she was the original Betty Crocker spokeswoman hired for television by General Mills (1949–64).

HEATTER, Gabriel. b. Sept. 17, 1890, New York, N.Y.; d. Mar. 30, 1972, Miami, Fla. *Ah, there's good news tonight!* Heatter insisted as he came on the air for three decades with *Gabriel Heatter News and Comment* (1935–65) over the MBS hookup. Born into a family of Jewish immigrants, he never acquired a high school diploma because he didn't pass his math tests. Yet at 16 he was drumming up crowds on street corners for William Randolph Hearst's gubernatorial bid, dubbed "the boy orator." It seemed an omen for what lay ahead. In the same era he took a part-time reporting job with *The New York Record* followed by a full-time reporting job with *The Brooklyn Times*. He added Hearst's *The New York Journal* as a part-time chore to his litany of literary tasks. Heatter was a political correspondent at the Albany state house in his early 20s, then suffered depression and a nervous breakdown, leaving him unemployed for two years. He gained a fleeting publicity job in the Warren G. Harding presidential campaign and penned freelance articles for *Forest and Stream* and *The Nation*. A couple of guest shots on New York's WMCA Radio in the early 1930s netted an offer to be a seven-night-a-week quarter-hour news commentator at $40 weekly. In the throes of the Great Depression he accepted it, moving a few months later to WOR for similar duties at $75 per quarter-hour broadcast. That humble start eventually led him to earn $400,000 annually as 196 MBS stations carried him six nights weekly. From 1937 to 1941, Heatter also hosted CBS's acclaimed human interest feature *We, the People*. Furthermore he appeared in two Hollywood films in the middle of the 20th century. In 1951, he relocated to Miami Beach and persisted with his nightly commentaries on MBS. Heatter also penned a column for *The Miami Beach Sun*, performed on Miami's WIOD Radio, and briefly attempted TV.

HERLIHY, Edward Joseph. b. Aug. 14, 1909, Dorchester, Mass.; d. Jan. 30, 1999, Manhattan, N.Y. For about five years (1943–48), in addition to scores of amusing series he introduced to national radio audiences, Herlihy was a network newscaster. One would hardly know it, however, for he's far better recalled as the commercial spokesman for Kraft Foods on NBC Radio and Television as well as having presented legions of aural shows from the 1930s to the 1950s: *America's Town Meeting of the Air, The Big Show, Dick Tracy, The Falcon, Grand Central Station, The Great Gildersleeve, The Horn and Hardart Children's Hour, Information Please, Inner Sanctum Mysteries, Just Plain Bill, The Martin and Lewis Show, Mr. District Attorney, People Are Funny, Pickens Party, Truth or Consequences, Vic and Sade,* et al. Herlihy was the nephew of comedian Fred Allen. Ed's sibling, Walter, followed him into broadcasting, becoming a busy announcer at ABC Radio and TV. While in stage productions at Boston College, Ed Herlihy got on the air at WLOE Radio (1932) followed by an announcing job at WHDH. He moved to WEEI (1933) and left Boston altogether in 1935 for NBC in New York. He was on the air there some 63 years, 42 as commercial spokesman for Kraft, although not exclusively so. For 25 years he was the voice of Universal-International newsreels screened in movie theaters. His TV inventory included *Kraft Television Theatre, Your Show of Shows, The Perry Como Show,* and *Kraft Music Hall*. Herlihy also appeared in a trio of motion pictures while his voice was added to another quartet of films. His stints as a newscaster were, of course, all on NBC.

HERMAN, George. b. Jan. 14, 1920, New York, N.Y.; d. Feb. 8, 2005, Washington, D.C. In 1944, Herman took his bachelor's degree from Dartmouth College and master's degree in journalism from Columbia University and applied for a post at CBS. He was hired as a newswriter and interacted with legends of broadcast journalism: Winston Burdett, Charles Collingwood, John Daly, Larry Lesueur, Edward R. Murrow, Eric Sevareid, William L. Shirer, Robert Trout, etc. From the 1950s to the 1980s, Herman was one of those familiar names dispatching news over CBS Radio and TV. White House correspondent into the early 1960s, he covered the Supreme Court to the early 1970s. He's best recalled as moderator of CBS-TV's *Face the Nation* (1969–83), with a longer run there than anyone until Bob Schieffer took that chair in 1991. (In 2012, Schieffer was still there.) Herman's 43-year tenure at CBS ended with his retirement in 1987. He appeared at the first televised political conventions in 1948, provided CBS its initial overseas sound and film reports in 1949, and delivered the first report of the break-in at Democratic Party headquarters in the Watergate office building in 1972. That year his and journalist Jack Anderson's questions of *Face the Nation* guest Thomas Eagleton, Democratic candidate for vice president, revealed the guest's past bouts with depression. Shortly after that inquisition Eagleton was history, off the ticket, dramatically reshaping that race.

HICKS, George Francis. b. Aug. 26, 1905, Tacoma, Wash.; d. Mar. 17, 1965, Jackson Heights, Queens, N.Y. Hicks' formal education was about as mixed as his youthful methods of sustaining himself. Working at logging camps, sawmills, shipyards, door and pickle factories, a hardware store, and trucking firms, he also chased academia in that era: a year at the University of Washington, a year at Puget Sound College, and still later — after embarking on myriad adventurous voyages — at George Washington University in the nation's capital. In Washington in September 1928, Hicks applied and beat out 99 more aspirants for an announcing job at WRC Radio. Fourteen months hence he was hired by NBC as a staff announcer at its owned-and-operated flagship outlet, New York's WEAF. For a decade he developed light features for the chain at a time when he, Ben Grauer, Tom Manning, and Graham McNamee also covered the political campaigns and conventions of 1936. Once the Second World War was under way Hicks convinced the Blue web to add a daily series about servicemen. The human interest draw received plaudits from pundits. Hicks also led superiors to appoint him as the Blue's sole foreign correspondent (London, 1942) at a time when its shaky operation hardly had finances to support domestic news. Hicks nevertheless gained a cohort in London and struck out for the battlefront. A 10-minute tape of a German bombing raid made on D-Day, June 6, 1944, was a classic segment of unfolding wartime drama to radio audiences. "It significantly elevated Hicks's stature as a redoubtable newsman," read one opinion, "and won for him a National Headliners Club award." In the postwar epoch his daily quarter-hour newscasts for nearly a decade aired intermittently on ABC and NBC Radio. U.S. Steel Co. picked him as its chief spokesman for a primetime radio series that aired eight years (1945–53) and another decade on television (1953–55, ABC; 1955–63, CBS) known as *The U.S. Steel Hour*. Hicks also presided over *The U.N. in Action*, a live weekly public affairs telecast over CBS (1955–59). He also hosted a weekly half-hour ABC-TV religious series in 1961, *Directions*.

HIETT, Helen Annette. b. Sept. 23, 1913, Chenoa, Ill.; d. Aug. 22, 1961, Chamonix, France. After earning a political science degree from the University of Chicago in three years (1934), a disciplined Hiett set out for Europe on a summer scholarship. She stayed over for another year in Geneva to work at the League of Nations' research center. Studying in Rome (1936), she traveled in Greece and Italy before academic quests took her to the London School of Economics. In 1937, Hiett was exposed to more of the continent: briefly working at a German girls' labor camp and witnessing echoing effects of Spain's civil war. Hiett traversed the Balkans (1939), lectured in the U.S., dispatched shortwave broadcasts of her impressions from Paris, took another American speaking tour (1940), and joined NBC's European staff in Paris. In a lone season (1941–42) she did what few of her gender had the opportunity to do: with a quarter-hour of national radio time she delivered news and personal perceptions over NBC Blue at 10:15 Eastern weekday mornings. A critic explained, "As more men got drafted, we would begin to hear more women on the air in nontraditional roles." Hiett left Blue/ABC in the mid–1940s to be director of forums for *The New York Herald Tribune*. In 1948, she wed a San Francisco man (Theodore Waller) with a federal overseas post. Her quests came to an end as she was climbing in the French Alps one day and was fatally injured (1961).

HILL, Edwin Conger. b. April 23, 1884, Aurora, Ind.; d. Feb. 12, 1957, St. Petersburg, Fla. At 17, Hill was an Indianapolis newspaper reporter pursuing a bachelor's degree at Butler College. He subsequently transferred to a Cincinnati paper and, by 1904, to *The New York Sun*. He left to direct

Twentieth Century–Fox newsreels and to edit Fox movie scenarios (1923–27) before returning to print. Hill penned a trilogy of books, too (1925, 1933, 1934). Going on the air a newscaster over New York's WOR (1931), within a year he acquired a web slot of his own and kept it for two decades, at times airing as many as six quarter-hours weekly over three national chains. *The Human Side of the News*, a syndicated newspaper column he wrote, attracted a national following. Hill was depicted by a critic as "one of New York's best reporters, with a flair for human interest." On the air he "could express far better than printer's ink the movement, the color, and the emotion of his words," a cohort said. He gravitated from a liberal bent early in his career to a conservative stance in his later observations.

HILLMAN, William (né Vladimir Hillman). b. Sept. 5, 1895, New York, N.Y.; d. May 30, 1962, New York, N.Y. As careers go, it was late for Hillman to make the switch at age 46 from print to electronic journalism (although H. V. Kaltenborn did so as well as a few others). Hillman was a guest on NBC on July 7, 1940, and must have found it to his liking. He furnished foreign reports to radio (1940–41). Involved in wartime coverage in Europe in the years just prior to the war's outbreak, Hillman returned to the U.S. in 1941 seeking work. Washington's WMAL hired him as a newscaster. By 1942, the Blue chain paired him with Ernest K. Lindley for a quarter-hour joint appearance four nights weekly under the banner *News Here and Abroad*. A quadrennial later, Hillman moved on solo with a newscast on the MBS outlet in the capital, WOL (1946), soon beamed to the entire Mutual chain. Between the mid–1940s and 1962, he was a roving correspondent with the North American Newspaper Alliance, too. Hillman edited a compilation of President Harry S Truman's letters, diaries, and personal papers, *Mr. President* (1952). In so doing he helped the ex–chief executive compose his *Memoirs* and worked in other Truman literary and TV projects (1952–62). After journalism graduation from Columbia College (1917), Hillman enlisted in the army, was sent to France during the First World War, and rose to second lieutenant. He returned to invest himself in print, taking a newspaper appointment in 1926 sending him to Paris, Berlin, and London. From 1934–39, he was chief of the Hearst newspapers' foreign correspondents. In London, Hillman held several posts: administrative agent for King Features Syndicate, director of the British News Service, Ltd., European manager of International News Service, and European manager of *Collier's Weekly*.

HOLLENBECK, Don. b. Mar. 30, 1905, Lincoln, Neb.; d. June 22, 1954, New York, N.Y. Hollenbeck is one of few U.S. electronic journalists driven to suicide. A byproduct of the Sen. Joseph R. McCarthy-inspired witch hunt ferreting out public figures perceived to harbor Nazi or Communist sympathies in the mid–20th century, Hollenbeck's demise was a result of a chaotic obsession taken to extremes. Ill, hounded, and depressed by partisans—a few leading newspapers hammered him with doubts of his patriotism—Hollenbeck took his own life leaving a wife and daughter. His career began on a propitious note more than a decade earlier: Serving the U.S. Office of War Information in London, he joined NBC's London staff (1943). Returning to America after the war, Hollenbeck signed on as a newscaster and disc jockey at New York's WJZ, flagship outlet of newly-formed ABC (1945). In a dispute with a sponsor he was thrown off the air the following year. CBS picked him up and gave him a news slot; he was the first anchor of the quarter-hour daily *News of America* (1946). *Pathfinder* magazine dubbed him "the first newscaster to put the spotlight on drama from small towns." In the late 1940s, however, he lost that gig after criticizing McCarthy (R-Wis.) for his vengeance in tracking suspected anti–Americans. Hollenbeck suddenly moved to the forefront of potential traitors and a relentless effort ensued to extricate him. In the summer of 1950, he anchored *The Saturday News Special* for a quarter-hour on CBS-TV. As he became too hot a property for even that little national visibility, the badgered journalist was reduced to a weeknight newscast over WCBS-TV in New York—the web's flagship station—which he handled at the time of his death.

HOTTELET, Richard C. b. Sept. 22, 1917, Brooklyn, N.Y. Defying the odds, Hottelet was still with us in early 2012, more than 94 years after his birth, the last of the 11-member troupe identified by authors Stanley Cloud and Lynne Olson (*The Murrow Boys*, Houghton Mifflin, 1996). He served among that intrepid bunch from January 1944, the last to be so designated by CBS mentor Edward R. Murrow, who picked Hottelet after he was a prisoner of war in a German concentration camp. He was the only one of his cohorts so distinguished like that. A first generation American of German parentage, Hottelet studied philosophy at hometown Brooklyn College, earning a degree in 1937.

The next year, on learning the University of Berlin was concentrating in propaganda instead of education, he dropped his pursuit of a graduate degree to report for United Press International in Berlin. From a strategic vantage point he was an eyewitness to Adolf Hitler's preparations for global war, candidly reporting on them. The Gestapo was outraged. To suppress his unbridled tongue, he was arrested and placed in solitary confinement for suspected spying against the Third Reich (1941). To his amazement, he and another U.S. newsman were exchanged for two German journalists held by the Allies after spending four months in Alexanderplatz and Moabit prisons. Hottelet went to London and took a job with the U.S. Office of War Information but not to his liking. That's when Murrow added him to his staff of European reporters, albeit late in military pursuits (1944). The last in was the last out; Hottelet remained with CBS longer than the others, and also stayed behind to give listeners vivid word pictures from London, Moscow, Berlin, Bonn, and more locales after the war. From the mid–1940s to the mid–1980s, he was a contributor to aural features like the *CBS Morning News Roundup*, the *CBS World News Roundup* (a.k.a. *The World Tonight*), *Crisco Radio Newspaper*, *Richard C. Hottelet and the News*, *The World is Our Beat*, and *You Are There*. Dispatched to New York to cover the U.N. (1956), he subsequently anchored two daily CBS News programs on television (1957–61). Retiring from CBS in 1985, for a while Hottelet aided the U.S. ambassador to the U.N. As a broadcaster, he finished his professional career at National Public Radio moderating *America and the World* (1993), the last of the "Murrow Boys" to cast his voice broadly over the nation. Yet he persisted in writing op-ed pieces and traveling the lecture circuit. Hottelet penned some comments for *The Christian Science Monitor* (2001–05) and lectured at George Washington University in the present millennium. Cited by the National Press Club on Aug. 10, 2011, and given an award for his work — one of many over a long career — Hottelet received a standing ovation for the brevity of his response: "Thank you very much," said he. "I just want to tell you, I tried."

HOWE, Quincy. b. Aug. 17, 1900, Boston, Mass.; d. Feb. 19, 1977, New York, N.Y. *Quincy Howe Comments* was heard intermittently (but not continuously) from 1938–68 over MBS, CBS, and ABC. Some other enduring radio posts included *Invitation to Learning* as a panelist (1940–64) and *The World Today* as an analyst (1940–46). The Harvard grad edited for book publisher Simon and Schuster before finding radio work that often included five- and even six-night stints weekly. An observer admonished: "Howe helped to make analysis an accepted part of news reporting." Through myriad periodical inserts as well as *The News and How to Understand It* (Simon and Schuster, 1940), he told more about the nature of radio commentary "than any of his peers," according to one source. Howe penned other books, too. He was kicked off CBS after angering a sponsor in 1947 (a result often linked with that turf), leaving radio to teach journalism. But he was back on the air in 1953 at ABC, and some sources maintain that he persisted to 1968. Simultaneously the analyst filled many pithy public affairs and news-related spots over CBS and ABC television (1948–61). "Howe was a keen observer of the American scene and a perceptive historian," wrote radio pundit Luther Sies, citing him as "one of the most intellectually gifted and objectively honest news broadcasters."

HOWELL, Wayne Clay (né Wayne H. Chappelle). b. Feb. 16, 1921, Lexington, Ky.; d. July 8, 1993, Pompano Beach, Fla. Howell is remembered for many things but news isn't one of them. Nevertheless, between 1949 and 1951, during NBC servitude, he was on the air with *Wayne Howell and the News*. Surely the purists recall it. Howell left sportscasting at Charleston, S.C.'s WTMA in 1946 to join NBC–New York and introduce TV's first regularly scheduled late-night feature, *Broadway Open House* (1950–51). But he's better known for video work as interlocutor with quizmaster Hugh Downs on *Concentration* (1958–61) and emcee Bert Parks on the *Miss America Beauty Pageant* (1966–85). Howell retired from NBC in 1985. Aside from his radio news he also opened aural features like *Honeymoon in New York*, *The Martin and Lewis Show*, *Monitor*, *Name That Tune*, *The NBC Radio Theater*, *Pickens Party*, and *The $64,000 Question*. In 1950, he hosted *The Wayne Howell Show*, a disc jockey entry.

JACKSON, Allan Harry. b. Dec. 4, 1915, Hot Springs, Ark.; d. Apr. 26, 1976, New York, N.Y. In the early 1930s, Harry Jackson (the moniker he then used) studied at the University of Illinois and earned tuition announcing at Urbana's WILL. It gave him incentive to return to his hometown for the summer to emcee dance band remotes over KTHS, Hot Springs. (That's the station where Chester Lauck and Norman Goff launched the notorious hayseed characters *Lum and Abner* in 1930, incidentally, taking that property to NBC in Chicago the next year, persisting nationally to 1954.) Jackson was subsequently engaged at a litany of stations across hundreds of miles in myriad capacities before gaining nationwide recognition: WKZO, Kalamazoo, Mich. (1936); KTHS, Hot Springs (1937); WLW, Cincinnati; WHAS, Louisville; Texas State Network (1939); WMC, Memphis; and CBS News, New York (1943–75, then identified as Allan Jackson). From 1944–50, he was on the air weeknights with a quarter-hour for Met Life. When the insurer decided to go with Eric Sevareid at 6 o'clock instead, that didn't work out: Sevareid's caustic anti–Sen. Joseph R. McCarthy (R-Wis.) annotations troubled the sponsor, netting Sevareid's shift to 11 o'clock and a loss of a $1,200 weekly fee. Jackson, perceived as steady as a rock, was summoned to resume at 6 P.M. For the remainder of the golden age, his voice was reliable assurance on CBS, often on weekends as he related current events. Anchoring the *CBS Morning News Roundup* in the mid–1940s, he was also a regular on *The World Tonight* (appearing on both series to 1975) as well as the *Crisco Radio Newspaper* (1940s) and *Chevrolet Spotlights the News* (1950s). Jackson was cited for "crisp, cosmopolitan delivery" by *Who's Who in TV & Radio*. He moderated the CBS-TV public affairs *Youth Takes a Stand* (1953–54). On Nov. 22, 1963, he was the first network newsman to tell radio listeners of President John F. Kennedy's death, a fact confirmed a quarter-hour later by rival reporters and webs.

JORDAN, Max Arthur. b. Apr. 21, 1895, San Remo, Italy; d. Nov. 28, 1977, Illgau, Switzerland. Jordan, an ethnic German, is a fitting subject for a study in contrasts. On moving to the U.S. from Europe, he gained American citizenship and returned to Europe for his education and most of his livelihood! Earning a doctorate at Weimar, Germany's University of Jura, he signed with International News Service as a correspondent. His intimacy with German politics occasionally pressed him into service translating German broadcasts to English for NBC (1931–34). Jordan became the European rep for NBC, synchronizing continental coverage (1934). Based at Basel, Switzerland, he was linked with Fred Bate in London, the net's British correspondent, and they became a daunting duo. A historian observed: "Ever the aggressive journalist, Jordan prided himself on his reputation as 'Ubiquitous Max,' always on the scene when news was happening — and he made a special point of keeping ahead of the competition, keeping his supervisors in New York well advised on CBS activities and constantly suggesting strategies for maintaining NBC's advantages." In 1936, he was one of a few broadcasters heard in an initial multiple remote pickup. In 1938, he reported live from the scene as Germany invaded Austria, commencing war, something Jordan's CBS equivalent William L. Shirer missed (he reported from London). CBS president Bill Paley was livid; it resulted in launching a prototype of the *CBS World News Roundup* which was to lead CBS to vault over its rival. Jordan was nonplussed, gaining ground on CBS whenever he could. He hired Martin Agronsky to cover the war (1940), one of the arduous newsmen of the era. Jordan penned his only tome, an autobiographical *Beyond All Fronts: A Bystander's Notes to This Thirty Years' War* (Bruce, 1944) and was named NBC's director of religious programming in the same era. Those duties altered his views and set a new course for him: he gave his final report on the *NBC World News Roundup* Feb. 4, 1947, and retired from journalism. Jordan had scored one of his biggest scoops not long before, being in Switzerland on Aug. 14, 1945 — where exchanges between warring parties met — to report Japan's acceptance of the surrender terms proffered by the allies first, thus giving NBC an edge. On Dec. 7, 1952, he recorded a talk to air on Dec. 28 on NBC's *Catholic Hour*. By then he was the Reverend Max Jordan, a Benedictine priest. It was Jordan's last airing. Returning to Switzerland, he devoted a quarter-century to his order.

KALB, Marvin Leonard. b. June 9, 1930, New York, N.Y. A younger sibling of Bernard Kalb who likewise devoted many years to newscasting at CBS and NBC before he (Bernard) took his show on the road as press secretary at the U.S. State Department, Marvin Kalb spent three decades at the dual webs. He held the distinction as the last of a latter day troupe of "Murrow Boys" hired by legendary CBS newsman Ed Murrow. The younger Kalb joined those hallowed ranks in 1957 after a stint in Moscow begun in the previous year, the State Department having sent him there. He rose to become the two broadcasting networks' chief diplomatic correspondent and eventually moderated NBC's heralded public affairs forum *Meet the Press* (in that capacity alongside Roger Mudd, 1984–85, and solo thereafter, 1985–87). For years both Kalbs pursued similar courses, each one earning a bachelor's degree from the City College of New York in 1951 followed by a master's degree from Harvard University in 1953. Though Bernard — the eldest by eight years — also gave three decades to full-time journalism, his tenure encompassed CBS, NBC, and *The New York Times* prior to his 1985 governmental post. (It unraveled the following year when he abruptly quit, prompted by an alleged ethical snafu in Reagan administration communications.) Younger brother Marvin, meanwhile, devoted three decades to the transcontinental chains, reporting for dual webs on radio and TV. His investigations landed him on the infamous "enemies list" of the Nixon administration while he served CBS. He received numerous citations for covering diplomatic missions — two George Foster Peabody awards, Columbia University's E. I. DuPont Award, The National Press Club's Fourth Estate Award, and more than a half-dozen Overseas Press Club honors. If possible, Marvin Kalb seemed busier after leaving full-time broadcasting. He was instrumental in establishing Harvard's Joan Shorenstein Center on the Press, Politics and Public Policy and its first director. The center links journalists, scholars, and the public to research and instruction. From 1987 to 1999, he was Edward R. Murrow professor of practice and senior fellow at Harvard's Kennedy School of Government. Subsequently he became James Clark Welling fellow at George Washington University (GWU). Kalb now contributes to Fox News, America Abroad, and National Public Radio. For many years he has presided over *The Kalb Report*, a monthly discussion broadcast feature. Jointly sponsored by Harvard and GWU, it circulates from Washington's National Press Club, directed toward media ethics and accountability. Kalb is the author or coauthor of a dozen texts including two bestselling novels. He's been on the lecture circuit for decades and sundry news organizations solicit his opinion on topical issues.

KALISCHER, Murray, Jr. (Peter). b. Dec. 25, 1914, New York, N.Y.; d. July 7, 1991, New Orleans, La. For over two decades Kalischer posted reports from the Far East for diverse sources. His sojourn in Japan occurred as an officer in the Counter Intelligence Corps attached to Gen. Douglas MacArthur's headquarters (1945). After the war the newsman remained in Tokyo to report for United Press International, then *Collier's* magazine (1952–57), and finally CBS Radio and TV (1957–78). Kalischer traipsed thousands of miles across the Orient reporting eyewitness accounts of disputes involving the islands of Matsu and Quemoy and Syngman Rhee's regime collapse in South Korea. His travels were pointedly focused on Saigon, Vietnam, in the 1960s as he dispatched details of the U.S.A.'s pursuit of "an unwinnable war." Growing weary of it, at his request he was shifted to Paris (1966) as CBS's correspondent for Western Europe, Poland, the Middle East, Greece, and Turkey. Even in that distant outpost, however, he wasn't far from the Vietnam milieu that he hoped to leave: he was told to cover its stalled peace talks (1968–72). In 1963, Kalischer was awarded honors for best reporting in TV spot news by the Overseas Press Club of America. Retiring from CBS in 1978, he returned to the states to become associate professor of communications at Loyola University in New Orleans (1978–82), his last appointment.

KALTENBORN, Hans Von. b. July 9, 1878, Milwaukee, Wis.; d. June 14, 1965, New York, N.Y. One of the towering figures of early electronic journalists, Kaltenborn was middle-aged by the time radio was available to him. The son of German immigrants joined a broadcast exhibition on Newark's WJZ on Apr. 21, 1921, his first air date — the tenderfoot was then 42. Though his initial ongoing gig bowed over New York's WEAF on Oct. 23, 1923 (he was 45) — and he was on New York's WOR in 1927 at 49 — he was 52 by the time his voice was wafting beyond the confines of metropolitan Manhattan on a recurring daily newscast (1930, CBS). He and esteemed colleague Lowell Thomas shared the same audience but at different times over competing hookups. Kaltenborn, the elder statesman as they debuted, launched his network career over CBS. But he departed for what he thought was greener pastures (more freedom to speak his mind) in 1940. ("Be careful what you ask for....") He remained in NBC's employ until retiring at 77 in 1955. (Thomas, on the other hand, airing briefly over CBS in 1930, settled in for the long haul at NBC in 1931. But in 1947, he uprooted, persuaded to return to CBS where he hung out until 1976 at age 84.) Over his long stretch Kaltenborn was accorded many decorations including the label "dean of American commentators," a tag that may not be misplaced. His journalistic endeavors before radio were print-focused: at 14 he earned $5 weekly reporting for *The Merrill Advocate*, the paper in the tiny Wisconsin sawmill burg where he grew up; at 19, he left to fight with the Army in the Spanish-American War, yet dispatched eyewitness accounts of Wisconsin boys in an Alabama infantry camp to a trio of home state journals; with a truce signed before he saw action he returned home to be gifted as city editor of the *Advocate*. Kaltenborn was restless, however, and sought other prospects. The enterprising young man boarded a livestock barge from New York to Europe to debut as a foreign correspondent at $1 per article to the *Advocate*. He also attended the 1900 Paris World's Fair. Post-fair, he remained on the continent as a freelance journalist. Returning to America in 1902, he took a reporting job with *The Brooklyn Eagle* and enrolled at Harvard as a special student. In 1907, he left for Berlin as secretary of the Harvard Professional Exchange. Returning to Harvard to finish his studies, Kaltenborn grabbed honors for public speaking and debating and graduated cum laude (1909). Rejoining *The Brooklyn Eagle* in 1910, he gained greater accountability in time, boosted to associate editor in 1921. In that capacity he was invited to appear on WJZ. As his notoriety grew, the newsman received more invitations to the airwaves. In September 1938, Kaltenborn began 102 broadcasts from New York in an 18-day run for CBS. This was during the Munich crisis as Hitler and Chamberlain set the short-term course of Czechoslovakia's future. That gained him a sponsor, amplified his recognition, and confirmed his own sense of destiny. When CBS extended an offer (back in 1930) to join it full-time at $100 weekly, after almost three decades at the *Eagle* he resigned his post. But upon numerous run-ins with CBS news director Paul White over softening his stances, Kaltenborn pulled up stakes in 1940 to accept an NBC offer. During the war his average Hooper rating of 15.9 was second only to Walter Winchell's (who aired one night weekly to Kaltenborn's five). The latter solidified the Association of Radio News Analysts as its first president (1942) and penned eight volumes (1937–56). He narrated old newsreels on a syndicated TV documentary series (1953) and was a panelist on the tube version of *Who Said That?* (1954). He had appeared on its radio incarnation years earlier. Historiographer Luther Sies noted Kaltenborn's "rapid, staccato speech delivery that varied from 150 to 175 words per minute with occasional bursts of up to 200 words per minute." When CBS declared in 1939 that all news analysts should be neutral and objective, Kaltenborn said "no commentator could meet that standard." At times he appeared to possess more integrity than his profession could digest.

KAPLOW, Herbert. b. Feb. 2, 1927, New York, N.Y. Kaplow launched a career as a broadcast newsman over WCTC Radio, New Brunswick, N.J. After he received a master of science in journalism in 1951 from Chicago's Northwestern University, he joined NBC News in Washington, D.C., becoming a reporter three years later. One of his early assignments was to cover *Brown vs. the Board of Education* school desegregation conflict in May 1954. Kaplow reported from Atlanta, Birmingham, Clemson, S.C., Little Rock, Montgomery, New Orleans, and several more places in pursuit. Over a lengthy career he covered politics, reporting on 10 presidential campaigns between 1956 and 1992. He attended 19 presidential nominating conventions, too. Kaplow was also frequently sent on congressional, gubernatorial, and mayoralty election junkets. He traveled with Vice President Richard Nixon in 1958 on a Latin American tour, then with Nixon in 1964 to the Orient for a meeting with world leaders, and in 1968 with Nixon as he campaigned for president. Kaplow remained with NBC until 1972, when he switched to ABC as Washington correspondent. After a budget-cutting Capital Cities acquired ABC in 1985, hundreds of employees — some quite strategic — were shown the door. Kaplow, senior political correspondent then, received walking papers in 1986. He was able to discover some new opportunities at reduced levels. Among them he became senior editorial consultant for a debuting series at PBS (1997): veteran NBC newsman Bob Abernethy continues to host *Religion & Ethics Newsweekly*, although Kaplow left that PBS show some time ago. Over his professional tenure Kaplow pursued news events in 50 states plus 50 other nations. In 2012 he resided at Falls Church, Va., near the District of Columbia. He gained several honors for his involvement in ABC Radio projects: a Unity Award for "The Kennedy Years" (1983), Headliner and Unity awards for "The Dream Revisited" (1983), and an Emmy for the ABC Radio series *Directions*.

KENDRICK, Alexander. b. July 6, 1910, Philadelphia, Pa.; d. May 17, 1991, Philadelphia, Pa. Arriving at CBS in the late 1940s — too late to be one of the infamous "Murrow Boys" circling his late mentor (and clearly, idol) in the Second World War — Kendrick penned a warm memoir of his hero even so: *Prime Time: The Life of Edward R. Murrow* (Little, Brown, 1969). For him that period characterized "the fullest and most satisfying professional expression that any news staff has ever had." He had launched a journalism career with *The Public Ledger* in his hometown. Later switching to *The Philadelphia Inquirer*, he was dispatched to Europe at the war's start to cover the Murmansk Run where American freighters evaded Nazi U-boats ferrying supplies to the Soviet Union. While stationed in Russia, Kendrick became an eminent writer for *The Chicago Sun*. He crossed paths with Murrow in Rome following the war and was invited to join the CBS team. As a foreign correspondent Kendrick sent news from Moscow, Vienna, London, and many other cities on the continent. His reports aired irregularly on the daily *CBS World News Roundup*, *The World Tonight*, and *Edward R. Murrow and the News*. For the latter, CBS correspondents competed for time on Murrow's weeknight quarter-hour. A sponsor paid them $75 for each appearance, an enticement beyond exposure before millions. "Murrow treated them as experts," said one account. "He pitched unexpected questions to them while proffering himself as a rank novice, then sat back to listen while they exhibited their capacities." Is there any wonder why the colleagues doted on their icon? Dan Rather, future anchor of TV's *CBS Evening News*, followed Kendrick as bureau chief (1965). Kendrick went to Washington then and focused on writing. Beyond the Murrow biography he scored with *The Wound Within* (Little, Brown, 1974), an analysis of U.S. policy in the Vietnam War. He retired in 1976 from CBS and returned to his native Philadelphia.

KENNEDY, John Bright. b. Jan. 16, 1895, Quebec, Canada; d. July 22, 1961, Toronto, Canada. Airing in this country 1926–56, Kennedy isn't well remembered today among newscasters and commentators. He broadcast at discrete times on a pair of coast-to-coast chains (and perhaps a third). Kennedy first chased academia in a trio of nations: England, Canada, and the U.S. (St. Louis University here). Afterwards he entered print journalism full-time, initially for a horde of newspapers and later for some magazines. During the First World War, Kennedy managed the Knights of Columbus and edited its *Columbia* magazine followed by a decade at *Collier's* where he rose to managing editor. Although "just a sideline" to his editorial work, radio became a factor in Kennedy's life when he took a part-time post as announcer-newscaster at New York's WJZ (1926). On Jan. 1, 1927, WJZ became the flagship outlet of NBC's Blue web, projecting his voice far past the confines of Manhattan. As radio grew, options kept expanding. Kennedy accepted one in 1933, signing on full-time at NBC and putting print behind him. He transitioned to the newly separate Blue net in 1943, a web that became ABC two years hence. In 1950, he filled a commentary slot at ABC. In the meantime, he moonlighted at a couple of prominent New York stations: from April 1941 to January 1944, at WNEW as a newscaster, and later in that decade as a commentator at WOR, the flagship outlet of the MBS web. Kennedy's major series, *John B. Kennedy News*, a.k.a. *Looking Over the Week*, ran almost continuously (1933–51). In 1956, he co-anchored another entry, *John B. Kennedy-Edwin C. Hill News*. When not analyzing or reporting the news Kennedy's duties as an interlocutor saw him opening *The Collier Hour*, *General Motors Concert*, *The Magic Key*, *The Packard Hour*, *The People's Rally*, and *Radio City Party* among several entertainment features.

KURALT, Charles Bishop. b. Sept. 10, 1934, Wilmington, N.C.; d. July 4, 1997, New York, N.Y. At 14, Kuralt dispatched sports scores over Charlotte's ABC outlet, WAYS. He won a trip to Washington and met President Harry S Truman by taking first place in a high school American Legion essay competition. After graduating from Charlotte's Central High School he continued on to the University of North Carolina to earn a journalism degree (1955). UNC ultimately was so charmed by his accomplishments that in due course it recreated his office on its Chapel Hill campus near his interment site. Kuralt joined *The Charlotte News* as a reporter after leaving UNC. His offbeat human interest columns — an early indication of what he would undertake — gained him the Ernie Pyle Memorial Award (1956). And unable to get radio out of his system, he moved over to 50,000-watt WBT, Charlotte's CBS heavyweight, and — quickly discovered by the network — was summoned to New York to be one of its most prestigious reporters (1957). Kuralt went on the campaign trail following candidates bidding for the presidency in 1960, and then was appointed head of CBS's Latin America bureau in Miami. Named its principal West Coast voice in 1963, he was headed for a "career" as a roving correspondent (one of his superiors dubbed him "the next Ed Murrow," a tag Kuralt felt was over the top even if both he and Murrow were native Tar Heels). Following four eyewitness tours in Vietnam, Kuralt premiered a three-month trial of *On the Road* (1967), which struck a resounding chord with a large segment of his audience. He traveled over a million miles in fact, dispensing tales of people in American hamlets and behemoths. By then he was ready for another feather, a final one: on Jan. 28, 1979 — the debut of *Sunday Morning*, a CBS-TV newsmagazine — Kuralt anchored what was to be classified as "a crown jewel of the CBS News division," according to one critic. And when he retired at 60 in 1994, Kuralt was the longest tenured ethereal presence of CBS's news division.

Winning a trio of coveted George Foster Peabody awards over his 37 years there, Kuralt also gained 10 Emmys. He received the George Polk Memorial Award for national TV reporting (1981) and was cited as "Broadcaster of the Year" (1985) by the International Radio-Television Society. Kuralt penned a half-dozen books, some depicting his own journalistic tours. Gauging his career, CNN's Washington bureau chief Frank Sesno referred to "the most beautiful and vivid journalism that I've ever heard in broadcast." He continued: "His voice, his inflection, his delivery. Everything about him was just pure art." Indeed, "the next Ed Murrow"? Who could argue that?

LESUEUR, Lawrence Edward. b. June 10, 1909, New York, N.Y.; d. Feb. 5, 2003, Washington, D.C. Lesueur was born with ink in his veins. His father was a foreign correspondent for *The New York Sun* and *The New York Tribune*. His grandfather was newspaper publisher in the tiny burg of Tama, Iowa. From the outset Larry seemed likeminded, taking a post in Macy's advertising department after high school. Degreed by New York University in 1932, he became a private investigator, hated it, and went back to Macy's as a floorwalker. The journalism pedigree was overpowering however: he signed on at *Women's Wear Daily* as a reporter (1935). In 1936, he joined United Press (at $37.50 weekly, including workweeks that often ran 60 hours and above). Lesueur's predicament was about to improve. On the side — in the hours beyond 60 with UP — he submitted a few scripts to the producers of *We, the People* at CBS. They liked them and gave their new author some minor speaking roles too. Matching opportunity with appeal, Lesueur was soon departing for London after CBS invited him to join up (1939). As war hung on the horizon, he delivered human interest anecdotes from the British Isles. Not until then had anyone in his clan capitalized the "s" in the surname but he applied it (LeSueur). Newsman Edward R. Murrow added him to his roster of "Boys" to report continental war engagements. Lesueur went to the British Royal Air Force's command center in France in 1940, and returned to London as that nation fell to the Nazis. In autumn 1941, he was dispatched to Moscow and spent a couple of "miserably desolate" winters covering the battle. Lesueur's accounts were "some of the war's most pragmatic," pundits said. He toured factories, schools, hospitals, collective farms, Red Army encampments, prisoner camps, theaters, public gatherings, and ordinary Russian domiciles. His verbal expositions, short-waved to London and carried over the BBC, were transmitted to CBS in New York for airing in America. He encapsulated his efforts in *Twelve Months That Changed the World* (Knopf, 1943). Lesueur left Russia for New York as 1942 ended but was back in London by Murrow's side six months later. He remained in Europe to the Normandy invasion in 1945. Home again he launched an intermittent CBS Radio commentary (*Larry Lesueur and the News*, 1946–58). For two decades he was a presence on more aural series, including the CBS *World News Roundup*, *Chevrolet Spotlights the News*, and *The World Tonight*. He anchored newscasts over CBS's flagship video outlet, New York's WCBS-TV, the first journalist to do so recurringly (1946–47), preceding Douglas Edwards. His next post was as CBS United Nations rep. In the 1950s, Lesueur presided over a couple of CBS-TV series — *Chronoscope* (1953–55), a late-night world issues entry, and *The U.N. in Action* (1955–60), sporadically on Sunday mornings. The latter earned him a George Foster Peabody Award. After moving to the CBS bureau in the nation's capital, he resigned in 1963 to join the U.S. Information Agency's Voice of America. He stayed to 1983, retiring as White House correspondent. Some who chronicled the Murrow Boys activities — citing Lesueur's work as on a par with colleagues — emphatically stated that he gained few plaudits for his efforts. Labeling him CBS's "forgotten man," biographers Stanley Cloud and Lynne Olson noted: "Whenever CBS staged one of its commemorative extravaganzas extolling Murrow and the Boys, the people in charge always neglected to include Larry LeSueur." Those scribes dubbed him "the best and bravest of the 20th century's war reporters" with a standing that "earned him a permanent place in the network's pantheon." After 1963, Lesueur seldom went to New York where he invested all of his early working life beyond European soil. He died in the nation's capital four decades after moving to it.

LEVINE, Irving Raskin. b. Aug. 26, 1922, Pawtucket, R.I.; d. Mar. 27, 2009, Washington, D.C. If we could have seen him back in the day we would have always known Levine by the customary bowtie he traditionally wore to professional gigs (like work). This, of course, is beyond his highly identifiable nasal-toned measured delivery trademark branding at the close of every report: "Irving R. Levine ... NBC News ... Washington." The ellipses indicate some protracted pauses. We didn't know about the bowtie until he turned up on television after debuting on NBC Radio in 1950, of course. Levine was unique not simply in sight and sound but also tenure, persisting longer than almost any journalist, particularly with a single network. He reached 45 years at NBC by the time he went out to pasture in 1995. It may not have been a record but close. In time he moved from the Korean War into other provinces, yet was recognized from 1971 forward by insiders, listeners, and viewers as NBC's clearinghouse for economic news. One summary of his career proffered that — for nearly a quarter-century — Levine "explained the finer points of economics to millions of viewers." That designation allowed him to exceed 100 appearances on the public affairs forum *Meet the Press* and to ultimately contribute financial commentary weekly to derivative network MSNBC (1990–95). Over the long haul he covered more than 20 international economic summits with five U.S. presidents. Much earlier the bespectacled, bowtied Levine was invested in overseas assignments in far-flung places like Korea, Moscow, Vietnam, Algeria, Poland, and South Africa. From 1959 to 1970, with a brief time out in London (1967–68), he was NBC's bureau chief in Rome. As his web's correspondent to Russia (1955–59) — the first American reporter so accredited — he presided over a half-hour TV travelogue revealing the communist capital at the height of the Cold War in a way that Americans hadn't seen it. Highlights included an amusement park "not unlike Coney Island" and another park in which "old men played chess and mothers relaxed with their children." Swept up by the response, Levine followed with a book titled *Main Street, U.S.S.R.* (Doubleday, 1959) that bore a comparable premise. He also penned three other tomes. A first generation American of Ukrainian heritage, he fixated on being a foreign correspondent from a young age. After graduating from Brown University in 1944, he served in the U.S. Army Signal Corps during and after the Second World War. Following his release Levine enrolled in the journalism school at Columbia University, obtaining a master's degree in 1947. His professional pursuits commenced in 1940 — a decade before he arrived at NBC — with a home state newspaper while in college as he wrote obituaries for *The Providence Journal*. In 1947, he became a correspondent for the wire carrier International News Service and contributed to *The Times* of London. Initially sent to Vienna, he embarked on Korean War coverage in 1950. After offering some freelance reports to NBC he was invited to join the chain. Following retirement from it Levine joined the faculty of Lynn University, Boca Raton, Fla., as dean of the college of international communication. He retired there in 2004. From 1997 to 2008, he was a commentator on PBS's *Nightly Business Report*. On one occasion, he recalled with glee, NBC producers attempted to persuade him to shorten a piece for air by deleting the "R" in his habitually elongated signature sign-off "Irving R. Levine" complete with its lingering lapses. "I'd rather drop the 'B' in 'NBC,'" he quipped. He liked to poke fun at himself, a son allowed. When NBC newswoman Linda Ellerbee appeared as herself in the CBS-TV sitcom *Murphy Brown* in the 1990s, she started a rumor that the namesake character played by actress Candice Bergen "had the hots for Irving R. Levine." Daniel Levine, his offspring, recalled later, "Dad loved it."

LEWIS, Fulton, Jr. b. Apr. 30, 1903, Washington, D.C.; d. Aug. 21, 1966, Washington, D.C. When we think of electronic journalists who fell from grace, Lewis is unmistakably one. He toppled from his perch when a segment of the body politic turned on him long after he acceded as one of the shining stars in the nighttime ether. His outspokenness resulted in at least as many detractors as advocates. "Lewis was loved and hated with equal intensity," affirmed Booton Herndon in his biography *Praised and Damned: The Story of Fulton Lewis, Jr.* (Duell, Sloan and Pearce, 1954). In an epoch in which the nation was growing progressively liberal, Lewis reacted contrarily: he wasn't hesitant to push his radical conservative stance (for those times) down listeners' throats. Irving Fang included a mixed bag of reactions to Lewis in *Those Radio Commentators!* (Iowa State University Press, 1977) that underscored the love-hate tie with listeners: "One of the most dishonest reporters the American people have"; "Probably the most influential man of his profession on Capitol Hill"; "A fiendishly talented architect of mass intolerance and hate"; "One of the great patriots of the age." A contemporary observer said Lewis was "an erstwhile Rush Limbaugh ... the master of partisan smear who rarely strayed from GOP talking points." Abandoning his formal studies at the University of Virginia and George Washington University without degrees, Lewis reported for hometown paper *The Washington Herald* (1925). Two years later he added radio, reading news bulletins nightly over WMAL, owned by the paper. Rising to assistant city editor, he resigned in 1928 to join the conservative Universal News Service run by Hearst, soon becoming its local bureau chief. As he wed the GOP National

Committee chairman's daughter in 1929, looking on were First Lady Lou Hoover, Vice President Charles Curtis, Supreme Court justices, senators and a litany of GOP VIPs. Lewis dispatched a column, *The Washington Sideshow*, to 60 newspapers (1933–36) giving him wide exposure. WOL, the MBS affiliate in the nation's capital, hired him as a commentator in October 1937; he went coast-to-coast two months later. At his apex he was heard by 10 million over 500 MBS stations weeknights. He refused wire service connections to solicit his own news, also insisting that outlets carrying him engage their own sponsors. *Radio Days* said his try-outs on TV went nowhere ("simply not good television"). As the Sen. Joe McCarthy witch hunt heated up, Lewis enthusiastically signed on. When McCarthy's harangue ended in disgrace, the newsman waned. Though he persisted until a heart attack quelled him in summer 1966, his fans began to disperse. Fulton III, his son, attempted to succeed him but it wasn't the same. "The old magic," obsessed one pundit, "was gone."

MACK, Floyd (né Floyd Taft McLaughlin). b. Oct. 23, 1912, Ava, Oh.; d. Jan. 3, 1983, Newark, Oh. When his career is equated with most of his peers, Mack's often comes up short as a network newscaster. It lasted from 1942 to about 1945. Yet he was among a multitude of individuals pressed into service as replacements for the "A" teams by the major chains and stations, filling in for men called to overseas duty. Although his time delivering the headlines was pithy, he had a greater impact on the medium. Mack is more widely recognized as the enduring interlocutor of NBC's *Bell Telephone Hour*, where he exceeded the law of averages, performing for 18 years on radio (1940–58) plus a year of recorded encores (1968–69). Mack also acquired radio gigs presenting the music of Paul Whiteman and Everett Hoagland, *The Cavalcade of America*, and *X Minus One*. His radio introduction occurred at 17 at WALR, Zanesville, Ohio, where he was hired as an office boy (1930). He was asked to sub for an announcer one day and handled two shows so well that the owner promoted him to his announcing staff. A litany of similar jobs followed: WPAU, Portsmouth, Ohio (1934); WAIU, Columbus, Ohio (1934); WLW, Cincinnati (1935); NBC, Washington, D.C. (1936); MBS, Los Angeles (1937); MBS, New York (1939); and NBC, New York (1940). An enterprising fellow, Mack operated a recording business outside radio (1948–63). In 1963, he returned to his native Buckeye State to be special projects coordinator for funding and grants for a private venture. He also launched a local transportation service for seniors.

MACVANE, John Franklin. b. Apr. 29, 1912, Portland, Me.; d. Jan. 28, 1984, Brunswick, Me. A New Englander born and bred, MacVane was well educated with a bachelor's degree from Williams College, Williamstown, Mass., and a master's degree from Oxford (UK) University. He signed on to report for *The Brooklyn Daily Eagle* (1935) and the next year at *The New York Sun*, rising to rewrite editor. An eight-week summer away in 1938 kept him in Europe to 1945; he took a post as sub-editor at *The London Daily Express* which dispatched him to Paris to serve in its local bureau. He also worked for International News Service. Caught as the Nazi army invaded town, MacVane fled to London. He joined NBC there to report machinations of war to a U.S. audience (1940), observing from vantage points across Africa and Europe. He recalled it four decades later in *On the Air in World War II* (William Morrow, 1979). MacVane was the first broadcaster ashore at Omaha Beach on D-Day and the first U.S. newsman to enter Paris with Allied liberators in August 1944. After the war he became NBC's United Nations correspondent. Late in the 1940s, MacVane shifted his loyalty to ABC in the same post. From the early 1950s to the early 1960s, he contributed to a handful of ABC-TV series. At retirement in 1977, he left Westport, Conn., his hometown for more than two decades, to return to his native Maine.

MARBLE, Harry W. b. June 11, 1905, Brownville, Me.; d. Aug. 1, 1982, Damariscotta, Me. Although little remembered today, Marble was familiar to millions of radio listeners during the Second World War when he regularly presided over CBS Radio's *News of the World*, precursor of the CBS *World News Roundup*. Having begun his career at Boston's WORL and continued at Philadelphia's WCAU, Marble was a seasoned veteran of the ether when he moved to CBS in New York in 1941. As a staff announcer from the postwar era to 1955, he introduced a number of the chain's entertainment features (e.g., *Margaret Arlen, Matinee Theater, Radio Reader's Digest, Up for Parole*). Marble was a key figure in the CBS Radio and TV documentary *You Are There* for a few years in this period. He took his skills to Portland, Maine's WGAN Radio-TV in 1955, retiring from it in the early 1970s. For the last 27 years of his life he resided in Greenland Cove, Md.

MARVIN, Anthony (Tony) (né Marvin Sandusky). b. Oct. 5, 1912, New York, N.Y.; d. Oct. 10, 1998, Boynton Beach, Fla. When most people think of Tony Marvin they recall a deep bass voice, reserved yet gregarious, sophisticated — a performer habitually linked to a broadcasting icon: Arthur Godfrey. Marvin was the Old Redhead's interlocutor in the heyday of manifold daily and weekly variety series on CBS Radio-TV ("and now, here's that man himself"). He introduced other shows (*Casey, Crime Photographer*; *The Columbia Workshop*; *This Life Is Mine*; and more) while dispatching news, beginning Oct. 1, 1939. And what few people realize is that, while back in the day most Americans believed Marvin was of Italian ancestry and he didn't comment on it professionally, he was actually of Jewish heritage. His parents (Joseph and Ida "Marvin" Sandusky) were first generation Jewish Americans. Both extended from native Russian parents who immigrated to New York. Another stereotypical myth in radio's lineage of entertainers is put to rest with the disclosure. Attending hometown St. John's University in hopes of becoming a physician, the youth quit after two years in the throes of the Depression to help his family. After taking many other odd jobs like ushering in a theater he became a mechanic. He sang to himself one day and a limousine owner overheard him, was impressed, and offered to bankroll voice training for him. A coach tutored Marvin for a year and he performed with the New York Operatic Guild and won roles in comedy theater. In 1937, WNYC added Marvin to its staff as chief announcer. Dubbed "official voice" of the New York World's Fair, he joined CBS as announcer-newscaster (1939). The latter duty — prior to teaming with Godfrey (1945) — resumed when Marvin left CBS for MBS (1959). He earned the dubious honor as the last of the celebrated "Little Godfreys" cast standing (a difficult Godfrey had fired his performers or they had quit). In 1958, *The Tony Marvin Show*, a daily two-hour matinee DJ entry, bowed over New York's WABC, flagship of the ABC web. Marvin conducted a talk show later and did commercial voiceovers. In the 1950s, his was the broadcast voice of Tony the Tiger, an advertising emblem of cereal-maker W.K. Kellogg. One never knows how far a few voice lessons will go. A media historiographer conjectured: "For a decade-and-a-half he [Marvin] was the deep-voiced, reliably affable and erudite foil for emcee-humorist-vocalist Godfrey and his lighthearted repartee. Marvin's input contributed emphatically to Godfrey's multiple broadcast features in dual mediums."

MCCORMICK, Robert K. b. Aug. 9, 1911, Danville, Ky.; d. Sept. 4, 1984, New York, N.Y. This journalist, educated at George Washington University in the nation's capital, isn't the one by the same moniker who published *The Chicago Tribune* and also owned station WGN. While this one reached his summit in TV, he made his mark earlier in radio by conducting a daily NBC quarter-hour newscast (1947–49). He joined the web shortly after the start of the Second World War, and habitually signed off with "Robert McCormick ... NBC News ... Washington." In the same era he was one of a handful of newsmen at the first televised Democratic national political convention in Philadelphia (1948). Subsequently he worked as NBC's Washington manager of TV news and special events and later as the chain's Paris-based European TV correspondent. Although he was in Manhattan when he died, McCormick's retirement home was at Tarpon Springs, Fla.

MCNAMEE, Thomas Graham. b. July 10, 1888, Washington, D.C.; d. May 9, 1942, New York, N.Y. During his earliest days in broadcasting, McNamee could be considered a newscaster in modern parlance, reporting eyewitness events of monumental proportions as they occurred. But he is more fittingly recalled as a leading network announcer, emcee, and sportscaster for focusing the bulk of his efforts into myriad arenas after his first few years in the business. His transition from performing as a vocalist at public venues into radio announcing didn't occur until he was 35, out of work, and hurting, however. Hoping to return to concert tours rapidly, McNamee nevertheless accepted a blended post as announcer and baritone soloist at New York's WEAF (1923). He would rise to be, according to one contemporary critic, "the first announcer superstar." A radio historiographer observed: "Within a year McNamee would be the most famous man in radio — without question the most influential and hardest-worked announcer in the medium's first decade." Few might question it. In those days, however, "announcer" was often broadened to encompass far more than now. And "newscaster" could be considered a misnomer, too, for it seldom involved reading any prepared copy over the airwaves about what had transpired of interest to the listeners. Instead "news" was generally event-focused and consisted of telling the audience what was transpiring *right then*. McNamee reported on parades, political campaigns, inaugurations, airship arrivals, ceremonies honoring individuals for achievements or bravery, public park and library ribbon-cuttings, and the like. His signature broadcast opening, "Good evening, ladies and gentlemen of the radio audience," became a familiar axiom to listeners in the East. Typical examples of his assignments included the dual major party political conventions (1924), the launch of the National Broadcasting Company in which he was master of ceremonies during a four-hour gala (1926), and the triumphant return of aviator Charles Lindbergh following a heroic inaugural Atlantic crossing by air (1927). All of this in addition to scads of sporting events like the World Series, National Football League Thanksgiving football scrimmages, boxing matches, Rose Bowl, Kentucky Derby, and many more athletic competitions. What McNamee didn't know about individual sports that he covered he ultimately acquired. At the same time, he presided over a plethora of early programming fare (i.e., *The Atwater-Kent Hour*, *Believe It or Not*, *The Cities Service Orchestra*, *The Texaco Fire Chief*, *Elsa Maxwell's Party Line*, *Major Bowes' Original Amateur Hour*, *The Rudy Vallee Show*, *The Voice of Firestone*, *Vox Pop*, et al.). He was also penning a Sunday syndicated newspaper column, "Graham McNamee Speaking," with "interesting gossip of the broadcasting studio." And finally his tome, *You're On the Air* (Harper, 1926), was one of the very first to spotlight the electrifying new information and entertainment medium.

MORGAN, Edward Paddock. b. June 23, 1910, Walla Walla, Wash.; d. Jan. 27, 1993, McLean, Va. *The Seattle Star* engaged Morgan to report for it (1932) once he completed studies at his hometown Whitman College and Seattle's University of Washington. Later moving to United Press International, he was dispatched to cover war atrocities in Italy, Palestine, and more far-flung sites. He joined *The Chicago Daily News* and — after the war — *Collier's* magazine editorial staff. Hired by CBS in 1951, Morgan sporadically added reports to the nightly *Edward R. Murrow and the News*. By late 1954, he moved to ABC where he remained for two decades. Airing from the nation's capital, he secured a heritage with *Edward P. Morgan News and Commentary*, a weeknight quarter-hour. His composed manner contrasted markedly with the machine-gun deliveries of a few other commentators, critics attested. Furthermore his left-leaning opinions were diametrically opposed to the persuasions of a handful of earlier opinionated radio analysts. Morgan received a prestigious George Foster Peabody Award for his poignant reporting of the sinking of the passenger liner *Andrea Doria* in the north Atlantic on July 25, 1956. Though he did not state it then, he was convinced that his only child, 14, perished in that disaster. (She did not.) His analyses over the years won for him the Sidney Hillman Foundation Award (1959) and the Alfred I. duPont Award (1960). Throughout the 1950s and 1960s, Morgan was a key figure in many TV productions on ABC, CBS, and PBS (then NET). He retired from ABC in 1975, and curtailed a Newsday Syndicate column that year.

MUELLER, Merrill Frank. b. Jan. 27, 1916, New York, N.Y.; d. Nov. 30, 1980, Los Angeles, Calif. "Red" Mueller (so called by cohorts for his blazing hair) was a key member of NBC's overseas wartime deputation in the early to mid–1940s. Growing up in Westport, Conn., at 14 he was reporting for a local daily newspaper. Eventually, during the war, he offered pool coverage to all the audio webs by providing Americans with word pictures from the Allied central command of Gen. Dwight D. Eisenhower on June 6, 1944 (D-Day). In 1945, Mueller posted eyewitness accounts from the Pacific theater. He had been exposed to foreign soil well before the war, however. Formally educated at Paris' Sorbonne, at 20 he was a European correspondent for International News Service (1936). Soon he began contributing to *Newsweek* too, and in the late 1930s, worked his way up to chief of the newsmagazine's London bureau. While continuing there he also began broadcasting for NBC (1939). In 1943, Mueller accepted full-time correspondent duties with the network. Returning home following the ceasefire, he was one of NBC's prime news commentators, dispatching events for the chimes chain for a quarter-century. He regularly turned up for NBC's epic weekend marathon *Monitor* from the mid–1950s through the late 1960s, dispatching top-of-the-hour headlines plus occasional features in half-hour news specials aired within that series' framework. Though he was most often heard on radio, intermittently Mueller was called to duty for NBC-TV special events coverage. He was before the cameras on the day John F. Kennedy died (1963) and — with Jay Barbree — co-anchored multiple space launches in that decade. Shifting to ABC in 1968, Mueller anchored most of its radio Apollo 13 crisis coverage. Leaving ABC in 1976, he taught journalism for a year at Ohio University followed by a similar assignment at Syracuse University before retiring in 1979.

MURROW, Edward Roscoe. (né Egbert Roscoe Murrow). b. Apr. 25, 1908, Pole Cat Creek,

N.C.; d. Apr. 27, 1965, Pawling, N.Y. Of the handful of memorable names of newscasters-commentators in the halcyon days of chain radio — Heatter, Kaltenborn, Murrow, and Thomas foremost among them — two (Murrow and Lowell Thomas) settled in the tiny burg in the upscale Berkshire foothills township of Pawling, N.Y. (2010 pop. 8,463), some 60 miles north of the big city. And they died there. Adding to the irony, for multiple decades both were heard on CBS. While across the years others profoundly spoke into its microphones, indisputably it was Murrow who set the gold standard for CBS and all of broadcasting (some say since). He was the one so many peers and heirs preferred to copy. None carried his power and burden. He was the mentor, pal, and authority in setting basic patterns of electronic journalism during the earliest days of dual mediums. Primed at State College of Washington, Pullman, Murrow was initially introduced to the ether there, sportscasting over campus station KWSC, as he pursued a speech degree. Graduating in 1930, he was hired to run the National Student Federation of America in New York. His world vision broadened rapidly as he visited Europe multiple times, a continent where he would soon spend some years, that first time as coordinator of collegians on tour. CBS summoned him as director of talks in 1937, perceived as a non-broadcast role. He was sent back to Europe where he observed preparations for war. Murrow participated in a prototype of the *CBS World News Roundup* on Mar. 13, 1938, which was still airing in 2012. By Sept. 22, 1938, he was heard frequently in the states from London by shortwave radio (his familiar sign-on, "This is London," was emblematic for years). As war clouds darkened he was sanctioned to hire a cadre of correspondents to assist in reporting what was transpiring across Europe. Insiders dubbed his deputation of remarkably talented journalists the "Murrow Boys." Profilers Stanley Cloud and Lynne Olson assigned 11 reporters to the tribe: Mary Marvin Breckinridge, Cecil Brown, Winston Burdett, Charles Collingwood, William Downs, Thomas Grandin, Richard C. Hottelet, Larry Lesueur, Eric Sevareid, William L. Shirer, and Howard K. Smith. An appraisal of Murrow's significance in informing America during the war could entail many pages. Suffice it that many hints of his efforts appear in earlier pages. CBS Chairman William S. Paley prevailed on him to be VP for public affairs when the newsman came home after the war. It was a task Murrow neither sought nor desired. He gave up his airtime, anathema to his whole being. After a few months he returned to the ether, resuming the nightly *Edward R. Murrow and the News* (1942–44, 1947–59) with a platform he loved, securing an audience of millions for CBS. On Jan. 1, 1950, he launched what became an annual evaluation of the previous year's news events with a freewheeling, scholarly exchange among the legendary "Murrow Boys." As their leader fielded questions, turning the spotlight on colleagues, he let them bask in the glow he could have taken. It underscored their warm ties. Murrow's radio salary of $112,000 (highest in the industry) rose to about $250,000 as he added two CBS-TV series to his chores — the documentary *See It Now* (1951–58) and the interview feature *Person to Person* (1953–59). Nevertheless he was suspicious of TV, "a medium that depended more on pictures than words," never hiding his predilection for radio and sharply criticizing video at public forums. His most memorable telecast occurred Mar. 9, 1954, when Murrow directly challenged the diatribes of Sen. Joseph R. McCarthy (R-Wis.), a once respected lawmaker whose career had evolved into a fanatical witch hunt seeking Nazi and Communist sympathizers in high places. McCarthy's innuendo, often without validation, was exposed. The U.S. Senate later censured McCarthy for bringing "dishonor and disrepute" to their body. Earning prestigious George Foster Peabody awards four times (1943, 1949, 1951, 1954), Murrow ultimately fell out of favor with Paley and executive leadership at CBS in the late 1950s. He took a year's sabbatical in 1959–60, and departed the web forever in 1961 when President John F. Kennedy asked him to direct the U.S. Information Agency with accountability for the Voice of America. An extended illness and early death ended the further contributions Murrow might have made. The accolades at his passing, however, were hardly repressed, and he remains even now the model that many electronic journalists aspire for themselves.

NEWMAN, Edwin Harold. b. Jan. 25, 1919, New York, N.Y.; d. Aug. 13, 2010, Oxford, England. Marked by intellect, a droll wit, and a limitless fondness for puns, Newman — dubbed by one reporter as "a prince among men" — was a linguistic wizard with an obsession for defending legitimate applications of the Mother Tongue. "He made us feel like we had a very smart, classy friend in the broadcast news business," said NBC's Brian Williams, TV anchor and managing editor of the *Nightly News*. A line of books certifying Newman's zest for proper dialect emanated from his fertile pen: *Strictly Speak-*

ing: *Will America Be the Death of English?* (Bobbs-Merrill, 1974) reached first place on *The New York Times* non-fiction bestseller list, along with *A Civil Tongue* (Bobbs-Merrill, 1976), *Sunday Punch* (Houghton Mifflin, 1979), and *I Must Say: On English, the News, and Other Matters* (Warner, 1988). With identifying balding head and fierce dark eyebrows, a sly but grinning Newman was a fixture at NBC News from 1952 to 1984 as a radio correspondent. He also made inveterate appearances on all the chain's leading news and public affairs TV productions (*Meet the Press*, *Nightly News*, *Today*). That was but a start in calculating his gifts to manifold projects, several beyond the ether. Graduating from Manhattan's George Washington High School, Newman acquired a political science degree from the University of Wisconsin at Madison (1940). He took an active collegiate role at *The Daily Cardinal*, indoctrinating his veins with ink. (An older sibling, Morton Newman, was a reporter for *The Chicago Daily News*.) Though he briefly studied American government in grad school at Louisiana State University, Baton Rouge, Ed Newman departed academia to be a "dictation boy" at Washington's International News Service. Not there long either, he transferred to a wire competitor, United Press. For a dozen hours on Dec. 7, 1941—the day Pearl Harbor was attacked—he took dictation from UP reporters phoning in their stories. Although his apprenticeship was basic, it grounded him in the skills to last a lifetime. His UP work was interrupted for service as a signal officer in the Navy in Trinidad and at the Brooklyn Navy Yard (1942–45). Returning to UP the newsman soon left for the Washington bureau of the progressive New York newspaper *PM*, departing again for Washington's Tufty News Service. An altogether new sphere opened in 1947 as he joined the Washington bureau of CBS News. Newman's first couple of years in radio saw him help legendary CBS journalist Eric Sevareid prepare his daily on-air stints. Striking out on his own as a freelancer in London in 1949— often on behalf of NBC—Newman joined that web full time as a London-based correspondent three years hence. (The British obviously impressed him. Not only was his preoccupation with language intensified, the locale instigated a magnetic clutch that pulled him back as a resident in retirement.) In the 1950s he was NBC bureau chief in London, Rome, and Paris, finally settling in New York in 1961. His pursuits encompassed French President Charles de Gaulle's rise to power (1958), provided gavel-to-gavel coverage of the national political conventions every quadrennial (1960–84), added to myriad NBC-TV documentaries (1961–81), broke the news of President John F. Kennedy's death to NBC's radio audience (1963), anchored TV coverage of the Six Day Arab-Israeli War (1967) plus coverage surrounding the assassinations of Martin Luther King and Robert F. Kennedy (1968), as well as the Vietnam ceasefire (1973). In addition, he's recalled for moderating two presidential debates (Ford-Carter in 1967, Reagan-Mondale in 1984), conducting 250-plus hour-long interviews with public figures for his *Speaking Freely* radio show aired over New York's WNBC weekly and syndicated to other outlets (1967–76), and being the sole journalist to interview Japanese Emperor Hirohito prior to a diplomatically sensitive visit to the U.S. (1975). One of a quartet christened "The Four Horsemen of the Apocalypse" during political conventions starting in 1968 (including NBC's John Chancellor, Frank McGee, and Sander Vanocur), Newman roamed convention floors with a superior technological backpack that let him interview delegates live, a breakthrough novelty. As a music lover he hosted Boston Symphony concerts, contributed to NBC's religious affairs unit, relished assignments for sports broadcasts, and was a Broadway drama critic (1965–71). He won seven Emmys for his drama reviews at the network's flagship affiliate, WNBC-TV, New York, including hosting the local series *Speaking Freely*. For many years Newman was chairman of the usage panel of Houghton Mifflin's *American Heritage Dictionary*. A long run of syndicated newspaper columns for King Features ranged over U.S. politics, foreign policy, journalistic assignments, and the state of English. After leaving the network on Jan. 31, 1984, Newman was in demand as an interviewer, narrator, and moderator, and turned up on profuse numbers of PBS and cable channel shows. He went on the lecture circuit, currying the favor of audiences he addressed on language and journalism. Newman acted in multiple spoofs that gave him venues to exhibit a quirky sense of humor. They included a handful of films (*The Pelican Brief*, *Spies Like Us*, *My Fellow Americans*) and TV series (*Newhart*, *Mr. Belvedere*, *The Golden Girls*, *Wings*, *Murphy Brown*, *Saturday Night Live*). He received a prestigious George Foster Peabody Award in 1966. Newman and his wife moved to England in 2007 where their only child, a married daughter, lived.

O'CONNOR, Charles Peter. b. June 10, 1910, Cambridge, Mass.; d. Mar. 17, 1942, Douglastown,

N.Y. O'Connor's life was all too brief; his death at 31 removed one of the youngest promising newscaster-announcers of the national airwaves. For 11 years he was an NBC news correspondent (1931–42) and introduced features in the era like *The Court of Human Relations, Crime Doctor, Major Bowes' Original Amateur Hour*, and *Philip Morris Presents*. Giving a public recitation at age five put him before an audience early, possibly a prolonged influence. He quit school after a year at Boston College to tour the East with a stock company. In January 1931, Boston's WBZ hired O'Connor to announce as did NBC in New York later that year. He was one of 10 contenders (among 2,500 applicants in the Depression) to win NBC spots. On Mar. 1, 1932, O'Connor and a few cohorts set up a truck-mounted mobile transmitting apparatus to report from the Hopewell, N.J., Lindbergh baby kidnapping trial. On June 1, 1936, he covered a festive gala surrounding the New York arrival of the maiden voyage of the *Queen Mary*. He also handled many football scrimmages. Lapsing into alcoholic spates, O'Connor eventually was shunned by the networks, stations, and sponsors. An inability to maintain work resulted in his suicide.

OSGOOD, Charles (né Charles Osgood Wood, III). b. Jan. 8, 1933, New York, N.Y. Although few recall it, in his early days on the national airwaves CBS's "poet-in-residence" was a news correspondent at ABC. The man whose emblematic "See you on the radio" made him memorable, Fordham-trained (1954) Osgood rose to the vanguard with a litany of mounting tasks: program director and manager of WGMS Radio, Washington, D.C.; general manager of WHCT-TV, Hartford, Conn.; general assignment reporter at ABC, New York (1963–67); and anchor-reporter for WCBS, New York (1967–71). Joining CBS News in September 1971, he launched *The Osgood File* that year, one of the prevailing status symbols of radio with frequent lyrical interludes on disparately timely topics. In 2012, his brief recorded posts still aired throughout weekdays. After anchoring early morning and late evening news features on CBS-TV, Osgood became host of its 90-minute *Sunday Morning* magazine (1994). He was still doing that in 2012. Author of numerous humorous tomes and a syndicated column, he gained about every honor a broadcaster had a right to: no less than a dozen honorary degrees (mostly doctorates); impressive trustee- and director-ships; organ, piano and banjo gigs with the Mormon Tabernacle Choir, New York Pops, and Boston Pops; "Father of the Year" Award (1985); George Foster Peabody awards (1985, 1986, 1997); induction into the Radio Hall of Fame (1990); International Radio-TV Society honors (1999); five "Best in Business" awards of *The Washington Journalism Review*. As this is readied, the Radio Hall of Fame still claims online — as it has for many years — that he's "the voice of CBS News."

PEARSON, Andrew Russell (Drew). b. Dec. 13, 1897, Evanston, Ill.; d. Sept. 1, 1969, Washington, D.C. Earning a degree from Swathmore (Pa.) College in 1919, Pearson — for a couple of years — exhibited some of his Quaker instincts by assisting First World War refugees in present-day Montenegro and Serbia. Returning home he taught geography at the University of Pennsylvania followed by an 18-month global trek. It exposed him to the world and netted a syndicated column. Subsequent overseas trips provided spice for the lecture circuit. In his mid-twenties he resumed teaching geography at Columbia University followed by his hire as foreign editor of the *United States Daily*, forerunner of *U.S. News & World Report*. As the same time, Pearson joined *The Baltimore Sun* as diplomatic correspondent. Without any fanfare he shared in an illegal Irish Sweepstakes ticket smuggling venture that paid him $30,000 annually with a chauffeured Lincoln Continental as a perk. His involvement somehow went unnoticed, something his many critics would have capitalized on later had they known it. With *The Christian Science Monitor* Washington bureau chief Robert Allen, Pearson secretly released *Washington Merry-Go-Round* (Horace Liveright, 1931), an anthology of gossip about public figures. The *Sun* fired Pearson when it learned who was behind it. International News Service hired him but it, too, fired him after the pressure mounted. When the intrepid writing pair issued a sequel in 1932, all their employers let them go. Things were bleak in the short-term but not for long as a lifetime of notoriety sprung up. The duo sold a daily newspaper column, *Washington Merry-Go-Round*, to United Features Syndicate. Six papers initially subscribed but at its peak 620 papers ran it. "The column put the screws to those in the seats of power and in proper Washington society, too, making unflattering disclosures a practice," noted a source. Pearson disseminated it alone after Allen left for war (1941), curtailing their joint venture. Before the split, the infamous twosome sat before microphones to offer an engaging audio version of the outrageous treats in their column. After 1940, Pearson did that solo. He angered the far right during the Joseph R. McCarthy-inspired witch hunt seeking Communist and Nazi sympathizers at mid–20th century. Pearson sided with a more tolerant left although he was probably too successful to fire then. He fought the Ku Klux Klan in an era when doing so was unpopular, fervidly angered two presidents (Roosevelt and Truman), and cited many lawmakers and other public figures for their perceived shortcomings. An ABC-TV reporter during the 1952 political conventions, Pearson took his popular radio series to TV over ABC and then Dumont (1952–53). Further, he produced a syndicated TV feature, *Predictions of Things to Come* (1954–57). The commentator also penned the newsletter *Personal from Pearson* plus 10 books across his lifetime.

PIERPOINT, Robert Charles. b. May 16, 1925, Redondo Beach, Calif.; d. Oct. 22, 2011, Santa Barbara, Calif. Lauded for introducing the human interest factor into Korean War coverage, plus reporting the daily activities of a half-dozen of the nation's chief executives, Pierpoint was one of the most enduring journalists to serve a single network (CBS). "Few have trailed as many presidents as Pierpoint," a source affirmed. His yield from Eisenhower to Carter (1957–80) produced extraordinary detail on the executive branch. His tenure at CBS persisted past four decades and saw him at the site of several imposing moments in the country's history. Riding in the press bus during the Kennedy motorcade in Dallas in 1963, Pierpoint heard the fatal shots ring out and proceeded to Parkland Hospital where — for three hours — he telephoned comments to CBS on what he saw and heard. He literally became the eyes and ears of a nation transfixed by his every word. His Watergate coverage in the next decade was captivating as he got a close-up look at what was transpiring within the White House. After graduating from Whittier (Calif.) Union High School (1943) Pierpoint joined the navy but did not see action; his deployment was channeled into stateside readiness. Following his discharge two years hence, he enrolled in Pasadena's California Institute of Technology on the GI Bill. He completed a degree in 1948 at the University of Redlands (Calif.). A lifelong educational advocate, Pierpoint proceeded with graduate studies at the University of Stockholm (Sweden). In 1949, in a break from classes, he traveled to Finland while a Communist uprising occurred. Reporting the news to CBS, he was invited to become a stringer for the chain on his return to Stockholm. A subsequent chance meeting with CBS European chief Ed Murrow led him to a post as a full-time correspondent. Pierpoint was dispatched to Tokyo and was thereby in place to cover the looming Korean conflict. Speaking from Korea he contributed to Murrow's debuting CBS-TV series *See It Now* in November 1951, where he humanized personhood. "Pierpoint's report was among the very first on television to focus on the soldier in a more personal style, as opposed to the newsreel film style that featured battles and material over the story of the individual trooper," a contemporary report allowed. During a Christmas *See It Now* show in December 1953, Pierpoint interviewed U.S. troops stationed in Korea, persisting in the relevancy of the individual combatant. Covering the war intermittently on TV, most of Pierpoint's observations aired on CBS Radio's *World News Roundup* broadcasts weekday evenings. He continued giving coverage after the war to 1957 as CBS's Far East bureau chief. As a result of his pioneering Korean War reportage his voice was heard on the single most-watched TV episode in history: it occurred at the end of the *MASH* run in 1983, as 125 million viewers heard Pierpoint announce the ceasefire that ended the fighting. In 23 years at the White House, the newsman earned Emmys for reporting on the resignation of Vice President Spiro Agnew and backdrop on Charles G. ("Bebe") Rebozo, Nixon intimate. The memoir *At the White House: Assignment to Six Presidents* (Putnam, 1981) is introspective, giving his annotations on first families as well as how the head of state functioned politically while interacting as head of household. A CBS publicist maintained that "his biggest mark" at CBS News came as he covered the "political wars," presumably during the White House years. At the end of his run there in 1980, Pierpoint shifted to the State Department where he continued to report until he retired from CBS in 1990. He made frequent appearances on television's *CBS Evening News* with Walter Cronkite and *Sunday Morning* with Charles Kuralt. He ultimately donated a collection of professional and personal mementoes to his alma mater at Redlands, Calif. Included are photographs, reminiscences, speeches, correspondence, press badges, and presidential memorabilia (pens used by chief executives and commemorative items from visits abroad). In his last interview, appearing on Oct. 2, 2011 — three weeks before his death — in reference to that awful day in Dallas nearly a half-century ago, Pierpoint expressed a personal conviction to *The Santa Barbara News-Press*: "I didn't like what the priest said about a time to live and a time to die. It was not Kennedy's time to die."

POLK, George. b. Oct. 17, 1913, Ft. Worth, Tex.; d. May 1948, Greece. One of the few broadcast newsmen whose death overshadowed his significance as a journalist, Polk is remembered for vanishing in Greece 65 years ago on a CBS assignment, his body turning up a few days after that. A boatman discovered it floating in the bay of Salonika in northern Greece. Polk had been shot in the back of the head at point-blank range; his hands and feet were tied. He had flown to Salonika on Friday, May 7, and he was found Sunday, May 16, 1948. His disappearance and sighting became a subject of speculation and investigation without satisfactory conclusion. Although a trio of suspects was tried and convicted for his murder in May 1949, some decried the outcome as "a sham," insisting that unknown assailants were guilty. The episode is the theme of Elias Vlanton's volume *Who Killed George Polk?: The Press Covers Up a Death in the Family* (Temple University Press, 1996). Vlanton's is the most recent of a handful of late 20th century tomes exploring Polk's role in controversial news plus his death and the aftermath. The CBS newsman was reporting a Greek civil war and is alleged to have injected himself into hullabaloo between a right-wing government and communists, sparing no ridicule of both. Branding communist guerrillas "thugs," he labeled the Greek leaders "greedy" and "corrupt," depicted an ex-minister of public order as a gangster, and vilified America's buttressing of a tyrannical Grecian regime. The year following his murder, a series of news media high achievement honors was inaugurated in the U.S. Named the George Polk Award in Journalism, it's presented annually by Long Island (N.Y.) University and modeled after the Pulitzer Prize for outstanding efforts in print news. Radio journalists Don Hollenbeck, Peter Laufer, Edward R. Murrow, Daniel Schorr, Eric Sevareid, Howard K. Smith and many more have been Polk recipients. Polk earned a bachelor's degree at the University of Alaska (1938) before launching a journalistic quest. That was interrupted by serving in the marines during the Second World War in the Pacific. His claims of some wartime exploits were a topic of further controversy examined on the Internet in the present millennium. When Ed Murrow hired him for the CBS news staff in 1946, Polk was nevertheless described by a Murrow biographer as "a young decorated war veteran." He was assigned then to the Middle East.

PUTNAM, George Frederick (a.k.a. George Carson Putnam). b. July 14, 1914, Breckenridge, Minn.; d. Sept. 12, 2008, Chino, Calif. "Silvery, melodious and super-smooth" said *Time* in assessing Putnam's on-air performance. Columnist-commentator Walter Winchell said his was "the greatest voice in radio." Putnam carried that one to the bank, telling the daily Los Angeles *Metropolitan News-Enterprise* the endorsement "made his career." He was initially exposed to radio at Minneapolis' WDGY on his 20th birthday (1934) but three years elapsed before St. Paul's KSTP hired him as a sportscaster. After joining NBC in New York (1939), Putnam appeared on a trio of news series. He was a Movietone newsreel narrator in some of the war years too (1941–44). Drafted by the army in the Second World War, he transferred to the marines and became first lieutenant, overseeing links to the Armed Forces Radio Service (1944–46). Returning home, Putnam went on the air over MBS with daily newscasts on July 1, 1946. To avoid name chaos with another George Putnam then at NBC, he revised his taxonomy to "George Carson Putnam." In 1951, *TV Guide* reported he had "self-destructed," was heavily in debt and headed for divorce. Leaving his troubles behind, Putnam departed for Hollywood where KTTV-TV hired him as a newscaster (1951). He reverted to his true identity. Over several decades he became a hit in the L.A. market, newscasting and handling other chores at TV stations KTTV and KTLA and a quartet of radio outlets: KHJ, KCOP, KIEV, and KPLS. His video work is recalled with a star on the Hollywood Walk of Fame. "There has never been a more popular and influential newsman in Los Angeles television than Putnam," said columnist Roger Grace in the *News-Enterprise* in January 2003.

SAERCHINGER, Cesar Victor. b. Oct. 23, 1884, Aachen, Germany; d. Oct. 10, 1971, Washington, D.C. Emigrating to the U.S. at nine, Saerchinger joined *The New York Evening Post* as a foreign correspondent after the First World War (1920s). When a CBS newsman had to return home from London before an event being covered ended, he persuaded Saerchinger to fill in. He did so and afterwards offered to supply British officials for CBS interviews. In 1930, Saerchinger became "the pioneer and dean of this esoteric profession of foreign radio representatives" as CBS's first permanent European newsman. He literally inaugurated transatlantic broadcasts seven years before Ed Murrow's arrival. CBS, however, did not realize what it had. When Saerchinger told them he could get Adolf Hitler to the chain's microphone for $1,500 in 1932 — the same Hitler about to be German chancellor — he was snubbed with this cable: "Unwant Hitler at any price." The window for attracting a madman with visions of global domination soon closed. In 1937, everything changed: Saerchinger resigned at CBS to go with NBC which sent him to New York. CBS's replacement (Murrow) arrived in London that spring. The rest is history. Saerchinger gained a weekly quarter-hour commentary and was assigned other newscasting duties at NBC. He returned to Europe to participate in NBC's D-Day coverage June 6, 1944. An earlier analysis of his efforts reads: "Given the advantage of distance and time it seems evident that even Saerchinger himself did not fully appreciate the groundbreaking strides he made as a pioneering broadcast journalist. He resigned his European post in May 1937 because, according to a radio historian, he believed 'there was no future in it.' If Saerchinger failed to recognize the possibilities growing out of where he had been, others likely did too. None of that diminishes his extensive accomplishments, of course. Considering the foundation he laid, overseas reporting appeared to have begun where he left off."

ST. JOHN, Robert William. b. Mar. 9, 1902, Chicago, Ill.; d. Feb. 6, 2003, Waldorf, Md. St. John exhibited early signs of rabble-rousing that persisted for his whole life. Like many other youths he lied about his age to get into the navy (at 16) to fight overseas in the First World War. Subsequently enrolling at Trinity College, Hartford, Conn., he took a job during school reporting for *The Hartford Courant*. But his pursuits spelled trouble when he exposed the college president for censoring a faculty member, resulting in his dismissal from Trinity. St. John took more reporting posts in rapid fire order: *The Oak Leaves*, Oak Park, Ill. (1922), *The Chicago American* and *The Chicago Daily News* (both 1923), and *The Cicero Tribune* (1923–26). He and his brother bought the *Tribune*. At 21, Robert St. John was an editor and publisher! He persevered in his seditious acts, creating a stir among prohibitionists and divulging the sleaze of notorious mobster Al Capone. St. John's exposés caught up with him and he nearly lost his life. Ralph Capone, the gangster's sibling, almost beat the crusader senseless before some chums sent in a figurehead to wrest control of the *Tribune* from the brothers St. John. Robert continued his quests at *The Rutland* (Vt.) *Herald* as managing and then city editor (1927–29), *The Camden* (N.J.) *Courier* as reporter (1929), *The Philadelphia* (Pa.) *Record* as cable editor (1929–31), the Associated Press in New York as night city editor (1931–33), freelance author and farmer at Barnstead, N.H. (1933–39), and at the Associated Press again as Balkan correspondent (1939–41). When the Nazis bombed a troop train on which he was riding in Greece, St. John's right leg took shrapnel and he returned to New York. During his recovery, he penned *From the Land of the Silent People* (Doubleday, 1942), a bestseller on Yugoslavia, one of 23 tomes he was to author. The journalist joined NBC in 1942, briefly was a European correspondent based in London, and returned to New York in October 1942. An NBC publicist hinted that trouble followed him wherever he went: "Robert St. John is probably the only man in the world with scars on one leg from Chicago's gangster, Capone, and a bullet in the other leg from Germany's gangster, Hitler." Perhaps due to his ill-fated history NBC gave him a break in 1944: a mid-morning news commentary quarter-hour five days weekly. It lasted about three years. And that wasn't all: when anchor John W. Vandercook of the prestigious weekday evening *News of the World* was out of pocket, St. John usually supplied for him. St. John was tapped to cover the 1944 political conventions as well as the San Francisco premier of the United Nations in 1945. On one occasion he remained in the NBC newsroom 117 hours — sleeping just 10 of those hours — when the Japanese surrendered in August 1945 to end the Second World War. In fact, he was the first journalist to confirm their surrender on the air. Angered when he lost the enduring post at *News of the World* as Morgan Beatty succeeded Vandercook (the latter left NBC in 1946), followed by the loss of his (St. John's) own daytime gig in 1947, the newsman reverted to some incendiary episodes of earlier times. Leaving NBC in a fit of rage he stayed gone about two years and never permanently went back to its newsroom. When he did return to NBC in 1949, he was given sporadic TV assignments. But that didn't last long; NBC fired him after his name appeared in *Red Channels*, a pamphlet citing alleged Communist sympathizers in broadcasting. St. John's reliance on Communist sources for another book made him "a subconscious follower of the 'party line,'" said a *New York Times* book reviewer. His ethereal summit had passed. He was turning to full-time authorship as a principal pursuit. "He was an old-fashioned reporter who banged out his books with two fingers on a manual typewriter," an obituary scribe remembered years later. At the time of his death at 100, St. John was still writing. George Washington University had conferred an honorary doctorate on him less than a year earlier, commemorating eight decades in journalism.

SCHERER, Ray. b. June 7, 1919, Ft. Wayne, Ind.; d. July 1, 2000, Washington, D.C. NBC's White House correspondent during the presidencies of Truman, Eisenhower, Kennedy, and Johnson, Scherer was an imposing figure in that web's radio and TV news developments from the 1940s to the 1970s. Beyond that quartet of dignitaries he also covered the terms of Nixon and Ford although Scherer had left the White House by then. In addition, he helped arrange the first televised presidential press conference on Jan. 19, 1955. When Dwight Eisenhower spoke directly to the nation, communications from the President were altered forever. Beyond his concentration on the chief executive, Scherer also reported from the Pentagon and Congress. Earning a degree from Valparaiso (Ind.) University and serving in the navy during the Second World War, he returned to the classroom for a master's degree in international relations at the University of Chicago. In the mid–1940s, he was hired by *The Fort Wayne Journal-Gazette* as a feature writer. It was the paper he had delivered to local residents in his youth and the one for which his father was business manager. In 1947, the young journalist joined NBC as a newswriter, becoming an on-air reporter a short time later. Among the first in his field to comment from the White House live, Scherer was a TV pioneer. "At 6 foot 4 and 200 pounds," *The New York Times* recalled, "he had an on-screen presence that radiated authority in the early days of television news broadcasts." He was one of the first broadcasters to preside over a nationally telecast midday news program. Reports from the floor of the presidential nominating conventions were added to his expanding portfolio in 1956. A decade later he anchored the Saturday night telecast of the *Evening News*. From 1969 to 1973, NBC stationed him in London as its correspondent, after which he came home to be the senior reporter in Washington. During much of that epoch he was frequently heard on NBC's *Monitor*, the popular epic series that aired from 1955 to 1975, registering most of its teeming hours on Saturdays and Sundays. In 1975, Scherer left journalism altogether when he was elevated to a vice presidency with the Washington digs of NBC's parent firm, Radio Corporation of America. He retired from that post in 1986.

SCHOENBRUN, David Franz. b. Mar. 15, 1915, New York, N.Y.; d. May 23, 1988, New York, N.Y. Depending on which version one reads of the broadcasting pilgrimage of Schoenbrun and his peers, a distorted picture could emerge. In the reporter's own account a few colleagues are elevated (Cronkite, Edwards, Friendly, Murrow, and Rather gain propitious treatment) and few are vilified. He is never prideful or boastful. In the books of some other electronic journalists, however, Schoenbrun comes off as arrogant, self-aggrandizing, conceited, and inconsiderate of his peers. Dissension pervades the camp. With a degree from City College in 1934, Schoenbrun taught French and Spanish and began freelance writing. Enlisting in the army nine years hence, he went to Algiers, taking a shine to broadcasting there while working on a weekly United Nations radio feature. Unlike most contemporaries who were shaped in print media before leaping into the ether, Schoenbrun missed that practice. Yet he was ecstatic when Ed Murrow hired him in May 1947 to be chief of CBS's Paris bureau. "Nobody ever covered Paris and Charles de Gaulle as well as he," observed CBS producer Fred W. Friendly. Schoenbrun missed out, too, on being one of the "Murrow Boys," reporting news on foreign soil during the war, and he clearly harbored regrets for the inclusiveness they enjoyed. That never stopped him from considering Murrow to be his mentor as he almost fell at his feet ("I've never admired a man more in my life," he wrote). He nominated himself as one of a "second string" of Murrow protégés who replaced the original contingent when it left Europe for home. In late 1961, he was tapped to replace Howard K. Smith at CBS's Washington bureau dually as correspondent and coordinator. "Schoenbrun assumed that the cachet he brought with him from France would give him entrée into the inner circles of Camelot" during the Kennedy years, CBS profiler Gary Paul Gates disclosed. Not so, no matter how much the newsman tried. "That blow to his outsized ego only made him more determined to prove that he was every bit as important as he claimed." For years Schoenbrun had essentially run a one-man show in Paris, yet encountered teamwork in D.C. with the likes of George Herman, Roger Mudd, Robert Pierpoint, and more. And with that — trouble. Gates said the new environment never prevented Schoenbrun from trying "to hog the best assignments for himself." That was confirmed by some other historians. Friction was rampant. The bureau chief was angered by the ability of CBS-New York to leverage what went on the air, superseding decisions he made in

Washington. For a year starting in September 1962, he anchored the Sunday afternoon news analysis *Washington Report* on CBS-TV. When it ended CBS sent him packing to Europe as continental news chief, an assignment that left Schoenbrun an unhappy camper once more. In June 1964, he resigned from the web that he had professed his undying affection for on numerous occasions. (Mudd did the same when he split from CBS to join NBC in 1980. Some others adopted similar courses.) A disillusioned Schoenbrun, in the meantime, knocked on doors of Gotham broadcasters. WNEW Radio took him in as a news analyst as did some added Metromedia properties. Later he worked for WPIX-TV and its Independent Network News operation. For a brief while in the mid–1970s, Schoenbrun was a foreign affairs analyst for a Los Angeles public TV channel. He penned 10 volumes with themes pertaining to America, France, Israel, and Vietnam. His personal odyssey is recounted in *On and Off the Air: An Informal History of CBS News* (E.P. Dutton, 1989).

SCHORR, Daniel Louis. b. Aug. 31, 1916, New York, N.Y.; d. July 23, 2010, Washington, D.C. His greatest attainment in life, said Schorr, happened when he found himself on President Richard M. Nixon's hit list. The newsman was one of hundreds of political opponents, entertainers, and publications "hostile to the administration"—an enemies register that Schorr had seen his own name on (#17) as he read it aloud on the air ("the most electrifying moment of my career"). The infamous compendium was part of an eventual charge of impeachment against Nixon. While Schorr headlined no CBS Radio series, from the 1940s to the 1970s he contributed often to *Edward R. Murrow and the News*, *Washington Week*, *The World Is Our Beat*, *World News Roundup*, and *The World Tonight*, plus intermittent hourly newscasts. His steadfastness in journalistic integrity cost him several jobs: he resigned from CBS before he could be fired in 1976 after angering politicians, peers, and network officials in an imbroglio stemming from his release of a confidential congressional document; after a half-dozen years as a commentator for upstart cable network CNN (its first employee), Schorr's inability to bend in a contract dispute led to his departure (1985); a successive contract for a column in *The Des Moines* (Iowa) *Register and Tribune* was canceled by the paper after two years; and Schorr quit a teaching appointment in 1976–77 at the University of California, Berkeley, after a brief, disappointing engagement because students were "captivated by the notoriety" that swirled about his career. After an interlude of freelance writing, he appeared to grasp his niche at last: for a quarter-century he contributed occasional commentaries to NPR as senior news analyst while concurrently penning a column for *The Christian Science Monitor*. It seemed the best of print and electronic worlds. A native of the Bronx, Schorr was the son of Belorussian immigrants. In his memoir, *Staying Tuned: A Life in Journalism* (Pocket Books, 2001), he revealed an unhappy childhood. "Being poor, fat, Jewish, fatherless" made him feel "like an outsider." Through his writing he eventually "achieved identity." He got a taste of it early: in his puberty, a woman who lived in his apartment house jumped or fell from the roof and died. Schorr (then 12) telephoned the police and *The Bronx Home News*— gave the latter his first scoop – and gained $5 for his tip. It was an early harbinger of his future. Following his graduation from City College of New York, *The Jewish Daily Bulletin* and then the Jewish Telegraphic Agency hired him. Growing restive and with Europe at war, however, he joined Aneta, news agency of the Netherlands East Indies. Drafted into the army (1943) Schorr returned to Aneta in the Netherlands after the war. Witnessing postwar reconstruction, the Marshall Plan's effects, and creation of the NATO alliance, he sent dispatches from Western Europe to *The Christian Science Monitor* and added *The New York Times* later. He made a trip home in 1952 and impressed the *Times* with his skill. As details for a future post were ironed out, Schorr returned to the Netherlands "for a few weeks." He was soon contacted by legendary CBS newsman Edward R. Murrow and the *Times* opportunity vanished—"too many Jewish bylines might jeopardize coverage of the Mideast" he was informed—just as CBS hired him to work in Washington. But that was fleeting: Schorr made his mark as a foreign correspondent in the Soviet Union. Reopening the web's Moscow bureau in 1955 after Soviet premier Joseph Stalin closed it eight years earlier, he scored a coup when he got current leader Nikita Khrushchev to sit for his first TV interview as *Face the Nation* cameras rolled. Schorr defied Soviet censors repetitively, however. When he went home to the U.S. for a hiatus in late 1957, he was denied re-admission by the Soviets. At that juncture he became a Washington-based journalist for most of the rest of his life. When his "love-hate affair" (his term) with CBS News ended in 1976, Schorr went on the lecture circuit, where he was gamely embraced. Plaudits for his journalistic labors included a trio of Emmys for Watergate reporting (1972–74), a George Foster Peabody Award, and induction into the Society of Professional Journalists' Hall of Fame. Beyond his autobiography he penned several more books. Schorr's last appearance on NPR's *Weekend Edition*, where he discussed current events, aired two weeks before his death.

SEVAREID, Arnold Eric. b. Nov. 26, 1912, Velva, N.D.; d. July 9, 1992, Washington, D.C. A classic case of mike fright and camera-shy too, Sevareid never wholly conquered his fears of two of broadcasting's most common tools, the microphone and lens. He insisted he was a writer, not a performer. Some would agree with him. At his death an obit writer observed that he "wrote elegant commentaries that he delivered in grave and sonorous tones." Many more pundits—including colleagues—similarly appraised his hard-copy literary conquests. Beyond crafting commentaries for air Sevareid authored a half-dozen books plus a syndicated newspaper column and scores of articles for a variety of magazines. He is best recalled for breaking through the strictures of straight news reporting to pioneer editorial analysis on radio and TV, however. Two-minute nightly perspectives on current events brought honor not only to him but to anchormen Walter Cronkite and Dan Rather of the *CBS Evening News* where he was the resident scholar (1964–77) on legions of subjects. Born in rural North Dakota to parents of Norwegian ancestry (he kept a lifelong respect for Norway), Sevareid and his clan were forced by a 1920s drought to move to Minneapolis where he graduated high school (1930). His boyhood and early career are recounted in the memoir *Not So Wild a Dream* (Alfred A. Knopf, 1946). It covers tales from an epic youthful 2,200-mile canoe excursion from Minneapolis to Hudson Bay, wanderings among hoboes, a newspaper reporting apprenticeship, and his odyssey in wartime. Witnessing the terror of Nazism and anti–Semitism in Germany profoundly affected him. At 18, Sevareid was a copy boy at *The Minneapolis Journal*, obtaining reporting duties before graduating from the University of Minnesota (1935). Losing that job the next year, he and his wife struck out for Europe. He studied political science at the London School of Economics before enrolling at the Alliance Francaise in Paris. *The New York Herald Tribune* added him to its Paris staff (1938) and Sevareid was soon promoted to night city editor. He was also working at the time in the city's United Press bureau. Recruited by CBS newsman Edward R. Murrow, Sevareid chucked his dual tasks to focus on CBS Radio in August 1939. He thus became one of the renowned "Murrow Boys" that kept America informed as the war progressed across Europe. It was an ultra-satisfying liaison for all parties and Sevareid remained content at CBS until mandatory retirement kicked in at 65 (1977). (Several prominent peers made hasty retreats to ABC, CNN, NBC, NPR, OWI, PBS, VOA, local stations, and other media before their careers ended. Some left CBS of their own accord, yet disillusioned; some others after being fired for running afoul of expectations.) In the war years, Sevareid covered the French army and air force in Belgium, the Netherlands, and Luxembourg. He was the last American to air from Paris, barely escaping before the Nazis seized the city. Alongside Murrow, he broadcast from London during the bombing blitz before being dispatched to Washington in late 1940. Covering President Franklin D. Roosevelt until 1943, he then went to the China-Burma-India theater. The following year he pursued the campaign in Italy and Marshal Tito's partisans in Yugoslavia; he landed with the first wave of Americans in southern France, and traveled with them across the Rhine into Germany. In the postwar era Sevareid spent time in Washington, France, Germany, and Britain. He became a D.C.-based roving correspondent in 1964, when his nightly commentaries launched on CBS-TV. Throughout his career Sevareid was heard sporadically on CBS Radio on a variety of series: the daily *CBS World News Roundup* and *The World Tonight*, on his own weeknight newscast *Eric Sevareid and the News* (1947–51), the weekly panel show *Capitol Cloakroom* (1950–57), and a handful of added aural news and public affairs features. He returned to the airwaves on Dec. 7, 1991—14 years past retirement—for one more shot, a CBS-TV special titled *Remember Pearl Harbor*. It aired one-half century after U.S. peace was shattered. Defining himself as "a cultural conservative and a political liberal," Sevareid "followed in Murrow's footsteps" so an online evaluation said. At his last regular appearance on CBS-TV in 1977, the newsman allowed that Murrow was "the man who invented me." As such, he was one of the early critics of Sen. Joseph R. McCarthy's anti–Communism stimulus. During the early 1950s, Sevareid caught the notice of the FBI as it tried to root out American Communists. A British critic summarized: "Throughout 1953, in his thoughtful, late evening radio commentaries, he regularly took McCarthy to task for his unsubstantiated accusations of disloyalty and treachery. That was at a time when too many Washingtonians were running for cover." Sevareid won an Emmy and a George Foster Peabody Award for reporting excellence. In a eulogy at his funeral newsman Dan Rather affirmed Sevareid had "no equal in the history of broadcast journalism."

SHADEL, Willard Franklin (Bill). b. July 31, 1908, Milton, Wis.; d. Jan. 29, 2005, Renton, Wash. "You'll never be taken seriously on television unless you improve your on-camera appearance," a balding Shadel — who never looked up from what he was reading — was told by a producer for entertainer Arthur Godfrey. "My old bald head was all you could see," Shadel freely admitted. The newsman bought a toupee and wore it "the rest of the time he was on television," said a witness. And he began looking into the camera. Educated at Andrews University, Berrien Springs, Mich., and the University of Michigan, Ann Arbor (where he gained a master's in history), Shadel launched his career playing marimba in silent movie theaters. He carried the instrument to radio later. Accepting a correspondent's post with the National Rifle Association, he rose to the editorship of the group's *The American Rifleman*. Then he shipped himself to Europe to study the Second World War's use of rifles. In 1943, he met CBS newsman Edward R. Murrow there recruiting talent for a team of correspondents reporting the war to Americans tuning in to radio. When a job was proffered, Shadel accepted. While he wouldn't make the "Murrow Boys"—cohorts covering the war from its start identified by authors Stanley Cloud and Lynne Olson — the new hire was a vital cog among "second string" journalists. In his time at CBS, his reports were regulars on the *CBS World News Roundup*, *The World Tonight*, hourly newscasts, and added news and public affairs series. His most vivid wartime recollection came when he and Murrow saw Nazi death camps. They gave chilling details later of what they had witnessed at Buchenwald on Apr. 12, 1945. It was the day President Franklin D. Roosevelt died at the Southern White House at Warm Springs, Ga. "They [Murrow and Shadel] came by jeep and were swarmed by the starving and dying," a pundit allowed. "Shadel said it was the memory of the living, not the multitudes of dead that stayed with him." After Shadel died at 96, one of his sons noted: "Even last week, he said to me, 'I remember that atrocity as if I was there yesterday. It's almost as if nothing else happened.'" Less than a year before visiting the death camp, Shadel was one of a few CBS reporters to cover the D-Day invasion at Normandy, France on June 6, 1944. He subsequently reported from the Battle of the Bulge, the last unsuccessful Nazi attempt to push the Allies back from German home territory, Dec. 16, 1944, to Jan. 16, 1945. After the war he went to Washington and aired over CBS Radio before getting into video at CBS's WTOP-TV property. Shadel was on a local news show there anchored by Walter Cronkite. "He was a very bright reporter and a damn good writer," Cronkite observed. "He'd hunt stories that I thought were quite remarkable, and we were just a great team." There were some high watermarks in Shadel's Washington years. He was the original host of *Face the Nation* on CBS-TV, premiering Nov. 7, 1954, and still on the air in 2012. A few times he substituted for Eric Sevareid when stage fright — a dilemma he suffered all of his life — got the best of Sevareid. After 15 years, Shadel left CBS to switch chains in 1958, plucked by ABC-TV as a rotating anchor for its evening news, replacing John Charles Daly. Shadel was tapped to moderate a presidential debate between John F. Kennedy and Richard M. Nixon on Oct. 13, 1960, carried by all three networks. At the debate's finish the newsman was accused of favoring "the other side" by both camps. Nixon was incensed that Shadel hadn't enforced his (Nixon's) tenet against using notes — one his opponent hadn't agreed to. Kennedy partisans were angry that Nixon — in a studio across the country — was surrounded by reporters, a violation of that debate's rules. The aftermath led the trio of web presidents to challenge Shadel. "I don't need this," one can almost hear him mutter as he left broadcasting altogether not so long afterward. Prior to it he reached one more peak when he anchored 12 hours of ABC coverage as astronaut John Glenn flew three orbits around Earth in Friendship 7 on Feb. 20, 1962. In 1963, Shadel resigned ABC to be professor of communications at Seattle's University of Washington, retiring in 1975.

SHAW, Bernard. b. May 22, 1940, Chicago, Ill. One of the first African-American newscasters to rise to exalted recognition among his peers, Shaw attended the University of Illinois in his hometown (1963–68) following service as a corporal with the U.S. Marine Corps (1959–63). His interest in journalism stemmed from the time his family received four daily newspapers in their south side Chicago home while he was growing up. "I read them all," he said. Finagling his way into the 1952 and 1956 Democratic conventions held in his city, Shaw declared that when he looked up in that hall and witnessed the radio booths high above it, "I knew I was looking at the altar." His career launched at Chicago's WYNR/WNUS in 1963 as a reporter and anchor. Two years hence he joined the Windy City's WFLD as a newswriter, then WIND (1966–68), and moved to the Westinghouse Broadcasting Company as White House reporter (1968–71). At that juncture Shaw joined the Washington bureau of CBS News. He was with ABC News two years (1977–79), initially as Latin American bureau chief, then senior correspondent on Capitol Hill. Moving to CNN at its inception in 1980, he became its chief anchor. Shaw is recalled for moderating a presidential debate in 1988 (Bush-Dukakis) and vice presidential debate in 2000 (Cheney-Lieberman). He reported from the Gulf War site in 1991, and from many other strategic places where news of international import broke. He hosted CNN's *Inside Politics* from 1992 until he retired in 2001 to focus on writing. A member of the National Press Club and the Society of Professional Journalists, he is the recipient of numerous honorary degrees (Marion College, University of Chicago, Northeastern University) and awards (Lowell Thomas Electronic Journalism Award of the International Platform Association in 1988, four citations from the National Academy of Cable Programming, the Journalist of the Year Award given by the National Association of Black Journalists in 1989, and a George Foster Peabody Award in 1990). The University of Illinois established the Bernard Shaw Endowed Scholarship Fund to assist promising students "who share his interests and integrity."

SHIRER, William Lawrence. b. Feb. 23, 1904, Chicago, Ill.; d. Dec. 28, 1993, Boston, Mass. The first person of a string of journalists hired by CBS newsman Edward R. Murrow under war clouds in 1937, Shirer exited from that illustrious coterie a decade later but under the cloud of a broken friendship. The break from Murrow and CBS was one of the most patently visible in the industry. Though Shirer intimated in *A Native's Return, 1945–1988* (Little, Brown, 1990) that the pair had righted their overturned liaison, in the preface to her dad's *This Is Berlin: Reporting from Nazi Germany, 1938–40* (Simon & Schuster, 1993), Shirer's eldest daughter indicates that her father (who died shortly before the book's release) and Murrow never repaired the chasm. A few months before his own death in 1964, Murrow attempted reconciliation by inviting the Shirers to his farm at Pawling, N.Y. But Shirer didn't want to consider their strain while there. The rupture, Shirer said, occurred after J.B. Williams, a men's toiletries producer, abruptly withdrew sponsorship of Shirer's CBS news analysis after which he was pulled from the air. He felt it all stemmed from some liberal remarks that ultimately put him on a suspect list of Communist sympathizers which he fervently denied. When CBS chairman Bill Paley and Murrow — then Paley's hand-picked VP for public affairs (a job Murrow never wanted or liked) — made decisions limiting Shirer's status and career, he left. (He insisted he was fired by his former mentor but colleagues, defending Murrow, claimed poor ratings did him in.) Bleak times were ahead. With the exception of a few brief turns at MBS, Shirer was soon effectively silenced on the ether and in print. Ironically, until 1960, he was a victim of the blacklisting he put down that fueled his downfall. To make ends meet as he was raising a family, Shirer went on the college lecture circuit. "I spent almost five years when my sole income was from one-night stands at universities," he proclaimed. "They were almost the only place in the country in the 1950s that still had some respect for freedom of speech." From the early 1940s to his death he was a prolific writer, penning nearly 20 volumes. Active in protecting writers' rights in the 1950s, he was elected president of the Authors Guild. In 1960, meanwhile, his ship came in. Simon & Schuster released his massive 1,200-page book, *The Rise and Fall of the Third Reich: A History of Nazi Germany*. It was printed 20 times in its first year and sold more than a half-million copies by the Book of the Month Club. The tome won prestigious honors for nonfiction in 1961 including the National Book Award and Carey-Thomas Award. Life is filled with paradoxes and Shirer told *The New York Times* in 1977 that — had he not been blacklisted by the networks — he "would never have found the time to write" his best seller. His training and early experience prepared him for it. At age eight, Shirer lost to death "the most influential person" in his life — his dad, a U.S. attorney in Chicago. The man had already instilled a love of music, education, and literature in his son. Infinitely distraught, the youngster's sadness was compounded when his mother moved the family to Cedar Rapids, Iowa, within months to be close to her parents. The lad hated the shift from Chicago's bustle to the rural countryside. He grew to manhood exhibiting a nonconforming streak. He ran afoul with many of the expectations as a student at Coe College, a Presbyterian school in Cedar Rapids, where he earned a degree in 1925. After his death, a Coe magazine was oblivious to the college pranks he had carried out, to his drinking binges, and "thumbing his nose at everything the college held dear" according to its assessment. Apparently he "raised so much hell with his fraternity brothers that the Coe chapter was suspended for a year." He edited the school paper and made it "his personal forum," decrying all he felt were political travesties. After Coe gave Shirer its highest award in 1976, he announced that his manuscripts and personal papers would be sent there at his death for keeping. Shirer's first *real* job in journalism was as a sportswriter for *The Cedar Rapids Republican*. In summer 1925, he pitched hay on a British cattle freighter bound for Europe. He expected to return home at the end of summer. More than 15 years passed however. Not wanting any more small town U.S.A. he was hired on the copy desk at the Paris edition of *The Chicago Tribune* and eventually became the paper's European correspondent (1927–32). He enrolled in courses in European history at the College de France, too. After a skiing accident in the Alps cost him the sight in one eye in 1932, Shirer left the *Tribune* and spent a year freelance writing in a Spanish fishing village. Returning to Paris in 1934, he went to work for *The New York Herald Tribune*, leaving it the following year for Berlin where he was a correspondent for Universal News Service, a Hearst wire enterprise. That folded in 1937; he joined another Hearst property, International News Service, and that too ended within a few weeks. CBS's Murrow cabled from London the very same day and requested a meeting in Berlin. The rest is history with Shirer working for CBS in Berlin to 1940. His duties took him to Amsterdam, Berlin, Brussels, Geneva, Paris, Rome, Vienna, plus the Balkans, India, and the Middle East. He reported on the Munich Agreement and Hitler's march into Czechoslovakia before disclosing the German invasion of Poland signaling the start of the Second World War Sept. 1, 1939. On June 22, 1940, Shirer reported the signing of the German armistice with France to U.S. listeners six hours before any other news source. The day after their return from the Nazi prison camp in spring 1938, Murrow and Shirer were asked by CBS in New York to produce a European roundup, a 30-minute broadcast with live reports from five capitals: Berlin, London, Paris, Rome, and Vienna. Organized in eight hours using telephone and transmission apparatus of the day, the program was a major feat without a pattern and applied limited primitive facilities. The first roundup created a formula still used in broadcast journalism. The plan was the genesis of the *CBS World News Roundup* heard daily almost three-fourths of a century later.

SINGISER, Frank King, Jr. b. July 16, 1908, Montevideo, Minn.; d. May 28, 1982, Sudbury, Vt. Unlike most newscasters, Singiser arrived with overseas residency in his portfolio apart from military service. As an American Baptist preacher's kid, he grew accustomed to moving. His childhood carried him from Minnesota to Pittsburgh, Pa., and then to Rangoon, India, where the family patriarch shepherded a flock of English-speaking parishioners. After five years the clan returned to the U.S. and the youngster finished his education. At 19 in 1928, he obtained a degree from Brown University, Providence, R.I. The following year Singiser applied for work with the mammoth General Electric Company operations in Schenectady, N.Y., and was referred to WGY, its local radio outlet. After an audition the youth was hired to announce features, read the news, and do some writing and directing for broadcast. Shortly thereafter NBC officials in New York City became aware of Singiser's presence at their Schenectady affiliate. Impressed by his voice and versatility, they put him on in May 1929, transferring him to Manhattan. That fall he was beckoning listeners to several NBC programs, an inventory eventually including *The A & P Gypsies, Cavalcade of America, G. E. Circle*, and *General Motors Concerts*. In that same period independent New York broadcaster WOR collaborated with three stations in the Midwest to launch a fourth national radio chain. MBS first punctured the airwaves in autumn 1934. In November 1935, Singiser signed on for duty with WOR as a newscaster. No later than 1938, he was reading news reports to a much wider audience on "the network for *all* America" as MBS eventually touted itself. His newscasts were suspended during the Second World War when he was assigned to the U.S. Power Squadron (1942–44). With Singiser's return, however, a major oil producer underwrote a three-times-weekly MBS newscast for him, applying the banner *The Sinclair Headliner* (1944–46). Singiser continued to deliver MBS news and program features for another quarter-century. *The New York Times* noted in 1957 that Singiser could be heard on MBS newscasts twice daily. Simultaneously he was public relations director at Skidmore College, Saratoga

Springs, N.Y., while operating his own urological appliance firm, Ambutainer Company, since 1953. He retired from MBS at 63 in 1971.

SMITH, Howard Kingsbury, Jr. b. May 12, 1914, Ferriday, La.; d. Feb. 15, 2002, Bethesda, Md. His pronounced stands on segregation, Vietnam, fading commentaries, and untenable network directives led Smith to a falling-out at two national webs. One of few elite "Murrow Boys" in the Second World War at CBS who "went away sorrowful" (Matt. 19:22), Smith entered the trap not once but twice, deeply embittered by it each time. While his impact on electronic journalism was strikingly large, the stains of his inability to compromise left scars. *The New York Times* said he was "contentious"; though he physically appeared as a courtly Southerner, he was "tough and insightful, stubborn and opinionated and frequently clashed with his bosses." He let the chips fall without apologies. Smith vigorously buttressed the Vietnam War, endearing him to Richard M. Nixon. The president was then engaged in rebuking CBS, NBC, and a few newspapers. Smith, at ABC then, was granted an hour-long one-on-one interview with him in 1971, a coup d'état. Even so, he was the first commentator to call for Nixon's exit over Watergate. Born in the rural South, Smith had enduring resentment for racial segregation from the injustices of Jim Crow laws that he witnessed earlier, reinforced by the Nazi terrorism he saw in the war. His feelings were a trigger in his removal from CBS in late 1961 over a TV special, *Who Speaks for Birmingham?* Warned against inserting a line at the documentary's conclusion that CBS chairman Bill Paley believed was inflammatory, Smith refused to back down. It was the final straw in mounting dissension with CBS officials and — after two decades — he was history. He went on the air at ABC-TV in 1962 with news and public affairs specials before landing the top spot as co-anchor of the *ABC Evening News* (1969), initially beside Frank Reynolds and then another disillusioned CBS alumnus, Harry Reasoner. Smith persisted to 1975, when he shifted to the duty of on-air analyst at ABC. He grew angry as his commentaries were reduced, however. Approaching 65 in April 1979, he withdrew from the rat race that had plagued him since the late 1950s. On the way out he took potshots at a revamped format for ABC's *World News Tonight*. He lectured widely then and penned a memoir. The journalist prepared well for his career several decades earlier. Working his way through New Orleans' Tulane University, he earned a B.A. in 1936, specializing in French, German, and journalism. Winning a summer scholarship to Heidelberg (Germany) University, he traveled as a deckhand on a European-bound freighter. After that brief respite he returned to the Big Easy to work for *The New Orleans Item*. With a Rhodes scholarship in 1937, he took off for Oxford (UK) University's Merton College, completing a master's in two years. He also took an active role in campus politics, stridently objecting to Prime Minister Neville Chamberlain's ostensibly soft stance on Nazism. United Press in London gained Smith's services next and sent him to Berlin (January 1940). He augmented his income with sporadic dispatches to the major dailies *The New Orleans Item* and *The New York Times*. In Berlin, Smith impressed CBS's Edward R. Murrow who was corralling a cadre of reporters to feed news from the continent to America. Offered one of the coveted posts in spring 1941 (at five times his $25 weekly UP salary), Smith jumped at it, joining the gifted "Murrow Boys." At a later date he asked Paul White, CBS news director in New York, how he had faith in an unknown. "I knew you were well brought up from a top school," replied White. "Oxford?" Smith inquired. "United Press," White said. Smith visited Hitler's mountain retreat at Berchtesgaden and interviewed powerful Nazis including the fuehrer himself. Refusing to insert Nazi lingo in his reports, however, he got a harsh taste of the Gestapo which seized his notes and shut off communications. Smith hastily departed Germany for Switzerland on Dec. 6, 1941, the day before Pearl Harbor. His foresight made him one of the last out of Berlin before the U.S. declared war and everything changed for any reporters left behind. Smith's recall is in his best-selling *Last Train from Berlin: An Eye-Witness Account of Germany at War* (A.A. Knopf, 1942), re-released several times. He spent two-and-a-half years in Bern telling of underground movements in German-occupied terrain. In winter of 1944-45, he transmitted vivid tales of a German counterattack at the Battle of the Bulge; he crossed the Rhine with the Allies into Berlin and — in May 1945 — witnessed the German surrender to the Russians. CBS sent him to London as chief European correspondent (1946-57), replacing Murrow. Smith penned *The State of Europe* (A.A. Knopf, 1949), a 400-page nation-by-nation odyssey detailing the postwar climate in varied countries. He condemned American and Russian policies there. He was heard on CBS Radio's *World News Roundup* and *The World Tonight* and maintained a commentary under his own moniker that aired intermittently for a decade (1945–55). Smith added commentary to Douglas Edwards's evening CBS-TV newscast, moderated the first presidential debate between John F. Kennedy and Richard M. Nixon (1960), and a second between Jimmy Carter and Ronald Reagan (1980). "His star at CBS was on the rise," *The New York Times* averred, "and many network executives thought he would inherit the mantle of Ed Murrow." Smith anchored *CBS Reports* documentaries and received an Emmy, George Foster Peabody and George Polk awards for writing and narrating *The Population Explosion* (1960). He garnered DuPont awards (1955, 1963), a Sigma Delta Chi Award for radio journalism (1957), and an American Jewish Congress Award (1960). The University of Missouri presented him its Journalism Medal (1971). The newsman appeared — often as himself— in several films while authoring five books. In 1961, Smith was appointed chief correspondent and general manager of CBS's Washington bureau. Buying a home by the Potomac River in suburban Bethesda, Md. (1958), he resided there into this millennium. His advocacy of overseas welfare policies in *The State of Europe* (A.A. Knopf, 1949) also earned him a spot in *Red Channels*, a catalog of media types suspected as left-wingers at mid-20th century.

STRAWSER, Neil Edward. b. Aug. 16, 1927, Rittman, Oh.; d. Dec. 31, 2005, Washington, D.C. A 34-year CBS veteran, Strawser was chiefly in audio although he filled occasional spots in video. His most renowned contribution may have been anchoring CBS Radio's four-day coverage after the assassination of John F. Kennedy in November 1963. Strawser was linked to the president earlier by interviewing Jacqueline Kennedy on CBS-TV in 1960's campaign and in 1962 during the Cuban missile crisis. In the latter instance he was allegedly the first newsmen at Guantanamo Bay Naval Base. He also reported on space launches, civil rights developments in many places, and the 1973 "Saturday Night Massacre" as President Richard M. Nixon ordered the firing of a prominent Justice Department official in the Watergate inquiry. For many years Strawser anchored the web's weekend hourly newscasts and the Saturday airing of *CBS World News Roundup*. In the early 1980s, he was assigned to the White House beat. But Strawser first and foremost was considered "spokesman for Capitol Hill committees," *The Washington Post* asserted at his passing. When CBS announced massive job cuts in 1985, the newsman, 58, accepted early retirement to direct public affairs at the Joint Economic Committee. He was subsequently press officer for the House Budget Committee (1987–94). From the late 1940s until his affiliation with CBS in 1952, Strawser was an electronics technician in the U.S. Navy. He served with the Naval Reserve and worked as a radio disc jockey and local news anchor before hooking up with CBS as an editorial research assistant. For many years he kept a sideline post narrating Encyclopedia Britannica films bound for school classrooms. Strawser earned a bachelor's degree from Oberlin (Oh.) College (1951) and master's at George Washington (D.C.) University.

SWAYZE, John Cameron. b. Apr. 4, 1906, Wichita, Kan.; d. Aug. 15, 1995, Sarasota, Fla. "It takes a licking but keeps on ticking." If you recall Swayze, that catchphrase is as familiar to you now as it was when he introduced it through TV commercials for Timex watches. He's also remembered for "Glad we could get together" and "Hop-scotching in the world of headlines," both phrases he wore out on his NBC-TV newscast which began in February 1948 and lasted to 1956. Swayze grew up wanting to be a thespian, not a newscaster or game show player (he was ultimately active in both genres in dual mediums). He finally got to act but it was several decades after he started preparing for the footlights. He studied drama in New York City before returning to his native Sunflower State to enroll at the University of Kansas. He paid his tuition as a reporter for a small Kansas City radio station. After graduating, Swayze was hired by *The Kansas City Journal* as drama critic and columnist. In 1935, he was newscasting and commenting on current events at KMBC in Kansas City, Mo. He went over to competitor WHB in 1937, but returned to KMBC in 1940. Hosting a game show was added to his duties, the first of many guessing games, panel, quiz, and other audience participation features with which he would be identified into the 1950s. Swayze left the local stations in 1943 to join NBC in New York City as a radio newscaster. He was heard intermittently to 1958 on a newscast he headlined, sporadically on hourly newscasts, and bearing the headlines on *Monitor* after it cranked up in mid–1955. It's his nightly telecast of the news that most people recall however; it was NBC's first serious attempt to program a weekday news show. By any measure it was absolutely primordial when compared with the sophistication in technology and highly knowledgeable, skilled, resourceful support help available today. But they were breaking new turf and literally finding their way. Swayze was taken off the air in 1956 and replaced by the fresh duo of Chet Huntley and David Brinkley (who eventually toppled CBS's venerated Douglas Edwards). Swayze left NBC for ABC in 1958, where he was never considered a radio man but a television newscaster and narrator of sundry travelogues which were then in vogue. For two full years ABC-TV tried what was surely an "experiment." The web programmed the first triple-anchor weekday evening newscast in 1961 and 1962 with Swayze and a couple of unknowns (Bill Lawrence, Al Mann). Very late in his career Swayze appeared in a quartet of motion pictures (1956, 1957, 1968, 1985). His roles aren't memorable there although he finally graced a stage as a performer, harboring that dream since the 1920s.

SWING, Raymond Gram. b. Mar. 25, 1887, Cortland, N.Y.; d. Dec. 22, 1968, Washington, D.C. "He was the closest thing broadcasting ever had to a Walter Lippman" (1889–1974) — a Pulitzer Prize-winning print journalist, media critic, and philosopher — CBS News president (1964–66) Fred W. Friendly proclaimed at Raymond Swing's passing. As a radio commentator in the 1930s and 1940s identified on-air as "Raymond Gram Swing," wedded in 1921 to his second of four wives — Betty Gram, a militant feminist — the newscaster succumbed to her petitions to add "Gram" to his birth nomenclature. The taxonomy persisted as long as she did (divorced, 1944). His release by Ohio's Oberlin College for youthful pranks in his freshman year left him cashiering at a Lorain, Ohio, barber shop until he was hired by *The Cleveland Press* at 18. (Swing was embraced by Oberlin 35 years hence; his improved status earned him an honorary LL.D. and boosted him to the trustee board. What a difference time and a reputation make!) Swing's ascent in the ranks of journalists was little short of phenomenal. In five years he moved incrementally to more papers, sequentially *The Cleveland News*, *The Richmond* (Ind.) *Evening Item*, *The Indianapolis Star*, *The Cincinnati Times Star*, and *The Indianapolis Sun*— in the role of managing editor at the latter at 23! An uncle's wedding gift for his original nuptials (dissolved) was a year's European sojourn. Touring the continent solo Swing turned it to profit by affiliating with *The Chicago Daily News*. As its Berlin news bureau chief, he was at the right place at the right time as the Great (First World) War commenced. Afterward he gained a comparable post in London with *The Philadelphia Daily Ledger* and stayed for a decade. His contacts lifted him to frequent commentary in the 1930s over CBS Radio. It was a common practice for networks to rely on professional journalists for analysis of newsworthy events in the era. As a consequence Swing was offered full-time employment at CBS as director of talks. He demurred, taking a spot with Mutual's WOR in New York where he aired weekly in 1936. (An unknown with little radio familiarity and no newspaper training, Edward R. Murrow, filled the CBS post.) With Hitler on the rise in Europe, Swing's perceptions prompted MBS to enhance his presence with five broadcasts weekly. The newfound authority thrust him into esteem and affluence. He was enlisted by the BBC to speak across the British Empire weekly, explaining American stances to those listeners. Swing did so for nine years and recalled it later as "the most gratifying of my whole broadcasting experience." A biographer observed that his concurrent opportunities before Americans and Britishers may have given Swing "the largest audience of anyone on the air anywhere" in the epoch. The newsman transitioned from MBS to the more influential NBC Blue chain in 1942 where he dissected Second World War episodes. Following the war in 1945, Elmer Davis — who had presided over the then defunct Office of War Information — joined ABC (evolving from the Blue web). In what seemed a suitable pattern, Davis aired nightly quarter-hour commentaries Sunday, Monday, and Tuesday each week while Swing supplanted him Wednesday, Thursday, and Friday evenings in a single time zone. Swing left ABC in 1947 to devote more time to writing and lecturing. In the early 1950s, he turned up on the Liberty network, and then finished his career in the early 1960s with the Voice of America under the tutelage of none other than Ed Murrow. For Swing, what went around came around again.

TAYLOR, Henry Junior. b. Sept. 2, 1902, Chicago, Ill.; d. Feb. 24, 1984, New York, N.Y. Few radio commentators could say they spent part of their careers as U.S. envoys in a foreign land. Taylor could, however. His unmistakable ultra-conservative views may have contributed appreciably to his pick by President Dwight D. Eisenhower as ambassador to Switzerland in 1957, coinciding with Ike's second term. As Taylor offered his opinions on the General Motors-backed *Your Land and Mine* (1945–56), he expounded against big government and socialism. Taking popular GOP stances on most issues, he became a moving target on the national ether (MBS, 1945–48; ABC, 1948–54; NBC, 1954–56).

When his successive epoch in officialdom ended at age 59 (1961), Taylor mounted a new diversion as a syndicated columnist for United Features. He persisted for a couple of decades (1961–81). Graduating from Lawrenceville (Ill.) High School in 1920, he was degreed by the University of Virginia at Charlottesville in 1924. He was a foreign correspondent for the Scripps-Howard Syndicate (1941–45). In that capacity Taylor initially reported from Europe before his transfer to the Near East and Asia. Some of his reports in that period could be heard over New York's WHN Radio. In the late war years, meanwhile, that he affiliated with WJZ, the flagship outlet of what was in the process of transitioning to the Blue network (from NBC). By 1945, it had been renamed ABC. In addition to his professional duties on the air, for the wire services, and in governmental service, Taylor penned a novel and several nonfiction tomes.

THOMAS, Lowell Jackson. b. Apr. 6, 1892, Woodington, Oh.; d. Aug. 29, 1981, Pawling, N.Y. Volumes could be — and have been — written about this newscaster-commentator. Few back in the day achieved his stature in aural news history or acquired his level of perseverance. His nightly transmissions aired from the 1930s to the 1970s. In national durability Thomas has been surpassed by Paul Harvey alone. When it came to performance, trust, and respect, he was never exceeded. With the exception of Edward R. Murrow, no American radio newscaster reached the high watermarks he did in the multiple decades embracing the mid–20th century. Thomas was a world traveler too, traipsing the globe to every continent, airing his quarter-hour revelations from Taipei, Tunisia, Topeka, or Timbuktu. "If Lowell Thomas wasn't there to witness it, it wasn't worth hearing about," a critic surmised. His first quarter-century hinted at the wanderlust to envelope him. With his adolescence nurtured in two states (Ohio and Colorado) and stints in both twice each, he exhibited a couple of other absorptions early: a keen thirst for knowledge and a distinct fascination with journalism. The latter began as he toted two daily newspapers along carrier routes each morning at 10 years of age before attending school. By his mid-twenties he reported for five journals, including editing two small village dailies at 19! *The Denver Post* and *The Chicago Evening Journal* joined his repertoire of reportorial credentials. A parallel educational focus saw him degreed by the University of Northern Indiana at Valparaiso and the University of Denver (two degrees there), plus more study at Chicago-Kent College of Law and Princeton (N.J.) University. During that epoch he was already into intensive explorations of the planet, stockpiling photographic evidence to animate endless tours on lecture circuits of the future (for which he earned $40,000 in 20 stops). Of his many books, *With Lawrence in Arabia* (Doubleday, 1924), written in this period — recounting a journey with T.E. Lawrence over the Arabian Desert — became his most memorable. Sporadically, before the mid–1920s, Thomas shared his adventures with radio listeners at stations in some of the U.S. cities he visited. In so doing he acquired not only a taste for the new medium but a comfort level with it. Late in the 1920s, some jockeying for his services was evident between newly formed broadcasting rivals CBS and NBC. The journalist-author-lecturer caused enough stir to achieve some notoriety and both webs were stocking their inventories with figures with something to say. Although NBC secured Thomas first, an opportunistic Bill Paley, new owner of CBS, went after the rising star anyway. Paley was able to strike a deal with a sponsor to carry Thomas's newscasts on CBS in the West at the same time he was heard in the East on the NBC Blue hookup. Beginning Sept. 29, 1930, the pairing lasted six months, until Thomas segued into a nightly news show for a single nationwide network: Blue. Having had a taste of what he offered and observing the increasing size of his draw, Paley was determined to win back the prize he briefly experienced. It took him 16 years. The gallant newsman whose customary arrival was signaled by "Good evening everybody" and finish was the familiar "So long until tomorrow" carried his identifying trademarks to jubilation in timing. The 6:45 P.M. broadcast quarter-hour assigned him in the East was propitious. In tens of thousands of homes he aired the day's events as families gathered around supper tables. It guaranteed a huge audience and remained his for 45 years on four networks. From 1931 to 1943 he was heard exclusively on NBC Blue; from 1943 to 1945 on the separated Blue; from 1945 to 1947 on NBC (ex–Red); and then Bill Paley got into the act. He signed household and personal goods manufacturer Procter & Gamble Company to a pact that returned Thomas to CBS in his traditional 6:45 time zone. The newsman occupied it until he said "So long" for the last time on May 14, 1976. His was then the longest running transcontinental news program in America. During his heyday P&G compensated Thomas at $2,000 per show. Beyond that and the lecture circuit he was well paid for his services including 10 articles for major magazines annually along with a new book contract yearly, plus narrating two Fox Movietone newsreels for theaters weekly (1935–52) at $156,000 per year, along with investments in varied businesses outside radio. In his peak years Thomas's yearly take approached a projected $2 million. He received a George Peabody Foster Award and many more, plus 30 honorary doctorates, and inclusion in five halls of fame. A mountain range in Antarctica, an arctic island, schools in the Himalayas, on Long Island, and a sector of the University of Denver's law school were named for him. It's believed no other radio journalist may have achieved as many milestones.

THOMPSON, Dorothy Celene. b. July 9, 1893, Lancaster, N.Y.; d. Jan. 30, 1961, Lisbon, Portugal. In today's parlance Thompson might be dubbed an activist. Indeed, she devoted much of her life to crusades for social reforms along with appeals to rescue the unfortunates. Some of her favorite causes were woman's suffrage, the slums, and caring for refugees. The fact that she was a Methodist minister's progeny may have set her life's course early as she reveled in noble humanitarian efforts. Tenacious, brave, focused, and persevering, she set some records for achieving feats that no journalist had ever experienced. After she earned a degree from Syracuse University (1914), Thompson campaigned for social improvements. While representing causes for the National Social Unit Organization, she was sent to Europe (1919). There she freelanced some articles for the Jewish Correspondence Bureau and *The Philadelphia Public Ledger*. Soon *The Chicago Daily News* named her its Vienna correspondent and she accepted part-time duties in publicity for the American Red Cross. In 1924, however, she became the first U.S. woman to head a regional news bureau on foreign soil. It happened when *The New York Evening Post* and *The Philadelphia Public Ledger* jointly hired her in Berlin. For five years she tried to get in to Adolf Hitler's sanctuary to interview him (1926–31). At last invited to the fuehrer's lair, she was the first journalist to attain that chance. Her account appeared in *I Saw Hitler!* (Farrar & Rinehart, 1932). Two years after its release — once she had reported on the rapid, pervasive German arms buildup she personally witnessed — Thompson was deported at Hitler's command. Her usefulness to the Gestapo had dissipated. Going on the lecture circuit she warned Americans of the growing threat of unchecked Nazism and Fascism. She penned a thrice-weekly column for *The New York Tribune* as of 1936, eventually syndicated to 200 newspapers. When she supported Franklin D. Roosevelt's bid for a third term in 1940, however, the *Tribune* dropped her although most of the others continued. At the same time she contributed a monthly column to *The Ladies' Home Journal*, wrote 10 books (1928–57), lectured frequently, and resisted hundreds of speaking invitations (700 in one week in 1937). Thompson rebuffed CBS when it proffered an invitation for a radio commentary in the mid–1930s, yet accepted one at NBC. Her first weekly quarter-hour gig aired Aug. 6, 1837. In the next eight years, she broadcast intermittently over NBC, NBC Blue, Blue, ABC, and MBS. Some of the time she could be heard on two chains on different days. At her peak she attracted five million listeners while 10 million were reading her columns and articles. Few feminine journalists reached such a lofty perch in the 1930s and 1940s. *Time* put her on a 1939 cover and termed her "the second most popular woman in America, just behind first lady Eleanor Roosevelt." Thompson had already won the Nobel Prize for literature in 1930. The National Institute of Social Sciences gave her its gold medal in 1938 for her "distinguished service to humanity." It was representative of the crusades she had pursued while earning an income as a feminine journalist.

TOMLINSON, Edward. b. Sept. 27, 1892, Stockton, Ga.; d. Dec. 29, 1973, Fairfax, Va. Intending to become a concert pianist, Tomlinson — a native of south central Georgia just above the Florida line — pursued music studies for eight years, initially at Georgia Normal College and then at Scotland's University of Edinburgh. When his ambition wasn't realized, after a couple of years with British and American armed services in the First World War, the young man found his way into journalism virtually by accident. He delivered some educational talks on British staff operations that enlarged a developing attraction he nurtured for global affairs. A newspaper column for *The New York Herald Tribune* that he penned was eventually syndicated to more Scripps-Howard journals. At the same time, he contributed magazine articles to *Colliers, Cosmopolitan, Crowell,* and *Reader's Digest*. Tomlinson became a seasoned raconteur and turned up on the lecture circuit across America, Canada, and the Pan American states. Hired by NBC as a commentator in the mid–1930s, he became the network's South American correspondent (1936–43). His commentaries were steadily aired by the chain from 1935 to 1949, however. Tomlinson often used his broadcasting platform to urge Americans to develop strong ties with their neighbors living in the southern hemisphere. In 1936, the newsman gave his listeners an eyewitness account of the maiden voyage of the first clipper ship sailing from Miami to Buenos Aires. A fraternal group, the League for Political Education, picked him as its official South America lecturer and his expertise on the geographical region was often sought and widely quoted.

TOWNSEND, Dallas Selwyn, Jr. b. Jan. 17, 1919, New York, N.Y.; d. June 1, 1995, Montclair, N.J. The superlatives documenting Townsend's career are legion. In a 44-year span with CBS (1941–85) he covered every Democratic and Republican national convention between 1948 and 1980, including nominations of presidents Truman, Eisenhower, Kennedy, Johnson, Nixon, Carter, and Reagan. A 1968 print ad picturing him alongside CBS colleague Robert Trout bore the headline: "Dallas Townsend and Robert Trout have been to more Republican Conventions than most Republicans." The inaugurations of Eisenhower and Kennedy were among his impressive broadcast credentials. Townsend also covered the Vietnam peace talks in Paris (1968) and many United Nations sessions. He reported the Japanese peace conference (1951) plus two Mercury space flights, four Gemini missions, two Apollo launchings — every space launch, in fact, from 1962 to 1980 — along with the atomic tests in Nevada in the early 1950s. But his sonorous base intonations were most familiar to millions in the audience for his anchoring of the *CBS World News Roundup* — the nation's most enduring radio news broadcast — for a quarter-century (1956–61, 1963–82). His tenure was briefly interrupted for a couple of years while he presided over CBS's *The World Tonight* evening roundup. On graduating from Montclair (N.J.) Kimberley Academy in 1936, Townsend earned a bachelor's degree from Princeton (N.J.) University in 1940, plus a graduate degree in journalism from New York's Columbia University in 1941. Working briefly as a news editor at WQXR Radio in the Big Apple, he soon joined CBS. Entering the Second World War later with the U.S. Army, Townsend rose to captain. He was assigned to signal and communications in New Guinea, the Philippines, and Japan. In the post–Japanese surrender epoch of 1945, Townsend launched advance signal centers in Tokyo and Yokohama. Returning to CBS, he successively performed as a news editor, director of special events, and manager of TV news broadcasts. He was picked as a news correspondent in 1954; two years hence he began writing, editing, and anchoring the morning *Roundup* quarter-hour broadcasts. For many years Townsend also anchored CBS Radio top-of-the-hour newscasts between 6 and 10 A.M. In his final three years prior to retiring (1982–85), he anchored varied radio newscasts at random hours. Townsend's labors earned many plaudits including the Alfred I. DuPont-Columbia University Award in Broadcast Journalism, George Foster Peabody Award for Journalism Excellence, and a Radio Pioneer Award. "No other newsman of our day has had a broader acquaintance with news nor communicated it with more economy and precision," the jurors awarding him the DuPont tribute allowed in 1983. His trademark, they said, was "intelligent, incisive reporting and editing." Although Townsend retired to Sarasota, Fla., he died following a fall at 76 during a return hiatus in New Jersey.

TROUT, Robert (né Robert Albert Blondheim). b. Oct. 15, 1909, Washington, D.C.; d. Nov. 14, 2000, New York, N.Y. He was the first in a long line of daunting newscasters at CBS during radio's golden age, one of its memorably enduring voices, and one of few preceding Edward R. Murrow's addition to an impending sacrosanct coterie. It was Trout, in fact, who coached Murrow, sharing his broadcasting tips with a man who had never encountered anything like them (he arrived sans journalism fluency). Trout helped the future legend rise and supersede him and all other luminaries in CBS's soon-to-be stockpile of "name" newsmen. Trout's own launch was like that of most others — of fairly humble circumstances. Born to a footwear salesman in the District of Columbia, the lad didn't grow up hoping to be a newsman. He confessed to being a lethargic school pupil, dreaming of global jaunts that might result in his acknowledgment as a respected scribe. Upon graduation from Washington's Central High School (1927), he set sail to Europe on a summer hiatus aboard a passenger liner, earning his way as a cabin boy. That curtailed his wanderlust for a while. Never attending college, he earned a living in a series of odd jobs ranging from soda jerking to taxi driving. He shuffled between employers until 1931 when a nearby Alexandria, Va., radio station, WJSV, hired him as handyman. One day when the newscaster didn't report for his gig the new hire was pressed into service. He became a regular interlocutor and taught the rudimentary basics of broadcasting to himself. Beyond writing news scripts he dispensed household hints and offered up tips to hunters and fishermen. At 22 in 1932, Blondheim altered his professional moniker to Trout, adopting the surname of a pal. That same year (October 1932) WJSV joined the Columbia Broadcasting System. CBS shifted the station's operations to Washington and adjusted its call letters to WTOP. Trout transitioned with it and soon joined the fledgling chain's pioneering news crew in New York. By the time Ed Murrow showed up at CBS in 1937 as director of talks, Trout was clearly recognized as the web's premier newscaster. For a few years he remained so, persisting as an imposing on-air presence for decades. Trout's deep baritone intonations became familiar to CBS listeners early when — in the 1930s and 1940s — he introduced President Franklin D. Roosevelt's "Fireside Chats" to the nation. (The newsman is mistakenly cited with naming that application; it correctly goes to WJSV manager Harry Butcher.) Some more highlights of Trout's durable broadcasting pursuits include numerous political conventions and inaugurations, funerals of public figures, 35 broadcasts on D-Day (June 6, 1944) during the Allied invasion of France with one of his eyewitness accounts running more than seven continuous hours, and — on V-E Day (May 8, 1945) — relaying the long-awaited news flash to Americans signaling "the end of the Second World War." Trout's reportage embraced many more momentous global events in an expanse occupying nearly seven decades of airtime. Most of it was on CBS although he departed for NBC following an internal dispute at CBS (1947–52), worked for ABC in the early 1980s as a foreign correspondent reporting from his retirement digs in Madrid, and finished his career creating essays for *All Things Considered* at NPR. In the postwar era of 1946–47, Trout filled the venerable evening quarter-hour newscast that was better connected to Murrow after he (Murrow) balked over a CBS public affairs vice presidency he had been pushed into. Murrow's return to the air ignited a tiff with Trout (he took Trout's newscast) and the latter left abruptly. Trout badly missed CBS in the five years he was away, however, and when the fences were mended he returned. In 1964, when NBC's Chet Huntley and David Brinkley overwhelmed CBS's Walter Cronkite on TV during the Republican National Convention, CBS chairman Bill Paley ordered a pair of co-anchors to handle the looming Democratic National Convention. Paley picked Roger Mudd and Trout — the young and the restless. Had it gone smoothly it might have foretold replacements for Cronkite on television's *CBS Evening News*. But it was a train wreck and ended Trout's ambitions for a permanent spot on national TV. He delivered daily CBS Radio newscasts in the 1960s while presiding over local news on WCBS-TV, the network's flagship station in New York, as his time before the national cameras diminished. "His swarthy complexion and mustache reminded one CBS executive 'of an Armenian rug dealer,' so he was seen less and less," noted a history encyclopedia. Trout still earned many accolades across his tenure including a prestigious George Foster Peabody Award for reporting (1980). Following his death *The New York Times* described him as "famously self-deprecating," a trait similarly applied by several other journalists as well.

VAN, Lyle (né Dennison Van Valkenburgh). b. Sept. 10, 1904, Troy, N.Y.; d. July 22, 1997, Clearwater, Fla. The lad's public debut occurred in a boys' choir at Old St. Paul's Episcopal Church in Baltimore, the city where he grew up. Following prep school graduation he hurried to Key West, Fla., hoping to make a killing in a real estate flurry. It didn't happen for him, however, and — then broke — he signed on as a U.S. deputy marshal pursuing bootleggers. In that job he traveled to Atlanta regularly transporting prisoners to a federal penitentiary. Auditioning at WSB during one trip to the Peach Capital he was hired as a featured singer. Leaving radio to open a retail store some time later didn't work out for him either; once again he lost his shirt. Van subsequently applied at Atlanta's WGST and became its program director. When he auditioned as an NBC announcer in New York, he joined the big time in 1934. Most of his professional efforts were focused from then on in newscasting. Van aired for NBC to the mid–1940s, switching to MBS where he persisted throughout the following decade. Bill Jaker, Frank Sulek, and Peter Kanze provide a glimpse into the journalist's tenure at WOR, the MBS flagship outlet, in *The Airwaves of New York* (McFarland, 1998): "Through the 1950s Lyle Van's 6:00 P.M. newscast concluded with a fatherly 'good night, little redheads,' featured a Wednesday 'midweek moment of meditation,' and even originated occasionally from a WOR auditorium studio so that faithful listeners could come watch Van read the news, responding with applause such as no other newscaster ever heard." It was indeed a different age.

VANDERCOOK, John Womack. b. Apr. 22, 1902, London, England; d. Jan. 6, 1963, Delhi, N.Y.

Despite the fact he was given but six decades on earth, Vandercook crammed a whole lot into the time he had. His journalistic pedigree emanated from both sides of his American family — at John's birth his father was European manager of a press association, then editor of *The Cincinnati Post*, finally founder and first president of United Press Association (1906); his mother authored hundreds of tomes for girls and young ladies (*Red Cross Girls, Ranch Girls Series, Campfire Girls Series*). When the family ultimately left Britain to return to the U.S.A. in 1919, the youngster was enrolled at St. Paul's School, Garden City, N.Y., graduating there. He went off to Yale but quit after a year complaining of "too damn many Republicans." For a year Vandercook took bit parts in stage plays including some on Broadway. In a quest for a permanent niche he pursued his family's tradition in print journalism. Yet he filtered in fairly rapid succession through *The Columbus* (Oh.) *Citizen, The Washington News, The Baltimore Post*, Macfadden Publications, and *The New York Graphic*. None brought him lasting contentment. In 1925, still only 23, Vandercook went for something altogether unconventional. For 15 years he combed the globe through 73 nations, sharing his eyewitness interpretations caught on camera lens and in an imaginative mind via reams of books and magazine articles. Radio historiographer Irving Fang proffered that he "lived the life kids dream of." Vandercook's *Black Majesty: The Life of Christophe, King of Haiti* (Harper, 1928) became a bestseller while his *Murder in Trinidad: A Case in the Career of Bertram Lynch, P.C.B* (Doubleday, Doran & Co., 1933) was turned into a popular celluloid attraction featuring actors Nigel Bruce, Heather Angel, and Victor Jory. One day in 1940, as the adventurer conversed with an old chum — a VP at NBC, in that official's office — news arrived that the Allies had signed an accord to establish some West Indies bases. Vandercook had been there many times in 15 years and was asked to be a guest that evening on NBC's *News of the World*. Shortly thereafter he was appearing there *every* evening as anchor of the pivotal quarter-hour roundup of daily events. His personal observations contributed color to the broadcasts. In 1944, *Time* labeled his "the most elegant voice on the U.S. air." With the exception of a brief hiatus in the late 1940s, the journalist was a nightly airwaves fixture for a couple of decades, initially on NBC (to 1946), then MBS, Liberty Broadcasting Company, and finally ABC (the latter 1953–60). A stroke two years before his death forced Vandercook to relinquish his nightly analysis at ABC. He also suffered a series of heart attacks. The newsman was known to verbally disparage television news as he was an unflinching champion of radio although he did occasionally appear on TV. Vandercook's early demise removed from the microphones what might have been an even more enduring impact on listeners.

VANOCUR, Sander (né Sander Vinocur). b. Jan. 8, 1928, Cleveland, Oh. For nearly five decades, beginning in 1954, Vanocur was an active presence on the media stage as a radio correspondent for CBS, NBC, ABC, and PBS, and in varied posts in television for broadcast and cable channels. He faded from the dials and screens in recent years to focus on a consultancy. After graduating from Chicago's Northwestern University in 1950 as a political science and speech major, Vanocur enrolled for graduate study at the London School of Economics. Following a two-year stint in Germany with Uncle Sam as a first lieutenant in the Army (1952–54), he returned to London to report for *The Manchester Guardian*. In the same epoch, Vanocur contributed to *The New York Times*, United Press, CBS News, and the British Broadcasting Corporation. From 1955–57, he was on the *Times*' city staff, moving to NBC News (1957–71). In those years he was the chain's White House correspondent (1961) and weekend co-anchor (1961–65). Vanocur was senior correspondent for PBS (1971–77) and television columnist for *The Washington Post* (1975–77). He finished his full-time career at ABC (1977–92) in multiple capacities that often saw him perform executive tasks as well as be on the air. Intermittently, Vanocur appeared on the History Channel (1995–2002). He continued to offer services in early 2012 as a media consultant, operating Old Owl Communications from Santa Barbara, Calif. He briefly taught communications at Duke University, Durham, N.C., and consulted with the Center for the Study of Democratic Institutions. Vanocur once depicted the Kennedy clan as "the Irish mafia" and some of his other revelations earned him a place on the "enemies list" of the Nixon administration. Vanocur's dad, Louis Vinocur — born in Russia in 1899 — spoke Yiddish and immigrated to the U.S. in 1906. His wife Rose, born in Iowa in 1900, was of Russian parentage. All were Jewish. Upon divorcing in 1941, Mrs. Vinocur took Sander and his sister Roberta to Michigan to live, altering their surname to Vanocur.

WILE, Frederic William. b. Nov. 30, 1873, La Porte, Ind.; d. Apr. 7, 1941, Washington, D.C. Typical of actions in radio's earliest days, Wile was recruited from print journalism where he had been a reporter for a handful of prominent dailies. His heritage prepared him to be celebrated as one of radio's first news commentators. Here was a guy whose veins didn't merely flow with printer's ink but virtually drowned in it. He wanted to be a journalist from an early age as he "published" *The Wile Evening Journal*, a pencil-written exposé of family activities that was circulated to members of his clan. The attraction never subsided. Although Wile attended Indiana's Notre Dame University (1886–90), he didn't graduate but received the LL.D. degree later for his "brilliant journalistic career." His vocation formally began when he was added as a cub reporter to *The Chicago Record* in 1898. His stock rose astonishingly in two years for — at the turn of the century — the *Record* and *The Chicago Daily News* sent him to London to live as a foreign correspondent. For a half-dozen years he worked for those papers in tandem until he was named chief German correspondent for *The Daily Mail* of London, dispatched to Berlin to reside (1906–18). He picked up more duties there reporting for *The Chicago Tribune* and *The New York Times*. During that period Wile emerged as a book author, too. He produced no fewer than seven expositions starting in 1909, principally themed with European political issues. The tomes culminated in *News Is Where You Find It: Forty Years' Reporting at Home and Abroad* (Bobbs-Merrill, 1939). That memoir shortly before his death is one of the earliest abstracts we have reviewing a life that combined print and electronic journalism. Arrested by the Germans as a British spy as First World War hostilities activated in 1918, Wile escaped to England "with difficulty" through direct intervention by the U.S. ambassador. Subsequently returning to America, he proceeded on a speaking tour before settling in Washington as chief of the capitol bureau of *The Philadelphia Public Ledger* (1920–23). The year 1923 was a big one for the journalist: he founded the Frederic William Wile News Service, launched a syndicated column ("Washington Observations") distributed to *The Washington Star* and other newspapers, began penning editorials for the *Star*, and went on the air as one of the nation's first news commentators. In the latter province he offered his reflections to WRC listeners in the District of Columbia. The Calvin Coolidge presidency was just beginning, times were largely prosperous for Americans, and Wile had much to ruminate over with the European crisis settled. It included what he himself had witnessed. His prominence in print and then on radio no doubt led NBC to add him to its stable of "stars" as it organized in 1926. *The Political Situation in Washington Tonight*, unwieldy nomenclature that designated Wile's pronouncements, became a weekly feature of the NBC Blue chain in its earliest days (1926–29). Nevertheless in February 1929, Wile signed an exclusive contract with CBS for which he was paid for his ethereal views for the first time. His political analysis for NBC's rival debuted on the topic of Herbert Hoover's inauguration. It was Sunday evening Mar. 3, 1929, the eve of Hoover's investiture. Wile also became CBS's original foreign correspondent, albeit briefly. In January 1930, he and NBC's William Hard traveled with a U.S. delegation to London for a five-power naval disarmament summit. CBS aired 32 broadcasts from the meetings, some with Wile speaking and all put together by him. He set a precedent for many more journalists who would follow including — seven years hence — Edward R. Murrow, the most distinguished reporter of radio's golden age. Wile continued airing on CBS into the late 1930s, creating a legacy for a deluge of commentators who were arriving on all the chains and local stations as well. His veins and his voice never really ran dry.

WILLS, W. R. (Bud) (né Walter Ray Baranger). b. June 10, 1893, Raton, N.M.; d. July 1977, Indianapolis, Ind. A colorful character whose widely reported exploits exceeded his tenure with CBS, Wills was in a strategic geographical zone at a critical period in international relations. From his surveillance in the Far East as Japan was engaging our nation in the Second World War, he added to Americans' understanding of what was transpiring half a world away. At 16 he had already selected advertising as his vocational choice, a direction that ultimately would lead him into print and broadcast journalism. Facts are vague surrounding his military service but it's clear that by 1916, turning 23, he was engaged in a partnership that was foundational to his later achievements. Headquartered in Los Angeles with offices in San Francisco and Seattle, his Baranger-Weaver Company represented newspaper advertising sales clients. Three years hence he was secretary-treasurer of ad sales for a West Coast newspaper syndicate whose title was soon altered to W.R. Baranger Company. The early 1920s were life-changing for the young executive. Not only did he alter his nomenclature to W.R. (Bud)

Wills, he abandoned his mother (who had lived with him), his spouse (since 1914), and infant son (born May 5, 1921). Sans family, in the mid–1920s Wills was appointed ad manager of Harley-Davidson motorcycles. In 1927, he assumed that task for Japan's Harley-Davidson outfit and then joined the business staff of Tokyo's *Japan Advertiser* in 1929. In 1932, Wills left the newspaper to open a Tokyo branch of filmmaker Twentieth Century–Fox. In 1935, he launched the Oriental-American Booking agency to sign American artists for a Yokohama Exposition. Two years hence *Japan News-Week* premiered under his auspices, the same year he became a CBS correspondent, providing onsite coverage from China, Japan, and more countries of the Orient. Wills picked a Canadian newswoman, Phyllis Elta Argall, to be managing editor of *Japan News-Week* in December 1940. She was an ex-missionary and foreign correspondent who lived in the Land of the Rising Sun for more than two decades. On Dec. 8, 1941—the day following the Japanese attack on Pearl Harbor—that nation's secret police arrested Wills and Argall and charged them as enemy civilians. Allegedly they were spies that violated the National Defense Act and were confined for months under severe hardship and tortuous treatment. The duo was repatriated Aug. 25, 1942 aboard a Swedish liner. On Sept. 3 they wed at St. Thomas, Ont., Canada, and by 1943 they were living in St. Louis, Mo. Hired as a news analyst by KMOX, the CBS-owned affiliate, Wills got into trouble there, too. He related an incident surrounding a shamelessly profligate meal aboard the Baltimore & Ohio Railroad in September 1944 served to a handful of U.S. senators. (Accompanying the senators on their journey, Wills was mistakenly served the disproportionate fare, too, by dining car staff thinking he was a senator.) His comments angered KMOX management which ordered him to submit future scripts in advance for preview. That was unacceptable to Wills who quit and returned to print journalism to 1954 for yet another fling, buying *The Steelville* (Mo.) *Ledger*. He and his wife subsequently moved to Indianapolis, Ind. Phyllis Wills passed at 67 in 1977, four months prior to his death at 85. Long before, she had detailed their time as guests of the Japanese government in *My Life with the Enemy* (Macmillan, 1944).

Winchell, Walter (né Walter Winchel). b. Apr. 7, 1897, New York, N.Y.; d. Feb. 20, 1972, Los Angeles, Calif. Winchell's career encompassed a whole lot of venues, affording him opportunities to perform as a stage actor, columnist, commentator, newscaster, and print journalist for several leading organs (*Billboard, The New York Daily Mirror, The New York Graphic, Vaudeville News*, plus a syndicated column carried by hundreds of U.S. chronicles). His best recognized forum nevertheless was radio where millions tuned in on Sunday nights to hear him dispatch the news in a rapid-fire quarter-hour gig. They listened as much, however, for the latest Hollywood showbiz exposés which his many sources gathered for his broadcasts. Winchell fought tenaciously against some rivals in a cutthroat business (mainly Louella Parsons, although he wanted to trounce Jimmy Fidler, Sheilah Graham, Hedda Hopper, and others of their trade as well). "It is hard to imagine the power he possessed and the ruthlessness with which he used it," assessed radio historiographer Luther Sies. Raised in Harlem by an 80-year-old grandma after abandonment by his parents, Winchell—a grade school dropout—sang with a performing ensemble in boyhood before turning to journalism as a career at 25. For a quarter-century (1932–57) he attracted a national audience to his late-breaking revelations on the ether, eventually making the rounds of a trio of transcontinental webs (NBC, ABC, MBS). While he wasn't a regular at CBS, Winchell alerted that chain to a morning DJ on WJSV in the nation's capital that had impressed him: Arthur Godfrey. The rest, as they say, is history.

Notes

Introduction

1. *British Mercury*, July 30–August 2, 1712.

Chapter 1

1. http://www1.assumption.edu/ahc/1770s/pprinttoryloyal.html.
2. Mitchell Stephens, *A History of News: From the Drum to the Satellite* (New York: Viking, 1988), p. 201.
3. James W. Carey, "The Internet and the End of the National Communications System: Uncertain Predictions of an Uncertain Future," *Journalism Quarterly*, Spring 1998, p. 28.
4. John V. Pavlik, *Journalism and New Media* (New York: Columbia University Press, 2001), p. xii.
5. Christopher Harper, *And That's the Way It Will Be: News and Information in a Digital World* (New York: New York University Press, 1998), p. 5. Adapted from W. Russell Neuman, *The Future of Mass Audience* (New York: Cambridge University Press, 1995).
6. Michael Emery, Edwin Emery, and Nancy L. Roberts, *The Press and America: An Interpretive History of the Mass Media*, 9th ed. (Boston: Allyn and Bacon, 2000), p. 1.
7. Ibid., pp. 1, 3.
8. "Long before there was an alphabet, there were thriving civilizations of people who found ways to communicate with each other.... Ancient people had to memorize thousands of writing signs and spend perhaps twelve years learning to use them correctly. Because of the alphabet, we can take written communication for granted" (Lois Warburton, *The Beginning of Writing* [San Diego: Lucent Books, 1990], p. 9).
9. Emery, Emery, and Roberts, p. 3.
10. Ibid.
11. Jim Cox, *The Daytime Serials of Television, 1946–1960* (Jefferson, N.C.: McFarland, 2006), p. 4.
12. "Of all mankind's inventions ... nothing has proved more useful or led to more innovations than the alphabet.... With the printing press we finally encounter a technology whose impact on the use of the alphabet is so great that it must be ranked in importance with the alphabet itself" (Robert K. Logan, *The Alphabet Effect: The Impact of the Phonetic Alphabet on the Development of Western Civilization* [New York: William Morrow, 1986], pp. 17–18, 177).
13. Emery, Emery, and Roberts, p. 7.
14. The Middle Ages is defined as the middle period between the decline of the Roman Empire and the Renaissance. The early Middle Ages are often branded as the Dark Ages, also dubbed as the Medieval age. Dates extend from the Battle of Hastings (1066) to the inception of the English Renaissance and the Tudor dynasty (1485) (http://www.middle-ages.org.uk/).
15. Emery, Emery, and Roberts, p. 8.
16. Ibid., pp. 17, 19.
17. Often overlooked in citations regarding Ben Harris's exploit in Boston is that, 11 years earlier in London, he launched another newspaper, *Domestick Intelligence Or News Both from City and Country*. The date was July 7, 1679. He was imprisoned for what he said there, and his track record as a publisher was suspect when he fled to America in 1686 (Stephens, pp. 2, 183–184).
18. "Harris got into trouble with the local authorities ... because he printed the truth as he saw it" (Emery, Emery, and Roberts, p. 23).
19. Nearly 14 years passed before the colonists read another locally produced journal. On April 24, 1704, Boston postmaster John Campbell began issuing his weekly *Boston News-Letter*, a single sheet with two columns of news and ads on both sides. Unlike its precursor, Campbell's paper gained British endorsement and lasted 72 years (Stephens, p. 184; James Playsted Wood, *The Great Glut: Public Communication in the United States* [Nashville: Thomas Nelson, 1973], p. 21; John Clyde Oswald, *Printing in the Americas* [New York: Hacker Art Books, 1968], p. 9; Frank Luther Mott, *American Journalism: A History of Newspapers in the United States Through 250 Years, 1690–1940* [New York: Macmillan, 1941], pp. 11–14; Frederic Hudson, *Journalism in the United States, from 1690 to 1872* [New York: Harper & Brothers, 1873], pp. 52–58).
20. Michael A. Longinow, "News Gathering," *American Journalism: History, Principles, Practices*, W. David Sloan and Lisa Mullikin Parcell, eds. (Jefferson, N.C.: McFarland, 2002), p. 145.

21. Victor Rosewater, *History of Cooperative Newsgathering in the United States* (New York: D. Appleton, 1930), p. 9.
22. Emery, Emery, and Roberts, pp. 517–518.
23. In the first Industrial Revolution, roughly between 1760 and 1840, technological, socioeconomic and cultural shifts occurred in spades. Power-driven machinery replaced manual labor and animal-driven effort. Textile production was mechanized; iron-making skills advanced, netting fabrication of machinery; improved waterways and roads resulted; steam power and railroads were introduced (Jim Cox, *Rails Across Dixie: A History of Passenger Trains in the American South* [Jefferson, N.C.: McFarland, 2011], p. 11).
24. Multiple individuals working individually contributed to many of these innovations, altering dates that mark specific achievements. Some of these occurred beyond the timeframe stated.
25. Tim Wu, *The Master Switch: The Rise and Fall of Information Empires* (New York: Alfred A. Knopf, 2010), pp. 5–6.
26. Two decades prior to Hertz's discovery, in 1864, a Scot, James Clerk Maxwell, worked out the theory of the transmission of electromagnetic waves — vibrations moving through space without physical support (Pierre Miquel, *Histoire de la radio et de la télévision* [Paris: Perrin, 1984]).
27. Also credible in arriving at Marconi's ultimate achievements are the experiments of Michael Faraday (1845), Maxwell (1864–73), Hertz (1887), Edouard-Eugène Branly (1890), and Aleksandr Stepanovich Popov (1896) (Henri-Jean Martin, *The History and Power of Writing* [Chicago: University of Chicago Press, 1994], p. 473).
28. Edward Bliss, Jr., *Now the News: The Story of Broadcast Journalism* (New York: Columbia University Press, 1991), p. 2.
29. The facts herewith are from Michael Jay's *The History of Communications: Advances That Have Changed the World* (New York: Thomson Learning, 1995), pp. 20–21.
30. Martin, p. 474.
31. Oddly, Robert Slater's chronicle of CBS dismisses the MBS announcement of the Japanese bombing of Pearl Harbor, citing instead CBS newsman John Daly's disruption of a network program at 2:25 P.M. ET (three minutes later) to announce the event. Slater embellishes further as if other chains weren't involved which, of course, may imply a blind side on the issue (Robert Slater, *This ... Is CBS: A Chronicle of 60 Years* [Englewood Cliffs, N.J.: Prentice-Hall, 1988], p. 95).
32. Stephens, p. 278.
33. Bob Edwards, *Edward R. Murrow and the Birth of Broadcast Journalism* [Hoboken, N.J.: John Wiley & Sons, 2004], p. 41.
34. Stephens, pp. 278–279.

Chapter 2

1. Recreational radio operators are often dubbed as radio amateurs or hams. They don't ply their craft as a commercial or professional trade but usually as an enriching or gratifying pastime.
2. Edward Bliss, Jr., *Now the News: The Story of Broadcast Journalism* (New York: Columbia University Press, 1991), p. 13.
3. Richard Butsch, *The Making of American Audiences: From Stage to Television, 1750–1990* (Cambridge: Cambridge University Press, 2000), p. 175.
4. A much smaller segment of radiomania deems August 31, 1920, as electronic journalism's intro. That day Detroit's 8MK (renamed WWJ in October 1921) aired a Michigan primary election to a few hundred listeners. One historian allowed: "Regular broadcasting of news was born that night" (Mitchell V. Charnley, *News by Radio* [New York: Macmillan, 1948], p. 1). 8MK launched broadcasts on August 20, 1920, after *The Detroit News* put a transmitter in its facility, becoming the first U.S. newspaper with a station (Bliss, pp. 6–7). Following that milestone, *The Detroit News* reported in its September 1, 1920, editions: "The sending of the election returns by the Detroit *News* radiophone on Tuesday night was fraught with romance and must go down in the history of man's conquest of the elements as a gigantic step in his progress. In the four hours that the apparatus, set up in an out-of-the-way corner of the *News* building, was hissing, and whirring its message into space, few realized that a dream and a prediction had come true. The news of the world was being given forth through this invisible trumpet to the unseen crowds in the unseen marketplace."
5. Experimenter/inventor Lee De Forest, touting his innovations and dubbing himself the *Father of Radio*, the title of his memoir, argued it was *he* who dispatched inaugural election returns, ahead of Detroit and Pittsburgh spokesmen. In 1916, from a trial transmitter on a bank of New York's Harlem River, De Forest read returns in a close presidential race between Woodrow Wilson and Charles Evans Hughes. By 11 P.M. when he quit he opined that Hughes would win. Hughes lost. De Forest's autobiography reported it was "the first use of [the] radiotelephone for broadcasting news of general interest," taking pride that it was heard by a few thousand amateur radio operators within 200 miles and four years before the heralded KDKA broadcast (Bliss, pp. 4–5).
6. Jim Cox, *This Day in Network Radio: A Daily Calendar of Births, Deaths, Debuts, Cancellations and Other Events in Broadcasting History* (Jefferson, N.C.: McFarland, 2008), p. 200. Though often credited singularly, Conrad's participation wasn't altogether of his own making. Westinghouse official Harry P. Davis, maybe a superior to Conrad, had "an epiphany" in 1920. Amateur radio transmission broadcasts from a garage piqued Davis' imagination. It led him to ponder matters like confining radio contacts from ship to shore, between war planes and bases, and amateur radio operators with one another. Davis concluded that "the efforts ... to develop radio telephony as a confidential means of communication were wrong, and ... its field was really one of wide publicity" (Harry P. Davis, "The History of Broadcasting in the United States," an address to Harvard University Graduate School of Business Administration, April 21, 1928). In other words he realized radio could (and perhaps should) gather a crowd.
7. Michael Emery, Edwin Emery, and Nancy L. Roberts, *The Press and America: An Interpretive History*

of the Mass Media, 9th ed. (Boston: Allyn and Bacon, 2000), p. 270.

8. Lest we lose sight of it, it's worthwhile to mention that as early as 1894 — fully 26 years before KDKA aired its now infamous election returns — the Chicago Telephone Company delivered local and state election results to an estimated 15,000 patrons. Widely proclaimed experiments of several legendary inventors, in fact (including Armstrong, De Forest, Dolbear, Edison, Fessenden, Hertz, Marconi, Stone, Stubblefield, more), were exalted in publicity that overshadowed the phone firm's feat (Emery, Emery, and Roberts, p. 268).

9. Rosenberg, certified as one of radio's first announcers, left the medium in 1925 to join the Chicago ad agency Lord & Thomas (renamed Foote, Cone & Belding in 1942). Retiring in 1961, he remained a FCB consultant another 15 years. He died at age 92 on September 5, 1988.

10. Rosenberg's correspondence to Edward Bliss, Jr., appears in Bliss's *Now the News*, p. 8.

11. While *Detroit News*-owned competing station 8MK (the future WWJ) was also airing Harding-Cox returns that night, those reports were directed to radio hams advised a leading radio historian. Westinghouse, on the other hand, "presented the activity as something for everyone, a social delight for home and country club." By then KDKA was authorized to provide the general public with a regular service — that night, journalism. For more, see Erik Barnouw, *A Tower in Babel: A History of Broadcasting in the United States*, Vol. I — to 1933 (New York: Oxford University Press, 1966), p. 70.

12. Mitchell Stephens, *A History of News: From the Drum to the Satellite* (New York: Viking, 1988), p. 276.

13. In 1977, after examining histories of four contenders for the title of "oldest station in America," investigators Joseph E. Baudino and John M. Kittross published their findings in the venerated *Journal of Broadcasting*. Their opinion was that KDKA merited the honor, adding, "We hesitate to say that our conclusion will stand for all time." See the *Journal of Broadcasting*, 21:1, Winter, 1977, pp. 61–83.

14. "Wireless Telephone Spreads Fight News Over 120,000 Miles," *The New York Times*, July 3, 1921, p. 6.

15. Tim Wu, *The Master Switch: The Rise and Fall of Information Empires* (New York: Alfred A. Knopf, 2010), pp. 33–35.

16. Many added beneficial experiments were coming to fruition in this period. In the 1870s, Thomas A. Edison proved that electric sparks could be produced from a distance. In the early 1880s, over a mile-long distance Amos Dolbear sent messages by wireless telephone. By 1892, John Stone tested voice transmission techniques after first applying a high-frequency wave to modulate the human voice. Also in 1892, Kentucky melon farmer Nathan B. Stubblefield rigged a wireless telephone and demonstrated talking to a chum across some distance. After later sending a voice message from ship to shore near the nation's capital, Stubblefield acknowledged to journalists that his invention would be applied in the "transmission of news of every description" some day. All of these achievements, while solitary in themselves, were useful in advancing radio's creation (Emery, Emery, and Roberts, p. 268).

17. By 1925, nearly half of the radio sets in use on earth were owned by Americans — 5.5 million in the U.S. (Stephens, p. 276).

18. Emery, Emery, and Roberts, pp. 267–268.

19. Kaltenborn nevertheless maintained his regular job as an editor at the *Brooklyn Eagle* to 1930, seemingly unsure if "this radio thing" would fly. Not until CBS signed him did he resign his day spot. The weeknight work was steady; moving to NBC in 1940, he stayed to retirement in 1955 (Stephens, p. 277; Cox, *This Day in Network Radio*, p. 129).

20. For more on this station see Chapter 8 in this text.

21. Bliss, p. 13.

22. J. Fred MacDonald, *Don't Touch That Dial! Radio Programming in American Life, 1920–1960* (Chicago: Nelson-Hall, 1979), p. 281.

23. Alfred Balk, *The Rise of Radio: from Marconi through the Golden Age* (Jefferson, N.C.: McFarland, 2006), p. 128.

24. Charnley, p. 79.

25. Bliss, p. 16.

26. Erik Barnouw, *The Golden Web: A History of Broadcasting in the United States*, Vol. II — 1933 to 1953 (New York: Oxford University Press, 1968), p. 17.

27. Intending to study medicine, Klauber attended the University of Louisville and the University of Pennsylvania without earning a degree from either, fascinated by journalism instead. His uncle, Adolph Klauber, drama critic of *The New York Times*, was likely influential in his vocational choice. He helped his nephew gain his first news post. For much more on Klauber see Christopher H. Sterling, ed., *Encyclopedia of Radio*, Vol. 2 (New York: Routledge, 2003).

28. One of Klauber's harshest critics noted that "he was anything but popular to those who worked for him" at the *Times*. "In a pattern that would later become familiar at CBS, Klauber became a hated boss — taciturn in mood, quick to criticize (often in front of others), and slow to give compliments."

29. "Yellow Press" is based on distortion of facts to attempt to make news exciting and entertaining when it could otherwise possibly net little interest. Classified as "biased opinion masquerading as objective fact," it involves sensationalism, distorted stories, and misleading images. Its purpose is to draw a wider audience (readers, listeners, viewers). It's also dubbed "Yellow Journalism." See http://iml.jou.ufl.edu/projects/Spring03/Dyal/page2.htm and http://library.thinkquest.org/CO111500/spannamer/yellow.htm for greater detail.

30. David Schoenbrun, *On and Off the Air: An Informal History of CBS News* (New York: E.P. Dutton, 1989), p. 23.

31. Robert Slater, *This ... Is CBS: A Chronicle of 60 Years* (Englewood Cliffs, N.J.: Prentice-Hall, 1988), p. 32.

32. Sterling. Klauber moved on to the Office of War Information as associate director to Elmer Davis, whom he had hired at CBS. He played the same hatchet man and organizational guru there that he had at CBS, having developed a niche.

33. Emery, Emery, and Roberts, p. 321.

34. An Episcopal vicar's son, Glover was born July 31, 1898, at Brooklyn, New York. Married later and the father of a daughter and son, he signed on with WJZ's announcing staff in 1925, joining CBS in 1929 as a sports announcer, often broadcasting with Ted Husing. Subsequently Glover became manager of events broadcasts (1930), director of news broadcasting (1931), and director of CBS News (1933), also assigned the chain's football schedule in the latter year.

35. Much more introduction of White will appear presently.

36. After writing publicity releases and editing news broadcasts, Gude, a Brown University grad, left CBS in 1944 to join Thomas L. Stix and form Stix & Gude, a talent agency representing many prominent figures in broadcasting and publishing, e.g., Edward R. Murrow, Walter Cronkite, William L. Shirer, Andy Rooney, Fred W. Friendly, Elmer Davis, Howard K. Smith, and James Thurber. Gude produced *I Can Hear It Now*, a recording of historic events conceived by Friendly and narrated by Murrow. Its success led to a CBS Radio series, *Hear It Now*, then *See It Now* on CBS-TV (1952–55) (*The New York Times*, October 26, 1998, p. 19).

37. Correspondence with Bliss on April 2, 1982, a half-century after the fact, appearing in Bliss's text, p. 27.

38. Gary Paul Gates, *Air Time: The Inside Story of CBS News* (New York: Harper & Row, 1978), p. 98.

39. Ibid., pp. 98–99.

40. "Paul White Dies; Radio Newsman," *The New York Times*, July 10, 1955. White's departure from CBS was shameful but inevitable. Bliss provides an account: "When, in 1946, Robert Trout succeeded Douglas Edwards as anchor of 'The World Today' ... the program was so important that White wanted to speak.... This was a fateful decision. Ever since Murrow's promotion, White had been drinking heavily. There had been embarrassing scenes, some in public, and the situation was becoming intolerable. Now on this night, perhaps to overcome the nervousness that speaking into a microphone invariably caused him, he went again to the bottle. He may not have drunk a great deal — his tolerance was low — but he obviously was intoxicated, and Murrow fired him. So ended, tragically, a brilliant 15-year career at CBS, a period in which the mold for much of broadcast journalism was cast" (p. 184). Ex-newsman John Daly would later label White, Ed Klauber, and Murrow "a hell of a triumvirate" (Bliss, p. 185).

41. Roger Mudd, *The Place to Be: Washington, CBS, and the Glory Days of Television News* (New York: PBS Public Affairs, 2008), p. 248.

42. An incorrigible and unrepentant prankster, some of the tales of Gibbons' incessant practical jokes — particularly during his adolescent and young adult years — are recounted in Irving E. Fang's *Those Radio Commentators!* (Ames: Iowa State University Press, 1977), pp. 45–62.

43. NBC had signed Gibbons earlier to spin yarns about his overseas exploits on a weekly half-hour, *Headline Hunters*. He is credited for the first remote network aircast: he toted a shortwave transmitter to the landing site of the German dirigible *Graf Zeppelin* at Lakehurst, N.J., in 1929. Hoisting an antenna, Gibbons' voice was fed to NBC for sharing with the nation.

44. Fang, pp. 55–56.

45. Norman H. Finkelstein, *Sounds in the Air: The Golden Age of Radio* (New York: Charles Scribner's, 1993), p. 92.

46. A summary of the transfixing background of CBS's early development appears in Jim Cox's *American Radio Networks: A History* (Jefferson, N.C.: McFarland, 2009), pp. 45–51.

47. Ibid. An account of NBC's early days is reported on pp. 16–25.

48. Lewis J. Paper, *Empire: William S. Paley and the Making of CBS* (New York: St. Martin's Press, 1987), p. ix.

49. Schoenbrun, pp. 20–21.

50. Ibid., p. 22.

51. In the meantime, however, one of Paley's key innovations engaged the network-affiliate link. Networks supplied their stations with features of two types of "sponsored" material paid by advertisers and "sustaining" programs paid by the chains. Under its original plan, NBC allowed outlets to choose among its offerings, paying them to carry sponsored programs and charging for sustaining programs. Under Paley's system, CBS offered sustaining programs at no charge — during the Depression years, a huge benefit for stations, furnishing about 15 hours of programs sans cost. In return, Paley got an option on any part of the affiliates' schedules for the net's hours of sponsored programs without payment to a local station. The option gave CBS a marketing edge, enabling it to pledge sponsors time on as many stations as they desired without local clearance issues. By the mid 1930s, CBS hurtled ahead of NBC in profitability although not in total power of station affiliates (Paul Starr, *The Creation of the Media: Political Origins of Modern Communications* [New York: Basic Books, 2004], p. 354); Sally Bedell Smith, *In All His Glory: The Life of William S. Paley, the Legendary Tycoon and His Brilliant Circle* (New York: Simon and Schuster, 1990), pp. 62–67; Barnouw, *The Golden Web*, p. 251.

52. For details, see *American Radio Networks*, p. 38.

53. As one indicator, at the start of 1950, CBS owned 80 percent of network radio's top 20 Nielsen-rated shows, substantially lifting CBS's audience levels over NBC's. It translated into a $7 million commercial revenue loss in a single year. Jim Cox, *Say Goodnight, Gracie: The Last Years of Network Radio* (Jefferson, N.C.: McFarland, 2002), p. 24.

54. Joining Bing Crosby and Groucho Marx (the latter didn't stay put long) from ABC at CBS were ex–NBC legends Ozzie and Harriet (Nelson) and Harold Peary (*The Great Gildersleeve*).

55. Adapted from Barnouw, *The Golden Web*, p. 150; and Paul W. White, *News on the Air* (New York: Harcourt, Brace, 1947), pp. 8–9.

56. Emery, Emery, and Roberts, p. 319.

57. Schoenbrun, p. 34.

58. A contemporary historian cited Thomas' triumphs by focusing on impressive ratings early in his ethereal career: "Radio's growing importance as a news source was personified by Blue's Lowell Thomas, whose Crossley average had increased 35 percent and placed his Sun Oil newscast in the Top Ten every night

of its broadcast during the 1933–34 season. It was the beginning of Thomas' unmatched record of 13 straight years in the nightly Top Ten, all five nights a week" (Jim Ramsburg, *Network Radio Ratings, 1932–1953: A History of Prime Time Programs Through the Ratings of Nielsen, Crossley and Hooper* [Jefferson, N.C.: McFarland, 2012], p. 38).

59. Slater, p. 34.

60. From 1952 to 1973, he operated a PR firm, Schechter Associates, Inc., which he sold to Hill and Knowlton, Inc. He remained a board member of the latter agency until he retired in 1979.

61. *The New York Times*, May 26, 1989, p. 18; *The Chicago Tribune*, May 27, 1989, p. 7.

62. Cox, *American Radio Networks*, p. 31.

63. John Dunning, *On the Air: The Encyclopedia of Old-Time Radio* (New York: Oxford University Press, 1998), p. 486.

64. Balk, p. 129.

65. Ibid.; MacDonald, p. 283.

66. Cox, *Say Goodnight, Gracie*, p. 46.

67. Stanley Cloud and Lynne Olson, *The Murrow Boys: Pioneers on the Front Lines of Broadcast Journalism* (Boston: Houghton Mifflin, 1996), p. 260.

68. Ibid.

69. David Schoenbrun, *On and Off the Air: An Informal History of CBS News* (New York: E.P. Dutton, 1989), pp. 4, 5.

70. Bob Edwards, *Edward R. Murrow and the Birth of Broadcast Journalism* (Hoboken, N.J.: John Wiley & Sons, 2004), pp. xi, 23.

71. Mudd, p. 378.

72. Edwards, p. 4.

73. Emery, Emery, and Roberts, p. 367.

74. Robert A. Rutland, *Newsmongers: Journalism in the Life of the Nation* (New York: Dial Press, 1973), p. 335.

75. Llewellyn White, *The American Radio* (Chicago: University of Chicago Press, 1947), p. 66.

76. Presumably considering radio stations as well as chains, one scholar insisted, "News gained, and would maintain, a position second only to music as a staple of radio programming" (Stephens, p. 277).

77. Emery, Emery, and Roberts, p. 321.

78. MBS instigators: WGN, Chicago; WLW, Cincinnati; WXYZ, Detroit; and WOR, New York.

79. At the time MBS was superseded by ABC, a reorganized NBC Blue, by then owning multiple networks totaling 1,561 outlets. NBC had 268 at the time; CBS had 278 (Cox, *American Radio Networks*, p. 79).

80. A. A. Schechter with Edward Anthony, *I Live on Air* (New York: Stokes, 1941), pp. 156–157.

81. "Radio Pioneers Organize," *The New York Times*, May 24, 1951, p. 32.

82. "Radio-TV Notes," *The New York Times*, September 20, 1952, p. 21.

83. Gerald Nachman, *Raised on Radio: In Quest of The Lone Ranger, Jack Benny, Amos 'n' Andy, The Shadow, Mary Noble, The Great Gildersleeve, Fibber McGee and Molly, Bill Stern, Our Miss Brooks, Henry Aldrich, The Quiz Kids, Mr. First Nighter, Fred Allen, Vic and Sade, The Cisco Kid, Jack Armstrong, Arthur Godfrey, Bob and Ray, The Barbour Family, Henry Morgan, Joe Friday, and Other Lost Heroes from Radio's Heyday* (New York: Pantheon Books, 1998), p. 399.

84. Charnley, p. 11.

85. Schechter and Anthony, p. 1.

86. Radio ad sales doubled between 1930 and 1933 as soap and cigarette makers embraced broadcasting. Newspaper ad revenues plummeted 45 percent (Rutland, p. 335).

87. Gary W. Larson, "Radio Journalism," in W. David Sloan and Lisa Mullikin Parcell's *American Journalism: History, Principles, Practices* (Jefferson, N.C.: McFarland, 2002), p. 278.

88. Charnley, pp. 16–17.

89. Attending: William S. Paley, president, CBS; M. H. Aylesworth, president, NBC; Roy Howard, Scripps-Howard Newspapers; Harry Bitner, Hearst Newspapers; J. H. Gortatowsky, INS; Karl Bickel, president, UP; Lloyd Stratton, executive assistant to general manager Kent Cooper, AP; Alfred J. McCosker, president, NAB; L. B. Palmer, general manager, ANPA; and four ranking members of the ANPA radio committee led by E.H. Harris, editor, *The Richmond* (Indiana) *Palladium* (Charnley, p. 17).

90. "Radio-News Program in Final Stage," *Broadcasting*, February 1, 1934, p. 7.

91. The Press-Radio Bureau officially began in March 1934, corralling 245 subscribers in its first year. It was doomed from the start however. It was unrealistic, yet spawned other newsgathering agencies outside the accord. Five competing news services surfaced paced by Herbert Moore's Transradio Press Service that attracted 230 radio clients and a few newspapers by 1937. In 1935, UP and INS were released from the pact to meet Transradio's threat by selling full news reports to stations. UP launched a wire report for radio that AP matched in 1940, the year the Press-Radio Bureau dissolved. Transradio lasted to 1951 (Emery, Emery, and Roberts, p. 321).

92. Faced with the cutoff of press association news in 1933, Edward Klauber of CBS persuaded General Mills, Inc., to put up half the money the network needed to create a Columbia News Service, direct predecessor of CBS News (Sterling, *Encyclopedia of Radio*, Vol. 2).

93. Larson, in Sloan and Parcell, p. 279. The British Broadcasting Corporation began the world's first scheduled TV service on November 2, 1936, however (Emery, Emery, and Roberts, p. 327).

94. In 1994, AP expanded its radio news service by launching a 24-hour news network for stations unable to afford the ever-increasing cost of producing their own all-news format. Times supposedly change everything.

95. James Playsted Wood, *The Great Glut: Public Communication in the United States* (Nashville: Thomas Nelson, 1973), pp. 118–119.

96. Jim Upshaw, "Characteristics of Journalists," in Sloan and Parcell, eds., p. 72.

97. Ibid. Beyond the *Detroit News* and *Pittsburgh Post*, previously cited, stalwarts such as the *Kansas City Star*, *Milwaukee Journal*, *Chicago Tribune*, *Los Angeles Times*, Louisville *Courier-Journal*, *Atlanta Journal*, *Dallas News*, and *Chicago Daily News* joined the ranks of station owners.

98. Bliss, p. 14.

99. Jim McPherson, "Mergers, Chains, Monopoly, and Competition," in Sloan and Parcell, eds., p. 120.

100. Edwin Emery, *History of the American Newspaper Publishers Association* (Minneapolis: University of Minnesota Press, 1950), chapter 13.
101. Alfred N. Goldsmith and Austin C. Lescarboura, *This Thing Called Broadcasting* (New York: Henry Holt, 1930), p. 71.
102. Charnley, p. 28.
103. Ibid.

Chapter 3

1. Susan J. Douglas, *Listening In: Radio and the American Imagination, from Amos 'n' Andy and Edward R. Murrow to Wolfman Jack and Howard Stern* (New York: Times Books, 1999), p. 175.
2. Ibid., pp. 175, 176, 180.
3. Gerald Nachman, *Raised on Radio: In Quest of The Lone Ranger, Jack Benny, Amos 'n' Andy, The Shadow, Mary Noble, The Great Gildersleeve, Fibber McGee and Molly, Bill Stern, Our Miss Brooks, Henry Aldrich, The Quiz Kids, Mr. First Nighter, Fred Allen, Vic and Sade, The Cisco Kid, Jack Armstrong, Arthur Godfrey, Bob and Ray, The Barbour Family, Henry Morgan, Joe Friday, and Other Lost Heroes from Radio's Heyday* (New York: Pantheon Books, 1998), p. 399.
4. Bob Edwards, *Edward R. Murrow and the Birth of Broadcast Journalism* (Hoboken, N.J.: John Wiley and Sons, 2004), p. 6.
5. Erik Barnouw, *A Tower in Babel: A History of Broadcasting in the United States*, Vol. 1 — to 1933 (New York: Oxford University Press, 1966), p. 250.
6. This figure and others in these examples are from Mitchell V. Charnley's *News by Radio* (New York: Macmillan, 1948, p. 43).
7. Mitchell Stephens, *A History of News: From the Drum to the Satellite* (New York: Viking, 1988), p. 56. Within two decades of the end of radio's golden age, radio historiographers were professing that daily newspapers were "beginning to underplay breaking news about yesterday's events (already old news to much of their audience) in favor of more analytical perspectives on those events." They maintained that dailies of that era were "moving in the direction toward which weeklies retreated when dailies were introduced." More: Gerald Lanson and Mitchell Stephens, "'Trust Me' Journalism," *Washington Journalism Review*, November 1982, pp. 43–47.
8. Charnley, p. 49.
9. Ibid., pp. 49–50.
10. See pp. 50–51 of Charnley's text for comparisons and specific discoveries.
11. Stephens, p. 278.
12. Eugene Lyons, *David Sarnoff: A Biography* (New York: Harper & Row, 1966), p. 79.
13. Ernst Alexanderson, a Swedish immigrant, perfected an alternating current generator he designed for Reginald A. Fessenden's use at Brant Rock, Massachusetts. Alexanderson's original made it possible to dispatch the human voice, singing and violin music for long distances across the sea to ship operators on Christmas eve 1906. By 1914, on-air tests were conducted daily between the GE lab in Schenectady and a GE plant at Pittsfield, Mass. using a successor to the initial alternator. GE had patented Alexanderson's creation earlier. A 50,000-watt model installed for the Marconi Co. at New Brunswick, N.J., subsequently played a vital role for the U.S. Navy during the First World War (Barnouw, *A Tower in Babel*, pp. 19–20, 48–49).
14. Ibid., p. 148.
15. Gene Smith, *When the Cheering Stopped: The Last Years of Woodrow Wilson* (New York: William Morrow, 1964), pp. 223–228; Clyde D. Wagoner, *Reminiscences*, unpublished, 1950, p. 25, housed in New York City in the Columbia University Oral History Collection.
16. Joseph M. Barnett, *Reminiscences*, unpublished, 1951, p. 28, housed in New York City in the Columbia University Oral History Collection.
17. Barnouw, *A Tower in Babel*, p. 196.
18. For a summary of this famous trial, go to http://www.u-s-history.com/pages/h1438.html.
19. While other pilots crossed the Atlantic earlier, Lindbergh was the first to do it nonstop and solo.
20. A summary of Lindberg's life appears at http://www.charleslindbergh.com/history/index.asp.
21. A brief but stimulating account of Lindbergh's trip appears in Edward Bliss, Jr., *Now the News: The Story of Broadcast Journalism* (New York: Columbia University Press, 1991), pp. 20–21.
22. You may view highlights of the fight at http://www.youtube.com/watch?v=-OeeCfbahwQ.
23. Alfred Balk, *The Rise of Radio: From Marconi through the Golden Age* (Jefferson, N.C.: McFarland, 2006), pp. 128–129.
24. At that time newly-elected presidents weren't inaugurated until March 4 of every quadrennial.
25. Said one source: "The events in Miami were significant for two reasons. First, many in the country were uncertain of what to expect from the man who would become president several weeks later; some were outspokenly fearful, but FDR's calm and compassion during the incident offered a large measure of reassurance to an anxious public. Second, the assassination attempt underscored the fact that the response of the overwhelming majority of Americans to the hardships of the Depression was orderly and lawful. Giuseppe Zangara was not a socialist or Communist, but a deranged individual. Leftist groups that were critical of American capitalism did grow during the 1930s, but their numbers remained consistently small. The vast majority of citizens were confident that the existing system of government would eventually find the answers to the nation's ills" (http://www.u-s-history.com/pages/h1516.html).
26. Nachman, p. 8.
27. Stephens, p. 278; http://en.wikipedia.org/wiki/Hindenburg_disaster. It took some well known entertainers, namely singer Bing Crosby, comic quizmaster Groucho Marx, and comedienne Eve Arden, among them, to break down the networks' longstanding opposition to airing shows recorded earlier. That didn't occur until Crosby broke the ice in the fall of 1946 over ABC, the newest of the national chains (in name, at least). *The New York Times* observed: "Mr. Crosby has delivered a major, if not fatal, blow to the outworn and unrealistic prejudice against the recorded program." By then the camel's nose was in the tent; it was a matter of time before his whole body was inside.

Translation: *everybody* would make transcriptions (Jim Cox, *Music Radio: The Great Performers and Programs of the 1920s through Early 1960s* [Jefferson, N.C.: McFarland, 2005], pp. 70–77).

28. Jim Cox, *This Day in Network Radio: A Daily Calendar of Births, Deaths, Debuts, Cancellations and Other Events in Broadcasting History* (Jefferson, N.C.: McFarland, 2008), pp. 131, 198–199; http://history 1900s.about.com/od/1930s/a/warofworlds.htm.

29. All over the U.S. people were phoning newspapers to ask what to do. *The New York Times* received 875 calls. Police stations were swamped with calls. Priests had calls from people seeking confession. But many weren't waiting to make phone calls. By 8:30 cars were racing along highways between New York and Philadelphia. Police were helpless. Some people dug old gas masks out of closets. Sailors on shore leave in New York were summoned back to their ships. In Indianapolis a woman rushed into a church service screaming that the world was coming to an end. The service broke up hurriedly. A power failure in a town in Washington state convinced inhabitants that the end had arrived. Some people claimed they had seen the Martians. It was a brilliantly produced broadcast, with an impact not foreshadowed by anything in radio experience. Its relation to war fears was avidly discussed. Dorothy Thompson called it "the news story of the century — an event which made a greater contribution to an understanding of Hitlerism, Mussolinism, Stalinism, and all the other terrorisms of our time than all the words about them that have been written by reasonable men." The event was in ways a reenactment of *The Fall of the City*: men rushed to prostrate themselves before an empty visor (adapted from Erik Barnouw, *The Golden Web: A History of Broadcasting in the United States*, Vol. 2 — 1933 to 1953 [New York: Oxford University Press, 1968], pp. 87–88).

30. "Radio stations received hundreds of telephone calls from people hysterically inquiring about the Martians' landing near Princeton. The FCC found nothing amusing about these public fears, nor did the network presidents. In Washington it was agreed that no further radio programs would use a 'news broadcast' type of presentation ... radio networks felt that they must be more careful to control the content of their programming, apparently believing that bad news, real or otherwise, was unacceptable" (David Holbrook Culbert, *News for Everyman: Radio and Foreign Affairs in Thirties America* [Westport, Conn.: Greenwood Press, 1976], pp. 75–76).

31. In 1924, Americans listened to election returns on three million radio sets; four years later they tuned to eight million sets. Michael Emery, Edwin Emery, and Nancy L. Roberts, *The Press and America: An Interpretive History of the Mass Media*, 9th ed. (Boston: Allyn and Bacon, 2000), p. 276.

32. Robert Hardy Andrews, "A Voice in the Room," adapted from *Legend of a Lady: The Story of Rita Martin* (New York: Coward-McCann, 1949), pp. 111–112.

33. Nachman, p. 405, who affirms Stanley Cloud and Lynne Olson's *The Murrow Boys: Pioneers on the Front Lines of Broadcast Journalism* (Boston: Houghton Mifflin, 1996).

34. Despite such figures scholars with contrary data or bias say otherwise. In the first chapter of his memoir an enduring CBS-TV reporter references the early 1960s with "As a young newspaperman in those days when most Americans got their news from newspapers...." Partiality for an early career in print may have supplanted some stats (Bob Schieffer, *This Just In: What I Couldn't Tell You on TV* [New York: Berkley, 2003]).

35. Ned Midgley, *The Advertising and Business Side of Radio* (New York: Prentice-Hall, 1948), pp. 19–20.

36. Cloud and Olson, p. 103.

Chapter 4

1. Sally Bedell Smith, *In All His Glory: The Life of William S. Paley, the Legendary Tycoon and His Brilliant Circle* (New York: Simon & Schuster, 1990), pp. 65, 132.

2. Ibid., pp. 134–135.

3. The Federal Communications Commission established in 1934 currently with about 1900 federal employees (2011) and underwritten totally by regulatory fees projected a budget for 2012 of $354.2 million (http://en.wikipedia.org/wiki/Federal_Communications_Commission).

4. For more detail see Web sites like http://en.wikipedia.org/wiki/Federal_Communications_Commission and http://transition.fcc.gov/omd/history/ or text by Jim Cox, *American Radio Networks: A History* (Jefferson, N.C.: McFarland, 2009), pp. 116–121.

5. Christopher H. Sterling and John M. Kittross, *Stay Tuned: A Concise History of American Broadcasting*, 2d ed. (Belmont, Calif.: Wadsworth, 1990), p. 66.

6. "In the earliest years, self-regulation meant little other than 'silent nights.' Time-sharing was mostly voluntary, but ..., there was always the threat of government action. In technical matters, broadcasting clearly needed a governmental traffic cop..." (Ibid., p. 88).

7. Ibid.

8. Passed by Congress on February 18, the Radio Act of 1927 was signed into law by President Calvin Coolidge on February 23 of that year.

9. Alfred Balk, *The Rise of Radio: From Marconi through the Golden Age* (Jefferson, N.C.: McFarland, 2006), p. 68.

10. Public Law No. 632, 69th Congress, Sec. 29.

11. The Dill-White bill of 1923, based on legislation introduced by Rep. Wallace White of Maine and Sen. Clarence C. Dill of Montana, became the radio law, giving licensing control to an independent bipartisan commission of five members for a period of one year to bring order out of chaos. After a year the licensing authority was to revert to the Secretary of Commerce or so the law anticipated. "But I knew," Senator Dill said, "if we ever got a commission, we would never get rid of it." Later amendments prolonged the life of the commission; its work never seemed finished (Erik Barnouw, *A Tower in Babel: A History of Broadcasting in the United States*, Vol. 1 — to 1933 [New York: Oxford University Press, 1966], p. 199).

12. Charles A. Siepmann, *Radio's Second Chance* (Boston: Little, Brown, 1947), pp. 6–7.

13. Cox, *American Radio Networks*, p. 120.

14. Supreme Court *Report on Chain Broadcasting*, Appendix v, 1940.
15. Susan Smulyan, *Selling Radio: The Commercialization of American Broadcasting, 1920 to 1934* (Washington, D.C.: Smithsonian Institution Press, 1994), p. 103.
16. Barnouw, *A Tower in Babel*, p. 154.
17. Cox, *American Radio Networks*, p. 124.
18. Barnouw, *A Tower in Babel*, p. 155.
19. Gleason L. Archer, *History of Radio, to 1926* (New York: American Historical Society, 1938), pp. 288–289.
20. Edgar H. Felix, *Reminiscences*, 1962, p. 29; William E. Harkness, *Reminiscences*, 1951, p. 64 — both housed in New York City in the Columbia University Oral History Collection.
21. Barnouw, *A Tower in Babel*, pp. 157–158.
22. William Peck Banning, *Commercial Broadcasting Pioneer: The WEAF Experiment 1922–1926* (Cambridge: Harvard University Press, 1946), pp. 108, 147–150.
23. Francis Chase, Jr., *Sound and Fury: An Informal History of Broadcasting* (New York: Harper & Brothers, 1942), pp. 135–136.
24. In 1932, the Federal Radio Commission noted paid advertising's mounting presence by observing that the form was underwriting 33.8 percent of NBC's schedule and 21.94 percent of CBS's. "The sponsored programs were getting the best hours and the main attention from radio columns and fan magazines," a source acknowledged. Advertising was depicted as "brief, circumspect, and extremely well-mannered" (Cox, *American Radio Networks*, p. 128).
25. Siepmann, *Radio's Second Chance*, p. 134.
26. Chase, p. 131.
27. Ibid., p. 133.
28. Corydon B. Dunham, *Fighting for the First Amendment: Stanton of CBS vs. Congress and the Nixon White House* (Westport, Conn.: Praeger, 1997), pp. xii, xiii, 5, 6.
29. Ibid., pp. 172–182.
30. Ibid., p. 178.
31. Ibid., p. 201.

Chapter 5

1. Robert D. Heinl, "Radio and the Next War," *Radioland*, September 1933, pp. 12–15.
2. *Variety*, July 29, 1942, p. 25.
3. J. Fred MacDonald, *Don't Touch That Dial! Radio Programming in American Life from 1920 to 1960* (Chicago: Nelson-Hall, 1991), pp. 304–305.
4. The Office of Censorship remained in operation until three months after President Harry S Truman declared "voluntary censorship of the domestic press and radio at an end" on August 15, 1945 (Ronald Garay, "Office of Censorship," in Donald G. Godfrey and Frederic A. Leigh, eds., *Historical Dictionary of American Radio* [Westport, Conn.: Greenwood Press, 1998], p. 70).
5. Edward Bliss, Jr., *Now the News: The Story of Broadcast Journalism* (New York: Columbia University Press, 1991), p. 138.
6. Sally Bedell Smith, *In All His Glory: The Life of William S. Paley, the Legendary Tycoon and His Brilliant Circle* (New York: Simon & Schuster, 1990), p. 159.

7. In 1972, the Fairness Doctrine was broadened, adding cable systems that generated programming. The FCC voted to repeal the doctrine in 1987, and a federal appellate court upheld the FCC's power to do so in 1989. Since 1987, Congress debated amending the *Communications Act* to include the Fairness Doctrine, thereby making it impossible for the FCC to alter the law. This failed, however, aided by President Ronald Reagan's veto in 1987 (Dom Caristi, "Fairness Doctrine," in Donald G. Godfrey and Frederic A. Leigh, eds., *Historical Dictionary of American Radio* [Westport, Conn.: Greenwood Press, 1998], p. 149).
8. MacDonald, p. 70.
9. Ibid., p. 71.
10. One account recorded: "Sensitive to strong isolationist sentiments in America, radio newscasters were hard pressed to remain objective as they reported the spread of Nazi militarism. Although journalistic ethics placed a premium on reporting news in a vocabulary free from prejudice, it must have been a strain for network correspondents to remain implacable in the face of unchecked fascist aggression" (MacDonald, pp. 302–303).
11. Bob Edwards, *Edward R. Murrow and the Birth of Broadcast Journalism* (Hoboken, N.J.: John Wiley and Sons, 2004), pp. 46–47.
12. David Schoenbrun, *On and Off the Air: An Informal History of CBS News* (New York: E.P. Dutton, 1989), p. 42.
13. Shortly before both died, David Schoenbrun wrote: "Edwards was a natural. He had a warm, melodious voice and flawless phrasing. Doug was completely at ease in front of a microphone or camera. He never flubbed, was never flustered, never missed a beat, and maintained a rhythmic delivery easy to listen to. They could hand him a script with a minute to go to air and, without having read it in advance, Edwards would sit down, face the camera, smile, and in his rich, baritone voice deliver the script without a glitch. He was and has remained for fifty years the consummate newsreader in the history of radio and television" (p. 44). It sounded well to have a colleague who believed as much too.
14. Reuven Frank, *Out of Thin Air: The Brief Wonderful Life of Network News* (New York: Simon & Schuster, 1991), p. 110.
15. Philip Seib, *Going Live: Getting the News Right in a Real-Time, Online World* (Lanham, Md.: Rowman & Littlefield, 2001), p. 16.
16. Mitchell V. Charnley, *News by Radio* (New York: Macmillan, 1948), p. 308.
17. David Holbrook Culbert, *News for Everyman: Radio and Foreign Affairs in Thirties America* (Westport, Conn.: Greenwood Press, 1976), p. 27.
18. *Variety*, June 18, 1941, p. 25.
19. Culbert, p. 28.
20. Ibid.
21. There are multiple references to Klauber to be found in Chapter 2 of this volume that introduce him more comprehensively.
22. *Variety*, January 25, 1939, p. 121.
23. The radio networks policed their own entertainment performers in that age just as they did newscasters. Particularly was this true of a handful of comics, whose jests sometimes spelled trouble by stir-

ring the ire of advertisers, audiences and federal autocrats. Routinely kept on short leashes by their chains were Fred Allen, Bob Hope, Henry Morgan and more of similar persuasion. Groucho Marx, with a penchant for ribald asides, got around censorship by taping his shows with far more material than could be aired in 30 minutes, then having it rigorously edited to fit the allowed format — and meet network censors' approval.

24. MacDonald, p. 71.

25. In the Second World War correspondents largely went along with censorship because they thought it was in the nation's interest. On a practical level they could only go to the front if they abided by censorship rules, thus motives other than patriotism existed. They allowed military reps to examine their dispatches before sending. The atomic bomb is an excellent example of how well voluntary censorship worked. Some journalists were aware the bomb was being developed but wrote little about it until it was used on August 6, 1945, at Hiroshima (Debra Reddin Van Tuyll, "The Press and War," in W. David Sloan and Lisa Mullikin Parcell, eds., *American Journalism: History, Principles, Practices* [Jefferson, N.C.: McFarland, 2002], p. 232).

26. MacDonald, p. 306.

27. Bringing self-censorship closer, a 2000 Pew Research Center inquiry revealed that more than 40 percent of modern journalists felt a need to self-censor their work by avoiding certain topics or softening the exhibitions they pursued to benefit interests of the organizations that employed them ("Self-Censorship: How Often and Why: Journalists Avoiding the News," April 30, 2000, Pew Research Center for the People and the Press; http://www.people-press.org/reports/display.php3?ReportID=39).

28. Commentary and editorializing aren't identical. Commentary is the expression of an individual's views; editorializing encompasses views of the station itself, e.g., a licensee and management.

29. The Mayflower Decision history in essence is this: Prior to 1941, Boston's WAAB, owned by Mayflower Broadcasting Corp., supported causes and advanced chances of political candidates it favored. Persons of differing persuasions weren't afforded equal opportunities. Following complaints to the FCC and a full investigation, that body issued an edict that a licensee, "by virtue of his privileged access to a public domain," wasn't justified in using it as if it were his "private property." Thus, a "licensee shall not be advocate," said the FCC. After review in 1949, the FCC issued a revised ruling that "empowered radio licensees to editorialize as long as the 'other side' of questions thus treated was also given" (Charles A. Siepmann, *Radio, Television and Society* [New York: Oxford University Press, 1950], p. 219).

30. *Radio Daily*, September 16, 1943; H. V. Kaltenborn, *Reminiscences*, unpublished, 1950, p. 207.

31. Giraud Chester, *The Radio Commentaries of H. V. Kaltenborn: A Case Study in Persuasion*, unpublished Ph.D dissertation, University of Wisconsin, 1947, pp. 504–545.

32. Barnouw, *The Golden Web*, p. 136.

33. Ibid.

34. *Variety*, January 21, 1942, p. 25.

35. Bliss, p. 138.

36. John Chancellor, "From Normandy to Grenada: A Veteran Reporter Looks Back," *American Heritage*, June/July 1985, p. 32.

37. Culbert, pp. 25–26.

38. Douglas, p. 198.

39. In mid 20th century, McCarthy pursued a witch-hunt to reveal perceived — and often unsubstantiated — subversives. People in government, professions, and performing arts were targets as "McCarthyism" exposed Communist and Nazi sympathizers. Hundreds in radio-TV employ were named (Cox, *American Radio Networks*, p. 59).

40. Douglas, p. 198. The episode also had lingering effects for Murrow so a biographer claims. Though he exposed McCarthy as a despot and bully, "the triumph of that accomplishment was short-lived ... and in some ways marked the beginning of the end for Murrow at CBS" (Edwards, p. 4).

41. Edwards, p. 7.

42. Ibid., p. 107.

43. Emery, Emery, and Roberts, pp. 369–370.

44. William D. Leahy, *I Was There* (New York: Whittlesey House, 1950), p. 127; Robert Klara, *FDR's Funeral Train: A Betrayed Widow, A Soviet Spy, and a Presidency in the Balance* (New York: Palgrave Macmillan, 2010), p. 95.

45. Irving E. Fang, *Those Radio Commentators!* (Ames: Iowa State University Press, 1977), p. 35.

46. *Variety*, May 5, 1943, p. 52.

47. MacDonald, p. 72.

48. Self-censorship is still perceived as a threat among news practitioners. As recently as the turn of the century a respected interpreter of the industry allowed: "The truth about self-censorship is that it is widespread, as common in newsrooms as deadline pressure, a virus that eats away at the journalistic mission" ("The Truth About Self-Censorship," Columbia Journalism Review, May-June 2000; http://www.cjr.or./year/00/2/2/may-juneindex.asp).

49. Fang, pp. 9–10. The parameters of Paul White's professional career and his influence are discussed in Chapter 2.

50. *Variety*, October 13, 1943, p. 33.

51. Fang, p. 10.

52. Ibid.

53. Ibid.

54. While it's uncertain to what degree the ARNA was active in fighting for freedom to voice personal opinions on the airwaves, although it may well have done so, as one example of its efforts it registered complaints over middle commercial interruptions during broadcasts.

55. Edwards, p. 7.

56. Ibid., p. 3.

57. Ibid., pp. 40–41.

58. *Variety*, October 6, 1943, p. 27.

59. Edwards, p. 7.

60. *Variety*, December 15, 1943, p. 27.

61. Robert J. Landry, *This Fascinating Radio Business* (Indianapolis: Bobbs-Merrill, 1946), pp. 247–248.

62. Davis had been a praiseworthy radio commentator. Of the 1939–40 season a pundit affirmed: "Davis soon became one of the most widely heard newsmen in radio when CBS carved out a five minute slot for his news and comment seven nights a week at

8:55. The first five-minute news capsule in network prime time aired on September 18 [1939] and furthered the CBS News image to audiences of popular nighttime fare" (Jim Ramsburg, *Network Radio Ratings, 1932–1953: A History of Prime Time Programs through the Ratings of Nielsen, Crossley and Hooper* [Jefferson, N.C.: McFarland, 2012], p. 82).

63. Besides Elmer Davis, CBS vice president William B. Lewis also joined the Office of War Information. Jack Benny, George Burns and Gracie Allen, Nelson Eddy, Jean Hersholt, Kay Kyser, and other radio legends comprised a "Committee of 25" recruited in 1942 to coordinate fund-raising and morale-building activities on radio. Government officials were advised by insiders who wouldn't burden the chains with "disorderly programming or ponderous uninteresting propaganda." They gained staff skilled in managing national radio systems and top celebs whose reputations lent credibility to appeals for funds and patriotic statements (adapted from MacDonald, pp. 72–73).

64. *Variety*, February 17, 1943, p. 28.

65. Roger Burlingame, *Don't Let Them Scare You: The Life and Times of Elmer Davis* (Philadelphia: Lippincott, 1961), p. 200. Wartime correspondents vehemently criticized this form of federal censorship, reported in *Variety*, May 5, 1943, p. 32.

66. Raymond Gram Swing, *"Good Evening!" A Professional Memoir* (New York: Harcourt, Brace & World, 1964), pp. 225–226.

67. MacDonald, p. 73.

68. Ibid., p. 74.

69. Swing, pp. 194–211.

70. Smith, p. 161.

71. Susan J. Douglas, *Listening In: Radio and the American Imagination, from Amos 'n' Andy and Edward R. Murrow to Wolfman Jack and Howard Stern* (New York: Times Books, 1999), p. 172.

72. Ibid., p. 173.

73. http://www.un.org/en/documents/udhr/index.shtml. The UDHR was fabricated by a nine-member panel of global human rights representatives including the U.S.'s Mrs. Eleanor (Franklin D.) Roosevelt. The document is seen as "a road map to guarantee the rights of every individual everywhere."

74. Kyu Ho Youm, "Censorship," in Godfrey and Leigh, eds., *Historical Dictionary of American Radio*, p. 68.

75. Noble wanted a more commanding name than *Blue* and, in 1944, he acquired the rights to *ABC* from broadcaster George Storer (Cox, *American Radio Networks*, p. 205).

76. Balk, p. 258.

77. Cox, *American Radio Networks*, p. 95.

78. http://en.wikipedia.org/wiki/Hollywood_blacklist.

79. Rita Morley Harvey, *Those Wonderful, Terrible Years: George Heller and the American Federation of Television and Radio Artists* (Carbondale: Southern Illinois University Press, 1996).

Chapter 6

1. Erik Barnouw, *The Golden Web: A History of Broadcasting in the United States*, Vol. II —1933 to 1953 (New York: Oxford University Press, 1968), pp. 135–136.

2. Susan J. Douglas, *Listening In: Radio and the American Imagination, from Amos 'n' Andy and Edward R. Murrow to Wolfman Jack and Howard Stern* (New York: Times Books, 1999), p. 164.

3. Charles A. Siepmann, *Radio's Second Chance* (Boston: Little, Brown, 1947), p. 87.

4. J. Fred MacDonald, *Don't Touch That Dial!: Radio Programming in American Life, 1920–1960* (Chicago: Nelson-Hall, 1991), p. 282.

5. Siepmann, p. 100.

6. Figures from a May 15, 2002, report issued by Scarborough Research, a cooperative endeavor fostered by Arbitron, Inc., Columbia, Maryland, and VNU Media Measurement & Information, New York, N.Y.

7. http://www.americanprogress.org/issues/2010/03/ta031110.html.

8. Pew Project for Excellence in Journalism.

9. *Inside Radio*.

10. http://www.americanprogress.org/issues/2010/03/ta31110.html.

11. Ibid.

12. http://en.wikipedia.org/wiki/Progressive_talk_radio.

13. Eric Alterman, *What Liberal Media? The Truth about Bias and the News* (New York: Basic Books, 2003), p. 74.

14. Jim Cox, *American Radio Networks: A History* (Jefferson, N.C.: McFarland, 2009), p. 185.

15. Alterman, pp. 71–72.

16. *Broadcasting*, December 15, 1937.

17. Barnouw, *The Golden Web*, p. 135.

18. Douglas, p. 164.

19. Ibid., pp. 164, 165, 180

20. Edward Bliss, Jr., *Now the News: The Story of Broadcast Journalism* (New York: Columbia University Press, 1991), p. 107.

21. Douglas, p. 181.

22. Ibid., p. 183.

23. Stanley Cloud and Lynne Olson, *The Murrow Boys: Pioneers on the Front Lines of Broadcast Journalism* (Boston: Houghton Mifflin, 1996), p. 142; A.M. Sperber, *Murrow: His Life and Times* (New York: Freundlich Books, 1986), p. 123; *News of Europe*, September 7, 1939.

24. Edouard Daladier (1884–1970), France's minister of war earlier, was prime minister on three brief occasions: 1933, 1934, and 1938–40. He fled to Morocco early in the Second World War, was handed over to Germany, and imprisoned there 1942–45 (http://www.spartacus.Schoolnet.co.uk/2WWdaladier.htm).

25. Robert Slater, *This ... Is CBS: A Chronicle of 60 Years* (Englewood Cliffs, N.J.: Prentice-Hall, 1988), p. 67.

26. From a Murrow broadcast on September 20, 1939; he quoted from *The London Evening Standard* before adding his remarks designed to motivate his native countrymen.

27. Norman H. Finkelstein, *Sounds in the Air: The Golden Age of Radio* (New York: Charles Scribner's, 1993), p. 99.

28. David Holbrook Culbert, *News for Everyman: Radio and Foreign Affairs in America* (Westport, Conn.: Greenwood Press, 1966).

29. Cloud and Olson, p. 145.
30. Sherman H. Dryer, *Radio in Wartime* (New York: Greenberg, 1942), p. 239.
31. MacDonald, pp. 292, 293.

Chapter 7

1. You may read more about how this blueprint worked and indeed an overview of MBS itself in Jim Cox's *American Radio Networks: A History* (Jefferson, N.C.: McFarland, 2009), pp. 72–88.
2. John Dunning, *On the Air: The Encyclopedia of Old-Time Radio* (New York: Oxford University Press, 1998), p. 26.
3. Mark J. Heistad, "University of Chicago Roundtable," in Donald G. Godfrey and Frederic A. Leigh, eds., *Historical Dictionary of American Radio* (Westport, Conn.: Greenwood Press, 1998), p. 402.
4. Charles A. Siepmann, *Radio's Second Chance* (Boston: Little, Brown, 1947), pp. 120–121.
5. Francis Chase, Jr., *Sound and Fury: An Informal History of Broadcasting* (New York: Harper & Brothers, 1942), p. 218.
6. Ibid., p. 217.
7. Author Max Wylie delineated this when he chose one of the show's representations for inclusion in his *Best Broadcasts of 1938–39* (New York: Whittlesey House, 1939).
8. Dunning, *On the Air*, pp. 30–31.
9. Alfred Balk, *The Rise of Radio, from Marconi through the Golden Age* (Jefferson, N.C.: McFarland, 2006), p. 222.
10. Chase, p. 122.
11. John Files, "Martha Rountree, 87, a Creator of 'Meet the Press,'" *The New York Times*, August 25, 1999.
12. Marc Robinson, *Brought to You in Living Color: 75 Years of Great Moments in Television & Radio from NBC* (Hoboken, N.J.: John Wiley & Sons, 2002), p. 217.
13. John Dunning, *Tune in Yesterday: The Ultimate Encyclopedia of Old-Time Radio, 1925–1976* (Englewood Cliffs, N.J.: Prentice-Hall, 1976), pp. 404–405.
14. Some data is from http://www.tvweek.com/news/2007/04/making_tv_history_meet_the_pre.php.
15. Richard Severo, "Lawrence E. Spivak, 93, Is Dead; The Originator of 'Meet the Press,'" *The New York Times*, March 10, 1994.
16. Siepmann, *Radio's Second Chance*, p. 124.
17. Ibid., pp. 125–125.

Chapter 8

1. Mitchell Stephens, *A History of News: From the Drum to the Satellite* (New York: Viking Penguin, 1988), p. 56.
2. http://jeff560.tripod.com/chronol.html.
3. Ibid.
4. Ibid.
5. Ibid.
6. Jim Cox, *This Day in Network Radio: A Daily Calendar of Births, Deaths, Debuts, Cancellations and Other Events in Broadcasting History* (Jefferson, N.C.: McFarland, 2008), p. 200.
7. http://jeff560.tripod.com/chronol.html.
8. Stephens, p. 277.
9. Jim Cox, *American Radio Networks: A History* (Jefferson, N.C.: McFarland, 2009), pp. 12, 116, 178.
10. Cox, *This Day in Network Radio*, p. 200. There is a difference of opinion among historiographers as to which station was licensed first by federal authorities. Luther Sies maintains it was KDKA in January 1920, evidenced by a report in the U.S. Chamber of Commerce's *Radio Service Bulletin*. Laurie Lee says WBZ, Springfield, Mass., holds that honor, having received it September 15, 1921, 10 months after KDKA's infamous election night coverage. Sources: Luther F. Sies, *Encyclopedia of American Radio, 1920–1960*, 2d ed., Vol. 2 (Jefferson, N.C.: McFarland, 2008), p. 639; Laurie Thomas Lee, "Stations," in G. Godfrey and Frederic A. Leigh, eds., *Historical Dictionary of American Radio* (Westport, Conn.: Greenwood Press, 1998), p. 371.
11. http://jeff560.tripod.com/chronol.html.
12. http://www.wjag.com/Wjaghist.htm; http://en.wikipedia.org/wiki/WJAG. There are several more Web sites giving further detailed history of WJAG.
13. WLW, which began as 8CR and among the early "converted" radio stations when its license was granted March 2, 1922, still wasn't in the vanguard of transitions. Between October 27, 1920, when KDKA's call letters were assigned, and WLW's date with destiny, 60 or so outlets with three- or four-letter designations sans numerals were licensed to operate. Source: http://jeff560.tripod.com/chronol.html.
14. Michael Emery, Edwin Emery, and Nancy L. Roberts, *The Press and America: An Interpretive History of the Mass Media*. 9th ed. Boston: Allyn and Bacon, 2000, p. 322.
15. Smith is credited as an authentic pioneer of radio drama: http://en.wikipedia.org/wiki/Radio_drama.
16. For profound details of how *The March of Time* was executed see http://www.examiner.com/old-time-radio-in-national/time-marches-to-war-old-time-radio-... and/or http://www.otrr.org/FILES/Synopsis_txt/M_Series/March_Of_Time.htm.
17. http://jeff560.tripod.com/chronol.html.
18. Lawrence W. Lichty and Thomas W. Bohn, "Radio's *March of Time*: Dramatized News," *Journalism Quarterly*, LI (Autumn 1973), pp. 458–462.
19. One of the actors in a company of New York radio thespians in *The March of Time* news dramas was Orson Welles. On October 30, 1938, his production of "The War of the Worlds" on CBS's Mercury Theatre pursued the Smith formula of turning a newsmaking event into a dramatic offering, albeit fictional that time. It created a panic never foreseen as thousands and maybe millions of listeners took the invasion of America's East Coast by Martian spaceships as gospel despite disclaimers to the contrary.
20. John Dunning, *On the Air: The Encyclopedia of Old-Time Radio* (New York: Oxford University Press, 1998), p. 485.
21. Ibid.
22. Paley partially attempted to accomplish his aim by infusing the CBS schedule with some highbrow musical fare, sparring with his opposite number at NBC (David Sarnoff) in his quest. For details, see

"The Classics" section in Jim Cox's *Music Radio: The Great Performers and Programs of the 1920s through Early 1960s* (Jefferson, N.C.: McFarland, 2005), pp. 103–126.

23. Gary Paul Gates, *Air Time: The Inside Story of CBS News* (New York: Harper & Row, 1978), pp. 22–23.

24. Data from *The New York Times* radio page, January 2, 1930.

25. Data from *The New York Times* radio page, January 3, 1933.

26. Cox, *This Day in Network Radio*, p. 220.

27. Data from *The New York Times* radio page, January 2, 1935.

28. Data from *The New York Times* radio page, January 3, 1940.

29. Bill Jaker, Frank Sulek and Peter Kanze, *The Airwaves of New York: Illustrated Histories of 156 AM Stations in the Metropolitan Area, 1921–1996* (Jefferson, N.C.: McFarland, 1998), p. 170.

30. Harry Castleman and Walter J. Podrazik, *505 Radio Questions Your Friends Can't Answer* (New York: Walker, 1983), pp. 116, 121. As of Saturday, July 3, 1954, WABC (and presumably much of the network) programmed news at the top of 10 of 18 broadcast hours plus at five minutes before an eleventh hour. News appeared at the top of seven of 17 broadcast hours on Sunday, July 3, 1954, on WABC. Source: *The New York Times* radio pages.

31. Jim Cox, *Say Goodnight, Gracie: The Last Years of Network Radio* (Jefferson, N.C.: McFarland, 2002), p. 152. The media critics quoted are Christopher H. Sterling and John M. Kittross, *Stay Tuned: A Concise History of American Broadcasting*, 2d ed. (Belmont, Calif.: Wadsworth, 1990), p. 338.

32. For an intriguing and compelling examination of this monumental audio series the reader is directed to author Dennis Hart's *Monitor (Take 2): The Revised, Expanded Inside Story of Network Radio's Greatest Program*. New York: iUniverse, Inc., 2003.

33. The data does not reflect weekend programming when news and public affairs shows might have fallen or risen.

34. Data from *The New York Times* radio page, January 4, 1960.

35. Cox, *Say Goodnight, Gracie*, p. 147.

36. Sterling and Kittross, pp. 337–338.

37. Jim Cox, *The Great Radio Soap Operas* (Jefferson, N.C.: McFarland, 1999), pp. 131–132.

38. The soapy sagas were good for CBS too, 25 percent of whose programming in 1959 was in daytime serials, "the biggest audience-attracting block of programming in all network radio," according to CBS VP-sales John Karol. A lavishly produced promotional piece that year specified that those narratives were audience leaders in their time periods in nearly every major market where there was a CBS affiliate. Source: Cox, *Say Goodnight, Gracie*, p. 146.

39. MBS and NBC Radio effectively ended their broadcasting regimens in 1999. ABC Radio and CBS Radio persist today (2012). News is the prevailing feature of the existing webs. Source: Cox, *American Radio Networks*, pp. 43, 87.

40. Data from *The New York Times* radio page, December 29, 1960.

41. For a succinct overview of "Radio Specialization," see that section (similarly titled) in Sterling and Kittross, pp. 396–398.

42. http://xroads.virginia.edu/~ug00/3on1/radioshow/1920radio.htm.

43. John R. Broholm, "News Programming Criticism," in Godfrey and Leigh, eds., p. 286. Some of this material is adapted from Edward Connors' "They Still Call It Radio News" that ran in *Washington Journalism Review*, May 1, 1991, pp. 39–42.

44. NBC sent unmistakable signals of impending doom much earlier. "December 31, 1982, was something of a defining moment for NBC Radio. On that date it ended the news-and-features approach it had pursued since the end of the 1950s. In one fell swoop the chain scrubbed nearly all of its daily features and weekend public affairs programming.... All that was left ... was the hourly news, several two-minute weekday *Comments on the News* bits and *Meet the Press*, an audio rebroadcast of the popular TV ... series which aired every Sunday" (Cox, *Say Goodnight, Gracie*, p. 175).

45. ABC created other sub-webs in 1982, when its transmission was switched to satellite, allowing concurrent diffusion on sundry transponders (Phillip O. Keirstead, "ABC News Networks," in Godfrey and Leigh, eds., p. 2).

46. Cox, *Say Goodnight, Gracie*, p. 152; Castleman and Podrazik, pp. 117, 121.

Chapter 9

1. Homer Croy, "The Newspaper That Comes through Your Walls," Popular Radio, September 1922, pp. 11–16.

2. Even the major wire services like AP, UP, and INS weren't especially perplexed in the 1920s, and certainly not so very early in that decade, as broadcasters pilfered their efforts, particularly if on-air credit was extended. It wasn't until the early 1930s that grave consternation erupted between the joint wire-print media and the radio stations-networks. That resulted in the Press-Radio War (which began in 1922 but didn't hit a peak until 1933). Review it in Chapter 2.

3. Mitchell V. Charnley, *News by Radio* (New York: Macmillan, 1948), p. 4.

4. Much earlier in that decade the U.S. Department of Commerce became alarmed that too many stations, particularly of the amateur and experimental variety, were making broadcasts to the wide-ranging public. Effective December 1, 1921, rules were adopted to restrict public broadcasting to stations meeting precise criterion of a new broadcast service requirement (http://earlyradiohistory.us/sec018.htm).

5. Alas, these Americans needed the entrepreneurial spirit of *The Telephone-Hirmondo* innovators who devised a way to use party-lines so Budapest citizens could hear the news early instead of reading it later.

6. The original work by authors Rhey T. Snodgrass and Victor F. Camp has been reprinted in contemporary times by Nabu Press, Charleston, S.C.

7. http://xroads.virginia.edu/~ug00/3on1/radioshow/1920radio.htm.

8. Ibid.

9. http://www.californiahistoricalradio.com/100years.html.
10. www.ce.org/publications/books_references/digital_american/history/the_transistor.asp; www.etedeschi.ndirect.co.uk/tr.radio.history.htm.
11. http://jeff560.tripod.com/62.html. The original Western Electric sculpt, a 100-watt tower for what was to be WEAF, New York, flagship of the future NBC Red network, was installed on the 11th floor of WE's Engineering Department structure at 463 West Street. Although two more enterprises crafted transmitters at that time, they made them solely for their own stations. In 1922, the WE transmitters sold for $8,500 (100 watts) and $10,500 (500 watts (William Peck Banning, *Commercial Broadcasting Pioneer: The WEAF Experiment 1922–1926* [Cambridge: Harvard University Press, 1946], p. 74).
12. http://jeff560.tripod.com/62.html.
13. Erik Barnouw, *A Tower in Babel: A History of Broadcasting in the United States,* Vol. I — to 1933 (New York: Oxford University Press, 1966), pp. 108–109.
14. Ibid., pp. 117–119.
15. Hiram L. Jome, *Economics of the Radio Industry* (Chicago: A.W. Shaw, 1925), p. 70.
16. Ibid. This information is based on U.S. Department of Commerce data.
17. S.E. Frost, Jr., *Education's Own Stations: The History of Broadcast Licenses Issued to Educational Institutions* (Chicago: University of Chicago Press, 1937), p. 4. Another authoritative source illuminates further: "There are small discrepancies between various sets of statistics concerning this period." For an example and more elucidation see Erik Barnouw's *A Tower in Babel: A History of Broadcasting in the United States,* Vol. I — to 1933 (New York: Oxford University Press, 1966), p. 104, footnote 42.
18. http://library.thinkquest.org/27629/themes/media/md20s.html?tql-iframe.
19. http://jeff560.tripod.com/1930am.html.
20. Ronald P. Richards, "Montana's Pioneer Radio Stations: A Hobby Becomes an Industry," *Montana Journalism Review,* Spring 1963; Lyman Lloyd Bryson, *Reminiscences,* unpublished, 1951, p. 108. Bryson subsequently became educational counselor of the Columbia Broadcasting System.
21. H. V. Kaltenborn, *Reminiscences,* unpublished, 1950, p. 111.
22. Alfred Balk, *The Rise of Radio, from Marconi through the Golden Age* (Jefferson, N.C.: McFarland, 2006), p. 42.
23. Edward Bliss, Jr., *Now the News: The Story of Broadcast Journalism* (New York: Columbia University Press, 1991), p. 14.
24. Richards, Ibid.
25. http://library.thinkquest.org/27629/themes/media/md20s.html?tql-iframe.
26. *Broadcasting,* 1939 Yearbook, p. 11.
27. http://xroads.virginia.edu/~ug00/3on1/radioshow/1920radio.htm.
28. Charles Siepmann, "American Radio in Wartime," in Paul Lazarsfeld and Frank Stanton, eds., *Radio Research 1942–43* (New York: Duell, Sloan & Pearce, 1944), p. 119.
29. Susan J. Douglas, *Listening In: Radio and the American Imagination, from Amos 'n' Andy and Edward R. Murrow to Wolfman Jack and Howard Stern* (New York: Times Books, 1999), pp. 174–175.
30. Irving E. Fang, *Those Radio Commentators!* (Ames: Iowa State University Press, 1977), p. 13.
31. Herschell Hart, *Reminiscences,* unpublished, 1951, p. 6. Quoted in Barnouw, *A Tower in Babel,* p. 138. WCX subsequently became WJR.
32. Walter Chew Evans, *Reminiscences,* unpublished, 1950, 1951, p. 14.
33. The reference is to a crisis in September 1939 that resulted in the betrayal of Czechoslovakia by the principal powers of Europe. The Sudetenland territory on the Czech border was awarded to Germany in a misguided belief it would appease Hitler from aggression. Signed at Munich, Germany, the pact was instead a progenitor of the outbreak of war.
34. Charnley, p. 29.
35. Ibid., p. 9.
36. Ibid.
37. The previous examples are reported in Charnley, p. 236.
38. Charnley, p. 36.
39. *Broadcasting,* December 2, 1946.
40. These are from a long registry of citations in Charnley's text, pp. 260–264, and are adapted for use here.

Chapter 10

1. Mitchell V. Charnley, *News by Radio* (New York: Macmillan, 1948), p. 4.
2. Ibid.
3. Ibid., p. 14.
4. Ibid., p. 28.
5. Of 16 stations operating in 1922 in Pennsylvania, none was beamed from Indiana, Pa., and the closest and perhaps most active appears to have been KDKA with a transmitter at East Pittsburgh.
6. Davis and Grand theatres, jointly owned, existed in Pittsburgh from the early years of the 20th century lending plausibility to KDKA being the only station capable of reaching Indiana, Pa.
7. Duquesne University was a Pittsburgh institution, further hinting which station remained unidentified.
8. Personal communication to the author from Jim Widner on November 30, 2011. Used by permission.
9. Francis Chase, Jr., *Sound and Fury: An Informal History of Broadcasting* (New York: Harper & Brothers, 1942), pp. 135–136.
10. Ibid., p. 136.
11. Charles A. Siepmann, *Radio's Second Chance* (Boston: Little, Brown, 1947), pp. 256–257.
12. Charnley, p. 36.
13. A fascinating account of the family's activities is recorded in Marie Brenner's *House of Dreams: The Bingham Family of Louisville* (New York: Random House, 1988).
14. http://www.wave3.com/story/8897056/columnist-tom-dorsey-fired-from-courier-journal?cl....
15. "New Orleans newspaper retrenches," *The Tampa* (Fla.) *Tribune,* May 25, 2012, p. 3.
16. http://cup.columbia.edu/book/978-0-231-144

96-4/cbss-don-hollenbeck. The biography referenced here is Loren Ghiglione's *CBS's Don Hollenbeck: An Honest Reporter in the Age of McCarthyism* (New York: Columbia University Press, 2008).

17. Rita Morley Harvey, *Those Wonderful, Terrible Years: George Heller and the American Federation of Television and Radio Artists* (Carbondale: Southern Illinois University Press, 1996), p. 157.

Chapter 11

1. http://en.wikipedia.org/wiki.Fanzine; http://en.wiktionary.org/wiki/prozine.
2. http://en.wikipedia.org/wiki.Fanzine.
3. For more discussion on other fanzines beyond science fiction, see http://en.wikipedia.org/wiki/Fanzine. Included are these topics: media, comics and graphic arts, horror film, rock 'n' roll music, punk, mod, local music, role-playing game, war-gaming, and sport.
4. http://en.wikipedia.org/wiki/Zine.
5. http://en.wikipedia.org/wiki/Photoplay.
6. Ibid.
7. Ibid.
8. Certain style rules are followed by periodicals to assure that writing, grammar, and other facets of copy in which there may be confusion or variation will conform to stated methods or standards of expectation.
9. If the name *Patricia Ryan* seems familiar it may be because it was the moniker adopted by the late Mrs. Richard Nixon. Christened Thelma Catherine Ryan, she was nicknamed *Pat* by her dad because she was born the day before St. Patrick's Day. At college she began using *Pat Ryan* and *Patricia Ryan* although she never legally altered her taxonomy.
10. Fred Sammis obviously maintained editorial oversight over *Radio Mirror* in 1943 (and the specific issue cited) even though his tenure as editor there ended in 1941, his day-to-day responsibilities shifting to *Photoplay* at that time. He may have carried some duties for more than one of Macfadden's periodicals.
11. Based on *Redbook* magazine narratives by Rose Franken and William Brown Meloney, *Claudia and David* was introduced to radio audiences on the June 6, 1941, broadcast of *The Kate Smith Hour* where it was a recurring skit for a month prior to its separate summertime run.
12. The narrative returned to the air in 1947 as a five-times-weekly serial transcribed at Chicago's WGN but without the network leads in its cast (Jim Cox, *Historical Dictionary of American Radio Soap Operas* [Lanham, Md.: Scarecrow Press, 2005], p. 60).
13. "Double in White," *Radio Mirror*, March 1943, p. 16. Furthermore, Ryan expressed a desire "to go to England as a nurse." Several uncles, aunts, and cousins (from her mother's side of the family) were then members of the British Royal Air Force.
14. Robert Maley, "Inside Radio," *The Sunday Times-Signal*, Zanesville, Ohio, February 20, 1949, p. IV-6.
15. Born February 21, 1921, Ryan was but a few days shy of her 28th birthday.
16. http://www.findadeath.com/forum/showthreat.php?22492-Patricia-Ryan.
17. "Double in White," *Radio Mirror*, March 1943, p. 16.

Chapter 12

1. Jim Cox, *Sold on Radio: Advertisers in the Golden Age of Broadcasting* (Jefferson, N.C.: McFarland, 2008, pp. 13, 16). Wireless telegraphy, developed by Guglielmo Marconi, arrived some time from 1893 to 1897 (sources dispute the year).
2. A forerunner of the electrical telegraph, classified in sweeping terms the *optical telegraph*, appeared in France in 1792, and later made its way to more European nations and crossed the Atlantic to America and Canada. Developed by Claude Chappe and siblings, the invention was envisaged by English scientist Robert Hooke in 1684. The apparatus was also dubbed a *semaphore line* (applying visual telegraphy and signal arms or shutters), *flag semaphore* (using hand-held flags), *signal lamp* (for visual naval exchanges), and *heliograph* (visual communications applying reflected sunlight). Highly dependent on good weather and daylight, the devices required operators and towers every 20 miles and projected only a couple of words a minute. Useful to governments for military operations, it was too expensive for most commercial service. Jonathan Grout built the first optical telegraph in the U.S., a 104-kilometre line linking Martha's Vineyard with Boston, to send news about shipping. A key knoll in San Francisco, "Telegraph Hill," was the site of a semaphore in 1849, signaling ships' arrival in the Bay. Samuel F.B. Morse patented his electrical telegraph in 1837, complete with his infamous Morse Code. Morse's invention transmitted messages at a cost 30 times less that of semaphores, and the last of them vanished in 1880 in Sweden (http://www.en.wikipedia.org/wiki/Telegraphy; http://www.en.wikipedia.org/wiki/Semaphore_line).
3. FM was patented in 1933, however, by Edward Howard Armstrong (1890–1954) who is credited with its invention as his most memorable life's work (Jim Cox, *Say Goodnight, Gracie: The Last Years of Network Radio* [Jefferson, N.C.: McFarland, 2002], pp. 57–58).
4. Christopher H. Sterling and John M. Kittross, *Stay Tuned: A Concise History of American Broadcasting*, 2d ed. (Belmont, Calif.: Wadsworth, 1990), p. 145.
5. For a brief but beguiling account of evolving news transmittal on Earth, see Cox's *Sold on Radio*, pp. 7–16.
6. Mitchell V. Charnley, *News by Radio* (New York: Macmillan, 1948), p. 37. All of the examples presented are from this source.
7. Ibid.
8. An app is a tiny sophisticated program ("application") that turns a mobile phone from its original functionality to greater use. Powered by computer software, it engages technology for real-life circumstances (http://www.pocket-lint.com/news/31462/what-the-hell-are-apps).
9. Bob Tedeschi, "App Smart: Scanner Apps Turn the Phone Into a Fax Machine," *The New York Times*, February 2, 2012, p. B8.
10. Charnley, pp. 37–38.

11. http://www.merriam-webster.com/dictionary/ultrafax.
12. "Science: The Flying Words," *Time*, November 1, 1948.
13. Ibid.
14. Charnley, p. 38.
15. Robert Slater, *This ... Is CBS: A Chronicle of 60 Years* (Englewood Cliffs, N.J.: Prentice-Hall, 1988), pp. 219–220.
16. Hugo Gernsback, "Mileposts in Television," *Radio-Craft*, March 1938, pp. 576–577.
17. Cox, *Sold on Radio*, p. 16.
18. Some of the material on the three cited individuals is gathered from the following web sites: http://www.madehow.com/inventorbios/71/Paul-Gottlieb-Nipkow.html; http://www.what-when-how.com/.../nipkow-paul-gottlieb-1860-1940-german-electricale...; http://www.transition.fcc.gov/omd/history/tv/1880-1929.html; http://www.histv.free.fr/plessner/plessnereng.htm.
19. http://www.bbc.co.uk/history/historic_figures/baird_logie.shtml.
20. Marconi, cited as the "father of long distance radio transmission," instigated a radio telegraph system. He is sometimes cited as "the inventor of radio," sharing in the 1909 Nobel Prize in Physics with Karl Ferdinand Braun for "the development of wireless telegraphy." He was more successful than others in commercializing radio and its apparatus. Yet many of his radio transmission triumphs came by exploiting the accomplishments of previous experimenters like Hertz, Maxwell, Faraday, Popov, Lodge, Fessenden, Stone, Bose, and Tesla (http://www.wikipedia.org/wiki/Guglielmo_Marconi).
21. http://www.freewebs.com/paulpert/pioneers.htm.
22. TFT screens refers to thin film transistor liquid crystal display glass for improved image quality while CRT technology refers to the traditionally enduring cathode-ray tube projection.
23. Adapted from http://www.freewebs.com/paulpert/pioneers2.htm.
24. Eugene Lyons, *David Sarnoff, A Biography: The Extraordinary Story of an Immigrant Boy Who Became an Industrial Giant* (New York: Harper & Row, 1966), p. 121.
25. Ibid., pp. 124–125. The magazine article cited appeared in *The Saturday Evening Post*, August 14, 1926.
26. http://www.xroads.virginia.edu/~1930s/display/39wf/frame.htm; Lyons, p. 216.
27. Lyons, pp. 204–205.
28. In his comprehensive volume *The Encyclopedia of Daytime Television: Everything You Ever Wanted to Know About Daytime TV but Didn't Know Where to Look! From American Bandstand, As the World Turns, and Bugs Bunny, to Meet the Press, The Price Is Right, and Wide World of Sports, the Rich History of Daytime Television in All Its Glory!* (New York: Billboard Books, 1997), pp. viii–ix, Hyatt states that the NBC New York outlet went on the air in 1928. While NBC was granted a federal permit to operate a station that year, it didn't premier until July 1930. It launched by transmitting a fuzzy image of a fuzzy feline, Felix the Cat. See also Sally Bedell Smith, *In all His Glory: The Life of William S. Paley, the Legendary Tycoon and His Brilliant Circle* (New York: Simon & Schuster, 1990), p. 186.
29. Jim Cox, *American Radio Networks: A History* (Jefferson, N.C.: McFarland, 2009), pp. 169–170.
30. Some of this material is adapted from Jim Cox's *The Daytime Serials of Television, 1946–1960* (Jefferson, N.C.: McFarland, 2006), pp. 24, 25.
31. You may read a succinct version of this in Cox's *American Radio Networks*, pp. 65, 170–171, which posits: "Paley had fought valiantly to the end and — to his credit — only in the face of insurmountable odds did he finally throw in the towel. Radiophiles had to be in his debt, whether they recognized it or not."
32. Cox, *American Radio Networks*, p. 171.
33. David Halberstam, *The Fifties*. New York: Villard Books, 1993, p. 181.
34. Albert Abramson, *The History of Television, 1942 to 2000* (Jefferson, N.C.: McFarland, 2003), p. 18.
35. Ibid., p. 1.
36. Reuven Frank, *Out of Thin Air: The Brief Wonderful Life of Network News* (New York: Simon & Schuster, 1991), p. 7.
37. Ibid., pp. 7–8. While only nine cities were situated along the coaxial cable route in 1948, 18 U.S. cities actually had TV stations then. A day or two after live coverage aired, stations not on the cable received packages by U.S. Mail of edited kinescopes (films of TV pictures) of the earlier live coverage which they screened for their viewers. It was pioneer times and methods for sure (Frank, p. 9).
38. Ibid., p. 7.
39. Ibid., p. 8.
40. Jim Cox, *Radio Speakers: Narrators, News Junkies, Sports Jockeys, Tattletales, Tipsters, Toastmasters and Coffee Klatch Couples Who Verbalized the Jargon of the Aural Ether from the 1920s to the 1980s — A Biographical Dictionary* (Jefferson, N.C.: McFarland, 2007), p. 88.
41. Frank, pp. 31–32, 33.
42. David Schoenbrun, *On and Off the Air: An Informal History of CBS News* (New York: E.P. Dutton, 1989), pp. 12–13.
43. Slater, p. 317.
44. Dan Rather, *Rather Outspoken: My Life in the News* (New York: Grand Central, 2012).
45. *The New York Times*, September 5, 1986.
46. Slater, p. 315.
47. *The New York Times*, March 10, 1987.
48. Brian Stelter, "Youths Are Watching, But Less Often on TV," *The New York Times*, February 9, 2012, pp. B1, B9.

Chapter 13

1. Jim Cox, *Say Goodnight, Gracie: The Last Years of Network Radio* (Jefferson, N.C.: McFarland, 2002), p. 101.
2. Michele Hilmes, ed., *NBC: America's Network* (Berkeley: University of California Press, 2007), p. 13.
3. Bill Leonard, *In the Storm of the Eye: A Lifetime at CBS* (New York: G.P. Putnam's Sons, 1987).
4. The change in call letters occurred on November 2, 1946. Don't confuse this series with an earlier one also titled *This Is New York* aired by the CBS Radio

network from December 11, 1938, to March 19, 1939. Appearing Sunday nights for an hour at 8 P.M. ET the musical variety entry starred Danny O'Neil, Lyn Murray, and featured the Leith Stevens Orchestra. It was succeeded to August 31, 1946, by *The Danny O'Neil Show* while continuing to be identified intermittently as *This Is New York*. It never pursued the magazine fashion in that manifestation, however.

5. Bill Jaker, Frank Sulek, and Peter Kanze, *The Airwaves of New York: Illustrated Histories of 156 AM Stations in the Metropolitan Area, 1921–1996* (Jefferson, N.C.: McFarland, 1998), p. 51.

6. Ibid., adapted.

7. Randy Kennedy, "William Leonard, 78, Former Head of CBS News," *The New York Times*, October 24, 1994.

8. "William A. Leonard; TV News Innovator," *The Los Angeles Times*, October 24, 1994.

9. Leonard also was stepdad to far-right newsman Chris Wallace, ironically laboring in modern times at Fox News, labeled by at least one pundit as "the antithesis of CBS News" (http://donswaim.com/wcbsnewsradio88.html).

10. http://articles.latimes.com/1994-10-24/news/mn-54081_1_cbs-news-correspondent.

11. Mitchell V. Charnley, *News by Radio* (New York: Macmillan, 1948), p. 264.

12. Jaker, Sulek, and Kanze, p. 51.

13. Jerry Walker, *Editor & Publisher*, January 31, 1948.

14. Wingate would subsequently become a newsman at WABC, WOR, and WOR-TV.

15. Dennis Hart, *Monitor (Take 2): The Revised, Expanded Inside Story of Network Radio's Greatest Program* (New York: iUniverse, 2003), p. 7.

16. *Variety*, an entertainment trade paper, reported that when Cullen left his local morning radio show in 1961, he was being compensated at $112,000 annually for that one gig. In 2010 dollars, that's $807,073.

17. Bold in its promotional hoopla some radio historians said, *Pulse* (and the people behind it) spared little expense to tout the show like treasure hunts in 1956. These rewarded "a lucky listener who deciphered the clues and found an object hidden somewhere in the metropolitan area." It didn't matter that Cullen cautioned "'you don't have to move anything or disturb anything to find the hidden object." Listeners caused minor turmoil at suspected mystery sites. Most were friendly encounters as fans met one another. *The New York Times*, however, called it "childish" on its editorial page (Jaker, Sulek, and Kanze, p. 131).

18. WRCA's lineage includes WBAY (1922), WEAF (1922), WNBC (1946), WRCA (1954), WNBC (1960), WFAN (1988).

19. F. Leslie Smith, *Perspectives on Radio and Television: An Introduction to Broadcasting in the United States* (New York: Harper & Row, 1979), p. 68.

20. Cox, *Say Goodnight, Gracie*, p. 102.

21. William Lawrence (Bill) Cullen, born February 18, 1920, at Pittsburgh, Pa., seemed destined to run more TV game shows (1952–86) than anyone, including *Give and Take, Winner Take All, Who's There, Why?, Quick as a Flash, Down You Go, The Price is Right, Eye Guess, Three on a Match, Winning Streak, Blankety Blanks, Pass the Buck, The Love Experts, Chain Reaction, Blockbusters, Child's Play, Hot Potato*, and *The Joker's Wild*. Cullen was a panelist on CBS-TV's *I've Got a Secret* (1952–67), introduced *This Is Nora Drake* on radio (1947–51), and hosted 1940s-50s radio guessing games *Catch Me if You Can, Fun for All, Hit the Jackpot, Quick as a Flash, Stop the Music!, Walk a Mile*, and *Winner Take All*. He co-hosted CBS Radio's *It Happens Every Day* humor newsmaker citations daily in the 1950s. He died July 7, 1990 (Jim Cox, *This Day in Network Radio: A Daily Calendar of Births, Deaths, Debuts, Cancellations and Other Events in Broadcasting History* [Jefferson, N.C.: McFarland, 2008], p. 39).

22. Hart, p. xxv.

23. Jim Cox, *American Radio Networks: A History* (Jefferson, N.C.: McFarland, 2009), p. 19.

24. Reported by Douglas Gomery in "Talent Raids and Package Deals: NBC Loses Its Leadership in the 1950s," in Michele Hilmes, ed., *NBC: America's Network* (Berkeley: University of California Press, 2007, p. 161.

25. Gomery, in Hilmes, ed., p. 160.

26. "I won't come to NBC just to sell time to ad agencies," Weaver told NBC when it considered him for a position in 1949. "I'll come only if we can create our own shows and own them, and if we can sell every kind of advertising to support the program service" (http://www.answers.com/topic/pat-weaver).

27. Cox, *American Radio Networks*, p. 64.

28. Pat Weaver, with Thomas M. Coffey, *The Best Seat in the House: The Golden Years of Radio and Television* (New York: Alfred A. Knopf, 1994), p. 225.

29. In July 1955, MBS launched *Companionate Radio* and four months hence ABC's *New Sounds* debuted on weekday evenings. Both copied the magazine style but neither approached the longevity or success of the original they impersonated and vanished after brief runs.

30. http://www.monitorbeacon.net/patweaver.html.

31. *Monitor* factored hugely in staving off fiscal ruin at NBC Radio. With $1.4 million in billings prior to its premiere, its annual advertising take in 1959 was figured at $6 million by *Newsweek*. An aural series had never equaled that, "radio's biggest moneymaker" (http://www.monitorbeacon.net/patweaver.html).

32. Hart, pp. 7–8.

33. James F. Fleming (1915–96) was a CBS newsman (1938–49) before joining NBC-TV's *Today* as its first newscaster (1952–53). In the 1940s, he introduced soap operas *The Goldbergs, John's Other Wife, The Light of the World*, and *Vic and Sade* and was the enduring interlocutor of *Mr. Keen, Tracer of Lost Persons*. Fleming produced *The Morning Show* at CBS-TV (1956–57) and later many TV documentaries and specials (Cox, *Say Goodnight, Gracie*, pp. 76–77).

34. Transcription of live closed-circuit preview presentation to NBC Radio affiliates, April 1, 1955.

35. http://www.monitorbeacon.net/patweaver.html. Quoted from *Newsweek*, June 27, 1955.

36. In its first hour on the air, simulcast by NBC-TV, *Monitor* offered its audience a swing band in Los Angeles, a visit to California's San Quentin prison, double-speak artist A Kelly, Roscoe Drummond with political analysis, comments by Harvard University president Nathan Pusey, an oyster's sound, a stopover

at a summer theater in Bucks County, Pa., excerpts from a Jerry Lewis film, and a live pickup of a trans-Atlantic aircraft departing New York's Idlewild Airport. A smorgasbord indeed.

37. Gerald Nachman, *Raised on Radio: In Quest of The Lone Ranger, Jack Benny, Amos 'n' Andy, The Shadow, Mary Noble, The Great Gildersleeve, Fibber McGee and Molly, Bill Stern, Our Miss Brooks, Henry Aldrich, The Quiz Kids, Mr. First Nighter, Fred Allen, Vic and Sade, The Cisco Kid, Jack Armstrong, Arthur Godfrey, Bob and Ray, The Barbour Family, Henry Morgan, Joe Friday and Other Lost Heroes from Radio's Heyday* (New York: Pantheon Books, 1998), p. 489.

38. Edward Bliss, Jr., *Now the News: The Story of Broadcast Journalism* (New York: Columbia University Press, 1991), p. 190.

39. Rayburn's work notwithstanding, Cullen let it slip that he earned $500 per hour for his *Monitor* stints. That rate fattened some wallets big time (http://userdata.acd.net/ottinger/cullen/radio/pulse.html).

40. Not long after *Monitor* departed the aural airwaves, its moniker was pulled from NBC's mothballed inventory of unused names and applied to a Saturday night NBC-TV newsmagazine. A low-rated, low-budgeted *Monitor* on the tube didn't last long; the effort was soon re-titled *First Camera* and thrown against CBS's Sunday night stalwart *60 Minutes* where it also faltered. (Reuven Frank, *Out of Thin Air: The Brief Wonderful Life of Network News* (New York: Simon & Schuster, 1991), pp. 394–396.

41. http://en.wikipedia.org/wiki/History_of_CNN_(1980%E2%80%932003).

42. There may have been two colossal stumbles on Weaver's watch even though his intents were noble. In his treatise *Network Radio Ratings, 1932–1953: A History of Prime Time Programs Through the Ratings of Nielsen, Crossley and Hooper* (Jefferson, N.C.: McFarland, 2012), Jim Ramsburg pins the dismal outcome of NBC's *The Big Show* (1950–52) on Weaver although he notes Weaver didn't control radio programming until the fall of 1951 (p. 195). Was *The Big Show* his brainchild or did he merely inherit it? Wherever it originated, it was an inspired attempt to regain some of what NBC lost when *Amos & Andy*, Jack Benny, and Edgar Bergen defected to CBS, leaving large gaps in NBC's Sunday night agenda. Ramsburg may be right in dubbing it Weaver's "most expensive blunder in network radio." He calls it Weaver's "biggest" blunder, too. While it may be Weaver's baby, emptying the daytime schedule of programming entrenched for decades now "seems" a much worse gaffe, especially as so much of that audience never returned.

43. There is much more detail on this topic appearing in Jim Cox's *Say Goodnight Gracie*, pp. 110–112.

44. At its helm were four hosts on *Weekday*, paired for two multiple-hour matinee shifts. Walter Kiernan and Martha Scott comprised a team; Margaret Truman and Mike Wallace filled the other. They offered a diet of news, culinary tips, mini dramas, and interviews with "scintillating and provocative personalities."

45. In his memoir, Weaver allowed: "That was not a big shock to me. I had always known that Bobby would one day become president. It didn't really bother me as long as I could continue to wield the power of the chief executive officer. Then came the bad news. I was to lose not only my title but my authority. Bobby was obviously embarrassed about this. The troubles I had with his father had never affected my relations with him. I can't remember a time when there was any serious difference between us" (Weaver and Coffey, p. 268).

46. All this time Weaver and Bobby Sarnoff's relationship was cordial, warm, and heartening, as intimated in Weaver's autobiography. Good terms also brought more advantages. Another observer commented: "Nepotism was a word often heard in NBC corridors, and often spoken with resentment — but not by Weaver. His attitude, always free-swinging and jovial, was that nepotism was as useful to him as to the General. When major plans needed approval, he took them first to Bobby, who became the spokesman when they went to his father" (Erik Barnouw, *The Image Empire: A History of Broadcasting in the United States*, Vol. III — From 1953 [New York: Oxford University Press, 1970], p. 59).

47. Reporting on an article in *The Denver Post* in 1960, an author noted that Weaver continued to express irritation at how the networks were run, citing the early 1950s as TV's golden age. "Management doesn't give the people what they deserve," he insisted. "I don't see any hope in the system as it is" (William Boddy, *Fifties Television: The Industry and Its Critics* [Champaign: University of Illinois Press, 1992]).

48. In early 2012, under the broad brush of Westwood One, five news networks are aligned, including the final vestiges of NBC's aural product: CBS Radio News, CNBC Business Radio, CNNRadio, MarketWatch Radio Network, and NBC News Radio. For background on how this transpired see Cox's *American Radio Networks*, pp. 42–44. For samples of broadcasts:, visit http://affiliates.westwoodone.com/news/cnnradio.asp.

49. From a telephone dialogue with Charles Garment on August 4, 2001, by Dennis Hart for his book, p. 231.

50. http://en.wikipedia.org/wiki/Newsmagazine.

51. Ibid.

52. Michael Emery, Edwin Emery, and Nancy L. Roberts, *The Press and America: An Interpretive History of the Mass Media*, 9th ed. (Boston: Allyn and Bacon, 2000), p. 486.

53. William A. Henry III, "Don Hewitt: Man of the Hour," *Washington Journalism Review*, May 1986, p. 25; Judy Flander, "Hewitt's Humongous Hour," *Washington Journalism Review*, April 1991, p. 26.

Chapter 14

1. Mitchell V. Charnley, *News by Radio* (New York: Macmillan, 1948), p. 243.

2. The arm-twisting in giving local stations greater voice in their futures is enticing to the serious student of vintage radio history. See more details in Jim Cox's *Say Goodnight, Gracie: The Last Years of Network Radio* (Jefferson, N.C.: McFarland, 2002), pp. 73–74, 113, 114–115, 116, 117, 121, 128, 145–147.

3. Ibid., p. 117.

4. Ibid., pp. 10, 79–80, 184. For much more see also Jim Cox, *Music Radio: The Great Performers and*

Programs of the 1920s through Early 1960s (Jefferson, N.C.: McFarland, 2005), pp. 28–29, 145–148.

5. Cox, *Say Goodnight, Gracie*, p. 155.

6. Adapted from Ibid., pp. 173–175.

7. For more on the utopian hypothesis of NIS, see Edward Bliss, Jr., *Now the News: The Story of Broadcast Journalism* (New York: Columbia University Press, 1991), pp. 193–194.

8. Ibid., pp. 190–191.

9. http://www.bayarearadio.org/schneider/kjbs.shtml.

10. http://www.angelfire.com/zine/forty2/radiohistory.html.

11. Ibid.

12. http://www.radiohof.org/pioneer/gordonmclendon.html.

13. In a letter to *Broadcasting* appearing August 19, 1983, the president of WTAL, Tallahassee, Fla., Donald C. Keyes, acknowledged that he had designed the all-news format at XETRA.

14. http://en.wikipedia.org/wiki/All-news_radio.

15. Joshua Mills, "Development and Refinement of All-News Programming at Radio Stations and Networks," a paper presented at the annual meeting of the Association for Education in Journalism, Boston, August 1980, p. 3. Mills, of New York University, had completed a study of all-news operations.

16. Bliss, p. 191.

17. Ibid.

18. Edward Bliss, whose 500-page treatise is all over the topic of all-news radio, says KFAX, XETRA, WNUS, and WINS — in that order — formed the initial progression of outlets implementing the format.

19. A couple of WCBS's early reporters, Ed Bradley and Charles Osgood, would gain national status as network correspondents/hosts/anchormen.

20. http://en.wikipedia.org/wiki/WINS_(AM).

21. http://donswaim.com/clock-text2.jpg.

22. http://www.broadcastpioneers.com/kywstory.html.

23. To read more detail see Jim Cox, *Sold on Radio: Advertisers in the Golden Age of Broadcasting* (Jefferson, N.C.: McFarland, 2008), pp. 7–8, 15.

24. Adapted from http://www.broadcastpioneers.com/kywstory.html.

25. Jim Cox, *Music Radio*, p. 153.

26. The station has moved physical location several times since.

27. The Dodgers returned to KABC following the 2007 season; "All News, All the Time" returned to KFWB with that; yet in 2008, National Football League broadcasts were aired. By 2009, KFWB was broadcasting weekday baseball games of the Los Angeles Angels of Anaheim, and that year the station signed a multi-year pact to air the National Basketball Association's L.A. Clippers games.

28. http://en.wikipedia.org/wiki/KFWB.

29. http://worldfamouscbs.com/.

30. http://www.bayarearadio.org/schneider/kqw.shtml.

31. Irving E. Fang, *Those Radio Commentators!* (Ames: Iowa State University Press, 1977), p. 24.

32. http://en.wikipedia.org/wiki/KCBS_(AM).

33. Figures from New York's Radio Information Center appeared in *Broadcasting*, September 24, 1990.

34. Bliss, p. 193.

35. http://tunein.com/radio/WTOP-1035-s23234/.

Chapter 15

1. David Pogue, "State of the Art: Sampling the Future of Gadgetry," *The New York Times*, January 12, 2012, p. B7.

2. Ibid.

3. Mitchell Stephens, *A History of News: From the Drum to the Satellite* (New York: Viking Penguin, 1988), pp. 299–300.

4. Philip Seib, *Going Live: Getting the News Right in a Real-Time, Online World* (Lanham, Md.: Rowman & Littlefield, 2001), pp. 122–123.

5. "WXYC's groundbreaking internet simulcast is now 10 years old," http://wxyc.org/about/first/, November 12, 2004.

6. "We got here first. Sort of," http://www.wrek.org/?q=wreknet-first.

7. Olga Kharif, "The Last Days of Internet Radio?" *Business Week*, March 7, 2007.

8. Joe Lensky and Bill Rose, "The Infinite Dial 2008: Radio's Digital Platforms," http://www.arbitron.com/downloads/digital_radio_study_2008.pdf.

9. "Weekly online radio audience increases from 11 percent to 13 percent of Americans in last year, according to the latest Arbitron/Edison media research study," http://www.redorbit.com/news/technology/1334023/weekly_online_radio_audience_increases_from_11_percent_to_13/index.html.

10. David Kusek and Gerd Leonhard, *The Future of Music: Manifesto for the Digital Music Revolution* (Boston: Berkley Press, 2005), p. 72.

11. Amy Chozick, "After a Year, Tablet Daily Is a Struggle," *The New York Times*, February 6, 2012, pp. B1, B3.

12. Brian X. Chen, *Always On: How the iPhone Unlocked the Anything-Anytime-Anywhere Future — and Locked Us In* (Philadelphia: Da Capo Press, 2011), pp. 10, 131.

13. Apple, the device's manufacturer, reportedly sold 17 million iPhones in fourth quarter 2011 (http://www.venturebeat.com/2012/01/04/verizon-iphone-sales/).

14. Seib, p. 16.

15. Some would argue that TV news didn't seriously begin to threaten radio news until the debut of CNN in 1980, however.

16. David Schoenbrun, *On and Off the Air: An Informal History of CBS News* (New York: E.P. Dutton, 1989), pp. 201–202.

17. Seib, p. 87.

18. Pavlik, pp. 3–4.

19. David Noack, "Extra! Extra! Read All about It! TV Web Site Acts Like a Newspaper," *Editor and Publisher Interactive*, June 13, 1997, p. 2.

20. Ibid., quoting Jason Primus of International Broadcasting Systems.

21. Seib, p. 87.

22. Seib, pp. 124–125. Adapted from "Stretching Past Streaming," *Communicator*, April 2000, p. 14. Since this appeared in print in the reference cited WTOP2 has been relabeled "Federal News Radio."

23. Chen, pp. 60–61.

24. Exchange between Brian Chen and John Ham on September 10, 2009.

Bibliography

Alterman, Eric. *What Liberal Media? The Truth About Bias and the News*. New York: Basic Books, 2003.

Andrews, Robert Hardy. "A Voice in the Room." *Legend of a Lady: The Story of Rita Martin*. New York: Coward-McCann, 1949.

Archer, Gleason L. *History of Radio, to 1926*. New York: American Historical Society, 1938.

Arnot, Charles P. *Don't Kill the Messenger: The Tragic Story of Welles Hangen and Other Journalistic Combat Victims*. New York: Vantage Press, 1994.

Balk, Alfred. *The Rise of Radio: From Marconi through the Golden Age*. Jefferson, N.C.: McFarland, 2006.

Banning, William Peck. *Commercial Broadcasting Pioneer: The WEAF Experiment 1922–1926*. Cambridge: Harvard University Press, 1946.

Barnett, Joseph M. *Reminiscences*. Unpublished. Columbia University Oral History Collection, 1951.

Barnouw, Erik. *The Golden Web: A History of Broadcasting in the United States*, Vol. II—1933 to 1953. New York: Oxford University Press, 1968.

_____. *The Image Empire: A History of Broadcasting in the United States*, Vol. III—From 1953. New York: Oxford University Press, 1970.

_____. *A Tower in Babel: A History of Broadcasting in the United States*, Vol. I—to 1933. New York: Oxford University Press, 1966.

Baudino, Joseph E., and John M. Kittross. *Journal of Broadcasting*. 21:1, Winter 1977.

Bliss, Edward, Jr. *Now the News: The Story of Broadcast Journalism*. New York: Columbia University Press, 1991.

Blue, Howard. *Words at War: World War II Era Radio Drama and the Postwar Broadcasting Industry Blacklist*. Lanham, Md.: Scarecrow Press, 2002.

Boddy, William. *Fifties Television: The Industry and Its Critics*. Champaign: University of Illinois Press, 1992.

Brenner, Marie. *House of Dreams: The Bingham Family of Louisville*. New York: Random House, 1988.

Bresee, Frank, and Bobb Lynes. *Radio's Golden Years: A Visual Guide to the Shows & the Stars*. Hollywood: Frank Bresee Productions, 1998.

Broadcasting. Feb. 1, 1934; Dec. 15, 1937; 1939 Yearbook; Dec. 2, 1946; Aug. 19, 1983; Sept. 24, 1990.

Broholm, John R. "News Programming Criticism." *Historical Dictionary of American Radio*. Westport, Conn.: Greenwood Press, 1998.

Brooks, Tim, and Earle Marsh. *The Complete Directory to Prime Time Network TV Shows, 1946–Present*, 4th ed. New York: Ballantine, 1988.

Bryson, Lyman Lloyd. *Reminiscences*. Unpublished, 1951.

Burlingame, Roger. *Don't Let Them Scare You: The Life and Times of Elmer Davis*. Philadelphia: Lippincott, 1961.

Butsch, Richard. *The Making of American Audiences: From Stage to Television, 1750–1990*. Cambridge: Cambridge University Press, 2000.

Campbell, Robert. *The Golden Years of Broadcasting: A Celebration of the First 50 Years of Radio and TV on NBC*. New York: Charles Scribner's, 1976.

Carey, James W. "The Internet and the End of the National Communications System: Uncertain Predictions of an Uncertain Future." *Journalism Quarterly*. Spring 1998.

Caristi, Dom. "Fairness Doctrine." *Historical Dictionary of American Radio*. Westport, Conn.: Greenwood Press, 1998.

Castleman, Harry, and Walter J. Podrazik. *505 Radio Questions Your Friends Can't Answer*. New York: Walker, 1983.

Chancellor, John. "From Normandy to Grenada: A Veteran Reporter Looks Back." *American Heritage*. June–July 1985.

Charnley, Mitchell V. *News by Radio*. New York: Macmillan, 1948.

Chase, Jr., Francis. *Sound and Fury: An Informal History of Broadcasting*. New York: Harper & Brothers, 1942.

Chen, Brian X. *Always On: How the iPhone Unlocked*

the *Anything-Anytime-Anywhere Future — and Locked Us In*. Philadelphia: Da Capo Press, 2011.

Chester, Giraud. *The Radio Commentaries of H. V. Kaltenborn: A Case Study in Persuasion*. Ph.D. dissertation, University of Wisconsin, 1947.

The Chicago Tribune. May 27, 1989.

Cloud, Stanley, and Lynne Olson. *The Murrow Boys: Pioneers on the Front Lines of Broadcast Journalism*. Boston: Houghton Mifflin, 1996.

Columbia Broadcasting System, Inc. *The Sound of Your Life*. New York: CBS, 1950.

Communicator. "Stretching Past Streaming." April 2000.

Connors, Edward. "They Still Call It Radio News." *Washington Journalism Review*. May 1, 1991.

Cox, Jim. *American Radio Networks: A History*. Jefferson, N.C.: McFarland, 2009.

_____. *The Daytime Serials of Television, 1946–1960*. Jefferson, N.C.: McFarland, 2006.

_____. *The Great Radio Soap Operas*. Jefferson, N.C.: McFarland, 1999.

_____. *Historical Dictionary of American Radio Soap Operas*. Lanham, Md.: Scarecrow Press, 2005.

_____. *Music Radio: The Great Performers and Programs of the 1920s Through Early 1960s*. Jefferson, N.C.: McFarland, 2005.

_____. *Radio Speakers: Narrators, News Junkies, Sports Jockeys, Tattletales, Tipsters, Toastmasters and Coffee Klatch Couples Who Verbalized the Jargon of the Aural Ether from the 1920s to the 1980s — A Biographical Dictionary*. Jefferson, N.C.: McFarland, 2007.

_____. *Rails Across Dixie: A History of Passenger Trains in the American South*. Jefferson, N.C.: McFarland, 2011.

_____. *Say Goodnight, Gracie: The Last Years of Network Radio*. Jefferson, N.C.: McFarland, 2002.

_____. *Sold on Radio: Advertisers in the Golden Age of Broadcasting*. Jefferson, N.C.: McFarland, 2008.

_____. *This Day in Network Radio: A Daily Calendar of Births, Deaths, Debuts, Cancellations and Other Events in Broadcasting History*. Jefferson, N.C.: McFarland, 2008.

Culbert, David Holbrook. *News for Everyman: Radio and Foreign Affairs in Thirties America*. Westport, Conn.: Greenwood Press, 1976.

Davis, Harry P. "The History of Broadcasting in the United States." Address to Harvard University Graduate School of Business Administration, April 21, 1928.

DeLong, Thomas A. *Radio Stars: An Illustrated Biographical Dictionary of 953 Performers, 1920 Through 1960*. Jefferson, N.C.: McFarland, 1996.

Dickerson, Nancy. *Among Those Present: A Reporter's View of 25 Years in Washington*. New York: Random House, 1976.

Douglas, George H. *The Early Days of Radio Broadcasting*. Jefferson, N.C.: McFarland, 1987.

Douglas, Susan J. *Listening In: Radio and the American Imagination, from Amos 'n' Andy and Edward R. Murrow to Wolfman Jack and Howard Stern*. New York: Times Books, 1999.

Dryer, Sherman H. *Radio in Wartime*. New York: Greenberg, 1942.

Duncan, Jacci, ed. *Making Waves: The 50 Greatest Women in Radio and Television*. Kansas City: Andrews McMeel, 2001.

Dunham, Corydon B. *Fighting for the First Amendment: Stanton of CBS vs. Congress and the Nixon White House*. Westport, Conn.: Praeger, 1997.

Dunning, John. *On the Air: The Encyclopedia of Old-Time Radio*. New York: Oxford University Press, 1998.

_____. *Tune in Yesterday: The Ultimate Encyclopedia of Old-Time Radio, 1925–1976*. Englewood Cliffs, N.J.: Prentice-Hall, 1976.

Edwards, Bob. *Edward R. Murrow and the Birth of Broadcast Journalism*. Hoboken, N.J.: John Wiley & Sons, 2004.

Emery, Edwin. *History of the American Newspaper Publishers Association*. Minneapolis: University of Minnesota Press, 1950.

Emery, Michael, Edwin Emery, and Nancy L. Roberts. *The Press and America: An Interpretive History of the Mass Media*, 9th ed. Boston: Allyn and Bacon, 2000.

Evans, Walter Chew. *Reminiscences*. Unpublished, 1950, 1951.

Fang, Irving E. *Those Radio Commentators!* Ames: Iowa State University Press, 1977.

Fates, Gil. *What's My Line? The Inside History of TV's Most Famous Panel Show*. Englewood Cliffs, N.J.: Prentice-Hall, 1978.

Felix, Edgar H. *Reminiscences*. Columbia University Oral History Collection. 1962.

Finkelstein, Norman H. *Sounds in the Air: The Golden Age of Radio*. New York: Charles Scribner's, 1993.

Flander, Judy. "Hewitt's Humongous Hour." *Washington Journalism Review*. April 1991.

Frank, Reuven. *Out of Thin Air: The Brief Wonderful Life of Network News*. New York: Simon & Schuster, 1991.

Frost, Jr., S.E. *Education's Own Stations: The History of Broadcast Licenses Issued to Educational Institutions*. Chicago: University of Chicago Press, 1937.

Garay, Ronald. "Office of Censorship." *Historical Dictionary of American Radio*. Westport, Conn.: Greenwood Press, 1998.

Gates, Gary Paul. *Air Time: The Inside Story of CBS News*. New York: Harper & Row, 1978.

Gernsback, Hugo. "Mileposts in Television." *Radio-Craft*. March 1938.

Ghiglione, Loren. *CBS's Don Hollenbeck: An Honest Reporter in the Age of McCarthyism*. New York: Columbia University Press, 2008.

Godfrey, Donald G., and Frederic A. Leigh, eds. *Historical Dictionary of American Radio. Westport, Conn.: Greenwood Press, 1998.

Goldenson, Leonard H., with Marvin J. Wolf. *Beating the Odds: The Untold Story of the Rise of ABC: The Stars, Struggles, and Egos That Transformed Network Television By the Man Who Made It Happen.* New York: Charles Scribner's Sons, 1991.

Goldsmith, Alfred N., and Austin C. Lescarboura. *This Thing Called Broadcasting.* New York: Henry Holt, 1930.

Gomery, Douglas. "Talent Raids and Package Deals: NBC Loses Its Leadership in the 1950s." *NBC: America's Network.* Berkeley: University of California Press, 2007.

Halberstam, David. *The Fifties.* New York: Villard Books, 1993.

_____. *The Powers That Be: Within the Kingdom of the Media: How Luce's Time, Paley's CBS, the Grahams' Washington Post, and the Chandlers' Los Angeles Times Became Rich and Powerful and Changed Forever the Shape of American Politics and Society.* New York: Andrew A. Knopf, 1979.

Harkness, William E. *Reminiscences.* New York: Columbia University Oral History Collection. 1951.

Harper, Christopher. *And That's the Way It Will Be: News and Information in a Digital World.* New York: New York University Press, 1998.

Hart, Dennis Hart. *Monitor (Take 2): The Revised, Expanded Inside Story of Network Radio's Greatest Program.* New York: iUniverse, 2003.

Hart, Herschell. *Reminiscences.* Unpublished, 1951.

Harvey, Rita Morley Harvey, *Those Wonderful, Terrible Years: George Heller and the American Federation of Television and Radio Artists.* Carbondale: Southern Illinois University Press, 1996.

Heinl, Robert D. "Radio and the Next War." *Radioland.* September 1933.

Heistad, Mark J. "University of Chicago Roundtable." *Historical Dictionary of American Radio.* Westport, Conn.: Greenwood Press, 1998.

Henry, III, William A. "Don Hewitt: Man of the Hour." *Washington Journalism Review.* May 1986.

Herndon, Booton. *Praised and Damned: The Story of Fulton Lewis, Jr.* New York: Duell, Sloan & Pearce, 1954.

Hickerson, Jay. *The Third Ultimate History of Network Radio Programming and Guide to All Circulating Shows.* Hamden, Conn.: Presto Print II, 2005.

Hilmes, Michele, ed. *NBC: America's Network.* Berkeley: University of California Press, 2007.

Howe, Quincy. *The News and How to Understand It.* New York: Simon & Schuster, 1940.

Hudson, Frederic. *Journalism in the United States, from 1690 to 1872.* New York: Harper & Brothers, 1873.

Hyatt, Wesley. *The Encyclopedia of Daytime Television: Everything You Ever Wanted to Know About Daytime TV But Didn't Know Where to Look! From American Bandstand, As the World Turns, and Bugs Bunny, to Meet the Press, The Price is Right, and Wide World of Sports, the Rich History of Daytime Television in All Its Glory!* New York: Billboard Books, 1997.

Jaker, Bill, Frank Sulek, and Peter Kanze. *The Airwaves of New York: Illustrated Histories of 156 AM Stations in the Metropolitan Area, 1921–1996.* Jefferson, N.C.: McFarland, 1998.

Jay, Michael. *The History of Communications: Advances That Have Changed the World.* New York: Thomson Learning, 1995.

Jome, Hiram L *Economics of the Radio Industry.* Chicago: A.W. Shaw, 1925.

Jordan, Max. *Beyond All Fronts: A Bystander's Notes to This Thirty Years' War.* Milwaukee: Bruce, 1944.

Kaltenborn, H.V. *Reminiscences.* Unpublished, 1950.

Kendrick, Alexander. *Prime Time: The Life of Edward R. Murrow.* Boston: Little, Brown, 1969.

_____. *The Wound Within: America in the Vietnam Years, 1945–1974.* Boston: Little, Brown, 1974.

Kharif, Olga. "The Last Days of Internet Radio?" *Business Week.* March 7, 2007.

Klara, Robert. *FDR's Funeral Train: A Betrayed Widow, A Soviet Spy, and a Presidency in the Balance.* New York: Palgrave Macmillan, 2010.

Kusek, David, and Gerd Leonhard. *The Future of Music: Manifesto for the Digital Music Revolution.* Boston: Berklee Press, 2005.

Landry, Robert J. *This Fascinating Radio Business.* Indianapolis: Bobbs-Merrill, 1946.

Larson, Gary W. "Radio Journalism." In W. David Sloan and Lisa Mullikin Parcell, eds. *American Journalism: History, Principles, Practices.* Jefferson, N.C.: McFarland, 2002.

Lazarsfeld, Paul, and Frank Stanton, eds. *Radio Research 1942–43.* New York: Duell, Sloan & Pearce, 1944.

Leahy, William D. *I Was There.* New York: Whittlesey House, 1950.

Lee, Laurie Thomas. "Stations." *Historical Dictionary of American Radio.* Westport, Conn.: Greenwood Press, 1998.

Leonard, Bill. *In the Storm of the Eye: A Lifetime at CBS.* New York: G.P. Putnam's Sons, 1987.

Lesueur, Larry. *Twelve Months That Changed the World.* New York: Alfred A. Knopf, 1943.

Levine, Irving R. *Main Street, U.S.S.R.* New York: Doubleday, 1959.

Lichty, Lawrence W., and Thomas W. Bohn. "Radio's *March of Time*: Dramatized News." *Journalism Quarterly.* LI (Autumn 1973).

Logan, Robert K. *The Alphabet Effect: The Impact of the Phonetic Alphabet on the Development of Western Civilization.* New York: William Morrow, 1986.

Longinow, Michael A. "News Gathering." In W. David Sloan and Lisa Mullikin Parcell, eds. *American Journalism: History, Principles, Practices.* Jefferson, N.C.: McFarland, 2002.

The Los Angeles Times. "William A. Leonard; TV News Innovator." Oct. 24, 1994.

Lyons, Eugene. *David Sarnoff, A Biography: The Extraordinary Story of an Immigrant Boy Who Became an Industrial Giant.* New York: Harper & Row, 1966.

MacDonald, J. Fred. *Don't Touch That Dial! Radio Programming in American Life, 1920–1960.* Chicago: Nelson-Hall, 1979.

MacVane, John. *On the Air in World War II.* New York: William Morrow, 1979.

Maltin, Leonard. *The Great American Broadcast: A Celebration of Radio's Golden Age.* New York: Penguin Putnam, 1997.

Martin, Henri-Jean. *The History and Power of Writing.* Chicago: University of Chicago Press, 1994.

McNamee, Graham. *You're On the Air.* New York: Harper, 1926.

McNeil, Alex. *Total Television: The Comprehensive Guide from 1948 to the Present*, 4th ed. New York: Penguin, 1996.

McPherson, Jim. "Mergers, Chains, Monopoly, and Competition." In W. David Sloan and Lisa Mullikin Parcell, eds. *American Journalism: History, Principles, Practices.* Jefferson, N.C.: McFarland, 2002.

Midgley, Ned. *The Advertising and Business Side of Radio.* New York: Prentice-Hall, 1948.

Mills, Joshua. "Development and Refinement of All-News Programming at Radio Stations and Networks." Paper presented to Association for Education in Journalism, Boston, August 1980.

Miquel, Pierre. *Histoire de la radio et de la télévision.* Paris: Perrin, 1984.

Mott, Frank Luther. *American Journalism: A History of Newspapers in the United States Through 250 Years, 1690–1940.* New York: Macmillan, 1941.

Mudd, Roger. *The Place to Be: Washington, CBS, and the Glory Days of Television News.* New York: PBS Public Affairs, 2008.

Nachman, Gerald. *Raised on Radio: In Quest of The Lone Ranger, Jack Benny, Amos 'n' Andy, The Shadow, Mary Noble, The Great Gildersleeve, Fibber McGee and Molly, Bill Stern, Our Miss Brooks, Henry Aldrich, The Quiz Kids, Mr. First Nighter, Fred Allen, Vic and Sade, The Cisco Kid, Jack Armstrong, Arthur Godfrey, Bob and Ray, The Barbour Family, Henry Morgan, Joe Friday, and Other Lost Heroes from Radio's Heyday.* New York: Pantheon Books, 1998.

Neuman, W. Russell. *The Future of Mass Audience.* New York: Cambridge University Press, 1995.

Newman, Edwin. *A Civil Tongue.* Indianapolis: Bobbs-Merrill, 1976.

_____. *I Must Say: On English, the News, and Other Matters.* Anderson, Ind.: Warner Press, 1988.

_____. *Strictly Speaking: Will America Be the Death of English?* Indianapolis: Bobbs-Merrill, 1974.

_____. *Sunday Punch.* Boston: Houghton Mifflin, 1979.

The New York Times. Jan. 2, 1930; Jan. 3, 1933; Jan. 2, 1935; Jan. 3, 1940; July 3, 1954; Jan. 4, 1960; Dec. 29, 1960; Sept. 5, 1986; March 10, 1987; May 26, 1989; Oct. 26, 1998.

_____. "After a Year, Tablet Daily Is a Struggle." Feb. 6, 2012.

_____. "App Smart: Scanner Apps Turn the Phone Into a Fax Machine." Feb. 2, 2012.

_____. "Lawrence E. Spivak, 93, Is Dead; The Originator of 'Meet the Press.'" March 10, 1994.

_____. "Martha Rountree, 87, a Creator of 'Meet the Press.'" Aug. 25, 1999.

_____. "Paul White Dies; Radio Newsman." July 10, 1955.

_____. "Radio Pioneers Organize." May 24, 1951.

_____. "Radio-TV Notes." Sept. 20, 1952.

_____. "State of the Art: Sampling the Future of Gadgetry." Jan. 12, 2012.

_____. "William Leonard, 78, Former Head of CBS News." Oct. 24, 1994.

_____. "Wireless Telephone Spreads Fight News Over 120,000 Miles." July 3, 1921.

_____. "Youths Are Watching, But Less Often on TV." Feb. 9, 2012.

News of Europe. Sept. 7, 1939.

Noack, David. "Extra! Extra! Read All about It! TV Web Site Acts Like a Newspaper." *Editor and Publisher Interactive.* June 13, 1997.

Oswald, John Clyde. *Printing in the Americas.* New York: Hacker Art Books, 1968.

Paper, Lewis J. *Empire: William S. Paley and the Making of CBS.* New York: St. Martin's Press, 1987.

Paulson, Roger C. *Archives of the Airwaves*, Vols. 1–7. Boalsburg, Pa.: BearManor Media, 2005–2006.

Pavlik, John V. *Journalism and New Media.* New York: Columbia University Press, 2001.

Pew Research Center for the People and the Press. "Self-Censorship: How Often and Why: Journalists Avoiding the News." April 30, 2000.

Pierpoint, Robert. *At the White House: Assignment to Six Presidents.* New York: Putnam, 1981.

Radio Daily. Sept. 16, 1943.

Radio Mirror. "Double in White." March 1943.

Ramsburg, Jim. *Network Radio Ratings, 1932–1953: A History of Prime Time Programs through the Ratings of Nielsen, Crossley and Hooper.* Jefferson, N.C.: McFarland, 2012.

Rather, Dan. *Rather Outspoken: My Life in the News.* New York: Grand Central, 2012.

Report on Chain Broadcasting. Washington, D.C.: U.S. Supreme Court, 1940.

Richards, Ronald P. "Montana's Pioneer Radio Stations: A Hobby Becomes an Industry." *Montana Journalism Review.* Spring 1963.

Robinson, Marc. *Brought to You in Living Color: 75 Years of Great Moments in Television & Radio from NBC.* Hoboken, N.J.: John Wiley & Sons, 2002.

Rosewater, Victor. *History of Cooperative Newsgath-*

ering in the United States. New York: D. Appleton, 1930.

Rutland, Robert A. *Newsmongers: Journalism in the Life of the Nation.* New York: Dial Press, 1973.

St. John, Robert. *From the Land of the Silent People.* New York: Doubleday, Doran, 1942.

Schechter, A. A., with Edward Anthony. *I Live on Air.* New York: Stokes, 1941.

Schieffer, Bob. *This Just In: What I Couldn't Tell You on TV.* New York: Berkley, 2003.

Schoenbrun, David. *On and Off the Air: An Informal History of CBS News.* New York: E.P. Dutton, 1989.

Schorr, Daniel. *Staying Tuned: A Life in Journalism.* New York: Pocket Books, 2001.

Seib, Philip. *Going Live: Getting the News Right in a Real-Time, Online World.* Lanham, Md.: Rowman & Littlefield, 2001.

Settel, Irving. *A Pictorial History of Radio: The Complete Story of Radio Broadcasting in America from Crystal Sets to Transistors with All the Stars, All the Great Shows of Radio's Golden Age.* New York: Grosset & Dunlap, 1967.

Sevareid, Eric. *Not So Wild a Dream.* New York: Alfred A. Knopf, 1946.

Shirer, William. *A Native's Return, 1945–1988.* Boston: Little, Brown, 1990.

Siegel, David S., and Susan Siegel. *Radio and the Jews: The Untold Story of How Radio Influenced America's Image of Jews, 1920s-1950s.* Yorktown Heights, N.Y.: Book Hunter Press, 2007.

Siepmann, Charles A. "American Radio in Wartime." *Radio Research 1942–43.* New York: Duell, Sloan & Pearce, 1944.

_____. *Radio, Television and Society.* New York: Oxford University Press, 1950.

_____. *Radio's Second Chance.* Boston: Little, Brown, 1947.

Sies, Luther F. *Encyclopedia of American Radio, 1920–1960*, 2d ed., Vols.1, 2. Jefferson, N.C.: McFarland, 2008.

Shirer, William L. *A Native's Return, 1945–1988: 20th Century Journey.* Boston: Little, Brown, 1990.

Slater, Robert. *This ... is CBS: A Chronicle of 60 Years.* Englewood Cliffs, N.J.: Prentice-Hall, 1988.

Slide, Anthony. *Great Radio Personalities in Historic Photographs.* Vestal, N.Y.: Vestal Press, 1982.

Sloan, W. David, and Lisa Mullikin Parcel. *American Journalism: History, Principles, Practices.* Jefferson, N.C.: McFarland, 2002.

Smith, F. Leslie. *Perspectives on Radio and Television: An Introduction to Broadcasting in the United States.* New York: Harper & Row, 1979.

Smith, Gene. *When the Cheering Stopped: The Last Years of Woodrow Wilson.* New York: William Morrow, 1964.

Smith, Howard K. *Last Train from Berlin: An Eye-Witness Account of Germany at War.* New York: Alfred A. Knopf, 1942.

Smith, Sally Bedell. *In All His Glory: The Life of William S. Paley, the Legendary Tycoon and His Brilliant Circle.* New York: Simon & Schuster, 1990.

Smulyan, Susan. *Selling Radio: The Commercialization of American Broadcasting, 1920 to 1934.* Washington, D.C.: Smithsonian Institution Press, 1994.

Snodgrass, Rhey T., and Victor F. Camp. *Radio Receiving for Beginners.* New York: Macmillan, 1922.

Sperber, A.M. *Murrow: His Life and Times.* New York: Freundlich Books, 1986.

Starr, Paul. *The Creation of the Media: Political Origins of Modern Communications.* New York: Basic Books, 2004.

Stephens, Mitchell. *A History of News: From the Drum to the Satellite.* New York: Viking, 1988.

Sterling, Christopher H., and John M. Kittross. *Stay Tuned: A Concise History of American Broadcasting.* 2nd ed. Belmont, Calif.: Wadsworth Publishing, 1990.

Sterling, Christopher H., ed. *Encyclopedia of Radio*, Vol. 2. New York: Routledge, 2003.

Summers, Harrison B., ed. *A Thirty-Year History of Programs Carried on National Radio Networks in the United States, 1926–1956.* New York: Arno Press and *The New York Times*, 1971.

The Sunday Times-Signal. "Inside Radio." Zanesville, Ohio, Feb. 20, 1949.

Swing, Raymond Gram. *"Good Evening!" A Professional Memoir.* New York: Harcourt, Brace & World, 1964.

The Tampa Tribune. "New Orleans newspaper retrenches." May 25, 2012.

Thomas, Lowell. *With Lawrence in Arabia.* Garden City, N.Y.: Garden City Publishing, 1924.

Thompson, Dorothy. *I Saw Hitler!* New York: Farrar & Rinehart, 1932.

Time. "Science: The Flying Words." Nov. 1, 1948.

Upshaw, Jim. "Characteristics of Journalists." In W. David Sloan and Lisa Mullikin Parcell, eds. *American Journalism: History, Principles, Practices.* Jefferson, N.C.: McFarland, 2002.

Van Tuyll, Debra Reddin. "The Press and War." In W. David Sloan and Lisa Mullikin Parcell, eds. *American Journalism: History, Principles, Practices.* Jefferson, N.C.: McFarland, 2002.

Variety. Jan. 25, 1939; June 18, 1941; Jan. 21, 1942; July 29, 1942; Feb. 17, 1943; May 5, 1943; Oct. 6, 1943; Oct. 13, 1943; Dec. 15, 1943.

Vlanton, Elias. *Who Killed George Polk? The Press Covers Up a Death in the Family.* Philadelphia: Temple University Press, 1996.

Wagoner, Clyde D. *Reminiscences.* Unpublished. Columbia University Oral History Collection, 1950.

Warburton, Lois. *The Beginning of Writing.* San Diego: Lucent Books, 1990.

Weaver, Pat, with Thomas M. Coffey. *The Best Seat*

in the House: The Golden Years of Radio and Television. New York: Alfred A. Knopf, 1994.

White, Llewellyn. *The American Radio.* Chicago: University of Chicago Press, 1947.

White, Paul W. *News on the Air.* New York: Harcourt, Brace, 1947.

Wile, Frederic William. *News Is Where You Find It: Forty Years Reporting at Home and Abroad.* Indianapolis: Bobbs-Merrill, 1939.

Wolfe, Charles Hall. *Modern Radio Advertising.* New York: Printers' Ink, 1949.

Wood, James Playsted. *The Great Glut: Public Communication in the United States.* Nashville: Thomas Nelson, 1973.

Wu, Tim. *The Master Switch: The Rise and Fall of Information Empires.* New York: Alfred A. Knopf, 2010.

Wylie, Max. *Best Broadcasts of 1938–39.* New York: Whittlesey House, 1939.

Youm, Kyu Ho. "Censorship." *Historical Dictionary of American Radio.* Westport, Conn.: Greenwood Press, 1998.

Index

The A&P Gypsies 46, 214
Abbott, Bud 119
ABC Close-Up! 151
ABC Evening News 215
ABC Movie of the Week 183
ABC World News Tonight 215
Abernathy, Bob 196
Abie's Irish Rose 120
Academy Awards 114
Acme Newspictures 125
Acta Diurna 6
actuarii 6
Adams, Cindy 147
Advance Publications, Inc. 110
Adventure (periodical) 180
The Adventures of Ellery Queen 120
The Adventures of Helen and Mary 118
The Adventures of the Thin Man 118
Advertising Age 116
advertising agencies' control of network programming 146
advertising as means of underwriting radio 42, 43, 46–47
Adweek 116
African-American 212
Agnew, Spiro 206
Agronsky, Martin 63, 81, 171, 172, 194
Akron (dirigible) 186
A.L. Alexander's Mediation Board 120
Albert Lasker Award 141
Alcoholics Anonymous (AA) 176, 185
The Aldrich Family 118
Alexanderson, Ernst F.W. 33
Alexanderson, Verner 33
Alfred I. DuPont Award 172, 202, 216, 220
all-music format 93
all-news format 93, 156
all-talk format 93, 153–164
All Things Considered 149, 150, 221
Allen, Fred 132, 190
Allen, Gracie 15, 20
Allen, Mel 147

Allen, Robert 119, 205
Alliance Française, Paris 211
Alterman, Eric 67
Ambutainer Company 215
America Abroad 195
America and the World 193
America Overnight 155
America United 81
American Association for Adult Education 74
American Association of Retired Persons (AARP) 187
American Broadcasting Company (ABC) 26, 52, 60, 62, 63, 76, 90, 91, 93, 94, 125, 133, 151, 156, 158, 172, 174, 176, 178, 179, 181, 180, 182, 183, 184, 185, 186, 187, 189, 190, 191, 192, 193, 196, 197, 200, 202, 205, 206, 211, 212, 213, 215, 217, 218, 219, 221, 222, 224
American Civil Liberties Union (ACLU) 34
American Cultural Expeditions 178
American electronics manufacturing slips away 132–133
American Expeditionary Force 173
The American Forum of the Air 60, 73–74, 75
American Heritage Dictionary 204
American Jewish Congress Award 216
American Legion 197
American Mercury 79, 80
American Newspaper Publishers Association (ANPA) 28, 97, 104, 105
American Public Media (APM) 150
American Red Cross 219
The American Rifleman 212
American Telephone & Telegraph Company (AT&T) 34, 98, 99, 133
American Theater Wing 119
American Theatre (periodical) 116
American University 184
American Viewpoints 81

America's Town Meeting of the Air 74, 75, 76–78, 180, 186, 190
Amos 'n' Andy 11, 20
Anastos Media Group, Inc. 163
Anderson, Jack 191
Andrea Doria (seagoing vessel)
Andrews, Johnny 147
Andrews, Robert Hardy 37
Andrews University 212
Aneta (Netherlands East Indies news agency) 210
Angel, Heather 222
Anglo-American Press Association (AAPA) 172
Antiques (periodical) 80
Antoine, Josephine 119
AP Newsbreak 174
apazines 113, 114
Apollo (spaceship) 202
apps 167, 170
Aquaduct Park 186
Arbitron ratings system 159, 167
"arc-phone" 162
Archinard, Paul 171, 172
Argall, Phyllis Elta 224
Argonaut Broadcasting Company 156
Arlington, Charles 171, 172
Armed Forces Radio Service (AFRS) 172, 174, 207
Armistice Day 34, 172
Armstrong, Edwin 170
Armstrong Theater of Today 183
Arnot, Charles P. 188
Associated Press (AP) 23, 24, 27, 28, 50, 101, 102, 103, 110, 141, 158, 170, 173, 208
Association of Radio News Analysts (ARNA) 59, 196
The Atwater-Kent Hour 202
Aunt Jenny's Real Life Stories 118
Authors Guild 213
Aviation Weather 87

Backstage Wife 149, 177
Baird, John Logie 127–128, 129
Baker, Phil 15, 188

249

Balk, Alfred 99
Baltimore & Ohio Railroad 224
The Baltimore Post 222
The Baltimore Sun 205
Bamberger's dry goods store, New York City 34, 73
Banghart, Kenneth 171, 173
Bankhead, Tallulah 79
Baranger Company, W.R. 223
Baranger-Weaver Company 223
Barber, Red 147, 188
Barbree, Jay 202
Barnet, Charlie 119
Barnouw, Erik 61
Barrett, Raymond 171, 173
Barrett, Rona 111
Bartholomew, René 129
Bate, Fred 171, 172, 173, 194
Battle of the Ages 176
Battle of the Bulge 212, 215
Baukhage, H.R. 53, 171, 173–174, 184, 186
Beatty, Morgan 24, 147, 171, 174, 183, 208
"Beautiful Music" programming motif 156, 157
Becquerel, Alexandre Edmond 128
Believe It or Not 202
Bell, Alexander Graham 14
The Bell Telephone Hour 200
The Bellingham (Wash.) *Herald* 27
Bennett, Joseph 34
Benny, Jack 15, 20
Bergen, Candice 199
Bergen, Edgar 20
Berlin, Irving 79
Berlin Olympics 129
Bernard Shaw Endowed Scholarship Fund 213
Bernays, Edward L. 15, 40–41, 51
Berzelius, Jöns Jakob 128
Best Broadcasts of 1938–39 (book) 76
The Best Foods Boys 46
The Better Home Show 176
Betty Crocker 190
Bidwell, Shelford 128
The Big Broadcast of 1936 (film) 188
The Big Show 190
Billboard 116, 131, 224
Biltmore Agreement 27–28, 88, 108
biographies of radio news personnel in Appendix 2–3
The Birmingham (Ala.) *News* 110
"blacklisting" 48, 56, 63, 111, 213
blackout in New York City 173
Blair, Frank 147
Blake, Henry Ingraham 8
Block, Martin 160
Bloomberg L.P. 164
Blue Network 50, 60, 63, 184, 186, 191, 192, 197, 217, 218, 219
The Bob Mathias Story (film) 188
Bogart, Humphrey 69
Book of the Month Club 213
Boorts, Neil 67
Boston College 179, 190, 205
The Boston Pops Orchestra 186, 205

Boston Symphony 204
Bourgholtzer, Frank 171, 174
Bowes, Major Edward 176, 188, 202, 205
Boxoffice 116
Bradley, Bruce 147
Braun, Karl Ferdinand 128
The Breakfast Club 119
Breckinridge, John C. 175
Breckinridge, Mary Marvin 171, 174–175, 180, 203
Brewster, Eugene V. 114
Bride & Groom 120
The Bridgeport (Conn.) *Post-Telegram* 141
Brinkley, David 52, 133, 138, 147, 181, 221
British Broadcasting Corporation (BBC) 26, 39, 78, 198, 217, 222
British News Service, Ltd. 192
British Royal Air Force 198
broadcast journalism introduced 9
Broadcast News (film) 187
Broadcasting (trade paper) 124, 146
Broadcasting & Cable (trade paper) 116
Broadway Open House 193
Brokaw, Tom 80
Brokenshire, Norman ("Broke") 171, 175–176
The Bronx (N.Y.) *Home News* 210
Brooklyn College 192
The Brooklyn (N.Y.) *Daily Eagle* 176, 196, 200
The Brooklyn (N.Y.) *Times* 190
Brooks, Ned 80
Broun, Heywood 77
Brown, Cecil 171, 176, 203
Brown, Ted 147, 148
Brown University 183, 188, 199, 214
Brownell, Herbert, Jr. 80
Bruce, Nigel 222
Bryan, William Jennings 34–35
Bryson, Lyman 78, 99
Burdett, Winston 171, 176–177, 181, 191, 203
Burns, George 15, 20
Busch, Ed 155
Bush, George H.W. 213
Butcher, Harry 221
Butler College 191

Cable News Network (CNN) 36, 77, 147, 148, 150, 153, 155, 158, 198, 210, 211, 213
California Institute of Technology 206
California State Polytechnic University 176
Calling America 187
Calmer, Ned 58, 171, 177
Calvary, Inc. 164
The Camden (N.J.) *Courier* 208
Camel News Caravan 52, 135
Campnell-Swinton, Alan Archibald 128
Canham, Erwin 171, 177
Cantor, Eddie 15, 69, 176

Capital Cities Corporation 196
Capitol Cloakroom 81, 181, 211
Capitol Close Up 79
Capitol Opinions 81
Capone, Al 208
Capone, Ralph 208
Captain Kangaroo 155
Carey, George Roswell 127
Carey-Thomas Award 213
Carnegie, Andrew 46
Carpenter, Ken 188
Carpentier, Georges 13, 14, 31
Carr, Mitch 155
Carter, Harold Thomas Henry ("Boake") 15, 53, 61, 62, 68, 69, 141, 171, 177
Carter, Jimmy 204, 206, 216, 220
Casablanca (film) 69
Casey, Crime Photographer 201
Cashbox 116
The Catholic Hour 194
Catholic University 180
The Cavalcade of America 119, 200, 214
Caxton, William 6
The CBS Evening News 136, 137, 138, 141, 197, 206, 211, 221
CBS Morning News Roundup 193, 194
CBS News Radio LA 161
The CBS Radio Mystery Theater 183
CBS Reports 141, 216
CBS-TV News 133, 182
CBS Views the Press 111
CBS World News Roundup 24, 59, 176, 177, 182, 193, 194, 197, 198, 200, 203, 206, 210, 211, 212, 214, 215, 216, 222
The Cedar Rapids (Iowa) *Republican* 214
censorship 47–48, 54, 56, 60, 61–62, 63–64
Center for the Study of Democratic Institutions 222
Cermak, Anthony J. 36
Chamberlain, Neville 215
Chancellor, John 204
The Charlotte News 197
Charnley, Mitchell 32, 33, 53
Chauvenet, Louis ("Russ") 113
Chen, Brian 167, 170
Cheney, Dick 213
Chess Records 157
Chevrolet Spotlights the News 194, 198
The Chicago American 208
The Chicago Daily News 187, 202, 204, 208, 217, 219, 223
The Chicago Evening American 160
The Chicago Evening Journal 218
Chicago-Kent College of Law 218
Chicago Opera Company 159
The Chicago Record 223
The Chicago Sun 196
The Chicago Sun-Times 111
The Chicago Tribune 9, 34, 177, 185, 201, 214, 223
The Chicago World 185
The Children's Hour 118, 188

Childs, Marquis 189
The Christian Science Monitor 189, 193, 205, 210
Chronicle 178
Chronoscope 198
Churchill, Winston 182
The Cicero (Ill.) *Tribune* 208
The Cincinnati Post 222
The Cincinnati Times Star 217
The Cisco Kid 172
The Cities Service Orchestra 202
citizen journalists 170
City College of New York 186, 194, 209, 210
Civilian Conservation Corps (CCC) 77
Clarke College 180
Claudia and David 118
clear-channel status 42
The Cleveland News 217
The Cleveland Press 217
The Cliquot Club Eskimos 46
Close, Upton 171, 177–178
Cloud, Stanley 176, 177, 192, 198, 203, 212
CNBC cable network 150
CNN Entertainment (periodical) 116
Coast-to-Coast on a Bus 118
Code of Ethics (NAB) 55
Code of Wartime Practices for American Broadcasters 55
Coe College 214
Cohan, George M. 35
Cold War 174, 199
College de France 214
The Collier Hour 197
Collier's Weekly 192, 195, 197, 202, 219
Collingwood, Charles 63, 138, 171, 178, 191, 203
Collum, Blanquita 67
Collyer, Clayton ("Bud") 120
Columbia (periodical) 197
Columbia Broadcasting System (CBS) 15, 16, 17, 18, 19, 20, 22, 23, 24, 25, 26, 31, 35, 36–37, 38–39, 40–41, 48, 49, 50, 51, 52, 53, 54, 55, 56, 57, 58, 59, 60, 61, 66, 68, 69, 70, 73, 78, 79, 81, 86, 88, 89, 91, 92, 93, 94, 101, 102, 111, 118, 125, 131, 132, 133–135, 137, 138, 141–142, 143, 146, 149, 150, 151, 155, 158, 159, 161, 162, 163, 164, 172, 173, 174, 175, 176, 177, 178, 179, 180, 181, 182, 183, 184, 186, 187, 188, 189, 190, 191, 192, 193, 194, 195, 196, 197, 201, 202, 203, 204, 205, 206, 207, 208, 209, 210, 211, 212, 213, 214, 215, 216, 217, 218, 219, 220, 221, 222, 223, 224
Columbia College 192
Columbia University 17, 78, 184, 188, 190, 195, 199, 205, 220
The Columbia Workshop 201
The Columbus (Oh.) *Citizen* 222
Combs, George Hamilton 59, 171, 178

commentator defined 53
commentators in radio's golden age 53, 58, 59, 68–69, 71
Communication Day based on 24-hour day 5–6
Communications Act of 1934 43
Como, Perry 190
Concentration 193
Confidentially Yours 187
Congressional Record 74
Conrad, Frank 12, 170
Considine, Bob 171, 178–179
Consolidated Press Association 173
control of the airwaves 41, 42, 43, 48, 49, 50
Cooke, Dwight 78, 79
Coolidge, Calvin 35, 175, 223
corantos 7
Corpus Christi College 189
Cosmopolitan 219
Costello, Lou 119
Coughlin, Charles E. 68
The Count of Monte Cristo 172
Counter Intelligence Corps 195
The Courier-Journal, Louisville 29, 108–109
The Court of Human Relations 205
Cox, James M. 12, 14, 31, 84, 154
Crandall, Brad 147
Cravens, Kathryn 171, 179
Crime Doctor 205
Crisco Radio Newspaper 193, 194
Cronkite, Walter 25, 133, 137, 138, 141, 150, 178, 181, 182, 206, 209, 211, 212, 221
Crookes, Sir William 128
Crosby, Bing 188
Crosby, John 111
Crosby, Lou 120
Crosley Broadcasting Corporation 158
Crowell (periodical) 219
Crowell-Collier Broadcasting Company 160
Croy, Homer 95
crystal radio set 14, 97–98, 106, 162, 168
Cuban missile crisis (1962) 216
Cuddihy, R.J. 22
Culbert, David Holbrook 70
Cullen, Bill 143, 144, 147
A Current Affair 151
Curtis, Charles 200

D-Day 32, 185, 186, 191, 200, 202, 208, 212, 221
The Daily 167
The Daily Cardinal 204
The Daily Kansan 181
The Daily Mail, London, UK 223
Daladier, Edouard 69
Daly, James 147
Daly, John Charles 16, 138, 151, 171, 179–180, 182, 186, 191, 212
Daniel, Dan 147
Darrow, Clarence 34
Dartmouth College 141, 183, 190
Dateline 151
David Harding, Counterspy 184

Davis, Elmer 16, 53, 59, 60, 63, 89, 170, 171, 176, 180, 217
Davis, John W. 31
Death Valley Days 190
Declaration of Independence 5, 46
de Forest, Lee 170
de Gaulle, Charles 204, 209
Dempsey, Jack 13, 14, 31, 35
Denny, Charles 146
Denny, George V., Jr. 76, 77, 78
The Denver Post 218
The Des Moines Register and Tribune 210
Detours (periodical) 113
The Detroit Free Press 101
The Detroit News 101
Dewey, Thomas E. 32
Dick Tracy 184, 190
Dickerson, Claude Wyatt 181
Dickerson, Nancy 171, 180–181
Dieckmann, Max 128
digital video recorder (DVR) 138
Dingell, John 49
Directions 191, 196
disc jockey (DJ) mania/format/participants 90, 153, 154–155, 156, 160, 162, 173, 176, 193, 201, 216, 224
Don Lee Network 162
Dornan, Bob 67
Douglas Edwards with the News 52, 133–135, 18, 216, 217
Downs, Bill 171, 181, 203
Downs, Hugh 147, 151, 193
Drake, Galen 171, 181–182
Dreier, Alex 171, 182
Dublin Daily Express 9
Dukakis, Michael S. 213
Duke University 222
DuMont, Allen B. 131
Dumont Television Network 125, 133, 176, 206
DuPont, Alfred I. 172, 202, 216, 220

E! Online 116
Eagleton, Thomas 191
earbud headphones 168
Earhart, Amelia 35
Earl Godwin and the News 185–186
Early, Steve 56
Eastman Kodak Company 125
The Eddie Cantor Show 176
Editor & Publisher (trade paper) 142
educational television 173
Edward P. Morgan News and Commentary 202
Edward R. Murrow and the News 197, 202, 210
Edwards, Bob 25, 51–52
Edwards, Douglas 52, 133–135, 138, 150, 171, 178, 179, 182, 184, 198, 209, 216, 217
Eichmann, Adolf 172
8XK, Pittsburgh 12, 84
Eisenhower, Dwight Dowd 185, 202, 206, 209, 217, 220
electronic device proliferation 83
Eliot, George Fielding 58, 59
Ellerbee, Linda 199

Elliott, Bob 147
Elsa Maxwell's Party Line 176, 202
Emory University 182
Empire Broadcasting Company 164
Empire State Building opening 35
Encyclopedia Britannica films 216
Entertainment Today 116
Entertainment Weekly 116
Eric Sevareid and the News 211
Ernie Pyle Memorial Award 197
Ethridge, Mark 29
Eveready Hour 47, 108
Eye on New York 141
e-zines 113, 114

Face the Nation 79, 80–81, 181, 191, 210, 212
facsimile broadcasting/transmission 123, 124, 130
facsimile newspaper 124
Fadiman, Clifton 147
Fairmont Office Tower, San Jose, Calif. 162
Fairness Doctrine 51, 54, 68
The Falcon 190
Family Theatre 172
Famous Fortunes 190
Fang, Irving 177, 183, 199, 222
fanzines 113–121
Farnsworth, Philo T. 129
Farrington, Fielden 171, 183
Fates, Gil 180
Fawcett Publications 118
Feder, Robert 111
Federal Communications Commission (FCC) 43, 45, 51, 53, 54, 58, 61, 62, 63, 68, 73, 124, 131, 160, 186
Federal Radio Commission (FRC) 42–43, 45, 160
Fessenden, Reginald 170
Fibber McGee & Molly 120
Fidler, Jimmy 111, 224
"Fifth Estate" 48
Film of the Year 114
"Fireside Chats" 31, 36, 100, 221
Fisher Communications 164
Fleet Motion Picture Office 190
Fleming, Art 147
Fleming, Jim 147
Fleming, Sir John Ambrose 128
Flipboard 167
Fly, James L. 58, 59
FN, San Jose, Calif. 162
Fontainebleau School of Music 187
Ford, Art 147, 148
Ford, Gerald R. 189, 204, 209
Ford, Glenn 119
Ford, Henry 18
Ford Foundation 173
The Ford Show 188
The Ford Summer Theater 183
Fordham University 205
Forest and Stream (periodical) 190
Fort Myers Broadcasting Company 164
The Fort Wayne Journal-Gazette 209
Fortune 30, 32
48 Hours 150

Foster, Cedric 26, 171, 183
"Fourth Estate" 49
Fox cable network 150
Fox Movietone newsreels 178, 207, 219
Fox News 181, 195
Frank, Reuven 52, 133, 135
Franklin College 180
Fraser, Gordon ("Jack") 147, 171, 183
Frazier, John 13
The Fred Allen Show 190
Frederic William Wile News Service 223
Frederick, Pauline 24, 171, 183–184
Freed, Alan 159
Freeman, Florence 171, 184
Frequency Modulation (FM) 123, 124
Friendly, Fred W. 209, 217
Friendship 7 (spaceship) 212
Front Page Farrell 187
Funt, Allen 147
Fust, Johann 6

Gabriel Heatter News and Comment 190
Gahn, Johan Gottlieb 128
Gallop, Frank 147
Gangbusters 184
Garagiola, Joe 147
Gardiner, Don 63, 171, 184
Gardner, Hy 111
Garment, Charles 149
Garroway, Dave 144, 147
Gates, Gary Paul 134, 177, 182, 209
G.E. Circle 214
General Electric Company 214
General Foods Corporation 61, 177
General Mills Corporation 190
General Motors Concert 197, 214
General Motors Corporation 107, 214, 217
George Foster Peabody Award 17, 26, 74, 76, 141, 172, 176, 178, 180, 181, 182, 184, 187, 195, 198, 202, 203, 204, 205, 211, 212, 213, 216, 219, 220, 221
George Polk Award in Journalism 198, 207, 216
George VI (King of England) 36
George Washington University 177, 178–179, 191, 193, 195, 199, 201, 208–209, 216
Georgetown University 180, 184
Georgia Normal College 219
Gernsback, Hugo 126, 127
Gernsback's Electro Importing Company 126
Gettysburg College 187
Gibbons, Floyd 17–18, 22, 28, 170, 171, 184–185
Gibbons, Jim 174
Gibson, George Robert 119
Gimbel's dry goods store, New York City 73, 158
Glage, Gustav 128
Glen Gray and His Casa Loma Orchestra 135
Glenn, John 212

global village 168
Globe Wireless, Ltd. 125
Glover, Herbert B. 16
Goddard, Don 171, 185
Godfrey, Arthur 140–141, 201, 212, 224
Godwin, Earl 171, 185–186
Goff, Norman 193
The Gold Dust Twins 46
Goldberg, Danny 67
The Goldbergs 188
The Golden Girls 204
Goldwyn, Samuel 18, 79
Good Morning America 138
Goodrich, B.F. 175
The Goodrich Silver Masked Tenor 46
Gordon, Gale 120
Gordon, Gloria 120
Gotham Broadcasting Corporation 158
Gould, Jack 111
Goulding, Ray 147
Grabovsky, Boris Pavlovich 129
Grace, Roger 207
Graham, Michael 67
Graham, Sheilah 111, 114, 224
Graham McNamee Speaking (syndicated column) 202
Gram, Betty 217
Grand Central Station 118, 186, 188, 190
Grandin, Thomas 171, 186, 203
Granik, Theodore 73–74
Grant, Bob 67
Grant, Taylor 171, 186
Grauer, Ben 147, 171, 186–187, 191
Gray, Glen 135
Great Depression 2, 87, 88, 100, 190, 201, 205
The Great Falls (Mont.) *Tribune* 99
The Great Gildersleeve 190
The Green Hornet 183
Gregory, David 80
Grinnell College 187
Gude, John George ("Jap") 16
The Gulf Headliners 176
Gulf War 213
Gunther, John 171, 187
Gutenberg, Johann 6

Hackes, Peter 171, 187
Hale, Arthur 56, 171, 187
Hall, Monty 147
Hallmark Playhouse 188
ham (amateur) operators 12, 14, 84, 85, 96, 104, 107, 126, 162
Ham, John 170
Hamblin, Ken 67
Hamilton, Gene 147
Hamilton, Wayne 147
Hancock, Don 171, 188
hand-held devices capture media 165–170
Handyman 176
Hangen, Welles 171, 188
Hanlon, Tom 171, 188
Hannity, Sean 67
The Happiness Boys 46

Hard, William 223
Hard Copy 151
Harding, Warren G. 12, 14, 31, 33–34, 42, 84, 101, 154, 190
Harkness, Richard 171, 188–189
Harley-Davidson Company 224
Harper's Bazaar 175, 180
Harriman, Averell 178
Harris, Benjamin 7, 8
Harsch, Joseph C. 171, 189
Hart, Herschell 101
Hart, Maurice 160
The Hartford (Conn.) *Courant* 208
The Hartford (Conn.) *Times* 183
Hartmann, Thom 67
Harvard Professional Exchange 196
Harvard University 78, 130, 176, 193, 194, 195, 196
Harvey, Paul 63, 88, 171, 189, 218
Harvey, Rita Morley 63
Hauptmann, Bruno Richard 36
Hawk, Bob 120
Hawley, Adelaide 190
Hawley, Mark 171, 189–190
Hawthorne, Nathaniel 119
Hayes, Bill 147
Headline Hunters (aka *The Headline Hunter*) 22, 179, 185
Hearst, William Randolph 158, 190
Hearst Corporation 16, 158, 192, 199, 214
Heatter, Gabriel 26, 28, 88, 171, 190, 203
Heidelberg University 215
Henry, Patrick 58
The Herb Jepko Show 155
Herlihy, Ed 171, 190
Herlihy, Walter 190
Herman, George 81, 171, 190–191, 209
Herndon, Booton 199
Herrold, Charles David 161–162, 170
Herrold, Sylvia 161–162
Herrold College of Engineering and Wireless 161–162
Hershey, Burnett 59
Hertz, Heinrich Rudolf 9, 170
Hewitt, Don 150
Hicks, George 171, 191
Hiett, Helen 171, 191
high-definition (HD) radio 167
Hill, Edwin C. 15, 36, 88, 89, 171, 191–192, 197
Hill, Frank Ernest 74
Hillman, Sidney 202
Hillman, William 171, 192
Himmler, Heinrich 174
Hindenburg (dirigible) 36
Hirohito, Emperor 204
History Channel 25, 222
Hitler, Adolf 175, 193, 196, 207–208, 215, 217, 219
HLN cable network 150
Hoagland, Everett 200
Hodges, Charles 59
Hogan, John V.L. 90
Hollenbeck, Don 111, 171, 192, 207
Holles, Everett 58
Hollywood Magazine 114

The Hollywood Reporter 116
Hollywood Star Playhouse 176
Hollywood Walk of Fame 207
Home 91, 145
Honeymoon in New York 193
Hooper ratings system 196
Hoover, Herbert 35, 40, 42, 44, 45, 79, 223
Hoover, Lou 200
Hopper, Hedda 111, 114, 224
The Horn and Hardart Children's Hour 190
Hottelet, Richard C. 171, 192–193, 203
House Budget Committee 216
Housman, A.E. 9
Howe, John 75
Howe, Quincy 58, 59, 171, 193
Howell, Wayne 171, 193
Hubbard Broadcasting Company 164
The Human Side of the News 15, 192
Hummert, Anne 177
Hummert, Frank 177
Hunting and Fishing (periodical) 80
Huntley, Chet 52, 133, 138, 181, 217, 221
The Huntley-Brinkley Report 52, 181, 217, 221
The Huntsville (Ala.) *Times* 110

Imus, Don 67, 93, 147
In Touch Weekly 116
Independent Network News 210
The Indiana (Pa.) *Evening Gazette* 105–106
Indiana Symphony 188
The Indianapolis Star 111, 217
The Indianapolis Sun 217
Industrial Revolution (second) 9
Industry on Parade 26
Information Age 5, 6
Information Highway 83
Information Please 186, 187, 190
Ingraham, Laura 67
Inner Sanctum Mysteries 190
Inside book series 187
Inside Edition 151–152
Inside Politics 213
Inside Radio (trade periodical) 116
Inside Washington 181
Intermountain Radio Network 183
International Consumer Electronics Show (ICES) 165
International News Photos 125
International News Service (INS) 27, 101, 102, 103, 116, 125, 158, 176, 185, 192, 194, 199, 200, 202, 204, 205, 214
International Olympics (Summer and Winter) 37
International Platform Association 213
International Radio-Television Society 198, 205
Internet/online reception 5, 8, 66, 83, 113, 123, 138, 164, 166–167, 168, 169, 207

Interstate Commerce Commission 43
The Invention of Love 9
inventions that improved communications 9
Invitation to Learning 193
The Ipana Troubadours 46
iPhone 167–168, 170
Irish Sweepstakes 205
It Happens Every Spring (film) 188

The Jack Smith Show 188
Jackson, Alan 171, 193–194
Jaker, Bill 221
Jane Endicott, Reporter 188
Japan Advertiser, Tokyo 224
Japan News-Week 224
Jarvis, Al 160
Jarvis, Bert 33
Jefferson, Thomas 5
Jenkins, Charles Francis 129
Jepko, Herb 155
The Jergens Journal 186
Jewish Correspondence Bureau 219
The Jewish Daily Bulletin 210
Jewish Telegraphic Agency 210
John B. Kennedy–Edwin C. Hill News 197
John B. Kennedy News 197
John Gunther's High Road 187
Johnson, Joseph French 9
Johnson, Julian 114
Johnson, Lyndon Baines 181, 209, 220
Johnstone, G.W. ("Johnny") 26
Joint Economic Committee 216
Jolson, Al 15
Jordan, Max 171, 194
Jory, Victor 222
Joyce Jordan, Girl Interne 118
Junior League (periodical) 175
Just Plain Bill 118, 149, 183, 190

Kalb, Bernard 194
Kalb, Marvin 80, 171, 194–195
The Kalb Report 195
Kalischer, Murray, Jr. ("Peter") 171, 195
Kaltenborn, Hans von 14, 15, 16, 24, 26, 28, 53, 54–55, 57, 58–59, 62, 99, 100, 141, 162, 170, 171, 180, 183, 192, 195–196, 203
The Kansas City (Mo.) *Journal* 216
Kansas City School of Law 178
Kanze, Peter 221
Kaplow, Herbert 24, 171, 196
Kaufman, Murray the K 147, 159
Kay Kyser's Kollege of Musical Knowledge 186
KCBS-AM-FM, San Francisco 161, 162, 164
KCET-TV, Los Angeles 176
KCOP, Los Angeles 207
KDKA, Pittsburgh 12, 13, 31, 84, 99, 105, 107, 154
KDYS, Great Falls, Mont. 99
Keep Posted 79
Keeshan, Bob 155
Kellogg Company, W.K. 201

Kendall College 179
Kendrick, Alexander 63, 171, 196–197
Kennedy, Jacqueline 216
Kennedy, John B. 171, 197
Kennedy, John F. 49, 126, 194, 196, 202, 203, 204, 206, 209, 212, 216, 220, 222
Kennedy, Robert F. 204
Kentucky Derby 37, 202
Kesten, Paul 40
KFAB, Lincoln, Neb. 102
KFAX, San Francisco 156–157
KFI, Los Angeles 188
KFMB, San Diego 17
KFML, Denver 183
KFOX, Long Beach, Calif. 181
KFWB, Los Angeles 159, 160–161
KGCX, Vida, Mont. 99
KGO, San Francisco 63
KHJ, Los Angeles 160, 207
Khrushchev, Nikita 210
Kiernan, Walter 147
KIEV, Los Angeles 207
Kilgallen, Dorothy 111, 114
Kill the Umpire (film) 188
kinescope 129
King, Larry 93, 155
King, Martin Luther 204
King Features Syndicate 192, 204
KJBS, San Francisco 156
Klauber, Edward A. 15–16, 17, 22, 40, 51, 54, 55, 69
Kline, George 102
KLIV, San Jose, Calif. 164
KMBC, Kansas City, Mo. 216
KMOX, St. Louis 179, 224
KMPC, Beverly Hills, Calif. 102
KNEL, Brady, Tex. 103
Knights of Columbus 197
KNX, Los Angeles 161, 164, 178, 181, 182, 188
KOIN, Portland, Ore. 14
Kollmar, Richard 118
KOLO, Reno 190
KOMO-AM-FM, Seattle 164
Koop, Ted 50
KPAB, Laredo, Tex. 103
KPIX-TV, San Francisco 162
KPLS, Los Angeles 207
KQV, Pittsburgh 164
KQW, San Jose, Calif. 162
Kraft Foods Company 188, 190
Kraft Music Hall 188, 190
Kraft Television Theatre 190
Krebsbach, Ed 99
KRLA, Los Angeles 160
KRLD, Dallas 164
KROI-FM, Houston 164
KSD, St. Louis 34
KSFO, San Francisco 162
KSL, Salt Lake City 155
KSOO, Sioux Falls, S.D. 27
KSTP, St. Paul, Minn. 207
KTHS, Hot Springs, Ark. 193, 194
KTLA-TV, Los Angeles 207
KTLN, Denver
KTTV-TV, Hollywood, Calif. 207
Ku Klux Klan 34, 206

Kuralt, Charles 151, 171, 197–198, 206
KUT, University of Texas 84
KVOD, Denver 183
KVOO, Tulsa 189
KVOS, Bellingham, Wash. 27
KWK, St. Louis 179
KWSC, Pullman, Wash. 203
Kyser, Kay 186
KYSM, Mankato, Minn. 102
KYW, Chicago/Philadelphia/Cleveland 93, 101, 107, 159, 160, 164

Labor-Liberal FM Network 189
Laconia (seagoing vessel) 185
The Ladies' Home Journal (periodical) 219
LaGuardia, Fiorello H. 74, 80
Lamarr, Hedy 120
Larry Lesueur and the News 198
Lasker, Albert 141
Lauck, Chester 193
Laufer, Peter 207
Laughter, Victor 84
Law for the Layman 73
Lawrence, Bill 217
Lawrence, David 53
Lawrence, T.E. 218
The Leading Question 181
League for Political Education 76, 220
League of Nations 34, 178, 191
Leahy, William D. 57
Leave It to the Girls 79
LeBlanc, Maurice 128
Lenman and Mitchell ad agency 15
Leonard, Bill 140, 141, 142, 143
LeSueur, Larry 39, 171, 188, 191, 203
Let's Pretend 118
Levine, Daniel 199
Levine, Irving R. 24, 171, 198–199
Levy, Estelle 118
Lewis, Fulton, Jr. 26, 28, 53, 62, 89, 171, 199–200
Lewis, Fulton, III 200
Lewis, Jerry 190, 193
Lewis, John L. 80
Liberty Broadcasting System 157, 217, 222
Liddy, G. Gordon 67
Lieberman, Joseph 213
Life 173, 175
Life Can Be Beautiful 188
Limbaugh, Rush 67, 93, 199
Lincoln, Abraham 175
The Lincoln (Neb.) *Star* 102
Lindbergh, Charles A. 35–36, 177, 202, 205
Lindbergh, Charles A., Jr. 35–36, 177, 205
Lippman, Walter 217
Literary Digest 17, 22
"Little Godfreys" 201
Little Women 118
Loews, Inc. 136
The London Daily Express 24, 200
London School of Economics 191, 211, 222
Long, Huey 68

Long Island University 207
Look 173
Looking Over the Week 197
Lorenzo Jones 149
Los Angeles City News Service 158
Los Angeles Dodgers 160
The Los Angeles Times 182
Louisiana State University 204
Love of Life 188
Lowe, Jim 147, 148
Lowell Thomas and the News 22, 88, 218
Lowell Thomas Electronic Journalism Award 213
Loyola University 195
Lucerne Music Festival 175
The Lucky Strike Dance Band 46
Lum and Abner 120, 193–194
Lux Radio Theater 188
Lynn University 199

Ma Perkins 92
MacArthur, Douglas 23, 195
Macfadden, Bernarr 114
Macfadden Publications, Inc. 114, 115, 118, 222
Mack, Floyd 171, 200
MacLeish, Archibald 60
Macmillan Publishing Company 118
The MacNeil-Lehrer News Hour 25
MacVane, John 171, 200
Macy's dry goods store, New York City 73, 198
Magazine (TV series) 141
Magazine/cafeteria programming motif 139, 140, 142, 143, 144, 145, 146–147, 148–149, 150, 151, 152
The Magic Key 197
Maizlish, Harry 160
Major Bowes' Original Amateur Hour 176, 188, 202, 205
Make Believe Ballroom 160
Malloy, Mike 67
Man on the Go 182
The Manchester (UK) *Guardian* 222
Manhattan at Midnight 118, 120
Mann, Al 217
Manning, Tom 191
Marble, Harry 171, 200
March, Hal 147
The March of Time 15, 86, 172, 180
Marconi, Guglielmo 9, 10, 14, 21, 127, 170
Marconi Company 33
Margaret Arlen 200
Marion College 213
Marketplace 150
Marshall Plan 210
Martin, Dean 66, 190, 193
The Martin and Lewis Show 190, 193
Marvin, Tony 172, 201
Marx, Groucho 79
MASH 206
Mason, Julian 77
Mathias, Bob 188
Matinee Theater 200
Mature Focus 187

Index

Maxwell, Elsa 176, 202
May, Joseph 128
Mayer, Louis B. 18
Mayflower pronouncement 54
McCarthy, Joseph R. 48, 56, 172, 192, 194, 200, 203, 206, 211
McClelland, M.C. 13
McCormick, Robert 172, 201
McCrary, Tex 80
McDevitt, Ruth 119
McEvoy, Denis 59
McGee, Frank 147, 204
McLendon, Gordon 157–158
McMahon, Ed 147
McManus, John T. 111
McNamee, Graham 31, 35, 172, 175, 191, 201–202
McNeill, Don 119
Medical Horizons 185
Medved, Michael 67
Meet the Press 26, 79–80, 81, 94, 138, 186, 194, 204
Memphis Turtles 84
Men of the Land, Sea, and Air 120
Merlin Media 163
The Merrill (Wis.) *Advocate* 195–196
Merton College 215
Metropolitan Life Insurance Company 194
The Metropolitan News-Enterprise, Los Angeles 207
The Metropolitan Opera Auditions of the Air 186
The Miami Beach Sun 190
The Miami Herald 124
Michael Shayne 172
Miller, Irving 120
Miller, Stephanie 67
The Milwaukee Free Press 185
The Milwaukee Sentinel 185
The Minneapolis Daily News 184–185
The Minneapolis Journal 211
The Minneapolis Tribune 185
Misericordia Hospital, Manhattan, N.Y. 119
Miss America Beauty Pageant 193
Miss Radio News 116
Mr. Belvedere 204
Mr. District Attorney 186, 190
Mr. Keen, Tracer of Lost Persons 186
"Mr. Safety" 144, 145
The Mobile (Ala.) *Press-Register* 110
Mondale, Walter F. ("Fritz") 204
Monday Morning 151
Monday Morning Headlines 184
Monitor 52, 91, 94, 146–148, 155, 173, 179, 181, 183, 186, 187, 193, 202, 209, 216
"monkey trial" 34–35
Monks, Edward 68
Monroe, Bill 80
Monroe, Vaughn 119
Montgomery, George 120
Moore, Garry 120
Morgan, Edward P. 172, 202
Morgan, Henry 147, 148
Morgan, Robert W. 147
Mormon Tabernacle Choir 205

Morning Edition 150
Morrison, Herbert 36
Morse Code 10, 84, 85
Motion Picture (periodical) 116
Motion Picture Magazine 114
Motion Picture Story 114
Movie Mirror 115, 116
MSNBC cable network 150, 199
Mudd, Roger 17, 25, 80, 194, 209, 210, 221
Mueller, Merrill 24, 172, 173, 202
Murphy Brown 199, 204
Murray the K 147, 159
Murrow, Edward R. 16, 17, 22, 24, 28, 30, 31, 38, 39, 51, 52, 53, 56, 57, 58, 59, 61, 62, 68–70, 86, 100, 111, 136–137, 138, 141, 150, 170, 172, 173, 175, 176, 180, 181, 182, 183, 186, 189, 191, 192, 193, 194, 195, 196, 197, 198, 202–203, 206, 207, 208, 209, 210, 211, 212, 213, 214, 215, 216, 217, 218, 220, 221, 223
Murrow, Janet 175
"Murrow Boys" 24, 38, 57, 70, 137, 175, 176, 178, 181, 182, 186, 192, 193, 194, 196, 198, 203, 209, 211, 212, 213, 214, 215
Music Box (periodical) 116
Music Vendor (trade periodical) 116
Musical News 85
Mutual Broadcasting System (MBS) 10, 23, 26, 33, 50, 51, 52, 53, 54, 56, 60, 63, 73, 79, 88, 89, 91, 94, 155, 172, 174, 176, 177, 178, 179, 180, 181, 182, 183, 187, 190, 192, 193, 195, 197, 200, 201, 207, 213, 214, 217, 219, 221, 222, 224
The Mutual Forum Hour 73, 74

Name That Tune 193
narrowcasting audience segments 84, 93
NASA 187
The Nation (periodical) 190
National Academy of Cable Programming 213
National Academy of Television Arts and Science 180
National Academy of Vocal Arts 186
National Association of Black Journalists 213
National Association of Broadcasters (NAB) 29, 50, 55, 56, 108, 124
National Book Award 213
National Broadcasting Company (NBC) 15, 16, 17, 18, 19, 20, 21, 22, 23, 24, 25, 26, 27, 31, 35, 36, 40, 45, 49, 50, 51, 52, 53, 54, 55, 57, 58, 61, 62, 63, 69, 73, 74, 75, 76, 79, 80, 81, 86, 88, 89, 91, 93, 94, 118, 119, 125, 129, 130, 131, 133, 135, 143, 144, 145, 146, 147, 148–149, 150, 151, 155, 156, 160, 161, 172, 173, 174, 175, 176, 178, 179, 180, 181, 182, 184, 185, 186, 187, 188, 189, 190, 191, 192, 193, 194, 195, 196, 197, 198, 199, 200, 201, 202, 203, 204, 205, 207, 208, 209, 210, 211, 214, 215, 216, 217, 218, 219, 220, 221, 222, 223, 224
National Defense Act 224
National Education Television 202
National Emergency Council 178
The National Farm and Home Hour 173
National Football League 202
National Headliners Club 181, 191
National Institute of Social Sciences 219
National Opinion Research Center (NORC) 32
National Press Club 193, 195, 213
National Public Radio (NPR) 149, 150, 184, 193, 195, 210, 211, 221
National Rifle Association 212
National Social Unit Organization 219
National Sportsman (periodical) 80
National Student Federation of America 203
NBC News of the World 172, 174, 183, 208, 222
NBC News on the Hour 91, 155
NBC Nightly News 203, 204, 208
The NBC Radio Theater 193
The NBC Symphony Orchestra 186
NBC World News Roundup 194
Nebel, Long John 155
Nelson, Barry 147
Nelson, Lindsey 146
New Deal 54, 61, 68, 73
New England Paladium 8
The New Orleans Item 215
The New Orleans Times-Picayune 110
The New York Daily Mirror 111, 179, 224
The New York Daily News 111
The New York Evening Bulletin 17
The New York Evening Post 207, 219
New York Giants 84
The New York Graphic 222, 224
The New York Herald Tribune 9, 111, 177, 188, 191, 211, 214, 219
The New York Journal 190
The New York Journal-American 111
The New York Mirror 176
New York Operatic Guild 201
New York Pops 205
The New York Post 90, 167
New York Publishers Association 47, 108
The New York Record 190
The New York Sun 191, 198, 200
The New York Sunday World 17
The New York Telegram 47, 108
The New York Times 15, 16, 36, 79, 87, 88, 89, 90, 91, 106, 107, 111, 136, 145, 176, 180, 188, 195, 204, 208, 209, 210, 213, 214, 215, 216, 221, 222, 223
The New York Tribune 198, 219
New York University 198

The New York World 15, 23, 185
New York World's Fair, Flushing Meadows, N.Y. (1939) 28, 125, 130, 131, 183, 186, 201
New York Yankees 84
The New Yorker 61, 180
Newhart 204
Newman, Edwin 172, 203–204
Newman, Morton 204
News and Information Service (NIS) 155
News and Views 174
news around the clock 153–164
News at Noon 185
News Corporation 167
News for Everyman: Radio and Foreign Affairs in Foreign America (book) 70
News of America 192
News of the World 200, 208
News on the Air 17
news on the hour (NOTH) 89, 90, 91, 94
news operations at local stations 14–15
NewsActing 86
The Newscaster (trade periodical) 116
NewsCasting 86
Newsday Syndicate 202
newspaper criteria 7
"The Newspaper That Comes Through Your Walls" 95
newspapers' conflict with radio 27–28
Newsweek 147, 202
Nielsen research agency 138
Nightcap 155
Nightline 189
Nightly Business Report 199
Nighttalk 155–156
9XM, Madison, Wis. 84
9YV, Manhattan, Kan. 84
Nipkow, Paul Gottlieb 127
Nipkow disk 127
Nixon, Richard M. 48, 49, 181, 195, 196, 206, 209, 210, 212, 215, 216, 220, 222
Nobel Prize 219
Noble, Edward J. 63
The Norfolk (Neb.) *Daily News* 85
North, Oliver 67
North American Newspaper Alliance 184, 192
North Atlantic Treaty Organization (NATO) 210
Northeastern University 213
Northwestern University 196, 222
Norville, Deborah 151
Notre Dame University 223
Novins, Stuart 81

The Oak Leaves, Oak Park, Ill. 208
Oberlin College 216, 217
Oboler, Arch 70–71
O'Brian, Jack 111
O'Connor, Charles 172, 204–205
Ohio State University 176
OK! Magazine 116

O'Keefe, Walter 189
Old Owl Communications 222
Olney (Md.) Theatre Summer Playhouse 173
Olson, Lynne 176, 177, 192, 198, 203, 212
On the Line (syndicated column) 178
On the Line with Considine 179
On the Road 197
Oriental-American Booking agency 224
Osgood, Charles 151, 172, 205
The Osgood File 205
Our Barn 118
Overseas Press Club 181, 188, 195
ownership of the airwaves 41
Oxford University 178, 200, 215

The Packard Hour 197
Paducah Plantation 188
Paige, Raymond 119
Paley, William S. (Bill) 16, 18, 19–20, 22, 23, 40–41, 51, 61, 68, 69, 86, 101, 131, 132, 136, 140, 146, 170, 190, 194, 203, 213, 215, 218, 221
Paley's attempts to save radio 132
The Palmolive Hour 46
Paramount Studios 18
The Paris Herald 177
The Paris Tribune 177
The Parker Family 118
Parks, Bert 147, 193
Parsons, Harriet 111
Parsons, Louella 111, 114, 224
Pathé newsreels 172, 190
Pathfinder (periodical) 192
Patterson, Jeff 175
Paul Harvey News and Comments 189
Paul Pert Screen Collection 127
Paul White Radio-TV News Directors Association Award 184
Pauley, Jane 151
paying for radio's operation 44
payola scandal 154–155
Peabody, George Foster 17, 2, 74, 76, 141, 172, 176, 180, 181, 182, 184, 187, 195, 198, 202, 203, 204, 205, 211, 212, 213, 216, 219, 220, 221
Peabody Players 179
Pearl Harbor 10, 31, 33, 50, 70, 89, 173, 179, 204, 215
Pearson, Drew 53, 172, 205–206
Pearson, Leon 147
Penner, Joe 15
Pentagon Reports 174
People 116
People Are Funny 190
The People's Platform 75, 78–79
The People's Rally 197
The Perry Como Show 190
Person to Person 178, 203
Personal from Pearson (newsletter) 206
Peter Hackes Award 187
Pfeiffer, Bob 92

PGA Championship 37
The Phil Baker Show 188
The Philadelphia Daily Ledger 217
The Philadelphia Daily News 177
The Philadelphia Evening Bulletin 177
The Philadelphia Inquirer 188, 196
Philadelphia Phillies 84
The Philadelphia Public Ledger 104, 219, 223
The Philadelphia Record 208
Philco Corporation 61, 177
Philip Morris Presents 205
Phillips, Stone 151
Photoplay 114–115, 116, 118
Photoplay and TV Mirror 115, 117
Photoplay Gold Medal 114
Photoplay Medal of Honor 114
Pickens Party 190, 193
Pierpoint, Robert 24, 172, 206, 209
Pittsburgh Corsairs 84
The Pittsburgh Post 12, 13
platforms of many persuasions proliferate 165–170
PM, New York City (periodical) 111, 204
podcasts 167
The Political Situation in Washington Tonight 223
Polk, George 172, 198, 207, 216
Popular Radio 95
portability impacts radio listening habits 139, 147, 149
Postmaster General 43
Predictions of Things to Come 206
Premiere (periodical) 116
Press, Bill 67
Press Conference 79
Press-Radio News 88
Press-Radio War 27–28, 85, 104, 105
Pressman, Gabe 146
Price, Byron 50
The Pride of St. Louis (film) 188
Primetime Live 151
Princeton University 218, 220
Printer's Ink 44
printing press invention 6, 122
Probst, George 75
Procter & Gamble Company 218
The Providence Journal 23, 199
prozines 113, 114, 116, 117
Public Broadcasting System (PBS) 25, 172, 181, 196, 199, 202, 204, 211, 222
public domain 27
The Public Ledger, Philadelphia, Pa. 196
Public Radio International (PRI) 150
Publick Occurrences, Both Forreign and Domestick 7
Puget Sound College 191
Pulitzer Prize 207, 217
Pulse 143, 144, 145, 146
Pure Oil Company 189
Putnam, George 172, 207
Putnam, George Carson 207

Queen Mary (seagoing vessel) 205
Queen's College, Oxford 180
Quincy Howe Comments 193
Quirk, James R. 114

radio: conflict with newspapers and wire services 27–28; escalation as news source 38; first sportscast 13; impact on America 10–11; introduction 10; logs in print 104, 105–108; proliferation 13, 42; reliance on newspapers 12, 23
Radio Act of 1927 13, 40, 42, 43, 44, 50
Radio Age 116
Radio and Television Executives Society, Inc. 26
Radio and Television Mirror 117, 131
Radio and Television News Association 136–137
Radio Broadcast (trade paper) 33, 44
Radio Business Report (trade paper) 116
Radio City Party 197
Radio Corporation of America (RCA) 18, 19, 21, 26, 40, 62, 125, 129, 130, 131, 132, 144, 145, 209
Radio-Craft (trade paper) 116, 126
Radio Days 200
The Radio Dealer (trade paper) 45
radio-equipped vehicles proliferate 139–140
Radio Executives Club 58
Radio Guide 116, 180
Radio Hall of Fame 157, 205
"radio halls" 13, 31
Radio Ink 116
Radio Mirror 74, 116, 117, 118–120, 131, 179
Radio News 116
Radio One, Inc. 164
Radio Pioneer Award 220
Radio Pioneers 26
Radio Press International 178
Radio Reader's Digest 200
Radio Receiving for Beginners (book) 98
Radio Service Bulletin (trade periodical) 96
Radio Television Digital News Association 187
Radio-TV Mirror 117
Radio World 116
Raphael, Sally Jessy 156
Rather, Dan 25, 136, 137–138, 141, 150, 197, 209, 211, 212
Rayburn, Gene 147, 148
Reader's Digest 219
Reagan, Michael 67
Reagan, Ronald 68, 195, 204, 216, 220
Reasoner, Harry 150, 178, 215
Rebozo, Charles G. ("Bebe") 206
Red Barber Sports 188
Red Channels 56, 208, 215
The Register 174

The Register-Guard, Eugene, Ore. 68
Reinheart, Alice 119
Religion & Ethics Newsweekly 196
religious radio 157
HMS *Repulse* (seagoing vessel) 176
The Rest of the Story 189
Reuther, Walter 80
Reynolds, Frank 215
Rhodes, Randi 67
Rhodes scholarship 215
Rice, Grantland 84
Richard C. Hottelet and the News 193
The Richard Harkness Show 189
The Richmond (Ind.) *Evening Item* 217
The Right to Happiness 149
RKO Corporation 155
Roadshow 143, 144–145
Roberts, Peter 147
Rockefeller Center 144
Rolling Stone 116
Rollins College 183
The Romance of Helen Trent 183, 188
Roosevelt, Eleanor 219
Roosevelt, Franklin Delano (FDR) 31, 32, 36, 43, 50, 51, 54, 56–57, 61, 68, 74, 79, 174, 177, 178, 179, 180, 182, 184, 186, 188, 206, 211, 212, 219, 221
Root, Waverly 59
Rose Bowl 37, 202
Rosenberg, Leo Henry 12, 13
Rosing, Boris 128
Rotten Tomatoes 116
Rountree, Martha 79–80
Royal Institute, London 127
The Rudy Vallee Show 202
Russell, Don 147
Russert, Tim 79, 80
Rutgers University 172
The Rutland (Vt.) *Herald* 208
Rutledge Books 118
Ryan, John Harold 50
Ryan, Patricia 118–119

Saerchinger, Cesar 172, 207–208
St. John, Adela Rogers 114
St. John, Robert 172, 182, 208–209
St. John's University 201
St. Louis University 197
Sammis, Edward R. 118
Sammis, Frederick Rutledge 118
Sammis, John 118
Sammis, Kathy 118
The San Diego Journal 17
The San Francisco Chronicle 111
Sanger, Elliott 90
The Santa Barbara News-Press 206
Sarnoff, David 18, 19–20, 21, 22, 125, 129, 130, 131, 145, 148, 149, 170
Sarnoff, Robert W. (Bobby) 26, 145, 148, 149
satellite's impact 123, 155, 167, 168
The Saturday News Special 192

Saturday Night Live 204
"Saturday Night Massacre" (1973) 216
The Saturday Review of Literature 180
Savage, Michael 67
Schechter, Abraham A., Jr. 23, 24, 26, 27
Scherer, Ray 172, 209
Schieffer, Bob 81, 191
Schlesinger, Laura 67
Schoenbrun, David F. 24–25, 52, 172, 209–210
Schorr, Daniel 172, 207, 210–211
Schultz, Ed 67
Scopes, John T. 34
Scott, Frank W. 9
Screen Life 114
Scripps-Howard newspaper syndicate 47, 218, 219
The Seattle Post-Intelligencer 27
The Seattle Star 202
The Seattle Times 27
Second Sunday 187
The Secret Storm 188
See It Now 56, 203, 206
The Selling of the Pentagon 48
Senate Foreign Relations Committee 180
Senlecq, Constantin 127
Sesno, Frank 198
Sevareid, Eric 38–39, 53–54, 69, 70, 137, 141, 172, 186, 191, 194, 203, 204, 207, 211–212
Shadel, Bill 81, 172, 212
The Shadow 188
Sharbutt, Del 119
share-time radio stations on single frequency 42
Shaw, Bernard 158, 172, 212–213
Shenandoah (dirigible) 34
Shepard, Dick 147
Shirer, William L. 16, 58, 59, 62, 63, 68–69, 141, 170, 172, 189, 191, 194, 203, 213–214
"shock jocks" 93
Shockley, Marion 120
Shore, Dinah 120
shortwave radio broadcasting 173, 203
Show Business 116
Sidney Hillman Foundation Award 202
Sieberling Singers 47, 108
Siepmann, Charles A. 78
Sies, Luther 193, 196, 224
Sigma Delta Chi 179, 216
"silent nights" 42
Simon & Schuster book publishers 193, 213
The Sinclair Headliner 214
Singiser, Frank 172, 214–215
Six Day Arab-Israeli War (1967) 204
The $64,000 Question 193
60 Minutes 138, 141, 142, 150, 151
6XE, San Jose, Calif. 162
6XF, San Jose, Calif. 162
SJN, San Jose, Calif. 162

Skelton, Red 20
Skidmore College 214
Skolsky, Sidney 114
Slater, Bill 80
Smith, Al 35
Smith, Fred 85–86
Smith, Howard K. 63, 81, 172, 203, 207, 209, 215–216
Smith, Jack 188
Smith, Kate 118, 119
Smith, T.V. 75
Smith, Willoughby 128
Society of Professional Journalists 174, 179, 211, 213
Something for Everyone 86
Sorbonne, Paris 202
"sound like water" 167
Speak Your Mind 189
Speaking Freely 204
Special Features Plan wartime propaganda 59–60
Special Investigator 118
spectaculars (TV) 145
The Spirit of St. Louis (aircraft) 35
Spivak, Lawrence E. 79, 80
Sport (periodical) 118
sportscasting inception 84
Sputnik I (spaceship) 173
Stage Door Canteen 119
Stahl, Lesley 81
Stalin, Joseph 210
Stanford University 182
Stanton, Frank 48, 49, 81, 134
Star Magazine 116
Stars & Stripes (armed services periodical) 173
Stassen, Harold 79
State College of Washington 203
State University of New York 184
Steel, Johannes 59
Steele, Ted 147, 148
The Steelville (Mo.) *Ledger* 224
Stella Dallas 149
Stepmother 188
Stern, Howard 67, 93
Stop the Music! 188
Stoppard, Tom 9
Strawser, Neil 172, 216
streaming radio/video 166–167, 169, 170
Stringer, Howard 141–142
Stubblefield, Nathan 170
The Studebaker Champions 186
Sulek, Frank 221
Sullivan, Ed 111
summer stock 173
Sun Oil Company 61
Sunday Morning 141, 151, 197, 205, 206
surfing the airwaves 14
Swathmore College 205
Swayze, John Cameron 52, 133, 135, 138, 147, 172, 216–217
The Sweeney and March Show 188
Swing, Betty Gram 217
Swing, Raymond Gram 26, 28, 53, 59, 60–61, 89, 170, 172, 217
Syracuse University 172, 175, 202, 219

Taft, Robert A. 74, 79
Takayanagi, Kenjiro 129
talk radio format 66–68, 93, 155, 163, 189
Talknet 156
Talkradio 156
The Tampa Tribune 79
Tarzan 172
Taylor, Henry J. 172, 217–218
Taylor, Tony 147
The Taystee Loafers 46
telectroscope 127
Telenews 125, 135
The Telephone-Hirmondo, Budapest 95
telephone party line 97
Television Broadcasters Association (TBA) 131
Television Corporation of America 181
Television Today 116
television's impact in news delivery 125, 126–138
The Texaco Fire Chief 202
Texas State Network 194
"theater of the mind" 37–38
Theater of Today 120
The Theatre Guild on the Air 176
30 Minutes 141
This Is New York 141, 142, 144
This Is Nora Drake 144
This Life Is Mine 201
Thomas, Ann 119
Thomas, Lowell 15, 22, 23, 24, 28, 59, 88, 89, 170, 172, 174, 178, 183, 189, 195, 203, 213, 218–219
Thomas, William 12
Thomas Cook & Sons travel agency 172
Thompson, Dorothy 53, 74, 79, 80, 172, 219
Those Wonderful, Terrible Years (book) 63
Tihanyi, Kálmán 129
Time 15, 17, 77, 86, 147, 207, 219, 222
The Times, London, UK 199
Times Square 186
Timex Watch Company 216
Tisch, Laurence 136, 138
Tito, Marshal 211
Today 23, 91, 145, 147, 149, 150, 181, 204
Tomlinson, Edward 172, 219–220
Tomorrow's Headlines 184
Tonight 91, 145, 149, 150
The Tony Marvin Show 201
Tony the Tiger (advertising figure) 201
"Top 40" programming motif 156, 157, 160
Town & Country (periodical) 175
The Town Crier 101
Town Hall, Inc., New York City 76
Townsend, Dallas 172, 220
Tracy, Eric 155
transistor radio 139, 149, 167, 168
Transradio 176

Trinity College 208
Trout, Robert 16, 31, 68–69, 141, 170, 172, 177, 180, 183, 191, 220–221
True Story Theater 120
Truman, Harry S 74, 174, 192, 197, 206, 209, 220
Truth or Consequences 190
Tucker, J.B. 147
Tuesday Morning 151
Tufty News Service 204
Tulane University 215
Tunney, Gene 35, 79
TV Guide 116, 207
TV Mirror 117
TV-Radio Mirror 115, 117, 131
20th Century–Fox 179, 192, 224
Twenty Thousand Years in Sing-Sing 186
20/20 151

Uncle Don 176, 187
United Features Syndicate 205, 218
United Nations 79, 178, 184, 186, 188, 191, 193, 198, 200, 208, 209, 220
U.N. Correspondents Association 184
U.N. General Assembly 62
The U.N. in Action 191, 198
United Press International (UPI) 17, 27, 86, 101, 102, 103, 124, 125, 158, 178, 181, 182, 188, 193, 195, 198, 202, 204, 211, 215, 222
U.S. Army 175, 185, 188, 195, 207, 209, 210, 220, 222
U.S. Army Air Corps 173
U.S. Army Ambulance Corps 173
U.S. Army Reparations Commission 173
U.S. Army Signal Corps 199
U.S. Coast Guard 62
United States Daily 205
U.S. Department of Agriculture 84
U.S. Department of Commerce 42, 99, 107
U.S. Department of Interior 74
U.S. Department of Justice 160
U.S. Information Agency 198, 203
U.S. Library of Congress 125, 174
U.S. Mail 85
U.S. Marine Corps 185, 207, 212
U.S. Marketing Bureau 84
U.S. Merchant Marine 120
U.S. Navy 12, 26, 36, 141, 173, 178, 190, 204, 206, 208, 209, 216
U.S. Navy Reserve 187, 216
U.S. News & World Report 173, 174, 184, 205
U.S. Office of Facts and Figures 60
U.S. Office of Radio Research (ORR) 30
U.S. Office of War Censorship 50, 55, 58
U.S. Office of War Information (OWI) 50, 60, 120, 180, 192, 193, 211, 217
U.S. Power Squadron 214

U.S. State Department 175, 178, 181, 187, 194, 206
U.S. Steel Corporation 176, 191
The U.S. Steel Hour 176, 191
U.S. Supreme Court 27, 43, 63, 68, 191
U.S. War Department 187
Universal Declaration of Human Rights (UDHR) 62
Universal-International movie newsreels 190
Universal News Service 185, 199, 214
University of Alabama 182
University of Alaska 207
University of Berlin 193
University of California 99, 210
University of California at Los Angeles 181
University of Chicago 173, 191, 209, 213
The University of Chicago Round Table 74–76
University of Denver 218, 219
University of Edinburgh 219
University of Geneva 188
University of Georgia 182
University of Grenoble 187
University of Illinois 193, 212
University of Indiana 174
University of Iowa 187
University of Jura 194
University of Kansas 181, 216
University of Maine 183
University of Michigan 178, 212
University of Minnesota 211
University of Missouri 130, 178, 216
University of North Carolina 197
University of Northern Indiana 218
University of Ohio 202
University of Pennsylvania 205
University of Redlands 206
University of Stockholm 206
University of Texas 84
University of Tulsa 179, 189
University of Virginia 188, 199, 218
University of Washington 178, 191, 202, 212
University of Wisconsin 84, 180, 204
Up for Parole 200
Us (magazine) 115
Us Weekly 116
Ustream 170
Utley, Garrick 80

vacuum tube radios 97, 98
Vallee, Rudy 24, 202
Valparaiso University 209
Van, Lyle 172, 221
Vandercook, John W. 28, 59, 172, 208, 221–222
Vanocur, Sander 172, 204, 222
Variety 46, 50, 51, 53, 54, 66, 70, 116, 131
vaudeville 175

Vaudeville News 224
V-E Day 179, 180, 185, 221
Vic and Sade 190
Victrola 13
Vietnam War 215, 220
Villa, Pancho 17
V-J Day 32, 185
Vlanton, Elias 207
Vogue (periodical) 175
A Voice in the Room 37
Voice of America (VOA) 180, 187, 198, 202, 203, 211, 217
The Voice of Firestone 46, 180
Voorhis, Westbrook Van 26
Vox Pop 202
Voyage of the Scarlet Queen 172

WABC, New York City 88, 91, 93, 140, 141, 142, 156, 159, 175, 201
WAGF, Dothan, Ala. 182
Wagner, Rob 114
WAIR, Winston-Salem, N.C. 184
WAIU, Columbus, Oh. 200
Walker, Jerry 142
Walker, Jimmy 35
The Wall Street Journal 167
Wallace, Chris 80
Wallace, Mike 150
Waller, Judith 76
Waller, Theodore 191
WALR, Zanesville, Oh. 200
Walters, Barbara 151
War of the Worlds 36–37
Warner, Sam 160
Warner Brothers Studios 160
The Washington Evening Star 185
Washington Exclusive 79
The Washington Herald 179, 199
The Washington Journalism Review 205
Washington Merry-Go-Round (syndicated column) 205
Washington Monument 35
The Washington News 222
Washington Observations (syndicated column) 223
The Washington Post 179, 216, 222
Washington Report 189, 209
The Washington Sideshow (syndicated column) 200
The Washington Star 184, 223
The Washington Times 185
Washington Week 210
Watch the World Go By 186
Watergate imbroglio 191, 206, 211, 215, 216
Wayne, David 147
Wayne, Frances 119
Wayne Howell and the News 193
The Wayne Howell Show 193
WAYS, Charlotte 197
WBBM, Chicago 161, 163
WBBR, New York City 164
WBIC, Bay Shore, L.I., N.Y. 176
WBNY, Buffalo, N.Y. 103
WBT, Charlotte 197
WBYN, Brooklyn, N.Y. 176
WBZ, Boston, Mass. 163, 205
WBZ, Springfield, Mass. 107

WCAP, Washington, D.C. 34
WCAU, Philadelphia 161, 175, 177, 186, 200
WCBS, New York City 91, 93, 111, 141, 142, 143, 159, 161, 164, 173, 205
WCBS-TV, New York City 141, 192, 198, 221
WCTC, New Brunswick, N.J. 196
WCX, Detroit 101
WDGY, Minneapolis 207
WDRC, Hartford 173
We Love and Learn 183
We the People 188, 190, 198
WEAF, New York City 14, 34, 162, 175, 185, 191, 195, 201
weathercasting 84
Weaver, Sylvester Barnabee (Pat) 91, 145, 146–147, 148–149, 150
Wednesday Morning 151
WEEI, Boston 190
Weekday 149
Weekend Edition 150, 211
Weekly Review, Shanghai, China 177
Weems, Ted 120
WEHS, Chicago 157
Weiller, Lazare 128
Welles, Orson 36–37
Wells, H.G. 36–37
Wells, Linton 59
Wells College 184
Wendy Warren and the News 182, 184
WENR, Chicago 63, 189
West 57th St. 150
Western Electric Company 98
Westinghouse Broadcasting Corporation 158, 159, 161, 213
Westinghouse Electric and Manufacturing Company 12, 13, 84, 93, 106, 159, 162
WFAA, Dallas 99
WFBH, New York City 175
WFIL, Philadelphia 124
WFLD, Chicago 213
WFOY, St. Augustine, Fla. 102
WGAN, Portland, Me. 200
WGBS, New York City 73, 158
WGHF-FM, New York City 124
WGMS, Washington, D.C. 205
WGN, Chicago 34, 185, 189, 201
WGST, Atlanta 221
WGY, Schenectady 33, 107, 214
WHA, Madison, Wis. 84
WHAS, Louisville 194
WHB, Kansas City, Mo. 216
WHCT-TV, Hartford 205
WHDH, Boston 190
When a Girl Marries 184
When Love Awakens (play) 86
WHET, Troy, Ala. 182
WHFC, Chicago 157
White, J. Andrew 13
White, Paul Welrose, Jr. 16, 17, 26, 58, 66, 70, 86, 180, 184, 186, 189, 196, 215
White, Steve 143, 146
White House Correspondents Association 185

Whiteman, Paul 200
Whitman College 202
WHN, New York City 91, 98, 159, 218
Who Said That? 180, 196
Who's Who in TV & Radio 194
WICC, Bridgeport, Conn. 187
Wide, Wide World 145
Wile, Frederic William 53, 172, 223
The Wile Evening Journal (family periodical) 223
Wiley, Fletcher 181
WILL, Urbana, Ill. 193
Willard Storage Battery Company 156
Williams, Armstrong 67
Williams, Brian 174, 203
Williams, Bruce 155
Williams, Walter 9
Williams College 189, 200
Williams Company, J.B. 213
Willkie, Wendell 55, 188
Wills, Phyllis Elta Argall 224
Wills, W.R. ("Bud") 223–224
Wilson, Big 147
Wilson, Woodrow W. 33, 34, 185
WIMG, Medford, Wis. 103
Winchell, Walter 24, 28, 53, 58, 59, 63, 68, 111, 114, 172, 196, 207, 224
WIND, Chicago 161, 213
Wingate, John 143, 146
Wings 204
WINK, Fort Myers, Fla. 164
WINR, Binghamton, N.Y. 102
WINS, New York City 91, 158, 159, 161, 164, 185
WIOD, Miami 155, 190
WIQI-FM, Chicago 163
wire services' conflict with radio 27–28
Wireless Age 13
"wireless telegraph" 10, 14, 104
Wireless Telegraph and Signal Company 9
wirephoto 124
WJAG, Norfolk, Neb. 14, 85
WJSV, Washington, D.C. 180, 220, 221, 224
WJTN, Jamestown, N.Y. 103
WJZ, Newark/New York City 14, 63, 84, 85, 88, 106, 107, 175, 183, 192, 195, 196, 197, 218
WKBI, Chicago 157
WKZO, Kalamazoo, Mich. 194
WLOE, Boston 180, 190
WLS, Chicago 36

WLW, Cincinnati 85, 86, 194, 200
WMAK, Buffalo, N.Y. 190
WMAL, Washington, D.C. 176, 192, 199
WMAQ, Chicago 75, 161, 182
WMAZ, Macon, Ga. 102
WMBD, Peoria, Ill. 102
WMC, Memphis 194
WMCA, New York City 89, 90, 159, 183, 184, 185, 190
WMGM 159
WNBC, New York City 93, 143, 148, 188, 204
WNBC-TV, New York City 204
WNEW, New York City 176, 179, 197, 210
WNUS, Chicago 157, 158, 213
WNYC, New York City 201
WOL, Washington, D.C. 79, 200
Wolfe, Thomas 137
Wolfman Jack 147
Woman's Christian Temperance Union (WCTU) 185
Women's National Radio Committee (WNRC) 78
Women's Wear Daily 198
WOMT, Manitowoc, Wis. 14, 89
WOR, New York City 34, 73, 86, 88, 91, 176, 178, 183, 187, 190, 192, 195, 197, 214, 217, 221
WORL, Boston 200
The World 150
The World Is Our Beat 193, 210
World News Today 183
World News Tonight 215
World Series 31, 37, 84, 202
The World Tonight 176, 177, 193, 194, 197, 198, 210, 211, 212, 215, 220
World War I ("The Great War") 12, 17, 22, 26, 84, 172, 173, 175, 178, 185, 187, 192, 197, 205, 207, 208, 217, 219, 223
World War II 2, 10, 16, 23, 24, 31–32, 33, 38, 50, 59–60, 62, 69–70, 79, 86, 89, 102, 116, 118, 123, 131, 172, 173, 174, 176, 181, 182, 185, 190, 191, 196, 199, 200, 201, 207, 208, 209, 211, 212, 214, 215, 217, 220, 221, 223
World Wide Web 122, 123, 166, 167, 169
WOW, Omaha 103
WPAC, Patchogue, L.I., N.Y. 176
WPAU, Portsmouth, Oh. 200
WPEN, Philadelphia 177
WPG, Atlantic City, N.J. 175
WPIX-TV, New York City 210

WQXR, New York City 89–90, 91, 220
WRAL-TV, Raleigh, N.C. 169
WRC, Washington, D.C. 173, 175, 184, 188, 191, 223
WRCA, New York City 91, 143, 144, 146, 148, 173
WREK-FM, Atlanta 167
WSB, Atlanta 182, 221
WSLB, Ogdensburg, N.Y. 103
WSTP, Minneapolis-St. Paul 103
WTG, Manhattan, Kan. 84
WTHT, Hartford 183
WTMA, Charleston, S.C. 193
WTOP-AM-FM, Washington, D.C. 161, 163, 164, 170, 189, 221
WTOP-TV, Washington, D.C. 212
WTOP2.com, Washington, D.C. 169–170
W2XAB, New York City 131
WUAM, Albany, N.Y. 163
WVON, Chicago 157
WVP, Bedlow's Island, N.J. 106–107
WWJ, Detroit 101, 164
WXYC-FM, Chapel Hill, N.C. 167
WXYZ, Detroit 182, 183
Wyandotte College 181
Wylie, Max 76
Wynn, Ed 15
WYNR, Chicago 158, 213

X Minus One 200
XEAK, Tijuana, Mex. 157
XETRA, Tijuana, Mex. 157–158
XTRA News 157

Yale University 186, 222
Yankee Network 183
Yokohama Exposition 224
York, Cal 114
You Are There 193, 200
Young, Agnes 119
Young Men's Christian Association (YMCA) 77, 175
Young Widder Brown 184
Your Hit Parade 186
Your Land and Mine 217
Your Show of Shows 145, 190
Youth Takes a Stand 178, 194

Zachary, George 120
Zangara, Giuseppe 36
zines 113, 114, 116
Zuker, Adolph 18
Zworykin, Vladimir Kosma 128–129

JIM COX HAS ALSO WRITTEN
THE FOLLOWING BOOKS PUBLISHED BY MCFARLAND

Sold on Radio: Advertisers in the Golden Age of Broadcasting (2008; paperback 2013)

The Great Radio Sitcoms (2007; paperback 2012)

Musicmakers of Network Radio: 24 Entertainers, 1926–1962 (2012)

Radio Speakers: Narrators, News Junkies, Sports Jockeys, Tattletales, Tipsters, Toastmasters and Coffee Klatch Couples Who Verbalized the Jargon of the Aural Ether from the 1920s to the 1980s — A Biographical Dictionary (2007; paperback 2011)

Music Radio: The Great Performers and Programs of the 1920s through Early 1960s (2005; paperback 2011)

Mr. Keen, Tracer of Lost Persons: A Complete History and Episode Log of Radio's Most Durable Detective (2004; paperback 2011)

Rails Across Dixie: A History of Passenger Trains in the American South (2011)

The Daytime Serials of Television, 1946–1960 (2006; paperback 2010)

Radio Crime Fighters: More Than 300 Programs from the Golden Age (2002; paperback 2010)

The Great Radio Audience Participation Shows: Seventeen Programs from the 1940s and 1950s (2001; paperback 2009)

American Radio Networks: A History (2009)

The Great Radio Soap Operas (1999; paperback 2008)

This Day in Network Radio: A Daily Calendar of Births, Deaths, Debuts, Cancellations and Other Events in Broadcasting History (2008)

Frank and Anne Hummert's Radio Factory: The Programs and Personalities of Broadcasting's Most Prolific Producers (2003)

Say Goodnight, Gracie: The Last Years of Network Radio (2002)

www.ingramcontent.com/pod-product-compliance
Lightning Source LLC
Chambersburg PA
CBHW081547300426
44116CB00015B/2782